Where to watch birds in

Central America, Mexico, and the Caribbean

THE *WHERE TO WATCH BIRDS* SERIES

Where to watch birds in Africa
Nigel Wheatley

Where to watch birds in Asia
Nigel Wheatley

Where to watch birds in Australasia and Oceania
Nigel Wheatley

Where to watch birds in Central America, Mexico, and the Caribbean
Nigel Wheatley and David Brewer

Where to watch birds in Europe and Russia
Nigel Wheatley

Where to watch birds in South America
Nigel Wheatley

ALSO AVAILABLE FROM PRINCETON UNIVERSITY PRESS

A Guide to the Birds of the West Indies
Herbert Raffaele, James Wiley, Orlando Garrido, Allan Keith, and Janis Raffaele

A Guide to the Birds of Panama: With Costa Rica, Nicaragua, and Honduras
Robert S. Ridgely and John A. Gwynne

A Guide to the Birds of Colombia
S. L. Hilty and W. L. Brown

A Guide to the Birds of Venezuela
R. M. de Schauensee and W. H. Phelps, Jr.

A Guide to the Birds of Puerto Rico and the Virgin Islands
H. A. Raffaele

Where to watch birds in

Central America, Mexico, and the Caribbean

Nigel Wheatley and David Brewer

Princeton University Press

Princeton and Oxford

This book is dedicated to the memory of Terry Pratt, who trod many
trails and introduced so many people to the natural beauties and
wildlife of Central America; tragically killed in an aircraft accident on
the flanks of Volcán Arenal, Costa Rica, August 26 2000.

Published in the United States, Canada, and the Philippine Islands by
Princeton University Press, 41 William Street, Princeton, New Jersey 08540

In the United Kingdom and the European Union,
published by Christopher Helm (Publishers) Ltd, a subsidiary of
A & C Black (Publishers) Ltd, 37 Soho Square, London W1D 3QZ

Library of Congress Control Number 2001094365

ISBN 0-691-09515-9

This book has been composed in Cheltenham Light

www.birds.princeton.edu

Printed and bound in Great Britain by
Creative Print and Design (Wales), Ebbw Vale

1 3 5 7 9 10 8 6 4 2

CONTENTS

Contents

Contents

Contents

Contents

ACKNOWLEDGEMENTS

David Brewer (Central America)

One of the amiable and pleasant characteristics of bird-watchers is their willingness to help others afflicted by the same obsession; help which runs all the way from offering useful hints to providing hospitality and accommodation to total strangers. One way in which bird-watchers provide useful assistance to others is by writing up detailed accounts of their own experiences with regard to good bird-watching locations. This book is a compendium of such experiences, many of them on the part of the two authors, but many others distilled from the altruistic provision of information by many colleagues.

The junior author, who was responsible for that part of the book dealing with Central America, would like to thank the following who sent him copies of write-ups on sites or helped in many other ways: Maria Allen, Robert Ballard, Bob Bates, Dennis Beall, Jan-Joost Bouwman, Tom Brooks, Peter Browne, Richard Carlson, Adriana de Castro, Doug Danforth, Marcus England, Dodge and Lorna Engleman, David Ferry, Steve Ganley, Pedro Gasca, Mark Gawn, Brian Gee, Paul Grant, Clive Green, Tom Harding, Brian Henshaw, Mark Howells, Gene Hunn, Greg Jackson, Marcel Kok, Ronald Larkin, Nick Leatherby, Ofelia Lozano, Bill McDonald, Mark Oberle, Richard Palmer, Bill Porteous, Hein Prinsen, Chris Risley, Steve Russell, Andres Sada, Eric and Lorna Salzman, Graham Speight, Richard Stern, Mary Thompson, Jan Toland, Francis Toldi, Sandra de Urioste, Bruce Webb, Jack Whetstone, Bret Whitney, Terry Witt, Valerie Wyatt, and Howard Youth.

Information was also abstracted from reports and write-ups, some published or privately circulated in paper copy, and some available on the web, from the following contributors: Yvonne Alström, Björn Anderson, Bruce Barrett, Mark Beevers, Ron and Marcia Braun, Paul Bristow, Michael de Boer, Craig Faanes, Emery Froehlich, Chris Gibbins, Michael Gochfield, A.G. Goodwin, Tom and Heleen Heijnen, Henk Hendriks, Jim Hengeveld, Sue Hughes, Jim Hully, Peter Joost, David Lauten, Kevin Loughlin, Greg Links, Daniëlle Maatman, David Matson, John Regan, David Sargeant, J. Stratford, Chris Sykes, Sonja Tausch-Treml, Rainer Tempel, and Jan Vermeulen. All of these people have performed a signal service to other bird-watchers by making available the fruits of their experiences. I also thank Steve Whitehouse, Ib Huysman, the Dutch Birding Travel Report Service and Jan Vermeulen for their help in obtaining some of the reports by the above authors and the www. service provided by Blake Maybank.

There are a number of other people who deserve to be singled out for special acknowledgement for their extensive assistance for particular areas; these are David Agro (Panama), Peter Burke (Panama), Martin Cody (Nicaragua), Juan Fernando Hernández (Guatemala), Alan Gehret (Belize), Jon Hornbuckle (several countries), Lee Jones (Belize), Oliver Komar (El Salvador), Wilberto Martínez (Panama), Darién Montañez (Panama), Pat O'Donnell (Costa Rica) and David Wiedenfeld (Nicaragua). I am especially indebted to them for their help and kindness.

Finally, I must thank my co-author, Nigel Wheatley, for his advice, patience and for his hospitality during my latest visit to my favourite island; and, above all others, my wife Margaret for a huge amount of mind-blowing and tedious labour in turning my script into a workable document.

Nigel Wheatley (Caribbean)

It would have been impossible to produce this section of the book without the help of the many birders who have not only travelled to the Caribbean in search of birds, but also been unselfish enough to record their experiences for the benefit of others. Most of these have made their information generally available, and, to me, are some of the pillars of the birding world. I would therefore like to express my heartfelt thanks to the following birders and organisations who have generously permitted me to use their information and/or covered some country, archipelago and/or island accounts in red ink: J Atherton, Giff Beaton, BirdLife International, Patricia Bradley, Chris Bradshaw, Andy Brown, Pete Clement, David Cooper, Mike Flieg, Nick Gardner, Brian Gee, Ian Green (Greentours), Megan Hall, Henk Hendriks, Mike Hicks, Charles Hood, Jon Hornbuckle, Ib Huysman (Dutch Birding Travel Report Service), Brenda Kay, Guy Kirwan, Dave Lambert, Harry Lehto, Steve Lister, Chet McGaugh, Jonathan Meyer, Dominic Mitchell (*Birdwatch* magazine), Steve Mlodinow, Barry Nicholson, Mark Oberle, David Porter, Francisco Rivas, Dave Sargeant, Dave Smith, Tony Smith, Sunbird, Ann and Robert Sutton, Jan Vermeulen, Kate Wallace, Steve Whitehouse (Foreign Birdwatching Reports and Information Service), Paul Whiteman, Ithel (Taff) Williams, Rob Williams, Paul Willoughby (Bird Holidays) and Barry Wright.

Naturally, many thanks also go to the birders who accompanied these people in the field, helped find the birds, and doubtless contributed information to the trip reports. I have also spoken to numerous people on the telephone, in the field and in the pub about birding in the Caribbean, who I may have unwittingly omitted from the above list. I sincerely hope they will accept my profuse apologies if I have failed to acknowledge their help in this edition, and hope they will let me know before the next one!

Unfortunately, it must be said at this juncture that there are some birders, including a few with a wealth of Caribbean experience, who have never written a trip report! Or, if they have done so, their information has not been made widely available. Fortunately such people are few and far between, and sharing information comes naturally to the vast majority of birders. Writing trip reports can be a very enjoyable undertaking, enabling the authors to relive their experiences and cement the birding and other memories, hence I can only say to those who don't bother, have a go next time.

When I conceived the idea of 'Where to watch birds in the World' in 1991 I had to convince a publisher it was a project the growing number of birders who travel abroad would be interested in, and therefore worthy of publication. Fortunately Robert Kirk, the editor at Christopher Helm (Publishers) Ltd at the time, was aware of the potential and deserves thanks for developing the original idea. When I started compiling the basic information for the books it seemed as though every bird had at least three different names. This major headache was cured by James Clements, to whom I am very grateful for permitting me to use his superb world checklist of species (and now races) as the baseline for the series.

11

Acknowledgements

Finally, I thank my birding companions in the Caribbean, without whom I would never have seen so many great birds and the wild places they inhabit, and who made the birding more enlightening, entertaining and enjoyable. They are Angelito (Angel) and Orestes (El Chino) Martinez Garcia, Brian Field and Barry Stidolph.

INTRODUCTION

We should start off by admitting that the title of this book, *Where to Watch Birds in Central America and the Caribbean,* is something of a misnomer. A considerable section of the book is devoted to Mexico, which strictly speaking is not usually considered to be part of Central America. However, for the purposes of this book it will be treated as if it were. The two regions covered are very disparate. Central America has a large admixture of the original Amerindian population, without any recent legal or cultural attachments to any of the European powers. Faunistically, it is a fascinating bridge between the Nearctic and the enormous riches of the Neotropics. Conversely, the Caribbean is largely a creation of colonising European states, equally split among the English, French and Spanish languages, with only a tiny remnant of its aboriginal population. It has a fauna combining elements of all the adjacent landmasses with a few novelties flung in for good measure. Either is worthy of a lifetime's study, and some of the most distinguished scholars in modern ornithology—Skutch and Bond, to name only two—have done just that. For the visiting bird-watcher, typically from Europe or North America, there is an embarrassment of riches, the main problem being one of selection—so many birds, so little time! We hope that this book will help a little by making whatever choice is finally made as productive as possible.

With increasingly affordable airfares and a generally improved infrastructure on the ground, Central America has become very accessible in recent years to visiting bird-watchers, who now get off the plane and find themselves suddenly immersed in a whole new fauna. This was not the case for DB; all of his early forays into the area were by road, in some ways more tedious but much more educational. Crossing the US border into a new country and a novel culture, and then, not many hours later, seeing a Magpie Jay flying across the road, its tail undulating in a series of sine waves, was a memorable experience. This was quickly followed by more new sights—a flock of White-crowned Parrots, a covey of Elegant Quail, some unfamiliar hummingbirds—and all of this on the first day. Another day brought us to San Blas, where the Neotropics really start to make their presence felt, with new families—woodcreepers, cotingas—and spectacular new sights—a flock of Military Macaws, saltators, unfamiliar tanagers and flycatchers, tiger-herons and anhingas, around every corner. All of this without a practical field-guide, since the only book was Emmet Blake's *Birds of Mexico,* a monumental work in its time, but with only one-third of the species illustrated and then only in black and white—and often only the head!

At about that time Peter Alden wrote a pioneering little book, with colour illustrations and site-maps, on where to find birds in the three Mexican states south of the Arizona border. Now the whole area is covered by field-guides of the highest quality, superbly illustrated and well-researched, but the second aspect of Peter's work, the site information, is only patchily available for much of the region. It was to rectify this omission and to provide, in one volume, an overall guide to these two distinct regions that we undertook this work. Anyone who has taken part in an intensive—or not so intensive—bird-watching trip to a new

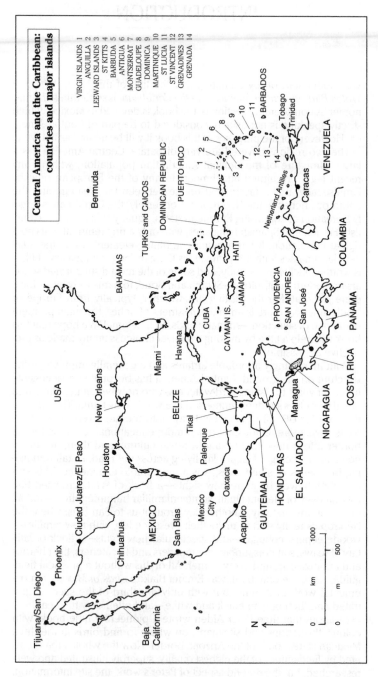

Central America and the Caribbean: countries and major islands

VIRGIN ISLANDS 1
ANGUILLA 2
LEEWARD ISLANDS 3
ST KITTS 4
BARBUDA 5
ANTIGUA 6
MONTSERRAT 7
GUADELOUPE 8
DOMINICA 9
MARTINIQUE 10
ST LUCIA 11
ST VINCENT 12
GRENADINES 13
GRENADA 14

area will realise that the key to success is good information and good planning. The planning is yours, but we hope to provide the information. Equally, we realise that our work is only as accurate as the information that we have received, although we have taken all reasonable

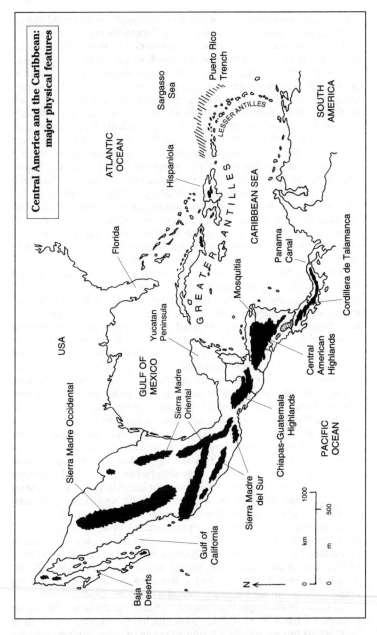

Central America and the Caribbean: major physical features

Sierra Madre Occidental

USA

GULF OF MEXICO

Florida

ATLANTIC OCEAN

Sargasso Sea

Puerto Rico Trench

LESSER ANTILLES

Hispaniola

GREATER ANTILLES

SOUTH AMERICA

CARIBBEAN SEA

Mosquitia

Panama Canal

Cordillera de Talamanca

Central American Highlands

Yucatan Peninsula

Sierra Madre Oriental

Chiapas-Guatemala Highlands

Sierra Madre del Sur

PACIFIC OCEAN

Gulf of California

Baja Deserts

N

1000

500

0

km

m

0

steps to verify the precision of the input we have obtained for sites not personally known to us. Also, areas change. Because most changes are to the detriment of wildlife habitat there are many sites known to us over the years which are simply no longer worth visiting. We do welcome updated trip-reports or comments about inaccuracies and omissions.

When Chino instructed us to leave the metal punts we had used to navigate the deep, narrow channel into the Zapata Swamp, Cuba, he was met with open mouths, for we were surrounded by water. This is usually the case in December we were informed, so we had no choice but to plunge in up to our knees, barefoot in my case because I didn't want to get my only pair of trainers wet, and start tramping through the swamp, complete with biting water-beetles, eight-foot high sawgrass and, worst of all, invisible limestone sink-holes where the water was considerably deeper. After a few hundred yards, Helen, one half of the couple from Belgium who were accompanying Barry, Brian, Chino, his brother Angel and myself, Nigel Wheatley, muttered something about birders, birding and divorce papers, but we still had some way to go before Angel started playing the Zapata Wren tape. He waded even further into the marsh with his hand-held speaker aloft, blasting out the recording of the wren's loud warble. After what seemed an age we heard one responding from the dim, distant backwaters of the swamp, and prepared to move on. We were not keen on the idea but knowing that this was the only place on earth where the Zapata Wren occurs there appeared to be no two ways about it, we would have to wade on.

However, Chino told us to stay put, much to Helen's delight, for the bird, he confidently explained, would come to us, albeit in about 40 minutes, and now we should concentrate on looking for Zapata Sparrow. After about fifteen minutes and a couple of false alarms (just Common Yellowthroats) a bird appeared in one of the small buttonwood bushes, which are liberally sprinkled throughout the swamp, and proved to be one of up to four rather confiding Zapata Sparrows. They were not the most beautiful birds we had seen on our trip to Cuba but, nevertheless, one of the rarest in the world and therefore a solid start to the day.

There was still no sign of the wren though, or for that matter Angel, who could have disappeared forever down a sink-hole for all we knew, so Chino decided to try calling up a Zapata Rail. He produced a noise which resembled the sound made by a basketball bouncing at ever-decreasing heights, having been thrown high into the air, and to his surprise and our amazement a real rail responded almost immediately, from a clump of sawgrass about fifty sploshes away. We could scarcely believe it because there we were, up to our knees in water, having seen Zapata Sparrow, awaiting the arrival of a Zapata Wren and within striking distance of one the hardest birds to see on the planet! All thoughts of wrens were replaced with whispered wishes as we carefully moved in on the calling rail, for we now had a chance of completing an almost impossible hat trick. So, when a Spotted Rail started calling, even closer than the Zapata, and Chino turned to ask "Zapata or Spotted?" he required no verbal response, for the five of us moving as quietly as we could behind him were already zooming in on the Zapata!

Then, just as we began thinking that we might actually see the rail up popped a Zapata Wren. It didn't look much different from many other large wrens but we watched it sing a couple of times, long enough for the rail to shut up and for us to lose the scent. We heard another rail a little later, but it was buried in a distant clump of dense sawgrass and Chino said there was absolutely no chance of seeing it, so we made our way back to the punts, frustrated by the rail but happy having seen two of the most range-restricted birds on earth.

Back on dry land it was a joy to walk without fear of falling into a waist-high sink-hole full of water. Chino escorted us to a small patch of woodland near his village, Santo Tomás, and helped us see our first Grey-headed Quail-Dove, a far more beautiful bird than any of the field guides portray, and then to a glade at the edge of a wood where, he told us, "Pájaro mosca lives". He pointed into the canopy and after a few seconds said "There", as his forefinger followed its movement. This scene was repeated two or three times but we still couldn't see the damned thing, even though our eyes were by now on stalks. Fortunately, the seemingly invisible creature then perched in one place for a moment longer, enabling Chino to show us the smallest bird on earth, a male Bee Hummingbird. The tiny mite throbbed with life, moving its head sideways every milli-second or so, raising its crown feathers constantly, and shivering its wings and tail. One moment it was there, the next it was gone. In a flash the dot dashed from its perch a foot or so to zap some unseen aerial insect or take a brief sip of nectar from a nearby flowering climber, often returning sideways to its perch and landing with aplomb. Hyperactive, it simply could not sit still but when perched we did manage to see it through a telescope, albeit for only a few seconds at a time. The bundle of energy looked tiny even through the 'scope but with binoculars it looked no bigger than a large bee, and with the eye it was virtually impossible to see, perched or in flight.

Although the Pájaro mosca was a male it possessed only a small patch of red on the throat, not the full red hood and cape it acquires later in the year. Had it been in full breeding splendour it may have been *the* bird of the trip, but even then it may have struggled to compete with the other major contenders for that title. What the Caribbean lacks in quantity it more than makes up for in quality, and by the end of our trip to Cuba it was the waves of wonderful New World warblers, including the likes of Yellow-headed, Yellow-throated, Black-and-white and Black-throated Blue, and two other beautiful birds which were foremost in our minds. We saw Cuban Trogons virtually everywhere and everyone was a beauty, but the Caribbean is the only region in the world where it is possible to see todies and, for me at least, these cracking birds make going there a must. The confiding Cuban species, which has a fantastic combination of glowing green upperparts, scarlet throat and carmine flanks, is common and widespread, and therefore, for once, the bird of the trip was an almost daily delight.

These personal memories and the hope of many more have inspired us to research and compile the information contained within this book, and in sharing this information we hope not only to encourage fellow birders to travel to Central America and the Caribbean but also help them establish where to search for the birds they dream of. It is, in fact, fairly easy to see most of the region's birds, time and funds permitting, but it is essential to prepare for any trip thoroughly, hence we have aimed to include all the birding information needed to assist birders to plan their own successful and enjoyable birding trips to the region. Unlike another 'Where to watch' guide for which the author states, in his tour company's newsletter, 'some of our favourite niches are not included on the sensible grounds that we want to keep them to ourselves', this guide has no such policy and we have included every hotspot known to us, or to the many other birders who have helped us to produce the book.

Birders planning a trip to Central America and the Caribbean will probably want to know, first and foremost, where to look for certain birds, in which case, those which may catch the eye in the Central American field guides include the likes of the tinamous, Agami and

Boat-billed Herons, tiger-herons, Jabiru, Harpy Eagle, Ornate Hawk-Eagle, guans and curassows, Ocellated Turkey, wood-partridges, wood-quails, wood-rails, Sungrebe, Sunbittern, Northern Jacana, Double-striped Thick-knee, quail-doves, Scarlet and other macaws, Rufous-vented Ground-Cuckoo, owls such as Crested, potoos, Greater and Lesser Swallow-tailed Swifts, hummingbirds, trogons, Resplendent Quetzal, kingfishers, motmots, jacamars, puffbirds, Red-headed and Prong-billed Barbets, toucans, woodcreepers, Beautiful Treerunner, foliage-gleaners, leaftossers, antshrikes, antthrushes and antpittas, cotingas, Purple-throated Fruitcrow, Bare-necked Umbrellabird, Three-wattled Bellbird, manakins, tody-flycatchers, spadebills, Royal Flycatcher, Sapayoa, Thrush-like Schiffornis, tityras, Sharpbill, silky-flycatchers, solitaires, nightingale-thrushes, gnatwrens, gnatcatchers, jays, Chestnut-sided Shrike-Vireo, Rufous-browed Peppershrike, New World warblers such as Olive, Flame-throated, Red and Pink-headed, and Red-breasted and Grey-throated Chats, tanagers, euphonias, chlorophonias, honeycreepers, orioles and oropendolas.

In the Caribbean dream birds may include Red-billed and White-tailed Tropicbirds, Bridled and Sooty Terns, Brown Noddy, quail-doves, the endemic parrots, lizard-cuckoos, owls, nightjars, hummingbirds, including the streamertails and Bee Hummingbird, Cuban and Hispaniolan Trogons, the five endemic todies, the endemic woodpeckers, Golden Swallow, the endemic and monotypic Palmchat, Zapata Wren, the endemic thrashers, tremblers and thrushes, Rufous-throated Solitaire, passage migrant and wintering New World warblers such as Cape May, Black-throated Blue and Prairie, endemic warblers such as Olive-capped, Adelaide's, Elfin-woods and Whistling, and the endemic orioles.

Once birders have decided which birds they would most like to see, further questions may arise, such as which country, island, archipelago or region supports the best selection of these birds? Is it a safe place to visit? When is the best time to go? Which are the best sites? How easy is it to travel between them? How much time will be needed at each? What other species occur at these sites? Which birds should I concentrate on? The list goes on.

Such questions require careful consideration if the proposed birding trip is going to be an enjoyable success, and without months of painstaking preparation a trip may not be anywhere near as exciting as it could be. Hence, this book's major aim is to answer those questions birders may ask themselves before venturing to Central America and the Caribbean for the first or fortieth time. It is not meant to direct you to every bird in the minutest detail, but to be a first point of reference, an aid to your own research and planning, a guiding light. It is no substitute for up-to-date trip reports and we urge readers to seek these (see Useful Addresses, p. 414), and to write up their own experiences, which will then, hopefully, be made generally available. Sharing information is, after all, one of the joys of birding.

Birders are notoriously hard to please, so compiling this book has been all consuming. We began by compiling a list of sites and the species recorded at them, using every imaginable source. Reports written by independent birders were a major gold mine and without the generous permission of their writers the book would have been immeasurably poorer (see Acknowledgements, p. 10). When compiling the site lists it quickly became apparent that many species had more than one

English name, hence we needed a baseline species list to cure what was fast becoming a severe headache. Thus we searched for the world list that we thought was the most logical, easy to use and popular, in terms of individual species names and taxonomic order; it did not take long to settle on *Birds of the World: A Checklist* by James Clements (now in its fifth edition, complete with races), and we are most grateful to James for kindly permitting us to use it. Some of the names James uses do differ however from those used in other books and birders trip reports covering the region, hence we have included a table to compare these (see p. 421). In addition, where names used by James are significantly different from those in common use by most birders we have retained these popular names.

Although the 'English' names of New World birds should be spelt in the American way (e.g. 'colored' should be used instead of 'coloured', and 'gray' instead of 'grey'), we have written all bird names in 'the English way', simply because our busy fingers refused to miss out the 'u' in 'coloured' or to press the 'a' in 'grey' instead of the 'e', while whizzing, no, stumbling, across the keyboard.

By using our own experiences, birders trip reports and many other sources, most of the best birding sites for the endemic and near-endemic species, birds which are hard to see beyond the region's boundaries, and any other popular birds, have been included, albeit in varying detail. Absolute coverage and precision would have resulted in the staggered publication of several thick volumes! The major sites, of which there are over 000, are listed in the Site Index (p. 000) and all species mentioned in the text are covered within the Species Index (p. 000).

The Layout

During the course of compiling the information for the book it more or less acquired its own format. Countries, islands and archipelagos are, on the whole, divided according to political boundaries and treated alphabetically, with details for each as follows.

The **Introduction** to each country, island or archipelago includes:
a brief **summary** of the features discussed below;
size of the country, island or archipelago in relation to England and Texas;
the basics of **getting around** and the range of **accommodation and food** available;
details relating to **health and safety** where, although general advice is given, it is still important to check the latest information on vaccination requirements and personal safety levels, before travelling;
a section on **climate and timing**, where the best times to visit are given (these are summarized in the Calendar, p. 411);
an outline of **habitats**;
a brief outline of **conservation** issues;
bird families, the number of regularly occurring families is presented for Central American countries;
a list of **endemics** (where the phrase 'relatively common' means that a certain species is common relative to others. Use of 'common' to describe a species' status can be misleading because very few species are as common as formerly, and many survive in far smaller numbers than in the past);
a list of **near-endemics**;

the total number of **bird species** recorded (where known), followed by a short list of notable species intended to give a brief taste of what to expect (rarely seen species are not usually included in this brief list);
and **expectations**, where an idea of how many species it is possible to see, usually on a short trip lasting 1–3 weeks, is given.

Some sections may be very brief, or missing altogether, for the less well-known destinations, and details for all countries, islands and archipelagos on getting around, accommodation and food, and health and safety, are intended to be as brief as possible because there appears to be little point in repeating the wealth of information available within numerous general travel guides. In this book, it makes more sense to save room for more information on the birds and birding.

At the start of each country, island or archipelago account there is a map showing the major cities and towns, main road routes and sites. The sites are then discussed in detail, after the introduction: along a more or less logical route through the country; or in 'bunches' for specific regions. Naturally, different birders will prefer their own routes, but we felt this was more practical than dealing with them alphabetically because those birders intending to follow the same 'route' we use, or visit just one area of a country, island or archipelago, will find all sites they intend to visit within the same section.

The **Sites** accounts within each country, island or archipelago include:

The **site name**, which usually refers to the actual site, or, if it involves a number of birding spots in close proximity, the name used is that of the most convenient city, town or village from which to explore all of these.

The **site introduction** includes a brief breakdown of the site's general location, size, main physical characteristics, habitats and most notable birds (i.e. those most worth concentrating on at the given site).

Next is a **Species** list, including **Endemics** (to the country, island or archipelago, not the site), **Near-endemics**, **Localised Specialities** (species that are not site specialities, but have (i) restricted ranges across country boundaries; (ii) broader distributions throughout Central America and the Caribbean, but are generally scarce, rare, or threatened with extinction; or (iii) have rarely been mentioned in the literature consulted in preparing this book), **Others** (widely distributed species that are uncommon, spectacular or especially sought after for a variety of reasons), and **Other Wildlife** (notable mammals and, if appropriate, a reference to other flora and fauna).

The Others section is not designed to be comprehensive and many more species than those listed may have been recorded at a given site. Such species are relatively common or widespread in small numbers and therefore occur at many sites throughout the relevant country, island or archipelago, or indeed across much of the region. By restricting the number of species listed under Others we have sought to avoid repetition, and save a considerable amount of space, not least in the Species Index. Species not normally listed include the following:

Central America Eared and Pied-billed Gebes, Brown Pelican, Neotropic Cormorant, most herons also occurring in North America, most migrant North American ducks, Black and Turkey Vultures, Northern

Harrier, Sharp-shinned, Cooper's Red-shouldered, Broad-winged, Swainson's and Red-tailed Hawks, American Kestrel, Merlin, Scaled, Gambel's and California Quail, Virginia and Sora Rails, Common Moorhen, American Coot, most migrant shorebirds (waders), most non-breeding gulls and terns, Rock and Mourning Doves, Black-billed and Yellow-billed Cuckoos, Groove-billed Ani, Great Horned, Long-eared and Short-eared Owls, Lesser and Common Nighthawks, Chimney and Vaux's Swifts, Ruby-throated, Black-chinned, Anna's, Costa's, Rufous and Allen's Hummingbirds, Belted Kingfisher, Acorn, Gila and Hairy Woodpeckers, all sapsuckers and flickers, most migrant flycatchers, Blue-grey Gnatcatcher, all bluebirds and migrant thrushes, Northern Mockingbird, Grey Catbird, American Pipit, Cedar Waxwing, most migrant North American vireos, some common North American warblers, Summer and Scarlet Tanagers, Northern Cardinal, Rose-breasted, Black-headed and Blue Grosbeaks, Indigo, Lazuli and Painted Buntings, Rufous-sided, Spotted, Canyon and California Towhees, most migrant North American sparrows and finches, House Finch, Dark-eyed Junco, most migrant North American icterids, House Sparrow.

Caribbean Least and Pied-billed Grebes, Brown Pelican, Brown Booby, most egrets and herons, Turkey Vulture, Red-tailed Hawk, American Kestrel, most shorebirds, Laughing Gull, most terns, Mourning Dove, Common Ground-Dove, Smooth-billed Ani, Grey Kingbird, Barn Swallow, Northern Mockingbird, Black-whiskered Vireo and Bananaquit.

No one, not even the most experienced observer, is likely to see all of the species listed under each site in a single visit, or over a period of a few days, or even, in some cases, during a prolonged stay of weeks or more! This is because a number of species, even some which are relatively common and widespread, are very thin on the ground or highly elusive and thus difficult to find, especially in a short space of time.

Although you may not wish to take this book into the field once you have decided on your destination and itinerary, it, or a photocopy of the relevant section, may prove useful if you are prepared to scrawl all over it. For, by crossing out those species you have seen on a previous trip, or at a previously visited site, or already at the site you are at, you will be able to see what species you still need to look for. It is all too easy, in the haze of excitement generated by birding in a new country or at a new site, to see a lot of good birds and be satisfied with your visit, only to discover later that you have missed a bird at that site which does not occur at any other, or that you have just left a site offering you the last chance to see a certain species (on your chosen route) and are unable to change your itinerary.

Within the lists of species those marked with an asterisk (*) have been listed as threatened, conservation dependent, data deficient, or near-threatened by BirdLife International/IUCN in *Threatened Birds of the World* by Stattersfield, A. J. & Capper, D. R. 2000. BirdLife International's Threatened Birds Programme aims to gather the most up-to-date information on these species, raise awareness of their plights among governments, decision-makers and the public, and initiate action to protect them. It is therefore important to report all records of these species to BirdLife International, Wellbrook Court, Girton Road, Cambridge CB3 0NA, UK. The excellent BirdLife book treats, in detail, Central America and the Caribbean's rarest and often most spectacular species, hence all birders planning a trip to the region should seriously consider consulting it as part of their pre-trip research.

The sites accounts also include details of **Access**, where directions to the site from the nearest large city, town, village or previous site, are usually given, followed by more detailed information on where to search for the birds, especially those which occur at few, if any, other sites. Distances are usually given to the nearest km because speedometers and tyres vary so much, and directions are often described from points of the compass rather than left or right, so as not to confuse those travelling from a different direction. If the access details appear scant this is usually because most species are easily seen, or one or more endangered species are present at the site, and we have considered it wise to avoid presenting specific details on their whereabouts. The directions are aimed at birders with their own transport, as this is the most effective mode of travel in most of the region. We have decided not to repeat the vast amount of information available about public transport, in order to permit more room to 'talk birds'.

Accommodation recommended by birders for reasons such as safety, economy, comfort, location and, in some cases, opportunities for birding in the grounds is also listed. Once again, in order to save space and avoid repeating the very detailed descriptions to be found in the plethora of travel guides, we have not listed all types of accommodation available at every site. In some cases prices of accommodation (per person per night) are graded as follows: (A) = Over £10/US$15 (usually a long way over!); (B) = £10/US$8–15; (C) = Below £5/US$8. In a few cases these price codes have been used to indicate other costs, such as boat hire and guide fees.

There are many good birding sites and numerous nooks and crannies where some scarce and difficult birds can be found, which have not been included in this book, due to a lack of space. If you find it impossible to find certain species, even with the help of this book, it is time to put your exploring boots on and track them down. If successful please send the details to us for inclusion in the next edition (see Request, p. 410).

Where appropriate, at the end of each country, island or archipelago account there is a section of **Additional Information**, including **Books and papers**, recommended for further reading, research and field use, and **Addresses** to contact for more information, permits, booking accommodation in advance, and so on.

Finally, it is important to remember that this book is not an up-to-the-minute trip report. Some sites will have changed when you get there, some may not even be there, and new ones will be discovered. Still, a little uncertainty is what makes birding so fascinating. It would be a poor pastime if every bird was lined up on an 'x' on the map, and while some are 'teed up' like that in this book, we hope there are not too many! We have aimed to provide just the right amount of guidance to help you to plan a successful and enjoyable birding trip to Central America and the Caribbean, and, hopefully, left enough leeway for you to 'find' your own birds.

INTRODUCTION TO BIRDING IN CENTRAL AMERICA

Species Diversity

South America is, of course, *the* bird continent, with over 3000 species recorded, almost one third of the world's total. By comparison all other areas pale. For its size, however, Central America does possess some very respectable totals. Approximately 1350 species have been recorded in the region's eight countries, or about 14% of the world total; but Central America, including Mexico, is only 1.5% of the world's land mass and Central America proper is only 0.3%. Mexico alone has a list of about 1050 species, 100 more than the entire Palearctic region, an enormous area which stretches from Iceland and the Azores to Kamchatka and Japan. Panama, which is smaller than many European countries, holds over 900.

Of the 1350 species, approximately 340 are endemic to Central America, while a further 47 are near-endemics, mostly species which just reach the Río Grande delta, the mountains of southern Arizona or extreme northwest Colombia.

There are several reasons for this species richness. One is the highly diverse range of habitats in the area. Central America is very mountainous: the highest peaks, in Mexico, have permanently snow-covered summits above 5000 m, and between sea level and these altitudes lie a great variety of habitats, their diversity enhanced by differences in precipitation caused by the orientation of prevailing moist winds. It is thus possible, within a few km, to pass from a humid to dry habitat, even at comparable altitudes, but with a corresponding and far greater diversity caused by altitude itself. Furthermore intervening lowlands isolate many mountain ranges. This, coupled with the lack of a severe winter necessitating much migration, lends itself to greater endemism.

FIGURE 1: SPECIES LISTS OF THE WORLD'S AVIFAUNAL REGIONS
(The figures below relate to regularly occurring species, are approximate and based on *Birds of the World: A Checklist* (Fifth Edition) by James Clements, which recognizes 9748 species.)

Region	Species list	% of world total
CARIBBEAN	430	4
NORTH AMERICA	666	7
EUROPE and RUSSIA	688	7
CENTRAL AMERICA	1350	14
AUSTRALASIA and OCEANIA	1563	16
AFRICA	2313	24
ASIA	2689	28
SOUTH AMERICA	3083	32

Family Diversity

Though South America is much richer than Central America in terms of numbers of species, when it comes to members of families Central America holds its own. It supports representatives of 94 of the world's 204 families, the same number as South America (see Fig. 10, p. 31). The majority of the Neotropical families occur in the region; only nine families—rheas, screamers, Hoatzin, trumpeters, seriemas, Magellanic Plover, seedsnipes, gnateaters and plantcutters—are wholly restricted to South America. Fourteen families, mostly of Nearctic or Holarctic origin, occur in Central America, at least as far as Mexico, but not in South America: loons, turkeys, cranes, auks, kinglets, silky-flycatchers, waxwings, long-tailed tits (Bushtit), titmice, nuthatches, creepers, penduline tits (Verdin), shrikes and Olive Warbler. Fig. 3 presents the number of families found in each country; unsurprisingly, Mexico has the highest total. Second place is taken by Nicaragua, as several Nearctic families reach the southern limit of their ranges in its northern mountains.

FIGURE 2: BIRD FAMILIES IN CENTRAL AMERICA including Mexico (Based on *Birds of the World: A Checklist* (Fifth Edition) by James Clements, which recognizes 204 families.)

Tinamous
Loons (Divers)
Grebes
Albatrosses
Shearwaters and Petrels
Storm-Petrels
Tropicbirds
Pelicans
Boobies and Gannets
Cormorants
Anhinga (and Darter)
Frigatebirds
Herons
Storks
Ibises and Spoonbills
Flamingos
Ducks, Geese and Swans
New World Vultures
Osprey
Hawks, Eagles and Kites
Falcons and Caracaras
Guans, Chachalacas etc.
Turkeys
New World Quail
Cranes
Limpkin
Rails etc.
Sungrebe (and Finfoots)
Sunbittern
Jacanas

Oystercatchers
Avocets and Stilts
Thick-knees
Plovers
Sandpipers etc.
Skuas
Gulls
Terns
Skimmers
Auks etc.
Pigeons
Parrots
Cuckoos
Barn-Owls
Typical Owls
Oilbird
Potoos
Nightjars
Swifts
Hummingbirds
Trogons
Kingfishers
Motmots
Jacamars
Puffbirds
Barbets
Toucans
Woodpeckers
Ovenbirds
Woodcreepers

Typical Antbirds
Antthrushes and Antpittas
Tapaculos
Cotingas
Manakins
Tyrant Flycatchers
Larks
Swallows
Wagtails and Pipits
Kinglets
Silky-flycatchers
Waxwings
Dippers
Wrens
Mockingbirds and Thrashers
Thrushes
Gnatcatchers
Long-tailed Tits (Bushtit)

Chickadees and Tits
Nuthatches
Creepers
Penduline Tits (Verdin)
Shrikes
Crows etc.
Starlings (introduced)
Old World Sparrows (introduced)
Vireos
Finches
Olive Warbler
New World Warblers
Bananaquit
Tanagers
New World Sparrows etc.
Saltators, Cardinals and allies
New World Orioles

FIGURE 3: COUNTRY FAMILY LISTS

Mexico	93
Nicaragua	84
Guatemala	83
Panama	82
Costa Rica	78
Belize	75
El Salvador	75
Honduras	74

FIGURE 4: COUNTRY NEOTROPICAL FAMILY LISTS

Costa Rica, Panama	17
Mexico, Belize, Guatemala, El Salvador, Honduras, Nicaragua	13

(The same four families, Oilbird (vagrant), barbets, tapaculos and Sharpbill, occur in Panama and Costa Rica but not further north.)

Representatives of two families (Penguins and Old World Warblers) have occurred only as vagrants and two (Starlings and Old World Sparrows) only as introduced species. Now that the enigmatic Wrenthrush has been subsumed into the New World Warblers, there are no families which are exclusively endemic to Central America; the closest thing to an endemic family is the Silky-flycatchers, where one species only, the Phainopepla, breeds north of the US–Mexican border, the other three being Central American. In the above list, families in bold face are Neotropical in distribution (the Neotropics being defined to include the

West Indies), although a number of families such as the guans and tanagers are only weakly represented in North America.

Habitat Diversity

A detailed analysis of the habitat types to be found in Central America
would be a lengthy and complex essay, beyond the scope of this book.
For Mexico alone, Howell and Webb (1995) list 16 types, without entering into excessive detail. Habitat is largely a function of two factors, altitude and precipitation. The Atlantic or Caribbean coastline has generally more abundant rainfall than the Pacific, both in quantity and dura-
tion. Hence, at low altitudes the habitat on the Caribbean drainage
(where it remains) frequently includes rich broadleaf tropical forests,
one of the biologically richest habitats in the world; on corresponding
Pacific slopes the vegetation is more arid, often with a predominance of
deciduous thorn forest. At the extreme, in northwest Mexico, is some of
the harshest desert in the continent, with sparse rainfall occurring in a
period of a few weeks each year. As one moves south along the Pacific
coast the extreme aridity declines, so that the Osa peninsula of Costa
Rica, for example, is very lush.

The mountain ranges of Central America introduce a great degree of
complexity into the habitat types. Firstly, altitude causes major changes
in forest type, ultimately at the highest altitudes producing páramo. Secondly, the quantity of precipitation also dramatically effects forest type.
The abundance of epiphytes, plants that grow upon other plants without actually being parasitic, increases within or near the tropics. Cloud
forest, a specialized habitat that is usually enclosed in mountain mists,
is found mostly in tropical parts of Central America. Finally, the rain
shadow effect of mountain ranges can create areas at mid or high altitudes that are much more arid than corresponding areas on the other
side of a mountain range. All create specific habitat, frequently separated from similar areas by broad belts of different habitat; as a result
there is a much higher proportion of endemism than in corresponding
areas of North America or Europe.

Country Lists

While Central America cannot compare to South America in its sheer
abundance of species, in comparison to most other areas of the world,
for its size, its avifauna is rich. The areas of the countries covered by this
book are as follows.

FIGURE 5: COUNTRY SIZES (UK = 244,082 km^2, Texas = 688,681 km^2)

Mexico	1,972,545 km^2
Nicaragua	130,000 km^2
Honduras	112,088 km^2
Guatemala	108,890 km^2
Panama	77,082 km^2
Costa Rica	51,100 km^2
Belize	22,965 km^2
El Salvador	21,041 km^2

FIGURE 6: COUNTRY SPECIES LISTS

Mexico	1049
Panama	907
Costa Rica	838
Guatemala	691
Honduras	690
Nicaragua	656
Belize	560
El Salvador	508

These figures are possibly a little misleading, as Mexico is so much larger than all the other countries combined. The greatest species abundance is in Costa Rica and Panama, although neither country has nearly the diversity of habitat types of Mexico. A more realistic comparison would be with the southernmost Mexican state, Chiapas, which reaches from sea level to 4000 m, within an area of about 70,000 km^2, and has a species list of 642. Secondly, countries such as Nicaragua have been sorely neglected, and their species lists would undoubtedly increase substantially with more fieldwork. As an example, the classic study of El Salvador by Dickey and Van Rossem, in 1938, produced 380 species, only 75% of the current total; the list for Belize now contains 95 species not recorded by Russell in 1964.

Site, Trip and Day Lists
The richest areas in Central America are, as might be expected, broadleaf forests in the southernmost regions. As an example, La Selva and Rara Avis in Costa Rica both have species lists in excess of 400, despite their relatively small size. By combining La Selva with a good highland area (such as the flanks of Volcán Poás, only 25 km away) this total could be augmented by at least a further 100 species, possibly substantially more. This is still many fewer than many single sites in South America, e.g. Manu National Park in Peru has probably in excess of 1000 species, and Noel Kempff Mercado in Bolivia 700, but is still very respectable in comparison to Canada at 625 species, or the United Kingdom at 542. It would be unrealistic for a short-term visitor to expect to see a large majority of all the available species on one visit (any more than a visitor to Britain could hope for 400 species in one trip), but large lists are possible. For example, a week's visit to Colima and Jalisco in Mexico could expect at least 250 species with perhaps 25 endemics, or to Belize, 250. A comprehensive three-week visit to all the major habitats of Costa Rica could easily yield well over 500 species.

A second measure of site, trip or day lists is to look at Christmas Count figures. Christmas Counts involve multiple observers operating independently, but on the same day and within a circle of 16 km diameter. Typical high counts under these restricted conditions range from about 200 species around Belize City, to 300 in Catemaco, Mexico, and consistently above 300, occasionally 350, in the Panama Canal Zone. The Christmas Counts occur at a time of maximum species diversity, when all the wintering North American species are present, but may not be the optimum time for observing breeding or endemic species.

27

Endemic Species

The concept of endemicity is rather artificial; one has to ask, endemic to what? The answer is always, of course, to a political geographic entity, a concept that has no biological validity except for those rare occasions (such as Madagascar or Australia) where political and zoogeographic boundaries coincide. Including offshore islands, the endemic species found in Central America are as follows.

FIGURE 7: COUNTRY ENDEMIC LISTS

Mexico	88
Panama	10
Costa Rica	6
Honduras	1
Guatemala	1 (extinct)
Belize	0
El Salvador	0
Nicaragua	0

The high number of endemics in Mexico is a function not only of the numerous areas of isolated habitat in the country, but also its sheer size. If the geographic range of such Mexican endemics as Red Warbler, Sinaloa Wren, or Rufous-capped Brush-finch were to be superimposed on a map of southern Central America they would stretch from Guatemala to Panama. Alternatively, the total range of some non-endemics, such as Volcano Junco, Timberline Wren, or Flame-throated Warbler could comfortably fit into a couple of the larger Mexican states. A short visit to the centres of high endemism in Mexico could easily result in 25–30 of the country endemics, but equally a similar number of species of highly restricted, but not endemic, distribution could be found in a short trip to Costa Rica.

Exploration

It is now unlikely (though certainly not impossible) that species new to science will be discovered in Central America—in contrast to South America, where undescribed species are still being found regularly—but there are still great opportunities for exploration and new discoveries in Central America. This is especially true in the less accessible areas of Honduras and Nicaragua, where large areas of lowland forest must surely conceal surprises for any diligent investigator. Even if new species for a country or area cannot be found, the opportunities for genuine advancement of knowledge, even by the casual visitor, are immense. For example, for very many species in Central America the nest has never been described. The nest of Yucatan Wren is easily found (DB located five in an hour near Celestún), but the eggs are undescribed. For large numbers of species the known details of breeding are sketchy or non-existent; one does not have to be a professional ornithologist to make significant contributions.

INTRODUCTION TO BIRDING IN THE CARIBBEAN

Species Diversity

Approximately 430 species regularly occur in the Caribbean, only 4.4% of the world's 9700 or so birds, but the relative lack of diversity is more than compensated for by a high level of endemism. It is pointless to compare the region's total with bird-rich South America, Asia and Africa, but it is worth comparing with those of other archipelagos elsewhere in the world, such as Japan (580+) and the Philippines (572), which are both higher, and New Zealand (320+) which is considerably lower.

Birders hoping to find the widest possible diversity of species on a short trip to the Caribbean should head for Cuba, where it is possible to see 140–180 species within a couple of weeks. Species diversity declines east through Hispaniola to the Lesser Antilles, where on most islands it is difficult to see more than 50 species in a short stay.

FIGURE 8: SPECIES LISTS OF THE WORLD'S AVIFAUNAL REGIONS

(The figures below relate to regularly occurring species, are approximate and based on *Birds of the World: A Checklist* (Fifth Edition) by James Clements, which recognizes 9748 species.)

Region	Species list	% of world total
CARIBBEAN	430	4
NORTH AMERICA	666	7
EUROPE and RUSSIA	688	7
CENTRAL AMERICA	1350	14
AUSTRALASIA and OCEANIA	1563	16
AFRICA	2313	24
ASIA	2689	28
SOUTH AMERICA	3083	32

Family Diversity

The Caribbean supports representatives of 63 naturally and regularly occurring bird families, 31% of the world's total of 204. Two families are endemic to the region, the brilliant todies, of which there are five species, and the strange Palmchat, which belongs to a family of its own. Todies are restricted to Cuba, Jamaica, Hispaniola (two species) and Puerto Rico, and the Palmchat is confined to Hispaniola, making the Dominican Republic, which occupies the eastern two-thirds of Hispaniola (the western third is Haiti, a much more difficult place to visit), the best place to see representatives of the region's unique families. The remaining families are widespread in the Americas or, in some cases, cosmopolitan. The total of 63 compares favourably with Europe's 69 and North America's 73, but it is well short of Central and South America which both host 94, while Asia, the most diverse region on earth for bird families, has 121, nearly twice as many as the Caribbean.

FIGURE 9: LIST OF THE 63 NATURALLY AND REGULARLY OCCURRING BIRD FAMILIES REPRESENTED IN THE CARIBBEAN (Based on *Birds of the World: A Checklist* (Fifth Edition) by James Clements, which recognizes 204 families.)

Grebes
Petrels and Shearwaters
Storm-Petrels
Tropicbirds
Pelicans (Brown)
Boobies
Cormorants
Darters (Anhinga—Cuba only)
Frigatebirds (Magnificent)
Egrets, Herons and Bitterns
Storks (Wood)
Ibises and Spoonbills
Flamingos (Greater)
Waterfowl
New World Vultures (Turkey)
Osprey
Kites and Hawks
Caracaras (Crested) and Falcons
New World Quails (Northern Bobwhite)
Cranes (Sandhill—Cuba only)
Limpkin
Rails
Jacanas (Northern)
Oystercatchers (American)
Avocets and Stilts
Thick-knees (Double-striped—Hispaniola only)
Plovers
Sandpipers
Skuas
Gulls
Terns
Skimmers (Black)
Pigeons and Doves
Parakeets and Parrots
Cuckoos
Barn Owls
Owls
Potoos (Northern—Cuba, Jamaica and Hispaniola)
Nightjars
Swifts
Hummingbirds
Trogons (Cuba and Hispaniola only)
Kingfishers

TODIES (Endemic to the Caribbean)
Woodpeckers
Tyrant Flycatchers
Swallows
Waxwings (Cedar)
PALMCHAT (Endemic to the Caribbean)
Wrens
Mockingbirds and Thrashers
Thrushes
Gnatcatchers
Nuthatches (Brown-headed—Grand Bahama only)
Crows
Vireos
Finches (Antillean Siskin and Two-barred Crossbill—Hispaniola only)
New World Warblers
Bananaquit
Tanagers
Grassquits, Seedeaters, New World Bullfinches and New World Sparrows
Saltators, New World Grosbeaks and New World Buntings
Icterids

Very rare visitors to the region include Great Northern Diver (Divers or Loons), American Pipit (Wagtails and Pipits) and Ruby-crowned Kinglet (Kinglets).

Introduced species include Rufous-vented Chachalaca (Guans) and House Sparrow (Old World Sparrows).

FIGURE 10: FAMILY LISTS OF THE WORLD'S AVIFAUNAL REGIONS
(The figures below refer to naturally and regularly occurring families, and are based on *Birds of the World: A Checklist* (Fifth Edition) by James Clements, which lists 204 families.)

Region	Family list	% of world total	Endemic families
CARIBBEAN	63	31	2
EUROPE	69	34	0
NORTH AMERICA	73	36	0*
CENTRAL AMERICA	94	46	0**
SOUTH AMERICA	94	46	9**
AUSTRALASIA and OCEANIA	102	50	23
AFRICA	111	54	16***
ASIA	121	59	6

* Olive Warbler, in a family of its own, is confined to North and Central America.
** 17 families are confined to Central and South America.
*** three 'African' families are restricted to Madagascar.

31

Habitat Diversity

For the purposes of this book the Caribbean region includes the Bahamas, the Cayman Islands, the Greater Antilles (Cuba, Jamaica, Hispaniola and Puerto Rico), the Lesser Antilles (the Virgin Islands south to Grenada), the islands of Providencia and San Andrés, off the east coast of Nicaragua, and the Swan Islands, off northern Honduras. While the Virgin Islands are geologically part of the cordillera that forms the Greater Antilles to their west they are ornithologically more akin to the Lesser Antilles to the south, and considered part of that archipelago in this book.

The total land area covered by the islands is about 233,100 km², the vast majority of which is occupied by Cuba and Hispaniola. The Caribbean islands extend in an arc for 4023 km, from Cuba in the northwest (140 km south of Florida and 200 km east of the Yucatán Peninsula in Mexico) to Grenada in the southeast (120 km north of Venezuela).

While some islands are little more than raised limestone coral reefs, which rarely reach heights in excess of 30 m, the larger Greater Antilles rise to 1974 m at Pico Turquino, in eastern Cuba, 2256 m in the Blue Mountains of Jamaica and 3175 m at Pico Duarte in the Dominican Republic, on Hispaniola, which is the highest peak in the region. The much smaller Lesser Antilles are situated at the interface of two tectonic plates so the volcanic landmasses in this chain soar steeply from the Caribbean Sea to heights of 1447 m at Morne Diablotin, on Dominica, and 1467 m at La Soufrière, on Guadeloupe. There are at least 17 active volcanoes (ten of which are on Dominica), between Saba in the northern Lesser Antilles and the submerged Kick 'Em Jenny volcano near Grenada in the south, and the one on Montserrat erupted in 1997, causing considerable damage to almost half of the island.

Many Caribbean islands are surrounded by tiny offshore islets and cays, as well as barrier reefs, one of which—the 225 km-long Tongue of the Ocean in the Bahamas—is the third longest on earth. The deep waters beyond the reefs reach a depth of 8648 m in the Puerto Rican Trench, north of Puerto Rico and the Virgin Islands, which is the deepest such fissure in the Atlantic Ocean. These islets, cays, reefs and deep waters support a rich and diverse marine life, from corals to seabirds and whales.

Although many islands are mountainous and well watered they are too small to support large rivers and consequently there are few estuaries in the Caribbean. However, the mangrove-lined mudflats, brackish lagoons and salt ponds present on many islands' coasts, support a wide variety of waterbirds, including, in places, numerous passage migrant and wintering shorebirds. Due to the small size and often steep terrain of many islands habitats change quickly and there is often only a matter of a few miles between coastal wetlands, beaches or cliffs through thorn scrub and woods, and coconut, coffee, fruit and, especially, sugarcane, plantations, to montane rain and/or Caribbean pine forests.

Particularly on the high Lesser Antilles the prevailing northeasterly trade winds force clouds up above the mountainous interiors, where they cool rapidly and release their rain virtually year-round, providing sufficient moisture to support montane rainforests and, on the most exposed slopes and ridges, elfin woods. The westward or leeward sides of such islands therefore lie in rain shadows and during the driest period of the year, usually January–June, the deciduous species growing in the thorn scrub and woods here shed their leaves.

Many of the most important habitats for the Caribbean's unique birds, notably the lowland woods and montane forests, have been destroyed or degraded as a result of conversion to agriculture. Only a few relatively large areas of remnant pristine vegetation survive, hence many endemic bird populations have been severely depleted. Nevertheless, given the small size of most islands, habitat diversity is still generally high, and birdlife fairly rich.

Island, Trip, Site and Day Lists

Cuba has the richest avifauna in the Caribbean. Its list of over 350 species and that of about 320 for the Bahamas are the only ones within the region to exceed 300, and only four other islands have lists which exceed 200. Jamaica is the nearest competitor with 265, followed by Puerto Rico (c. 250), the Dominican Republic (about 245) and Haiti (over 240). Way behind lie the Turks & Caicos Islands, Guadeloupe and Martinique, though around 190 species have been recorded on all three. The smaller Lesser Antilles of Dominica (c. 170) and St. Lucia (c. 160) are further behind, and Grenada (about 120) and St. Vincent (110+), at the southern end of the chain, possess even lower avian diversity.

It hardly seems fair to compare the cream of the Caribbean with the world's best country and island lists, for there are many places in the world with lists that not only exceed the best the region can muster, but also the total for the entire Caribbean. Indeed, the world's highest country list, Colombia's total of over 1,800, is well over 1,200 higher than the 600 ever recorded in the Caribbean, and even tiny Costa Rica boasts a list of around 840, nearly 250 more than the Caribbean.

As for Cuba and the Bahamas, their totals of over 300 are, however, higher than those for some other islands or archipelagos in the world, including Hawaii (275), while species lists for Jamaica (265) and Puerto Rico (about 250) match those of the Canaries (256) and Madagascar (255), and the Dominican Republic (about 245) and Haiti (over 240), which comprise the island of Hispaniola, are close behind. The small islands of the Lesser Antilles only muster totals of 100–200, but these match those for places such as the Galápagos Islands (138).

FIGURE 11: CARIBBEAN COUNTRY, ISLAND AND ARCHIPELAGO SPECIES LISTS

Country, island or archipelago
totals (approximate)

Cuba	350+
Bahamas	320
Jamaica	265
Puerto Rico	250
Dominican Republic	245
Haiti	240+
Guadeloupe	190+
Turks & Caicos Islands	190
Martinique	187
Cayman Islands	180

US Virgin Islands	180
Dominica	170
Leeward Islands	167
St. Lucia	160
Barbados	150
UK Virgin Islands	140
Grenada	120
St. Vincent	110+

Birders in search of the broadest possible range of species on a Caribbean trip should head to Cuba where 140–180 species can be seen on a short trip, although it is possible to see around 130 species on a trip combining Dominican Republic and Puerto Rico, and over 100 species on a trip to Jamaica or the Bahamas. In the Lesser Antilles, however, seeing over 50 species on a short trip to a single island may prove impossible, even on Dominica and St. Lucia where the avifauna is at the most diverse. These potential trip totals are among the lowest possible anywhere in the world, for even outside the tropics it is easy to see more than 200 species on short trips to Israel, Turkey, and Churchill and Manitoba, and in some parts of the world, especially South America and Africa, it is possible to see more during a few weeks than in a lifetime within the Caribbean. The world record species total for a month-long birding trip is 1040, set in Colombia during October 1997 by a team led by Paul Salaman. This shattered the previous best, held by a group from the Danish Ornithological Society who recorded 844 during a 27-day trip to Ecuador in 1992. The African record belongs to the trip led by Brian Finch that notched up 797 on a 25-day tour to Kenya in 1991.

Although such immense totals are usually achieved only by organised tours led by leaders equipped with immense experience and the latest high-tech tape-players to tease out the many skulkers, the great advantage of birding in the Caribbean, where so much more is known about the whereabouts of the birds, is that a thoroughly prepared team of independent birders can see almost every species possible, including the endemics, in their chosen destination.

The richest area for birds in the Caribbean is the Zapata Peninsula in Cuba, where over 170 species have been recorded and it is possible to see as many as 100 species within a single day. Over 100 species have also been recorded at many other sites in the region, including the Península de Guanahacabibes (about 150) in extreme western Cuba, around the Étang Saumâtre in Haiti, and at several sites with coastal wetlands in the Caribbean archipelago, where resident birds are joined by a wide variety of waterbirds during passage periods and in winter, even on the smaller islands. A good example of such a site is Salt River Bay, on the island of St. Croix, in the US Virgin Islands, where, during winter, it is possible to see over 75 species within a day. Nevertheless, Caribbean site lists are poor in comparison with many other parts of the world, a result of the islands' geographical isolation and small size among other factors. The Caribbean's top-site lists cannot begin to compete with the best in the world, such as in South America, where the richest area for birds, Manu Biosphere Reserve in Peru and adjacent Madidi National Park in Bolivia, supports an incredible 1000 species. Elsewhere, in Africa, well over 500 species have been recorded at

Ruwenzori National Park in Uganda, and in Asia, almost 480 species have occurred at Chitwan National Park in Nepal.

As for day lists don't expect to tot up many more than 30–40 species on the smaller islands of the Lesser Antilles such as Antigua or Grenada, although up to 50 species have been seen in a day at Barbuda. Larger totals are possible on the higher, more forested Lesser Antilles, such as Dominica and St. Lucia, but even an exceptional day on Andros in the Bahamas, where 100 may be possible, or on the Zapata Peninsula, in Cuba, where over 100 species has been achieved on a single occasion, will seem pathetic compared to the best day totals in the world. For example, it is possible to record over 180 species during a day's walk at Bharatpur in India or Lake Naivasha in Kenya, and even these impressive totals can be considered paltry when compared to the 331 species recorded during 24 hours at Manu Biosphere Reserve in Peru, in 1986—the world's top single-site day list! Even this is not the world day-list record, which belongs to Kenya, where with the aid of a small aircraft, a team recorded 342 species on a November day, also in 1986. Both of these amazing totals are on a par with Cuba's total list, let alone the Zapata Peninsula, but in the Caribbean it's a case of never mind the list enjoy the quality. During a day's walk around Playa Larga, at the base of the Zapata Peninsula, for example, it is possible to compile a day list that includes such memorable birds as Grey-headed, Key West, Ruddy and Blue-headed Quail-Doves, Bee Hummingbird, Cuban Trogon, Cuban Tody and a host of beautiful wintering New World warblers.

Endemic Species

Regions of the world with concentrations of restricted-range birds have been identified as Endemic Bird Areas (EBAs) in BirdLife International's *Endemic Bird Areas: Priorities for Biodiversity Conservation* (A. J. Stattersfield *et al.* 1998). Of the world total of 221 EBAs, the Caribbean has five, four more than North America, which shares its one EBA with northwest Mexico, but far fewer than South America, where there are an amazing 55. The five EBAs in the Caribbean are Cuba and the Bahamas, Jamaica, Hispaniola, Puerto Rico, and the Lesser Antilles.

A total of 159 species are endemic to the Caribbean, 108 of which are confined to single countries, islands or archipelagos, and 51 more widespread forms. This total—37% of the regularly occurring species—is impressive for a group of islands in close proximity to two major landmasses, hence the Caribbean's lack of general diversity is amply compensated by its high degree of endemism. However, although there are far more endemics here than in some of the world's other major archipelagos, including the Solomon Islands (70), there are substantially fewer than in the Philippines (185) and the Caribbean cannot compete with the most endemic-rich island on the planet; New Guinea, which possesses an amazing 330 endemics.

While many of the world's smaller islands and archipelagos may support more regularly occurring species than similar-sized landmasses in the Caribbean, the region's islands do support comparable numbers of endemics. For example: Jamaica and Hispaniola, which have the highest number of single-island endemics in the region, possess the same number of endemics as Java and Bali (28). The Lesser Antilles are on a par with the Galápagos (25) and Fiji (25), and Cuba's total of 24 is one greater than that of Sri Lanka (23). Puerto Rico has one less endemic than Taiwan (14), and the same number as Tasmania (13). Even the tiny islands of St. Lucia (three), Dominica (two) and St. Vincent (two) boast more endemics than Trinidad and Tobago (one), where the avifauna lacks a high endemic component to its avifauna due its close proximity to South America.

During a trip to a single island, country or archipelago within the Caribbean the highest number of the region's endemics can be found in Haiti (44), closely followed by Cuba (43), the Dominican Republic (43) and Jamaica (40). By combining the Dominican Republic with Puerto Rico (28), as many birders do, it is possible to see as many as 63. In the Lesser Antilles the best islands to visit for the highest possible number of Caribbean endemics are St. Lucia (20) and Dominica (19), both of which support ten of the 14 Lesser Antilles endemics which are not confined to single islands.

In order to see all 25 of the species restricted to the Lesser Antilles, 11 of which are confined to single islands, it is necessary to visit Montserrat (one), Guadeloupe (one), Dominica (two), Martinique (one), St. Lucia (three), St. Vincent (two) and Grenada (one). At the other end of the scale, the islands supporting the fewest Caribbean endemics are Martinique (17, including ten of the 14 widespread Lesser Antilles endemics), the Bahamas (16), Guadeloupe (15), St. Vincent (13), the Cayman Islands (nine) and, at the bottom of the pile, Barbados, with a paltry three.

FIGURE 12: THE 51 ENDEMIC BIRDS OF THE CARIBBEAN NOT RESTRICTED TO SINGLE ISLANDS

Widespread (6)

West Indian Whistling-Duck*	Bahamas, Greater Antilles, Cayman Islands, Virgin Islands, Antigua and Barbuda
Loggerhead Kingbird	Bahamas (northern), Greater Antilles and Cayman Islands
Bahama Mockingbird	Bahamas, cays off northern Cuba and southern Jamaica
Rufous-throated Solitaire	Jamaica, Hispaniola, Dominica, Martinique, St. Lucia and St. Vincent
Red-legged Thrush	Bahamas (northern), Cuba, Cayman Islands (Cayman Brac), Hispaniola, Puerto Rico and Dominica
Antillean Euphonia	Hispaniola, Puerto Rico, Barbuda, Antigua, Guadeloupe, Dominica, Martinique, St. Lucia, St. Vincent and Grenada

Bahamas and Cuba (4)

Great Lizard-Cuckoo	Bahamas (Andros, Eleuthera and New Providence) and Cuba
Cuban Emerald	Bahamas (Grand Bahama, Abaco and Andros) and Cuba
Cuban Pewee	Bahamas (northern) and Cuba
Olive-capped Warbler	Bahamas (Grand Bahama and Abaco) and Cuba

Bahamas and Turks & Caicos Islands (1)

Bahama Woodstar   Throughout

Bahamas, Cuba and Cayman Islands (3)

Cuban Parrot*   Bahamas (Abaco and Great Inagua),
                                   Cuba and Cayman Islands (Grand
                                   Cayman and Cayman Brac)
West Indian Woodpecker   Bahamas (Abaco and San Salvador),
                                   Cuba and Cayman Islands (Grand
                                   Cayman)
La Sagra's Flycatcher   Bahamas, Cuba and Cayman Islands
                                   (Grand Cayman)

Cuba and Cayman Islands (1)

Cuban Bullfinch   Cuba and Cayman Islands (Grand
                                   Cayman)

Cuba and Turks & Caicos Islands (1)

Cuban Crow   Cuba and Turks & Caicos (North and
                                   Middle Caicos. Rare on Providen-
                                   ciales)

Cayman and Swan Islands (1)

Vitelline Warbler*   Cayman and Swan Islands (western
                                   Caribbean)

Bahamas and Greater Antilles (2)

Key West Quail-Dove   Bahamas, Cuba, Hispaniola and
                                   Puerto Rico
Greater Antillean Bullfinch   Bahamas, Jamaica and Hispaniola

Greater Antilles (3)

Plain Pigeon*   Throughout
Antillean Palm-Swift   Cuba, Jamaica and Hispaniola.
Greater Antillean Grackle   Cuba, Jamaica, Hispaniola, Puerto
                                   Rico and Cayman Islands.

Cuba and Hispaniola (2)

Grey-headed Quail-Dove*   Cuba and Dominican Republic
Tawny-shouldered Blackbird   Cuba and Haiti

Jamaica and Hispaniola (4)

Vervain Hummingbird   Widespread on both islands
Greater Antillean Elaenia   Locally common on both islands
Stolid Flycatcher   Widespread on both islands
Golden Swallow*   Not reliably reported from Jamaica
                                   since the 1980s so this species may
                                   now be endemic to Hispaniola
                                   where it is still seen regularly in the
                                   Sierra de Baoruco in the southwest
                                   Dominican Republic

Jamaica and San Andrés (1)

Jamaican Oriole   The *bairdi* race endemic to the Cay-

man Islands (Grand Cayman) has
not been reported since 1967

Hispaniola, Puerto Rico and Virgin Islands (1)

Antillean Mango

Widespread on Hispaniola, local on Puerto Rico and rare on the Virgin Islands

Puerto Rico and Virgin Islands (2)

Puerto Rican Screech-Owl

Widespread on Puerto Rico but rare in the Virgin Islands

Puerto Rican Flycatcher

Widespread on Puerto Rico, but uncommon on St. John and rare on St. Thomas, Virgin Gorda and Tortola in the Virgin Islands

Puerto Rico and Lesser Antilles (5)

Bridled Quail-Dove

Puerto Rico, Virgin Islands, Barbuda, Antigua, St. Kitts, Nevis, Montserrat, Guadeloupe, Dominica, Martinique and St. Lucia

Green-throated Carib

Puerto Rico, Virgin Islands and throughout the Lesser Antilles

Antillean Crested Hummingbird

Puerto Rico, Virgin Islands and throughout the Lesser Antilles

Lesser Antillean Pewee

Puerto Rico, Guadeloupe, Dominica, Martinique and St. Lucia (considered to be three separate species by some taxonomists: Puerto Rican, Lesser Antillean and St. Lucia)

Adelaide's Warbler

Puerto Rico, Barbuda and St. Lucia (recently considered to be three separate species by the American Ornithologists' Union)

Lesser Antilles (14)

Lesser Antillean Swift

Guadeloupe, Dominica, Martinique, St. Lucia and St. Vincent

Purple-throated Carib

Antigua, Nevis, Montserrat, Guadeloupe, Dominica, Martinique, St. Lucia, St. Vincent and Grenada

Blue-headed Hummingbird

Dominica and Martinique

Grenada Flycatcher

St. Vincent, the Grenadines and Grenada

Lesser Antillean Flycatcher

Barbuda, Nevis, Dominica, Martinique and St. Lucia; rare on Guadeloupe

White-breasted Thrasher*

Martinique and St. Lucia

Grey Trembler

Martinique and St. Lucia

Brown Trembler

Nevis, Montserrat, Guadeloupe, Dominica, St. Lucia and St. Vincent; rare on Martinique and Grenada

Scaly-breasted Thrasher

Antigua, St. Kitts, Nevis, Montserrat, Guadeloupe, Dominica, Martinique,

	St. Lucia and St. Vincent; possibly extinct on Barbuda and Barbados, and rare on Grenada
Forest Thrush*	Montserrat, Guadeloupe and Dominica; rare on St. Lucia
Plumbeous Warbler	Guadeloupe and Dominica
Lesser Antillean Tanager	St. Vincent and Grenada
Lesser Antillean Bullfinch	Virgin Islands south to Grenada, but absent from the Grenadines
Lesser Antillean Saltator	Guadeloupe, Dominica, Martinique and St. Lucia

FIGURE 13: ENDEMIC AND NEAR-ENDEMIC TOTALS FOR THE MAIN CARIBBEAN COUNTRIES, ISLANDS and ARCHIPELAGOS

Country, island or archipelago	No. of single-island, country or archipelago endemics	No. of endemics not confined to single islands or countries (and sub-total)	No. of Caribbean near-endemics	Overall total
Hispaniola	28	17 (45)	9	54
Jamaica	28	12 (40)	8	48
Lesser Antilles	25	13 (38)	12	50
Cuba	24	19 (43)	8	51
Puerto Rico	13	15 (28)	10	38
St. Lucia	3	17 (20)	8	28
Bahamas	2	14 (16)	9	25
Dominica	2	17 (19)	9	28
St. Vincent	2	11 (13)	7	20
Grenada	1	9 (10)	7	17
Guadeloupe	1	14 (15)	10	25
Haiti	1 (28)	16 (44)	9	53
Martinique	1	16 (17)	9	26
Montserrat	1	8 (9)	8	17
San Andrés	1	1 (2)	6	8
Barbados	0	3 (3)	7	10
Cayman Islands	0	9 (9)	9	18
Dominican Republic	0 (27–28)	16 (43–44)		
Dominican Republic and Puerto Rico	39	23 (63)	11	74

FIGURE 14: LESSER ANTILLEAN ENDEMIC TOTALS

Island	Single-island endemics (11)	More widespread endemics (14)	Overall total (25)
St. Lucia	3	10	13
Dominica	2	10	12
Martinique	1	10	11
Guadeloupe	1	9	10
St. Vincent	2	7	9
Grenada	1	6	7
Montserrat	1	5	6
Barbados	0	2	2

In addition to the 159 species endemic to the Caribbean, the region also supports ten endemic genera: *Cyanolimnas* (Zapata Rail*), *Starnoenas* (Blue-headed Quail-Dove*), *Saurothera* (lizard-cuckoos), *Hyetornis* (Chestnut-bellied and Bay-breasted* Cuckoos), *Trochilus* (streamer-tails), *Cinclocerthia* (tremblers), *Calyptophilus* (chat-tanagers), *Melopyrrha* (Cuban Bullfinch), *Euneornis* (Orangequit) and *Loxigilla* (other Caribbean bullfinches).

Near-Endemic Species

Eighteen species are nearly endemic to the Caribbean, including three that breed only here and two with breeding ranges virtually restricted to the region. A few of these, notably Scaly-naped Pigeon, Thick-billed Vireo and Cuban Martin, are difficult to get to see elsewhere, and the best place in the Caribbean to see them is Cuba. The islands with the highest number of near-endemics are the Lesser Antilles (14), followed by Puerto Rico, the Virgin Islands and Guadeloupe, all of which support ten. The remainder of the major islands support between nine and seven.

FIGURE 15: THE 18 NEAR-ENDEMIC BIRDS OF THE CARIBBEAN

Caribbean Coot*	Hispaniola and Puerto Rico, has also bred on Antigua, Martinique and Guadeloupe; rare on Jamaica and Virgin Islands. Also occurs in southeast USA, Trinidad, Curaçao and Venezuela
White-crowned Pigeon	Bahamas, Cuba, Jamaica, Hispaniola, Puerto Rico, Cayman Islands, Virgin Islands, Anguilla, Antigua, San Andrés and Providencia; rare on Guadeloupe. Also occurs on the Florida Keys, in the southeast USA, and islands off Belize and Mexico
Scaly-naped Pigeon	Cuba, Hispaniola, Puerto Rico and

	most of the Lesser Antilles. Also occurs on islands off north Venezuela
Zenaida Dove	Throughout. Also occurs in Florida, and on the coast and associated islands of the Yucatán Peninsula, Mexico
Caribbean Dove	Jamaica, Cayman Islands and San Andrés, and introduced to New Providence, Bahamas. Also occurs in southeast Mexico, and on islands offshore from there to north Honduras
Caribbean Elaenia	Cayman Islands, Puerto Rico and Lesser Antilles, and rare on Providencia and San Andrés. Also occurs on islands off the Yucatán Peninsula (Mexico), Belize and north Venezuela
Pearly-eyed Thrasher	Bahamas (central and southern), Beata Island (off Hispaniola), Puerto Rico and Lesser Antilles south to St. Lucia. Also occurs on Bonaire off north Venezuela
Thick-billed Vireo	Bahamas, Turks & Caicos Islands, some cays off north Cuba, Cayman Islands, Île de la Tortue (off north Haiti), Islas Providencia and Santa Catalina. Also occurs on islands off east Nicaragua
Yucatan Vireo	Cayman Islands (Grand Cayman). Also occurs in coastal Belize, Honduras and southeast Mexico
Kirtland's Warbler*	Winters solely in the Bahamas and the Turks & Caicos Islands; breeds in Michigan, USA
Northern Stripe-headed Tanager	Bahamas, Cuba and Cayman Islands (Grand Cayman). Also occurs on Isla Cozumel, off Yucatán Peninsula, Mexico
Black-faced Grassquit	Throughout, except Cayman Islands and occurs on just one island off Cuba. Also occurs in South America
Carib Grackle	Lesser Antilles from Anguilla south to Grenada. Also occurs in adjacent South America

(Several races belonging to the *petechia* group of Yellow Warbler, collectively known as 'Golden Warbler', which is also nearly endemic to the Caribbean, occur throughout the region, as well as on Isla Cozumel, off the Yucatán Peninsula, Mexico, and the northern coast and associated islands of Venezuela)

Breeding Endemics

Black-capped Petrel*	Breeds early November to mid-May,

	mainly December–February, in mountains of southeast Haiti, Dominican Republic and probably Dominica. Also occurs along Gulf Stream off eastern USA, mainly April to October
Antillean Nighthawk	Present March–October, mainly May–August, in the Bahamas, Greater Antilles and Virgin Islands. Probably winters in South America
Cuban Martin	Present on Cuba late January–October, mainly March–September. Probably winters in South America

Breeding Near-Endemics

Caribbean Martin	Present on Jamaica, Hispaniola, Puerto Rico and Lesser Antilles January–September. Also breeds on Tobago and probably winters in South America
Black-whiskered Vireo	Throughout and present year-round on Hispaniola and the Lesser Antilles, but only February–August on Bahamas, Cuba, Jamaica, Puerto Rico and Cayman Islands. Also occurs in extreme southeastern USA and northern South America

Exploration

Fred Sladen is the only person who has made it widely known that he has seen over 400 species in the Caribbean. He had amassed an amazing 409 by the end of 2000, enough to keep his major competitors, few of which have seen over 350 species in the region, at bay for a while. Those keen to add the little-known and rarely seen species to their Caribbean lists, or those more interested in birding off the beaten track than compiling such a list, will be busy planning future trips to the region's remoter areas, having undertaken extensive and painstaking research into the old records and habitat preferences of certain species, and present-day distribution of the relevant habitats.

Surprisingly for such a supposedly well-known region remote and rarely visited areas do still exist, especially in Haiti, where birds such as Ridgway's Hawk*, a Hispaniola endemic, may be easier to find than in the adjacent Dominican Republic where it is very rare. Even on regularly visited islands it may be possible to shock the birding world. Take Jamaica for example, where the endemic *caribbaea* race of Black-capped Petrel*, known as Jamaican Petrel*, is believed to be extinct, but could still breed in remote cliffs high in the Blue and John Crow Mountains, and perhaps even the Jamaican Poorwill, the last specimen of which was collected in 1866, could have escaped detection in the dry limestone woods of the southern lowlands, particularly in the Hellshire Hills. Puerto Rican Nightjar* was known only from a single specimen, taken in 1888, and was presumed extinct for over 70 years prior to its rediscovery in 1961. Then there is Cuba, where, despite several unsuccessful attempts since the last confirmed sighting in 1987, someone bold and adventurous enough to scour the remotest forested valleys in the far east of the island could still be stunned by a magnificent Ivory-billed Woodpecker*. Rarely visited rugged terrain even exists on some of the small islands in the Lesser Antilles, where intrepid birders may wish to check if the critically endangered Black-capped Petrel* has returned to its old breeding haunts on Dominica and Guadeloupe. Those interested in rediscovery may also wish to head for the interior of St. Lucia, where the endemic Semper's Warbler* has not been seen since 1961.

The chances of finding a new species in the Caribbean appear slim, although Cameron Kepler and Kenneth Parkes managed to do so as recently as 1971 when they described Elfin-woods Warbler*. It is highly unlikely but birders who make time for extensive explorations in the Caribbean could return home with news of something previously overlooked. Perhaps a very drab vireo, or maybe even something totally outrageous like a brilliant new quail-dove. It's possible.

CONSERVATION

Central America

Some information concerning conservation and protected areas is given in the individual country accounts. Though all of the nations of Central America have established conservation programmes and various reserves and parks, the area as a whole has not been well treated by the 20th Century. Huge areas of forest are gone—and continue to disappear—while marshland and savanna are frequently under threat from the spread of agriculture. The driving force for the bulk of this destruction is a burgeoning human population; in the early 20th Century the population of Mexico was about 13 million, at its end, almost 100 million. In the face of such growth it is almost remarkable that so much good habitat survives, but the disagreeable fact remains that the flora and fauna are a poor shadow of what our grandfathers could have found. It is significant that the country with the smallest population and lowest population density—Belize—has the largest proportion of protected areas, while that with the highest population density—El Salvador—has the greatest amount of habitat destruction.

Having said this, readers of this book and travellers in Central America will still be impressed by the extensive areas of wild country, or at least excellent wildlife habitat, remaining. Visitors who study wildlife are ambassadors for conservation; for by providing sources of income to local people, through using local hotels and businesses, hiring local people and paying park entrance fees (sometimes even irregular ones) they give an incentive to local people to preserve areas from destruction.

Caribbean

Until the 16th Century the Caribbean islands had been inhabited for over 1000 years by Arawak and then Carib Indians. The vast majority of these people lived and farmed in the coastal lowlands, so the island interiors were still densely vegetated when the Europeans arrived. These invaders wiped out most of the native inhabitants and by the 1800s had destroyed much of the remaining natural vegetation as well. By the end of the 20th Century over 80% of the original forest cover on Cuba and over 60% on Hispaniola had been cleared, mainly for vast plantations of sugarcane. However, such devastation is not only a thing of the past. Even in the mid-1990s the deforestation rate on Jamaica was 5.3% per annum, one of the highest in the world. Those who write tourist brochures take great care not to inform potential customers that vast areas of natural vegetation in the Caribbean have been destroyed or degraded, and that much of what survives does so only because it grows on the least accessible steep mountain slopes and ridges.

Deforestation, together with hunting and trapping, are the major reasons for extinctions within the Caribbean since the 16th Century, including such beautiful birds as Cuban Macaw, and these factors, combined with the continued loss and degradation of habitats, are the main reasons why 64 of the extant bird species that occur in the region are now listed as threatened or near-threatened with extinction by the respected international conservation organisation, BirdLife International.

Other factors that have led to so many birds declining to critically low levels include: wetland drainage; charcoal production; poor forestry management and agricultural practices, leading to such problems as overgrazing and desertification; the introduction of alien predators (the endemic avifauna has evolved in the absence of terrestrial predators and therefore lack the ability to survive the effects of introduced species such as Small Indian Mongoose); increasing numbers of tourists and the development of resorts to accommodate them; damage to reefs and the subsequent decline in marine life that sustains the region's seabirds; pollution (intensive spraying to control mosquitoes is widespread and may be partially responsible for the almost complete absence of insectivorous birds on New Providence in the Bahamas); trapping, partly for the international pet trade; and shooting, which, especially on Barbados, Guadeloupe and Martinique, has reduced numbers of waterfowl, shorebirds, pigeons and doves, to fractions of their former levels.

There are many problems then and most need solving swiftly, for they are particularly poignant in this sensitive region where the vast majority of species threatened with extinction are island endemics, which mostly exist in small, isolated populations. Lose these and the species is gone forever. One reason why local authorities need to act fast is because the islands on which these species survive are subject to regular hurricanes and volcanic eruptions, which can destroy large areas of remaining natural habitat in a few hours. It is vitally important therefore not only to maintain bird populations at their highest possible levels, but also to conserve as much habitat in as many different places as possible, so there is a higher chance of some individual birds and some habitat surviving such natural disasters, and therefore the potential for the species to recover.

Natural phenomena aside, the main reason why the Caribbean's unique avifauna has and continues to be depleted is because of over population resulting, primarily, in the spread of housing developments and agricultural encroachment. Thus, the simple solution to virtually all of the problems that have led to the decline of so many birds in the Caribbean is to reverse resident human population growth and control visitor numbers. However, this appears impossible and indeed undesirable to some governments, who still believe population growth equals economic growth and that economic growth reduces poverty. In the future they will hopefully realise that these factors do not necessarily go hand-in-hand, and in the meantime under-funded local and global conservation organisations are desperately trying to save what little remains of the region's natural resources, with a variety of small-scale projects that include: campaigns to protect more areas; introduce environmental taxes, which can be used to purchase and manage protected areas; increase environmental awareness; implement existing, and introduce new, legislation, particularly with regard to development, hunting and trapping; undertake vital research into the requirements of individual species; and to encourage more ecotourism rather than provide even more resorts for sun-seekers.

Tourism is currently the most important source of revenue in the Caribbean and it is likely to be so for the foreseeable future, yet the potential of ecotourism has yet to be tapped. If it can be demonstrated to local people that birds are just as valuable to their local economies as, say, hunting, poor forestry or overgrazing, via the injection of visiting birders' cash, then they may be persuaded to manage their natural resources accordingly. An excellent model of the sustainable utilization of natural resources for the benefit of wildlife, the local people and visitors is provided by St. Lucia, where due to a combination of initiatives put in place by the island's government in consultation with the RARE Centre for Tropical Conservation, the population of the endemic St. Lucia Parrot* rose from about 100 in 1976 to approximately 450 in 1998, and the number of visitors keen to experience the natural environment on the island increased dramatically, providing a significant boost to the local economy without the need for substantial new development and agricultural encroachment. Hopefully, other islands in the Caribbean will realise the potential for sustainably exploiting their dwindling natural resources for ecotourism, and follow St. Lucia's example.

We hope this book, in its own small way, will encourage as many birders as possible to visit as many sites as possible in Central America and the Caribbean, and, ultimately, help those birders not only to enjoy the region's birds but also to contribute to their conservation. Independent travellers can make a much larger contribution to local economies than those on package tours, so, when visiting any of the sites described in this book please utilize local accommodation, local guides, local transport and local restaurants, and ensure local people know why you are there and why more birders will follow.

GENERAL TIPS

The following words of advice are by no means intended to be comprehensive. They are little more than a selection of miscellaneous points resulting from personal experience and birding tales shared between friends. However, they may help maximize the enjoyment and success of a birding trip to Central America and the Caribbean.

The best birding trips almost invariably result from extensive research and months of planning. Before embarking on a trip pinpoint the sites to visit, whether it's because they are where you are most likely to locate those species you primarily wish to see, because they are generally the best for birds, or because they are simply wonderful wild places worth birding. If a trip is to be successful, in terms of seeing the top birds in the best places for example, it is crucial to allocate sufficient time to each site and not to attempt too much, as this may seriously hamper your enjoyment of the trip, let alone its success. Once you have decided which sites to concentrate on and how long you wish to spend at each it is time to draft an itinerary. Great care needs to be taken on this and the first draft is very unlikely to be the last. Alter, adjust and adapt it because the more finely tuned the itinerary is the more likely the trip will be enjoyable and successful.

Before departure it is also important to do as much homework as possible. Read about how each species looks, sounds and behaves, which habitats they favour, and, perhaps most importantly, study the plates in the relevant field guides, so that even if you don't know the name of what you are looking at when you finally see it at least you may be able to remember which plate it is on!

In the Caribbean it is possible to see many single-island endemics within a day or a few days on each island, especially in the Lesser Antilles, so many visiting birders combine two or more islands on a single trip, making full use of the various airpasses on offer from companies such as LIAT. Though local people may humourously suggest that this acronym stands for 'Leave Island Any Time', to describe the vagaries of its service, its airpasses do enable several of the Lesser Antilles to be covered within a short space of time and at reasonable cost.

Though many good birdwatching sites can be reached by public transport, to access the majority of areas, especially in the early morning, a vehicle is very helpful. For visitors arriving by air this usually means hiring locally. Be sure to check the vehicle thoroughly, even when hiring from an international company: check brakes, lights, tyres (including the spare), jack etc. as well as the insurance situation. Ensure that any existing damage is carefully noted. Those driving in Latin America will also quickly become aware that the legendary Hispanic courtesy evaporates instantly behind a steering wheel; not for nothing are there plaintive and forlorn signs on Mexican roads stating, 'Esteemed señor motorist, traffic lights are not there just for decoration'.

Once in the field, walk quietly and slowly, using vegetation as cover for patient stalking, and, especially in dense forests, scan for birds with your eyes, because they have a broader field of view and a greater depth of focus than binoculars. These well-known basic field skills are all too easily forgotten in the frenzy of new and exciting birds.

47

Early morning is usually the best time for birding anywhere in the world and the Central America and Caribbean region is no exception, especially in the hot lowlands where there is often a lull in avian activity from mid-morning to late afternoon, during which time heat haze can spoil birding as well. The middle of the day is therefore a good time to move between sites, or, if this is inappropriate, to take a siesta before a late afternoon walk, the evening owl and nightjar search, and the appropriate celebration of another great day in the field. Some fanatical birders argue that it is still possible to see many birds around midday, especially given some shade or water, or in areas where it is relatively cool throughout the day, such as in damp montane forests, and that the hours of darkness, after the owls and nightjars have been seen, are best for moving from site to site. Travelling at night can be dangerous in some regions, especially where roads are bad, but overnight drives do help to avoid what may be numerous time-consuming stops for birds which are usually easy to see at the main sites. They also keep accommodation costs down and may produce a few otherwise unexpected birds and mammals. However, while a couple of night drives may save some money and be good fun, too many may result in over-tiredness that can take the edge off your enjoyment of the whole trip. It's not much fun returning home after a trip full of glorious moments only to discover that you can't remember them clearly because you were too tired at the time.

Forest birding can be very frustrating and several hours may pass without a decent view of a single bird, although many may be heard. However, roaming flocks of feeding birds, known as waves, are a thrilling feature of forest birding in Central America and the Caribbean, and can make all those empty hours seem a small price to pay. Bird waves often appear suddenly and disappear in what seems like a flash, but try sticking with the birds as long as possible, even after it appears that they have all moved on, because the stragglers can sometimes prove to be the more unusual species. The sudden unexpected appearance of a forest-floor skulker on the trail or track in front of you may be just as exciting as a bird wave, especially after a lengthy spell of patient stalking. Some shy species, such as quail-doves, will 'freeze' on being surprised and if you stay still for a few minutes will usually resume feeding, often in full view. Some otherwise shy species, notably cotingas, often perch on exposed, sunlit branches late in the day, to preen and warm up before going to roost. At least an hour before dusk therefore it may be best to leave the forest interior in favour of the forest edge or, better still, a viewpoint overlooking a forested slope.

Cotingas, along with pigeons, parrots, hummingbirds, barbets, toucans, thrashers, thrushes and tanagers are good examples of species that are attracted to flowering and fruiting trees. On first impression such trees may appear devoid of avian life, as the birds feed quietly, but by waiting in places with such trees they can slowly come alive. In some cases there may be so many birds visiting a particular tree or trees on a regular basis, that watching these for a couple of hours will probably prove more productive than a long, slow forest hike, or a frantic wander around a large area of forest.

Tracking down every unknown call is essential, but more often than not requires the patience of a saint. It is easy to use tape play-back machines in such a situation, but this devious birding method, which requires very little field skill, is inappropriate for use with threatened or near-threatened species (not knowing the call means it could be such a species), if any species at all. Taping birds out interrupts their behaviour, distracting them from defending their breeding and feeding territories, and inevitably affects food intake, a potentially lethal outcome if the bird is busy feeding young. Furthermore, birds that eventually stop responding to tapes may also stop responding to real intruders, in which case their food supply could be diminished and this may ultimately lead to them leaving the area altogether. Trying to clap eyes on a bird that you can hear but not see is extremely frustrating, but surely there is more joy and satisfaction to be gained from seeing the bird after a long, hard search than by standing next to a tape player waiting for the unfortunate creature to come and peck at it? Good birders don't need tapes: they use their own knowledge of birds' habitats and habits, and their field skills, to track down and watch them.

Throughout the region it is usually hot, sunny and rather humid in the lowlands, but cool and often damp in the forested mountains, so take a sun/rain hat and/or an umbrella. The latter may prove particularly useful in montane forests where many tanagers for example may be active during wet weather, but umbrellas can be awkward to hold when using binoculars so a light waterproof with a top-class hood may be a better option in the highlands. Although some birders swear by brightly coloured waterproofs and umbrellas, because they attract birds such as hummingbirds, others insist such clothing is a magnet to insects such as mosquitoes. Airtight, waterproof optical equipment is essential for birding in humid or damp conditions, and binoculars with very close focus are also invaluable in both dense lowland and montane forests, where birds of the understorey, such as antbirds, often appear at close range.

For most physically fit people the altitudes found in Central America will present few problems, though you may find yourself short of breath at times. On the highest mountains (e.g. Popocatépetl in Mexico) it is possible to acquire altitude sickness; the recourse is to cease vigorous physical activity and return to lower altitudes as soon as possible. At high altitudes severe sunburn can be a major problem, and appropriate clothing and protection should be worn.

English is not widely spoken in rural Central America (with the exception of Belize) hence a basic grasp of Spanish is enormously useful for conducting day-to-day affairs and in establishing a rapport with local people. It is a language of great beauty and subtlety, but for English-speaking people it has one disadvantage; it is a very easy language to speak *badly*. To speak elegantly and correctly requires a major dedication of time and a good ear, but Central Americans are, in the experience of this author, immensely courteous people who rarely snigger at the linguistic inabilities of the foreigner. We have also found them to be enormously kind and helpful, like the barber in Ciudad Mante who, when asked for directions, promptly closed his shop, jumped on his motorbike and guided DB through miles of unmarked streets to the Pan-American Highway.

Most, if not all, of the countries, islands and archipelagos in Central America and the Caribbean are some of the safest places in the world to go birding. Apart from petty crime the most likely form of danger is from local drivers, many of whom always seem to be in a hurry, whether they are on a straight, wide road in the lowlands or a narrow, twisting road with terrifying drop-offs and blind bends in the highlands. So keep your eyes on the road rather than potential new birds and you should survive to tell tales of brilliant birding in Central America and the Caribbean.

GLOSSARY

2WD: Two-wheel-drive vehicle.

4WD: Four-wheel-drive vehicle.

Afforestation: The planting of trees in areas not previously forested.

Cloud Forest: A forest often enveloped in damp cloud but which may be situated within an otherwise dry region.

Elfin Woods: High-altitude temperate areas of stunted trees, often on exposed ridges.

Endemic: Species or subspecies that occur only in specified areas. For example, the Bee Hummingbird occurs only on the island of Cuba and nowhere else on earth, so it is endemic to Cuba.

Gallery Forest/Woodland: Waterside (riparian) forest and woodland, usually where areas with trees merge into more open areas.

Re-afforestation: The planting of trees in areas that have been deforested.

Secondary: This term normally refers to forested or wooded areas that have been cleared but have since partly regenerated, albeit usually in fragments alongside newly established land-uses.

MAPS

Before embarking on a birding trip it is essential to obtain the best maps available of your intended destination. Detailed maps of Central America and the Caribbean can be obtained from various outlets, but to avoid missing the best available and to track down those covering more remote areas contact the specialist map sellers listed under Useful Addresses on p. 414.

Maps in this book are simplified, as they are intended to provide an impression of (i) how the major birding sites are distributed within a country, archipelago or island, and (ii) where the best places for birds are at individual sites, and how to reach them. Each country, island or archipelago account has a map at the beginning that shows the location of the major cities and towns, roads and birding sites. In some accounts there may be maps of regions within countries. These are intended to show how 'bunches' of sites are distributed and how a birder might tackle them. Most major site accounts are also accompanied by more detailed maps, with the location of the best tracks and trails etc.

When in the field, birders are more interested in finding and watching birds than making detailed notes on their location, notably distances and directions, so although every effort has been made to make the site maps in this book as precise as possible many are not perfect.

The **map symbols** used are as follows:

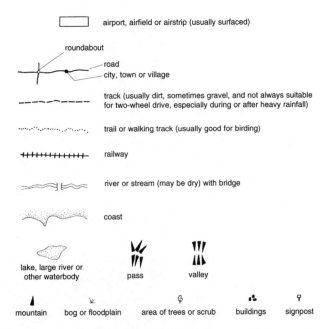

As the main purpose of the maps is to help birders orient themselves and to reach the best sites as easily as possible, more often than not 'direction-pointers' such as buildings, roads and rivers, and on-site detail such as trails, have been exaggerated, and are not usually drawn to scale.

It is also important to remember that details change. Signs may have fallen down or been removed, new signposts erected, trails may have become tracks, tracks become roads, buildings demolished or erected, marshes, lakes and rivers may have dried up or been drained, rivers may even have changed course, good habitats ploughed up, woods and forests felled, and new woodland planted, etc. Furthermore, some sites may no longer exist by the time you use these maps, so if you arrive at a site which looks totally different to your perception as a result of reading this book, or that site no longer exists, don't blame birders who have been before you or us, blame the planet's ever increasing human population.

BELIZE

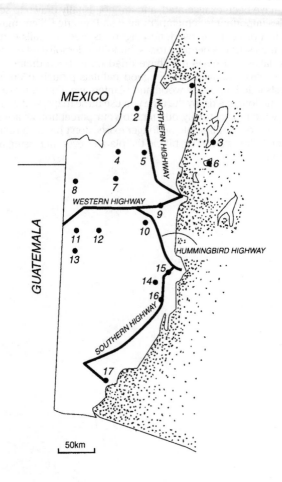

MEXICO

GUATEMALA

NORTHERN HIGHWAY

WESTERN HIGHWAY

HUMMINGBIRD HIGHWAY

SOUTHERN HIGHWAY

50km

1 Shipstern Nature Reserve
2 Blue Creek Rice Fields and the
   road to San Felipe
3 Ambergris Cay
4 Lamanai Outpost Lodge
5 Crooked Tree Wildlife Sanctuary
6 Cay Caulker (Cay Corker)
7 Hill Bank
8 Chan Chich Lodge and La Milpa
   Field Station
9 Belize Zoo and Monkey Bay

10 Blue Hole National Park
11 Mountain Pine Ridge
12 Pook's Hill
13 Caracol Natural Reservation
14 Cockscomb Basin Wildlife Sanc-
    tuary
15 Sites off the Southern Highway
    south of Dangriga
16 BFREE Protected Area and
    Bladen Reserve
17 Punta Gorda area

INTRODUCTION

Summary

Belize (former British Honduras) is unique in Central America: the only Commonwealth country in the isthmus, it is English-speaking (albeit with a dialect, when spoken rapidly, that is remarkably opaque to British and North Americans alike) and culturally has more in common with its Caribbean neighbours than with the republics that surround it. Faunistically it is very definitely Central American. The population is relatively small and concentrated in the lowlands, especially in the Belize River drainage. People of African extraction form the largest element of the population, but in some areas there is a substantial proportion of Mayan descent.

Size

Belize is approximately 23,000 km^2 in size, that is, about one-tenth the size of the United Kingdom; Mexico is 80 times larger and Texas 30 times.

Getting Around

Reasonable bus services link all the major towns and most villages, though these are run by a confusing array of companies. Some of the locations listed here are not served by public transport. Cars may be hired in Belize City. In many cases, four-wheel drive is desirable and for numerous locations essential during the wet season.

Accommodation and Food

Adequate food and accommodation are available in most towns. Prices tend to be rather higher than in Mexico or Guatemala, but are still very reasonable by North American or European standards. There are a number of ecologically oriented lodges that are either expensive or very expensive.

Health and Safety

Malaria is present throughout the country, at all altitudes and in urban as well as rural areas; suitable prophylactics are strongly recommended. Vaccinations against hepatitis A and typhoid are advised. Travellers arriving from areas where yellow fever is endemic must have a valid vaccination certificate.

Crime is a problem in urban areas, especially Belize City and Dangriga. In areas where tourists congregate, touts and drug dealers are abundant; the best technique to deter the latter is to thank them politely but say that you already have everything you need. A favourite scam is for someone to start telling you irrelevant information and then demand a 'guide fee'. Recently, the authorities have taken steps to discourage this type of harassment of visitors.

Drinking water in most areas is reliable, but in some rural localities the standard precautions should be taken. Police may be reached via any telephone by dialing 220-22.

Climate and Timing

Temperatures in Belize are not subject to very great annual variation; in Belize City mean daily maxima and minima are around 34°C and 22°C. Temperatures at higher elevations are slightly more moderate but there are no distinct altitudinal variations as in neighbouring Guatemala. Rainfall, in contrast, is distinctly seasonal; the dry season lasts from December or January to May, with 90% of rainfall in the other seven months. Within Belize there is considerable variation in the amount of precipitation, which increases southwards; at the northern border with Mexico annual rainfall is approximately 150 cm, in parts of the south it exceeds 500 cm. The most popular time to visit is late winter, when many North American migrants are present and rainfall is low. However, productive visits can be made at any time of year.

Habitats

In contrast to all neighbouring countries, Belize exhibits relatively little altitudinal variation, the highest elevations being a little over 1,100 m. There is thus much less altitudinally based habitat diversity than in, for example, Guatemala. Nevertheless there is a considerable variety of habitat types, including high humid forest (not, properly speaking, rainforest, as many of the trees are deciduous), dry tropical forest in the north, open pine forest (more properly pine-savanna) on sandy soils, as well as mangrove and savanna swamps, both fresh water and brackish. Offshore is a very extensive and beautiful system of small islands and cays (pronounced 'keys'), some holding major seabird colonies. There are very large areas of highly modified habitats, from rice-paddies to regenerating second-growth forest.

Conservation

Belize protects a greater proportion of its land area than any other country in the world; 40% is delimited as National Parks, Wildlife Sanctuaries or various types of reserve. In some cases enforcement against encroachment and illegal hunting is a problem.

Bird Families

Sixty-five families have been recorded in Belize. The two with the largest number of species recorded (over 40 each) are tyrant flycatchers and New World warblers; but whereas three-quarters of the flycatchers breed in the country, only six species of warbler do so.

Bird Species

Primarily due to its single coastline and lack of high mountains, Belize supports far fewer species than Guatemala or Honduras, with around 560 recorded, of which a little over 300 nest.

Endemics

Belize has no endemics, but shares with Mexico and Guatemala about 12 Yucatán Peninsular endemics, including such species as Ocellated Turkey*, Yucatan Poorwill, Yucatan Nightjar and Yucatan Jay.

Expectations

A well-planned trip to Belize can be expected to produce between 200 and 300 species.

SHIPSTERN NATURE RESERVE

An extensive area of saltwater lagoons and islands, some with large breeding colonies of Wood Stork and several species of heron; the area also has some interesting semi-deciduous, seasonally flooded, forest. There is a good trail system.

Specialities
Jabiru (rare), Yucatan Parrot, Yucatan Poorwill, Yucatan Woodpecker, Yucatan Jay, Yucatan Flycatcher, Black Catbird*, Grey-throated Chat.

Others
Thicket Tinamou, Bare-throated Tiger-Heron, Roadside Hawk, Crane Hawk, Collared Forest-Falcon, Plain Chachalaca, Purple Gallinule, Wilson's Plover, Royal Tern, White-tipped Dove, Ferruginous Pygmy-Owl, White-fronted Parrot, Aztec Parakeet, Squirrel Cuckoo, White-bellied Emerald, Cinnamon Hummingbird, Wedge-tailed Sabrewing, Black-headed Trogon, White-necked Puffbird, Collared Araçari, Rose-throated Becard, Masked Tityra, Boat-billed Flycatcher, Mangrove Swallow, Brown Jay, Spot-breasted and White-bellied Wrens, Mangrove Vireo, Altamira and Hooded Orioles, Red-throated Ant-Tanager, Olive Sparrow, White-collared Seedeater.

Access
Shipstern is located in extreme northeast Belize, east of Corozal, and can be reached by taking the road northeast from Orange Walk to Sarteneja and turning right at the sign 7 km before reaching Sarteneja; in total, it is 59 km from Orange Walk. There are buses (about two per day with an irregular schedule) from Orange Walk to Sarteneja; enquire as to times. Near the road there is a butterfly breeding facility from which further directions can be obtained. By walking for approximately 1.5 hours through very interesting habitat the northern shore of the lagoon can be reached. Boats can be hired to give closer access to the heron and stork breeding colonies, which are located on islands within the lagoon. The southern shore has more good habitat, but it is necessary to hire a guide (at Bz$5/hour) if you wish to explore the area.

Accommodation and kitchen facilities are available (bring a sleeping bag) in the Reserve Centre, which is rustic and comfortable, but you must bring your own food. Reserve staff are extremely friendly and helpful.

BLUE CREEK RICE FIELDS AND THE ROAD TO SAN FELIPE

An area of rice fields that can be remarkably productive for waterbirds, as well as other species. Probably best worked after the rice harvest in January–March, the area makes a convenient stop on the road between Chan-Chich and La Milpa.

Specialities
Jabiru, Yucatan Bobwhite, Yucatan Parrot, Yucatan Jay, Grey-crowned Yellowthroat.

Others

Wood Stork, many herons, Muscovy Duck, Black-bellied Whistling-Duck, Lesser Yellow-headed Vulture, White-tailed, Zone-tailed, Roadside and Short-tailed Hawks, Common Black-Hawk, Laughing and Aplomado Falcons, Limpkin, Sora, White-fronted Parrot, Acorn Woodpecker, Vermilion Flycatcher, Rufous-browed Peppershrike, Scrub Euphonia, Orange-billed and Olive Sparrows, Blue Grosbeak, White-collared Seedeater.

Access

Approximately 7 km west of the petrol station in Blue Creek (which is not really a village as such, but a scattered series of settlements), and 3.5 km east of the Río Bravo turn-off in Orange Walk District. The rice fields are situated about 8 km west of San Felipe, en route to Chan-Chich, near the rice mill, which is a grey building on a rise. The rice fields are private property and, if possible, ask (at the Hillside Bed & Breakfast) for permission to enter.

Accommodation: Hillside Bed & Breakfast, which is 8 km to the west of the area, i.e. 16 km west of San Felipe (Box 2, Orange Walk; tel. 501-03-30155, fax. 30158).

AMBERGRIS CAY

One of the largest offshore islands, the cay is an extension of the coastline of Quintana Roo state, Mexico. Though extensively developed for conventional tourism, it still supports several Yucatán Peninsula endemics, and is an excellent area for North American migrants, especially warblers.

Specialities

Caribbean Dove, Black Catbird*, Yucatan Vireo.

Others

Reddish Egret, Clapper Rail, Wilson's Plover, White-crowned Pigeon, White-winged Dove, Common Ground-Dove, Cinnamon Hummingbird, Mangrove (Yellow) Warbler, Prairie Warbler (winter), Yellow-backed and Altamira Orioles.

Access

By boat (see Cay Caulker for details) and air; both from Belize City. There is accommodation to suit all tastes and budgets. A bird enthusiast owns the Caribbean Villas; day visitors are permitted. There is a tower overlooking the canopy, which can sometimes be very productive.

LAMANAI OUTPOST LODGE

An area of enormously rich and varied habitat, which includes some very interesting Mayan ruins. The Outpost Lodge, which is extremely well appointed and comfortable, is definitely not for the budget birder, but the location is unparalleled. Currently 379 species have been recorded and this list is growing through ongoing fieldwork. Visitors are able to observe field research and mist-netting activities. Day visits are possible.

The Lodge also operates nocturnal excursions, which are extremely worthwhile, offering the chance of close-up views of such species as Agami Heron, Yucatan Nightjar and Northern Potoo.

Specialities
Jabiru, Agami Heron, Yucatan Nightjar, Black Catbird*, Grey-crowned Yellowthroat.

Others
Boat-billed Heron, King Vulture, Muscovy Duck, Snail Kite, Black-collared and Crane Hawks, Great Black Hawk, Collared and Barred Forest-Falcons, Laughing Falcon, Crested Guan, Great Curassow*, Limpkin, Sungrebe, Northern Jacana, Scaled and Red-billed Pigeons, Yellow-headed*, White-fronted and White-crowned Parrots, Scarlet Macaw, Crested Owl, Northern Potoo, Black-headed, Violaceous and Slaty-tailed Trogons, Emerald Toucanet, Ivory-billed and Olivaceous Woodcreepers, Great Antshrike, Red-capped Manakin, Eye-ringed Flatbill, Stub-tailed Spadebill, Northern Royal Flycatcher, Bright-rumped Attila, Spot-breasted and White-browed Wrens, Long-billed Gnatwren, Green Shrike-Vireo, Red-legged Honeycreeper, Crimson-collared and Grey-headed Tanagers, Olive-backed, Yellow-throated and Scrub Euphonias, Orange-billed, Olive and Botteri's Sparrows, Blue Bunting, Yellow-tailed Oriole.

Access
By road, from Belize City, head north on the Northern Highway for 77 km towards Orange Walk. Approximately 6 km before Orange Walk cross a toll bridge (Bz75c). Thereafter, look for a green sign in Orange Walk marked 'Lamanai Ruins 38 miles' and keep west. Turn left at a T-junction with a cemetery in front of you. Keep on this road, passing Yo Creek, San Lazaro, Trinidad and August Pine Ridge. In San Felipe keep straight, passing a concrete marker until the road makes a sharp left. Follow this road a further 18 km to the Lodge.

It is possible to visit independently by boat, which leaves from the toll bridge over the New River, 6 km south of Orange Walk. Arrangements can be made at the Crooked Tree Wildlife Sanctuary. Typically this tends to land you in Lamanai during the heat of the day, but is shorter than the car journey.

Accommodation: for those staying at the Lodge, transport by road, boat or by light aircraft can be provided. Arrangements can be made by calling, toll-free in North America, 1-888-733-7864, or local tel. 501-2-33578, fax. 2-12061, e-mail lamanai@btl.net, web page www.lamanai.org. Postal address is Box 63, Orange Walk, Belize.

CROOKED TREE WILDLIFE SANCTUARY

An excellent area of marsh, lagoons and open pine and hardwood forest, located just off the Belize City–Orange Walk road; Jabiru breeds here, as well as many herons and marshland raptors.

Specialities
Jabiru, Agami Heron, Yucatan Parrot, Yucatan Woodpecker, Yucatan Flycatcher, Yucatan Jay.

Others
American White Pelican, Bare-throated Tiger-Heron, Boat-billed Heron, Wood Stork, Lesser Yellow-headed Vulture, Muscovy Duck, Black-bellied and Fulvous Whistling-Ducks, Snail Kite, Black-collared and Grey Hawks, Aplomado Falcon, Ruddy Crake, Grey-necked Wood-Rail, Yellow-headed Parrot*, Rufous-breasted Spinetail, Streak-headed Woodcreep er, Rose-throated Becard, Northern Beardless Tyrannulet, Worm-eating Warbler (winter), Scrub Euphonia, Olive Sparrow.

Access
Leave Belize City on the Northern Highway and 48 km north of Belize City turn left (west) on the road to Crooked Tree. Within 3 km this road becomes a causeway over the lagoon, which is an excellent area for birding. Boats with a guide may be hired in the village beyond the causeway (look for signs); these are relatively expensive but can take up to half a dozen passengers to defray costs. Glen Crawford (the son of the owner of the Paradise Inn) and Sam Tillett are excellent knowledgeable guides. Jabiru is found on the Western Lagoon.

Other areas include a trail (the 'Trogon Trail') which runs for 9 km past the Post Office, though if water levels are high not all of it may be passable. This permits access to a large marshy field where Jabiru sometimes feed. A second worthwhile area is a pine savanna that has, among other species, Yucatan Jay. To reach this area walk back towards the village from the Paradise Inn, turn right onto the first track (after about 100 m) and after 60 m turn right again onto a sandy road. Walk past several plots to the savanna. The scrubby area behind the Paradise

CROOKED TREE WILDLIFE SANCTUARY

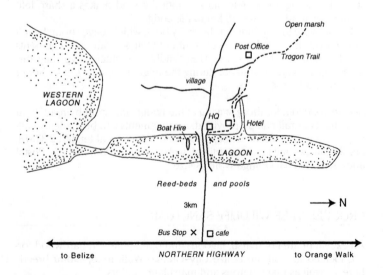

Inn holds such species as Yellow-billed Cacique and Thick-billed Seed-Finch.

There are hourly buses, from 6am onwards, from Belize City to Orange Walk and Chetumal (Batty's Bus Service, 54 E. Canal St.), which can drop you off at the Crooked Tree turn-off (make sure you get off at the *correct* turn-off!). There is also one bus daily from Belize City to Crooked Tree village (currently believed to leave at 4pm, but check).

Accommodation: locally available at the Paradise Inn, on the west side of the lagoon and north of the causeway, which is a rather basic but very friendly hotel with excellent food. Sam Tillett's Hotel is also recommended.

CAY CAULKER (CAY CORKER)

The cays off the Belize coast encompass the world's second largest coral reef and have superb scuba diving. Two cays have large colonies of seabirds, but access to these (they tend to be those farthest from shore) is usually extremely expensive. There are colonies of Magnificent Frigatebird and Brown Pelican on Man-of-War Cay, and Red-footed Booby on Half Moon Cay. Cay Caulker, while not supporting any seabird colonies, is much easier and cheaper to reach and holds a number of interesting 'Cay' species (as well as excellent snorkelling).

Specialities
Rufous-necked Wood-Rail, White-crowned Pigeon, Caribbean Elaenia, Black Catbird*, Yucatan Vireo, Bananaquit (of the race *caboti* which may be a separate species).

Others
Magnificent Frigatebird, Reddish Egret, Yellow-crowned Night-Heron, Common Black-Hawk, Sooty Tern, Cinnamon Hummingbird, Golden-fronted Woodpecker, Mangrove (Yellow) and Worm-eating (winter) Warblers, Hooded Oriole.

Access
Boats leave Belize City, from just east of the swing bridge and from one block west of the swing bridge, starting at 7am. These tend to leave only when full of passengers. The journey takes 50 minutes. There are also flights from Belize City airport. There is ample reasonable accommodation and food on the island. The northern half of the cay is most developed; at the southern end there are mangroves and littoral forest accessible from a trail south of the airstrip. The garbage dump (turn right at the airstrip) has lagoons and mangroves where Rufous-necked Wood-Rail occurs.

There is superb scuba diving and snorkelling offshore from the island; numerous boats are available for hire. One location is the Blue Hole, another Shark Ray Alley, where swimmers can get close to both sharks and rays.

HILL BANK

A large area owned and managed by the Programme for Belize (PfB), a non-profit conservation organisation. There are several different habitat types: about 70% is upland broadleaf forest, but there are also extensive areas of pine ridge and savanna, marsh (including mangrove swamp) and scrub. A total of 331 species has been recorded, but given more field work this will undoubtedly increase. Hill Bank offers a worthwhile alternative to some of the very expensive lodges located in nearby areas.

Specialities

Jabiru, Yucatan Bobwhite, Yucatan Parrot, Tody Motmot, Rose-throated Tanager.

Others

Great, Slaty-breasted, Little and Thicket Tinamous, Lesser Yellow-headed and King Vultures, White-tailed, Snail, Double-toothed and Plumbeous Kites, Crane, White, Grey and Short-tailed Hawks, Great Black Hawk, Ornate Hawk-Eagle, Laughing and Aplomado Falcons, Barred and Collared Forest-Falcons, Crested Guan, Great Curassow*, Ruddy and Uniform Crakes, Sungrebe, Pale-vented, Scaled, Red-billed and Short-billed Pigeons, Ruddy Quail-Dove, Olive-throated Parakeet, Brown-hooded, White-crowned, White-fronted, Red-lored, Mealy and Yellow-headed* Parrots, Vermiculated Screech-Owl, Mottled and Black-and-white Owls, Wedge-tailed Sabrewing, White-bellied Emerald, Black-headed, Violaceous and Slaty-tailed Trogons, American Pygmy Kingfisher, White-

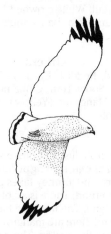

The spectacular White Hawk is a reasonably common sight in lowland rain-forest in Belize

whiskered Puffbird, Keel-billed Toucan, Black-cheeked, Chestnut-coloured, Lineated and Pale-billed Woodpeckers, Tawny-winged, Ruddy, Olivaceous, Northern Barred and Ivory-billed Woodcreepers, Dot-winged Antwren, Dusky Antbird, Ochre-bellied, Northern Royal, Sulphur-rumped and Yucatan Flycatchers, Northern Bentbill, Rufous and Speckled Mourners, Thrush-like Schiffornis, Red-capped Manakin, Mangrove

Vireo, Tawny-crowned and Lesser Greenlets, Green Shrike-Vireo, Spot-breasted and White-bellied Wrens, Tropical Gnatcatcher, Grey-throated Chat, Yellow-winged and Grey-headed Tanagers, Black-throated Shrike-Tanager, Red-throated and Red-crowned Ant-Tanagers, Olive and Green-backed Sparrows, Black-headed Saltator, Black-faced Grosbeak, Blue Bunting, Yellow-tailed Oriole, Montezuma Oropendola.

Access

There is no public transport to Hill Bank and road access requires a four-wheel-drive vehicle. Before planning a visit it is necessary to obtain permission from PfB (2 South Park Street, Box 749, Belize City, tel. 501-2-75616, fax. 2-75635, e-mail pfbel@btl.net). By road from Belize City, turn left (west) off the Northern Highway, approximately 8 km north of the airport road, towards Burrell Boom. On the latter keep straight, after which the road becomes dirt. Go a further 30 km to Rancho Dolores, cross Spanish Creek and after a sharp left bend take the first right to Yalbac Ranch, passing through broadleaf forest and pine savanna. After about 10 km there is a gate staffed by PfB personnel and 10 km further is the Yalbac access gate; approximately 2 km beyond here take a road heading north, which crosses into the Río Bravo Conservation and Management Area after a further 3 km. After 10 km turn east to Hill Bank.

From Orange Walk, take the road west through Yo Creek to San Felipe, continuing straight where the Blue Creek road goes right and after 2 km, where the road bends sharply to the left, take the first large road on the right (south). After approximately 30 km the road intersects the Gallon Jug road; turn east and go a further 1 km to reach Hill Bank.

CHAN CHICH LODGE AND LA MILPA FIELD STATION

An ecotourism centre located in the middle of more than 50,000 ha of private nature reserve, adjacent to an additional 100,000 ha of pristine forest managed by the Programme for Belize. The habitat is mostly dry upland rain forest, similar to that found in the Petén region of Guatemala. Though it is a very wild area it possesses an excellent system of foot trails. Approximately 350 species of birds as well as many mammals have been recorded.

Specialities

Ocellated Turkey*, Yucatan Poorwill, Yucatan Nightjar, Tody Motmot, Yucatan Jay, Rose-throated Tanager

Others

Great and Slaty-breasted Tinamous, Pinnated Bittern, Agami Heron, Jabiru, Lesser Yellow-headed and King Vultures, Muscovy Duck, Grey-headed, Hook-billed, Snail, Double-toothed and Plumbeous Kites, Crane, Bicoloured and White Hawks, Crested Eagle*, Black-and-white, Black and Ornate Hawk-Eagles, Bat Falcon, Great Curassow*, Crested Guan, Spotted Wood-Quail, Ruddy and Grey-breasted Crakes, Pale-vented and Short-billed Pigeons, Ruddy Quail-Dove, White-crowned, White-fronted, Red-lored, Mealy and Yellow-headed* Parrots, Vermiculated Screech-Owl, Spectacled, Mottled and Black-and-white Owls, Scaly-breasted Hummingbird, Canivet's Emerald, Azure-crowned Hummingbird, Slaty-tailed Trogon, American Pygmy Kingfisher, White-necked and White-whiskered Puffbirds, Smoky-brown and Chestnut-coloured Wood-peckers, Scaly-throated Leaftosser, Strong-billed Woodcreeper, Dot-winged Antwren, Black-faced Antthrush, Lovely Cotinga, White-winged and Grey-coloured Becards, White-collared and Red-capped Manakins, Thrush-like Schiffornis, Slate-headed Tody-Flycatcher, Stub-tailed Spade-bill, Mangrove Vireo, Green Shrike-Vireo, Yucatan Flycatcher, Couch's Kingbird, White-browed, Spot-breasted and White-bellied Wrens, North-ern Nightingale-Wren, Yellow-throated, Kentucky, Hooded, Magnolia and Black-throated Green Warblers, American Redstart (winter), Swain-son's Warbler, Grey-throated Chat, Golden-masked, Yellow-winged and Grey-headed Tanagers, Black-throated Shrike-Tanager, Olive-backed Euphonia, Red-crowned and Red-throated Ant-Tanagers, Blue Bunting, Black-faced Grosbeak, Green-backed Sparrow, Yellow-backed and Yel-low-tailed Orioles, Montezuma Oropendula.

Other Wildlife
Jaguar, Black Howler Monkey, Spider Monkey, Kinkajou, Morlet's Croc-odile, Fer-de-lance.

Access
Chan Chich is located close to the Guatemalan border and can be reached by charter flight from Belize City or by road. Road directions are as follows. Leave Belize City on the Northern Highway to Orange Walk (85 km). In Orange Walk, turn left two blocks after the Shell sta-tion to Yo Creek. In Yo Creek go south to San Felipe (30 km), where you should turn sharply right to the bridge over Booth's River (9 km), through Linda Vista (last chance for fuel) and turn left in another 6 km at Tres Leguas. Follow signs for Gallon Jug, passing the Río Bravo ent-rance gate (5 km), and continue a further 36 km to Gallon Jug. In Gal-lon Jug stay on the south perimeter road and turn left (west), following signs to Chan Chich.

Chan Chich has a dozen cabins located in prime habitat. It is defi-nitely not for the birdwatcher on a tight budget, but offers an excep-tional experience. Knowledgeable guides are available. For details, contact the US office, at Box 1088, Vineyard Haven, MA 02568, tel. toll-free 1-800-343-8009, fax. 508-693-6311, e-mail info@chanchich.com, web site www.chanchich.com.

It is essential to make prior arrangements before going to Chan Chich; at peak times the facilities may be booked months in advance.

La Milpa Field Station is located in the middle of the Río Bravo pre-serve, 65 km north of Chan Chich, and supports many of the same species. It offers simple but adequate accommodation, at substantially lower prices than Chan Chich. It is necessary to book in advance at the Río Bravo Conservation and Management Area, Box 749, Belize City, Belize; tel. (501)-2-75616, fax. 75635. There is a checkpoint on the ent-rance road and those who have not pre-arranged accommodation will not be admitted. Day visitors should also make prior arrangements.

BELIZE ZOO AND MONKEY BAY

A good area of pine forest, situated midway between Belize City and

Belmopan. It is the only known location in Belize for Blue Seedeater. Stygian Owl is also a possibility. Couch's Kingbird is an abundant winter visitor.

Specialities
Yucatan Bobwhite, Stygian Owl, Azure-crowned Hummingbird, Blue Seedeater.

Others
White-tailed Hawk, Aplomado Falcon, Yellow-headed Parrot*, White-tipped Dove, Buff-bellied Hummingbird, Acorn Woodpecker, Northern Beardless Tyrannulet, Vermilion Flycatcher, Couch's Kingbird (winter), Rose-throated Becard, Rufous-browed Peppershrike, Green Jay, White-bellied Wren, Yellow-throated (winter) and Grace's Warblers, Grey-crowned Yellowthroat, Hepatic Tanager, Thick-billed and Grassland Yellow-Finches, Olive and Botteri's Sparrows, Yellow-backed and Yellow-tailed Orioles.

Access
The area is located on the Western Highway, 46.5 km from Belize City, on the north side of the road. Monkey Bay is a further 4 km west of the zoo, on the left. It is possible to drive to the river at this point.

Accommodation is available, by prior arrangement, at the Tropical Education Centre, a rustic site set in pine savanna. There are two very good pub-restaurants a further 2 km west of Monkey Bay.

BLUE HOLE NATIONAL PARK

An excellent area with a good trail system, located near Belmopan. It is one of the few reliable locations in Belize for Northern Nightingale-Wren.

Specialities
Tody Motmot, Northern Nightingale-Wren.

Others
King Vulture, White and White-tailed Hawks, Barred Forest-Falcon, Short-billed Pigeon, White-tipped and Grey-fronted Doves, White-crowned Parrot, Squirrel Cuckoo, Vermiculated Screech-Owl, White-necked Jacobin, Slaty-tailed Trogon, Buff-throated Foliage-gleaner, Scaly-throated Leaftosser, Northern Barred Woodcreeper, Great Antshrike, Eye-ringed Flatbill, Stub-tailed Spadebill, Thrush-like Schiffornis, Cinnamon Becard, Band-backed and White-bellied Wrens, Variable Seedeater, Yellow-faced Grassquit, Orange-billed Sparrow, Black-faced Grosbeak.

Access
Turn south off the Western Highway 77 km from Belize City onto the Hummingbird Highway, passing the turn-off to Belmopan. The Visitor Centre is 20 km south of the Western Highway, to the west of the road.
    The 'Blue Hole' is a brilliantly coloured lake approximately 1.5 km south of the Visitor Centre. The nearest accommodation is in Belmopan.

MOUNTAIN PINE RIDGE

A beautiful area of pine-forested highland, which contains the highest waterfall in Belize, located south of Georgeville, which is near the Guatemalan border on the road to Tikal. The habitat, open pine forest on sandy soil, is quite different from the lush broadleaf tropical forest further east.

Specialities
Orange-breasted Falcon, Ocellated Turkey*.

Others
King Vulture, Swallow-tailed and Plumbeous Kites, Scaled Pigeon, Ferruginous Pygmy-Owl, White-collared Swift, Azure-crowned Hummingbird, Golden-olive and Acorn Woodpeckers, Greater Pewee, Black Phoebe, Plain Wren, Rufous-capped Warbler, Altamira, Yellow-backed and Yellow-tailed Orioles, Hepatic and Golden-hooded Tanagers, Black-headed Saltator, Rusty Sparrow.

Access
Take the Western Highway from Belmopan towards San Ignacio. Approximately 16 km east of San Ignacio, in Georgeville, turn south onto a very poor road. After a further 16 km there is a gate marking the boundary of the protected area. The area has a complicated series of dirt roads, but major attractions are signed; further directions can be obtained from the staff at the gate. The turn-off for Hidden Valley is 6 km beyond the gate. About 5 km past Hidden Valley Lodge is a turn-off to the left (dry season only) to Hidden Valley Falls, where Orange-breasted Falcon is regular.

The best area is around the old mining ghost town of Douglas de Silva (also known as Augustine), which is 22.5 km beyond the gate and 16.5 km past Hidden Valley Lodge. All lodge accommodation in the area is very expensive; however, with permission from the Forestry Department in Belmopan (which is 1.5 km along a dirt road from a traffic circle on the Western Highway), camping at Douglas de Silva is allowed.

Note that, especially after rain, many of the roads in the area are quite hazardous. It is possible to hire a taxi in San Ignacio for about $90/day.

Accommodation: Hidden Valley Lodge is one of several lodges in the area (e-mail info@hiddenvalleyinn.com).

POOK'S HILL

A 125 ha private reserve in the foothills of the Maya Mountains and bordering the 2000 ha Tapir Mountain Reserve, which is largely out of bounds to non-professional visitors. The habitat is broadleaf forest, similar to that surrounding Chan Chich or La Milpa, but with a greater southern, wet forest component.

Others
Bicoloured and Roadside Hawks, Collared Forest-Falcon, Laughing and Bat Falcons, Pale-vented Pigeon, Spectacled Owl, Mealy, Red-lored and White-fronted Parrots, Lesser Swallow-tailed Swift, Azure-crowned Hum-

mingbird, Little and Long-tailed Hermits, White-necked Jacobin, Black-headed Trogon, Rufous-tailed Jacamar, Keel-billed Toucan, Black-cheeked Woodpecker, Dusky Antbird, Black-faced Antthrush, Thrush-like Schiffornis, Black Phoebe, Ochre-bellied Flycatcher, Spot-breasted and Band-backed Wrens, Wood Thrush (winter), Red-legged Honey-creeper, numerous wintering warblers including Hooded Warbler and Louisiana Waterthrush, Yellow-billed Cacique, Montezuma Oropendola, Olive-backed Euphonia, Red-throated Ant-Tanager, Black-headed and Greyish Saltators, Blue-black Grosbeak, Yellow-faced Grassquit.

Access
Located on the Western Highway approximately 8 km west of Bel-mopan, or 32 km east of San Ignacio. Turn south at mile marker 52.5, at Teakettle Village, at the sign for Pook's Hill. Go another 6 km along a poor dirt road and turn right at the sign for a further 1 km. Teakettle Village can be reached by bus from Belmopan and free transport from Teakettle Village can be arranged with the owners of Pook's Hill.

Accommodation: prior arrangements should be made with the owners of Pook's Hill (P.O. Box 14, Belmopan, Belize, tel. (501) 8-12017, fax. 8-23361).

CARACOL NATURAL RESERVATION

A huge Mayan archaeological site, exceeding Tikal in size, which is still largely unexplored and of very difficult and uncomfortable access. The habitat is a mix of the lower limit of the Mountain Pine Ridge-type conif-erous ecosystem, drier rain forest and broadleaf deciduous forest. There are a number of tracks leading to various sites and excavations which make good birdwatching trails.

Specialities
Ocellated Turkey*, Keel-billed* and Tody Motmots.

Others
Slaty-breasted Tinamou, King Vulture, Grey-headed, Hook-billed and Double-toothed Kites, Black-and-white and Ornate Hawk-Eagles, Crest-ed Guan, Great Curassow*, Spotted Wood-Quail, Scarlet Macaw, Mealy Parrot, Crested and Black-and-white Owls, Northern Potoo, Violet Sabre-wing, Brown Violet-ear, Slaty-tailed Trogon, White-whiskered Puffbird, Rufous-tailed Jacamar, Chestnut-coloured Woodpecker, Scaly-throated Leaftosser, Plain Antvireo, Sepia-capped Flycatcher, Stub-tailed Spade-bill, Rufous Mourner, Rufous Piha, Cinnamon Becard, Tropical Gnat-catcher, Louisiana Waterthrush (winter), Golden-crowned Warbler, Crimson-collared, Scarlet-rumped and Golden-hooded Tanagers, Thick-billed Seed-Finch, Orange-billed Sparrow, Black-faced Grosbeak, Blue Bunting, Yellow-tailed Oriole.

Access
See Mountain Pine Ridge. From Douglas de Silva go south for 35.5 km, pausing at Guacamayo Bridge over the McCall River (16 km), which is a site for Scarlet Macaw and Solitary Eagle. The road to Caracol is very

difficult and slow; 4WD is essential and in the wet season the road may not be passable. There is no accommodation at Caracol.

Crested Owls, found in humid evergreen forest, are usually detected by their deep growling calls

COCKSCOMB BASIN WILDLIFE SANCTUARY

The Cockscomb Basin Sanctuary has an area of almost 50,000 ha of subtropical wet rain forest on the eastern slopes of the Mayan Mountains. The Sanctuary has basic accommodation (bring your own food) and a good series of trails through excellent habitat and is well worth a stay of several days. Trails (often muddy) vary in length from less than 1 km to a rugged two-day hike up Victoria Peak (about 1100 m). The latter requires a guide.

Specialities
Tody Motmot.

Others
Great, Little and Thicket Tinamous, King Vulture, Grey-headed Kite, Bicoloured and White Hawks, Black-and-white Hawk-Eagle, Great Curassow*, Crested Guan, Plain Chacalaca, Ruddy Crake, Sungrebe, Brown-hooded, White-crowned, Red-lored and Mealy Parrots, Squirrel Cuckoo, Least Pygmy-Owl, Black-and-white and Spectacled Owls, Pauraque, Little and Long-tailed Hermits, Violet Sabrewing, Rufous-tailed Hummingbird, White-necked Jacobin, White-breasted Emerald, Amazon and Green Kingfishers, Blue-crowned Motmot, Keel-billed Toucan, Collared Araçari, Smoky-brown, Black-cheeked, Golden-olive, Chestnut-coloured and Pale-billed Woodpeckers, Tawny-winged, Ruddy and Ivory-billed Woodcreepers, Barred and Great Antshrikes, Dot-winged Antwren, Red-capped and White-collared Manakins, Social, Couch's and Sulphur-rumped Flycatchers, Northern Bentbill, Common Tody-Flycatcher, Bright-rumped Attila, Rufous Piha, Cinnamon and White-winged Becards, Brown Jay, Spot-breasted Wren, Lesser Greenlet, Green and Red-legged Honeycreepers, Yellow-tailed and Black-cowled Orioles, Chestnut-headed and Montezuma's Oropendolas, Melodious Blackbird, Crimson-collared, Scarlet-rumped, Blue-grey, Hepatic and Yellow-winged

Tanagers, Red-throated Ant-Tanager, Olive-backed Euphonia, Variable and White-collared Seedeaters.

Other Wildlife
Jaguar.

Access
The Sanctuary is approximately 50 km south-west of Dangriga. From there take the Southern Highway about 33 km to the village of Maya Centre. Turn right at the craft shop in the village; the Visitors' Centre is after another 9 km of poor road, sometimes impassable after rain. The Sanctuary has dormitory style accommodation with a gas stove etc. at very reasonable rates. There are also camping facilities. All food must be brought in; the closest store (with limited choice) is in Maya Centre.

By public transport, the Z bus service and the James Bus Line go from Belize to Dangriga and, with a change, to Punta Gorda. Be sure to tell the driver to let you off at Maya Centre. There is no transport from Maya Centre to the Sanctuary, but by inquiring at Julio Saqui's store in Maya Centre it may be possible to arrange a ride.

Accommodation: bookings should be made in Belize City at the Belize Audubon office (Box 1001, Belize City, tel. 02-34987, fax. 02-34985). Confirm reservations at Cockscomb itself. Failing this, there is food and accommodation in Maya Centre (Ernesto and Aurora Saqui's Nuch Che'il cottages). Accommodation is also available in Hopkins and in Dangriga; however, it is much better to stay within the Sanctuary itself.

SITES OFF THE SOUTHERN HIGHWAY SOUTH OF DANGRIGA

These areas are worth a stop, as they can conveniently be combined with a visit to Cockscomb Wildlife Sanctuary.

KENDALL BRIDGE

About 5 km north of Maya Centre the road crosses the Kendall River. The bridge and areas around provide good overlooks.

Others
King Vulture, White-tailed Kite, Yellow-headed Parrot*, Vaux's Swift, Black Phoebe, numerous wintering warblers, including Hooded and Louisiana Waterthrush, Black-cowled and Yellow-tailed Orioles.

RED BANK VILLAGE

Approximately 56 km south of Maya Centre on the Southern Highway, there is a sign at the turn-off to Red Bank stating that Red Bank loves its macaws. This is probably one of the best areas in Belize for Scarlet Macaw, which can be found from January to March feeding on fruiting trees in the area.

Specialities
Yucatan Bobwhite, Scarlet Macaw.

Others
King Vulture, Plumbeous Kite, White-tailed Hawk, Black-Hawk-Eagle, Yellow-headed Parrot*, Vermiculated Screech-Owl, Acorn and Ladder-backed Woodpeckers, Northern Barred Woodcreeper, Great Antshrike, Couch's Kingbird, Green Jay, Sedge Wren, Grace's Warbler, Grey-crowned Yellowthroat, Hepatic, Crimson-collared, Scarlet-rumped and Golden-hooded Tanagers, Variable Seedeater, Thick-billed Seed-Finch, Rusty and Grasshopper Sparrows, Yellow-backed Oriole.

Access
The best birdwatching is on the wooded slopes behind the village. Before entering the area it is necessary to check at the store opposite the school where a $5 entrance fee is payable. You may also be requested to hire a guide; as this gives the villagers an incentive to protect the area you should accept this.

Accommodation: there is a rustic guesthouse in the village, but bring your own food.

BFREE PROTECTED AREA AND BLADEN RESERVE

The Belize Foundation for Research and Environmental Education (BFREE) Protected Area supports pine and tropical broadleaf forest, and also has a lagoon and a canopy walkway.

Specialities
Agami Heron, Tody Motmot, Chestnut-headed Oropendola.

Others
King Vulture, Muscovy Duck, Grey-headed, Hook-billed and Double-toothed Kites, Bicoloured and White Hawks, Black-and-white, Black and Ornate Hawk-Eagles, Barred Forest-Falcon, Aplomado Falcon, Crested Guan, Great Curassow*, Short-billed Pigeon, Grey-fronted and Grey-chested Doves, Brown-hooded, Mealy and Yellow-headed* Parrots, Central American Pygmy-Owl, Striped Owl, Scaly-breasted Hummingbird, Violet-crowned Woodnymph, Purple-crowned Fairy, Collared and Slaty-tailed Trogons, Keel-billed Motmot*, White-whiskered Puffbird, Rufous-tailed Jacamar, Acorn, Black-cheeked, Ladder-backed and Chestnut-coloured Woodpeckers, Scaly-throated Leaftosser, Wedge-billed, Northern Barred and Streak-headed Woodcreepers, Great Antshrike, Sepia-capped and Ruddy-tailed Flycatchers, Eye-ringed Flatbill, Stub-tailed Spadebill, Rufous Mourner, Thrush-like Schiffornis, Rufous Piha, Cinnamon Becard, Sedge and Northern Nightingale-Wrens, Grace's and Golden-crowned Warblers, Grey-crowned Yellowthroat, Black-throated Shrike-Tanager, Red-crowned Ant-tanager, Hepatic, Crimson-collared, Scarlet-rumped and Golden-hooded Tanagers, Orange-billed Sparrow, Black-faced Grosbeak, Yellow-backed and Yellow-tailed Orioles.

Access

Coming from the north, go south on the Southern Highway for 91 km from the Hummingbird Highway. Cross the Bladen Branch Bridge and after 6.1 km turn right (west) onto a poor road. There is a sign at this intersection but it is easy to miss.

From the south, cross the bridge at Medina Bank and take the turn (left) after 7.5 km. There is rustic accommodation and camping is permitted. The adjacent Bladen Reserve has no facilities.

PUNTA GORDA AREA

Punta Gorda is the southernmost town in Belize. There are several worthwhile sites close to the town.

Specialities

Tody Motmot, Western Slaty Antshrike, Paltry Tyrannulet, White-vented Euphonia, Chestnut-headed Oropendola.

Others

Great, Little, Thicket and Slaty-breasted Tinamous, Lesser Yellow-headed Vulture, Muscovy Duck, Black Hawk-Eagle, Barred Forest-Falcon, Spotted Wood-Quail, Ruddy and Grey-breasted Crakes, Sungrebe, Short-billed Pigeon, Grey-fronted and Grey-chested Doves, Brown-hooded Parrot, Vermiculated Screech-Owl, Striped Owl, Band-tailed Barbthroat, Scaly-breasted Hummingbird, Violet Sabrewing, Purple-crowned Fairy, Collared and Slaty-tailed Trogons, Keel-billed Motmot*, White-whiskered Puffbird, Scaly-throated Leaftosser, Wedge-billed, Northern Barred and Streak-headed Woodcreepers, Sepia-capped Flycatcher, Rufous Mourner, Couch's Kingbird (winter), Thrush-like Schiffornis, White-winged Becard, Band-backed Wren and Northern Nightingale-Wren, Grey-throated Chat, Black-throated Shrike-Tanager, Red-crowned Ant-tanager, Crimson-collared, Scarlet-rumped and Golden-hooded Tanagers, Green Honeycreeper, Orange-billed Sparrow, Black-faced Grosbeak.

Access

Aguacaliente Swamp Now a National Park, also known as Lu Ha, a few km north of Punta Gorda; the swamp harbours such species as Jabiru, Wood Stork, Muscovy Duck, Sungrebe and Chestnut-headed Oropendola. To reach here leave Punta Gorda northwest on the Southern Highway, which bends sharply northeast at a petrol station 23 km from Punta Gorda. Approximately 5 km before this station, a road goes left (southwest) to the village of Laguna (4 km). In Laguna you can hire a guide to take you into the swamp. There is a rustic but pleasant guesthouse in the village; arrangements can be made in Punta Gorda. You eat with the local people.

Manfredi and Blue Creek Village Returning to the Southern Highway and continuing north, you reach a dirt road leading west from the petrol station; the paved highway turns sharply right at this point. The dirt road passes through rice fields (Grey-breasted Crake) and reaches Manfredi after 9 km. Go left here; within a further 10 km you reach Blue

Creek Village, where there is accommodation in a cheap guesthouse and also at a field station with cabins. If you stay at the latter you should enquire in advance as to the cost. There is primary rain forest on the Blue Creek River and a canopy walkway. Good habitat is easily accessible from the guesthouse.

Joe Taylor Creek This area has good marsh and forest edge. It is reached by heading north from Punta Gorda on a road running along the coastline. The creek is about 2 km out of town. Dugouts can be hired to take you along the creek.

Cattle Landing A further 1.5 km north along the coast the road reaches Cattle Landing, where it swings west away from the sea. Follow a trail along the coast northwards into primary forest. This is the best location for Western Slaty Antshrike.

VoA Station Less than 2 km from Punta Gorda is a Voice of America station. Enquire locally for directions. The transmitting equipment is located behind a fence but surrounding this is productive forest habitat.

ADDITIONAL INFORMATION

Addresses
Belize Audubon Society: P.O. Box 1001, 12 Fort Street, Belize City, Belize. Tel: 501-2-35004, fax. 501-2-34985.

Books and papers
A Guide to the Birds of Mexico and Northern Central America. Howell, S. N. G. and Webb, S. 1995. Oxford UP. (Covers Belize.)

A Distributional Survey of the Birds of British Honduras, Russell, S. M. 1964. Ornithological Monographs No.1, American Ornithologists' Union, Washington DC.

The birds of Hill Bank, Belize, Vallely, A. C. and Whitman, A. A. *Cotinga* 8: 39–49.

Status updates for selected bird species in Belize, including several species previously undocumented from the country, Jones, H. L. *et al.* 2000. *Cotinga* 13: 17–31.

The Landbird Monitoring Programme at Lamanai, Belize: a preliminary assessment, England, M. C. 2000. *Cotinga* 13: 32–43.

Five new bird species in Belize, Jones, H. L. *et al.* in press. *Cotinga* 16

Ornithology in Belize since 1960, Miller, B. W. and Miller, C. M. 1998. *Wilson Bull.* 110: 544–558.

A Field Guide to the Birds of Belize, Jones, H. L. and Gardner, D. In press. Oxford UP.

COSTA RICA

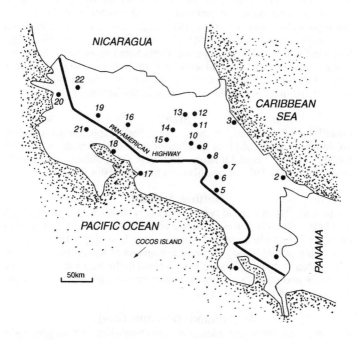

1 Wilson Botanic Gardens (Las Cruces)
2 Cahuita National Park and nearby areas
3 Tortuguero National Park
4 Península de Osa
5 Cerro de la Muerte
6 Tapantí Nature Preserve
7 Rancho Naturalista
8 Volcán Irazú National Park
9 Braulio Carrillo National Park
10 El Ceibo Ranger Station, Braulio Carrillo National Park
11 Rara Avis
12 La Selva Biological Station
13 Selva Verde
14 Colonia La Virgen del Socorro
15 Volcán Poás
16 Monteverde area
17 Carara Biological Reserve and Río Tárcoles
18 Chomes
19 Hacienda La Pacifica
20 Santa Rosa National Park
21 Palo Verde National Park and Dr Rafael Lucas Rodríguez Caballero National Wildlife Refuge
22 El Rincón de la Vieja National Park
Cocos Island

INTRODUCTION

Summary

Costa Rica has, for many years, been the most popular destination in all of Central America for visiting birdwatchers and other naturalists, with good reason. It is a small country, but with great diversity of habitat and a very rich fauna and flora. It is also the most mountainous of the Central American republics, with some spectacular scenery. Well served by an extensive road system (though many are of poor quality), the public transport is relatively good. Though there has been much habitat destruction, a major system of national parks and other publicly and privately protected areas has ensured that large parts of the country remain pristine. Perhaps most important and in sad contrast to most of its neighbours in Central and South America, Costa Rica has an enviable history of stable democracy and solid social government, with no armed forces and, for its region, high levels of expenditure on education and social services, making it the safest destination in the isthmus.

Size
Costa Rica, at 51,000 km², is the third smallest of the countries of Central America, exceeding only El Salvador and Belize. It is about one-fifth the size of the United Kingdom (but with a population only one-fifteenth that of the UK), or one-fifteenth the size of the Texas.

Getting Around
There is an extensive road system, but many rural roads are very rough and best suited for four-wheel-drive vehicles. Most towns and villages are served by public buses, and much of the best bird habitat is accessible using public transport, albeit not always at the times most desirable for birdwatchers. Cars are readily hired in the major urban centres. There are two railways, the trip to Limón on the Caribbean coast being recommended for its own sake.

Accommodation and Food
Both are available in abundance almost everywhere. Prices vary widely according to standard and location, being substantially higher in popular tourist areas; but by current European or North American standards, generally highly reasonable. A feature much more widespread in Costa Rica than in other Central American countries is the numerous lodges, or hotels specifically catering to visiting naturalists, sited within or very close to prime habitat. These tend to be more expensive but in many cases offer excellent value.

Health and Safety
A very safe country, without the banditry prevalent in some of its neighbours. Nevertheless, petty theft can be a significant nuisance, especially in some parts of San José as well as other locations. There is some malarial risk in the lowlands, especially the area bordering Nicaragua and on the Caribbean coast. For those visiting rural locations (i.e. birders), immunization against typhoid fever and viral hepatitis A is recommended.

Climate and Timing
The climate is greatly influenced by location and altitude. The northwest is dry to semi-arid, becoming steadily wetter as one nears Panama, while the Caribbean slope is much more humid. In the mountains that form the spine of the country the weather can vary from pleasantly warm to downright cold and wet. There are two seasons; confusingly, in local parlance, summer (*verano*) lasts from December to April and winter (*invierno*) the rest of the year. Rainfall is heavier in 'winter'; on

the Caribbean coast from mid-April to mid-December or late January, late April to November in the drier northwest. Rain tends to occur later in the day and into the night, with, even at the height of the rainy season, frequent clear mornings. The driest months are February and March, meaning that most bird tours visit during this period; an additional advantage being the occurrence of many wintering North American species. However, there are considerable arguments for visits at other times, for example in June, when many resident species are breeding. Back-country transport is, it should be said, more arduous in the wet season.

Habitats

For such a small country, Costa Rica has an astonishing variety of habitats. The Pacific lowlands are relatively narrow, with low limestone hills in many places and numerous offshore islands. In the north, in Guanacaste, the countryside is dry or semi-arid, with African-type savanna grassland interspersed by tropical deciduous forest that loses its leaves during the six-month dry season. In lower lying areas the woodland is less xeric in nature. Low limestone hills are often covered by dry scrub with cacti and other thorny plants. The short rainy season results in highly productive temporary wetlands in some river basins. Many dry-country species, such as White-throated Magpie-Jay and Stripe-headed Sparrow reach the southern limit of their ranges in this area.

As one progresses south along the Pacific coast the forest (where it remains) becomes steadily wetter, with the appearance of numerous species from further south. The Península de Osa has extensive evergreen wet forest.

The Caribbean lowlands are broader and more extensive. This was obviously a very rich habitat, as is evident from the huge species lists of those few locations where extensive original forest remains, but much has given way to the ubiquitous banana and rice plantations.

Along the spine of the country is a chain of mountains, with intermittent high, mainly volcanic, peaks, some still occasionally (or frequently) active. These support extensive forests, of varying character depending on altitude, with corresponding avifaunas. Much montane forest, especially at colder upper levels, still exists, although huge areas in the flatter Central Valley and elsewhere have long since gone. The mountains become steadily higher towards Panama with the Cerro de Chirripó reaching 3819 m, the highest peak in the country. None is sufficiently high to be permanently snow-capped, but the upper levels of the highest peaks have páramo, a high-altitude moorland with stunted, scattered bushes. Below the páramo are several different types of woodland, with varying levels of epiphytic growth and mix of tree species, each supporting a different avifauna.

Conservation

Costa Rica is fortunate in having a relatively small, and by Latin American standards, comparatively stable human population. Though large areas of the country have been cleared for agriculture and forestry, very extensive areas remain, much now preserved within National Parks, Biological Reserves and privately owned. Outside the protected areas there is continued pressure on habitat, especially forest. Another habitat under major pressure is coastal mangrove swamp, which is often converted to shrimp ponds. Recent efforts have concentrated in providing contiguous protected areas with extensive altitudinal ranges, in recognition of the importance of vertical migration to many species.

Tourism is now the second-largest earner of foreign currency in Costa Rica, and a large proportion of this is brought by the habitat, scenery and wildlife, bringing a positive incentive to habitat preservation.

Bird Families

About 80 of the 90 or more families that occur in Mexico and Central America are found in Costa Rica. The most notable absences are a number of essentially North American or Holarctic families, such as titmice, nuthatches and creepers, which occur in the high mountains of Mexico and no further south, and some seabirds. In compensation, Costa Rica is the northern limit of such typically South American families as tapaculos and Sharpbill. The family with the greatest number of species in Costa Rica is the tyrant flycatchers, with 78 species, but there are also 51 hummingbirds, 50 tanagers and allies, and 30 antbirds.

Bird Species

With a list of nearly 850 species, Costa Rica is second in the region only to Panama and to Mexico, a country 40-fold larger; in fact, the Costa Rican avifauna has more species than Canada and the USA combined. With 50 species of tanager, ten trogons including the indescribable Resplendent Quetzal*, ten manakins and 16 parrots there is no shortage of spectacular species.

Endemics

Mainland Costa Rica has only three endemics—Mangrove Hummingbird*, Coppery-headed Emerald and Black-cheeked Ant-Tanager*—plus, possibly, the mysterious Alfaro's Hummingbird, known from one specimen collected in 1895 and unrecorded since. The 24 km² Cocos Island, situated 300 km off Costa Rica's Pacific coast, has three more—a cuckoo, a flycatcher and a finch. There are, however, a very large number of near-endemics, species whose range crosses, especially, the Panamanian border, often by only a few kilometres, in these countries' shared highlands. This group includes abundant species such as Long-tailed Silky-Flycatcher, Collared Redstart, Volcano Junco and Sooty Robin, as well as some very interesting ones, including Peg-billed Finch, Timberline Wren and the enigmatic Wrenthrush or Zeledonia.

Expectations

A well-planned trip covering the major habitat-types—dry and wet lowlands, some of the wetland areas and a reasonable cross-section of highland habitats—should have no problems in finding 400 species. Some very intense three-week tours have recorded up to 550 species.

WILSON BOTANIC GARDENS (LAS CRUCES)

Run by the Organisation for Tropical Studies, near San Vito on the Panamanian border. Although little original forest remains, the area has a substantial species list and is an excellent location for seeing some of the specialties of southern Costa Rica, such as Fiery-billed Araçari and Chiriqui Yellowthroat. About 350 species have been recorded on site.

Specialities
Beryl-crowned Hummingbird, White-tailed Emerald, Fiery-billed Araçari, Chiriqui Yellowthroat.

Others
Little Tinamou, Black Hawk-Eagle, White-throated Crake, Grey-necked Wood-Rail, Ruddy Quail-Dove, Scaled and Short-billed Pigeons, Fork-tailed Emerald, Snowy-bellied Hummingbird, Purple-crowned Fairy, Violet Sabrewing, Black-throated, Violaceous and Collared Trogons, Olivaceous Piculet, Red-crowned Woodpecker, Brown-billed Scythe-bill, Pale-breasted and Red-faced Spinetails, Russet and Black-hooded Antshrikes, Blue-crowned and White-ruffed Manakins, Thrush-like Schiffornis, Turquoise Cotinga*, Grey-capped, Bran-coloured, Ruddy-tailed, Sulphur-bellied and Sulphur-rumped Flycatchers, Plain, Riverside and Rufous-breasted Wrens, Southern Nightingale-Wren, Wilson's Warbler (winter), White-vented, Spot-crowned and Thick-billed Euphonias, Scarlet-thighed Dacnis, Speckled, Silver-throated, Bay-headed, Golden-hooded and Crimson-collared Tanagers, Red-crowned Ant-Tanager, Chestnut-capped Brush-Finch.

Other Wildlife
Agouti, Kinkajou, otters, White-faced Capuchin.

Access
There is now a bridge crossing the Río Térraba just beyond Paso Real, about 86 km from San Isidro (to the nostalgic regret of those of us who remember the old ferry, a wondrous contrivance of oil-drums and planks, propelled by an outboard motor). Cross the river (looking for Mangrove Swallow and otters at this point) and proceed about 45 km to the pleasant town of San Vito. Turn south (sharp right) in San Vito towards Ciudad Neilly (Route 16 or 137). The entrance to the gardens is about 7 km out of town on the right-hand side. For early-morning birding (the gate opens at 8am), on-site accommodation is best (see below). Once in the Gardens, acquire a trail map. The river trail to the Río Jaba is especially good. Some trails are closed to casual visitors, but ask the administration for details. The Gardens themselves are about 10 ha, and are very good for hummingbirds; a further 150 ha of forest (mostly regenerating second growth) is adjacent.

East of San Vito a road goes to Sabalito on the Panamanian border. Just before the airstrip (about 2 km) is a marshy area on the left, and some ponds on the right. This is a good location for Chiriqui Yellowthroat. A few hundred metres beyond the airstrip there is a pond on the left with an observation tower. This marsh has Chiriqui Yellowthroat, White-throated Crake, Bran-coloured Flycatcher, Ruddy-breasted Seedeater and Purple Gallinule. Common Yellowthroat also winters here.

When driving from San Isidro de El General to the Río Terraba bridge, stop at El Brujo, about 10 km south of the turn-off to Buenos Aires. After crossing the Río General, take a right after 1.4 km along a rough track, or walk. Wedge-tailed Grass-Finch is found in an open area less than 1 km along this track.

There are several daily buses from San José to San Vito, some of which are slower than others. One daily bus from San Vito passes the entrance to the Gardens.

Accommodation: by arrangement with the Organisation for Tropical Studies you can stay within the Gardens, three daily meals included, in comfortable dormitory-style buildings (contact Las Cruces Biological Station, Apartado 73-8257, San Vito, Costa Rica. Tel. (506) 773-4404, fax. 773-3665, e-mail lcruces@hortus.ots.ac.cr; North American office: Box 90630, Durham, NC 27708-0630, USA. Tel. (919) 684-5774, fax. 684-5661, e-mail nao@duke.edu). A cheaper alternative is to stay in San Vito and pay the daily entrance fee to the Gardens.

CAHUITA NATIONAL PARK AND NEARBY AREAS

An extensive area of coastal lowland forest, with a magnificent offshore reef full of incredible fish. The park itself and some adjacent areas are good locations for several lowland and Caribbean specialties not easily found elsewhere.

Specialities
Green Ibis, White-crowned Pigeon, Snowy and Lovely Cotingas, Purple-throated Fruitcrow (roadside fruiting trees), Canebrake Wren, Plain-coloured Tanager.

Others
Common Black-Hawk, Hook-billed Kite, White-throated Crake, Sungrebe (river crossings), Pale-vented Pigeon, Crimson-fronted and Olive-throated Parakeets, Blue-headed and White-crowned Parrots, Long-tailed and Bronzy Hermits, Crowned Woodnymph, Blue-chested Hummingbird, Slaty-tailed Trogon, Amazon, Green and American Pygmy Kingfishers, White-necked Puffbird, Collared Araçari, Chestnut-coloured, Cinnamon, Black-cheeked and Pale-billed Woodpeckers, Northern Barred, Buff-throated and Streak-headed Woodcreepers, Western Slaty-Antshrike, White-collared Manakin, Cinnamon Becard, Long-tailed and Yellow Tyrannulets, Black-capped Pygmy-Tyrant, Band-backed, Bay, Black-throated and Stripe-breasted Wrens, Blue Dacnis, Olive-crowned Yellowthroat (roadside scrub), White-vented, Yellow-crowned and Olive-backed Euphonias, White-lined and White-shouldered Tanagers, Black-headed Saltator, Thick-billed Seed-Finch, Yellow-faced Grassquit, Black-striped Sparrow, Scarlet-rumped Cacique, Black-cowled Oriole.

Access
Cahuita is located on Highway 36, 42 km south of Limón. When travelling the coast road check river crossings for Sungrebe. The Park headquarters are on the road to Puerto Vargas, a further 5 km south. There are also public buses from Limón to Puerto Viejo de Talamanca (to distinguish it from the numerous other Puerto Viejos). Much of the forest in Cahuita is flooded and difficult of access, with many mosquitoes. There is a footpath along the shore, which crosses a couple of rivers; these areas are good for Sungrebe, and White-crowned Pigeon occurs along here. The road to the headquarters and fruiting trees beside Highway 36 can be quite productive. Two trails on the west side of Highway 36, one shortly after the turn-off to Cahuita, the second by a bus shelter further south, lead to good habitat.

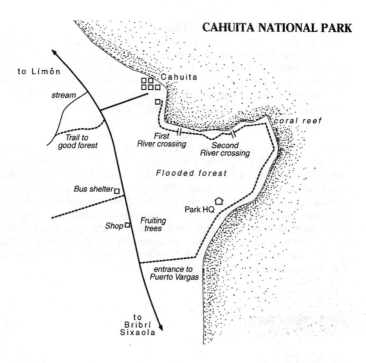

CAHUITA NATIONAL PARK

Accommodation is plentiful in Cahuita (weekends best avoided), and camping is possible at the Park headquarters; supplies can be bought in Cahuita. There is an entrance fee to the Park. An earthquake damaged the reef in 1991. There have been consistent reports of thefts and muggings, and recently a murder, in Cahuita, which appears to have something of a drug problem. Appropriate caution should be exercised.

Other Areas

Bribrí, a further 19 km south on Highway 36, has good habitat and could make a useful supplement to Cahuita. Most species found in Cahuita also occur in Bribrí, along with Crested Guan, Red-footed Plumeleteer and Black-chested Jay. There is good forest near the road, with some trail access, as well as disused railway tracks leading west.

Approximately 13 km south of the turn-off to Cahuita town, and about 6 km before Bribrí, there is a dirt road to the left to Puerto Viejo and Manzanillo. Just before Manzanillo this road accesses very good lowland forest, by Punta Uva on the coastline. There are several possible trails. Ask for permission where it appears appropriate. The road from Bribrí to Punta Uva can be difficult after rain.

TORTUGUERO NATIONAL PARK

A large area (20,000 ha) of lowland rainforest on the northern Caribbean coast. It is not easily accessed, but well worth the trouble. Once in the area, a network of streams and canals gives unique access to excellent habitat.

Others

Slaty-breasted Tinamou, many herons including Agami Heron and Bare-throated Tiger-Heron, Sungrebe, Red-lored Parrot, Great Green Macaw*, Great and Northern Potoos, Short-tailed Nighthawk, Green-and-rufous and American Pygmy Kingfishers, Chestnut-mandibled Toucan, Snowy Cotinga, Purple-throated Fruitcrow, White-collared Manakin, Scarlet-rumped, Palm and Blue-grey Tanagers.

Access

There are several methods of reaching Tortuguero. Boats, of varying degrees of reliability, leave from Moín (a suburb of Puerto Limón), travelling 70 km via the internal coastal waterway, an interesting trip that takes over six hours. In some cases local people may get precedence in buying tickets. Several tour agencies in San José offer packages including lodging and transportation. There are several choices in Tortuguero itself, ranging from fairly expensive lodges to cheaper, more basic, hotels. Motor boats and canoes can be rented in Tortuguero and offer the best way to explore and bird. Note that Fer-de-lance is common in the area; especial care should be taken after dark.

PENÍNSULA DE OSA

RINCÓN DE OSA

Located at the base of the Península de Osa, Rincón de Osa is a roadside village, easily accessible and with good forest and mangroves. Up to 140 species have been recorded in a single day here, including the endangered Yellow-billed Cotinga, which is apparently numerous in the area.

Endemics
Mangrove Hummingbird*.

Specialities
Scarlet Macaw, Fiery-billed Araçari, Yellow-billed Cotinga.

Others
Great Curassow*, Marbled Wood-Quail, Blue Ground-Dove, Mangrove Cuckoo, Band-tailed Barbthroat, Beryl-crowned Hummingbird, White-necked Puffbird, Black-striped Woodcreeper, Yellow-crowned Tyrannulet, Turquoise Cotinga*, Red-capped Manakin, Pale-breasted Spinetail, Spot-crowned Euphonia.

Access
Public buses to Puerto Jiménez pass Rincón de Osa; from San José to Puerto Jiménez is about 10 hours. The turn-off to Rincón de Osa is about 20 km south of Palmar Norte on the Pan-American Highway. Good forest habitat, both primary and secondary, occurs along the roadside. La Palma is a small town between Rincón de Osa and Puerto Jiménez, surrounded by pasture and second growth. The road to the Los Patos entrance of Corcovado National Park (frequently very difficult and some-

times impassable due to high stream crossings) joins this road. Red-breasted Blackbird and Yellow-breasted Seedeater occur along here. The road continues to Puerto Jiménez; in winter the harbour frequently holds many shorebirds. Around the town is mostly second growth; a road to Doña Leta's bungalows passes through mangrove forest with species such as Grey-necked Wood-Rail, American Pygmy Kingfisher and wintering Prothonotary Warbler.

Accommodation and food is available at the Cabañas de Golfo Dulce. Right behind these is mangrove with the endemic Mangrove Hummingbird*.

White-necked Puffbirds, which occur all the way from Mexico to Argentina, are quite common in broken forest in Costa Rica

CARATE AND LUNA LODGE

Luna Lodge is a private lodge with bungalows, not for the budget birder but excellently situated on a steep hill overlooking forest. There is a good trail system through primary and secondary rainforest, the best trail being the 'Ridge Trail', as well as a good overlook for raptors. There have been unconfirmed reports of Harpy Eagle* in this vicinity.

Endemics
Black-cheeked Ant-Tanager*.

Specialities
Ornate and Black-and-white Hawk-Eagles, Tiny Hawk, Scarlet Macaw, White-tipped Sicklebill, White-crested Coquette, Fiery-billed Araçari, Bicoloured Antbird, White-throated Shrike-Tanager

Others
Crested Guan, Marbled Wood-Quail, King Vulture, Swallow-tailed Kite, White Hawk, Barred and Collared Forest-Falcons, Bat Falcon, Spectacled Owl, Ruddy Quail-Dove, Beryl-crowned Hummingbird, Blue-throated Goldentail, Baird's*, Slaty-tailed, Black-throated and Violaceous Trogons, White-necked Puffbird, Rufous-tailed Jacamar, Golden-naped

Woodpecker, Long-tailed and Black-striped Woodcreepers, Pale-breasted Spinetail, Black-hooded and Russet Antshrikes, Black-faced Antthrush, Scaly-throated Leaftosser, Ruddy-tailed Flycatcher, Golden-crowned Spadebill, Turquoise Cotinga*, Rufous Piha, Red-capped and Blue-crowned Manakins, Southern Nightingale-Wren, Grey-headed Tanager.

Access

A truck leaves Puerto Jiménez for Carate each day at 6am, returning at 11 am; in the rainy season it may not make it the whole way. Luna Lodge is about 3 km along a poor road by the river, followed by a steep climb onto the ridge where the Lodge is situated. Transport can be provided from Carate to the Lodge by prior arrangement.

CERRO DE LA MUERTE

The Pan-American Highway reaches its highest point in Costa Rica as it crosses the Cerro de la Muerte, passing through excellent high-altitude forest as it does so. The combination of weird-looking, epiphyte-draped trees, often in dense cloud, and some spectacular or highly restricted species makes the Cerro an unforgettable location.

Specialities

Barred Parakeet, Red-fronted Parrotlet*, Maroon-chested Dove (Villa Mills), Volcano Hummingbird, Resplendent Quetzal* (several locations, including km 66 and km 97), Black-capped Flycatcher, Ochraceous Pewee, Timberline and Ochraceous Wrens, Yellow-winged Vireo, Wrenthrush, Volcano Junco, Blue Seedeater, Peg-billed Finch.

Others

Black-chested Hawk, Spotted Wood-Quail, Band-tailed and Ruddy Pigeons, Bare-shanked Screech-Owl, Sulphur-winged Parakeet, Dusky Nightjar, White-bellied and Purple-throated Mountain-gems, Magnificent and Fiery-throated Hummingbirds, Green Violet-ear, Band-tailed Barbthroat, Acorn and Hairy Woodpeckers, Spot-crowned Woodcreeper, Ruddy Treerunner, Buffy Tuftedcheek, Mountain Elaenia, Silver-throated Jay, Grey-breasted Wood-Wren, Mountain Robin, Sooty Robin (abundant), Black-billed Nightingale-Thrush, Long-tailed and Black-and-yellow Silky-Flycatchers, Slaty Flowerpiercer, Collared Redstart, Flame-throated, Black-cheeked and Black-throated Green (winter) Warblers, Spangle-cheeked Tanager, Sooty-capped Bush-Tanager, Golden-browed Chlorophonia, Large-footed Finch, Yellow-thighed Finch, Yellow-bellied Siskin.

Other Wildlife

Not spectacular, but the Cerro has small endemic salamanders.

Access

Leave San José on the Pan-American Highway and fork right to San Isidro de El General before entering Cartago. There are several stops along the road.

At km 66.6, a private dirt road leads to the right; the gate is usually locked, but access by foot appears permissible. This track winds downhill through excellent forest. Species include Resplendent Quetzal*, Black-billed Nightingale-Thrush, Collared Redstart, Black-cheeked Warbler, Sooty-capped Bush-Tanager and Golden-browed Chlorophonia.

Just beyond km 80 a road on the right (south) side of the highway descends to San Gerardo de Dota. It is worth walking the section about 3 km from the Pan-American Highway. Most of the species mentioned can be found here, and quetzals are frequent. Another good spot on the Highway itself is km 88.5, where there are a couple of ponds and a track leads to the north (left).

Restaurant La Georgina, located at km 95, is a legendary stop. Most of the buses travelling between San José and San Isidro stop here, often for a food break. The restaurant can be full one minute and deserted the next. Forest reaches right to the back of the restaurant, and Volcano Hummingbird, Yellow-winged Vireo and Black-capped Flycatcher can be seen from the window. A little further on the road to San Isidro, from La Georgina, is a track leading to the left. Once away from the road this is an excellent location, with Fiery-throated Hummingbird, Large-footed Finch, Ochraceous and Timberline Wrens, and many others. Behind La Georgina is a cut area for some electrical lines which provides further access; further along the road at about km 97 a track leads to the left via a locked gate. This land is private but there appears to be access, if possible ask permission. After passing through some cleared areas the track leads into oak forest where quetzals, Silver-throated Jay and Ochraceous Pewee have been seen. Further along the road to San Isidro a side road leads to the right, to an area with a soccer pitch and some houses. The forest edge here is sometimes productive and Maroon-chested Dove has been seen. Close to the summit of the pass, a steep road leads to some radio masts on the right; although possibly too steep for ordinary cars, this track leads into true páramo.

The Resplendant Quetzal, arguably one of the world's most spectacular birds, is still quite common in numerous locations in Costa Rica

Accommodation: Restaurant La Georgina offers good food and cheap, not luxurious, lodging; the staff is used to birders. It can be very cold at night. The name Cerro de la Muerte—Mountain of Death—arises from early travellers on foot, who sometimes succumbed to hypothermia on the pass. More expensive, at km 62, is the Albergue de Montaña Tapantí. The area around this lodge-type establishment offers good birding in its own right, with Flame-coloured Tanager, Flame-throated Warbler and Long-tailed Silky-Flycatcher. Access to the Cerro by public transport is easy; there are numerous daily buses between San José and San Isidro. There is a pay telephone at La Georgina.

TAPANTÍ NATURE PRESERVE

A superb area of montane forest originally preserved to protect the watershed of a reservoir, but now a reserve in its own right with a system of trails. Easily accessed from Cartago or San José.

Specialities
Rufous-rumped Antwren.

Others
Black Guan*, Red-fronted Parrotlet*, Black-bellied Hummingbird, White-bellied and Grey-tailed Mountain-gems, Purple-crowned Fairy, Green Hermit, Prong-billed and Red-headed Barbets, Black-banded Woodcreeper, Streaked Xenops, Lineated and Buff-fronted Foliage-gleaners, Dark Pewee, Yellowish Flycatcher, Lovely Cotinga, Barred Becard, Black-headed Nightingale-Thrush, Black-faced Solitaire, Slate-throated Redstart, Blue-and-gold*, Black-and-yellow, Silver-throated, Spangle-cheeked, Bay-headed, Crimson-collared and White-winged Tanagers, Blue-hooded Euphonia, Yellow-throated and Chestnut-capped Brush-Finches, Chestnut-headed Oropendola.

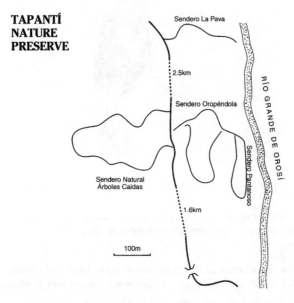

TAPANTÍ NATURE PRESERVE

Sendero La Pava

2.5km

Sendero Oropéndola

RÍO GRANDE DE OROSÍ

Sendero Pantanoso

Sendero Natural Árboles Caídas

1.6km

100m

Access

Take the road to Turrialba from Cartago and, at the western end of Paraíso turn south to Orosí. The Park headquarters is about 12 km beyond Orosí after passing Río Macho and Purisil. After passing the Park headquarters, the road continues for several km. There are several excellent trails (senderos) accessible from this road. Mist and rain, especially at higher levels frequently shroud Tapantí.

Accommodation: there is ample lodging in Cartago and some (rather basic) in Orosí. Buses run from Cartago to Orosí.

RANCHO NATURALISTA

A private 50 ha reserve a few km southeast of Turrialba with an impressive bird list (more than 400 species here and in adjacent areas). It is a good location for a number of difficult-to-find species such as Purplish-backed Quail-Dove and Snowcap. Capacity is quite limited and consequently the lodge has a more personal nature than larger establishments. Usually, competent guides are available.

Endemics
Coppery-headed Emerald.

Specialities
Purplish-backed Quail-Dove, Black-crested Coquette, Snowcap, Grey-headed Manakin, Ashy-throated Bush-Tanager.

Others
Great Tinamou, Barred and Collared Forest-Falcons, White-throated Crake, Red-headed Barbet, Yellow-eared Toucanet, Chestnut-mandibled Toucan, eight woodpeckers including Rufous-winged, Lineated, Pale-billed and Smoky-brown, 33 hummingbirds including Green-fronted Lancebill, White-necked Jacobin, Violet-headed, Steely-vented and

The uniquely-plumaged Snowcap is nowhere abundant, but Costa Rica offers some of the best chances to see this exotic species

Black-bellied Hummingbirds, Green Thorntail, Garden Emerald, Red-footed Plumeleteer, Green-crowned Brilliant and Purple-crowned Fairy, Collared, Black-throated and Violaceous Trogons, Broad-billed, Rufous and Blue-crowned Motmots, ten woodcreepers including Northern Barred, Spotted, Streak-headed and Brown-billed Scythebill, Slaty and Red-faced Spinetails, Fasciated and Russet Antshrikes, Plain Antvireo, Checker-throated and Dot-winged Antwrens, Dusky, Dull-mantled, Immaculate and Bicoloured Antbirds, Black-headed and Fulvous-bellied Antpittas, Barred, Cinnamon and Black-and-white Becards, White-crowned, White-ruffed and White-collared Manakins, Thrush-like Schiffornis, Bright-rumped Attila, Golden-bellied, Tufted, Ruddy-tailed, Tawny-chested* and Sulphur-rumped Flycatchers, Black-headed Tody-Flycatcher, White-throated Spadebill, Rufous-browed Tyrannulet, Rufous Mourner, Band-backed, Plain, Stripe-breasted, Bay, Black-throated and Song Wrens, Southern Nightingale-Wren, Black-faced Solitaire, Black-headed Nightingale-Thrush, Long-billed Gnatwren, Rufous-browed Peppershrike, Green Shrike-Vireo, Lesser Greenlet, Slate-throated Redstart, Golden-crowned, Rufous-capped and Buff-rumped Warblers, 40 species of tanager including White-shouldered, Dusky-faced, Black-and-yellow, Emerald, Speckled, Silver-throated, Golden-hooded, Scarlet-rumped and Olive, Golden-browed Chlorophonia, Tawny-capped, White-vented, Yellow-crowned and Yellow-throated Euphonias, Scarlet-thighed Dacnis, Black-faced and Black-thighed Grosbeaks, Thick-billed Seed-Finch, Yellow-throated and Chestnut-capped Brush-Finches, Orange-billed and Black-striped Sparrows, Prevost's Ground-Sparrow, Scarlet-rumped Cacique.

Access
Leave Turrialba southeast on Highway 10, after 7 km turn right to La Suiza and Tuis. Bypass Tuis and fork right about 1.5 km beyond the town; about 1 km further, a steep road leads to Rancho Naturalista. A bus also travels along this road to Tayutic (marked Platanillo on some maps, not to be confused with another Platanillo, within the Chirripó Indian Reserve). Daily costs including three meals, guiding, etc. are $135; three-day packages with transport from San José are also available. Telephones: San José 267-7138, Lodge 284-5894, North America 1-800-593-3305. At the time of writing (April 2000) a change of ownership is in process, but it is anticipated that previous policies will continue. Present (April 2000) e-mail: johnerb@sol.racsa.co.cr.

VOLCÁN IRAZÚ NATIONAL PARK

At 3400 m, Volcán Irazú is considerably higher than Volcán Poás. The upper levels are as yet largely uncolonised by plants and resemble a lunar landscape. On clear days there are spectacular views across the valley to Cerro de la Muerte, Volcán Turrialba and Volcán Poás. While not nearly as productive as Poás, Irazú is a reasonably reliable location for Volcano Junco.

Access
Head east from San José on the Pan-American Highway and take the left fork to Cartago (a pleasant town worth a visit). Shortly after the Cartago turn-off and before entering Cartago itself, a second left fork

(signed Irazú) leads upwards, via a paved road, to the summit. Most of the countryside is given over to agriculture and is relatively birdless, apart from the ubiquitous Rufous-collared Sparrow. However, in several places the road crosses wooded gullies where from the bridges species such as Green Violet-ear, Long-tailed Silky-Flycatcher and Black-billed Nightingale-Thrush can be seen. Shortly after entering the park (fee), a narrow road, initially dirt but then paved, leads downhill to the right. This road, which has no traffic, is worth walking for juncos and hummingbirds.

Accommodation: the trip can be made in half a day from San José; there is food and accommodation in Cartago, and a small hotel on the left-hand side part way along the road to the summit.

BRAULIO CARRILLO NATIONAL PARK

A superb area of mountain forest, about 45,000 ha in extent, now readily accessible from San José by a fast toll road. There is sufficient variation in altitude within the park to give several life zones, with a resulting large species list—at least 400 species are known including Tiny Hawk, Lanceolated Monklet and Sharpbill.

Specialities
Solitary Eagle, Tiny Hawk, Rufous-fronted Wood-Quail, Purplish-backed Quail-Dove, Black-crested Coquette, White-tipped Sicklebill, Snowcap, Lanceolated Monklet, Dull-mantled Antbird, Sharpbill, Stripe-breasted Wren.

Others
Great Tinamou, Swallow-tailed Kite, Ornate Hawk-Eagle, White Hawk, Black Guan*, Black-breasted Wood-Quail, Ruddy and Band-tailed Pigeons, Ruddy and Buff-fronted Quail-Doves, Barred Parakeet, White-col-

The most spectacular species of a spectacular genus, the tiny Black-crested Coquette is generally rare throughout most of its range

lared Swift, Green Hermit, Violet Sabrewing, Magnificent and Black-bellied Hummingbirds, Purple-throated Mountain-gem, Resplendent Quetzal*, Lattice-tailed and Collared Trogons, White-whiskered Puffbird, Emerald and Yellow-eared Toucanets, Red-headed and Prong-billed Barbets, Golden-olive Woodpecker, Ruddy Treerunner, Spotted Barbtail, Lineated and Spectacled Foliage-gleaners, Streak-breasted Treehunter, Red-faced Spinetail, Spotted Woodcreeper, Scaled Antpitta, Silvery-fronted Tapaculo, Long-tailed Tyrant, Golden-bellied, Tufted, Slaty-capped, Olive-striped and Yellowish Flycatchers, White-throated Spadebill, Torrent Tyrannulet, Scale-crested Pygmy-Tyrant, Three-wattled Bellbird*, Grey-breasted Wood-Wren, Ochraceous Wren, Slaty-backed and Ruddy-capped Nightingale-Thrushes, Mountain Robin, Black-faced Solitaire, Black-and-yellow Silky-Flycatcher, Azure-hooded Jay, Black-cheeked and Three-striped Warblers, Collared and Slate-throated Redstarts, Louisiana Waterthrush (winter), Tawny-capped Euphonia, Golden-browed Chlorophonia, Common Bush-Tanager, Spangle-cheeked, Black-and-yellow and Flame-coloured Tanagers, Black-thighed Grosbeak, Chestnut-capped Brush-Finch, Sooty-faced and Yellow-thighed Finches.

Access
Via the new San José–Limón road (Highway 32), the site is about 40 minutes from San José. There are a number of excellent stops along this road; km zero is the toll station (c. 2.5 km before the Zurqui tunnel). Right and left refer to directions when travelling towards Guápiles from San José. While a car is useful, there are frequent buses along Highway 32 between San José and Guápiles or Limón.

Stream trail About km 5, immediately below a series of high slopes on the right-hand (east) side. Park in a lay-by about 300 m further on. This trail winds down to a stream.

Administration Centre trail Km 10. Stop at the administration centre. A trail of about 2 km, with a lookout above the tunnel, goes left from the road here; a second trail forms a loop off this trail.

La Montura Km 10.9. The trails here may be difficult to find.

There is a steep trail on the right at about km 13, and a further one (Sendero de la Salta) at about km 18.3, also on the right. Sooty-faced Finch occurs here.

Sendero de la Botella (Ridge trail) About km 20. On the left-hand side of the road are some disused buildings with a trail leading along the ridge, with a further trail branching to the left down to a stream. This area can harbour an impressive array of tanagers.

The main road turns east and heads to a crossing of the Río Sucio; look for Torrent Tyrannulet at this point. About 3–4 km beyond the river is a ranger station on the right-hand side of the road at Quebrada González. There is an entrance fee for the trails. Several species occur here, such as Purplish-backed Quail-Dove, which are difficult to find elsewhere.

We have received consistent warnings from several different sources of thefts from cars and actual robberies along this road, especially in the area near the tunnel. Clearly, more than usual caution is advisable.

Accommodation is available in Guápiles. It may also be possible to stay at the Administration building at the San José end of the road.

EL CEIBO RANGER STATION, BRAULIO CARRILLO NATIONAL PARK

An access point to the less-visited western side of Braulio Carrillo, with many of the same species that are found at Quebrada González. A good location for the Great Green Macaw* (at least in the rainy season) and a good variety of tanagers.

Others

White and Barred Hawks, Ornate and Black Hawk-Eagles, Bat Falcon, Barred Forest-Falcon, Rufous-fronted Wood-Quail, Great Green Macaw*, Broad-billed Motmot, Yellow-eared Toucanet, Torrent Tyrannulet, numerous tanagers.

Access

About 15–20 km south and west of Puerto Viejo de Sarapiquí (on the road to Cariblanco and Vara Blanca), turn east at a stop called 'La Virgen' (not to be confused with the turn-off to La Virgen del Socorro, which is further along the same road but south of Cariblanco). Cross the Río Sarapiquí and fork right to San Ramón (about 16 km from the river). At San Ramón continue 8 km to El Ceibo. Pass the soccer pitch and follow the road to the left, then to the right and ford a second stream. El Ceibo station is about 1 km along a right-hand turn beyond the second stream. 4WD is helpful, and possibly necessary, for this journey.

The Yellow-eared Toucanet is resident throughout the foothills of the Caribbean slope of Costa Rica

Accommodation: it may be possible to stay and eat at the Ranger Station by arrangement with the staff. Failing that, the closest accommodation is Selva Verde. Public transport goes only as far as La Virgen.

RARA AVIS

A superb area of foothill forest now preserved privately, with accommodation and guiding services provided, abutting Braulio Carrillo.

Endemics
Coppery-headed Emerald.

Specialities
Tiny Hawk, Great Green Macaw*, White-tipped Sicklebill, Snowcap, Black-bellied Hummingbird, Red-headed Barbet, Yellow-eared Toucanet, Snowy Cotinga, Bare-necked Umbrellabird*, Black-and-yellow Tanager.

Others
Four hundred species have been recorded, including 22 raptors, eight pigeons, nine parrots, 29 hummingbirds, six trogons, five toucans, ten furnariids, 11 woodcreepers, 22 antbirds, 50 flycatchers and nine wrens.

Access
Located at the end of about 14 km of very bad road leading from Los Horquetas, which is situated on the Puerto Viejo–Guapiles road, and easily accessible from San José via Braulio Carrillo. The office in San José (tel. 506-764-3131 or 253-0844, fax 764-4187 or 256-4876) will arrange for transportation from San José to Los Horquetas, which is also accessible by bus.

Transport from Los Horquetas is via a very poor road (not passable in most vehicles) by one of two methods: a tractor-drawn cart or (much more pleasant) by horse. Those who are not expert equestrians should not be intimidated from using the latter method; the horses are all torpid, somnolent beasts apparently well beyond pensionable age and not in any way shaped for sportive tricks. Just sit on top and watch the countryside pass by (rather slowly). Luggage is taken by tractor.

The bizarre Bare-necked Umbrellabird* is generally uncommon, but quite easy to see at Rara Avis

Accommodation (at various prices) is available at Rara Avis, from a rather basic type at El Plastico, more suitable for students, to the cabins located further on. Prices include meals, guiding and transport from Los Horquetas. There is a good system of trails. Rubber boots are necessary and provided. For further information and current prices there is a web site at www.rara-avis.com/lodges_and_prices.htm, e-mail raraavis@sol. racsa.co.cr, postal address 8105-1000 San José, Costa Rica.

LA SELVA BIOLOGICAL STATION

A lowland area of tremendous species diversity, hinting at what most of Central America must have been like before the advent of agriculture. This 1500 ha reserve on the banks of the Río Puerto Viejo is administered by the Organisation for Tropical Studies (OTS). Aside from its great faunal richness, La Selva is very well set-up for birding, with a large series of unobtrusive trails giving access to prime forest habitat. The total list for the reserve stands at more than 400 species, though realistically a casual visitor can only expect half that number; it is, however, quite easy to see 100 species in a day. To do La Selva justice requires a visit of several days.

Specialities
Great and Slaty-breasted Tinamous, Tiny Hawk, Black Hawk-Eagle, Great Green Macaw*, White-tipped Sicklebill, Green Thorntail, Checker-throated Antwren, Spectacled Antpitta, Purple-throated Fruitcrow, Bare-necked Umbrellabird*, Canebrake Wren, Olive-backed Euphonia, Slate-coloured Grosbeak.

Others
Tinamous (three species), herons (12), raptors (37), guans (three), jacanas (two), pigeons (11), parrots (eight), cuckoos (six), owls (seven), swifts (seven), hummingbirds (24), trogons (five), kingfishers (six), motmots (two), puffbirds (four), toucans (five), woodpeckers (seven), woodcreepers (eight), furnariids (five), antbirds (21), cotingas (11), manakins (five), tyrant flycatchers (44), wrens (nine), thrushes (eight), vireos and allies (eight), warblers (31), tanagers (26), grosbeaks, finches and allies (18), orioles and cowbirds (12).

Access
By road from San José, either via that over the flank of Poás (see La Virgen del Socorro) or across Braulio Carrillo to Highway 4, north to Puerto Viejo de Sarapiquí. About 0.7 km west of Puerto Viejo turn south at a bar-restaurant on the road to Río Frío and Guápiles. After 2–3 km (passing a civil guard training camp on the left), turn right by some farm buildings onto a dirt road that in less than 1 km reaches the Río Puerto Viejo. A footbridge gives access to the reserve.

By prior arrangement with OTS (Apartado 676-2050, San Pedro, Costa Rica. Tel. (506) 766-6565, fax. 766-6535, e-mail laselva@sloth.ots.ac.cr; North America, OTS, Box 90630, Durham, NC, 27708-0630, USA. Tel. (919) 684-5774, fax. 684-5661, e-mail nao@duke.edu) one can stay at the station. By Costa Rican standards this is very expensive (*bona fide* students get a good rate), but by far the best solution. It is also possible to purchase day permits, if you wish to use cheaper accommodation in Puerto Viejo. In all cases advance reservation is strongly recommended; preference in accommodation is given to research workers rather than casual visitors.

SELVA VERDE

An alternative to the larger and more expensive OTS operation at La Selva, the Albergue Selva Verde is situated in productive lowland forest, and has many (but not all) of the species found at La Selva. Some species, such as Black-and-white Owl and Great Green Macaw*, are more easily found here.

Specialities
Sunbittern, Great Green Macaw*, Black-and-white Owl, Snowy Cotinga.

Others
See list for La Selva.

Access
Located on the main road from Puerto Viejo de Sarapiquí to San José, via Cariblanco and Vara Blanca, about 7 km west of Puerto Viejo near the village of Chilamarte. The entrance is on this road, within the only remaining forest. There are numerous buses from San José to Puerto Viejo. The best birding is around the lodge itself, with the best location for Black-and-white Owl a patch of forest on the opposite side of the road with a butterfly garden and cabins. Between Selva Verde and Puerto Viejo a road on the right crosses the river; this is a good location for Sunbittern and Snowy Cotinga. This road ultimately goes to La Selva in about 11 km. Immediately after crossing the river, a trail (request permission) alongside the river passes through good habitat. Boat-billed Heron roosts on the riverside and the bridge is a good location for Great Green Macaw* in the evening.

Accommodation: Selva Verde offers very comfortable lodging, including three meals (tel. 766-6077, fax. 766-6011, Aptdo. 55, Chilamarte, Heredia, Costa Rica). Cheaper accommodation is available in Puerto Viejo.

COLONIA LA VIRGEN DEL SOCORRO

A superb area of mid-altitude forest, now (with improvements to the road) readily accessible from San José. A classic location for one Costa Rica's endemics, Coppery-headed Emerald.

Endemics
Coppery-headed Emerald.

Specialities
Emerald Tanager, Tawny-capped Euphonia.

Others
Swallow-tailed Kite, Broad-winged Hawk, Red-billed and Short-billed Pigeons, Squirrel Cuckoo, White-collared Swift, Long-tailed, Little and Green Hermits, Collared Trogon, Emerald Toucanet, Collared Araçari, Wedge-billed, Olivaceous and Spotted Woodcreepers, Brown-billed Scythebill, Spotted Barbtail, Tufted Flycatcher, Scale-crested Pygmy-Tyrant, Black-headed Tody-Flycatcher, Yellow-olive, Yellow-margined and Slaty-capped Flycatchers, Torrent and Rufous-browed Tyrannulets, Azure-hooded Jay, American Dipper, Northern Nightingale-Wren, Bay Wren, Clay-coloured and Mountain Robins, Lesser Greenlet, Buff-rumped and Three-striped Warblers, Slate-throated Redstart, Silver-throated,

Bay-headed, Blue-and-gold*, Black-and-yellow and Crimson-collared Tanagers, Golden-browed Chlorophonia, Green Honeycreeper, Buff-throated Saltator, Slate-coloured, Black-faced and Black-thighed Grosbeaks, Sooty-faced Finch.

Access
Go north on Highway 126, passing through Vara Blanca after the turn-off to Poás. (The oak forest around Vara Blanca is a good location for Flame-throated Warbler). About 16 km from Vara Blanca, the road descends a hill and crosses a stream; just before this a dirt road on the right angles back sharply from the main road. If you come to a toll gate you have gone about 500 m too far. This road is just passable to normal vehicles, but it is much better to park and walk through good forest to a rickety bridge over the Río Sarapiquí, and up the opposite side, or along riverside trails near the bridge. Buses to Puerto Viejo also access this site. There is no local accommodation, but there are several places to stay in Vara Blanca.

Further Suggestions
About 1 km north of Cariblanco a dirt road goes west, via Angeles, to Laguna Hule, which has some good forest surrounding it. This area would be well worth further exploration.

On the road to La Virgen, about 2 km north of Vara Blanca, a trail goes right to Montaña Azul. This is well worth walking, if not shrouded in fog and drizzle, being an excellent location for Resplendent Quetzal* and several species of tanager including Spangle-cheeked and Silver-throated.

VOLCÁN POÁS

A spectacular volcano just north of San José and very easily accessible via paved roads. It makes a good introduction to the highland fauna of Costa Rica, and is not to be missed from the point of view of scenery. A reliable location for the near-endemic Peg-billed Finch.

Specialities
Bare-shanked Screech-Owl, Resplendent Quetzal*, Yellow-winged Vireo, Peg-billed Finch.

Others
Black Guan*, Buffy-crowned Wood-Partridge, Spotted Wood-Quail, Dusky Nightjar, Fiery-throated, Magnificent, Scintillant and Volcano Hummingbirds, Green Violet-ear, Black-capped Flycatcher, Mountain Elaenia, Ochraceous and Timberline Wrens, Sooty and Mountain Robins, Black-billed Nightingale-Thrush, Long-tailed and Black-and-yellow Silky-Flycatchers, Slaty Flowerpiercer, Collared Redstart, Flame-throated and Black-cheeked Warblers, Sooty-capped Bush-Tanager, Large-footed and Yellow-thighed Finches, Volcano Junco.

Access
A good paved road (Highway 125 and 9) leads north from Alajuela (towards Vara Blanca and Puerto Viejo). Approximately 25 km north of Alajuela turn left towards Poasito on Highway 120, keeping to the right

(uphill) in Poasito itself (a second access, Highway 146, via San Pedro, joins 120 in Poasito). The park entrance, which opens at 8am, is a few km further along the road. It is possible, at least on Sundays, to reach the park by bus from San José or Alajuela, but birding visits to Poás on Sundays, or (especially) public holidays, are not recommended as the area can become very crowded. For the same reasons and because cloud and fog tend to cloak the area by noon, an early visit is strongly advised. Alternatively, a taxi can be hired in Alajuela.

There is a parking lot at the visitor centre. Walk the closed road to the crater lookout (which offer spectacular views of the blue lake and yellow sulphur deposits); the bushes along here are good for Peg-billed Finch. A second major footpath leads up through good forest to a mountain lagoon, set in woodland. This, and smaller footpaths below and behind the visitor centre, are well worth investigating. If you arrive at the park entrance before it is open, there is good forest to search beside the road while you wait.

Accommodation: there are numerous hotels and restaurants in Alajuela. Close to the park entrance, on the left-hand side of the road, there is accommodation at La Providencia Cabinas y Restaurante (tel. 231-7884), and Laguinillas Lodge, both situated a little way off the road in quite good habitat.

Note: there have been numerous recent reports of thefts from cars in the parking lot near the visitor centre.

MONTEVERDE AREA

One of the prime birdwatching locations in Costa Rica and Central America. The system of reserves totals about 20,000 ha, straddling the Cordillera de Tilarán, with a maximum altitude of about 1850 m. A good trail network accesses superb habitat; more than 450 species have been seen in the general area. The protected areas consist of the Cloud Forest Reserve, 11,000 ha, administered by the Tropical Science Center of Costa Rica; the Children's Rainforest Preserve (El Bosque Eterno de los Niños), 7000 ha adjacent to the main reserve; and the Santa Elena Reserve, 360 ha. There is also excellent birdwatching in partially cleared farmland on the roads leading to the Reserve.

The area has sufficient variation in altitude and aspect to possess several distinct biotic communities. Usually about four are recognised. These are: Elfin Forest, a weird, sculpted area of short, dense, waxy leafed trees on the crest of the ridge, shaped by constant winds from the Caribbean. Cloud Forest, below the ridge tops and sheltered from the worst of the wind, is constantly shrouded in fog, which results in a riotous growth of epiphytes. Middle Zone Forest, lower down on the Pacific slope, is characterised by tall trees with moderate epiphytic growth. Tall Multi-layered Forest, is considerably drier, with fewer epiphytes and a more open understorey. To do these different habitats full justice requires a visit of several days.

Endemics

Coppery-headed Emerald.

Specialities

Ornate Hawk-Eagle, Black Guan*, Chiriqui Quail-Dove, Great Green Macaw*, Barred Parakeet, Bare-shanked Screech-Owl, Prong-billed Barbet, Brown-billed Scythebill, Red-faced Spinetail, Silvery-fronted Tapaculo, Three-wattled Bellbird*, Bare-necked Umbrellabird*, Azure-hooded Jay, Ochraceous Wren, Wrenthrush, White-eared Ground-Sparrow, Slaty, Peg-billed and Sooty-faced Finches.

One of the characteristic sounds of Monteverde is the loud and inelegant call of the Three-wattled Bellbird*

Others

Bicoloured and White Hawks, Barred and Collared Forest-Falcons, Crested Guan, White-throated Wood-Quail, Short-billed and Ruddy Pigeons, Buff-fronted Quail-Dove, Crimson-fronted, Orange-fronted and Orange-chinned Parakeets, Red-fronted Parrotlet*, Brown-hooded, White-crowned, White-fronted and Red-lored Parrots, Lesser Ground-Cuckoo, Black-and-white Owl, 30 species of hummingbird including White-tipped Sicklebill, Long-tailed, Green and Little Hermits, Green-fronted Lancebill, Violet Sabrewing, Fork-tailed Emerald, Violet-crowned Woodnymph, Fiery-throated and Stripe-tailed Hummingbirds, White-bellied and Purple-throated Mountain-gems, Purple-crowned Fairy, Magenta-throated Woodstar, Scintillant Hummingbird, and Green-crowned Brilliant, Resplendent Quetzal*, Slaty-tailed, Lattice-tailed, Collared, Orange-bellied and Black-throated Trogons, Broad-billed, Keel-billed*, Rufous and Blue-crowned Motmots, Red-headed Barbet, Yellow-eared Toucanet, Keel-billed Toucan, Hoffmann's, Smoky-brown and Golden-olive Woodpeckers, nine species of woodcreeper including Strong-billed, Northern Barred and Black-banded, Slaty Spinetail, Spotted Barbtail, Ruddy Treerunner, Lineated Foliage-gleaner, Streak-breasted Treehunter, Tawny-throated and Grey-throated Leaftossers, 15 species of antbird including Russet Antshrike, Plain Antvireo, Slaty Antwren, and Immaculate and Bicoloured Antbirds, Black-faced and Rufous-breasted Antthrushes, Scaled Antpitta, Barred and Black-and-white Becards, Sharpbill, Long-tailed and White-ruffed Manakins, 50 species of flycatcher including Golden-bellied, Dusky-capped, Yellow-ish, Tufted, Sulphur-rumped, Slaty-capped and Olive-striped Flycatch-ers, Dark Pewee, White-throated and Golden-crowned Spadebills, Eye-ringed Flatbill, Black-headed and Common Tody-Flycatchers, Scale-crested Pygmy-Tyrant, Mountain Elaenia, Mistletoe and Zeledon's Tyrannulets, Brown and Azure-hooded Jays, American Dipper, Plain, Rufous-and-white, Bay and Black-throated Wrens, Grey-breasted Wood-Wren, Northern Nightingale-Wren, Black-faced Solitaire, Black-headed, Slaty-backed, Ruddy-capped and Orange-billed Nightingale-Thrushes, Tawny-faced Gnatwren, Black-and-yellow Silky-Flycatcher, Rufous-browed Peppershrike, Green Shrike-Vireo, Lesser Greenlet, 31 species of warbler including Worm-eating and Kentucky, Tropical Parula, Olive-crowned and Grey-crowned Yellowthroats, Slate-throated and Collared Redstarts, and Three-striped, Golden-crowned, Rufous-capped and Buff-rumped Warblers, Slaty Flowerpiercer, 32 species of tanager including Golden-browed Chlorophonia, Tawny-capped, Yellow-crowned and Yellow-throated Euphonias, Silver-throated, Spangle-cheeked, Scarlet-rumped, Crimson-collared, Blue-and-gold*, Black-and-yellow and Olive Tanagers, Scarlet-thighed Dacnis, and Common and Sooty-capped Bush-Tanagers, Black-faced and Black-thighed Grosbeaks, Variable Seedeater, Yellow-faced Grassquit, Yellow-thighed Finch, Yellow-throated and Chestnut-capped Brush-Finches, Orange-billed and Black-striped Spar-rows.

Other Wildlife

Three-toed Sloth, Tayra, Margay, Spider and Howler Monkeys, Baird's Tapir.

Access

Head north on the Pan-American Highway and 32.4 km north of the turn-off to Puntarenas (at km 149), turn right (east) onto a gravel road, just before the bridge over the Río Lagartos. This road is signed Mon-teverde or La Montana Hotel. At Guacimal (15.7 km) keep straight, then take a left fork at 22.1 km, and a right turn at km 32.3. Parts of this road are very bad; it should be noted that some car hire agencies in San José specifically prohibit the use of their vehicles on this road and on the road to Volcán Arenal. The road from the Pan-American passes mainly through agricultural areas, but it is still worthwhile to stop at patches of trees and bush to search for lower altitude species. After the turn at km 32.3 (the left-hand turn goes to Santa Elena, which has hotels, restau-rants and a bank outlet) it is about 3 km to Monteverde (usually defined as the 'cheese factory' or lechería). From here to the park entrance is a further 3 km. There are daily buses from San José to the cheese factory leaving at 6.30am from Calle 14, Avenidas 9/11, taking about 5 hours, as well as daily buses from Puntarenas, Liberia and Tilarán. Enquire as to current schedules.

There are numerous good birding areas, not all in the Reserve itself. For instance it is worth walking the final 3 km from Monteverde to the Park entrance as much of this is through partially cleared pasture with some massive trees that harbour a good variety of species in an easily observable situation.

Once at the Park entrance (daily entrance fee) there are several trail options; it is necessary to enquire which are currently open to the pub-lic. At the Park entrance and adjacent buildings there are usually hum-

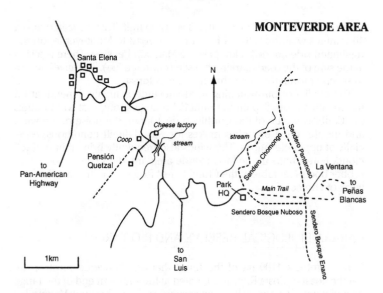

MONTEVERDE AREA

mingbird feeders. Up to ten species can be seen here, including the endemic Coppery-headed Emerald. Check Vervain hedges for hummingbirds as well.

Guided tours are also available from the Reserve Visitors' Centre, at 8am and 7.30pm (tel. 645-5212 for details). Many of the guides are extremely expert and knowledgeable, and you may consider these tours a good investment.

The main trail, formerly a road, climbs through excellent habitat to the Continental Divide at La Ventana, which offers a view to the right of the elfin forest atop the Caribbean-facing ridge. This trail, being fairly broad, has good vantages over the slopes below; on narrower trails birds in the canopy are more difficult to see. The trail from La Ventana winds down the Caribbean slope to Peñas Blancas. There are several refuges on this trail, which is often very muddy. About 8 km from La Ventana is the Portland-Audubon Center where, with the approval of the Field Station at Monteverde, it is usually possible to stay. The best location for Bare-necked Umbrellabird* is near here; there is a lekking area further downhill from the Center. They call only immediately after dawn; the best time is late March. If you intend to descend from La Ventana it is wise to consider at least one overnight stay, but enquire at the Field Station before committing yourself.

There are now numerous places to stay in Monteverde; however, the area has become very popular in recent years and in peak periods (such as March) reservations may be difficult. In Santa Elena, which is about 6 km from the park entrance, there are also several places to stay. Food and accommodation tend to be cheaper here. During peak times the trails within the Reserve may also be quite busy. There are some alternatives in these cases. The Santa Elena Reserve (360 ha) is located about 5 km out Santa Elena, on a road that branches to the right past town; a taxi can take you to the entrance. This Reserve reaches over 1,700 m and is less visited than the Cloud Forest Reserve, but has many of the same species. There is a canopy observation tower, and a modest admission charge. Open 7am to 5pm.

Another good alternative is the Bajo Tigre trail. This is located about 40 minutes walk from Santa Elena on the road to Monteverde, on the right-hand side about 1.5 km past the Manakin Pensión. There is a sign at the side of the road marking the site (entrance fee). This gives access to several productive trails through humid forest.

The quality of birdwatching in Monteverde is highly dependent on the weather. From September until February a strong east wind buffets the Caribbean face of the Cordillera de Tilarán; the noise of the wind and the thrashing branches makes for very difficult conditions, especially at upper elevations. The winds also frequently bring rain or thick cloud. Forest trails in the Monteverde area are often very muddy, and rubber boots (rentable at the Cloud Forest Reserve Centre) are the footwear of choice.

CARARA BIOLOGICAL RESERVE AND RÍO TÁRCOLES

Carara protects 4700 ha of the forest that once covered most of the Pacific coast of Costa Rica. It is located at the southern end of the range of dry-country Guanacaste species such as White-throated Magpie-Jay and Stripe-headed Sparrow, and at the northern end of those found in more humid areas, such as Fiery-billed Araçari and Black-bellied Wren, making for an impressive overall species list. The trail system is not very well developed, and can become quite busy, especially at weekends and later in the day. It is relatively easy to record 125 species in a day's birdwatching in this area.

Endemics
Mangrove Hummingbird* (Tárcoles).

Specialities
Scarlet Macaw, Fiery-billed Araçari, Hoffmann's Woodpecker, Black-hooded Antshrike, Orange-collared Manakin, Panama Flycatcher.

Others
Great Tinamou, Bare-throated Tiger-Heron, Pinnated Bittern, Boat-billed Heron, Muscovy Duck, King Vulture, Crane Hawk, Spectacled Owl, White-crowned, Red-lored, Yellow-naped and Mealy Parrots, Long-tailed and Little Hermits, Rufous-tailed, Steely-vented and Scaly-breasted Hummingbirds, Blue-throated Goldentail, Black-throated, Baird's*, Black-headed, Violaceous and Slaty-tailed Trogons, White-necked and White-whiskered Puffbirds, Chestnut-mandibled Toucan, Olivaceous Piculet, Golden-naped and Lineated Woodpeckers, Tawny-winged, Streak-headed, Wedge-billed, Northern Barred, Black-banded and Black-striped Woodcreepers, Giant and Barred Antshrikes, Dusky and Chestnut-backed Antbirds, Spectacled Antpitta, Rufous Mourner, Rufous Piha, White-winged Becard, Long-tailed and Red-capped Manakins, Grey-capped, Ruddy-tailed, Ochre-bellied and Sulphur-rumped Flycatchers, Stub-tailed Spadebill, Slate-headed Tody-Flycatcher, Rufous-naped, Black-bellied and Riverside Wrens, Shining, Red-legged and Green Honeycreepers, Blue Dacnis, Golden-hooded, Bay-headed, Scarlet-rumped and White-winged Tanagers, Thick-billed Euphonia, Orange-billed and Black-striped Sparrows.

CARARA BIOLOGICAL RESERVE
AND RÍO TÁRCOLES

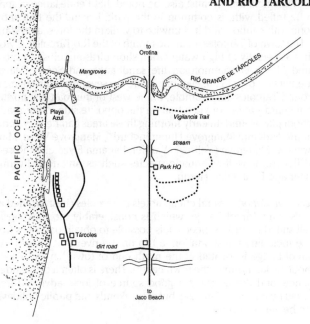

Other Wildlife
American Crocodile (Río Tárcoles).

Access
By road from San José via Orotina, south on Highway 34. The road crosses the Río Tárcoles (or Río Grande de Tárcoles) about 17 km south of Orotina. The reserve starts immediately after the bridge, on the left-hand side.

There are several trails into the reserve. The bridge over the Río Tárcoles provides a good overview; Collared Plover can be seen on the sand banks and American Crocodile occurs in the river.

A trail called 'La Vigilancia' or 'The River Trail' starts at a gate approximately 500 m south of the river. This is one of the most productive sites in the Reserve, but permission should be sought at the HQ before entering. Shortly after leaving the road, on this trail there is a lek of Orange-collared Manakin on the right-hand side along a short path. After about 2 km from the road there is an overgrown oxbow lake where Boat-billed Heron, Bare-throated Tiger-Heron, Purple Gallinule and various herons, egrets and shorebirds occur. The trail covers about 7 km before entering farmland and is well worth a comprehensive visit.

From the HQ (admission fee), located on the east side of the road about 2.5 km south of the river, a circular trail enters the forest, with a second trail branching off to a stream. This trail can become quite crowded with non-birders so an early start is advisable. Scarlet Macaw is frequent here. Before entering the trail look at the fruiting and flowering bushes near the HQ.

There have been recent occurrences of theft from vehicles parked at the Vigilancia trail. It must also be noted that Fer-de-lance, a snake not to be trifled with, is common in the park; leaving the trail should be done with caution and it is unwise to walk in the forest after dark.

The town of Tárcoles, near the mouth of the Río Tárcoles, is worth visiting, especially at high water when shorebirds are close to shore. Collared Plover is common on the sandbanks and Scarlet Macaw frequently flies over in the evening. There are several patches of mangrove around Tárcoles; for example, to the west of the road just north of the civil guard station, or via a trail on the opposite side of the road to the school playground. In early morning these areas can be very good: look for the endemic Mangrove Hummingbird*, Mangrove Vireo, Mangrove Swallow, Mangrove (Yellow) Warbler, Panama Flycatcher, Rose-throated Becard as well as aquatic species such as American Pygmy Kingfisher and Boat-billed Heron.

Accommodation: several cheap hotels in Tárcoles (best avoided at peak times) and Tárcol Lodge, which is considerably more expensive but well suited to birders' needs. It is possible to obtain packages from San José including transportation, a trip on the river and a visit to Carara. Tárcol Lodge is located at the north end of town beyond Playa Azul, about 4.5 km north of the town centre. There is often a bird guide in residence, and the Lodge is a good source of local advice. Tárcoles is served by bus from San José, but at weekends and public holidays these can be very crowded.

CHOMES

An area of shrimp ponds just off the Pan-American Highway about 25 km north of the Puntarenas junction. A good location for many migrant shorebirds and worth a stop if you are passing.

Others
Most Costa Rican herons and egrets, Roseate Spoonbill, terns, gulls, most North American migrant shorebirds. Grey Gull has occurred as a vagrant.

Access
Turn left (south) off the Pan-American Highway, approximately 25 km north of the Puntarenas turn-off, or about 44 km south of Cañas (signed Chomes). The small town of Chomes is about 8 km from the main highway. On entering town turn left towards the shrimp ponds. Request permission before entering the area. Best at high tide.

HACIENDA LA PACIFICA

A strategically situated ranch, about 130 km from San José airport north on the Pan-American Highway. There is excellent gallery forest beside the Río Corobici and the area boasts a list of more than 200 species, including many of the dry-country species that do not extend much further south in Costa Rica.

Specialities
Boat-billed Heron, Spot-bellied Bobwhite, Long-tailed Manakin.

Others
Collared Forest-Falcon, Grey-necked Wood-Rail, Orange-fronted Parakeet, White-fronted Parrot, Pacific Screech-Owl, Steely-vented and Cinnamon Hummingbirds, Plain-capped Starthroat, Black-headed Trogon, Turquoise-browed Motmot, White-necked Puffbird, Nutting's Flycatcher, White-throated Magpie-Jay, Rufous-naped and Banded Wrens, White-lored Gnatcatcher, Stripe-headed Sparrow.

Access
The hacienda is on the right (east) side of the Pan-American Highway, about 5 km north of Cañas. There are numerous buses along this road. Cabin-style accommodation and a restaurant are available on site, although both are fairly expensive by Costa Rican standards. There is quite good birding around the cabins (with species such as Pacific Screech-Owl and Black-headed Trogon). However the best area is the riverside, which is reached by walking along the track behind the cabins. (Look for Spot-bellied Bobwhite.) Boat-billed Heron is frequent in the riverside forest.

SANTA ROSA NATIONAL PARK

A large and readily accessible park in dry northwestern Costa Rica, protecting habitat that elsewhere has been converted to cattle ranches and cotton fields. Many species reach the southern limits of their range in Guanacaste Province, and Santa Rosa is a good place to find them. Much of the park has the air of an East African savanna, albeit without large mammals.

Specialities
Great Curassow* (road to Playa Naranjo), Crested Guan, Spectacled Owl, Elegant Trogon.

Others
Thicket Tinamou (dusk, behind the administration building), Bare-throated Tiger-Heron (mangrove at Playa Naranjo), King Vulture, Grey and Roadside Hawks, Plumbeous Kite, Collared Forest-Falcon, Plain Chachalaca, Spot-bellied Bobwhite (along entrance road), Double-striped Thick-knee (in fields just beyond park entrance), Red-billed Pigeon, White-tipped, Inca and White-winged Doves, Common Ground-Dove, Orange-fronted Parakeet, White-fronted and Red-lored Parrots, Yellow-naped Parrot (on track to beach area), Mangrove and Striped Cuckoos, Lesser Ground-Cuckoo, Cinnamon and Rufous-tailed Hummingbirds, Blue-throated Goldentail, Plain-capped Starthroat, Little Hermit, Black-headed Trogon, Turquoise-browed and Blue-crowned Motmots, Hoffmann's, Pale-billed and Lineated Woodpeckers, Northern Barred, Ruddy, Streak-headed and Ivory-billed Woodcreepers, Plain Xenops, Long-tailed Manakin, Brown-crested, Nutting's, Streaked, Yellow-olive and Northern Royal Flycatchers, Bright-rumped Attila, White-throated Magpie-Jay, Rufous-naped and Banded Wrens, White-lored

Gnatcatcher, Lesser Greenlet, Chestnut-capped Warbler, Grey-crown-ed Yellowthroat, Grey-headed Tanager, Western Tanager (winter), Red-legged Honeycreeper, Stripe-headed and Olive Sparrows, Spot-breasted and Streak-backed Orioles.

Other Wildlife

Leatherback Turtle (after dark at Playa Naranjo), Pacific Green Turtle, Ridley Turtle, Jaguar, Margay, Puma.

Access

Go north 37 km from Liberia on the Pan-American Highway; the ent-rance to Santa Rosa, which is signed, is on the left (west) side. There is an entrance fee. A paved road leads to the visitor centre and historic site (where Costa Ricans repelled one of several unwanted incursions from Nicaragua led by a very obnoxious American adventurer, William Walk-er, who later came to a sticky end at the hands of the British and Hon-durans in the Bay Islands), about 15 km from the Pan-American. The road leads through open grassland, where a lookout should be kept for thick-knees and bobwhites. There are patches of forest, especially where the road dips, which are highly productive. Several trails enter this forest, for example about 13 km from the Pan-American (or 2 km from the his-toric site). Once at the headquarters there are several areas worthy of exploration. Behind the administration building is a short circular trail (Sendero Natural). Heading northwest from the paved access road past the headquarters is a rough track leading through grassland to Laguna Escondida, a good location for Grey-crowned Yellowthroat. From the historic area, a road leads west. It is posted only 4WD, but with care and some disrespect for one's exhaust is probably negotiable by car and since it leads to excellent habitat it is a pity not to try it. Approximately 2.5 km along this road is a trail on the left (Sendero de los Patos), which

SANTA ROSA NATIONAL PARK

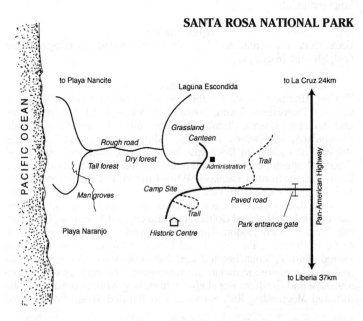

leads 1.2 km to a lookout in dry *Acacia* forest, where it is possible to observe an interesting relationship between Rufous-naped Wren and the aggressive stinging ant *Pseudomyrex*, which live symbiotically within the *Acacia*; wren nests acquire vicarious protection from White-faced Monkeys. Further on, the road forks, the south fork going to Playa Naranjo, where Mangrove Cuckoo and Bare-throated Tiger-Heron occur in the mangroves. Before reaching the coast there are open areas, good for thick-knees, and some excellent forest. Two trails are located off this road: Sendero Palo Seco on the right, about halfway to the coast, and Sendero Carbona, further along on the left. Great Curassow* can be found along this section of the road. Sendero Palo Seco crosses the bed of the Río Nispersal, which is worth exploring, especially if water is present.

A further section of Santa Rosa is accessible by a paved road to the north. About 9 km north of the turn-off to the main park entrance, turn left (west) off the Pan-American towards Cuajiniquil. Just past the village is the park entrance.

Accommodation: by far the best birding in Santa Rosa is in the very early morning; making it advantageous to camp in the park. A campsite near the historic site has toilets and showers, and there are basic campsites at Playa Naranjo and Playa Nancite, on the northern fork of the rough road to the coast. Enquire at the park entrance for up-to-date information. Food may be available at the administration, but it is wise to check ahead of time. Accommodation and food can be found in Liberia, and numerous buses will drop you at the park entrance; thereafter you will have to walk or hitch hike.

PALO VERDE NATIONAL PARK AND DR RAFAEL LUCAS RODRÍGUEZ CABALLERO NATIONAL WILDLIFE REFUGE

A large area of seasonally flooded lowlands, bordering the Río Tempisque. Although the area no longer appears to be as productive as formerly and many marshy areas are now overgrown, it is still one of the best areas for aquatic birds in Costa Rica.

Specialities
Jabiru (rare; look in paddyfields)

Others
Thicket Tinamou, Anhinga, Bare-throated Tiger-Heron, Cattle, Snowy and Great Egrets, Little Blue Heron, Wood Stork, Roseate Spoonbill, Black-bellied and Fulvous Whistling-Ducks, Muscovy Duck, Short-tailed, Bay-winged and Crane Hawks, Great Black Hawk, Yellow-headed Caracara, Crested Guan, Northern Jacana, Double-striped Thick-knee, Pale-vented and Red-billed Pigeons, Orange-fronted Parakeet, White-fronted and Red-lored Parrots, Mangrove Cuckoo, Common Pauraque, Steely-vented and Cinnamon Hummingbirds, Plain-capped Starthroat, Blue-throated Goldentail, Black-headed Trogon, White-necked Puffbird, Hoffmann's Woodpecker, Scissor-tailed, Streaked, Dusky-capped, Brown-crested and Nutting's Flycatchers, Mangrove Swallow, White-throated Magpie-Jay, Brown Jay, Rufous-naped and Banded Wrens, Scrub Euphonia, White-collared Seedeater, Stripe-headed Sparrow, Streak-backed Oriole.

Other Wildlife
Howler and White-faced Monkeys, iguanas, Collared Peccary.

Access
Former access, from Cañas via Bebedero, is apparently no longer possible. Therefore, leave the Pan-American Highway at Bagaces along a bad road that heads due south past Hacienda Tamarindo. The Park headquarters is about 25 km from Bagaces. Road conditions are variable, but a high-clearance four-wheel-drive vehicle is a distinct asset, especially after rain. The road to the Biological Station continues to the Río Tempisque; shortly beyond the station there is a marshy area on the left with an observation tower. Further marshy areas exist closer to the river. There are several trails north of the road, west of the Biological Station. Sendero Cerros Calizas gives some elevation above the lowlands and holds White-throated Magpie-Jay and Banded Wrens. Further west is Sendero Querque. At about km 23 on the road from Bagaces (i.e. east of the Biological Station) there is a road signed to the left 'Parque Nacional Palo Verde 7 km'; the main road to the Biological Station and river is on the right, signed 'Refugio Fauna Silvestre'. The left-hand turn, after crossing a bridge, leads to some further marshy areas on the left.

There is no public transport to the park, though you may be able to persuade a taxi driver in Bagaces to take you. There is no public accommodation, but with prior arrangement you may be able to stay at the Biological Station (tel. 240-6696, fax. 240-6783, e-mail pverde@ots.ac.cr. North American office: OTS, Box 90630, Durham, NC, 27708-0630, USA, tel. (919) 684-5774, fax. 684-5661, e-mail nao@duke.edu). There are several camping areas. It is wise to bring your own supplies.

It may be possible, by enquiry in Cañas or Bagaces, to arrange for a boat trip on the Río Tempisque, giving better access to some wetland habitat.

EL RINCÓN DE LA VIEJA NATIONAL PARK

A National Park not far south of the Nicaraguan border, which has been rather neglected by birdwatchers. An area of active vulcanism, with several eruptions in recent years, and hot springs and bubbling mud at Los Pailes. The two peaks, Volcán Santa María and Volcán Rincón de la Vieja, are just under 2000 m in altitude.

Endemics
Coppery-headed Emerald.

Specialities
Buff-fronted and Chiriquí Quail-Doves, Lesser Ground-Cuckoo, Three-wattled Bellbird*.

Others
Crested Guan, Sunbittern (streams on Los Pailes trail), Orange-fronted Parakeet, Brown-headed and White-fronted Parrots, Crested Owl (water ditch trail), Green Hermit, Stripe-tailed Hummingbird, Magenta-throated Woodstar, Orange-bellied Trogon, Blue-crowned Motmot, Collared Araçari, Yellow-eared Toucanet, Keel-billed Toucan, Olivaceous Wood-

creeper, Spectacled Antpitta, Streak-crowned Antvireo, Long-tailed Manakin, Nutting's, Yellowish and Sulphur-rumped Flycatchers, Golden-crowned Spadebill, Brown Jay, White-throated Magpie-Jay, Rufous-naped, Plain and Rufous-and-white Wrens, Rock Wren (very different from North American races, heavily barred), White-throated Thrush, Grey-crowned Yellowthroat, Rufous-capped Warbler, Grey-headed and Rufous-winged Tanagers, Yellow-throated and Scrub Euphonias, Olive and Rusty Sparrows, Montezuma Oropendola.

Access

From Liberia go north along a dirt road towards Colonia La Libertad. After about 25 km a road goes to the left, probably signed to the National Park, along which the Park headquarters are reached after 3 km. We have no recent information concerning road conditions but previously they were very rough and difficult, with 4WD a definite asset. A second means of access is via a poor dirt road to Curubandé. The turn-off for this is a few km north of Liberia. This road crosses private land and a toll may be charged. There is a daily entrance fee to the Park itself.

Once in the park there are some good trails. From the headquarters a trail goes to the 'water ditch' (Spotted Antbird, Golden-crowned Spadebill, Sulphur-rumped Flycatcher). In the other direction, a track that crosses a couple of streams joins another to Los Pailes, whence a very long and arduous trail leads to the summit. This passes through good forest with Sunbittern possible at stream crossings. There are also some trails on the road to Colonia La Libertad, beyond the Park entrance. El León trail is to the right, about 4 km from the entrance road; further on, on the left-hand side just beyond the second major dip in the road, a trail goes to a clearing.

EL RINCÓN DE LA VIEJA NATIONAL PARK

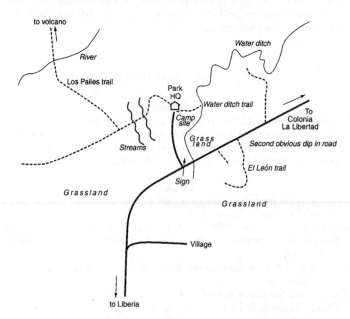

Accommodation: it may be possible to stay and eat at the Park head-quarters; camping is permitted. There is a very infrequent jeep bus service from Liberia to La Libertad; enquire in Liberia for the schedule, such as it is.

COCOS ISLAND

The most remote part of Costa Rica, a National Park located about 600 km southwest of Puntarenas. Notable for three endemic species, as well as a number of seabirds not found elsewhere in Costa Rica that breed there, and many pelagic species that have been seen in the vicinity or on boat trips to the island.

Endemics
Cocos Cuckoo*, Cocos Flycatcher*, Cocos Finch*.

Others
Breeding: Red-footed Booby, Great Frigatebird, Brown and Black Noddies, White Tern. Non-breeding: Dark-rumped Petrel, Pink-footed and Wedge-tailed Shearwaters, Band-rumped Storm-Petrel.

Access
The island can be visited only on an organised trip. Okeanos Aggressor runs about 30 departures a year from Puntarenas, each visit lasting 9–10 days. These trips are aimed at divers, but with prior arrangement birders can be landed on the island on a daily basis, weather permitting. Current prices (including transportation from San José, one night's accommodation in San José and food) are in the $2800–$3000 region. For details contact Okeanos at Box 1470, Morgan City LA 70381, tel. (toll free in North America 1-800-348-2628) or (504) 385-2416, fax. (504) 384-0817, e-mail okeanos@aggressor.com.

ADDITIONAL INFORMATION

Addresses
Richard Garrigues maintains a web site devoted to birding in Costa Rica, at www.angelfire.com/bc/gonebirding/, where you can also subscribe to his regular e-mail bulletin, *The Gone Birding Newsletter*, which details news about recent sightings in the country.

Books
A Guide to the Birds of Costa Rica, Stiles, F. G. and Skutch, A. F. 1989. Cornell UP, Ithaca. (Essential.)

A Naturalist in Costa Rica, Skutch, A. F. 1971. University of Florida Press, Gainesville. (A beautifully written book by the father of Costa Rican ornithology.)

Costa Rica: A Natural Destination, Sheck, R. S. 1990. John Muir Publications, Santa Fe.

A Travel and Site Guide to Birds of Costa Rica, Sekerak, A. D. 1996. Lone Pine Publishing, 202A 1110 Seymour St., Vancouver BC, Canada and

16149 Redmond Way #180, WA 98052.
A Birder's Guide to Costa Rica, Taylor, K. 1993. Keith Taylor, 4295 Carey Road #5, Victoria BC Canada V8Z 4H1.
Costa Rica National Parks, Boza, M. A. 1988. Incafo, Madrid. (Superb colour photographs.)
Costa Rican Natural History, Janzen, D. H. (ed.) 1983. University of Chicago Press.

COSTA RICA ENDEMICS (6)

Cocos Cuckoo*	Cocos Island
Mangrove Hummingbird*	Pacific coastline from the Golfo de Nicoya south to Golfo Dulce
Coppery-headed Emerald	Caribbean slope (mostly) of central massif from Cordillera de Guanacaste to the Río Reventazón
Cocos Flycatcher*	Cocos Island
Black-cheeked Ant-tanager*	Península de Osa
Cocos Finch*	Cocos Island

NEAR-ENDEMICS

Species shared with Panama (29) are defined as those occurring only in the two western provinces, Bocas del Toro and Chiriquí.

Chiriqui Quail-Dove	Cordillera de Tilarán to west Panama
Sulphur-winged Parakeet	Cordillera Central to west Panama
Red-fronted Parrotlet*	Cordillera de Guanacaste to west Panama
Dusky Nightjar	Cordillera de Talamanca to west Panama
White-crested Coquette	Cordillera de Tilarán to west Panama
Fiery-throated Hummingbird	South Pacific from Atenas to west Panama
Grey-tailed Mountain-gem	Pacific foothills: Carara to west Panama
Scintillant Hummingbird	Pacific slope from Río Tárcoles to west Panama
Fiery-billed Araçari	Foothills of Caribbean slope north to Río Sarapiquí; western Panama
Turquoise Cotinga*	Cordillera de Tilarán south to west Panama
Yellow-billed Cotinga	Cordillera de Guanacaste to west Panama
Bare-necked Umbrellabird*	Cordillera de Talamanca to west Panama
Dark Pewee	Cordillera Central to west Panama
Ochraceous Pewee	Cordillera Central (Irazú) to west Panama
Black-capped Flycatcher	Cordillera Central to west Panama
Riverside Wren	South Pacific slope from Carara to west Panama
Timberline Wren	Highlands from Volcán Irazú to west Panama
Sooty Robin	Highlands from Cordillera Central to west Panama

Black-billed Nightingale-Thrush	Cordillera Central to west Panama
Long-tailed Silky-Flycatcher	Cordillera Central to west Panama
Black-and-yellow Silky-Flycatcher	Cordillera de Tilarán to west Panama
Yellow-winged Vireo	Cordillera Central to west Panama
Flame-throated Warbler	Cordillera Central to west Panama
Wrenthrush	Cordillera de Guanacaste to west Panama
Nicaraguan Grackle	Lowlands of north Costa Rica (Río Frío, Lago Caño Negro); south Nicaragua
Spot-crowned Euphonia	Pacific slope in foothills, north to Carara; west Panama
Peg-billed Finch	Cordillera de Tilarán south; recently discovered in west Panama
Large-footed Finch	Cordillera Central to west Panama
Yellow-thighed Finch	Cordillera de Tilarán to west Panama
Volcano Junco	Cordillera Central to west Panama

EL SALVADOR

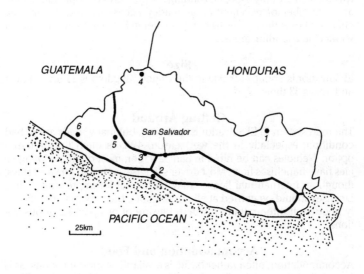

1 Perquín and Cuenca del Río Sapo   4 Montecristo National Park
2 Walter Deininger National Park   5 Cerro Verde and Volcán Santa Ana
3 Finca La Geralda   6 El Imposible National Park

INTRODUCTION

Summary

El Salvador is the smallest of the Central American countries and at present is rather a rare destination for birdwatchers. Ironically, it was the subject of one of the earliest detailed surveys of the birds of the region—the classic study of Dickey and Van Rossem in 1938—but several factors militate against it as a popular birdwatching destination. First and foremost is the widespread degradation of habitat: some estimates place the destruction of natural forest as high as 95%, although this gives an unrealistically gloomy picture, as the extensive shade-coffee plantations are often excellent habitat. El Salvador is the most densely populated country in the region, being a little smaller than Belize with a population 25 times greater. Until recently a chronic political instability led to cycles of unrest, followed by reprisal and repression, giving the country an unsavoury reputation and doing little to encourage tourism of any type.

However, having stated the above, it should be said that the neglect of El Salvador by birdwatchers is a great pity. It is a country of astounding natural beauty with some of the most spectacular volcanoes and mountain lakes anywhere in Central America. The population is not jaded by some of the excesses of tourism, which occur elsewhere in parts of Central America, and is friendly, courteous and helpful. The political situation has stabilized since 1992 with a corresponding improvement in security. Notwithstanding the pressures of population, there are a number of excellent areas readily accessible and, finally, the chance of new discoveries is much greater in El Salvador than in better worked surrounding areas.

Size
El Salvador is about 21,000 km^2; the United Kingdom is 11 times larger and Texas 33 times.

Getting Around
The road system in El Salvador is extensive, but many roads are in bad condition, especially in the wet season. 4WD is often the preferred option. Vehicles can be hired in San Salvador; most of the major agencies have franchises here. Most driver's licenses are valid for short stays, though an international license may be helpful for impressing police. Licenses should be carried at all times. Public bus services are relatively frequent if often rather crowded. Beware of pickpockets at bus stations.

Accommodation and Food
Accommodation, often rather basic, is available at most locations, as is food (albeit often rather heavily influenced by the black bean). However, excellent seafood is widely available on the Pacific coast. Prices tend to be very moderate.

Health and Safety
Malaria is present around Santa Ana and in the border regions of Guatemala, but currently chloroquine-resistant malaria has not occurred. Recommended vaccinations include hepatitis A and, for those going to rural areas, typhoid. There is a substantial and serious crime problem in San Salvador and other cities, and theft is frequent, even away from cities. The usual commonsense precautions should be taken.

Climate and Timing
Having only one coastline, El Salvador has less variation of climate than other Central American countries, altitude being the principal determining factor. The wet season (which complicates road travel) lasts from mid-May to mid-October. Probably the prime time to visit is at the end of the dry season, in April, when many North American migrants are still present.

Habitats
Originally El Salvador had very diverse habitats, as it ranges from sea level to 2730 m. On the Pacific coastal plain there were extensive swamp forests, humid and dry tropical forests, mangrove swamps and freshwater lagoons. Humid forest and cloud forest is present on the higher volcanoes; the interior valley has different forest types, and pine and pine–oak forest occurs in the central cordillera. For a detailed study see Komar (1998, 2001).

Conservation

'In all, 254 species (>50% of the avifauna) are threatened by habitat loss, pollution, hunting and exploitation for the pet trade. Of these, 117 are in danger of extinction at the national level and three are believed already extirpated' (Komar 1998). The National Park system is a recent creation in El Salvador, the first park being established as recently as 1987. The current protected area includes eight sites totalling 11,000 ha or 0.5% of the country. A proposal to increase this to 2.4% is current.

Bird Families

About 67 families (depending on taxonomy) occur in El Salvador, including 44 species of warbler (of which only seven breed), 41 flycatchers (19 breeding), 22 hummingbirds (11 breeding) and 10 wrens (all breeding). The proportion of proven breeders will doubtless increase with additional research.

Bird Species

508 species had been recorded in El Salvador by 1998, a rather low total compared to the number for less mountainous Belize (almost 550). With more fieldwork this total will undoubtedly increase.

Expectations

A visit that concentrated on the remaining habitat types, at a time when North American migrants are present, might expect 200–250 species. We are unaware of anyone who has carried out such an exercise recently.

PERQUÍN AND CUENCA DEL RÍO SAPO

One of the few remaining extensive areas of mid-altitude pine forest in El Salvador, and now the only site in the country for several species such as Plain Chachalaca and Mountain Trogon. Although not officially protected, it is one of the largest natural areas in El Salvador.

Others

King Vulture, Swallow-tailed Kite, Zone-tailed and White-breasted Hawks, Plain Chachalaca, Red-throated Parakeet, White-fronted Parrot, Common Nighthawk, Azure-crowned Hummingbird, Mountain Trogon, Acorn Woodpecker, Red-shafted (Guatemalan) Flicker, Greater Pewee, Painted Redstart, Hepatic Tanager, Black-headed Siskin, Yellow-backed Oriole.

Access

Situated in northern Morazán province, close to the border of Honduras. Head north from San Miguel through San Francisco Gotera on Highway 7. The road quality degenerates near Perquín. The Hotel Perkin Lanca, an excellent base, occupies a rise overlooking the road, approximately 1 km south of Perquín. The Quebrada de Perquín forest is within walking distance from the hotel.

Another good area is the Llanos del Muerte. Take the only road that leads east from Highway 7 (about 2 km south of the hotel) and proceed for about 4 km. 4WD is necessary in the rainy season. Park at the marked turn-off for Río Negro and walk 3 km north to the river, which is the Honduran border, or walk south to some waterfalls (the land owner charges a small fee for access).

Accommodation: Hotel Perkin Lanca.

WALTER DEININGER NATIONAL PARK

An easily accessible park located at the intersection of the coastal plain and foothills of the Sierra del Bálsamo, about one hour's drive from San Salvador. The protected area is about 730 ha in size.

Others
Grey-headed Kite, Grey Hawk, Laughing Falcon, Orange-fronted Parakeet, Lesser Ground-Cuckoo, Blue-throated Goldentail, Violaceous and Elegant Trogons, Collared Araçari, Black Phoebe, Rose-throated Becard, Red-throated Ant-Tanager.

Access
Leave San Salvador on Highway 4 and turn east on Highway 2. It is necessary to call the Salvadoran Tourism Institute (503)-222-8000 for permission to enter the park.

Accommodation: there is ample food and accommodation in Puerto La Libertad and Playa San Diego.

The Collared Araçari occurs in humid lowlands in El Salvador

FINCA LA GERALDA

A shade-coffee plantation situated in a 70 ha valley, two-thirds of which is natural forest. The plantation is being developed to cater for birdwatchers, with an ecotourism lodge and restaurant. Thus far 110 species of bird have been recorded but this will clearly increase with further work.

Specialities

Buffy-crowned Wood-Partridge, Greater Swallow-tailed Swift, Prevost's Ground-Sparrow.

Others

Rufous-necked Wood-Rail, Lesser Swallow-tailed Swift, Rufous Sabre-wing, Salvin's Emerald, Lineated Woodpecker, Paltry Tyrannulet, Long-billed Gnatwren, Orange-billed Nightingale-Thrush, Red-legged Honey-creeper, White-winged Tanager, White-eared Ground-Sparrow, Bar-winged Oriole.

Access

Leave San Salvador west on the Pan-American Highway (Highway 1). At the west end of the city of Santa Tecla, where the east and west lanes of the highway merge, turn south (making a U-turn across the eastbound lane just beyond a Shell station) onto a residential street. Immediately take the next right. At the end of the houses this street becomes a narrow paved road, to Comasagua, known as Carretera de la Cumbre (Summit Road), as it follows the ridge top of the Sierra del Bálsamo. After about 13 km the entrance to Finca La Geralda is 50 m before the turn-off to Comasagua. The road to the Finca itself requires 4-wheel drive but cars can be parked at the entrance. Visitors should make prior arrangement with the management (e-mail ecomillenium@hotmail.com).

MONTECRISTO NATIONAL PARK

Located on the border with Honduras, Montecristo has some of the best habitat remaining in El Salvador. The National Park covers approximately 2000 ha and protects some excellent cloud forest and pine–oak forest. It is rarely visited by overseas ornithologists and the species list for the area (currently about 230) will surely increase. For 26 species, Montecristo is now the only known location in El Salvador; in addition several species of large mammal which have largely or entirely disappeared from the rest of the country are found here.

Specialities

Highland Guan*, Fulvous Owl, Resplendent Quetzal*, Black-capped Swallow, Bushy-crested Jay.

Others

Amethyst-throated and Garnet-throated Hummingbirds, Collared Trogon, Blue-throated Motmot, Scaly-throated and Ruddy Foliage-gleaners, Tawny-throated Leaftosser, Black-throated and Unicoloured Jays, Slate-coloured Solitaire, Spotted Nightingale-Thrush, Golden-browed, Olive and Grace's Warblers, Slate-throated and Painted Redstarts, Yellow-backed and Black-vented Orioles, Hooded Grosbeak.

Other Wildlife

Puma, Black Spider Monkey, Agouti.

Access

The Park is 14 km northwest of Metapán along a road for which 4WD is often helpful. There is no public transport. Some visitors have been able to negotiate a ride from locals in Metapán. The Hotel San José (tel. 442-0556) apparently arranges trips—for a price—for its guests. There is a small admission charge to the park. During the wet season (April–September) areas of the park are closed to visitors to permit undisturbed breeding, though this policy may be relaxed in the future. Conventional vehicles can reach higher elevations during the dry season.

CERRO VERDE AND VOLCÁN SANTA ANA

Scenically beautiful, with spectacular views over Lago de Coatépeque and several volcanic peaks, the Cerro Verde area is one of the best pieces of relatively pristine habitat remaining in El Salvador. It is easily accessible from San Salvador by road. Volcán Santa Ana is 2365 m in altitude and possesses productive montane forest and cloud forest. It is the only easy location in El Salvador for many montane forest specialists, including an endemic race of Rufous-browed Wren.

Specialities
Black Hawk-Eagle, Rufous-browed Wren, Blue-and-white Mockingbird, Rufous-collared Robin.

Others
Barred Forest-Falcon, Emerald-chinned, Wine-throated and Magnificent Hummingbirds, Emerald Toucanet, Spot-crowned Woodcreeper, Scaled Antpitta, Eye-ringed Flatbill, Yellowish Flycatcher, Black Robin, Ruddy-capped Nightingale-Thrush, Brown-capped Vireo, Cinnamon-

CERRO VERDE AND VOLCÁN SANTA ANA

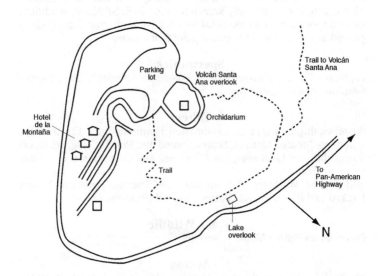

bellied Flowerpiercer, Blue-crowned Chlorophonia, Blue-hooded Euphonia, Yellow-throated Brush-Finch, Rufous-collared Sparrow.

Access
From San Salvador proceed northwest along Highway 1 (the Pan-American) towards Santa Ana. The best road appears to be that from El Congo, which skirts the south side of Lago de Coatépeque, and leads to the Hotel de la Montaña. There is a trail, which leads to the lake from a location known as El Jicote, which is approximately 4 km along the road to Cerro Verde from its intersection with the road skirting the lake from El Congo. The trail is about 10 km-long. A bus (number 348) goes from Santa Ana to Cerro Verde. Another trail leads from near the Hotel de la Montaña to the peak of Volcán Santa Ana, a hike that takes about three hours without long stops for birdwatching.

Accommodation and food are available at the Hotel de la Montaña. Early reservation (tel. 222-3241) is advised. The hotel was built to afford good views of nearby Volcán Izalco, which had been spewing spectacular hot lava for 200 years. Remarkably just as the hotel was completed the volcano became inactive and has been sitting in sulky silence ever since. Camping (with permission) is possible on Finca San Blas. There is also a variety of accommodations in Santa Ana (population 240,000).

EL IMPOSIBLE NATIONAL PARK

The largest National Park in El Salvador, being 5000 ha in extent. Its name derives from its inaccessibility, a feature that also explains its survival in a relatively untouched state. Located on the rocky slopes of the Cordillera de Apaneca, it contains more than 300 species of tree, while the bird list currently stands at 277. It is also home to several species of large mammal.

Specialities
Black Hawk-Eagle, Crested Guan, Great Curassow*, Black-and-white Owl.

Others
King Vulture, White Hawk, Ruddy Quail-Dove, Pale-billed Woodpecker, Ruddy, Olivaceous, Ivory-billed and Spotted Woodcreepers, Long-tailed Manakin, Greenish Elaenia, Stub-tailed Spadebill, Northern Bentbill, Bright-rumped Attila, Banded Wren, Lesser Greenlet, Blue Bunting.

Access
Take Highway 2 northwest towards the Guatemalan border. About 40 km from the intersection with Highway 12 (just north of Acajutla), at km 106, turn north (right) onto a gravel road on the west side of the bridge over the Río Ahuachapio. Proceed 13 km to the park entrance at the former San Benito hacienda. A permit from SALVANATURA headquarters (www.salvanatura.org, or tel. (503)-263-111) is required.

ADDITIONAL INFORMATION

Books and papers

A Guide to the Birds of Mexico and Northern Central America, Howell, S. N. G. and Webb, S. 1995. Oxford UP. (Covers El Salvador.)

The Birds of El Salvador, Dickey, D. R. and Van Rossem, A. J. 1938. Field Museum of Natural History, Zoological Series No. 7, Chicago. (Not a field guide.)

Avian diversity in El Salvador, Komar, O. 1998. *Wilson Bulletin* 110: 511–533.

Contribuciones a la avifauna de El Salvador, Komar, O. 2001. *Cotinga* 16

On Your Own in El Salvador, Brauer, J., Smith, J and Wiles, V. 1995. On Your Own Publications, Charlottesville. (Full of useful information on history, accommodation and transport.)

GUATEMALA

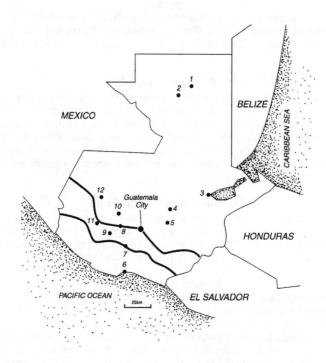

1 Tikal
2 Cerro Cahui Reserve
3 Bocas del Polochic Wildlife Refuge
4 Mario Dary Rivera Reserve (Biotopo de Quetzal)
5 Motagua Valley

6 Monterrico Natural Reserve
7 Royal Palm Drive
8 Sierra de Tecpán
9 Lago de Atitlán
10 Santa Cruz del Quiché (Utatlán)
11 Fuentes Georginas and km 197
12 Todos Santos Cuchumatán

INTRODUCTION

Summary

Guatemala, a country of spectacular beauty and infinite sorrows, is the northernmost of the Spanish-speaking republics of Central America. Within a relatively small area it is an extraordinarily diverse country. Though little more than one-twentieth the size of Mexico, it harbours 700 species of birds, almost two-thirds the Mexican total. The human population is also highly diverse. More than 50% are of more or less pure Mayan descent, and 21 local languages are spoken. Local costume, varying from village to adjacent village, is still routinely worn and there are colourful local markets in many towns. For almost a third of a century, following a US-inspired coup in 1954, a state of near civil war of fluctuating intensity and frequent savagery rendered the country a less than desirable location for visitors. A peace accord was signed in 1996.

Size

Guatemala has an area of 109,000 km², making it the second-largest country in Central America after Nicaragua. Slightly smaller than England, it is about the same size as the state of Virginia, or one-seventh the size of Texas.

Getting Around

Southern Guatemala has a good network of roads, but many are extremely rough. The northern part of the country, especially the extensive forested lowlands of the Petén have few roads and no good ones. There is a local air service to such places as Flores (Santa Elena) for Tikal and Puerto Barrios on the Caribbean coast. Car hire can be arranged in larger urban centres. There is an extensive system of public buses, which can be very crowded.

Accommodation and Food

Accommodation is readily available in virtually all towns of any size, as well as in some smaller centres. Quality varies from very luxurious to extremely basic. Food is easily available. Generally prices in Guatemala are very low, except in a few very popular places like Tikal.

Health and Safety

Malaria is present in lowland areas including Tikal. Chagas disease may also occur below 500 m. Immunizations against typhoid and viral hepatitis are recommended. Drinking water is frequently suspect.

Guatemala has the reputation of being a dangerous country; common sense, local enquiry and consultation with your embassy for the most recent information are all strongly advised. There has been, to our knowledge, at least one serious recent incident at Cerro Cahui, when a birdwatcher was shot, almost fatally. An especially distressing feature of this case was that local people, including hoteliers and park officials, were aware of the danger and failed to warn visitors. Theft is a considerable problem.

Climate and Timing

Climate in Guatemala is very much a function of location and elevation. The Pacific lowlands are hot and humid, with a rainy season in May–October, and the Caribbean lowlands are very similar, with rainfall more generally distributed throughout the year; e.g. the city of Cobán, in north-central Guatemala, has only one guaranteed dry month, April. In the Central Highlands the climate is frequently very pleasant, ranging to genuinely cool at higher elevations. Rainfall in Guatemala City occurs mostly in May–October. During the wet season high-altitude locations can be very cold and foggy. Most species breed in March–August; however, in September–April species diversity is augmented by winter migrants from North America, including many species of warblers and vireos.

Habitats

Guatemala is divided by a spine of high mountains, punctuated by volcanic peaks. Either side of the central chain are lowlands of rather different characters. The Caribbean lowlands and Petén are the richest areas in Guatemala, with more than 300 species recorded, including almost 100 that do not occur elsewhere in the country. The Caribbean lowlands are loosely divided into the Tropical Dry Forest zone, in northern Petén, and the Tropical Moist Forest zone in southern Petén and elsewhere. The Pacific lowlands have suffered more intense deforestation and habitat destruction than the Caribbean side, and possess far fewer specialities. Where habitat remains the Pacific lowlands vary from Tropical Dry Forest, at the lowest elevations, to Tropical Moist Forest in the foothills. In eastern Guatemala, especially in the Motagua Valley, northeast of Guatemala City, there is a seasonal arid zone, which though boasting a fauna poorer in overall species numbers harbours a number of dry-country species not found elsewhere in the country.

The central highlands are a continuation of the massif that rises in Chiapas, Mexico. Being isolated by lower elevations it holds a number of species confined to Mexico and Guatemala, such as the bizarre and rare Horned Guan*, the spectacular Pink-headed Warbler, Azure-rumped Tanager* and Rufous-collared Thrush. The highlands of Guatemala contain some of the most visually stunning scenery in Central America, ranging from high mountain lakes to geometrically precise volcanoes.

Conservation

Like all of Central America, Guatemala has suffered significantly from deforestation and general habitat destruction, and several formerly profitable sites known to us are no longer worth visiting. Conservation became a difficult and often dangerous theme to pursue during the civil war. Nevertheless Guatemala has more than 30 protected areas, including National Parks and Biological Reserves; a further 40 have been proposed, giving protection, at least on paper, to 15% of the country. The largest reserve in Guatemala is the Reserva de la Biosfera Maya, which covers almost 2 million ha, not including contiguous protected areas in Mexico and Belize. A law passed in 1989 established reserves and gave new hope for the future of conservation in Guatemala.

Bird Families

About 75 of the approximately 90 (depending on taxonomy) bird families found in Mexico and Central America occur in Guatemala. While Guatemala has no true endemics (if one neglects the flightless Atitlan Grebe, which probably no longer survives in a genetically pure state), there are a number of near-endemics and several species of restricted range most easily found in the country.

Expectations

A very determined birdwatcher could, in a few weeks, probably see 400 species in Guatemala, and we know of some observers who have amassed more than 350 in less than a fortnight. More realistically a total of 300–350 species is attainable.

TIKAL

For birdwatchers and non-birdwatchers alike, a trip to Guatemala that does not include Tikal on the itinerary is simply inconceivable. Leaving aside the spectacular ruins, Tikal is an accessible example of the forest that formerly covered most of northern Guatemala and southern Yucatán. Over 300 species of bird have been found within 20 km of Tikal. For several years, prior to the publication of more geographically comprehensive works, F. B. Smith's *The Birds of Tikal* (AMNH, 1966) was the only illustrated book dealing with the lowland birds of northern Guatemala and adjacent areas.

Specialities

Great Tinamou, Ornate Hawk-Eagle, Spotted Wood-Quail, Great Curassow*, Ocellated Turkey* (common, tame and wild), Black-and-white Owl, Canivet's Emerald, Wedge-tailed Sabrewing, Tody Motmot, Yucatan Poorwill, White-browed Wren, Olive-backed Euphonia, Black-throated Shrike-Tanager.

Others

Little and Slaty-breasted Tinamous, Bare-throated Tiger-Heron (Aguada Tikal), King Vulture, Barred and Collared Forest-Falcons, Bat and Orange-breasted Falcons, Hook-billed and Plumbeous Kites, Black Hawk-Eagle, Great Black Hawk, White Hawk, Crested Guan, Plain Chachalaca, Limpkin (airstrip ponds), Grey-necked Wood-Rail, Ruddy Crake, Scaled Pigeon, Blue Ground-Dove, Grey-headed and Ruddy Quail-Doves, Olive-throated Parakeet, White-crowned, White-fronted, Red-lored and Mealy Parrots, Mottled Owl, Vermiculated Screech-Owl, Little Hermit, White-bellied Emerald, Purple-crowned Fairy, Rufous-tailed Hummingbird, Black-headed and Slaty-tailed Trogons, Pygmy Kingfisher (airstrip

The Keel-billed Toucan, the largest member of its family in Guatemala, is quite common in suitable forest

ponds), Blue-crowned Motmot, White-necked (Mirador) and White-whiskered Puffbirds, Keel-billed Toucan, Emerald Toucanet, Collared Araçari, Golden-fronted, Pale-billed, Black-cheeked, Chestnut-coloured and Smoky-brown Woodpeckers, Olivaceous, Barred, Tawny-winged, Ivory-billed and Ruddy Woodcreepers, Buff-fronted Foliage-gleaner, Plain Xenops, Plain Antvireo, Dot-winged Antwren, Black-faced Antthrush, Dusky Antbird, Grey-collared Becard, Red-capped Manakin, Thrush-like Schiffornis, Rufous Mourner, Sulphur-bellied, Brown-crested, Ruddy-tailed, Piratic, Northern Royal, Yellow-olive, Sepia-capped and Sulphur-rumped Flycatchers, Eye-ringed Flatbill, Yellow-bellied Tyrannulet, Stub-tailed Spadebill, Spot-breasted and White-bellied Wrens, Tawny-crowned and Lesser Greenlets, Mangrove and Yellow-green Vireos, Prothonotoary, Worm-eating and Kentucky Warblers, Louisiana Waterthrush (winter), Grey-breasted Chat, Yellow-throated Euphonia, Yellow-winged, Golden-hooded and Grey-headed Tanager, Red-crowned and Red-throated Ant-Tanagers, Black-faced Grosbeak, Blue and Painted Buntings, Black-headed Saltator, Green-backed Sparrow, Yellow-backed and Black-cowled Orioles.

Other Wildlife

Jaguars are quite frequently seen, especially in the early morning and, appropriately, often near the Hotel Jaguar, but inappropriately, feeding on their rubbish tip. Howler and Spider Monkeys are common. Coatis, agoutis and peccaries also occur.

Access

Road access from Guatemala City—Highway 5 through Cobán, then Highway 13 from Modesto Mendez, or alternatively Highway 9 to La Ruidosa, thence north on Highway 13 to Flores—is a long, uncomfortable and dusty drive. There are buses from Guatemala City to Flores. However, you should be aware that the comforts of this ride are so imaginary that in Flores they sell T-shirts inscribed 'I took the bus to Tikal and survived'. Not all do. There are also daily air services between Guatemala City and Flores, and Belize City and Flores. Cars may be hired from several different agencies at Flores Airport and at the Hotel San Juan in Santa Elena. Daily buses for Tikal leave the major hotels in both Santa Elena and Flores several times each morning and return in the evening. Taxis can be hired from the airport, or in Flores and Santa Elena, for about $40 return. The road journey from Flores to the entrance of the Tikal complex takes 1–1.5 hours.

Tikal is worth a visit of several days. The ruins are, of course, indescribable. Birdwatchers will want to spend the earliest part of the day in

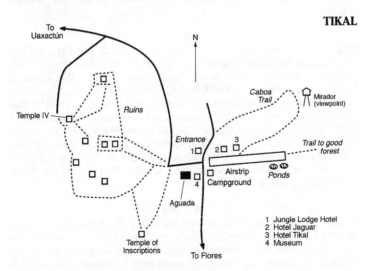

TIKAL

To Uaxactún

N

Caboa Trail · · · ⌂ Mirador (viewpoint)

Temple IV

Ruins

Trail to good forest

Entrance

3

Airstrip
Ponds

Campground

Aguada

Temple of Inscriptions

To Flores

1 Jungle Lodge Hotel
2 Hotel Jaguar
3 Hotel Tikal
4 Museum

the forest, which is fairly open (making for easy observation), before climbing one or more of the temples for a view over the canopy. Some structures are still covered in vegetation and are especially worth ascending. Raptors tend to rise over the forest canopy as the day warms up and are best observed from the tops of the temples; the view from Temple IV is particularly recommended. Outside the main temple areas there are several ponds and wet areas, good for rails and crakes, as is the Aguada, opposite the Jungle Lodge hotel. The airstrip itself is worth investigating. North of the airstrip, the Caboa trail leads from near the Hotel Jaguar and is well worth exploring. The lookout point (Mirador) is also worthwhile. From the eastern end of the airstrip another trail goes east. The road to Uaxactún and the road looping back to Temple IV should also be investigated.

Because hunting is prohibited, many of the large gamebirds, such as Ocellated Turkey* (which is common), Great Curassow* and Crested Guan are much easier to observe at Tikal than almost anywhere else.

Accommodation: at Tikal there are several hotels at assorted prices; however, they are frequently fully occupied by tour groups. Food is readily available. Prices for accommodation and meals in Tikal are high by Guatemalan standards. There is also an official campground, near the disused airstrip, and a private campground at the Hotel Jaguar. An entrance fee to the whole Tikal complex is payable.

CERRO CAHUI RESERVE

A small reserve on the northern shore of Petén Itzá. A visit can be conveniently combined with Tikal, which is only 33 km away.

Specialities
Tody Motmot (Los Ujuxtes trail), White-browed and White-bellied Wrens, Grey-throated Chat, Black-throated Shrike-Tanager, Olive-backed Euphonia.

Others
Snail and Double-toothed Kites, Great Black Hawk, Bat Falcon, Plain Chachalaca, Red-billed Pigeon, Blue Ground-Dove, Little Hermit, Fork-tailed and White-bellied Emeralds, Purple-crowned Fairy, Black-headed and Violaceous Trogons, Golden-olive and Golden-fronted Woodpeckers, Tawny-winged, Olivaceous, Northern Barred, Ivory-billed and Wedge-billed Woodcreepers, Plain Antvireo, Sulphur-bellied, Sulphur-rumped, Northern Royal, Yellow-Olive and Sepia-capped Flycatchers, Eye-ringed Flatbill, Spot-breasted Wren, White-bellied Wood-Wren, Tawny-crowned and Lesser Greenlets, Yellow-winged Tanager, Red-throated and Red-crowned Ant-Tanagers, Black-headed Saltator, Black-faced Grosbeak, Blue Bunting, Black-cowled Oriole.

Access
Usually visited in combination with Tikal. Regular flights from Guatemala City go to Flores airport. Flores (Santa Elena) is also served by buses from Guatemala City, some overnight. This is a long (12 hours) and unpleasant journey. By road, head north from Guatemala City on High-

way 5, then Highway 13. Turn right at Santa Elena towards Tikal; the entrance road leading to the park is opposite the 'Gringo Perdido' restaurant in El Remate. There are at least two daily buses from Santa Elena to El Remate (currently leaving at 6.30am and 1pm), which is approximately one hour's journey.

The reserve has two good trails, one approximately 3 km long (El Tzulunte) and the other 1.5 km (Los Ujuxtes). There is a $5 entrance fee to the reserve. The south shore of the lake has some marshy areas. Boat trips on Lago Petén Itzá can be arranged in Flores, either by negotiating with boat owners at the waterfront, going to the Santa Elena end of the causeway linking Flores to the mainland, or by asking at the Bar Las Puertas in Flores. It is advisable to inspect the boat you hire for seaworthiness. There is, incidentally, an endemic crocodile in the lake (Petén Crocodile *Crocodylus moreletti*). The mouth of the Río Ixpop in the southeast corner of the lake is the best area for waterbirds. The road along the north shore of the lake is extremely rough and the habitat very cut over; however, some semi-regenerated areas exist, which may be worthwhile visiting.

Note. At the time of writing, this area remains closed as a result of the shooting incident mentioned in the introduction, the perpetrators being apparently still at large.

Accommodation is available in Santa Elena. The Hotel El Gringo Perdido on the north shore of the lake near the park entrance is the most expensive; the Restaurant El Gringo Perdido in El Remate has basic cabins, and camping is possible. Food tends to be expensive by Guatemalan standards.

BOCAS DEL POLOCHIC WILDLIFE REFUGE

A very large (235 km^2) wetland at the western end of Lago de Izabal. Approximately 6400 ha are permanently flooded and a further 14,000 ha is seasonally flooded. There are several lagoons within the refuge area, as well as areas of permanently flooded forest.

Specialities
Agami Heron, Muscovy Duck (common in Sep).

Others
Bare-throated Tiger-Heron, Wood Stork, Black-bellied Whistling-Duck, Northern Jacana, Purple Gallinule, Grey-necked Wood-Rail, Limpkin.

Access
Access to the refuge is only by boat: these may be hired in El Estor (Sr. La Paz, Hotel Vista al Lago, El Estor), or in Mariscos, on the south shore of the lake. El Estor is on Highway 7E, which joins Highway 5 south of Cobán.

Accommodation: there are cabins at the Refuge with bunk beds, kitchen, etc. To rent these contact in advance the Fundación Defensores de la Naturaleza, Ave. 19, 0-89 Zona 15 Vista Hermosa 11, Guatemala City 01015, tel. 369-777, e-mail defensores@pronet.net.gt.

MARIO DARY RIVERA RESERVE (BIOTOPO DE QUETZAL)

A superb cloud forest reserve, of approximately 1100 ha at an altitude of about 2000 m, with a good system of trails and convenient accommodation. It is an excellent place to see a great variety of highland species including Resplendent Quetzal*.

Specialities
Highland Guan*, Barred Parakeet, Resplendent Quetzal* (most easily seen in February–March when displaying).

Others
Green-throated Mountain-Gem, White-eared and Garnet-throated Hummingbirds, Blue-crowned Motmot, Spotted, Strong-billed and Spot-crowned Woodcreepers, Scaly-throated Foliage-gleaner, Tawny-throated Leaftosser, Scaled Antpitta, Bushy-crested, Azure-hooded, Black-throated and Unicoloured Jays, Yellowish, Pine and Tufted Flycatchers, Grey Silky-Flycatcher, Blue-and-white Mockingbird, Spotted Nightingale-Thrush, Rufous-collared and Mountain Robins, Slate-coloured and Brown-backed Solitaires, Cinnamon Flowerpiercer, Crescent-chested, Rufous-capped, Hermit and Grace's Warblers, Slate-coloured Redstart, Blue-crowned Chlorophonia, Flame-coloured Tanager, Yellow-throated and Chestnut-capped Brush-Finches, Black-headed Siskin.

MARIO DARY RIVERA RESERVE

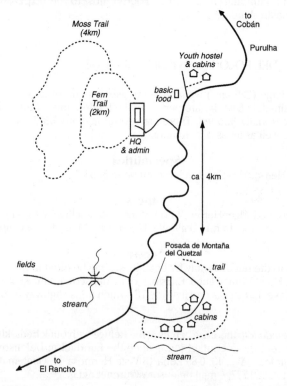

Access

Take Highway 9 from Guatemala City to El Rancho Junction and then turn left (west) onto Highway 17 (Cobán); at La Cumbre fork right onto 14 (Purulha). The park headquarters is at km 160.5. Buses from Guatemala City to Cobán take about 3.5 hours; ask the driver for Biotopo de Quetzal at km 160.5.

Once in the reserve (daily access 6am to 4pm) there are several trails; the 'Fern Trail' is 2 km long, the 'Moss Trail' 4 km. The road itself is good for birding. On the road to the Biotopo de Quetzal, a few km before El Rancho, a track to the right signed 'El Jicaro 14 km', and a turn-off 200 m on the right, access some dry-country habitat, where it is possible to find Blue-tailed and Cinnamon Hummingbirds, White-lored Gnatcatcher, and Altamira and Streak-backed Orioles.

Accommodation: comparatively expensive accommodation is available at Posada de Montaña del Quetzal, a hotel with cabins (and good birding in the vicinity) about 4 km south of the headquarters, and more basic accommodation just beyond the entrance in the Hospedaje (Youth Hostel). Quetzals are often seen in the trees opposite the Hospedaje in the early morning. Food is available at the Posada and at the Hospedaje. It may be possible to camp at the park headquarters. It can become very cold at night. For more information, contact Centro de Estudios Conservacionistas, Avenida de la Reforma, 0-63 Zona 10, 01010 Guatemala City. Tel. 334-6064, e-mail cecon@usac.edu.gt.

MOTAGUA VALLEY

A semi-arid area that can conveniently be visited en route to Mario Dary Rivera Reserve; it is a location for dry-country species.

MOTAGUA VALLEY

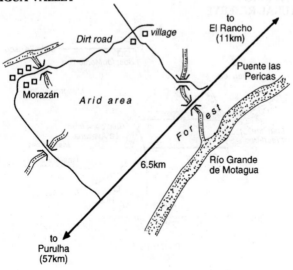

125

Others

Lesser Ground-Cuckoo, Lesser Roadrunner, Squirrel Cuckoo, Turquoise-browed and Russet-crowned Motmots, Golden-fronted Woodpecker, Bushy-crested Jay, White-throated Magpie-Jay, Rufous-naped and Plain Wrens, White-lored Gnatcatcher, Black-headed Saltator, Rusty and Stripe-headed Sparrows, Streak-backed, Hooded and Altamira Orioles.

Access

Take Highway 17 west from El Rancho. About 15 km from the latter a dirt road branches north (right) to Morazán. Stop and bird suitable habitat along this road before reaching Morazán. Shortly after the turn-off from Highway 17 a stream crosses the road and Highway 17 itself; the banks possess some good forest. The road loops through Morazán and rejoins Highway 17 approximately 7 km west of the river crossing.

MONTERRICO NATURAL RESERVE

A nature reserve on the south coast, about 35 km east of Puerto San José. There are good areas of mangroves and extensive reedbeds.

Others

Jabiru, Lesser Yellow-headed Vulture, Muscovy Duck, Zone-tailed Hawk, White-bellied Chachalaca, Black Skimmer, Orange-fronted and Orange-chinned Parakeets, Yellow-naped Parrot, American Pygmy Kingfisher, Barred Antshrike, Rose-throated Becard, Rufous-naped and Banded Wrens, Mangrove Vireo, Scrub Euphonia, Yellow-winged Tanager, Painted Bunting, Blue Grosbeak, White-collared and Ruddy-breasted Seedeaters, Stripe-headed Sparrow, Melodious Blackbird, Black-vented, Yellow-throated and Streak-backed Orioles.

**MONTERRICO
NATURAL RESERVE**

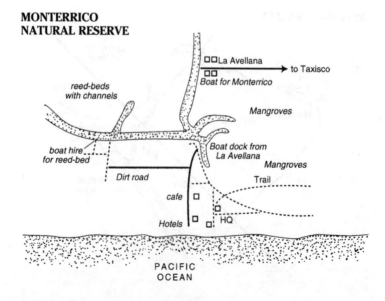

126

Other Wildlife
Sea turtles.

Access
Leave the Pan-American Highway on Highway 16 just east of Cuilapa, then turn west on Highway 2 just south of Chiquimulilla, and south in Taxisco (La Avellana). Alternatively go to Escuintla on Highway 9, then east on Highway 2 to Taxisco. In La Avellana, a 20-minute boat ride takes you to the docks in Monterrico. The reserve headquarters is east of the post office; from there a trail leads along the edge of the mangrove swamp. West of town, a long straight dirt road leads through fields; turn north at its end. Boats to enter the reedbeds may be hired here. For the best views of the mangroves a boat can be hired at the main dock. Buses run from Guatemala City to Chiquimulilla (3 hours). Get off at Taxisco and catch a local bus (35 minutes) to La Avellana. This area becomes very crowded at weekends. About 20 km west of Monterrico is the village of Iztapa (access via Escuintla and Puerto San José). Just west of Iztapa there are shrimp ponds with a selection of terns, herons, spoonbills and shorebirds. Mangrove Swallow also occurs here.

Accommodation: both food and accommodation are available in Monterrico and Puerto San José, and basic accommodation in Iztapa.

ROYAL PALM DRIVE

A road leading to a hydroelectric scheme just north of Escuintla accesses a good location for several Pacific-coast species.

Others
Grey Hawk, Band-tailed Pigeon, Orange-fronted Parakeet, Squirrel Cuckoo, Long-billed Starthroat, Turquoise-browed and Blue-crowned Motmots, Sulphur-bellied Flycatcher, Green Jay, Rufous-naped Wren.

Access
Five km north of Escuintla on Highway 9, turn right towards the hydroelectric station. There are some caves nearby (Grutas San Pedro Mártir).

SIERRA DE TECPÁN

A readily accessible area of highland pine–oak forest, made famous by the studies of Alexander Skutch, which supports a good selection of those species endemic to the Chiapas–Guatemalan massif.

Specialities
Blue-throated Motmot, Black-capped Swallow, Rufous-browed Wren, Rufous-collared Thrush, Pink-headed Warbler.

Others
Amethyst-throated and Garnet-throated Hummingbirds, Mountain Trogon, Hairy Woodpecker, Spot-crowned Woodcreeper, Tufted Flycatch-

er, Greater Pewee, Pine and Dusky-capped Flycatchers, Steller's Jay, Black-eared Bushtit, Brown Creeper, Golden-crowned Kinglet, Brown-backed Solitaire, Clay-coloured Thrush, Hutton's Vireo, Crescent-chested, Townsend's (winter), Grace's (winter), Wilson's (winter) and Mac-Gillivray's (winter) Warblers, Painted and Slate-throated Redstarts, Golden-browed, Red-faced (winter) and Olive Warblers, Common Bush-Tanager, Spotted Towhee, Cinnamon Flowerpiercer, Rusty and Rufous-collared Sparrows, Yellow-eyed Junco, Black-headed Siskin.

Access

Leave Guatemala City west on Highway 1 through Chimaltenango and take the second turn-off to the town of Tecpán (at the eco-hotel complex). After several blocks a dirt road veers to the left; if in doubt ask for the road to the antennas. It has a few bad patches where 4WD may be helpful, especially after rain, and ascends to the ridge at 3000 m, where commanding views of up to ten volcanoes may be had on a clear day. There are various trails through the woodland; the road is little travelled and makes a good birding site in its own right.

Accommodation: food and moderately priced accommodation is available in Tecpán.

LAGO DE ATITLÁN

A stunningly beautiful large mountain lake surrounded by high volcanoes. Formerly the only location of the Atitlan Grebe, whose status in a 'pure-blooded' form is presently obscure. Nearby volcanoes support the rare and near-endemic Horned Guan*.

Endemics
Atitlan Grebe.

Specialities
Horned Guan*.

Unlike its smaller cousin the Great Swallow-tailed Swift has a very restricted range, from Mexico to northern Nicaragua

Others

White-breasted Hawk, Red-billed Pigeon, Greater Swallow-tailed Swift, Green Violet-ear, Sparkling-tailed Woodstar, Rufous Sabrewing, Slender Sheartail, White-eared and Magnificent Hummingbirds, Guatemalan (Red-shafted) Flicker, Acorn Woodpecker, Spotted Woodcreeper, Grey-collared and Rose-throated Becards, Greater Pewee, Nutting's and Buff-breasted Flycatchers, Bushy-crested and Brown Jay, Black-eared Bush-tit, Band-backed, Spot-breasted, Rufous-browed, Plain and Rock Wrens, Blue-and-white Mockingbird, Cinnamon Flowerpiercer, Rufous-capped, Worm-eating (winter), Hooded (winter) and Townsend's (winter) Warblers, Rufous-browed Peppershrike, Blue-hooded Euphonia, Yellow-winged, Flame-coloured and Blue-grey Tanagers, Yellow-throated Brush-Finch, Prevost's Ground-Sparrow, Rusty Sparrow, Black-headed and Bar-winged Orioles.

Access

The Pan-American Highway (No. 1) skirts the northeast of the lake, passing through the resort town of Panajachel. South of San Andrés Semetabaj a surfaced road (No. 11) forks right toward San Lucas Tolimán, whence a very poor road continues to Santiago de Atitlán. An area of reedbeds 2 km northwest of Santiago is where grebes, of whatever ancestry, are found. This is accessible by negotiating boat hire in Santiago, or taking the road towards San Lucas (30 minutes on foot) to the park entrance (signed Pachaval). There is some forest on the road to San Pedro west of Santiago. Boat access is also available between Panajachel and Santiago.

There are several other worthwhile locations in the area. South of the lake are two volcanoes, Volcán Tolimán (3158 m) and Volcán Atitlán (3537 m), both of which harbour Horned Guan* and many other species. Access from Santiago is difficult; there are trails from near San Lucas,

LAGO DE ATITLÁN

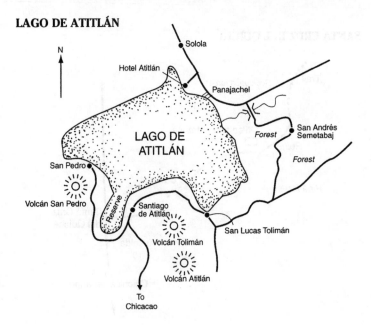

but local advice and guidance is necessary. There have also been reports of guerrilla activity in the area; again, local advice is essential. Volcán San Pedro, west of the lake, is more accessible but apparently has no Horned Guans*.

The road between Panajachel and San Andrés Semetabaj crosses a stream east of Panajachel. There are some good patches of forest on either side of the road before and after San Andrés. Another good birding area is accessible via a poor road southeast from Santiago de Atitlán (junction west of Santiago) towards Chicacao. After several km of climbing there is a picnic area (Mirador) on the right; approximately 100 m before this there is a steep trail on the left side which starts between two sandbanks and enters subtropical forest. This is a location for Resplendent Quetzal* and Black Chachalaca. Local enquiry as to conditions and safety is recommended. Belted Flycatcher* has been recorded between Santiago and Volcán Tolimán.

Buses from Guatemala City to Panajachel take three hours. There is a bus from Panajachel (leaving the pier area at 9 am) to Santiago (one hour). There are also buses between the lakeside villages and San Lucas.

Accommodation and food are available in Panajachel and Santiago. The Hotel Atitlán, on the north shore of the lake (turn west off Highway 1 west of Panajachel) also has a garden and adjacent woodland that may prove productive.

SANTA CRUZ DEL QUICHÉ (UTATLÁN)

This hilltop Mayan ruin is not especially spectacular archaeologically, but possesses some interesting forest surrounding the site.

SANTA CRUZ DEL QUICHÉ

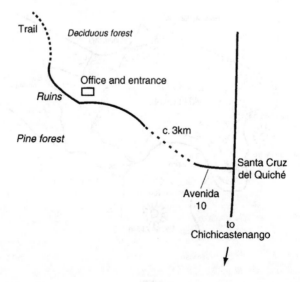

Others
Spot-crowned Woodcreeper, Pine Flycatcher, Band-backed Wren, Red-faced Warbler (winter).

Access
Santa Cruz del Quiché is located 33 km north of the tourist town of Chichicastenango, which is well worth visiting for its market. In Santa Cruz turn left (west) on Avenida 10 and proceed for about 3 km on a dirt road to the site entrance. Around the ruins are pine and deciduous forests, which are worth investigating.

FUENTES GEORGINAS AND KM 197

An area of hot springs, at approximately 2500 m altitude, with patches of remnant montane forest which, although small, are highly productive for some of the endemic species of the Chiapas–Guatemalan massif. Formerly, at least, a location for Horned Guan*; the present status of this species here is uncertain.

Specialities
Horned* and Highland* Guans, Singing Quail, Resplendent Quetzal*, Maroon-chested Dove, Blue-throated Motmot, Black-capped Swallow, Rufous-collared Thrush, Pink-headed Warbler, Azure-rumped Tanager*, Slaty Finch.

Others
Fulvous Owl, Green-throated Mountain-Gem, Wine-throated, Garnet-throated and Amethyst-throated Hummingbirds, Mountain Trogon, Black-banded Woodcreeper, Rufous-browed Wren, Blue-and-white Mockingbird, Ruddy-capped and Spotted Nightingale-Thrushes, Black and Mountain Robins, Cinnamon-bellied Flowerpiercer, Crescent-chested and Golden-browed Warblers, Yellow-eyed Junco, Chestnut-capped and Yellow-throated Brush-Finches.

Access
Reached by 8 km of dirt road from Highway 9 between Quetzaltenango (known locally as Xela, 'She-la') and Retalhuleu. The turn-off is at km 212, opposite the town of Zunil, approximately 20 km south of Quetzaltenango. Take a right fork part way along this road. There are good patches of forest along the entrance road, especially at stream crossings. At Fuentes there are several productive paths, as well as a steep and slippery trail, which ascends the ridge opposite the restaurant and terrace, across the stream. Pink-headed Warblers can be seen along this trail. Horned Guan* has been seen in the trees opposite the cabins, on the left-hand side as one enters, some way before the restaurant. Fuentes Georgina is a popular holiday spot for Guatemalans and can be quite noisy and crowded at weekends.

There are several other sites nearby. Returning to the Quetzaltenango–Retalhuleu road, turn left (south). At km 197 (Finca Pantonil) a jeep track leads off to the right. This is a relatively consistent location for Azure-rumped Tanager*; other species include Tawny-throated Leaftosser and Spotted Nightingale-Thrush. Take local advice before visiting this

FUENTES GEORGINAS AND KM 197

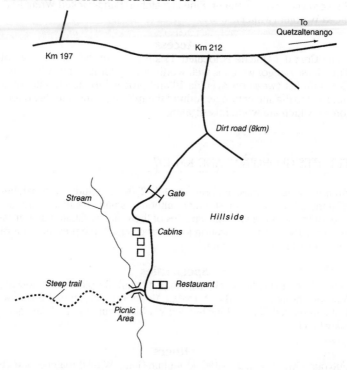

site though because there have been recent reports of bandit activity. Azure-rumped* and Yellow-winged Tanagers have also been seen further along the road, around km 183–185.

The Pan-American Highway, between the junction of Highway 1 north of Quetzaltenango (Cuatro Caminos) and Nahuala, passes through spectacular country including the highest point (3670 m) on this road. There are some residual patches of forest in this area, for example at km 172, where Pink-headed Warbler, Violet Sabrewing, Amethyst-throated Hummingbird and Cinnamon Flowerpiercer have been seen.

Accommodation: cabins at Fuentes can be rented very reasonably; food is also available.

TODOS SANTOS CUCHUMATÁN

A pleasant, traditional Mayan village situated at 2450 m in the heart of the Cordillera de los Cuchumatanes, the most extensive area of high-altitude habitat in Guatemala. Pink-headed Warbler, White-breasted Hawk, White-faced Quail-Dove, Grey Silky-Flycatcher, Black-capped Swallow, Rufous-browed Wren, Rufous-collared Robin and Spotted Nightingale-Thrush have been seen along the trail to San Juan Atitán. Southeast of Todos Santos, about 20 km from the village, near a junction known as Tres Caminos is an area of altiplano, which is a location for Black-capped Siskin and the local race of Audubon's Warbler, known as 'Goldman's Warbler' (which may be a separate species).

Others
White-breasted Hawk, White-faced Quail-Dove, Black-capped Swallow, Grey Silky-Flycatcher, Rufous-browed Wren, Spotted Nightingale-Thrush, Rufous-collared Robin, Pink-headed Warbler, Black-capped Siskin.

Access
Leave Huehuetenango north towards Chiantla and La Capellania, then northeast on Highway 9N. Todos Santos is about 40 km from Huehuetenango, from where there are four daily buses. In winter, nights in Todos Santos can be very cold. There are local tracks accessing highland habitat. Enquire on site for directions to these.

Accommodation: clean, very reasonable, but basic accommodation is available in Todos Santos (Casa Familiar) and there is a small restaurant nearby.

ADDITIONAL INFORMATION

Books
A Guide to the Birds of Mexico and Northern Central America, Howell, S. N. G. and Webb, S. 1995. Oxford UP. (Covers Guatemala.)

Birds of Guatemala, Land, H. C. 1970. Livingston, Wynnewood PA. (Not as useful as Howell and Webb, but contains more detailed distribution information.)

The Distribution of Bird-Life in Guatemala, Griscom, L. 1932. American Mus. Nat. Hist. Bull. 65. (Very outdated now, but nonetheless an interesting reference.)

HONDURAS

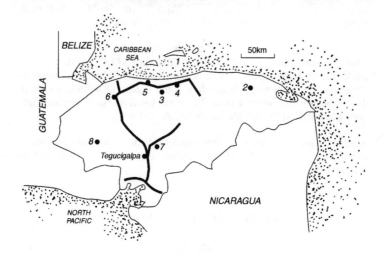

1 Bay Islands
2 La Mosquitia (Mosquito Coast)
3 Pico Bonito National Park
4 Olanchito

5 Cuero y Salado Wildlife Refuge
6 Marandón, San Pedro Sula
7 La Tigra National Park
8 Celaque National Park

INTRODUCTION

Summary

Honduras is the poorest of the Central American republics and is distinctly off the usual tourist routes. It is, rather unfairly, somewhat neglected by birdwatchers, which is a shame as it possesses some excellent habitat, albeit not especially easy of access, and a cheerful and friendly populace who have not been soured by overexposure to the excesses of the tourist trade.

Size

Honduras is about 112,000 km^2 in size, almost exactly half the area of the United Kingdom and one sixth that of Texas. The population is approximately six million, or only one-tenth that of Britain, and large areas of the country, especially in the Caribbean lowlands, have a very low population density.

Getting Around

There are three international airports in Honduras, serving the capital Tegucigalpa, San Pedro Sula and La Ceiba, the last two being on the Caribbean coast. There are several border crossings from the adjacent republics, some of which are open only during daylight hours. Within Honduras there are generally good bus services, though often operated by different companies from different terminals. Vehicles can be hired in major centres. Road conditions vary, but many country routes are very poor, especially during the rainy season.

Accommodation and Food

Accommodation of variable standard is available in most towns; in smaller centres it can be rather basic. Prices by European or North American standards are very low. Food is readily available and principally constitutes rice, tortillas and beans, but there is excellent seafood on both coasts. Honduras also has several good home-brewed beers.

Health and Safety

Malaria is present in much of the country including Tegucigalpa. Chagas disease occurs in areas below 1500 m. Vaccinations against viral hepatitis A and typhoid are strongly recommended. Cholera is present and the usual precautions against infection should be observed. Tap water throughout the country is highly unreliable; always drink and use purified water. Milk should not be drunk without being boiled.

Although considerably safer than either Guatemala or Nicaragua, Honduras does have a problem in both cities and rural areas with theft and outright robbery. Sensible precautions should be taken. The border regions with Nicaragua and Guatemala have a particularly poor reputation.

Climate and Timing

Climate is affected greatly by altitude and location. Lowland regions are hot year-round, with a marked wet season usually lasting from May to October. The Caribbean slope is substantially wetter than the Pacific. Even on the highest mountains freezing temperatures are rare.

The prime time to visit is at the end of the dry season, March–April, when many North American migrants are still present. Transportation becomes more problematical in the rainy season.

Habitats

Honduras has a broad variety of habitats. Lowland rain forest occupies much of the Caribbean lowlands, though in the northeast there are extensive areas of lowland pine savanna. In mountainous regions in the centre of the country there is montane rain forest and cloud forest, and in other areas highland pine and pine–oak associations. In the south there are areas of thorn forest and arid scrub.

Conservation

The country has suffered from significant habitat destruction for agriculture and forestry, but still has a relatively low population density. In 1987 the Honduran government declared 15 areas of cloud forest as protected. In total there are (actual and proposed) about 80 protected areas, including National Parks, Wildlife Refuges and Biological Reserves.

Bird Families

About 74 families of birds occur in Honduras. Well represented are parrots (15 species), hummingbirds (39 species), antbirds (19 species), cotingas (12 species), tyrant flycatchers (55 species), wrens (15 species) and New World warblers (53 species, but only 15 breed).

Bird Species

Approximately 690 species have been recorded in Honduras. Spectacular species include Scarlet Macaw, Ornate Hawk-Eagle, Snowcap and Blue-throated Motmot. One of the great mysteries of Honduran ornithology centres around a large swift, resembling the White-naped Swift of Mexico, which has been seen in the Caribbean lowlands, often in large flocks, but has never been collected or described.

Endemics

Honduras has one, the Honduran Emerald*. Formerly regarded as very rare, more recently it has been shown to be quite common in the upper valley of the Río Arguán. Green-breasted Mountain-gem is shared with northwestern Nicaragua.

Expectations

A well-organised trip to Honduras, covering all of its major habitats, might expect to record 300 or more species.

BAY ISLANDS

The Bay Islands lie in the Caribbean off the northern coast of Honduras. They have endured a long and complex history, alternating between Spanish and British rule. Today a large proportion of the local population speaks English as a first language. Faunistically the islands have some interesting features, notably a population of the distinctive (and endangered) *caribaea* race of Yellow-naped Parrot and an endemic race of Yucatan Woodpecker. The latter is found only on the island of Guanaja, which also harbours most of the remaining parrots. The Bay Islands have a number of typically Caribbean species such as White-crowned Pigeon and Caribbean Dove. In the lists below the following abbreviations are used to denote those islands on which a species occurs: U = Utila, R = Roatán, G = Guanaja.

Specialities

Rufous-necked Wood-rail, White-crowned Pigeon, Caribbean Dove (Barbareta Island, off R), Yellow-naped Parrot (R, G).

Others

Roadside and Grey Hawks, Great Black Hawk, Bat Falcon (R), Plain Chachalaca (U), Yucatan (R) and Red-lored Parrots (U, R, G), Mangrove Cuckoo (U, R), Barn Owl (R, G), Northern Potoo (R), Green-breasted Mango, Canivet's Emerald, Mangrove and Yucatan Vireos, Mangrove (Yellow) Warbler, Yellow-backed Oriole (R).

Access

The largest island, Roatán (pronounced Row-tan), with a population of about 15,000, has a runway that can accommodate jet aircraft; there are regular flights from La Ceiba, San Pedro Sula, Tegucigalpa and Houston, Texas. There are also airstrips on Utila (population c. 1500) and Guanaja (5500 people) with flights to La Ceiba. For a more interesting journey, however, there are boats from La Ceiba several times a week.

Roatán has several wildlife refuges: Barbareta Wildlife refuge, a separate island at its east end, has the largest remaining patch of tropical rain forest, as well as mangroves and a coral reef; other reserves are the West End Wildlife Refuge and Port Royal National Marine Park. Most recent reports of Yellow-naped Parrot have come from the dry ridges between French Harbour and Punta Gorda.

Guanaja is the easternmost island and has substantial areas of forest. Virtually the entire population lives in the town of Bonacca, leaving most of the island remarkably quiet.

Accommodation: the Bay Islands possess magnificent scuba diving and consequently are far more attuned to tourists than most of Honduras. By Honduran standards accommodation tends to be very expensive. However, by searching around cheaper rooms can be found. There are abundant places to eat. On Guanaja, especially, prices tend to be high, although it is possible to camp in some places with local permission.

LA MOSQUITIA (MOSQUITO COAST)

A large block of lowland tropical rain forest in northern Honduras that is only rarely visited by birdwatchers and undoubtedly capable of yielding many new discoveries for travellers willing to live rough and get off the beaten track.

Access

Apart from a limited number of dirt roads of very basic quality (e.g. from Puerto Lempira beside the Río Coco), ground transport is almost entirely by water. Several communities are served by air and can be used as bases for further travel into the interior. There are flights from La Ceiba to the small community of Palacios, on the Caribbean coast approximately 200 km to the east. From Palacios a motorboat accesses a number of villages on Laguna de Ibans, from where motorized dugout canoes proceed further upstream to the Indian community of Las Marías, a journey of about eight hours. There is little remaining productive riverside habitat, but with a lengthy hike some areas of forest are accessible. One worthwhile walk is the three-hour hike to Cerro Zapote.

A much lengthier excursion that permits access to far more pristine habitat is to follow the Río Platano by raft. This is not a trivial undertaking. It starts at the southern end of the Río Platano Biosphere reserve. Transport can be arranged from Tegucigalpa to the headwaters of the Río Platano, the last section by mule. It then takes about 10–12 days to travel downstream to Las Marías and the coast. Much of the journey is through unspoiled rain forest. We are unaware of any birdwatchers who have recently attempted this journey, but it is obviously highly worthwhile: species reported include Harpy Eagle*, Ornate Hawk-Eagle, Sunbittern, and Scarlet and Great Green Macaws*, as well as Jaguar, Puma, Tapir, River Otter and alligators.

Up to date information can be obtained from the Honduran Institute of Tourism, Box 140458, Coral Gables FL 33114, or in Canada and the US by calling 1-800-410-9608, e-mail gohondurastourism@compuserve. com.

PICO BONITO NATIONAL PARK

An area of cloud forest just south of La Ceiba. We do not have any recent reports or bird lists from the area but it obviously is very worthwhile. The area is accessible (with some substantial effort) by public transport.

Others
Sunbittern, Aztec Parakeet, Pale-billed Woodpecker, Dot-winged Antwren, Olive-backed Euphonia.

Access
From La Ceiba go to Armenia Bonito (buses from the Parque Central in La Ceiba), or take the bus to Tela and get off at the Río Bonito. It is also possible to reach Armenia Bonito relatively cheaply by taxi. From Armenia Bonito a dirt road leads uphill, petering out into a track. Follow this to the Campamiento del CURLA where there is a deserted visitor centre, from which trails lead uphill into excellent forest. A recently opened visitor centre is located on the road between La Ceiba and Yaruca, where up to date information on trails is available. Several local agencies run tours into Pico Bonito. Omega Tours has a basic but comfortable lodge situated on the road to Yaruca, just before Las Mangas. Recent reports suggest that a new lodge is set to open in El Pino, west of La Ceiba and on the northern edge of Pico Bonito.

OLANCHITO

This area is a location for the country's only endemic species, the Honduran Emerald*.

Endemics
Honduran Emerald*.

Others
White-winged Dove, Cinnamon Hummingbird, Brown-capped Flycatcher, White-lored Gnatcatcher, White-bellied Wren, Blue-black Grassquit.

Access
Olanchito is inland of La Ceiba. A direct route leads south via Yaruca, passing through beautiful scenery, or a better quality road exists through Jutiapa and Saba. Using the latter, after crossing the Río Arguán and entering Saba, bear right for Olanchito (40 km). From the Texaco station in Olanchito proceed west for approximately 2 km and turn left (west) at an inverted Y junction and continue for another 4.9 km, at which point there is a double fence on the right. After a further 100 m there is a second double fence line heading north. Walk the trail between the fences to a thorn forest. Honduran Emerald* is reportedly quite common at this location.

CUERO Y SALADO WILDLIFE REFUGE

A large area of coastal habitat, 13,000 ha in extent, which was originally established to protect a population of manatees. There are extensive
salt and freshwater lagoons. Approximately 200 species have been
recorded here, but this total could doubtless increase.

Specialities
Jabiru, Boat-billed Heron, Bare-throated Tiger-Heron, Sungrebe.

Other Wildlife
Jaguar, Manatee and White-faced Capuchin.

Access
The area is managed by FUCSA (Fundación Cuero y Salada) who will
arrange transport into the area and, if necessary, overnight accommodation at a cabin within the park. The FUCSA office is located in the
Standard Fruit Company's office in Masapán district. Transport into the
park is by 'burra', a hand-powered cart running along a railway line.
Guided entry by canoe is available at a very reasonable daily price.

To reach the park by public transport, take the bus from La Ceiba to
La Unión. In the latter ask for Doña Tina whose house is next to the railway and can arrange the 9-km trip by burra into the park. By road from
La Ceiba, take a right-hand turn off the Tela road at the police station at
km 169. From the end of the railway, at Campamiento Salado, is a
FUCSA office where several different boat trips into the refuge can be
arranged; there is also a trail.

*The Sungrebe, the only New World member of the Finfoot family, is
found beside slow-moving forest streams*

MARANDÓN, SAN PEDRO SULA

A protected watershed just outside the city of San Pedro Sula.

Others
Bare-throated Tiger-Heron, Grey and Roadside Hawks, Plain Chachalaca, Red-billed Pigeon, Grey-chested and Inca Doves, Ruddy and Plain-
breasted Ground-Doves, Olive-throated Parakeet, Squirrel Cuckoo, Fer-

ruginous Pygmy-Owl, White-collared Swift, Long-tailed and Little Hermits, Cinnamon Hummingbird, Blue-crowned and Turquoise-browed Motmots, Olivaceous Piculet, Golden-fronted Woodpecker, Greenish and Yellow-bellied Elaenias, Ochre-breasted Flycatcher, Masked Tityra, Plain, Rufous-naped and Spot-bellied Wrens, Clay-coloured Robin, Tawny-crowned and Lesser Greenlets, Rufous-capped Warbler, Blue-grey Tanager, Red-throated Ant-Tanager, Greyish and Black-headed Saltators, Grassland Yellow-Finch, Spot-breasted and Altamira Orioles, Montezuma Oropendola.

The Turquoise-browed Motmot (uncharitably called Pájaro Bobo—stupid bird—in Spanish) is frequently seen on roadside telephone wires

LA TIGRA NATIONAL PARK

A forested watershed ridge north of Tegucigalpa, which is a location for the near-endemic Green-breasted Mountain-gem.

Specialities
Crested Guan, Lesser Roadrunner, Red-billed Azurecrown, Amethyst-throated, Wine-throated and Garnet-throated Hummingbirds, Green-breasted Mountain-gem, Resplendent Quetzal* (near the summit).

Others
Plumbeous Kite, Singing Quail, Whip-poor-will, Greater Swallow-tailed Swift, Vaux's Swift, Green Violet-ear, White-eared Hummingbird, Spotted and Spot-crowned Woodcreepers, Tawny-throated Leaftosser, Scaled Antpitta, Rufous Mourner, Yellowish Flycatcher, Bushy-crested and Black-throated Jays, Rufous-browed and Plain Wrens, Ruddy-capped and Orange-billed Nightingale-Thrushes, Slate-coloured Solitaire, Cinnamon Flowerpiercer, Crescent-chested Warbler, Flame-coloured Tanager, Black-headed Saltator, Yellow-throated and Chestnut-capped Brush-Finches, Rusty Sparrow, Yellow-backed Oriole.

Access

Directions and distances are from the Hotel Posada del Angel in Tegucigalpa. Go north on the road to San Juancito, which can be reached
from Tegucigalpa by bus. After two blocks bear left at a fork in the road.
At 2 km the surfaced road ends. Bear left at 4 km at a fork with a large
sign 'FHIS'. At 10.2 km turn left off the highway at a small sign pointing
to La Tigra National Park. At 11.5 km bear right at an intersection in the
town of San Juancito, and at 12.5 km bear right and cross a small bridge
in the centre of town. Turn right after crossing the bridge, then at 12.6
km take a sharp left. The road degenerates at this point. At 14.9 km the
road takes a sharp right at a house selling food, which has a sign for the
National Park. You must park at 15.1 km and proceed on foot as only
local residents may drive further. There is an entrance fee (about $10
for foreigners). Continue straight along the road. Fork right (initially
downhill) just after the road makes a sharp left. A walk of 30–60 minutes
through agricultural land and second growth brings you to cloud forest.
There are trails into the forest from this point; one goes to the Cascades.
The elevation is 1800–1900 m. Another park entrance road is accessible
from Tegucigalpa past the US Ambassador's residence and via the El
Picacho road through El Hatillo and Jutiapa.

LA TIGRA NATIONAL PARK

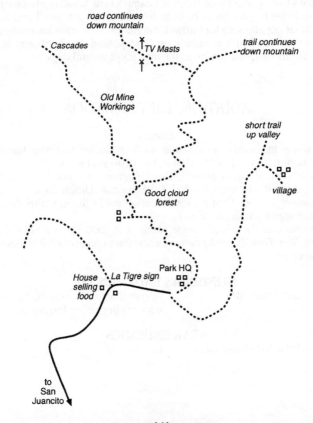

Accommodation: camping is allowed but a permit, obtainable only in Tegucigalpa, is required. It may also be possible to stay in buildings near the park entrance.

CELAQUE NATIONAL PARK

A beautiful area of upland cloud forest, created to protect the area around Cerro Los Minos, at 2849 m the highest peak Honduras, which covers more than 30,000 ha. It is relatively rarely visited by birdwatchers.

Access

Accessible from Gracias, the capital of Lempira Department, located on Highway 6 in western Honduras. To reach the park, walk towards the cemetery behind the fort on the hill. Keep to the left of the cemetery, fork right and bear right at a church with pink steeples. The park boundary is about two hours' walk along a dirt road; the Visitor's Centre, with basic accommodation, is half an hour further. There is a very small daily charge for park entry and accommodation. From the Visitor's Centre to the summit is a long hike. About three hours along the trail is a small hut with bunks (no mattresses or bedding), key available at the Visitor's Centre; further on there is a camp site at Naranjo, above which cloud forest begins. From Naranjo to the summit is about three hours (all times not allowing for birdwatching stops). The trails are marked by plastic ribbons but it is quite easy (and potentially disastrous) to get lost. To do adequate justice to the area takes several days.

ADDITIONAL INFORMATION

Books
A Guide to the Birds of Mexico and Northern Central America, Howell, S. N. G. and Webb, S. 1995. Oxford UP. (Covers Honduras.)
A Distributional Survey of the Birds of Honduras, Monroe B. L. Jr., 1968. Occasional Monographs No. 7, American Ornithologists' Union, Washington DC. (Not an identification guide but contains detailed information on distribution.)
Honduras and Bay Islands Guide, Panet, J. P. 1996. Open Road Publishing, New York. (Useful practical information on accommodation and transport.)

HONDURAS ENDEMICS (1)
Honduran Emerald*	Apparently quite common in the upper valley of the Río Aguán

NEAR-ENDEMICS
Green-breasted Mountain-gem	La Tigra NP

MEXICO

MEXICO (EAST)

1 Isla Cozumel	7 Celestún	13 Tuxtla Gutiérrez
2 Felipe Carrillo Puerto and the Vigia Chico road	8 Calakmul	14 El Sumidero
	9 Río Usumacinta Marshes	15 Arriaga
3 Cobá	10 Palenque	16 El Triunfo
4 Chichén Itzá	11 San Cristóbal de las Casas	17 Colonia de Cuauhtémoc
5 Uxmal		18 The Isthmus road
6 Progreso and Chicxulub	12 Lagunas de Montebello National Park	19 Catemaco area

INTRODUCTION

Summary

Mexico is a country of enormous diversity and spectacular scenery, with a rich fauna and a large number of endemic species. The highly varied terrain and country's vast size provides a wide variety of habitats, including such extremes as harsh desert, arid scrub, tropical deciduous forests, lowland rain forests, mid- and high-altitude oak and pine forests, cloud forest, páramo, permanent snow and sea-level mangrove swamps. Given such exceptional diversity the great richness of the Mexican fauna is scarcely a surprise. For North American birders Mexico is often the first taste of Latin America, as the border is no more than 2–3 days drive from most of the US and southern Canada, and Mexican endemics, and specifically Neotropical families, appear a further few hours south.

Size

Mexico occupies almost 2 million km^2 or eight times the size of the UK, but only one-fifth the size of the USA. Mexico is also five times the size of all six Central American countries (Belize to Panama) combined. Note that, strictly speaking, Mexico is not considered part of Central America.

Getting Around

There are numerous flights from North American and European points to a number of Mexican destinations, including occasionally very cheap fares to places such as Cancún or Acapulco, which while offering little

MEXICO (WEST)

20 Cerro San Felipe	29 Rancho Los Col-	38 Yécora and Highway
21 Monte Albán	orados	16
22 Amatlán	30 Cola de Caballo	39 Kino Bay (Bahía Kino)
23 El Cofre de Perote	31 Volcán de Fuego	40 Cape area
National Park	32 Autlán de Navarro	41 La Paz area
24 Teziutlán, Puebla	33 San Blas area	42 Puerto Escondido
25 Popocatépetl	34 Barranca Rancho	43 Isla Raza
26 La Cima, Huitzilac	Liebre	44 Parque Sierra de San
and Coajomulco	35 Alamos	Pedro Mártir
27 Mexico City	36 Isla Huivulai	45 Puerto Peñasco
28 Tlanchinol	37 Guaymas	(Rocky Point)

in themselves to a birdwatcher give ready access to superb hinterland. Within Mexico there is an efficient network of internal flights between major urban centres. The main road system in Mexico has improved beyond recognition within the last generation, and fast (rather expensive) toll (Cuota) expressways now cover much of the country; often a perfectly adequate and more interesting free alternative is available. Secondary roads vary in quality and many rural areas are really only accessible by high-clearance four-wheel-drive vehicles. Cars are readily hired in urban centres; charges are relatively high by North American standards. Those driving from North America should note that most insurance policies do not cover Mexico; appropriate daily coverage should be purchased at a reputable agency on the border. Gasoline is readily available, but in some locations only lower grades; always top up when possible with high grade in more remote areas.

Mexico has a very good system of public transport with fast, comfortable first-class buses on all the major routes, along with slower second-class buses for local travel, and a variety of socially interesting, if not exactly luxurious, (*colectivos*) means of transport to villages.

Accommodation and Food

Depending on location, a wide variety of accommodation is available. Most large towns have hotels that vary in price and comfort over the complete spectrum. In smaller centres there may be only very basic accommodation. Similarly for restaurants. Prices are usually considerably cheaper than either North America or Europe, except in resort areas and the centres of major cities.

Health and Safety

For those (such as birders) who are likely to spend time in rural and remote areas, immunization against typhoid and viral hepatitis A is recommended. Malarial risk is present in lowland areas on both coasts, and in lower parts of central Mexico, with falciparum malaria present in some southern parts of the country. Drinking water in much of the country is highly unreliable; bottled water is readily available.

Driving after dark in Mexico is not recommended. Aside from unmarked potholes, rocks on the road, wandering livestock and vehicles with defective lights, Mexicans have devised a technique for discouraging speeding in towns and villages, with obstacles known as *topes* which are situated across the road at either end of urban areas and near schools. These vary in ferocity, but passing over some examples at speed will result in a brief aerial excursion, with interesting results to the nether regions of both vehicle and driver on returning to earth. *Topes* are usually marked, but frequently not and are difficult to see after dark. Robberies reportedly occur at *topes*, taking advantage of slow-moving vehicles.

Certain parts of Mexico have an unsavoury reputation for banditry. Theft is widespread and the usual precautions should be taken. Some areas, such as parts of Sonora, have recently become more hazardous due to drug trafficking. For some considerable time there has been major unrest in the southern state of Chiapas, with government military operations being generally more hazardous than rebel ones. Since local situations change, enquiry as to current conditions is very advisable.

Having stated this, in 35 years of travel in Mexico this author has only once encountered any unpleasantness, in that instance a minor case of theft.

Climate and Timing

Almost any climate on earth occurs somewhere in Mexico. In the desert regions of the northwest summer temperatures can remain in excess of 40°C for weeks on end, while there is permanent snow on the highest mountains. Similarly, annual rainfall varies from less than 250 mm in parts of Baja California to more than 5000 mm in Chiapas, the southernmost state. Annual rainfall can change dramatically over short distances, giving rise to sudden changes in avifauna on, for example, opposite sides of a mountain range. Rainfall tends to occur from April/May to October/November, with longer wetter periods in some highlands. Baja California, by contrast, receives most of its limited rain in winter, in November–April. Almost any time of year is good for birdwatching, but back roads can become problematical after prolonged rain. Over much of Mexico the prime time to visit is March–April, when many birds are approaching breeding activity or actually breeding, rainfall is generally light and many North American migrants are still present.

Habitats

Mexico probably has a greater variety of habitats than any other country in the Americas, the US included. Chief causes of variation are rainfall and altitude. The outstanding geographic features of the country are two great chains of mountains in the north, the Sierra Madre Occidental and Oriental, which enclose a high central plateau. Further south are other ranges of rather different character, with several isolated volcanic peaks, some still active. Depending on location relative to prevailing winds and mountain ranges, precipitation varies markedly in different parts of Mexico. In the northwest, and Baja California, true desert (of varied vegetational types) occurs, with rainfall very restricted seasonally and limited in total. The Yucatán peninsula is also very arid although the vegetation is quite different from that in Baja California and there are surprisingly few common species. Arid areas also occur in rain shadows in the Mexican mainland, often with endemic species.

The mountain ranges, according to altitude and location, are typically heavily forested. In the north there tend to be pine and pine–oak associations. More humid forest, with a greater preponderance of epiphytes, occurs further south, and there are extensive areas of humid lowland forest in the south of the country. Cloud forest, a habitat characterised by abundant year-round moisture, much of it derived from the continuous presence of cloud and fog and with a rather specific fauna, occurs at various altitudes. The highest peaks protrude above the tree line into páramo, which in Mexico is mostly characterised by coarse grasses, while very highest elevations are permanently snow-covered. Other forest types, with characteristic and often endemic-rich faunas, are the deciduous woodland or thorn forest, where trees lose their leaves in the dry season (extensive areas of which occur in the Pacific northwest and Yucatán), and semi-deciduous forest, which is slightly better watered. Other habitats include savannas, often with scattered pines or palms, mangrove swamps in coastal areas, and marshes, both coastal and inland.

Conservation

Mexico has suffered and continues to suffer from a catastrophic destruction of habitat, fuelled by a rapidly expanding population, which has grown from 19 million in 1921 to 96 million in 1999. Wholesale clearance of forests of all types, drainage of marshes and degradation of pasture by gross overgrazing are rampant. Unsurprisingly this has resulted in major faunal losses, both birds and other animals. Three endemic species (Guadelupe Storm-Petrel*, Imperial Woodpecker* and Slender-billed Grackle) have become extinct this century, while the Socorro Dove survives only in captivity. Many others are in a parlous state, due to habitat destruction, uncontrolled hunting and capture for the cage bird trade; globally Mexico ranks in the top ten countries for threatened restricted-range species. Fortunately some progress is being made, even though many so-called reserves offer little protection due to inadequate enforcement. Conservation centres around National Parks (often created for recreational purposes), special Biosphere Reserves (usually rather small but of great significance) and larger Biosphere Reserves. A number of conservation organisations exist in Mexico; it is very clear that a local ethos of conservation will be essential to prevent further catastrophic losses of species in the next generation. Visitors can assist by making it plain that their presence (and the economic benefits it brings) is dependent on the existence of wildlife and wildlife habitat.

Bird Families
Depending on taxonomy, approximately 89 families are found in Mexico; only about five families found in Central America (two marginally) do not occur in Mexico.

Bird Species
Currently 1049 species have occurred in Mexico, a total that will certainly grow with more fieldwork; approximately 150 more than have ever been recorded in the whole of North America. This includes spectaculars like the Resplendent Quetzal* and Harpy Eagle*, though more sophisticated birdwatchers will be 'taken' by endemic beauties like the Red Warbler.

Endemics
The total number of Mexican endemics is subject to debate, being highly dependent on taxonomic opinion. Clements (2000) lists 96, while Howell and Webb (1995) list about 100. In the Americas, only Brazil (at least 190) and Peru (104) have larger totals. The high level of endemism in Mexico is mainly due to the existence of numerous areas of habitat which are isolated by intervening obstacles (be they areas of lowland or mountain ranges) from similar habitat; in addition, several habitat types do not possess close equivalents in neighbouring countries. Mexico also has several island groups supporting endemic species or races.

Expectations
Mexico is a very large country and in a typical two- or three-week visit only a portion of its numerous habitats can be sampled. To give some idea of the possibilities, the San Blas Christmas Count, a procedure where a large number of birdwatchers count birds and species within a ten-mile radius on a single day, has recorded almost 300 species on occasion, and routinely records 250, while the Mexico City count, an area without extensive wetlands, may acquire half that number, a significant proportion of which are not common to San Blas. A well-organised trip visiting three or more widely divergent habitat types—for example northwestern desert, high-altitude pine–oak forests and lowland tropical rain forest—could easily amass 500 species.

YUCATÁN PENINSULA

The Yucatán peninsula consists of the three states of Campeche, Yucatán and Quintana Roo as well as adjacent parts of Tabasco, northern Guatemala and northern Belize. It is for the most part a low-lying limestone plain covered in scrub forest, drier and sparser in the north, becoming much lusher and wetter in the south. The whole area is sparsely inhabited apart from a few cities. Because of the availability of cheap flights from North America and Europe to holiday resorts such as Cancún, some see it as a good place to start a Mexican visit. There are about 20 endemic species on the peninsula, as well as a number of Caribbean species not otherwise found in Central America. On the coast there are several major wetland areas, and substantial seabird colonies occur on some offshore islands. The Yucatán has some of the most spectacular archaeological sites in the New World and only a totally culturally illiterate birdwatcher would wish to miss them; besides, some of the best birding on the peninsula is, in fact, right around some of the ruins.

Endemics
Endemic to Yucután, not Mexico: Ocellated Turkey*, Yucatan Bobwhite, Yucatan Parrot, Yucatan Poorwill, Yucatan Nightjar, Mexican Sheartail, Yucatan Woodpecker, Yucatan Flycatcher, Yucatan Jay, Yucatan Wren, White-browed Wren, Black Catbird*, Yucatan Vireo, Rose-throated Tanager, Orange Oriole.
   (Isla Cozumel only: Cozumel Emerald, Cozumel Wren, Cozumel Thrasher*, Cozumel Vireo.)

Specialities
Ornate Hawk-Eagle, Ruddy and Yellow-breasted Crakes, White-crowned Pigeon, Canivet's Emerald, Caribbean Elaenia, Grey Kingbird, Northern Rough-winged Swallow (ridgwayi), White-lored Gnatcatcher, Mangrove Vireo, Grey-throated Chat, Northern Stripe-headed Tanager (Cozumel only), Blue Bunting.

ISLA COZUMEL

The largest of the Yucatan offshore islands, Cozumel measures about 45 x 15 km and is about 15 km from the mainland. Because of its size and isolation, it contains four endemic species, as well as being the only Mexican site for several West Indian species. The name, incidentally, comes from the Mayan Cuzamil, "Land of Swallows".

Endemics
Cozumel Emerald, Cozumel Wren, Cozumel Thrasher*, Cozumel Vireo.

Specialities
Yucatan Parrot, Caribbean Elaenia, Black Catbird*, Rose-throated and Northern Stripe-headed Tanagers.

Access
There are direct international flights to Cozumel airport. Otherwise, there is a frequent passenger ferry from Playa del Carmén, and a slow-

ISLA COZUMEL

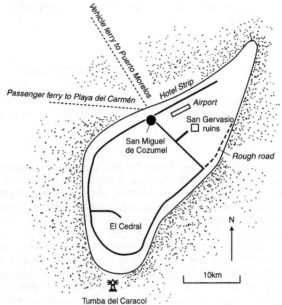

Vehicle ferry to Puerto Morelos

Passenger ferry to Playa del Carmén

Hotel Strip

Airport

San Gervasio ruins

San Miguel de Cozumel

Rough road

El Cedral

N

10km

Tumba del Caracol

er (3.5 hours), once-daily vehicle ferry from Puerto Morelos ($50 each way). Departure times vary depending on day of the week. Cars may be hired on the island; also motor scooters. Competence in the operation of the latter does not appear to be a prerequisite for hire.

A paved road runs south from San Miguel around the coast and returns across the centre of the island. A very poor road runs along the northeast side. Good habitat for most of the endemic species is accessible via paved roads. South of San Miguel, a paved road runs east for about 3 km to the small ruins of El Cedral. There is almost no traffic on this road, especially in the early morning. The section just short of the small village of El Cedral offers good habitat. The beach road in San Miguel passes north out of town, past the airport and eventually into partially disturbed habitat, ending at the waterworks. There is little traffic on this road. At the southern tip of the island a rough road leads to the lighthouse at Tumba del Caracol. From here a rough road goes a further 1–2 km, passing good coastal lagoons, with numerous shorebirds, herons etc.

A paved road leading north off the road that crosses the waist of the island (entrance fee) reaches the ruins at San Gervasio. There are numerous tracks and dirt roads leading off this road before the ruins are reached; any of these are worth investigating. Most of the comparatively few recent records of Cozumel Thrasher* have been in this area. The gates (at the junction with the cross-island road) open at 8am but it would doubtless be possible to walk in earlier.

Accommodation on Cozumel is expensive; however, with local enquiry clean, moderately priced hotels may be found (e.g. Hotel López in the main square of San Miguel). There is one town on the island, San Miguel de Cozumel, which is a popular holiday resort of little interest to bird-watchers. However, much of the island is relatively untouched by the recent developments.

FELIPE CARRILLO PUERTO AND THE VIGIA CHICO ROAD

An area of excellent and largely undisturbed forest habitat, easily accessible, leading to the very large (100 km x 60 km) Sian Ka'an Biosphere Reserve.

Others

Thicket Tinamou, Ocellated Turkey*, Great Curassow*, Crested Guan, Plain Chachalaca, Ornate Hawk-Eagle, Wedge-tailed Sabrewing, Canivet's Emerald, Black-headed and Collared Trogons, Turquoise-browed Motmot, Collared Araçari, Smoky-brown and Pale-billed Woodpeckers, Tawny-winged, Ruddy and Northern Barred Woodcreepers, Plain Xenops, Rose-throated Becard, Bright-rumped Attila, Northern Royal Flycatcher, White-throated Spadebill, Northern Bentbill, Greenish Elaenia, Ochre-bellied Flycatcher, Spot-breasted and White-bellied Wrens, Northern Waterthrush (winter), Long-billed Gnatcatcher, Rose-throated Tanager, Red-throated Ant-Tanager, Yellow-throated Euphonia, Grey-throated Chat, Rufous-browed Peppershrike, Green-backed Sparrow, Blue Bunting.

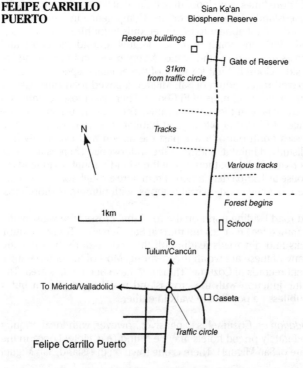

FELIPE CARRILLO PUERTO

Sian Ka'an Biosphere Reserve

Reserve buildings

Gate of Reserve

31km from traffic circle

N

Tracks

Various tracks

Forest begins

1km

School

To Tulum/Cancún

To Mérida/Valladolid

Caseta

Traffic circle

Felipe Carrillo Puerto

Access

At the northern end of the town of Felipe Carrillo Puerto on Highway 307 there is a traffic circle with a bust of a local dignitary in the centre. Signed Mérida to the west, Tulum/Cancún to the north and Vigia Chico to the east, take the latter; 0.6 km beyond the circle the pavement ends at a stop sign, with a police caseta on the right. Turn half left along a dirt road. At km 1.6 there is a school on the right, thereafter the road enters forest with many trails on either side. At about km 25 the road enters the Biosphere Reserve and at km 31 there is a locked barrier with the reserve guard's residence and some accommodation for visiting scientists on the left. The road continues through the reserve to the now-defunct village of Vigia Chico. To enter the reserve prior permission from SEMARNAP is required; office in Cancún, tel. (98) 83-05-63, fax 83-06-01; office in Felipe Carrillo Puerto on Avenida Constuyente 582, tel. 40265. However, there is much excellent forest before the reserve and very good birding is to be had within walking distance of the town. For those without transportation an option might be to take a taxi a few km along the road and walk back; there is almost no traffic.

Accommodation: there are several hotels in Felipe Carrillo Puerto varying from moderate in price and facilities to very basic. There are plenty of places to eat. For *bona fide* scientists accommodation may be available at km 31. Enquire from SEMARNAP.

COBÁ

A very large and still only partially explored Mayan site within excellent forest habitat and with an interesting lake nearby.

Yucatán Endemics
Yucatan Woodpecker, Yucatan Flycatcher, Yucatan Jay.

Specialities
Snail Kite (lake), Barred Forest-Falcon, Ruddy Crake, Spotted Rail, Wedge-tailed Sabrewing, Canivet's Emerald, Cinnamon and Fawn-breasted Hummingbirds, Citreoline and Olivaceous Trogons, Tawny-collared Nightjar, Turquoise-browed Motmot, Grey-collared Becard, Yucatan and Mangrove Vireos, Red-throated Ant-Tanager, Green-backed Sparrow, Blue Bunting.

Access
A good paved road joins Highway 307 at Tulúm and Highway 180 at Nuevo Xcan. Cobá is about 3 km off this road on a side road located 43 km from each end. All turns are clearly signed. Highway 180 is in fact two roads; an expensive toll (cuota) divided highway and a perfectly good free (libre) paved road. Buses run from Tulúm, Playa del Carmen and Nuevo Xcan; not all take the turn to Cobá itself. Once in Cobá village all attractions, ornithological or archaeological, are within walking distance.

There are two main birdwatching areas at Cobá: the lake and the ruins. The main street through the village forks at the lake, the left fork going to the ruins, the right to the Villas Arqueológicas. Right in front are

COBÁ

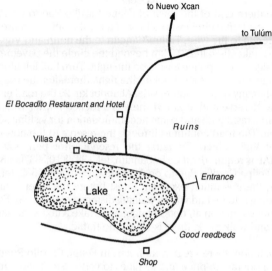

some reeds with numerous Ruddy Crake and, occasionally, Spotted Rail. Continuing to the left is the parking lot and entrance (fee) to the ruins. A network of footpaths goes through forest. The ruins themselves provide good overviews of the forest. Cobá is not such a popular destination for general tourists as Chichén Itzá or Palenque but visits early in the day are still best to avoid crowds.

Accommodation: on the main street of Cobá is a very basic but clean and cheap hotel, El Bocadito, very much more expensive is the Villas Arqueológicas on the lakeshore. There are several reasonable and cheap restaurants on the village street just before the lake.

CHICHÉN ITZÁ

No reasonable person would visit Yucatán without seeing Chichén Itzá. The scenic woodland around the ruins can be excellent for birding, especially in the cool of the morning.

Yucatán Endemics
Yucatan Woodpecker, Yucatan Flycatcher, Yucatan Jay, Orange Oriole.

Others
Canivet's Emerald, Buff-bellied Hummingbird, Turquoise-browed Motmot, Golden-fronted Woodpecker, Mangrove, Northern Rough-winged (ridgwayi) and Cave Swallows, Spot-breasted and White-bellied Wrens, Grey-throated Chat, Orchard Oriole.

Access
Easily accessible from either Mérida or Cancún, either via the expensive new toll (Cuota) road (180D) or the more interesting and perfectly ade-

quate old free (libre) 180. There are numerous buses from either town. There is an entry fee (except on Sundays). The ruins are situated within an area of scrubby forest that is surprisingly birdy. Good areas are the track southwest of the Nunnery to Viejo Chichén and between the Observatory (El Caracol) and Xtoloc Cenote. These are good locations for Yucatan Woodpecker, which are, however, less common than Golden-fronted. The Pyramid of Kukulcán (El Castillo) offers good views over the forest, although the area is not especially good for raptors; but you will want to climb El Castillo anyway.

In the early morning (gates open at 8am) the site can be remarkably quiet, suddenly becoming knee-deep in tourists by mid-morning when the buses arrive. Despite this it is possible to find secluded areas with bird activity away from the main attractions.

Accommodation: there are several places to stay and eat within a few km of the site. The Hotel Dolores Alba, about 3 km east of the eastern entrance to the ruins (km 122) is opposite a patch of forest, in which there is an impressive cenote with a substantial colony of Cave Swallow. In 1997 this was being developed for tourist access, but the swallows remained. Camping is possible at the Pirámide Inn and Trailer Park, on the eastern edge of the nearby town of Piste.

UXMAL

An impressive ruin complex set in low hills. One of the best locations for Yucatan Jay.

Yucatán Endemics
Yucatan Poorwill, Yucatan Flycatcher, Yucatan Jay, White-browed Wren, Orange Oriole.

Others
Yucatan Nightjar, Canivet's Emerald, Cinnamon and Buff-bellied Hummingbirds, Turquoise-browed Motmot, Couch's Kingbird, Northern Rough-winged (ridgwayi) and Cave Swallows, Spot-breasted and White-bellied Wrens, Grey-throated Chat.

Access
Uxmal is located on Highway 261 about 80 km south of Mérida, and about 12 km south of Ulema. Just before reaching the archaeological site there are good patches of deciduous thorn forest. The site itself is worthwhile for birds, especially away from the most crowded areas. There is good habitat near the parking lot. About 4 km north of the entrance is Rancho Uxmal; explore any tracks through the brush between this and the site entrance; the two caprimulgids may sometimes be found along this road.

Accommodation: there are several places to stay and eat in the vicinity; prices are high for the area.

PROGRESO AND CHICXULUB

A rather scruffy area on the north side of the Yucatán peninsula, which is nevertheless a good location for some local endemics such as Mexican Sheartail and Yucatan Wren.

Yucatán Endemics
Yucatan Bobwhite, Mexican Sheartail, Yucatan Wren.

Others
American White Pelican, Reddish Egret, Roseate Spoonbill, numerous other shorebirds and herons, Royal and Gull-billed Terns, Buff-bellied and Cinnamon Hummingbirds, Canivet's Emerald, White-lored Gnatcatcher.

Access
A fast, recently constructed road leads due north out of Mérida to Progreso. Approximately 20 km north of Mérida take a right at a gas station along a road that crosses some malodorous mangrove lagoons, which can be excellent for shorebirds. Reaching the coast road, go east (right) and watch for patches of low scrub, accessible by tracks, to the south of the road, which are good locations for Yucatan Wren. Mexican Sheartail also occurs in flowering areas along this road.

Accommodation: there is public transport from Mérida to Progreso, and food and lodging in the latter. Progreso can become very crowded at weekends.

CELESTÚN

A small, pleasant seaside town on the west coast of the Yucatán peninsula, located within the Flamingo Méxicano de Celestún National Park. There are large numbers of the American race of Greater Flamingo, American White Pelican and various herons on the Celestún River. North of the town is extensive bush country harbouring some Yucatán specialities.

Yucatán Endemics
Mexican Sheartail, Yucatan Wren.

Specialities
Plain Chachalaca, Golden-fronted Woodpecker, Yucatan Woodpecker, Cinnamon Hummingbird, Mangrove Vireo, White-lored Gnatcatcher, Hooded Oriole, Yellow-faced Grassquit.

Others
American White Pelican, Greater Flamingo, Green Kingfisher.

Access
Celestún lies at the end of Highway 281 from Mérida. There are fairly frequent first- and second-class buses from the latter. Just before entering town the road crosses a river (actually an inlet of the Gulf of Mexico). On the far side on the left is a parking lot and small restaurant where

CELESTÚN

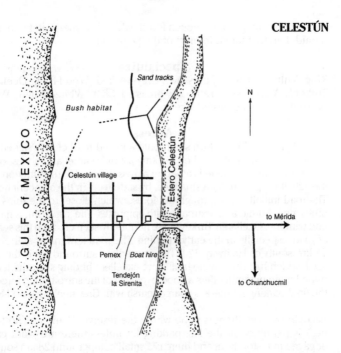

boat rides can be arranged to view flamingos, herons, Green Kingfisher etc. The boat trip to the north is best for flamingos and costs about $25; the trip to the south visits some petrified forests, takes longer and is rather more expensive.

To access good coastal scrub habitat with the species listed above, go north on the third street east of the Pemex station. For the first 2 km the road passes through an area of decrepit huts but finally enters bush habitat with a network of driveable sand tracks. Mangrove Vireo and Yucatan Wren are two of the commonest species.

Accommodation: there are several pleasant, reasonably priced hotels in Celestún e.g. the Hotel María del Carmén. Calle 12, on the seafront. Camping is permitted on the beach and is doubtless possible in the bushy area north of town. Note that the Pemex station in Celestún sells only low-grade gas.

Further Suggestions
About 21 km east from the bridge on Highway 281 a paved but almost deserted road goes south (signed Chunchucmil) The first 10 km passes through good undisturbed dry forest which would be well worth investigating, especially in the rainy season when birds are breeding.

CALAKMUL

A largely unexcavated Mayan ruin in the south-central Yucatán peninsula, surrounded by a very large Biosphere Reserve. The ruins lie 65 km south of the only east–west road in southern Yucatán, between Chetumal and Escarcega, in unbroken forest, which is lusher, taller and more humid than that found in most of the peninsula.

Specialities

King Vulture, Great Curassow, Grey-necked Wood-Rail, Ocellated Turkey*, Mangrove Vireo, Grey-breasted Chat, White-bellied, White-browed and Spot-breasted Wrens.

Access

Take Highway 120 and turn south onto a paved road clearly signed Calakmul, 51 km west of Xpujil or 101 km east of Escarcega, just west of the village of Conhuas. There is a barrier across the road at the junction with the 120. It is opened, for a small fee, by staff living in the adjacent house. The road initially runs through dry forest, which closer to the ruins becomes more humid and luxuriant, with epiphytes. The last 30 km is narrow and winding. Ocellated Turkeys* are frequently seen crossing this section of road, especially in the early morning. The road terminates at the ruins 64 km south of Highway 120. The immediate surrounds and the road itself, which has virtually no traffic, are excellent birding sites; the largely ruined main pyramid offers a good overview of the surrounding forest. At the final parking lot there is a large marsh with Grey-necked Wood-Rail.

Accommodation: there is none within the reserve. Camping (no facilities) is permitted at the last parking lot unless there are work crews engaged in restoration, and there is a small campground 28 km south of Highway 120. In Xpujil there are a couple of basic hotels. The Maya Mirador, on the western edge of the village, has clean, basic cabins and a good inexpensive restaurant. About 20 km west of Xpujil, at Chicanná, is the Ramada Ecovillage, which is very expensive but a modest amount of bargaining is possible.

RÍO USUMACINTA MARSHES

Seasonally flooded marshes with many species of herons and other waterbirds. Formerly a good location for Jabiru; this species now seems to be very scarce.

Specialities

Jabiru.

Others

Least Grebe, Olivaceous Cormorant, Pinnated Bittern, Bare-throated Tiger-Heron, Boat-billed Heron, White and Glossy Ibises, Fulvous and Black-bellied Whistling-Ducks, Muscovy and Masked Ducks, Lesser Yellow-headed Vulture, Snail Kite, Common and Great Black Hawks, Black-collared Hawk, Aplomado Falcon, Ruddy Crake, Grey-necked Wood-Rail, Purple Gallinule, Northern Jacana, Limpkin, Sungrebe, Rufous-breasted Spinetail, Fork-tailed Flycatcher, Grassland Yellow-Finch.

Access

Highway 186, the main road from Villahermosa to Escarcega, passes through marshes for several km. Some of the best areas are between km

The elegant Fork-tailed Flycatcher is a common sight on roadside fences in lowland agricultural areas in southern Mexico.

160 and km 175; essentially drive until you reach good habitat on either side of the road. A major problem is that the road is on a causeway, usually with no good lay-bys, and traffic can be heavy, fast and uninhibited. Where possible take a side road. A good and less busy alternative is to turn off the 186 to Emiliano Zapata and then turn right to La Libertad, and again look for roadside habitat.

PALENQUE

An essential stop for any visitor to southern Mexico, birdwatcher or not. The ruins are superb and spectacular, and the surrounds have retained their forest, in contrast to most of the nearby area. This is one of the best locations for many species that reach the northern end of their range in southern Mexico. About 250 species have been seen in the vicinity of the ruins.

Specialities

White-bellied Emerald, Stripe-tailed Hummingbird, Tody Motmot, Black-faced Antthrush, Red-capped Manakin, Yellow-winged Tanager.

Others

Great and Slaty-breasted Tinamous, Hook-billed, Double-toothed and Plumbeous Kites, White and Great Black Hawks, Collared and Barred Forest-Falcons, Ruddy Crake, Short-billed and Pale-vented Pigeons, Grey-headed and Grey-chested Doves, Crested and Black-and-white Owls, Central American Pygmy-Owl, Lesser Swallow-tailed Swift (nests in ruins), Wedge-tailed and Violet Sabrewings, Long-billed Starthroat, Black-headed, Violaceous, Collared and Slaty-tailed Trogons, Blue-crowned Motmot, White-necked Puffbird, Black-cheeked, Golden-fronted, Smoky-brown, Golden-olive, Chestnut-coloured and Lineated Woodpeckers, Rufous-breasted Spinetail, Tawny-winged, Olivaceous, Wedge-billed, Barred, Ivory-billed and Streak-headed Woodcreepers, Dot-winged Antwren, Dusky Antbird, Scaled Antpitta, about 30 species of flycatcher including Ochre-bellied, Sepia-capped, Northern Royal, Sulphur-rumped and Piratic, Stub-tailed Spadebill, Slate-headed Tody-Flycatcher, Grey-collared Becard, Masked and Black-crowned Tityras, Lovely Cotinga (snags overlooking forest), Band-backed, Spot-breasted and White-bellied Wrens, Green Shrike-Vireo, Grey-crowned Yellowthroat, Golden-hooded Tanager, Green and Red-legged Honeycreepers, Olive-backed, Yellow-throated and Scrub Euphonias, Black-throated Shrike-Tanager, Red-crowned and Red-throated Ant-Tanagers, Grey-headed, Crimson-collared and Scarlet-rumped Tanagers, Green-backed and Orange-billed Sparrows, Chestnut-headed and Montezuma Oropendolas.

Black-faced Antthrushes are commonly heard around Palenque.
Seeing them is another matter

Access

The town of Palenque is on a paved highway (199) running from Highway 86 to San Cristóbal de las Casas. The ruins are about 7 km from the town; take the road to Ocosingo and fork left a little way past the Mayan Head (a large statue in the middle of the road); this leads straight to the ruins. There is a regular minibus service from town to the ruins, which starts early in the day. As the road approaches the ruins, it climbs sharply with a couple of hairpins. At the bend of this road just before the steep hill a trail leads to the right down to a stream, where Scaled Antpitta and Orange-billed Sparrow are found. The forest on either side of the road can be very productive in the early morning. The ruins are not open until 8am. It may be possible to pay the previous day and birdwatch in the morning on-site but away from the ruins, especially on the trail that descends from the ruins to the road near the museum. Park staff are not pleased to find people wandering among the ruins outside hours. Otherwise it may be best to spend the early morning outside the site boundary. When you enter, philistine as this may appear, the best thing to do is to ignore the ruins and explore the trails that lead up the hillside behind the site, returning later in the morning. In the late morning the ruins offer a good vantage point for observing raptors; search sheltered parts of the buildings for the curious sock-shaped nests of Lesser Swallow-tailed Swifts.

Accommodation: in Palenque there are numerous places to stay and eat, at various levels. Near the ruins there is a campground and trailer park. A superb place to stay and eat is Misol-ha, about 20 km from Palenque on the road to Ocosingo. It is located about 1.5 km down a dirt road, and has a restaurant and cabins tucked away in the forest, while a couple of hundred metres away is a lake and a spectacular waterfall over 35 m high.

At 60 km from Palenque on the Ocosingo road is the extraordinary cascade complex of Agua Azul (Blue Water, well named as the river is a

PALENQUE

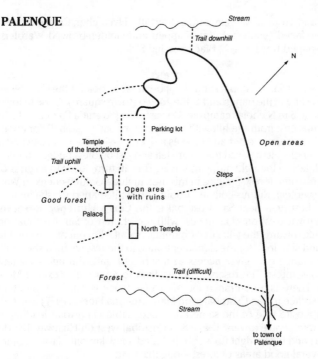

vivid turquoise-blue colour). There is some reasonable forest around the cascades.

There have been reports of recent thefts and outright robberies at this location. Caution is obviously advised. Before proceeding into the highlands towards Ocosingo and San Cristóbal de las Casas it would be wise to enquire as to the current political situation; at the time of writing things are pretty quiet, but this was not the case five years ago, and the future is unpredictable.

SAN CRISTÓBAL DE LAS CASAS

A beautiful highland city in the mountains of Chiapas, with some superb colonial architecture and a colourful Indian heritage. It gives access to a number of excellent birdwatching sites where most of the endemic species of the Chiapan–Guatemalan massif can be found fairly easily.

Specialities
Bearded Screech-Owl*, Blue-throated Motmot, Guatemalan (Red-shafted) Flicker, Black-capped Swallow, Rufous-browed Wren, Rufous-collared Thrush, Golden-cheeked* (winter) and Pink-headed Warblers.

Others
Singing Quail, Unspotted Saw-whet Owl, Green Violet-ear, White-eared, Amethyst-throated, Garnet-throated and Magnificent Hummingbirds, Strong-billed and Spot-crowned Woodcreepers, Steller's and Unicoloured Jays, Band-backed Wren, Grey-breasted Wood-Wren, Blue-and-

white and Tropical Mockingbirds, Grey Silky-Flycatcher, Crescent-chested, Red-faced (winter), Rufous-capped and Golden-browed Warblers, White-naped Brush-Finch, Black-headed Siskin.

Access

The town of San Cristóbal should not be missed; look for the Cave Swallows nesting in the bandstand at the *zócalo* (town square). Close to town is Rancho San Nicholas campsite. Go east along Avenida Francisco León (this runs east from the hill with the church of San Cristóbal) for about 2 km. This becomes dirt and crosses a river, passing the campsite and a quarry until it hits a paved road. Turn left and just before a bridge a muddy track leads to the right along the river. This, in turn, leads to a series of trails into pine forest. Species in this area include Golden-cheeked Warbler* (winter), Rufous-collared Robin and White-naped Brush-Finch.

The best area near San Cristóbal is the **Cerro Huitepec Reserve**. Leave town west on Mazariegos, with the church of San Cristóbal on your left, towards the village of Chamula. About 4 km out of town on the left-hand side look for the signed entrance to the reserve up a short hill. The entrance gate gives access to a series of trails through excellent pine–oak forest. The reserve is open 9am to 4pm daily (except Mondays). There is an entrance fee. Cerro Huitepec is run by Pro-Natura whose office in San Cristóbal is on Maria Adelina Flores ((967)-8-40-69). The opposite side of the same hill is accessible via a road leading to some microwave towers. Leave San Cristóbal west on Highway 190 (to Tuxtla) and take a right up a cobbled road a few km out of town. There are several good areas of forest along this road.

The road to Ocosingo passes through some good forest with many of the Chiapan massif endemics. Leave San Cristóbal on Highway 190 towards Comitán and turn left after 13 km on Highway 199 to Ocosingo. This road leads through semi-open pine forest; getting off it can be a problem, but about 2 km from the 190 a driveable track (with some low muddy spots) leads to the right. A second turn-off (about 10 km from the 190), also on the right, leads ultimately to the village of Chanal; take a left at a T-junction a little way off the 199 and stop at any good forest patches.

San Cristóbal is served by a variety of first- and second-class buses, connecting it with Tuxtla Gutiérrez, Oaxaca, Mérida, Palenque, Villahermosa and other centres. There are several daily buses to Ocosingo.

Accommodation: there are numerous hotels and restaurants to suit all budgets in the town.

This area of Chiapas has been in a state of political ferment in recent years, with open insurgency in the mid-1990s. The local people view outsiders with some suspicion, more than amply justified in many cases. Caution in travelling (and local enquiry as to recent conditions) is strongly advised. In particular, visitors should be sensitive to local feelings when photographing; always ask permission first.

LAGUNAS DE MONTEBELLO NATIONAL PARK

A beautiful area of scenic lakes set in low hills with good areas of forest. One of the few regions of Mexico where Resplendent Quetzal* still occurs.

Specialities

White-breasted Hawk, Singing Quail, White-faced Quail-Dove, Lesser Roadrunner, Resplendent Quetzal*, Tufted Flycatcher, Black-capped Swallow, Black-throated Jay, Rufous-collared Robin, White-naped Brush-Finch.

Others

Thicket and Slaty-breasted Tinamous, White-tailed Kite, Barred Forest-Falcon, Highland Guan*, Plain Chachalaca, Spotted Wood-Quail, Limpkin, Ruddy Crake, Barred Parakeet, White-crowned Parrot, Violet Sabrewing, Emerald-chinned, Azure-crowned, Amethyst-throated, Garnet-throated, Stripe-tailed and Wine-throated Hummingbirds, Slender Sheartail, Green-throated Mountain-gem, Sparkling-tailed Woodstar, Mountain Trogon, Smoky-brown, Golden-olive and Pale-billed Woodpeckers, Guatemalan (Red-shafted) Flicker, Scaly-throated Foliage-gleaner, Strong-billed Woodcreeper, Black-faced Antthrush, Northern Bentbill, Eye-ringed Flatbill, Yellowish, Pine and Sulphur-bellied Flycatchers, Azure-hooded and Unicoloured Jays, Band-backed, Spot-breasted and Plain Wrens, Brown-backed and Slate-coloured Solitaires, Black-headed and Spotted Nightingale-Thrushes, Black Robin, Blue-and-white and Tropical Mockingbirds, Grey Silky-Flycatcher, Crescent-chested, Golden-cheeked* (winter), Rufous-capped and Golden-browed Warblers, Blue-crowned Chlorophonia, Yellow-winged, Flame-coloured and White-winged Tanagers, Prevost's Ground-Sparrow, Black-headed Siskin, Hooded Grosbeak.

Access

South from Comitán on Highway 190: 15 km from Comitán turn left onto a paved road running due east. After about 35 km there is an archway over the road; there may be park personnel at this entrance. The paved road goes to Laguna Bosque Azul, with a parking lot about 3 km from the entrance. Around the lake is mostly pine forest with some broadleaf woodland. The best areas are in the vicinity of the bridge across a small stream just below the campsite, and the track that continues where the paved road ends. Species here include Lesser Roadrunner, Tufted Flycatcher, Unicoloured Jay and White-naped Brush-Finch. There are several other good tracks through the forest accessible from the parking lot.

After passing through the archway, look for a dirt road on the right. This leads to the pleasant village of Tziscao and several lakes with excellent forest nearby. Tziscao is on the shores of Laguna Tziscao, which has Ruddy Crake and Limpkin. About 1 km before the turn-off to Tziscao (i.e. 9 km from the archway) a track on the left goes to Laguna Pojoj. The forest here is mainly temperate broadleaf. Quetzals have been seen here, most easily in March–April when they are more vocal. Beyond the turn-off to Tziscao the road passes other patches of forest including some cloud forest.

About 7 km before the archway (i.e. 29 km from Highway 190) a signed dirt road goes left (north) about 1.5 km to the Mayan ruins of Chinkultic. There may be an entrance fee to this area. Birds around the ruins include White-tailed Kite, Plain Chachalaca, Azure-crowned Hummingbird, Slender Sheartail, Brown-backed Solitaire and Black-headed Siskin.

By public transport, buses and *colectivos* go from Comitán (2 Pte. Sur 17B) to the Lagunas (or Lagos) de Montebello; some buses also go to Tziscao.

LAGUNAS DE MONTEBELLO
NATIONAL PARK

N
Broadleaf forest
Laguna Pojoj
Tziscao
Albergue Turístico
GUATEMALA
dirt road
3km
Laguna Tziscao
Pine forest
campsite Paved road
Trails
Park entrance archway
Laguna Bosque Azul
Paved road
La Orquidea Cabins and restaurant
Hidalgo
Chinkultic Ruins
to Comitán

Accommodation: there are several places to stay; best known and probably the best is La Orquidea, 0.5 km beyond the turn-off to the Chinkultic ruins. In Tziscao village is the Albergue Turístico, and there is camping here or (free) at Laguna Bosque Azul. Rowing boats may be hired at Laguna Tziscao.

This area is on the border of Guatemala (in fact the eastern bank of Laguna Tziscao is Guatemalan). In recent years the area has been subject to civil unrest, both home grown and imported. Local enquiry is recommended before proceeding; this especially applies to the road that goes for many km beyond the Tziscao turn-off.

TUXTLA GUTIÉRREZ

Most people pause at Tuxtla on their way to El Sumidero or San Cristóbal de las Casas; however, the Zoológico Miguel Alvárez del Toro (named after one of Mexico's most distinguished ornithologists), located on a forested hill a few km south of town, can be very productive, though is best avoided at weekends. The zoo specializes in the fauna of Chiapas, and several (totally wild) species of cracids can be found, ridiculously tame, wandering around.

Specialities
Great Curassow*, Highland* and Crested Guans.

Others
Plain Chachalaca, Grey-necked Wood-Rail, Squirrel Cuckoo, Lesser Ground-Cuckoo, Lesser Swallow-tailed Swift, Canivet's Emerald, Stripe-tailed Hummingbird, Collared Trogon, Rufous-crowned Motmot, Collared Araçari, Green Jay, White-throated Magpie-Jay, Banded Wren, Clay-coloured Robin, Black-headed and Buff-throated Saltators, Streak-backed Oriole.

Access
Served by buses signed 'Cerro Hueco' that leave at 20-minute intervals from the corner of Calle 1 Oriente Sur and Avenida 7 Sur Oriente. The journey takes 20 minutes. The zoo is free, open from 8am to 5.30pm and has an excellent selection of local fauna. Closed on Mondays.

EL SUMIDERO

A large canyon carved by the Río Grijalva, which is easily reached from the state capital of Tuxtla Gutiérrez. A reasonable road winds through the area, giving spectacular views of the canyon on several occasions and accessing dry and semi-dry forest. One of the classic sites for the highly localized Belted Flycatcher*.

Specialities
Great Swallow-tailed Swift, Green-fronted Hummingbird, Slender Sheartail, Belted* and Flammulated Flycatchers, Northern Rough-winged Swallow (ridgwayi), Bar-winged Oriole.

Others
Bat Falcon, Plain Chachalaca, Red-billed Pigeon, White-winged, White-tipped and Inca Doves, Pheasant Cuckoo, Lesser Ground-Cuckoo, Lesser Roadrunner, Vermiculated Screech-Owl, Canivet's and White-bellied Emeralds, Azure-crowned and Buff-bellied Hummingbirds, Blue-crowned and Russet-crowned Motmots, Golden-fronted and Golden-olive Woodpeckers, Ivory-billed Woodcreeper, Greenish Elaenia, Nutting's and Sulphur-bellied Flycatchers, Grey-collared and Rose-throated Becards, Band-backed and Banded Wrens, Blue-and-white Mockingbird, Worm-eating (winter), Fan-tailed and Rufous-capped Warblers, Red-breasted Chat, Yellow-throated, Scrub and Blue-hooded Euphonias, Yellow-winged Tanager, Blue Bunting, Blue-black Grassquit, Yellow Grosbeak, Black-vented, Streak-backed and Altamira Orioles.

Access
From the centre of Tuxtla Gutiérrez take the road to San Cristóbal de las Casas (Avenida 14 de Septiembre), then turn north (left) onto 11A Ori-

ente Norte. After passing a park, look for signs to El Sumidero. This road climbs through degraded dry habitat to the park entrance. From the entrance to the end of the road (at a spectacular overlook, with a restaurant) is about 22 km. Once in the park it is worth stopping wherever there is suitable habitat and the road permits. The lower reaches are substantially more arid, with Lesser Roadrunner, White-throated Magpie-Jay and White-lored Gnatcatcher. Apart from the end of the road, there are four lookouts, all of which are worthwhile. Belted Flycatcher* occurs at km 22 and also at several locations further down, especially Mirador la Robla; Great Swallow-tailed Swift can be seen in and above the gorge from about km 16 upwards.

Colectivos run from Tuxtla Gutiérrez to near the park entrance, and by privately paying the driver you may be able to persuade him to take you to km 22. Alternatively, Transportes Cañon del Sumidero (tel. 2-06-49) runs two-hour minibus tours, but this is a sightseeing trip with limited time for birding. El Sumidero is best avoided at weekends. There have been several recent reports of robberies, especially at the first two lookouts.

The canyon can also be seen, spectacularly, by boat; in Chiapa de Corzo, a small historic colonial town about 12 km east of Tuxtla on the Río Grijalva, go two blocks from the west end of the *zócalo* to the dock. This trip is recommended, but not especially birdy.

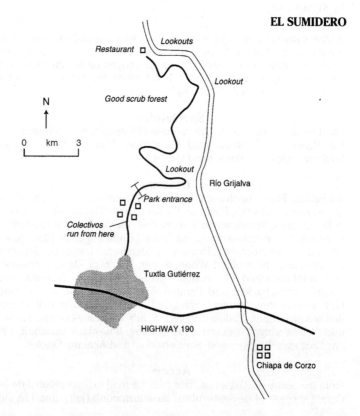

EL SUMIDERO

ARRIAGA

Arriaga is a small industrial town on the hot Soconusco Plain. It is not exactly a tourist destination. However the surrounding countryside, which is dry scrubland, does harbour a number of species not easily found elsewhere.

Endemics
Giant Wren, Rosita's* and Orange-breasted Buntings, Yellow-winged Cacique.

Others
Pacific (Green) Parakeet, Yellow-naped Parrot*, Ferruginous Pygmy-Owl, Russet-crowned Motmot, Golden-fronted Woodpecker, Long-tailed Manakin, Scissor-tailed Flycatcher, Thick-billed Kingbird, White-throated Magpie-Jay, Banded Wren, White-lored Gnatcatcher.

Access
Leave Arriaga north on the road to Tuxtla Gutiérrez and pull off in areas of good habitat. One such place is about 3 km north of Arriaga, where a track leads to the right through arid scrub.

South of Arriaga on the coast is the pleasant town of Puerto Arista. The road to Puerto Arista passes through mainly agricultural (pasture) land but patches of scrub should be checked for Giant Wren. East of Puerto Arista is a further area of pasture with scattered trees and brushy areas that may be worth checking for the same species.

EL TRIUNFO

A famous location in the Sierra Madre de Chiapas, especially noteworthy for two highly restricted and spectacular species, Horned Guan* and Azure-rumped Tanager*, but also a very good site for numerous other highland species.

Specialities
Horned Guan*, Rufous Hermit, Green-throated Mountain-gem, Wine-throated Hummingbird, Black-throated Jay, Azure-rumped Tanager*.

Others
White-breasted Hawk, Highland Guan*, Singing Quail, White-fronted Quail-Dove, Barred Parakeet, Mottled and Fulvous Owls, Emerald-chinned, Berylline and Amethyst-throated Hummingbirds, Mountain Trogon, Blue-throated Motmot, Scaly-throated Foliage-gleaner, Spotted and Spot-crowned Woodcreepers, Tufted Flycatcher, Black-capped Swallow, Unicoloured Jay, Rufous-browed Wren, Grey-breasted Wood-Wren, Black and Mountain Robins, Blue-and-white Mockingbird, Grey Silky-Flycatcher, Chestnut-sided Shrike-Vireo, Crescent-chested Warbler, Yellow-winged and Flame-coloured Tanagers, Blue-crowned Chlorophonia, Blue-hooded Euphonia.

Access
Not easy. El Triunfo is south of Tuxtla Gutiérrez, by the road south

The weird Horned Guan is an endangered species found in a very few locations in Chiapas and Guatemala

through Revolución Méxicana and Jaltenango de la Paz. However, while independent access to the reserve is perfectly possible, it is much better to make prior arrangements with the Instituto de Historia Natural (IHN) in Tuxtla (Calzada de los Hombres de la Revolución, Aptdo. Postal 6, Tuxtla Gutiérrez 29000. Tel. (011-52) 961-23663 or 23754, fax 961-29943). There is an entrance fee of $100. IHN can also, for an additional charge, arrange transport from Tuxtla Gutiérrez, as well as making arrangements to reach the reserve; this can, if you wish, include a guide, a mule to carry personal gear and food. There is sleeping accommodation within a basic dormitory in the reserve and camping is permitted. If you decide to make your own way be warned that the road from Jaltenango is poor and finding your way to the camp at El Triunfo may not be obvious. Prior permission to visit the reserve is required.

COLONIA DE CUAUHTÉMOC

The easiest location for the highly restricted (and endangered) Nava's Wren*.

Endemics
Green Parakeet, Long-tailed Sabrewing*, Nava's Wren*.

Others
Great and Slaty-breasted Tinamous, White and Grey Hawks, Common Black-Hawk, Crested Guan, Red-billed and Short-billed Pigeons, White-crowned, Red-lored and Mealy Parrots, Long-billed Starthroat, Black-headed and Violaceous Trogons, Blue-crowned Motmot, Black-cheeked, Golden-fronted, Smoky-brown and Chestnut-coloured Wood-peckers, Rufous-breasted Spinetail, Tawny-winged, Ivory-billed and Streak-headed Woodcreepers, Black-faced Antthrush, Greenish and Yellow-bellied Elaenias, Slate-headed and Common Tody-Flycatchers,

Stub-tailed Spadebill, Sulphur-rumped Flycatcher, Masked Tityra, Northern Rough-winged Swallow (ridgwayi), Band-backed and Spotted Wrens, White-breasted Wood-Wren, Red-legged Honeycreeper. Yellow-winged Tanager, Black-throated Shrike-Tanager, Scarlet-rumped, Crimson-collared and White-winged Tanagers, Blue-black Grosbeak, Orange-billed Sparrow, Montezuma Oropendola.

Access

Turn east off Highway 200 at km 174.5 in the village of Boca del Monte (marked on some maps as Sarabia). The turn is opposite Restaurante Ixtepeji (km 0). The road passes below an archway labelled illegibly 'Puerta de Uxpanapa'. The road is paved but is badly potholed. At about km 18 cross a toll bridge (5 pesos, good for return journey same day); the road becomes unpaved and passes through the village of Colonia de Cuauhtémoc; at km 25.9 (about 4 km past Cuauhtémoc) take a right signed 'Río Amaco 20 km'. About 400 m beyond this fork there are several weirdly sculpted limestone outcrops with forest; Nava's Wren* is found here. Shortly after crossing the toll bridge there are some reasonable patches of forest on both sides of the road. If, instead of turning to Río Amaco, you continue on the same road you reach Veracruz state, where from km 35–40 there are further patches of forest with another chance for the wren, and other species.

Please bear in mind that Nava's Wren* is an endangered species: persistent use of a tape recorder is detrimental to breeding success and should not be countenanced by ethical birdwatchers.

Accommodation: there are numerous cheap hotels in Matías Romero, about 25 km south of Boca del Monte. The closest is the Hotel Liesa, clean and cheap, with restaurant, on Highway 200 about 15 km south of Boca del Monte. Colonia Cuauhtémoc can be reached by minibus or *colectivo* from Matias Romero. There are several places to eat in Cuauhtémoc but we are not aware of any place to stay.

THE ISTHMUS ROAD

Highway 200, which becomes Highway 185, runs north–south across the narrowest part of Mexico, from Juchitán de Zaragoza to Acayucán. Although much of the habitat has been comprehensively destroyed, there are good locations along this road where regional endemics such as the spectacular Rosita's* and Orange-breasted Buntings, and Sumichrast's Sparrow* can be found.

Endemics

Rosita's* and Orange-breasted Buntings, Sumichrast's (Cinnamon-tailed) Sparrow*.

Others

Common Black-Hawk, Grey-headed Dove, Orange-fronted Parakeet, Lesser Roadrunner, Golden-fronted Woodpecker, White-throated Magpie-Jay, White-lored Gnatcatcher, Stripe-headed Sparrow, Altamira Oriole, Yellow-winged Cacique.

Access

At about km 229 (south of Matías Romero) there are rough tracks on either side of the road leading to quarries. Both are worth walking. Sumichrast's Sparrows* occur in scrub alongside these tracks and Rosita's Buntings* in scrub at the end of the eastern track. There is reasonable accommodation in Matías Romero and Santo Domingo Tehuantepec.

CATEMACO AREA

The area around Catemaco has a number of attractions. The lake of Catemaco nestles within an area of uplands, the highest being two volcanoes about 1700 m above sea level. Being isolated from other upland areas by extensive lowlands, the area is a minor centre of endemism; depending on taxonomy, there may be up to three endemics species in this small area. Much of the original forest has been destroyed, but a good patch remains at the UNAM (Universidad Nacional Autónomo de México) Biological Station, and on the upper levels of the hills, which are, however, difficult to reach. Other worthwhile areas are around the lake itself and Laguna de Sontecomapán. The list for the whole area probably exceeds 400 species.

Endemics
Tuxtla Quail-Dove*, Long-tailed Sabrewing*.

Specialities
Agami Heron, Muscovy Duck, Northern Potoo, Black-crested Coquette, Canivet's Emerald, Black-faced Antthrush, Lovely Cotinga, Black-throated Shrike-Tanager, Chestnut-capped Brush-Finch.

Others
Great, Thicket and Slaty-breasted Tinamous, Boat-billed Heron, Black-bellied and Fulvous Whistling-Ducks, Lesser Yellow-headed Vulture, Bicoloured, White and Grey Hawks, Great Black Hawk, Ornate Hawk-Eagle, Red-billed and Short-billed Pigeons, Blue Ground-Dove, Grey-headed Dove, Brown-hooded and Red-lored Parrots, Spectacled and Mottled Owls, Long-tailed and Little Hermits, Violet Sabrewing, White-bellied Emerald, Azure-crowned, Rufous-tailed and Buff-bellied Hummingbirds, Collared and Slaty-tailed Trogons, Blue-crowned Motmot, Ringed, Amazon, Green and American Pygmy Kingfisher, Keel-billed Toucan, Black-cheeked, Smoky-brown, Chestnut-coloured and Pale-billed Woodpeckers, Tawny-winged, Northern Barred and Ivory-billed Woodcreepers, Rufous-breasted Spinetail, Yellow-bellied Tyrannulet, Ochre-bellied, Sepia-capped, Yellow-olive, Boat-billed, Sulphur-rumped and Sulphur-bellied Flycatchers, Northern Bentbill, Eye-ringed Flatbill, Stub-tailed Spadebill, Bright-rumped Attila, Grey-collared Becard, Masked and Black-crowned Tityras, Red-capped Manakin, Mangrove Swallow, Band-backed and Spot-breasted Wrens, White-breasted Wood-Wren, Slate-coloured Solitaire, Tawny-crowned and Lesser Greenlets, Green Shrike-Vireo, Rufous-browed Peppershrike, Worm-eating, Orange-crowned, Magnolia and Kentucky Warblers, Northern (winter) and Louisiana (winter) Waterthrushes, Grey-crowned Yellowthroat, Golden-crowned and Rufous-capped Warblers, Blue-crowned Chlorophonia,

Scrub, Yellow-throated, Blue-hooded and Olive-backed Euphonias, Yellow-winged, White-winged and Crimson-collared Tanagers, Red-crowned and Red-throated Ant-Tanagers, Black-faced Grosbeak, Blue Bunting, Rusty Sparrow, Black-cowled, Yellow-tailed and Altamira Orioles, Montezuma Oropendola.

Access

The town of Catemaco (25,000) is located on Highway 180 from San Andrés Tuxtla. Laguna Catemaco is about 16 km long. Leave the town, on Hidalgo, in an easterly direction; if lost ask for Hotel Playa Azul or Sontecomapán. The Playa Azul is located on the lakeshore. 2.1 km beyond the Playa Azul there is a fork in the road. The right-hand fork goes to Coyame and the bottling plant. Take this, and in a further 1.5 km there is some forest on the right. This section of the lake, if you can gain access, is a classic location for Sungrebe. There are two tracks on the right; the first about 1.4 km past the Sontecomapán fork to the bottling plant (ask permission), and the second, about 2.5 km from the fork, to some good forest, probably signed La Jungla. Further on the same road, past the town of Coyame, a very poor road leaves the small village of Tebanca to the left and climbs the lower lopes of Volcán Santa Marta. There is good forest further up this road, but access is very rough.

The left-hand fork goes to Sontecomapán and the coast. About 2 km beyond the fork a poor road goes right, with some reasonable forest about 4 km up. In Sontecomapán, visit the dock and negotiate for a boat to explore Laguna de Sontecomapán. Be sure to fix the price before set-

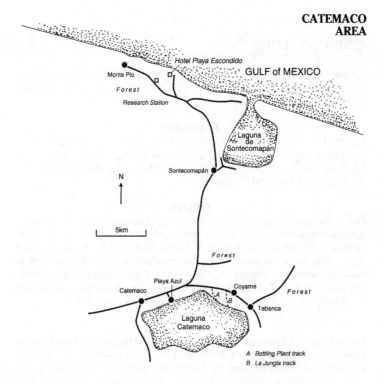

CATEMACO
AREA

A Bottling Plant track
B La Jungla track

ting out and explain to the boatman that you are interested in birds and don't wish to roar around the lake at breakneck speed. The boat gives good access to mangroves, with Bare-throated Tiger-Heron, Pinnated Bittern, Lesser Yellow-headed Vulture and Grey-necked Wood-Rail.

Continue on the same road, asking for Monte Pio or the University Research Station. The road degenerates and there was one very dubious bridge, about whose condition we have no very recent information. There is still some worthwhile forest along this road, but by far the best location is the Research Station Forest at about km 28. The 500 ha is one of the best examples of extant lowland forest on the Caribbean coast of Mexico. There are several trails, some of which may at any time be restricted to research workers. Be sure to obtain permission before entering.

Accommodation: there are numerous places to stay in Catemaco; the Playa Azul is also a good birding location, with Blue-crowned Motmot, Amazon and Green Kingfishers, Band-backed Wren and Yellow-winged Tanager. Beware of falling trees. There are a couple of basic places to stay beyond Sontecomapán: the Playa Escondida is located at the end of a right-hand turn before the Research Station, and there is a comfortable cheap hotel in Monte Pio. Buses serve Catemaco from Veracruz and local buses from San Andrés Tuxtla. Between Catemaco and Monte Pio there are regular camionetas, which are essentially utility trucks with wooden benches in the back.

There have been several reports, both recent and several years old, of robberies in the Playa Escondida area.

CERRO SAN FELIPE

A very fine area of upland forest, easily accessible from Oaxaca City, and one of the best location for endemics such as Grey-barred Wren (abundant) and Dwarf Jay*.

Endemics
Long-tailed Wood-Partridge, Mountain Pygmy-Owl, Dusky and Bumble-bee Hummingbird, Dwarf Jay*, Grey-barred Wren, Aztec Thrush, Russet Nightingale-Thrush, Golden, Dwarf and Slaty Vireos, Red Warbler, Bridled Sparrow, Collared Towhee.

Others
Great Swallow-tailed Swift, White-eared, Amethyst-throated, Garnet-throated and Magnificent Hummingbirds, Mountain Trogon, Spot-crowned Woodcreeper, Pine and Tufted Flycatchers, Brown-throated Wren, Grey-breasted Wood-Wren, Black-eared Bushtit, Mexican Chickadee, Brown-backed Solitaire, Black Robin, Ruddy-capped Nightingale-Thrush, Grey Silky-Flycatcher, Olive, Rufous-capped and Golden-browed Warblers, Chestnut-capped Brush-Finch, Black-headed Siskin.

Access
Leave Oaxaca City on the Pan-American south (Highway 190 to Tehuantepec). Turn left (north) on Highway 175 to Tuxtepec, about 5 km out of town and 500 m beyond the Motel Internacional. The road climbs,

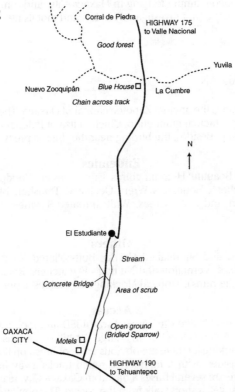

CERRO SAN FELIPE

passing the Black Tank (see below) and at about km 21 comes to a small settlement called La Cumbre (i.e. The Summit). In La Cumbre dirt roads go to the right (signed Yuvila 7) and to the left (signed Corral de Piedra 14). The Yuvila road leads to some small patches of forest, but the left-hand turn is much more productive. Usually there is a chain across this road, with someone charging a fee to open it. The legality of this may be debatable, but pay anyway, it gives the locals an incentive to prevent illegal logging. If the chain is padlocked, knock on the door of the blue house on the left-hand side just before the barrier. This dirt road winds through excellent forest for more than 10 km. There is very little traffic and good birding from the road itself. Especially productive spots are where streams cross the road. After about 7 km there is a fork; to the right to Corral de Piedra (RMO Teococuilco), and to the left to Nuevo Zooquipán. Both are worth exploring. Mountain Pygmy-Owl has been found near the end of the left-hand track, taking a further right turn at 9.1 km from the barrier and going past an open area on the right.

Route 175 and the Black Tank. The road from Highway 190 to La Cumbre passes through mostly agricultural land, heavily overgrazed and of little interest. However, some good habitat remains. About 6–7 km from Highway 190 (about km 208 on Highway 175) the road crosses a concrete bridge over a stream. Opposite (east) of this is a patch of scrub that has Dusky Hummingbird, Golden, Dwarf and Slaty Vireos, and Bridled Sparrow (all endemic). Beware of the dog.

Accommodation: ample lodging in Oaxaca City, and a number of reasonable-looking (not investigated) hotels and motels near the intersection of 190 and 175.

MONTE ALBÁN

Monte Albán is the ancient Zapotec capital of Oaxaca. The ruins do not have the spectacular grandeur of Chichén Itzá or Palenque but are well worth visiting. Besides, the birding near the ruins is pretty good!

Endemics
Dusky and Beautiful Hummingbirds, Grey-breasted Woodpecker, Pileated Flycatcher*, Boucard's Wren, Ocellated Thrasher, Blue Mockingbird, Dwarf and Slaty Vireos, White-throated Towhee, Oaxaca Sparrow*.

Others
White-tailed and Short-tailed Hawks, Buff-collared Nightjar, Berylline Hummingbird, Vermilion and Nutting's Flycatchers, Rock Wren (sings from atop the ruins), Tropical Mockingbird, Rufous-capped Warbler.

Access
Head towards Mexico City on Highway 135D and look for signs to the left. Monte Albán is located on a large flat hilltop (admission charge). From the parking lot there are obvious areas of brush on the downward-sloping hillsides, with a number of rough tracks away from the busy areas. There are several buses a day from Oaxaca City, leaving from the Hotel del Angél, a short walk from the *zócalo*. The obvious downside is that these tend to arrive later than most birders would prefer. Taxis are readily found in Oaxaca City. It is particularly important to be at this site early in the day; not only is it very hot later, but the whole area becomes very busy and noisy by mid-morning. The site opens at 8am, but beside the road there is accessible good brush, and you can park outside and scout the hillsides below the ruins.

Highway 90 from Oaxaca City to Izúcar de Matamoros passes through rolling semi-desert country. This is one of the easiest locations for Grey-breasted Woodpecker, a highly localised west Mexican endemic; for example, near the village of La Peña.

Accommodation: abundant accommodation at various levels of comfort and cost in Oaxaca City.

AMATLÁN

An interesting area of forest, by no means pristine, located on karst limestone with an open understorey. Probably the easiest location to see the highly restricted endemic Sumichrast's Wren*.

Endemics
Sumichrast's Wren*.

Others
Red-lored Parrot, Blue-crowned Motmot, Emerald Toucanet, Collared Araçari, Golden-olive and Golden-fronted Woodpeckers, Olivaceous Woodcreeper, Masked Tityra, Brown Jay, Band-backed Wren, Grey-breasted Wood Wren, Rufous-capped Warbler, Buff-throated Saltator.

Access
From Córdoba: at the intersection of Avenida 11 and Calle 7, go south on Avenida 11 and fork right at a large Pemex station. After crossing a two-track railway there is a five-way intersection; turn half (not full) left here and cross several other railway tracks, go past a sugar-cane processing plant on left, cross the autopista and enter Amatlán; if lost, head for the church spire. Enter the *zócalo* and exit at the opposite corner (i.e. the road by the church, not alongside it but away from it to the left) along Calle Matamoros. After 200 m turn right at a T-junction onto Calle Allende which curves to the left. About 150 m past Tortilleria los 3 Reyes turn right onto a cobbled street which becomes a driveable dirt track running for 1.4 km through cane fields. Ignore side tracks and drive to the edge of a wooded area where the driveable track ends. A footpath leads to the left at this point and within 150 m reaches the karst escarpment; the path winds for 2–3 km through the forest past a shrine. Wrens have been seen at the beginning of the path and again at 0.5 km and 1 km. Sumichrast's Wren* is classified as Vulnerable. Tape recorders should only be used with extreme caution to avoid disturbance to territorial birds.

Accommodation: there are many choices of food and accommodation for varied budgets in Córdoba.

EL COFRE DE PEROTE NATIONAL PARK

An interesting area of high-altitude forest, with road access to 4200 m, though apparently not much visited by birdwatchers. The species list is similar to that of other highland areas such as Popocatépetl, to which El Cofre de Perote would make a good alternative in the event of a volcanic eruption.

Access
In the town of Perote, exit southeast (signed Altonga, Teziutlán), next to the bus station. Proceed to the *zócalo*, turn right, first left on Ignacio Altimiran, right at end, pass the pink church and follow Calle Allende (half-right turn). A very wide rough road leads uphill. About 2 km from the church fork left at a large crucifix and peculiar yellow building. The road improves once out of town and may be followed by a normal vehicle to the microwave towers (24 km from Perote). The area is agricultural at first but shortly gives way to high-altitude coniferous forest. An intersection about halfway to the summit accesses further forest. There is one bus daily from Perote to the small village of El Conejo which is about two-thirds of the way up.

Accommodation: numerous places to stay in Perote, e.g. Hotel El Centro, Pino Suarez 17, near the pink church, is clean, friendly, with off-street parking and is reasonably priced.

TEZIUTLÁN, PUEBLA

A residual patch of cloud forest, giving a hint of what much of highland eastern Mexico must have been like many years ago, which is a location (at least formerly) for Bearded Wood-Partridge*.

Endemics
Bearded Wood-Partridge*.

Specialities
Azure-hooded Jay, Black Robin.

Others
Amethyst-throated and Garnet-throated Hummingbirds, Olivaceous, Spotted and Spot-crowned Woodcreepers, Unicoloured Jay, American Dipper, Grey-breasted Wood-Wren, Brown-backed and Slate-coloured Solitaires, Grey Silky-Flycatcher, Chestnut-sided Shrike-Vireo, Crescent-chested, Golden-browed and Rufous-capped Warblers, Blue-hooded Euphonia, Common Bush-Tanager, Flame-coloured Tanager, Black-headed Saltator, Hooded Grosbeak.

Access
Leave Teziutlán on Highway 129 (Nautla). At km 4.8 there is a major fork on the right (Perote) and at 5.2 an 'Automotel' on the right. At km 8.8 there is a small white shrine on the left (ignore other shrines looking like a blue dog kennel and a confessional). At about km 9.4 the road passes through a short cutting; until this point there is a high bank on the right and a deep valley on the left. Directly behind this cutting, beyond a barbed wire fence, a narrow muddy path leads steeply down into the valley. Both sides of the valley possess good forest, although for how much longer is unknown. After the cutting, there is a 10 km sign, and at km 10.4 high-voltage wires cross the road, while at km 10.6 there is a pink shrine with barred gates set into the bank on the right. Coming from Nautla, look for the shrine and wires and reverse the directions. In good weather the birding from the road is worthwhile (though busy). It is not easy to access the valley except by the one footpath described. Ownership of the land is apparently in dispute.

The author's most recent visit to this area was in March 1998; shortly after this there were major floods and landslides in Teziutlán, which caused substantial damage and loss of life. We have no more recent information.

Accommodation: food and accommodation in Teziutlán.

POPOCATÉPETL

Two spectacular volcanoes, Popocatépetl and Iztaccihuatl, both over 5000 m and permanently snow-covered, lie about 80 km from Mexico City. A good road leads to the col between them (Paso de Cortés), while side roads at the pass lead further up each slope. Road access is changeable at short notice, as Popocatépetl is presently active. Enquire in Amecameca as to the current situation. The road from Amecameca starts in agricultural land and passes through coniferous forest to tussock grassland at high altitude.

Endemics
Russet Nightingale-Thrush, Red Warbler, Green-striped Brush-Finch, Striped Sparrow (tussock grassland at pass)

Others
White-eared Hummingbird, Strickland's Woodpecker (higher pine forests near col), Brown-throated Wren, Steller's Jay, Slate-throated Redstart, Olive Warbler, Mexican Chickadee.

Access
Leave the *zócalo* in Amecameca at the western corner (below an arch, opposite the church). Fork left at 2.2 km at a Pemex station (signed Tlamacas). Follow this road to the Paso de Cortés at 25.8 km. There are numerous good pull-offs on this road; just before the pass there is an entrance fee (5 new pesos). Apart from the two side roads mentioned above the road continues over the pass to Cholula, becoming unpaved but still good. As it descends it passes through excellent forest. The road to the pass can be very busy on weekends; the road to Cholula is always very quiet and offers good birding.

POPOCATÉPETL

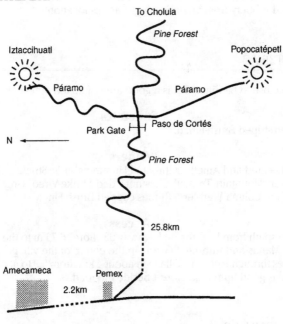

Accommodation: reasonable accommodation and food in Amecameca. Before the present round of volcanic activity it was possible to camp in the park; whether this is still possible is presently unknown.

LA CIMA

Probably the best-known location for one of Mexico's most restricted endemics, the Sierra Madre Sparrow*, although much of the area has been converted to agricultural fields.

Endemics
Grey-barred Wren, Red Warbler, Sierra Madre* and Striped Sparrows.

Others
Broad-tailed and White-eared Hummingbirds, Strickland's Woodpecker, Buff-breasted and Tufted Flycatchers, Mexican Chickadee, Olive Warbler, Rufous-capped Brush-Finch.

Access
From Mexico City take the old free (libre) Highway 95 to Cuernavaca. Between km posts 43 and 44 there is a rusty and almost illegible sign on the right-hand side 'La Cima'; this is about 1.4 km after passing under a railway bridge. There are two poor tracks off to the right just past the sign; the first leads past a wooded hill on the right. The sparrows are found in coarse bunch grass within an open, rough rocky volcanic field. The second track, on the same side, is beside a sign 'Curva peligrosa 300 m' and leads to some forest with Strickland's Woodpecker. The wooded hill mentioned above has a cobbled track leading up through good woodland. Note: there has been a recent serious incident of an armed robbery from an ornithologist at this location.

HUITZILAC

Very close to La Cima, this is a good area of mixed pine–oak forest.

Endemics
Green-striped Brush-Finch.

Others
White-eared and Amethyst-throated Hummingbirds, Strickland's Woodpecker, Mountain Trogon, Chestnut-sided Shrike-Vireo, Grey Silky-Flycatcher, Colima Warbler*, Rufous-capped Brush-Finch.

Access
Keep south from La Cima on Highway 95 (libre) 6.7 km to the village of Tres Marias and turn right (west) in the centre of the village. The road passes through Huitzilac Village in about 4 km; from 5.9 to about 7.6 km there is good humid oak forest beside the road.

COAJOMULCO

An area of relatively humid pine–oak forest, close to La Cima and Huitzilac.

Endemics
Long-tailed Wood-Partridge, White-striped Woodcreeper, Grey-barred Wren, Green-striped Brush-Finch.

Others
White-eared and Blue-throated Hummingbirds, Rose-throated Becard, Pine Flycatcher, Mexican Chickadee, Brown-throated Wren, Grey Silky-Flycatcher, Rufous-capped Brush-Finch.

Access
Continue south on free Highway 89 from Tres Marías. About 5 km from Tres Marías a road goes left to Coajomulco, and shortly afterwards a series of tracks leads to the right (west). If you can negotiate the turn-off it is possible to drive into the forest here, though there are some soft spots. There are quite extensive tracks, which can be walked, accessing good forest well away from the road.

MEXICO CITY

Mexico City is very large (nobody knows the precise population, but it may exceed 20 million), very noisy, very polluted and not most people's idea of a good birding location. Most birders will want to escape the city with all haste; fortunately there are some excellent locations (see sections on Popocatépetl, La Cima etc.) within easy reach. Having said that, there are also several sites in the greater city area with an attractive mix of species and which are easily accessible by public transport.

CONTRERAS VALLEY

A wooded valley on the southwest edge of the city, at an altitude of about 3400 m, with pine–oak woodland at lower levels and pine forest higher up, and open areas even lower down.

Endemics
White-striped Woodcreeper, Russet Nightingale-Thrush, Aztec Thrush, Blue Mockingbird, Red Warbler, Hooded Yellowthroat, Green-striped Brush-Finch, Striped Sparrow, Black-backed Oriole.

Others
Magnificent, Blue-throated and White-eared Hummingbirds, Strickland's Woodpecker, Green Violet-ear, Scaled Antpitta, Greater Pewee, Ruddy-capped Nightingale-Thrush, Cinnamon Flowerpiercer, Red-faced (winter), Crescent-chested, Rufous-capped and Golden-browed Warblers.

Access
By public transport, a *colectivo*, labelled 'Escuela de San Bernaba', leaves from opposite the San Angél metro station. Get off after about 5 km, 200 m beyond a yellow stone bridge over a small river. Take the road on the left and then the first road on the right. The road becomes cobbled and climbs steeply. At the top of this road (about 100 m) go up some steps and take a track to the left for 150 m, up some more steps and then at the top take the left road, downhill, for about 1 km. Turn left

at a circular gas storage building; the road leads to a track into the valley. After about 2 km this comes to an open area by the river. A trail leads off through woodland for about 200 m to another track.

BOSQUE DE TLALPAN

A substantial area of *pedregal* (a dry scrubland growing on larval bedrock) at the south end of Mexico City, with a number of good species, including the endemic Ocellated Thrasher.

Endemics
Rufous-backed Robin, Ocellated Thrasher, Blue Mockingbird, Hooded Yellowthroat, Black-backed Oriole.

Others
Magnificent, White-eared and Lucifer Hummingbirds, Greenish Elaenia, Northern Beardless Tyrannulet, Olive and Rufous-capped Warblers, Rufous-capped Brush-Finch, Black-chinned and Rufous-crowned Sparrows.

Access
Go south on Insurgentes, passing under the Periférico, turn right at the second set of lights and go about 750 m to a parking lot. There are a number of walking trails in this area.

UNIVERSITY BOTANIC GARDENS (JARDINAS BOTÁNICOS DE UNAM)

Closer to the centre of the city but still contains some worthwhile species.

Endemics
Rufous-backed Robin, Ocellated Thrasher, Blue Mockingbird, Hooded Yellowthroat.

Others
White-eared and Broad-billed Hummingbirds, Greater Pewee, Hammond's and Dusky Flycatchers, Scrub Jay, Canyon Wren, Curve-billed Thrasher, Rufous-crowned and Black-chinned Sparrows.

Access
From Paseo de la Reforma head south on Insurgentes for about 11 km, and exit at the University Stadium on the right; take a further left off this road and follow the signs. Opening hours are 9am to 5pm Monday to Saturday. By public transport, take any bus south on Insurgentes and get off at the stadium.

While the meek may inherit the earth, in Mexico City they do not usually command much road space; those of faint heart or with a pronounced sense of self-preservation may prefer to use public transport within the city. Note also that in Mexico City and sometimes in other major cities there may be daily restrictions on driving particular vehicles according to their license-plate numbers. This should be clarified when hiring a vehicle. Take special precautions against theft in Mexico City.

TLANCHINOL

An excellent and accessible area of cloud forest, situated on the humid slopes of the Sierra Madre Oriental near Xilitla, a site made famous in Fisher and Peterson's *Wild America*, but now largely destroyed. One of the best remaining locations for species such as Bearded Wood-Partridge.

Endemics
Bearded Wood-Partridge*, Green Parakeet, Bumblebee Hummingbird, Golden-olive Woodpecker, Hooded Yellowthroat, Hooded Grosbeak.

Others
White-crowned Parrot, White-bellied Emerald, Amethyst-throated Hummingbird, Collared and Mountain Trogons, Smoky-brown Woodpecker, Strong-billed and Spot-crowned Woodcreepers, Unicoloured Jay, Grey-breasted Wood-Wren, Slate-coloured and Brown-backed Solitaires, Black Robin, Grey Silky-Flycatcher, Crescent-chested Warbler, Blue-hooded Euphonia, Blue-crowned Chlorophonia, White-naped Brush-Finch.

Access
Head northeast from Pachuca (or southwest from Tampico) on Highway 105. About 4 km north of the town of Tlanchinol there is good roadside habitat with several overlooks. There are several indistinct trails leading west or northwest from the road to good habitat and distance you from traffic. Public buses run from Pachuca to Tlanchinol and beyond.

Accommodation: rather basic accommodation in Tlanchinol and a family restaurant about 4 km north of town where birdwatchers on previous occasions have been allowed to camp.

RANCHO LOS COLORADOS

A private ranch, northeast of Aldama (north of Tampico) on the Barro El Torro road, which is a study location for *Amazona* parrots.

Specialities
Red-crowned* and Yellow-headed* Parrots.

Others
Muscovy Duck, Great Black Hawk, Roadside Hawk, Great Curassow*, Plain Chachalaca, Red-billed Pigeon, Green Parakeet, Buff-bellied Hummingbird, Lineated, Pale-billed and Golden-fronted Woodpeckers, Rose-throated Becard, Brown Jay, Tamaulipas Crow, Grey-crowned Yellowthroat, Melodious Blackbird.

Access
It is necessary to make advance contact with Ernesto Enkerlin, Andromeda #258, Contay, Monterrey NL 64860. Accommodation may be available on site for a donation to parrot conservation.

COLA DE CABALLO

A famous location (and probably the only easy one) for the highly restricted Maroon-fronted Parrot*. Below and around the Parrot Cliffs is good forest with such species as Colima Warbler* and Crimson-collared Grosbeak. This area is apparently now protected.

Endemics
Maroon-fronted Parrot*, Golden-olive Woodpecker, Crimson-collared Grosbeak.

Others
Elegant Trogon, Pine Flycatcher, Brown-backed Solitaire, Spot-breasted Wren, Grey Silky-Flycatcher, Crescent-chested, Colima*, Golden-crowned and Rufous-capped Warblers, Painted Redstart, Black-crested Titmouse, Hepatic and Flame-coloured Tanagers, Audubon's Oriole.

Access
Leave Monterrey south on Highway 85, and after about 40 km turn right (west) on a road signed Cola de Caballo. The Hotel Cola de Caballo is 5.5 km from this junction and there is a waterfall at 6.9 km. The road passes through forest and gorges. At 34.9 km, in the village of San Isidro, turn sharp right at the village store onto a gravel road, signed S. José de Boquillas. Follow this, keeping right at an open gravel area at 35.4 km. At 38.5 km the Parrot Cliffs are visible south of the road. Maroon-fronted Parrot* is most readily seen here between late March and October, but is apparently absent in winter. The area is also accessible from Highway 57 south from Saltillo: turn left (east) at the signpost for Los Lirios, and left again in the village. This road is partly unpaved, but passes through good habitat.

Another good location in the area is near the Hotel Cola de Caballo. Take a track that goes south, leaving the road about 100 m uphill (west) from the hotel entrance, and walk past houses, crossing a stream, for several hundred metres. This is a good location for Crimson-collared Grosbeak. A reservoir (Presa Rodrigo Gómez) is on the east side of Highway 85, north of the Cola de Caballo turn-off. It is only accessible when travelling north on 85, and opportunities for U-turns are limited. It may hold good numbers of ducks in winter as well as Least Grebe and Ringed Kingfisher.

Accommodation: there is abundant food and lodging in Monterrey; more convenient is the Hotel Cola de Caballo (may be difficult at weekends). Camping below the Parrot Cliffs is also possible.

VOLCÁN DE FUEGO

The Volcán de Fuego is still active but good access to a variety of altitudinal habitats between 1300 m and 3300 m is available, with a number of species that are difficult to find elsewhere. Although much of the area is within a National Park, some of the best birdwatching sites are actually outside the park.

Endemics

West Mexican Chachalaca, Long-tailed Wood-Partridge, Banded Quail, Balsas Screech-Owl*, Eared Poorwill, Golden-crowned Emerald, Bumblebee Hummingbird, Golden-cheeked and Strickland's Woodpeckers, White-striped Woodcreeper, Grey-barred, Spotted, Happy and Sinaloa Wrens, Rufous-backed Robin, Aztec Thrush, Russet Nightingale-Thrush, Golden and Dwarf Vireos, Red Warbler, Red-headed Tanager, Green-striped Brush-Finch, Black-backed Oriole.

Apart from a few vagrant records in the US and El Salvador, the beautiful Aztec Thrush is endemic to the highlands of Mexico

Others

Grey and Short-tailed Hawks, Singing Quail, Lesser Roadrunner, Stygian Owl, Buff-collared Nightjar, Green Violet-ear, Broad-billed, White-eared, Berylline, Amethyst-throated, Magnificent, Calliope (winter), Lucifer (winter) and Rufous (winter) Hummingbirds, Mountain and Elegant Trogons, Russet-crowned Motmot, Acorn Woodpecker, Tufted, Pine, Buff-breasted and Nutting's Flycatchers, Grey-collared and Rose-throated Becards, Grey-breasted Jay, Mexican Chickadee, Brown-backed Solitaire, Grey Silky-Flycatcher, Chestnut-sided Shrike-Vireo, Crescent-chested, Rufous-capped and Golden-browed Warblers, Rufous-capped Brush-Finch, Cinnamon-bellied Flowerpiercer, Stripe-headed and Rusty Sparrows, Yellow-eyed Junco, Streak-backed Oriole, Black-headed Siskin.

Access

There is an expensive toll (Cuota) road and a free (libre) road from Colima. If using the free road (Highway 54), leave Colima towards Guadalajara; a few km out of town, take the free road and travel 48.7 km from the intersection with the toll road. Turn left onto a dirt road signed 'Telemex RMO Cerro Alto'. If you reach a lumber mill you have gone about 2 km too far. From Guadalajara the same road may be accessed via 54 (free) or 54D (toll). Take the exit to Atenquique, pass the pulp mills and look for the dirt turn-off and sign, which is located at a bend in the road.

The first 4 km from the highway is through agricultural land, which is nevertheless quite productive: Banded Quail, Lesser Ground-Cuckoo and Rusty-crowned Ground-Sparrow occur here. At km 8.9 the road passes a cattle trough. Long-tailed Wood-Partridge is found here. Pine–oak woodland starts at this point. A canyon at km 11 has Dwarf Vireo, Chestnut-sided Shrike-Vireo and White-striped Woodcreeper. At km

12.5 there is a road (on the right) to the microwave towers and an old logging road on the left. Species here include Balsas Screech-Owl*, Stygian Owl and Eared Poorwill. At km 18 the road enters more humid epiphyte woodland, the habitat of Crested Guan, Grey-barred Wren and Red Warbler. By km 25 the road is in coniferous forest. The road continues considerably further, the park boundary being at km 27.4, and the tree line at about km 29.

Road conditions are variable and can become very poor after heavy rain. Most visitors have been able to get at least part way up in passenger cars, but 4WD is obviously preferable. There is no public transport beyond Highway 54.

Accommodation: abundant accommodation in Colima and Ciudad Guzmán. Camping (there are several good places above the turn-off to the microwave station) would give access to the best habitat in the early morning, and make nocturnal birding easier.

AUTLÁN DE NAVARRO

A reasonably pleasant town on the road between Guadalajara and the coast at Barra de Navidad. Two roads leading to microwave towers give access to good habitat with some of the west Mexican specialities being quite easy to find.

Endemics
West Mexican Chachalaca, Long-tailed Wood-Partridge, Mexican Woodnymph*, Golden-cheeked and Grey-crowned Woodpeckers, White-striped Woodcreeper, San Blas Jay, Happy and Sinaloa Wrens, Blue Mockingbird, Golden Vireo, Orange-breasted Bunting, Green-striped Brush-Finch.

Others
Hook-billed Kite, Great Swallow-tailed Swift, Calliope (winter), Amethyst-throated and Berylline Hummingbirds, Ivory-billed Woodcreeper, Bright-rumped Attila, Brown-backed Solitaire, Orange-billed Nightingale-Thrush, Grey Silky-Flycatcher, Crescent-chested, Golden-crowned, Fan-tailed and Rufous-capped Warblers, Black-headed Siskin.

Access
One microwave tower is located to the west (right when coming from Guadalajara) off Highway 80, about 10 km before Autlán (at km 145). The road climbs through deciduous scrub. The second tower is reached by turning east (or left) off Highway 80, near the town of Puerto los Mazos; the turn-off is 15.7 km south of Autlán, at km 169, recognizable by a pull-off with a small store on the east side of Highway 80. The road passes through dry oak forest (at 1340 m), which becomes more humid at higher elevations (the towers are at 1660 m).

Accommodation: in Autlán (the Hotel Autlán is comfortable and reasonable), where there are several restaurants. There are buses from Guadalajara.

SAN BLAS AREA

The San Blas area is a must for any birding trip to western Mexico. Within a quite small area is a broad variety of different habitats; lowland tropical forest, subtropical forest, open farmland, sea coast with nesting marine species, and riverine forest, with some mangrove. For those travelling south by road from the western US it is one of the first locations where Neotropical families begin to form a substantial proportion of the fauna. The annual San Blas Christmas Count regularly produces 250 species in one day, sometimes 300. And, few small towns have an endemic species named after them!

Endemics

Elegant Quail, Lilac-crowned Parrot, Mexican Parrotlet, Colima Pygmy-Owl, Citreoline Trogon, Golden-cheeked Woodpecker, Purplish-backed and San Blas Jays, Sinaloa Crow, Happy and Sinaloa Wrens, Black-throated Magpie-Jay, Rufous-backed Robin, Blue Mockingbird, Golden Vireo, Audubon's, Black-throated Grey and MacGillivray's Warblers, Yellow-breasted Chat (winter).

Others

Blue-footed and Brown Boobies, Bare-throated Tiger-Heron, Boat-billed Heron, Muscovy Duck, Crane and Grey Hawks, Great Black Hawk, Collared Forest-Falcon, Rufous-bellied Chachalaca, Spotted Rail, Rufous-necked Wood-Rail, Collared Plover, Red-billed Pigeon, Ruddy Ground-Dove, Orange-fronted Parakeet, White-fronted Parrot, Mangrove and Squirrel Cuckoos, Lesser Ground-Cuckoo, Western Long-tailed Hermit, Golden-crowned Emerald, Berylline, Cinnamon and Violet-crowned Hummingbirds, Russet-crowned Motmot, Green Kingfisher, Ivory-billed Woodcreeper, Greenish Elaenia, Tufted and White-throated Flycatchers, Thick-billed Kingbird, Masked Tityra, Grey-breasted Martin, Mangrove Swallow, Black-capped* (winter) and Yellow-green Vireos, Grey-crowned Yellowthroat, Fan-tailed Warbler, Red-breasted Chat, Scrub Euphonia, Red-crowned Ant-Tanager, Flame-coloured Tanager, Rosy Thrush-Tanager, Yellow Grosbeak, Blue Bunting, Rusty-crowned Ground-Sparrow, Stripe-headed Sparrow, Black-vented and Streak-backed Orioles, Yellow-winged Cacique.

In addition, virtually all of the herons, shorebirds, gulls and terns of western North America have been recorded or occur regularly.

Access

San Blas village is located at the end of a paved road (Highway 54) which runs 36 km west from Highway 15, the main coastal road. There are numerous separate sites in the San Blas area. Coming from Highway 15 they are:

Huaristemba About 13 km from Highway 15, and 2 km beyond Navarrete, a track leads right (northwest) off the San Blas road, about 2 km to the village of Huaristemba. This track passes through patches of forest, one of the best locations for Lilac-crowned Parrot. Other species include Black-throated Magpie-Jay, Brown-crested Flycatcher, Painted Bunting, Stripe-headed Sparrow, Blue-black Grassquit and Ruddy-breasted Seedeater. The forest here is higher and slightly more temperate than in Singayta.

Singayta A small village approximately 10 km before San Blas prop-

SAN BLAS AREA

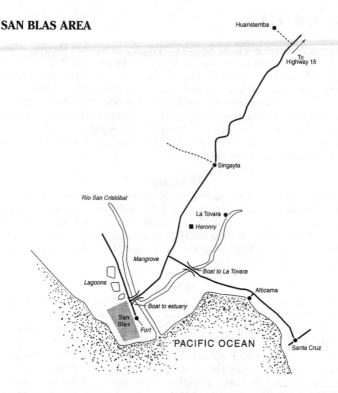

er. The road passes through excellent tropical forest here, especially above the village, and is a good birding site in its own right (though the traffic can be quite heavy and typically uninhibited). For about 3 km above the village the road winds through woodland that is excellent in the early morning. There are some short tracks off the road. Species include Lilac-crowned Parrot, Mexican Hermit, Ivory-billed Woodcreeper, Masked Tityra and San Blas and Purplish-backed Jays. In the village of Singayta a road goes right (north) off the San Blas road, passes through the village and goes on for several km further. Though dirt it is driveable, but worth walking, giving access to woodland, open pasture and marshy areas. Rosy Thrush-Tanager is found here, along with Mexican Parrotlet, White-crowned and Lilac-crowned Parrots, Citreoline Trogon and Russet-crowned Motmot.

The Heronry About 5 km from Singayta, or 4 km from the bridge over the Río San Cristóbal, there is an area of mangrove and open water. Wood Stork, various herons, Anhinga and Black-bellied Whistling-Duck occur here.

Road to Santa Cruz and boat trip to La Tovara Approximately 3 km from the San Cristóbal bridge, a road goes south (left) to Santa Cruz, after 3 km crossing a river at Matanchen. Boats can be hired at the bridge; the same section of river is also served by boats hired from near San Cristóbal bridge. La Tovara is a clear, freshwater spring much used by bathers, within a forested valley and is a good location for Boat-billed Heron, Bare-throated Tiger-Heron and (at dusk, arrange this with your boatman) Common Potoo. Further on, the Santa Cruz road gives access to the coast with various gulls, terns and shorebirds. From Santa

Cruz itself a road goes to Tepic: follow this for 9 km and then 3 km on a turn-off to the right. This habitat has San Blas and Purplish-backed Jays.

El Mirador del Aguila Not actually in San Blas; a famous stake-out for Military Macaw*. Continue south on the old (libre) Highway 15 to Tepic, for about 12 km after leaving the San Blas road. About 2 km south of the village of Buenos Aires there is a pull-off on the left, at about km 22, giving a view over a valley. Best in the early morning. The macaws can usually be located by their calls.

San Blas lagoons From the San Blas side of the bridge over the Río San Cristóbal a road (posted Guadeloupe Victoria) leads northwest from town with the river on your right. There are various ponds beside this road for several km. This an excellent area for herons, ibises, shorebirds, Roseate Spoonbills etc. About 7.5 km beyond the San Cristóbal bridge a dirt road to the right accesses more ponds. Landbirds here include Mangrove Vireo, Mangrove (Yellow) Warbler, Mangrove Cuckoo and Thick-billed Kingbird.

Cemetery and Fort Ruins (Cerro de la Contaduria) The old fort is on a hill overlooking San Blas and the ocean. Take the road opposite that to San Blas lagoons (above). The scrub and trees here have Mexican Parrotlet, Rufous-backed Robin, White-throated Thrush, Streaked-backed Oriole and, at dusk, Mottled Owl, Pauraque, Lesser Nighthawk, Buff-collared Nightjar (winter) and Collared Forest-Falcon.

River boat trips These leave upstream from the bridge over the Río San Cristóbal and give access to superb numbers of herons, ibises, various ducks (including sometimes huge flocks of Black-bellied and Fulvous Whistling-Ducks) and landbirds (including Mangrove Cuckoo and Mangrove Vireo). Most boatmen have a good idea of where to find the birds and some are very competent; be sure to impress upon them that you are a serious birder. Hire charges tend to be by the boat rather than per head, so it is advantageous to have several people. Boats also go from the same dock downstream, and to La Tovara.

Ocean Boat Trips These leave from Peso Island dock, at the west end of Campeche and Comonfort. A one-hour trip visits Virgin Rock, which is visible distantly from San Blas waterfront. Bridled Tern nests on the rock, and Brown and Blue-footed Boobies are easily seen. A longer trip can be arranged to Isla Isabel, also called Isla María Isabel, which takes at least four hours. Pelagics include Black and Least Storm-Petrels, Black-vented Shearwater*, Red-billed Tropicbird, Pomarine and Parasitic Jaegers and Red and Northern Phalaropes. It may be possible to camp on Isla Isabel with prior permission; enquire at the boat dock. There is no water on the island. Such trips are best taken as early as possible in the morning, before the wind gets up.

San Blas is readily accessible by public transport, with frequent first- and second-class buses to Guadalajara, Mazatlán, Mexico City and Puerto Vallarta. Local buses will drop off passengers at Singayta (or anywhere else on the San Blas Road), and can usually be persuaded to pick up passengers along the road.

Accommodation: there are numerous hotels and restaurants in San Blas.

One of the drawbacks of San Blas will quickly be discovered by anybody who camps out near the beach, or walks after dark: the small sandflies, known locally as *jejenes*, have extraordinary appetites. If staying in a hotel, ensure that there are window screens without holes.

BARRANCA RANCHO LIEBRE

The road (Highway 40) from Mazatlán to Durango passes through spectacularly beautiful scenery as it crosses the Sierra Madre Occidental. Famous as the most reliable accessible location for one of Mexico's most impressive (and most restricted) endemics, the Tufted Jay*, there are also many other exciting species in the area.

Endemics

Thick-billed Parrot*, Eared Trogon*, White-naped Swift, Grey-crowned Woodpecker, White-striped Woodcreeper, Purplish-backed and Tufted* Jays, Aztec Thrush, Red Warbler, Red-headed Tanager, Green-striped Brush-Finch.

Others

Blue-throated, Berylline and White-eared Hummingbirds, Mountain Trogon, Sparkling-crowned Woodstar, Strickland's Woodpecker, Pine Flycatcher, Mexican Chickadee, White-throated Thrush, Brown-backed Solitaire, Crescent-chested, Grace's, Townsend's, Hermit (both winter), Red-faced, Golden-browed and Olive Warblers, Painted and Slate-throated Redstarts, Hepatic Tanager, Rufous-capped Brush-Finch.

Access

Highway 40 is a good paved road. Coming from Highway 15, the junction is at Villa Unión just south of Mazatlán. The road passes through some dry deciduous thorn forest (Black-throated Magpie-Jay, Purplish-backed Jay) and then climbs into the Sierra Madre. Barranca Rancho Liebre is located between km 200 and 201, at a point where the road curves sharply. On the northwest side of the road is a pull-off with a restaurant (Comedor el Puente), as well as a track leading uphill. Keep to the right (northeast) of the stream and go about 2 km, crossing the stream and keeping right, until you reach a large rock overlooking the barranca. Further trails follow the left-hand side of the barranca. Tufted Jay* is found throughout the area, but the most famous site is the large rock. The jays (which have a peculiar system of cooperative breeding)

The splendid Tufted Jay* was only described to science in 1934, largely because of its tiny range

BARRANCA RANCHO LIEBRE

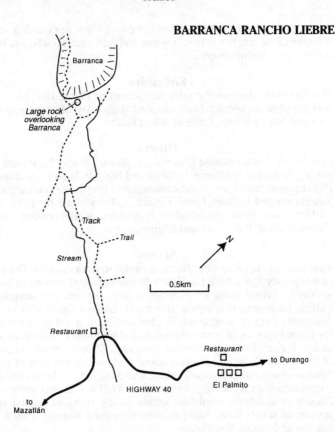

are usually found in flocks, in winter often with Steller's Jay. Other species in the area include Eared *and Mountain Trogons, Pine Flycatcher, Red-headed Tanager and Aztec Thrush.

There are buses from Durango to Mazatlán and vice-versa, permitting you to disembark where you want. Barranca Rancho Liebre is about 2 km west of the small village of El Palmito. There is no accommodation very close by; but a hotel in Capilla de Taxte, which is about 60 km from Highway 15 (i.e. 140 km from Barranca Rancho Liebre). Some birders have managed to beg sleeping space in El Palmito.

This area has a bad reputation following the armed robbery of some birdwatchers a number of years ago. We are unaware of any recent such incidents, but caution is obviously advised.

There are a number of other good sites along Highway 40; it is one of the best locations for the highly range-restricted White-naped Swift, which has been seen in flocks of 200 and more over some of the high valleys.

ALAMOS

Alamos is a pleasant little town situated on the paved road east from Navojoa, which is on the main coast road. Many species reach their northernmost extent in the Alamos area, and if you are coming south from the US border it is here where you feel that, faunistically, you have truly entered the neotropics.

Endemics

Elegant Quail, Mexican Parrotlet, Lilac-crowned Parrot, Blue Mockingbird, Purplish-backed Jay, Black-throated Magpie-Jay, Sinaloa Crow, Sinaloa and Happy Wrens, Rufous-backed Robin.

Others

Grey Hawk, Rufous-bellied Chachalaca, Military Macaw* (at least formerly), White-fronted Parrot, Buff-collared Nightjar, Lesser Roadrunner, Plain-capped Starthroat, Violet-crowned and Berylline Hummingbirds, Russet-crowned Motmot, Green Kingfisher, Thick-billed Kingbird, Tufted Flycatcher, Northern Beardless Tyrannulet, Scarlet-headed Oriole, Varied Bunting, Rufous-winged Sparrow.

Access

Turn east off Highway 15 in Navojoa, at the sign for Alamos. The road passes mostly agricultural land but with areas of deciduous thorn forest, worthy of investigating for Purplish-backed Jay and the magpie-jay (which frequently flies across the road). Elegant Quail also occurs beside the road in these areas. The town of Alamos is a good location for several species of hummingbird including Violet-crowned, as well as for Mexican Parrotlet. The best areas near Alamos are on the banks of the Río Cuchujaqui, which is about 5 km south and east of town. Road access is rather poor and worse after rain, but can be achieved in a conventional car, but high clearance or 4WD is a distinct advantage. Recent local advice would be useful. In the riverside habitat such species as Buff-collared Nightjar, Russet-crowned Motmot, Tufted Flycatcher and Happy Wren occur.

ISLA HUIVULAI

A very good location for ducks, shorebirds, herons and seabirds, easily accessible from the Hermosillo–Navojoa road.

Others

Pacific Loon, Blue-footed and Brown Boobies, Roseate Spoonbill, White Ibis, Snow Goose, Brant, Fulvous Whistling-Duck, American Oystercatcher, Gull-billed Tern, Black Skimmer, Mangrove (Yellow) Warbler; many species of shorebird and heron. (Several of these species only in winter or during migration.)

Access

Turn west off Highway 15 at the southern outskirts of Ciudad Obregón, by the brewery. After about 20 km (just before a radio tower) turn right and after another 1.6 km turn left. The road goes via a toll gate (small fee) onto a causeway that affords good views over the flats. The Gulf side of the island has good viewing points for seabirds including boobies and loons. Nearby mangroves have Mangrove (Yellow) Warbler.

GUAYMAS

Guaymas was formerly one of the best locations on the Sonora coast, but has been extensively developed, with attendant wholesale destruction of habitat, in the 35 years since this author first visited the area. It is probably not now worth visiting for its own sake, but if you are passing the harbour may still produce some interesting species such as Yellow-footed and Glaucous-winged Gulls. Mangrove Swallow reaches almost its northernmost limits here.

What still remains worthwhile is the seabirding, if you can arrange a boat trip by negotiating at the dock. March is a good time. Offshore, species seen include large numbers of Least and Black Storm-Petrels, Blue-footed and Brown Boobies, and Xantus' Murrelet*.

YÉCORA AND HIGHWAY 16

Yécora is a small town situated within pine forest at an altitude of about 1500 m in the Sierra Madre Occidental of northwestern Mexico. For travellers coming south from the USA it, and the road leading to it, is one of the northernmost locations for many Mexican species that do not extend north of the border, including several Mexican endemics.

Endemics
Grey-crowned Woodpecker, Spotted, Happy and Sinaloa Wrens, Blue Mockingbird, Russet Nightingale-Thrush, Black-throated Magpie-Jay.

Others
Military Macaw*, Mottled Owl, Lesser Roadrunner, Violet-crowned Hummingbird, Mountain Trogon, Green Kingfisher, Great Kiskadee, Tufted Flycatcher, Black-capped Gnatcatcher, Orange-billed Nightingale-Thrush, Brown-backed Solitaire, White-throated Thrush, Mexican Chickadee, Crescent-chested and Rufous-capped Warblers, Slate-throated Redstart, Flame-coloured Tanager, Rusty and Five-striped Sparrows, Black-headed Siskin, Black-vented Oriole.

Access
From the north, on the northern side of Hermosillo, at the first major intersection (with traffic lights and a Pemex station), turn left and take the eastern by-pass around the city. This skirts a reservoir worth checking for ducks, American White Pelican etc. Passing the prison, turn left (east) at a large intersection and almost immediately turn southeast onto Highway 16 (Tecoripa, Yécora, Chihuahua). After about 70 km, just before it enters the village of San José de Pima, the road crosses a stream. Green Kingfisher and Great Kiskadee occur here.

The town of Tecoripa is about 120 km from Hermosillo. About 27 km from the plaza in Tecoripa on Highway 16 look for a cattle guard on the south (right) side. Turn right over this, drive a short distance and cross a streambed, turn right down a track and park. This area is called Lo de Campa and is owned by Sr. Romeo Porchas, from whom permission should be obtained. The canyon downstream has such species as Violet-crowned Hummingbird, Happy and Sinaloa Wrens, Black-capped Gnatcatcher and Rufous-capped Warbler.

Continuing east on Highway 16, the road crosses the Río Yaqui near the town of Tonichi. 27.4 km east of the bridge (near km post 196) there is a fairly lush area of vegetation on the mountainside. Walking a short distance up the wash may produce Mottled Owl, Blue Mockingbird, Rufous-capped Warbler, Five-striped Sparrow and Black-vented Oriole. About 11 km further on (i.e. about 38 km from the Río Yaqui bridge) there is a steep-sided *barranca* where Military Macaw* is seen in the breeding season (Apr–Sep).

About 16 km past this point (10 km beyond Tecoripa) a road goes right (south) to Nuri and Cuidad Obregón. Keep left on Highway 16, setting the odometer to zero. About 24.9 km past the intersection there is a parking-space where truck drivers stop for water from a pipe in the cliff. There is a small *barranca* here which harbours Grey-crowned Woodpecker, Spotted Wren, Blue Mockingbird, Russet and Orange-billed Nightingale-Thrushes, Brown-backed Solitaire, White-throated Thrush, Slate-throated Redstart, Flame-coloured Tanager, Rufous-capped Brush-Finch, Rusty Sparrow and Black-headed Siskin. Just beyond the crest (about 4.5 km east of the *barranca*), at a small restaurant, a poor road leads south to Mesa Enmedio (or Mesa Campañero). After 1 km the road forks, the right fork leading to communication towers. Species here include Eared Poorwill, Mountain Trogon, Tufted Flycatcher and Crescent-chested Warbler, as well as the typical montane species of Arizona.

Accommodation: there is adequate food, fuel and accommodation in the town of Yécora. In recent years there have been reports of lawlessness in areas of Sonora, associated with the drug trade. Appropriate caution and local enquiry is advised.

KINO BAY (BAHÍA KINO)

An excellent area for shorebirds, herons and rails, readily accessible from Hermosillo.

Specialities
Yellow-footed Gull, Mangrove (Yellow) Warbler.

Others
Common and Pacific Loons, Western Grebe, Blue-footed and Brown Boobies, several species of heron including Reddish Egret and Yellow-crowned Night-Heron, Roseate Spoonbill, Clapper Rail, Harris' Hawk, Osprey, most western species of shorebirds including American Oyster-catcher, Black Turnstone, Surfbird, Wandering Tattler, and Snowy and Mountain* Plovers, Heermann's Gull*, Elegant Tern*, Ladder-backed and Gila Woodpeckers, Cactus, Canyon and Rock Wrens, Black-tailed Gnatcatcher, Varied Bunting, Black-throated Sparrow.

Access
Leave Hermosillo west on Highway 16, passing the airport turn-off and the towns of La Manga and Miguel Alemán. Most of the area along this road is agricultural but there are some patches of desert habitat left. The town of Bahía Kino is about 107 km from Hermosillo, and a few km before town there is an electrical switching station on the north side of the

road and a dirt road to the south which gives views of the mudflats of Laguna la Cruz. Further on, the road turns north along a sandy beach to the rapidly developing area of Kino Nuevo. A rocky promontory at the north end of the beach is a good overview for seabirds and Wandering Tattler, Black Turnstone and Surfbird are found on rocky parts of the shoreline.

There is a bus from Hermosillo to Kino Bay and adequate food and accommodation locally.

BAJA CALIFORNIA

Baja (or Lower) California is a 1300 km-long peninsula, separated from mainland Mexico by the Gulf of California. This isolation has given rise to a number of endemic species; currently the AOU recognizes three (Xantus' Hummingbird, Grey Thrasher and Belding's Yellowthroat*), though Howell and Webb add two more (Cape Pygmy Owl and Baird's Junco), and it is probable that the southern population of Le Conte's Thrasher will also achieve specific status under the name of Vizcaino Thrasher. Even the local race of American Robin is sometimes separated under the name of San Lucas Robin.

Formerly access to the southern tip of Baja California was difficult, involving the then-legendary Baja Road, which destroyed many a vehicle, but access is now vastly improved. Alternatively, there are numerous flights to La Paz and Los Cabos, both international or from other parts of Mexico. More interestingly, there are ferries from Pichilingue, just north of La Paz, across the Gulf of California to Topolobampo, near Los Mochis, Sinaloa, and to Mazatlán, Sinaloa. The Topolobampo ferry

Unlike many of its relatives, the Least Storm-Petrel is an inshore species that can sometimes be seen from land

runs east by day, returning in the dark. It offers some excellent seawatching, with Red-billed Tropicbird, Black-vented Shearwater*, Least and Black Storm-Petrels, Brown and Blue-footed Boobies and Yellow-footed Gull all possible. Prior booking on the ferries is essential, as truck drivers have precedence, and car drivers without reservations may get left behind on the dock. Tickets are sold only one-way. Another ferry, not investigated, runs between Guaymas, Sonora, and Santa Rosalia.

The areas around Cabo San Lucas, at the southern tip of the penin-sula, are popular holiday resorts, resulting in rather inflated prices; much more reasonable rates are found in La Paz.

CAPE AREA

The Cape area at the southern tip of Baja California is one of the best locations for most of the Baja endemics as well as many other dry-coun-try western species. Unfortunately the area is subject to rapid and uncontrolled development for the tourist trade.

Endemics
Cape Pygmy-Owl, Xantus' Hummingbird, Grey Thrasher, American (San Lucas) Robin, Belding's Yellowthroat*, Yellow-eyed (Baird's) Junco.

Others
Band-tailed Pigeon, Elf Owl, Nuttall's and Acorn Woodpeckers, Red-naped Sapsucker, Grey and Hammond's Flycatchers, Oak Titmouse, Grey Vireo (winter), Scott's Oriole, Varied Bunting.

Access
Leave La Paz south and fork left (east) to San José del Cabo approxi-mately 28 km after leaving town. Pass through San Antonio and turn right (west), onto a dirt road signed San Antonio de la Sierra; the catch is that the sign is only readable from the south. This turn-off is not marked on most maps and it is wise to obtain directions in San Antonio or San Bartolo. The road is negotiable in a passenger car and reaches a river after about 27 km. If you can negotiate the river bed the road con-tinues for about 4 km, at which point it may be possible to climb into higher habitat for Yellow-eyed (Baird's) Junco. At the river (where it is possible to camp) several endemics including Cape Pygmy-Owl, Xan-tus' Hummingbird and Grey Thrasher occur.

Belding's Yellowthroat* was formerly common in the Cape region; now much of its reedbed habitat has been destroyed. One area where it persists—precariously—is in Estero San José, south of San José del Cabo, which is northeast of Cabo San Lucas on Highway 1. East of the Hotel Presidente, which is near the beach, is a lagoon with some rem-nant reeds. As recently as January 1999 a few Belding's Yellowthroat* were present at the eastern end of the lagoon. In winter there are large numbers of Common Yellowthroat also present; doubtless locating a Belding's would be easier in the breeding season.

There is obviously good potential for oceanic species, such as Black-vented*, Pink-footed and Sooty Shearwaters, and Black and Least Storm-Petrels off the Cape. Fishing boats may be chartered in Cabo San Lucas. Rates begin at about $30 per hour, with a four-hour minimum, for a small boat. There are several agencies in Cabo San Lucas which hire out boats, but it is well to declare your purpose (most are oriented toward sport-fishing) and to agree on all charges before setting out.

LA PAZ AREA

The area near La Paz has two attractions: some good shorebird flats and excellent dry brushland habitat. For shorebirds, go (near high tide) to Ensenada La Paz. This is located just west of the airport turn-off, on Highway 1 west out of La Paz. Turn north off the highway, 700 m beyond the airport road, at the 'California Swap', taking a dirt road to the shore and mangroves. Large numbers of most of the western shorebirds can be found here, along with both species of pelican, at least five species of tern, White-faced and White Ibises and, in the mangroves, Mangrove (Yellow) Warbler.

For desert species, continue north on Highway 1 and after several km fork right towards San Juan de la Costa. Continue to the gate of the Centro de Investigaciones Biológicas and take a dirt road on the left. This leads onto the peninsula which divides Ensenada la Paz from Bahía la Paz, passing through desert scrub with typical species of the arid southwest, such as Harris' Hawk, Gila Woodpecker, Cactus Wren, Phainopepla, Pyrrhuloxia, California Towhee and Black-throated Sparrow, as well as the endemic Grey Thrasher.

The road which leaves La Paz northeast (Highway 11), going toward the ferry terminal at Pichilingue, skirts some good mangrove and lagoon habitat, with species such as White Ibis, Yellow-footed Gull and Mangrove (Yellow) Warbler. Further out Blue-footed and Brown Boobies may be seen roosting on buoys. California Gnatcatcher occurs in nearby desert scrub.

Accommodation: there are numerous places to stay and to eat in La Paz; prices tend to be more reasonable than in the Cape area.

PUERTO ESCONDIDO

A good location for Xantus' Hummingbird. Puerto Escondido is located on Highway 1, approximately 30 km south of the town of Loreto. Turn east off the highway towards the bay; on the left is a trailer park called El Tripue. There are usually several hummingbird feeders here that are frequently patronized by Xantus' Hummingbird. California Gnatcatcher also occurs.

ISLA RAZA

A small (1 km x 0.5 km) island, famous as the breeding location of between 90% and 95% of the world's Elegant Tern* population, which nest within a huge colony of Heermann's Gull* (evicting any gulls unwise enough to nest in the terns' chosen area).

Specialities
Elegant Tern*, Heermann's Gull*, Craveri's Murrelet*.

Others
Pink-footed and Black-vented Shearwaters*, Least Storm-Petrel, Blue-footed and Brown Boobies, Royal Tern, Yellow-footed Gull.

Access

It is possible to hire a boat in Bahía de Los Angeles, which is 68 km from Highway 1, and approximately 225 km south of El Rosario. Usually there are zoologists on the island during the breeding season. The boat trip is of itself worthwhile.

Please remember that gulls and terns are very susceptible to disturbance during the breeding season, and the integrity of Isla Raza is totally vital to the survival of the Elegant Tern*. Obey all instructions from resident staff.

PARQUE SIERRA DE SAN PEDRO MÁRTIR

The highest mountains in Baja California and the last Mexican location for California Condor; despite persistent rumours to the contrary, this species is most certainly extinct in Mexico and has been for many years. The San Pedro Mártir area contains few species not easily found in the USA but Grey Thrasher approaches its northernmost limit near here and the high-altitude parts of the park are the only Mexican location for several North American species such as Clark's Nutcracker and Mountain Quail. The road to San Pedro Mártir passes through numerous life-zones as it goes from sea level to over 3000 m.

Endemics
Grey Thrasher.

Others
Golden Eagle, Ladder-backed and Nuttall's Woodpeckers, Red-naped Sapsucker, Dusky Flycatcher, Pinyon Jay, Mountain Chickadee, Oak Titmouse, California Gnatcatcher, Wrentit, California Thrasher, Grey and Cassin's Vireos, (Sooty) Fox Sparrow, Tricoloured Blackbird.

Access
Turn east off Highway 1 at San Telmo de Abajo, south of km 140, through San Telmo de Arriba. From here to the park entrance is about 80 km via a dirt road that is usually negotiable, with care, by ordinary cars; after spring run-off it may be difficult in places. Initially the road passes through farmland and arid scrub where Grey Thrasher occurs. Approximately 50 km from Highway 1 is Rancho Meling with cottonwoods alongside a stream. At about 60 km the road enters pinyon pine. Species here include Mountain Quail, Grey Vireo and Black-chinned Sparrow. The park entrance is about 80 km from Highway 1. From the gate it is about 20 km to the Observatorio Astronómico Nacional, which is open on Saturday mornings; the gate giving access to the last 2 km of road is normally locked. The highest levels hold some species more typical of the mountains of the western USA such as Green-tailed Towhee and Cassin's Finch.

There is a bus service on Highway 1, but no public transport to the park.

Accommodation: camping is permitted in several areas of the park and lodging is available at Rancho Meling (rather expensive) and Mike's Sky Rancho, which is reached from Highway 3 via 35 km of dirt road. Food and accommodation are also available in Vicinte Guerrero, about 30 km south of the park turn-off on Highway 1.

PUERTO PEÑASCO (ROCKY POINT)

For visitors travelling by road from southern Arizona and nearby areas, Puerto Peñasco is the closest and most easily accessible part of the Gulf of California, with large numbers of shore and marine species. It is only four hours by road from Tucson and is a popular weekend destination for birders, but has little that cannot be found in abundance further south. Birding is worthwhile all year, but many species in the list below are winter visitors.

Specialities

Yellow-legged Gull, Le Conte's Thrasher, Savannah Sparrow ('Large-billed' rostratus race, sometimes regarded as a full species).

Others

Common and Pacific Loons, Western Grebe, Black-vented Shearwater*, Black and Least Storm-Petrels, Brown and Blue-footed Boobies, Reddish Egret, Surf Scoter, American Oystercatcher, Mountain Plover*, Black Turnstone, Surfbird, Wandering Tattler, Marbled Godwit, Glaucous-winged, Thayer's and Heermann's* Gulls, Elegant Tern*, Burrowing Owl, Ladder-backed and Gila Woodpeckers, White-necked Raven, Curve-billed Thrasher, Cactus Wren, Phainopepla, Black-throated and Sage Sparrows.

Access

There is now a good paved road (Highway 8) from the US border crossing at Lukeville/Sonoyta, which initially passes through good Organpipe Cactus habitat with the usual Sonoran Desert species. About 50 km south of Sonoyta the road curves at a small village with two bridges. A dirt road to the west goes to Pinacate National Park; this area should not be entered without a thoroughly reliable, preferably high-clearance, four-wheel-drive vehicle, a spare tyre, plenty of water and good local knowledge, as it can be savagely and unforgivingly hot in summer.

The habitat becomes much sparser nearer the Gulf, the cacti disappearing and giving way to sparse creosote bush. This is the habitat of Le Conte's Thrasher. About 85 km from Sonoyta, as you enter town, you pass under an arch announcing 'Bienvenidos Puerto Peñasco'. Approximately 600 m beyond this arch there is a dirt road going west. After 1.2 km it passes over a railway, and in another 5 km there is a left (south) turn-off to a sandy beach. There is a $3 entry fee to this road. Rocky outcrops at the shore are good for such species as Black Turnstone and Surfbird. The Cholla Bay road continues west to Punta Pelicán (Pelican Point). This is a good scanning point for boobies, loons and scoters, as well as shorebirds. Cholla Bay is also a good area for shorebirds; to reach it, take the road north off the Cholla Bay road, just behind the beach houses. Park at the head of the bay by a tall wooden pole and walk towards the bay (best at high water; the tide recedes a long way).

Species such as Wilson's and Snowy Plovers and Least and Elegant Terns* occur here.

The harbour of Puerto Peñasco town is worthwhile if there are recently returned fishing boats. The offal attracts gulls such as Glaucous-winged and Thayer's, while pelagic species such as shearwaters, petrels and boobies sometimes follow fishing vessels in.

Just after Highway 8 crosses the railway coming into Puerto Peñasco town, a paved road (Fremont Boulevard) goes east (left). The sea side of this road has a beach and a reef, exposed at low water, which is good for tattlers and turnstones. About 1.6 km further on, on the right-hand side is a partially hidden lagoon good for ducks, herons, gulls, phalaropes and other shorebirds. Approximately 1.2 km beyond here, near two small sand dunes, are some sewage ponds that frequently hold ducks and shorebirds. A further 2 km ahead, a side road goes to Estero Marua where there are mudflats and salt marshes. In winter Sage Thrasher and Sage Sparrow occur here.

Accommodation and food is available in Puerto Peñasco, and camping is possible at Sandy Beach. Avoid the area on American holiday weekends. Note that most car insurance policies issued in North America do not cover Mexico.

REVILLAGIGEDO ISLANDS

The Revillagigedo archipelago, situated some 500 km off the west coast of Mexico, has five endemic species (Socorro Parakeet*, Socorro Wren*, Clarion Wren*, Socorro Mockingbird* and Socorro Towhee) and a sixth, Socorro Dove, which is extinct in the wild but presently undergoing a reintroduction programme. There are, additionally, important colonies of breeding seabirds. Because of the remoteness of the archipelago and restictions on landing on the islands independent travel is not possible, though some tour agencies are investigating the possibility of visits. For current information contact Ornithology Expeditions (see p. 415).

ADDITIONAL INFORMATION

Books

Where to Watch Birds in Mexico, Howell, S. N. G. 1999. Cornell UP. (A very detailed, comprehensive and superbly-researched guide book.)

A Guide to the birds of Mexico and Northern Central America, Howell, S. N. G. and Webb, S. 1995. Oxford UP. (The best and most recent field guide to Mexican birds; also essential for Guatemala, Belize, Honduras and El Salvador.)

A Field Guide to Mexican Birds, Peterson, R. T. and Chalif, E. L. 1973. Houghton Mifflin. (Not as good as Howell and Webb, but pocket-sized.)

Mexican Birds, First Impressions, Sutton, G. M. 1951. University of Oklahoma Press. (A nostalgic read, for a Mexico that has largely gone.)

A Naturalists' Mexico, Wauer, R. H. 1992. Texas A. & M. UP. (Interesting travelogue accounts of journeys throughout much of Mexico in search of birds and other wildlife.)

A Distributional Survey of the Birds of the Mexican State of Oaxaca, Binford, L. C. 1989. AOU (Orn. Monogr. 43). (A superb example of a regional avifauna.)

Mexico: a Lonely Planet travel survival kit, Bernhardson, W. *et al.* 1995 (with frequent new editions). Lonely Planet Publications. (A fount of useful practical information.)

Many interesting papers on the distribution, taxonomy and status of

Mexican birds are published annually: journals such as the *Bulletin of the British Ornithologists' Club*, *Cotinga*, *Euphonia* (now defunct) and *Western Birds* are among the most frequent sources of such information.

MEXICO ENDEMICS (96)

Howell and Webb consider about a further dozen taxa to be endemic species, but taxonomy here follows Clements (2000).

Rufous-bellied Chachalaca	W, from Sonora to Nayarit
West Mexican Chachalaca	W, from Jalisco to W Chiapas
Long-tailed Wood-Partridge	W and south-central Mexico
Bearded Wood-Partridge*	E Mexico from San Luis Potosí to Veracruz
Banded Quail	W Mexico from Colima to Guerrero
Elegant Quail	NW Mexico (Sonora to Nayarit)
Purplish-backed Quail-Dove	Los Tuxtlas, Veracruz
Green Parakeet	Disjunct; S Sonora, E Mexico (Tamaulipas toVeracruz) Oaxaca and Chiapas
Socorro Parakeet*	Isla Socorro, Revillagigedo group
Thick-billed Parrot*	W Mexico from Sonora to Michoacán
Maroon-fronted Parrot*	NE Mexico (Coahuila to Tamaulipas)
Mexican Parrotlet	W Mexico from Sonora to Colima
Red-crowned Parrot*	NE Mexico (Tamaulipas to N Veracruz)
Lilac-crowned Parrot	W Mexico (Sonora to Oaxaca)
Balsas Screech-Owl*	Jalisco to W Puebla
Cape Pygmy-Owl	Cape region of Baja California
Colima Pygmy-Owl	W Mexico from Sonora to Oaxaca
Tamaulipas Pygmy-Owl	E Mexico (Tamaulipas to N Hidalgo)
Eared Poorwill	W Mexico from Durango to Oaxaca
Tawny-collared Nightjar	NE Mexico from Nuevo León to N Veracruz
White-naped Swift	Durango to Jalisco and disjunctly in Michoacán and Guerrero
Long-tailed Sabrewing*	Los Tuxtlas, Veracruz
Short-crested Coquette*	Guerrero
Golden-crowned Emerald	W Mexico from Durango to Oaxaca
Cozumel Emerald	Isla Cozumel, Quintana Roo
Mexican Woodnymph*	W Mexico (Nayarit to Colima)
Xantus' Hummingbird	Baja California Sur
Green-fronted Hummingbird	Guerrero, Oaxaca and Chiapas
Blue-capped Hummingbird*	Oaxaca
White-tailed Hummingbird	Guerrero and Oaxaca
Dusky Hummingbird	SW, from Jalisco to Oaxaca
Mexican Sheartail	Coastal Yucatán
Beautiful Hummingbird	South-central Mexico (Guerrero, Oaxaca)
Bumblebee Hummingbird	Central and S Mexico (Durango and Tamaulipas south to Oaxaca)
Citreoline Trogon	W and S Mexico from Sinaloa to Chiapas
Golden-cheeked Woodpecker	W Mexico from Sinaloa to Oaxaca

Grey-breasted Woodpecker	Guerrero and Oaxaca
Grey-crowned Woodpecker	W Mexico from S Sonora to Oaxaca
White-striped Woodcreeper	Montane S Sonora to México and Oaxaca
Pileated Flycatcher*	South-central Mexico (Michoacán to central Oaxaca)
Flammulated Flycatcher	W Mexico from Sinaloa to W Chiapas
Sinaloa Martin*	Sierra Madre Occidental from Sonora to Michoacán
Black-throated Magpie-Jay	W Mexico from central Sonora to Colima
Tufted Jay*	Restricted area of Durango, Sinaloa and Nayarit
Purplish-backed Jay	W Mexico from S Sonora to central Nayarit
San Blas Jay	W Mexico from Nayarit to Guerrero
Dwarf Jay*	Mountains of south-central Mexico (Veracruz, Puebla, Oaxaca)
White-throated Jay*	Mountains of Guerrero and Oaxaca (no sites)
Sinaloa Crow	NW, from Sinaloa to Nayarit
Grey-barred Wren	Mountains of south-central Mexico (Colima to Puebla and Veracruz to Oaxaca)
Giant Wren	Coastal Chiapas
Spotted Wren	W and central Mexico, disjunctly NE Mexico
Boucard's Wren	South-central Mexico (Guerrero, Puebla, Oaxaca)
Yucatan Wren	Coastal Yucatán
Sumichrast's Wren*	Tiny area of Veracruz and Oaxaca
Nava's Wren*	Tiny area of E Oaxaca, Veracruz and Chiapas
Happy Wren	W Mexico from S Sonora to W Oaxaca
Sinaloa Wren	W Mexico from central Sonora to W Oaxaca
Cozumel Wren	Isla Cozumel, Quintana Roo
Clarion Wren*	Isla Clarión, Revillagigedo group
Socorro Wren*	Isla Socorro, Revillagigedo group
Russet Nightingale-Thrush	Sierra Madre from Sonora and Nuevo León to Oaxaca
Rufous-backed Robin	W Mexico from S Sonora to Oaxaca
Aztec Thrush	Sierra Madre Occidental from Sonora to Oaxaca
Blue Mockingbird	W and central Mexico from Sonora and Tamaulipas south to Oaxaca
Socorro Mockingbird*	Isla Socorro, Revillagigedo group
Grey Thrasher	Baja California
Cozumel Thrasher*	Isla Cozumel, Quintana Roo
Ocellated Thrasher	South-central Mexico from Guanajato to Oaxaca
Vizcaino Thrasher	Central Baja California
Slaty Vireo	South-central Mexico from Jalisco to

	Oaxaca
Cozumel Vireo	Isla Cozumel, Quintana Roo
Dwarf Vireo	SW Mexico from Jalisco to Oaxaca
Golden Vireo	W Mexico from S Sonora to Oaxaca
Belding's Yellowthroat*	Baja California Sur
Ashy Storm Petrel*	E Mexico (Tamaulipas, N Veracruz)
Black-polled Yellowthroat*	Central Mexico (Michoacán, México)
Hooded Yellowthroat	East-central Mexico from Coahuila to Oaxaca
Red Warbler	Mountains from S Durango, Colima to Oaxaca
Red-headed Tanager	W Mexico from Durango to Oaxaca
Crimson-collared Grosbeak	NE Mexico (Nuevo León to N Veracruz)
Rosita's Bunting*	Tiny range in Oaxaca and Chiapas
Orange-breasted Bunting	W Mexico from Jalisco to W Chiapas
Green-striped Brush-Finch	W and central Mexico (Sinaloa to Nayarit and Jalisco to Puebla)
Rufous-capped Brush-Finch	Mountains from S Durango to Oaxaca
Collared Towhee	Central and S Mexico (Jalisco to Oaxaca)
Socorro Towhee	Isla Socorro, Revillagigedo Group
White-throated Towhee	South-central Mexico (Guerrero, Oaxaca)
Bridled Sparrow	South-central Mexico (Puebla to Oaxaca)
Black-chested Sparrow	SW Mexico (Jalisco to Puebla)
Sumichrast's Sparrow*	Tiny range in Oaxaca and Chiapas
Oaxaca Sparrow*	Oaxaca
Striped Sparrow	High altitudes of central Mexico (Durango to Puebla)
Worthen's Sparrow*	North-central Mexico (Coahuila, Zacatecas, San Luis Potosí)
Sierra Madre Sparrow*	Highlands of W (probably extirpated) and central Mexico (Distrito Federal and Morelos)
Guadelupe Junco*	Guadelupe Island, Baja California
Black-backed Oriole	Durango and Nuevo León to Michoacán and Veracruz

The following Mexican endemic taxa are treated as full species by Howell and Webb (1995) but not by Clements (2000).

Mexican (Western Long-tailed) Hermit	Pacific slope from Nayarit to Oaxaca
Doubleday's (Broad-billed) Hummingbird	Pacific slope from Guerrero to Chiapas
Cinnamon-sided (Green-fronted) Hummingbird	Oaxaca
Strickland's (Arizona) Woodpecker	Highlands from México to Veracruz
Bronze-winged (Golden-olive) Woodpecker	Nuevo León to Veracruz

Grayson's (Rufous-backed) Robin   Tres Marías Islands; possibly adjacent Nayarit
Baird's (Yellow-eyed) Junco   Cape area; Baja California

MEXICO NEAR-ENDEMICS

Horned Guan*	Chiapas and Guatemala
Ocellated Turkey*	Yucatán Peninsula; N Guatemala; N Belize
Yucatan Bobwhite	Yucatán Peninsula; Belize
Yucatan (Yellow-lored) Parrot	Yucatán Peninsula; N Belize
Yucatan Nightjar	Yucatán Peninsula and Isla Cozumel; Belize and N Honduras
Yucatan Poorwill	Yucatán Peninsula including N Guatemala and N Belize
Eared Trogon*	Sierra Madre Occidental from Sonora to Michoacán; Arizona
Yucatan Woodpecker	Yucatán Peninsula; N Belize
Belted Flycatcher*	Chiapas and Guatemala
Yucatan Flycatcher	Yucatán Peninsula, marginally into N Guatemala and Belize
Yucatan Jay	Yucatán Peninsula, N Guatemala, N Belize
Tamaulipas Crow	NE Mexico (Tamaulipas to N Veracruz; S Texas)
Mexican Chickadee	Mountains of Mexico from the US border to Oaxaca; S Arizona
Brown-throated Wren	Sierra Madre Occidental and Oriental from US border to Oaxaca
Rufous-collared Robin	Chiapas: Guatemala
Black Catbird*	Yucatán Peninsula; N Guatemala; N Belize
Black-capped Gnatcatcher	S Arizona, W Mexico south to Colima
Yucatan Vireo	E Yucatán Peninsula; N Belize
Chestnut-sided Shrike-Vireo	S Mexico from Jalisco disjunctly to Chiapas; Guatemala
Pink-headed Warbler*	Chiapas; Guatemala
Red-breasted Chat	W Mexico from Sinaloa to Chiapas; Guatemala (probably)
Azure-rumped Tanager*	Chiapas; Guatemala
Rose-throated Tanager	Yucatán Peninsula; N Guatemala, N Belize
Five-striped Sparrow	W Mexico (Jalisco to Sonora; S Arizona)
Audubon's Oriole	S Texas to Oaxaca
Orange Oriole	Yucatán Peninsula; N Belize
Yellow-winged Cacique	W Mexico from central Sonora to Chiapas, marginally W Guatemala
Hooded Grosbeak	Disjunctly, highlands of W Mexico (Durango to Nayarit); E Mexico (Tamaulipas to Oaxaca); Guatemala

NICARAGUA

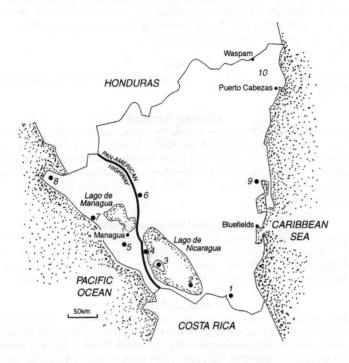

1 Refugio Bartola and Gran Reserva
  Río Indio-Maiz National Park
2 Isla de Zapote
3 Isla de Ometepe/Volcán Maderas
4 Volcán Mombacho
5 Volcán Masaya National Park and

6 Laguna Moyua
7 Salinas Grandes/Isla de Venados
8 Volcán Cosigüina
9 Río Kurinwas
10 Lowland Pine Savanna

INTRODUCTION

Summary
Nicaragua is the largest of the Central American republics, but ironically one of the least known or visited. There are several reasons for this.
For visitors from either North America or Europe it is a much less favoured destination than, for example, Costa Rica or Panama. It lacks the
high elevations of those countries to the south—the highest mountain
is below 1800 m—so consequently does not possess, for example, the
broad range of montane habitat in Costa Rica. Most important, the
social fabric of Nicaragua is less than ideal. For many years the country
was run as a private ranch by the Somoza family, who plundered the
treasury and neglected everything else. Following their overthrow
Nicaragua was the scene of prolonged civil war, with the US-backed

'contras' opposing the elected government. The situation is currently (August 2000) peaceful, but with a ruined economy and massive unemployment. This background is not exactly conducive to tourism. Nevertheless Nicaragua has some excellent lowland forest and the determined birdwatcher may find it rewarding. Since it is rarely visited the chance of new discoveries is substantial.

Size
Nicaragua is about 130,000 km^2, about half the size of the United Kingdom, or one-fifth that of Texas.

Getting Around
Most towns and villages are served by buses, many of them second-hand yellow school buses from North America. In some cases an express bus service, employing faster vehicles with functional shock absorbers, is available and well worth the small extra charge. Vehicles may be hired in Managua and elsewhere. Driving after dark is not recommended.

Accommodation and Food
In all of the larger towns there are adequate facilities for lodging and eating, albeit of highly variable standard. Prices by European or North American standards are extremely low. In smaller centres a certain amount of ingenuity and an ability to 'roll with the punches' is helpful.

Health and Safety
Appropriate precautions against malaria are essential. Inoculation against viral hepatitis A and typhoid are strongly recommended. Recent reports concerning personal security are varied. While some rural areas are relatively crime-free, the larger cities warrant sensible precautions, especially after dark. There have also been recent reports of banditry on some roads, with public buses being stopped and their passengers divested of valuables.

Climate and Timing
Basically there are two seasons, wet and dry. The driest months are March–May. The Caribbean coast is cooler than the Pacific but considerably wetter. Travel during the height of the rainy season can be difficult, especially in the Caribbean lowlands.

Habitats
Nicaragua has less altitudinal variation than either Honduras or Costa Rica, but does possess very large areas of largely uninhabited lowland forest, most of which are still in quite pristine condition. The bulk is located on the Caribbean drainage. One reason for the continued existence of such forest is the relative difficulty of access. Getting to good areas requires much patience and organisation; in the absence of roads, arrangements for boat hire must be made.

Conservation
Conservation in Nicaragua has always been a victim of political events, earlier efforts having been hampered by civil war and the US embargo. Nevertheless in 1989, with a change of government, Nicaragua commenced a vigorous plan to protect some areas. These include all vol-

canic peaks above 800 m on the Pacific coast. Currently there are 19 protected areas and 18 other potential reserves. Much of the Caribbean forest is protected by the currently bad access, a situation liable to change.

Bird Families
Approximately 70 families are found in Nicaragua. Several South American families, such as tapaculos, reach the northern limits of their range in Costa Rica and do not extend to Nicaragua.

Bird Species
About 656 species have been recorded in Nicaragua, a total that undoubtedly will increase with more fieldwork.

Endemics
None, but two, Green-breasted Mountain-gem and Nicaraguan Grackle, are almost so.

Expectations
A visit to Nicaragua encompassing all habitats might be expected to total 300 species. However, we have not heard of anyone attempting such an exercise recently.

REFUGIO BARTOLA AND GRAN RESERVA RÍO INDIO-MAIZ NATIONAL PARK

A huge area of pristine rain forest, the Refugio and National Park together exceed 500,000 ha, which is probably the largest area of lowland primary forest remaining in Central America. Virtually unknown to outside visitors, the current bird list of a little over 200 species is obviously merely scratching the surface when one considers that La Selva, not too far away in adjacent Costa Rica, has twice that number.

Specialities
Agami Heron, Great Green* and Scarlet Macaws, Crested Owl, Snowcap, Rufous-winged Woodpecker, Streak-chested Antpitta.

Others
Great Tinamou, Lesser Yellow-headed and King Vultures, Crested Eagle*, Great Curassow*, Rufous-fronted Wood-Quail, Sunbittern, Crimson-fronted, Olive-throated and Orange-fronted Parakeets, Blue-headed, Red-

Agami Herons are widely but sparsely distributed; Refugio Bartola offers one of the better chances for this enigmatic species

lored and Mealy Parrots, Rufous Nightjar, Black-bellied Hummingbird, Slaty-tailed, Black-throated and Violaceous Trogons, all six New World kingfishers, Broad-billed and Rufous Motmots, White-fronted Nunbird, Chestnut-mandibled Toucan, Black-striped Woodcreeper, Slaty Spinetail, Fasciated Antshrike, Bare-crowned and Wing-banded Antbirds, Black-faced Antthrush, Fulvous-bellied (Thicket) Antpitta, Cinnamon Becard, Purple-throated Fruitcrow, Red-capped, White-collared and Grey-headed Manakins, Thrush-like Schiffornis, Long-tailed Tyrant, Bright-rumped Attila, Golden-crowned Spadebill, Sulphur-rumped, Ruddy-tailed and Sepia-capped Flycatchers, Bay Wren, Tawny-faced Gnatwren, Green Shrike-Vireo, Northern Waterthrush, Canada (winter) and Buff-rumped Warblers, Olive-backed Euphonia, Scarlet-rumped, Crimson-collared, Olive, Tawny-crested and Grey-headed Tanagers, Black-faced Grosbeak, Pink-billed and Thick-billed Seed-Finches, Scarlet-rumped Cacique, Nicaraguan Grackle.

Other Wildlife
Southern Tamandua, Brown-throated Three-toed Sloth, Spider, Howler and White-faced Monkeys, Jaguarundi, Tayra.

Access
The Refugio is located on the northwest bank of the Río Bartola where it joins the Río San Juan (the border with Costa Rica), and the National Park starts on the opposite bank. Access is via San Carlos, which is at the southeast end of Lago de Nicaragua. San Carlos can be reached either

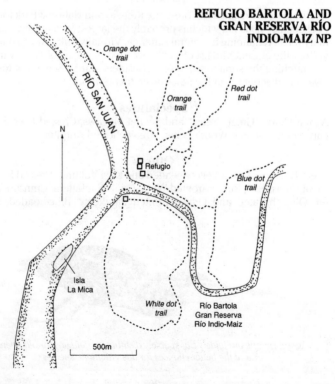

REFUGIO BARTOLA AND GRAN RESERVA RÍO INDIO-MAIZ NP

Orange dot trail

Orange trail

Red dot trail

RÍO SAN JUAN

N

Refugio

Blue dot trail

Isla La Mica

White dot trail

Río Bartola Gran Reserva Río Indio-Maiz

500m

by bus from Managua via Juigalpa (a tedious eight-hour journey, the last part on unpaved roads; robberies and banditry have recently been reported on this section), or by fast hydrofoil or slow boat from Granada (approximately 50 km south of Managua). It is also possible to fly from Managua (about $60 single). San Carlos is also accessible by boat from Los Chiles in northern Costa Rica; it is necessary to report to the Costa Rican authorities in Los Chiles, take a boat to San Carlos (about $7), reporting to Nicaraguan immigration authorities. From San Carlos a scheduled boat (about $5) goes downstream on the Río San Juan, or a boat may be chartered (about $50). The Refugio is located approximately 5 km downstream from the town of El Castillo de la Concepción. Accommodation, in a dozen small cabins, and food, is available at the Refugio. There is a well-developed system of trails leading from the Refugio buildings. In contrast, the National Park opposite has little in the way of facilities but is easily accessible by canoe from the Refugio. Arrangements at the Refugio should be made with Daniel Querol, Box 2715, Managua, Nicaragua, e-mail gme@tmx.com.ni.

Another similar area south of the Río San Juan is the Esperanza Reserve, which is located between the Ríos Frío and San Juan, south and east of San Carlos. This is an area of lowland wet forest, flooded during the rainy season. Like those areas around Refugio Bartola it has been little explored by outsiders and should harbour many of the species found at La Selva in Costa Rica. Access is by boat from San Carlos, which can be arranged by calling 283-0354 in San Carlos, or 266-8172 in Managua.

ISLA DE ZAPOTE

One of a group of islands (Archipiélago de Solentiname) located in Lago de Nicaragua about an hour by launch from San Carlos. These have become known for the balsa-wood carvings produced by their inhabitants. Isla de Zapote holds significant numbers of breeding waterbirds, mostly Olivaceous Cormorants, but also Anhingas, Wood Storks, White Ibises and Bare-throated Tiger-Herons. Boats may be hired by enquiring in San Carlos; it is as well to ensure that a firm agreement as to price and destination is reached before setting out.

ISLA DE OMETEPE/VOLCÁN MADERAS

A large island in Lago de Nicaragua with an inactive volcano cone at its southern end. Very scenic; it is a popular tourist/European backpacker destination. The island is unusual in being definitely on the Pacific slope but has a Caribbean slope character to its flora and fauna—probably because it is in the centre of the lake and humidity is relatively high. Volcán Maderas is about 1300 m. Nicaraguan Grackle occurs around Rivas and south along the road towards Costa Rica.

Specialities
Red-lored Parrot (Volcán Maderas is the only location on the Pacific slope of Nicaragua for this species), Nicaraguan Grackle.

Nicaragua

Others
Osprey, Green Parakeet, Yellow-naped Parrot, Mangrove Swallow, various wintering North American warblers such as Yellow, Black-and-white and Tennessee Warblers.

Access
From Rivas (about 2 hours drive south of Managua) take the road east to San Jorge on the shore of Lago de Nicaragua, after about 5 km. Take the ferry to Moyogalpa on the island. It is possible to take a vehicle onto the ferry. For foot passengers the cost is about $1.25 and the trip takes approximately an hour. The ferry runs several times a day each way, but watch the schedule. Hotels are numerous in Moyogalpa; El Pirata (about US$6.00 per night, but clean and nice, tel. 045-94262). In Moyogalpa a car and driver can be hired, but are not cheap; car rentals are not available. The drive to Mérida takes more than an hour without stops. From Mérida there are many trails up the slope of Volcán Maderas; all are good for birding. Above Mérida there is an old, formerly Somoza-owned, coffee plantation.

VOLCÁN MOMBACHO

A volcano which reaches 1300 m and an excellent birding area that is easily accessible from Granada, although the road can be relatively bad and require a 4WD. Good views of Lago de Nicaragua and Las Isletas can be had from the slope.

Others
Vaux's Swift, Yellow, Black-and-white and Tennessee Warblers, Rose-breasted Grosbeak, Summer Tanager and other North American migrants in season, Turquoise-browed Motmot.

Access
Travel south out of Granada towards hacienda El Cutirre, on the volcano's east slope. The road is not signed, so directions should be sought in Granada. Once on the road, there are no turns. Beyond the hacienda the road begins to switchback up the east side of the volcano, and fairly quickly enters more humid forest and coffee plantations. The drive from Granada takes about an hour, but higher up the road becomes rougher and requires 4WD. There are good hotels and pensions in Granada.

VOLCÁN MASAYA NATIONAL PARK AND LAGUNA MASAYA

An active volcano very close to Managua, which makes a nice place to visit due to the wonderful views. You can drive to the top of the volcano, walk to the edge and look into its glowing maw. It is not the best place for birding, however, having a low bird diversity, mainly grassland species, but is very close to Managua if you have only an hour or two to spare. Red-throated Parakeet, incredibly, roosts and nests inside the caldera, among the sulphurous fumes. Laguna Masaya, east of the volcano, has some arid scrub with typical species of the habitat.

Others

Red-throated Parakeet (especially Apr–Nov), Turquoise-browed Motmot, White-throated Magpie-Jay, Clay-coloured Robin, Blue Grosbeak (winter), Eastern Meadowlark.

Access

From Managua take the road to Masaya, about 13 km from the Plaza de Compras intersection, approximately 15 minutes drive. The park entrance is well-marked; there is a small entrance fee. Birding is best near the park headquarters where there are still some trees; the higher slopes are almost entirely grassland. The road within the park is all paved. To reach Laguna Masaya return to the main highway and turn towards Masaya (right at the park entrance). In Nindiri, the next town on the road, you will have to ask for directions, as there are no signs or other landmarks. Ask someone on the south side of the road at a place where you can see the Laguna Masaya. There are numerous good restaurants along the road between Nindiri and Managua.

LAGUNA MOYUA

A lake and marsh that host large numbers of waterfowl in season. The area includes several other smaller nearby lakes.

Others

Pied-billed Grebe, Black-bellied Whistling-Duck and Blue-winged Teal (large numbers), Osprey, Purple Gallinule, many other waterfowl and shorebirds, Orange-fronted Parakeet.

Access

The lagoon is situated along the main paved road linking Managua to Sébaco and Matagalpa. Take the road from Managua past Tipitapa, to km 73, about an hour's drive from Managua. There are no hotels nearby, only small restaurants. Most of the lake and marsh lies north of the road. A telescope is recommended to scan the lake and marsh.

SALINAS GRANDES/ISLA DE VENADOS

Coastal dry forest with salt pans and extensive mangroves, which are good for shorebirds. Isla de Venados is a protected reserve, encompassing a primarily mangrove-lined estuary and has a caretaker who lives at the mouth of the river.

Others

Peregrine Falcon (one of its few sites in Nicaragua, winter), Mangrove Swallow, Tropical Mockingbird (known from Nicaragua only since 1994). A wide range of waterfowl, herons and shorebirds can be quite numerous in season, while the mangroves serve as a roost for large numbers of White-fronted and Yellow-naped Parrots.

Access
The nearest hotels are in León. From there take the Panamerican Highway towards Managua; about 20 km from town turn south on a good dirt road towards Salinas Grandes. If coming from the direction of Managua, there are restaurants in La Paz Centro. The road passes through very arid dry forest. At the village of Salinas Grandes (the last high ground) turn north and cross the salt pans (look for shorebirds) to the beach and the estuary mouth. The beach is about 1.6 km from the village and the drive from León to the beach takes approximately an hour. You may be able to hire a boat at the caretaker's house, but most shorebirds can be seen from land, among the salt pans.

VOLCÁN COSIGÜINA

A symmetrical cone-shaped volcano with a crater lake and a reasonable area of deciduous forest on its flanks. There are spectacular views of the Golfo de Fonseca and three countries—Nicaragua, Honduras and El Salvador—from the summit.

Specialities
Scarlet Macaw (very low numbers).

Others
Great Black Hawk, Yellow-naped Parrot, Crested Bobwhite, Green-breasted Mango. During spring and fall migrations vast numbers of Lesser Nighthawks, Scissor-tailed Flycatchers and Barn Swallows occur in the lowlands surrounding the volcano.

Access
The nearest hotels are in Chinandega City. From there take the road toward Cosigüina, to the town of Potosí. The road is paved about 2/3 of the way and it is around 2 hours from Chinandega to Potosí. The Chinandega–Potosí road accesses mangrove, some areas of tropical deciduous forest and marshes. Marshy areas along the main road may also be productive. Use Potosí as a base; a guide can be hired if necessary. Potosí has a restaurant, but no hotel. The trail to the caldera begins at Potosí, but there are numerous routes up. The climb to the top of the volcano (800 m) from Potosí (sea level) takes about three hours of steady hiking and longer with birding stops.

RÍO KURINWAS

A remote area for the very hardy birder. It requires an expensive boatride (take 100 gallons of fuel) through Laguna de Perlas from Bluefields. The area is little inhabited and has no hotels or restaurants; bring camping gear. However, much of the area is pristine, with still extensive areas of lowland forest and swamp.

Specialities
Fulvous-bellied (Thicket) Antpitta.

Others

Green Ibis (unknown from Nicaragua until 1995), Sungrebe, White-crowned Parrot, Brown-hooded Parrot, Chestnut-mandibled Toucan, many lowland forest species.

Access

From Bluefields (accessible by air from Managua) hire a boat and an experienced boatman. The boat-ride, in a good fibreglass launch with 100 hp motor, takes about four hours—two hours through Laguna de Perlas (great seafood at the restaurant in the village of Laguna de Perlas) to the mouth of the river, and two hours upriver to Tortuguero, the uppermost extent of its navigable portion. Wear sunscreen, as the open boats have no shade. There is public transportation: a boat travels from Bluefields once a week or so, but it is very slow, uncomfortable and smelly. At Tortuguero there is a community, but no stores for food or supplies. With negotiation you may persuade someone to fix you a meal and let you sleep in an empty room or in the school.

LOWLAND PINE SAVANNA

The southernmost extent of Caribbean Pine forest in the lowlands of the New World is in eastern Nicaragua. This unique habitat forms a savanna almost untouched by human activity. It is a beautiful area, but access is difficult. The number of bird species is low, but many have limited distributions elsewhere in Central America. The avian community is unusual for Nicaragua, with many species more typical of areas further north.

Specialities

Black-throated Bobwhite, Botteri's Sparrow.

Others

Ladder-backed Woodpecker, Grace's Warbler, Eastern Meadowlark, Eastern Bluebird, Grey Catbird (winter), Hepatic Tanager, Black-headed Siskin, Red Crossbill, Chipping and Grasshopper Sparrows. Many lowland forest species extend into gallery forest within the savanna.

Access

Difficult. It is possible to drive from Managua to Puerto Cabezas in about 10 hours (in good weather). It is, however, more practical to take two days, spending the night in Siuna which has some decent hotels and restaurants. In the rainy season the road can become very bad and the ferry across the Río Wawa can be a nightmare. It is possible to fly from Managua to Puerto Cabezas, which is the largest town in the region and makes a good base, with some decent hotels and restaurants. If flying to Puerto Cabezas you will need to hire a vehicle there. The road to Waspam (northwest of Puerto Cabezas on the Honduran border) is good and traverses prime habitat: the total driving time is about two hours. Stop at stream crossings and look for birds. At Waspam there is a basic hotel and some decent restaurants. The pine savanna is beautiful, but birdwatching may be frustrating, because birds can be so scarce.

ADDITIONAL INFORMATION

Books and papers

Mexican and Central American Handbook, Cameron, S. and Box, B. 1999. Footprint Handbooks, 6 Riverside Court, Lower Bristol Road, Bath BA2 3DZ, England, UK and 4255 W. Tuohy Avenue, Lincolnwood IL 60646-1975, USA.

Let's Go Central America, Ellenberg, D. J. and Garston, B. D. 1999. St. Martin's Press, New York.

Both books are full of useful information on transport and accommodation; each is in a series updated annually.

Sight records of new species for Nicaragua and noteworthy records on range and occurrence, Wiedenfeld, D. A. *et al.* 2001. *Cotinga* 15: 53–57.

Two new species for Nicaragua, Cody, M. L. 2000. *Cotinga* 13: 65–66.

A Guide to the Birds of Costa Rica (see p. 106 for details).

A Guide to the Birds of Mexico and Northern Central America (see p. 196 for details).

NEAR-ENDEMICS

Green-breasted Mountain-gem	Northwest Nicaragua and central Honduras
Nicaraguan Grackle	Southwest Nicaragua and extreme north Costa Rica

PANAMA

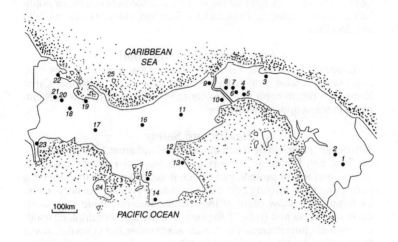

1 Cana, Darién
2 El Real, Darién
3 Nusagandi
4 Cerro Jefe
5 Tocumen Marsh
6 Canopy Tower
7 Madden Lake and Summit Gardens
8 Gamboa Pipeline Road
9 Middle Chagres
10 Cerro Campana National Park
11 El Cope
12 Ciénaga Las Macanas
13 Las Salinas de Chitré
14 Cerro Hoya
15 El Montuoso de Chepo
16 Santa Fé
17 Cerro Colorado
18 Fortuna Forest Reserve
19 Bocas del Toro
20 Boquete
21 Western Chiriquí Highlands
22 Changuinola
23 El Chorogo
24 Isla Coiba
25 Isla Escudo de Veraguas

INTRODUCTION

Summary

Panama is one of the most popular birding destinations in Latin America, with very good reason. It has a broad variety of habitats, from lush tropical rain forests to high-altitude páramo, a well-developed infrastructure of roads and accommodation, and it has been well studied, with its own excellent field guide. Panama's position, as the link between Central and South America, places it at the southernmost edge of the range of many species and the northernmost of many others.

Size

Panama is about 77,000 km², about one-third the size of the United Kingdom or one-ninth the size of Texas. Being a long, narrow country, distances are greater than the area implies.

211

Getting Around

The most effective way to access birding habitat is to hire a vehicle; for some areas 4WD is necessary. Most population centres can be reached by bus, but this frequently leaves the birdwatcher considerable distances from good areas. Internal flights are available between major population centres including Panama City, Santiago, David, Bocas del Toro and San Blas.

Accommodation and Food

Both are readily available. Prices by European standards tend to be very reasonable, at least away from the major cities near the former Canal Zone, although in comparison to countries such as Honduras or Nicaragua, Panama appears expensive.

Health and Safety

Anti-malarials should be taken in some lowland areas, including Bocas del Toro and Darién. In some places chloroquine-resistant malaria is present and recent professional advice is necessary as to the best drug to use. Travellers arriving from countries where yellow fever occurs may be required to show proof of inoculation. Recently there have been cases of cholera and typhoid. Reports as to the safety of drinking water are contradictory; Panama City has excellent water, but in smaller towns the standard precautions should be taken.

Some urban areas have significant crime problems—Colón and the Casco Viejo area of Panama City are frequently singled out in this respect—so obvious care should be taken. Recently the Darién area has seen an increase in general lawlessness.

Note that the electricity supply in Panama varies between 110 and 220 volts; check before plugging in!

Climate and Timing

The climate in Panama is very much a function of altitude and, to a lesser extent, whether you are on the Pacific or Caribbean slope. Temperatures in the lowlands vary remarkably little during the year, there being only a few degrees of difference between the mean maxima and minima: temperatures at Balboa, in the former Canal Zone, vary from a daily minimum of about 22°C to a maximum of about 33°C, with only 1–3°C year-round variation. At higher altitudes it is much colder and morning frosts are regular on the highest mountains on the Costa Rican border. Rainfall, by contrast, is much more seasonal, with a dry season in January–April and a wetter period during the rest of the year. However, on the Caribbean coast substantial rainfall can occur at almost any time of year. Rainfall tends to take the form of sudden torrential downpours, especially in the late afternoon. Even during the rainy season, dry periods may occur.

The most popular time for birdwatching visits is towards the end of the dry season, when roads are at their best and most North American migrants are still present. The early part of the wet season, when breeding activity is high, can also be very good.

Habitats

Because of its broad altitudinal range Panama is very rich in habitat types. Originally the country was largely forested, forest-type being more dependent on altitude than on geographic location. However, huge areas have now been deforested, with large open agricultural lands and, in some cases, second growth predominant. Páramo-type vegetation occurs at the highest altitudes in the west of the country, near the Costa Rican border. There are no large lakes, apart from those artificial ones created during the building of the Canal. In drier regions of the Pacific drainage there is some savanna, and extensive mangrove swamps exist on the Caribbean coast.

Conservation
Huge areas of natural habitat in Panama have been destroyed although for reasons of watershed maintenance, as well as for military reasons, much of the habitat in the former Canal Zone was preserved. With the transfer of sovereignty to the Republic of Panama there has been some destruction here, but recently a network of National Parks (Soberanía, Camino de Cruces, Chagres etc.) has been created in this region. There are several other National Parks, including the extensive La Amistad Park, which is shared with Costa Rica, as well as various forest reserves. The largest pristine area is the Darién National Park. Its remoteness and lack of access formerly protected the entire Darién, but this is now changing.

Bird Families
About 82 families (the precise number varies according to taxonomy) are found in Panama. Particularly well represented are tyrant flycatchers (85 species), hummingbirds (52), antbirds (38) and tanagers (54) but there are also 21 wrens, 21 parrots, 20 cotingas and 17 woodcreepers.

Bird Species
The total number of species recorded in Panama is over 950, with additions appearing on a regular basis. By comparison, Costa Rica, two-thirds of Panama's size, has approximately 50 fewer species and Colombia, 15 times larger, has about 1800 species.

Endemics
Panama has several endemics, the precise number varying according to taxonomy. Ridgely & Gwynne (*Birds of Panama*, 1976) list six—a hummingbird, a woodpecker, a treerunner, a flycatcher, a tanager and a finch—but other authorities recognise ten or more, classifying several forms previously regarded as races as full species.

Near-endemics
In addition, there are a number of near-endemics—species whose ranges extend only into adjacent Costa Rica, usually in the shared highland massif—and several which might be termed 'safety and security endemics'—species whose range extends into limited areas of Colombia but, given the lawless and chaotic state of affairs in many parts of that country, are largely inaccessible to birdwatchers with any sense of self-preservation.

Expectations
By covering both the eastern and western highland areas and lowlands in between a list of 400 or more species should be realistically attainable.

DARIÉN

Cana and El Real are in Darién, the easternmost, wildest and least accessible province of Panama, famous among birdwatchers as an area where many species, very difficult to find elsewhere, are readily encountered. *A Guide to the Birds of Panama* features a plate of Darién species with no fewer than 25 figures. Many of these are of primarily South American distribution and just reach Panama, but several are regional endemics whose distribution is very limited, such as Pirre Warbler*, Pirre Hummingbird* and Beautiful Treerunner*. Given the generally chaotic and dangerous state of much of Colombia, the Darién offers the best opportunity to find many of these species.

*Darién is the easiest and safest location to find the highly
restricted Dusky-backed Jacamar*

CANA

A superb area of forest located within the 500,000 ha Darién National Park, with a species list of at least 300. To do the area justice and, especially, to visit higher elevations, a stay of several days or more is necessary.

Endemics
Choco Tapaculo, Stripe-cheeked Woodpecker, Beautiful Treerunner*, Pirre Warbler*, Pirre Bush-Tanager, Green-naped Tanager*.

Specialities
Choco Tinamou*, Russet-crowned Quail-Dove*, Pirre Hummingbird*, Dusky-backed Jacamar, Black-billed Flycatcher*, Sooty-headed Wren, Varied Solitaire, Viridian Dacnis*.

Others
Crested Eagle*, Great Curassow*, Crested Guan, Tawny-faced Quail, Black-eared Wood-Quail, Great Green*, Blue-and-yellow, Red-and-green and Chestnut-fronted Macaws, Blue-fronted Parrotlet, Rufous-vented Ground-

Cuckoo, Vermiculated Screech-Owl, Chapman's Swift, White-tipped Sicklebill, Tooth-billed Hummingbird, Rufous-crested Coquette, Green Thorntail, Greenish Puffleg, Tody Motmot, Crimson-bellied Woodpecker, Double-banded Greytail, at least 30 species of antbird including Wing-banded Antbird, Black-crowned Antpitta, Speckled Mourner, Black-tipped Cotinga, Bronze-olive Pygmy-Tyrant, Sooty-headed Tyrannulet, Cinereous Becard, Yellow-browed Shrike-Vireo, White-headed and Stripe-throated Wrens, Slate-throated Gnatcatcher, Tropical Parula, Chestnut-sided, Blackburnian, Cerulean, Kentucky and Mourning Warblers, White-eared Conebill, Grey-and-gold, Lemon-spectacled and Scarlet-browed Tanagers.

Other Wildlife
Pale-throated Three-toed Sloth, Mantled Howler Monkey, Spider Monkey, Puma, Tayra.

Access
Only by air. Any trip must be planned well in advance, as all supplies must be flown in to a grass airstrip with few facilities, and which is not usable in poor weather. The facilities in Cana are maintained by the Asociación Nacional para la Conservación de la Naturaleza (ANCON), from whom permission to stay must be obtained. The simplest way to reach the area is to join a tour, or arrange a party of your own using a travel agent specializing in the area. To keep costs reasonable a group of 5–10 people is ideal. Such packages frequently include the services of a local guide.

Facilities at Cana are basic but adequate. Items to bring include good waterproof footwear, a flashlight, candles and a sleeping bag. There is a weight restriction of 25 lb (11 kg) on baggage for the flight.

Once at the airstrip, there are numerous areas to be explored on foot.

Trail to Boca del Cupe This is an Indian village about 40 km distant, which gives access to lower altitude forest. To treat this trail adequately would require camping further down, but the upper section near the airstrip is well worth investigating. The trail runs north from the airstrip.

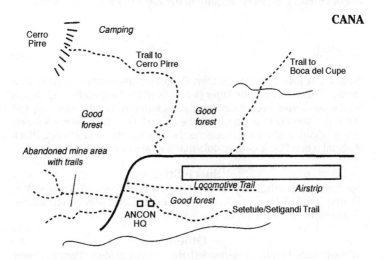

*The Grey-and-gold Tanager is mainly a South American species,
extending into Panama only in southern Darién*

Cerro Pirre An essential site, as many of the specialties are only found above 1000 m. A trail runs from the northwest corner of the airstrip towards the summit. A campsite (bring water) is located at about 1250 m; the hike is strenuous and may take up to eight hours, so it is worthwhile to make preparations for 2–3 nights stay. From the campsite, the ridge of Cerro Pirre is a further two hours. Species found here include Russet-crowned Quail-Dove*, Black-eared Wood-Quail, Blue-fronted Parrotlet, Greenish Puffleg, Tooth-billed and Pirre* Hummingbirds, Tody Motmot, Beautiful Treerunner*, Rufous-breasted Antthrush, Choco Tapaculo, Bronze-olive Pygmy-Tyrant, Pirre Bush-Tanager and Green-naped Tanager*. Choco Tinamou* occurs at lower levels on the same trail.

Trails near the mining camp The mines were abandoned many years ago but a series of trails lead from the ANCON camp through excellent habitat.

Setetule Trail This starts near the ANCON camp and runs alongside the stream and into secondary forest. It may be impassable after rain. This is a good area for Viridian Dacnis* and White-eared Conebill.

For current conditions enquire of the ANCON staff.

EL REAL

Situated at lower elevations than Cana and frequently regarded as a 'budget' alternative to the latter (which is indeed expensive), El Real is well worth a visit, even if Cana is also included within the itinerary, and if it is not, then El Real should not be missed. Due to its lower elevation it is a reliable site for some species such as Spectacled Parrotlet, Black Antshrike and Black Oropendola that are rare or absent at Cana.

Specialities
Spectacled Parrotlet, Grey-cheeked Nunlet, Spot-breasted Woodpecker, Double-banded Greytail, Black Antshrike, Yellow-breasted Flycatcher, White-eared Conebill, Black Oropendola.

Others
White-throated Crake, Blue-headed, Red-lored and Mealy Parrots, Green-

crowned Woodnymph, Olivaceous Piculet, Slaty Spinetail, Pygmy Ant-wren, Black-tailed, Northern Royal and Panama Flycatchers, Black-capped Pygmy-Tyrant, Cinnamon, Cinereous and White-winged Becards, Black-chested Jay, Black-bellied and Buff-breasted Wrens, Crimson-backed and Plain-coloured Tanagers, Orange-crowned Oriole, Yellow-rumped and Yellow-billed Caciques.

Access

Theoretically possible by road and canoe via Yaviza on the Pan-American Highway; more practically by air from Panama City (flights daily except Tuesdays). Baggage handling involves a wheelbarrow. There are three trails leading out of town. Best areas are as follows:

Around the airstrip Good location for White-throated Crake and Spectacled Parrotlet.

Trail to the river (Mercadeo Road) A trail leads north to an Indian village on the river bank. Some forest edge. Black Antshrike.

Pinogana trail Leads east from north of the airstrip. Greater Ani, Pale-bellied Hermit, Spot-breasted Woodpecker, Black Oropendola.

Pirre trail It is, theoretically, possible to reach Cerro Pirre on this trail; we are unaware if anyone has recently succeeded in doing this. Lower levels of the trail access the best forest in the area. The trail starts south of the school, passing a radio antenna and then a large concrete tank. The main trail crosses a river and a side trail goes left to a house; Black Antshrike occurs here. After about 3 km the trail passes a water tank. Riverine forest here holds Black Antshrike, Double-banded Grey-tail and White-eared Conebill.

All trails are very muddy and impassable after much rain.

Accommodation: there is a very basic hotel and nearby a restaurant, also very basic, in El Real. Entomologically the former is rather prolific.

EL REAL

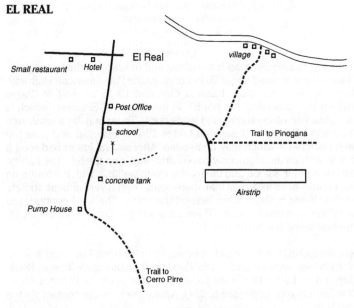

NUSAGANDI

An area of excellent forest, established as a reserve by the Kuna Indians to protect their land from squatters. It is a good location for a number of species normally associated with the Darién.

Specialities

Harpy Eagle*, Rufous-vented Ground-Cuckoo, Great Jacamar, Speckled Antshrike*, Green Manakin.

Others

Great Tinamou, Red-throated Caracara, Great Curassow*, Black-eared Wood-Quail, Mealy Parrot, Yellow-eared Toucanet, Black-crowned and Streak-chested Antpittas, Black-headed Antthrush, Long-tailed Tyrant, Broad-billed Sapayoa, White-thighed Swallow, Stripe-throated Wren, Rufous-winged and Tawny-crested Tanagers.

Terrestrial and secretive, the Streak-chested Antpitta is more often heard than seen

Access

Not easy; the access road is appalling and in places rather hazardous. Nusagandi is located about 20 km north of the Pan-American Highway. Take this road east from Panama City, and 10–15 km east of Chepo (which is bypassed to the north), in the village of El Llano (which is unsigned) an obvious dirt road leads north. There may be a small sign 'Pemasky'. To reach Nusagandi Lodge 4WD is essential and over the worst patches a winch may be needed. After several km of bad road a house with an incongruously paved driveway is on the left. The habitat from this point is good and the road is worth walking, which is fortunate as you may have to do just that, there being several very difficult stretches. The lodge is about 5 km beyond the house. The road continues to the Caribbean coast at Cartí. There are some good trails from the lodge, the best being the Ina Igar trail.

Accommodation is basic but comfortable with bunk beds and a separate kitchen, showers and toilets. Food must be brought with you. Bookings should be made. For the latest information visit the Panama Audubon Society web page (see p. 237). Alternatively, make contact via the

Institute for the Development for the Kuna Yala (IDIKY), Director Jesus Alemancia, IRIK Limnio Asistente, Avenida México, Calle 27, Panama City (e-mail idiky@sinfo.net). Daily charges are US$15. The site is guarded; it is a nice gesture to bring in a small present for the guards, like chocolate or beer.

CERRO JEFE

An area easily accessible from Panama City, and perhaps the easiest location for the near-endemic Tacarcuna Bush-Tanager, as well as many other foothill species.

Endemics
Stripe-cheeked Woodpecker.

Specialities
Black-eared Wood-Quail, Russet-crowned Quail-Dove*, Violet-capped Hummingbird, Spot-crowned Barbet, Tacarcuna Bush-Tanager, Black-headed Brush-Finch.

Others
King Vulture, Crested Guan, Rufous Nightjar, Green and Long-tailed Hermits, Garden Emerald, Snowy-bellied and Rufous-tailed Hummingbirds, Rufous Motmot, Yellow-eared Toucanet, Red-crowned and Crimson-crested Woodpeckers, Slaty-winged Foliage-gleaner, White-ruffed Manakin, Scale-crested Pygmy-Tyrant, Long-tailed Tyrant, Black-and-White, Blackburnian and Chestnut-sided Warblers (all winter), Three-striped Warbler, Blue-and-gold*, Black-and-yellow, Crimson-backed, Emerald, Speckled, Silver-throated, Rufous-winged, Olive, Sulphur-rumped and White-lined Tanagers, Scarlet-thighed and Blue Dacnises, Tawny-capped, Yellow-crowned, Fulvous-vented and White-vented Euphonias, Buff-throated and Streaked Saltators.

Access
Leave Panama City on Highway 1 (the Pan-American) towards Tocumen airport. Just west of the airport turn left (north) at the Riande Hotel. Take the second left in the centre of a small town at 6.6. km, and 1.9 km further take another left at the sign for Cerro Azul. Continue along this road for 17 km, where there is a small café that opens at 6am, and a nearby supermarket. The paved road peters out 19.8 km from the Cerro Azul sign. The road then requires 4WD or can be walked. At the summit are some radio towers surrounded by a fence. Beyond the fenced-off area is a 3-km-long broad track through good habitat, best reached by walking left at the fence and following it around. A second track leads to the right, about 800 m before the radio tower enclosure.

TOCUMEN MARSH

An interesting area of open country and marshland, near Panama City international airport.

Others

Bare-throated Tiger-Heron, White-necked Heron, Lesser Yellow-headed Vulture, Pearl Kite, Black-collared Hawk, Little Cuckoo, Greater Ani, Common Potoo, Pauraque, White-tailed Nightjar, Lesser Kiskadee, Pied Water-Tyrant, Northern Scrub Flycatcher.

Other Wildlife

Greater Grison.

Access

From the Riande Airport Hotel (which makes a convenient base to explore the southern section of the Canal Zone), take the Pan-American Highway east towards Chepo. After 6.8 km there is an intersection, with a Guardia station; turn right. After about 700 m there is a fork. Go left and after a further 2.7 km a dirt road goes to the left. Pass through a gate (which is locked in the afternoon). Keep right onto a maze of bumpy dirt roads. Ask for permission to proceed at the Maintenance Building; also ensure that you do not get locked in.

CANOPY TOWER

A unique lodge—surely the only converted radar station eco-lodge anywhere in the world!—located conveniently close to Panama City and its airport. Definitely not for the budget birder, but a very remarkable place, with a list of over 250 species.

Endemics

Yellow-green Tyrannulet.

Specialities

Tiny Hawk, Crested Owl, Great Potoo, Black-breasted Puffbird, Black-bellied Wren, Rosy Thrush-Tanager.

Others

Hook-billed Kite, Plumbeous Hawk*, Crested Guan, Vermiculated Screech-Owl, Mottled and Black-and-white Owls, Rufous-crested Coquette, Long-billed Starthroat, Green-and-rufous Kingfisher, White-whiskered Puffbird, Black-cheeked, Lineated, Crimson-crested and Cinnamon Woodpeckers, Tawny-throated Leaftosser, Spotted, Bicoloured and Ocellated Antbirds, Olivaceous Flatbill, Golden-crowned Spadebill, Purple-throated Fruitcrow, Blue Cotinga, Golden-collared, Blue-crowned and Red-capped Manakins, Green Shrike-Vireo, Bay-headed, Grey-headed and White-shouldered Tanagers, Slate-coloured Grosbeak.

Access

From Panama City take Gaillard Highway towards Miraflores Locks. Pass the entrance to the locks and continue beyond Paraíso. Go under a railway bridge and turn left, passing the main offices of Soberanía National Park on the right. Take the second right, after the entrance, to Summit Gardens and follow signs to Canopy Tower along Semaphore Hill Road.

Accommodation: for bookings, call 1-507-264-5720, or fax (in the US) 1-800-854-2597 (outside the US 1-507-263-2784). For information in the US or Canada, call Allen Hale at 1-800-722-2460, e-mail stay@canopytower.com.

MADDEN LAKE AND SUMMIT GARDENS

An area of forest just beyond the Continental Divide and easily accessible from Panama City and Colón. One of the best locations for the endemic Yellow-green Tyranulet; many other forest species such as Black Hawk-Eagle and Purple-throated Fruitcrow also occur.

Endemics
Yellow-green Tyrannulet.

Others
Boat-billed Heron, Black Hawk-Eagle, Grey-headed Chachalaca, Scaled Pigeon, Mealy Parrot, Snowy-bellied Hummingbird, Western Slaty Antshrike, White-bellied Antbird, Lance-tailed Manakin, Purple-throated Fruitcrow, Black-tailed Flycatcher, Rufous-and-white and Buff-breasted Wrens, Rosy Thrush-Tanager, Red-throated Ant-Tanager, Crimson-backed and Plain-coloured Tanagers, Red-legged Honeycreeper, Variable Seedeater, Thick-billed Seed-Finch, Streaked Saltator.

(Summit Gardens/Old Gamboa Road) Boat-billed and Capped Herons, Blue Ground-Dove, Great Jacamar, Great Antshrike, Jet Antbird, Yellow-olive, Yellow-margined and Bran-coloured Flycatchers, Yellow-bellied, Lesser, Forest and Greenish Elaenias, Pale-eyed Pygmy-Tyrant, Black-headed and Slate-headed Tody-Flycatchers, White-winged Becard, Rufous-capped Warbler, Rosy Thrush-Tanager.

Access
To reach Madden Lake head north along Gaillard Highway, passing the entrance to Fort Clayton (on the right), Pedro Miguel Locks and the town of Paraíso. Shortly beyond the golf course (on the right) you pass under a bridge. Keep right at the fork immediately beyond and access Madden Highway, one of the most beautiful paved roads near the city and one of the best places to get mugged while birdwatching. Leave the forest, passing the exit to a new highway on the right, pass under the Trans-Isthmian road (Colón to the left, Panama City on the right) and the town of Chilibre. Eventually Madden dam is reached; the road curves sharply left below the dam, and there is a parking area. Examine the trees here and overlook the lake. Birders have also been mugged in this parking lot, so be careful. The road continues for a few kilometres before joining the Trans-Isthmian road again.

Another interesting area is Summit Gardens/Old Gamboa Road. Go north on Gaillard Highway past Paraíso. With the golf course to your right, look for a small road that veers left just before a bus stop. This is the old road to Gamboa, a 4.4 km stretch of abandoned (and unpaved) road passing through a broad variety of habitats before joining the main road to Gamboa. Park at the golf course entrance, or preferably at Summit Gardens reached by staying on Gaillard Highway, then go under the railway bridge and turn left at the fork immediately beyond. About a km after the fork is the entrance to Summit Gardens on the right, with small parking lots either side of the road. Turn left at the entrance and cross the railway to a paved road that is Old Gamboa Road. Turn left to Summit Ponds, where Boat-billed Heron nests. The paved road to the right at the ponds goes to the Police Academy, but the best birding is along the blocked, unpaved road that extends in the same direction and eventually reaches the golf course.

A second interesting area is Summit Gardens. Go north on Highway 3 from Panama City and 7.2 km past the turn-off to Chiva Chiva there is a ruined building on the right. Opposite this is a broad track leading through patchy forest and grassland to a road by the Police Academy, with a couple of ponds at the junction. Alternatively take the Old Gamboa road to the left at 7.7 km past Chiva Chiva Road. The gardens (which are well worthwhile) are 1.5 km further along this road on the right. On the opposite side of the road from the gardens a turn-off leads (after crossing the railway) to the Police Academy road.

GAMBOA PIPELINE ROAD

A classic birdwatching location patronized by generations of birders and easily accessible from Panama City.

Others

Great Tinamou, King Vulture, Double-toothed Kite, White and Semi-plumbeous Hawks, Ornate and Black Hawk-Eagles, Great Curassow*, Pale-vented, Scaled and Short-billed Pigeons, Blue-headed, Red-lored and Mealy Parrots, Short-tailed Nightjar, White-necked Jacobin, Rufous-crested Coquette, Crowned Woodnymph, Sapphire-throated, Snowy-breasted and Violet-bellied Hummingbirds, Slaty-tailed, White-tailed, Violaceous and Black-throated Trogons, Broad-billed Motmot, Black-breasted, White-necked and Pied Puffbirds, Keel-billed and Chestnut-mandibled Toucans, Lineated, Black-cheeked and Cinnamon Woodpeckers, Long-tailed, Black-striped and Northern Barred Woodcreepers, Fasciated and Great Antshrikes, Spot-crowned Antvireo, White-flanked, Checker-throated and Dot-winged Antwrens, Chestnut-backed, Spotted

The Great Antshrike is a common inhabitant of forest-edge in the Canal Zone

and Ocellated Antbirds, Black-faced Antthrush, Purple-throated Fruit-crow, Blue Cotinga, Sirystes, White-ringed and Yellow-margined Flycat-chers, Southern Nightingale-Wren, Hooded and Mourning (both winter) Warblers, Shining Honeycreeper, Scarlet Dacnis, White-vented and Fulvous-vented Euphonias, Carmiol's, Tawny-crested, Sulphur-rumped, Dusky-faced, Golden-masked, Plain-coloured and Bay-headed Tanagers, Slate-coloured Grosbeak.

Access
Coming into Gamboa from the south, take a left turn (the main road goes right), immediately passing a line of buildings including a Guardia station. Shortly afterwards there is a large pond on the right (which is well worth examining, especially in the early morning, when White-throated Crake can be seen). The road curves right around the pond, up a hill, and then curves back left. The Pipeline Road leads off to the right at a point about 100–200 m past the pond and can be followed for about 17.5 km through excellent habitat. There is a gate, which may be locked; if it is, there is good habitat within walking distance, but ensure that your vehicle is secure. In some cases a day-permit may be required; also beware of the gate being locked behind you. There are several bridges of dubious negotiability and the road may be so heavily rutted as to require a high-clearance vehicle, especially after rain.

MIDDLE CHAGRES

An area easily accessible from Panama City that possesses a variety of habitats.

Endemics
Yellow-green Tyrannulet.

Specialities
Rufescent Tiger-Heron, Lesser Kiskadee, Orange-crowned Oriole (possibly introduced).

Others
Muscovy Duck, Amazon and American Pygmy Kingfishers, Northern Royal Flycatcher, Rufous-and-white and Rufous-breasted Wrens, Black-headed Saltator.

Access
Leave Panama City north on Highway 3 and 6.5 km beyond the turn to Madden Forest Reserve go right at Bodega Mario, reaching the Chilibre road within 200 m. Turn left and at 1.6 km take a paved road to the right (500 m short of Madden dam), then turn onto the Saddle dam road which passes through forest for several km and gives views over Lago Alajuela from a series of dams. If the gate to this road is locked you may still get access on foot.

Chagres River is interesting if you have a canoe. A good point to launch is Santa Rosa, accessible by turning south off Highway 3 at Gatuncillo. Within 2 km downstream of Santa Rosa there are small tributaries where American Pygmy and Amazon Kingfishers occur and marshy flats where Limpkin can be found. About 800 m further downstream the river widens to the Gamboa basin where reedbeds and shallows are good for ducks.

CERRO CAMPANA NATIONAL PARK

Panama's first National Park, located less than an hour's drive from Panama City. Its 4800 ha encompass Cerro Campana, which is a high bell-shaped peak, Cerro Trinidad, a three-peaked hill and the intervening foothills along the Continental Divide.

Others
White-tipped Sicklebill, Orange-bellied Trogon, Yellow-eared Toucanet, Plain Antvireo, Black-headed Antthrush, White-ruffed Manakin, Scale-crested Pygmy-Tyrant, White-throated Thrush, Silver-throated and Black-and-yellow Tanagers, Chestnut-capped Brush-Finch, Blue Seedeater, Wedge-tailed Grass-Finch.

Access
Go west out of Panama City on the Pan-American Highway and 6.3 km beyond the end of the autopista there is a gas station and Quesos Chela on the right. 4.9 km beyond this the road crests a hill and curves left. At the crest a road to the right (signed) leads to the National Park. If you reach Sajalices Motel you have gone 4.1 km too far.

After 4.1 km on the access road look for Wedge-tailed Grass-Finch. At 8.1 km there is a sharp right; it is possible to walk to the summit of Cerro Campana from this point. Otherwise stay on the road, passing Finca Las Estrellas on the left; at 8.9 km there is a sign for the administrative offices and a road to the right which leads into forest. This road forks in a further 200 m, the right fork accessing more forest. This area should be covered on foot.

EL COPE

A good area of mid-altitude habitat, which has some of the Chiriquí highland specialties as well as many foothill species. A high-clearance vehicle is required.

Specialities
White-tailed Sicklebill, Snowcap, Bare-necked Umbrellabird*, White-throated Shrike-Tanager.

Others
Barred Hawk, Purplish-backed Quail-Dove, Striped Owl, Tropical Screech-Owl, Red-fronted Parrotlet*, Brown Violet-ear, Green Thorntail, Green-crowned Brilliant, Purple-throated Mountain-gem, Orange-bellied Trogon, Red-headed Barbet, Yellow-eared and Emerald Toucanets, Golden-olive Woodpecker, Spotted Barbtail, Immaculate and Dull-mantled Antbirds, Russet Antshrike, Black-crowned Antpitta, White-throated Spadebill, Tufted and Slaty-capped Flycatchers, Three-wattled Bellbird*,

Stripe-breasted Wren, White-throated and Pale-vented Thrushes, Black-faced Solitaire, Buff-rumped Warbler, Golden-browed Chlorophonia, Blue-and-gold Tanager*, Yellow-throated Bush-Tanager, Crimson-collared Tanager, Black-thighed and Black-faced Grosbeaks. In the dry lowlands: White-tailed Hawk, Aplomado Falcon, Crested Bobwhite, Mouse-coloured Tyrannulet.

Other Wildlife
Tapir.

Access
Drive west along the Pan-American Highway from Penomoné. At 19 km, turn right onto a paved road posted 'El Cope 28 km' (about 1 km east of Río Grande bridge). Roadside scrub on the way to El Cope has Aplomado Falcon and Crested Bobwhite. Turn right on a gravel road just before El Cope. After 3 km there is a dirt track on the left, which leads to Cerro Peña Blanca. The track fords a river and comes to footbridges over the Ríos Colorado and Blanco. The trail continues through cut over land before reaching forest, but there are numerous side trails so it is best to ask directions and take care not to get lost in the forest. Higher altitudes hold western highland species such as Red-headed Barbet.

If you do not take the left-hand dirt track, the gravel road leads within 400 m to the Barrigón school clearing, and in a further 4 km (not suitable for low-clearance vehicles) to a disused sawmill on the Continental Divide, at 715 m altitude. The forest from this point on offers good birding; a trail on the right (on the Atlantic slope) has Snowcap.

Accommodation and food are available in Penomoné and, more basic, in El Cope.

CIÉNAGA LAS MACANAS

A large shallow lake, the remnants of the much larger Santa María marshes, now largely drained.

Others
Aplomado Falcon, Pearl Kite, Ferruginous Pygmy-Owl, Mangrove Cuckoo, ducks (especially during winter).

Access
Turn south off the Pan-American Highway at Divisa (about 20 km east of Santiago) onto Highway 2 towards Chitré. Pass through Santa María and 7.3 km from Divisa turn left onto a paved road to El Rincón. After 2.1 km pass the church, bear right on the paved road and fork right after 200 m at the Correguduria. After 1.3 km fork left, and after another 1.4 km turn left at a T-junction. After a further 1.4 km there is a place to park and an overgrown track on the left. Walk this track (muddy in rainy season), which passes through good bushy habitat.

A further 500 m beyond the track another rough road ends, after about 200 m, at the ciénaga. Returning to the road and proceeding a further 3 km brings you to a cattle loading station where the road ends. The Río Santa María is a short walk through the fields; keep an eye out for bulls.

LAS SALINAS DE CHITRÉ

An area of salt flats which has good shorebird habitat.

Specialities
Yellowish Pipit.

Others
Roseate Spoonbill, American Oystercatcher, numerous other shorebirds and gulls, Common Ground-Dove, Mouse-coloured Tyrannulet, Northern Scrub Flycatcher.

Access
Enter Chitré from the north, turn left on Avenida Herrera by the cathedral and continue 2.8 km to the airport. Yellowish Pipit occurs in the grass between the parking lot and the runway. Fork left 700 m beyond the airport and go 1.9 km to Agallito beach. Drive beyond the beach houses (to avoid the dogs) along a track that peters out and becomes a trail paralleling the mangroves. There are salt flats at the end of the paved road. On the road between the airstrip and Agallito beach there is an arch across the road; immediately before this is a dirt track, passable only when dry, which after 2–3 km joins the road to Retén Beach, which is good for shorebirds depending on the tide.

CERRO HOYA

A remote area at the southwest end of the Azuero Peninsula, which is relatively rarely visited and undoubtedly capable of producing some surprises. A recently described race of Painted Parakeet (sometimes regarded as a full species under the name Azuero Parakeet *Pyrrhura eisenmanni*) was discovered here.

Specialities
Painted Parakeet, Great Green Macaw*.

Others
King Vulture, White Hawk, Crested Guan, Brown-hooded Parrot, Spectacled, Mottled and Black-and-white Owls, Blue-throated Goldentail, Black-hooded Antshrike, Mountain Elaenia, Pale-eyed Pygmy-Tyrant, White-winged Becard, Three-wattled Bellbird*, Orange-billed Nightingale-Thrush, Rosy Thrush-Tanager.

Access
Not easy. By road from Panama City, turn south (probably best via Chitré and Las Tablas, but enquire locally about most recent conditions) to Cambutal at the southern tip of the peninsula. In Cambutal it may be possible to make arrangements to hire a boat to the small village of Cobachón. The only alternative from Cambutal is a long walk or horseback ride. Around Cobachón there is some remnant xeric forest. From Cobachón, a trail (local guides are available in the village) climbs to a location known as Cascajillaso, at about 650 m, where it is possible to camp; all water must be carried in. Above 650 m there are magnifi-

cent tall oak forests, on steep and rather difficult-to-access slopes. The best habitat appears to be the highest.

Access is also possible from the west side of the Azuero Peninsula by turning south off the Pan-American Highway, about 5 km east of Santiago, through Atalaya and driving south to Punta Restingue.

EL MONTUOSO DE CHEPO

An area of original forest readily accessible from the Pan-American Highway, preserved as an INRENARE reserve, with good trails.

Endemics
Brown-backed Dove*.

Others
Green Thorntail, Slaty Antwren, Orange-collared Manakin, Northern Royal Flycatcher, Black-throated Green (winter) and Golden-crowned Warblers.

Access
From the town of Las Minas, which can be accessed either from the Pan-American Highway, by turning south about 20 km east of Santiago (a few km west of the junction of the Pan-American and Highway 2) to Chitré at Divisa, or from Chitré itself.

At the opposite end of the Las Minas plaza from the church turn left and then turn right, onto a gravel road, at the first opportunity. After 17.5 km there is a church in the scattered settlement of Chepo. The road follows a ridge, parallel to the Montuoso and separated from it by a shallow, narrow valley. There are two access points: 1.5 km past the church there is a steep downhill road through pines to the school, where a vehicle may be left. Walk down to and ford the stream, then climb uphill through the forest. The second is by a large boulder with pre-Columbian stylistic designs, known locally as 'Caras Pintadas'. Continue on the same road 800 m beyond the school turn-off and turn left onto a narrow trail leading to an adobe house. The trail continues to the left of the house and enters disturbed woodland and, thereafter, good forest.

The area is an IRENARE reserve; it would be courteous to stop at the Vivero Florestal in Chepo to ask permission to enter.

SANTE FÉ

An interesting area of upland with some productive remnant forest where several rare species have been recorded recently, including Rufous-winged Woodpecker, which previously had not been recorded in Panama since 1920.

Endemics
Glow-throated Hummingbird* (perhaps only formerly).

Specialities
Solitary Eagle, Black-breasted Wood-Quail, Purplish-backed Quail-Dove, Snowcap, Lanceolated Monklet, Sharpbill, White-throated Shrike-Tanager.

Others
Harris' Hawk, Orange-breasted Falcon, Black Guan*, Sunbittern, Great Horned Owl, Yellow-eared Toucanet, Red-faced Spinetail, Spotted Barbtail, Immaculate Antbird, Scaled Antpitta, Slaty-capped Flycatcher, Scale-crested Pygmy-Tyrant, Eye-ringed Flatbill, Black-and-white Becard, Three-wattled Bellbird*, Black-chested Jay, White-breasted Wood Wren, Bay Wren, Black-faced Solitaire, Orange-billed and Slaty-backed Nightingale-Thrushes, Golden-crowned, Buff-rumped, Three-striped, Golden-winged (winter), Chestnut-sided (winter), Blackburnian (winter) and Bay-breasted (winter) Warblers, Silver-throated Tanager, Red-crowned and Red-throated Ant-Tanagers, Rosy Thrush-Tanager, Yellow-throated Bush-Tanager, Scarlet-rumped Cacique.

Access
Turn north onto a paved highway off the Pan-American Highway in Santiago, 1.1 km west of the Piramides Hotel/restaurant/gas station. If you pass below a white footbridge you have gone too far. Continue north to San Francisco (17 km), staying left at the police station at the entrance to the town (17.1 km). Pass through San Juan (26 km) and San José (33 km) to Santa Fé (56 km). Keep left upon entering town and about 500 m beyond a school on the right take the left fork to Altos de Piedra.

Approximately 4.4 km past Santa Fé there is the Altos de Piedra school on the right; 500 m beyond this a road goes off to the right, which passes through good second growth, and 500 m along this road on the right is a trail by a stream to a water catchment where Sunbittern has been seen. After another 200 m there is a parking area adjacent to a fenced-off meadow where Three-wattled Bellbird* and Crimson-collared Tanager occur. The road beyond the parking spot is worth walking; it is here that Rufous-winged Woodpecker has been seen.

From this point, via a confusing series of paths, it is possible to reach Cerro Tute (990 m), a location for Glow-throated Hummingbird* (at least formerly; we are unaware of any recent records). Starting at the left fork, the track becomes impassable to vehicles after about 1.5 km so take the track to the right, which crosses a stream, and keep straight for several hundred metres until you reach a dirt road; turn right onto this, and after about 1 km through pasture take a track on the right (through a gate), which leads to an abandoned bus. Just before the bus a narrow trail leads through orange groves to the summit of Cerro Tute. From the end of the passable road to the summit is about 5 km. Note that the land is private and permission (and, usefully, directions) should be asked for.

If instead of taking the left fork past the school you go right, within 400 m there is an abarroteria on the left where a vehicle may be safely left. A trail leads off here, starting through an orchard and then entering forest; as it does so it forks, following the contour line left and right. The left-hand trail leads to another trail, which continues for about 5 km and climbs from about 800 m to 1250 m. A branch trail goes to the left along a ridge before descending to the road. Species seen along here include Snowcap, Immaculate Antbird, both ant-tanagers, Slaty-capped Flycatcher, Eye-ringed Flatbill, Golden-crowned Warbler, Crimson-collared

Tanager, Yellow-throated Bush-Tanager and Yellow-eared Toucanet. Higher are Black Guan*, Black-faced Solitaire, Slaty-backed Nightingale-Thrush and Three-striped Warbler.

There is no problem with the road as far as Santa Fé; beyond this 4WD may be useful.

CERRO COLORADO

An interesting highland area which offers an alternative to some of the better known areas further west.

Endemics
Glow-throated Hummingbird*, Yellow-green Finch*.

Others
Fork-tailed Emerald, Black-bellied and Snowy-breasted Hummingbirds, Ruddy Treerunner, Silvery-fronted Tapaculo, Black-faced Solitaire, Black-and-yellow Silky-Flycatcher, Flame-throated, Golden-winged (winter) and Black-throated Green (winter) Warblers, Collared Redstart, Spangle-cheeked Tanager, Common and Sooty-capped Bush-Tanagers, Scarlet-thighed Dacnis, Slaty Flowerpiercer, Black-thighed Grosbeak.

Access
Turn north off the Pan-American Highway at San Felix (116 km west of Santiago and 74 km east of David). There is a gas station and restaurant at the intersection, and a hotel (Hotel Castillo) just west of San Felix. Nine km from the Pan-American is a bridge with gate and guard post where you may have to register; apparently no advance permit is required. Fork right at km 27 by some houses (Hato Chami). Beyond this the road leads to some good remnant habitat, although much has been destroyed. Yellow-green Finch* has been seen along a flatter stretch of the road just before a radio mast. The road is now in very poor condition, requiring 4WD. In the rainy season it can be very difficult. It may be best to hire the local four-wheel-drive truck whose driver knows the road very well.

FORTUNA FOREST RESERVE

A large (100 km²) area of forest, which has been protected to preserve the integrity of the watershed around the Fortuna reservoir and hydro-electric plant.

Access
The area is accessed via the Trans-Isthmian road, which runs from Chiriquí to Chiriquí Grande on the Caribbean coast. Turn right in the village of Chiriquí, which is on the Pan-American Highway 12 km east of David. After 16.8 km, you pass Gualaca, which is the last chance for petrol. At 33.2 km pass a road on the left to Los Planes and at 37 km there is a gravel road to Chiriquícito. Continue uphill on the paved road and, after 300 m, there is a sign indicating the boundary of the reserve.

One km past this, on the right, is Finca La Suiza where with ten days' advance notice accommodation can be arranged (fax to MONHE, S. A., c/o TRANSPORTES FERGUSON, David, 75-0113.). There is very good birding around the Lodge itself: Orange-billed Nightingale-Thrush, Blue-hooded Euphonia, Flame-coloured Tanager and Acorn Woodpecker are common, as well as several species of hummingbird.

There are several good sites in the general area.

Hillsides south of the watershed There is a trail to Cerro Pata de Macho (2000 m) accessed: (i) via the driveway into Finca La Suiza, about 100 m before the lodge; (ii) from the paved road 7.5 km beyond Los Planes (where the road makes a sharp curve to the left, with a gravel parking area on the right); or (iii) 9.2 km from Los Planes, where it is possible to descend a steep bank to the river, cross a footbridge and climb the opposite ridge to the trail. The two latter access points may be overgrown and it is best to stop at the IRHE office in Los Planes for recent information. Species recorded include Black Guan*, Chiriqui Quail-Dove, Violet Sabrewing, Prong-billed and Red-headed Barbets, Lineated Foliage-gleaner, Azure-hooded Jay and White-throated Spadebill.

The watershed The road through the watershed accesses good forest, especially where streams cross the road. A bridge crosses the reservoir; 1.2 km beyond here a gravel road goes sharp left off the paved road. Bare-necked Umbrellabird* has been seen here, as well as Lattice-tailed Trogon, Ruddy Foliage-gleaner and Black-and-white Becard.

The Continental Divide Road 5.6 km north of the road mentioned above, just beyond Quebrada Arena and before a guard shack, turn left onto a gravel road and descend to the creek. Do not take the creek but turn back to the right. The Continental Divide trail leaves the road to the left, as the road turns sharp right, between two hills. The trail ascends a 6 m-high bank before entering the forest. It is frequently very muddy. Species seen along here include Black Guan*, Black-bellied Hummingbird, Rufous-breasted Antthrush, Silvery-fronted Tapaculo, Bare-necked Umbrellabird*, Azure-hooded Jay, Black-and-yellow Silky-Flycatcher, Slaty-backed Nightingale-Thrush, Wrenthrush and Sooty-faced Finch.

'Espinilla's Place' This abandoned finca at the end of the Continental Divide Road, 4.6 km from its start, is a good place for soaring raptors, including Barred Hawk, Great Black Hawk and Ornate Hawk-Eagle. The roadside woodland here holds White-bellied Mountain-gem, Rufous-browed Tyrannulet, White-crowned Manakin, Pale-vented Thrush, Spangle-cheeked and Blue-and-gold* Tanagers, while Grey-breasted Crake occurs in the roadside grass.

Accommodation: if it is not possible to stay at Finca La Suiza, or this does not suit your budget, there is a wide variety of accommodation in David (air conditioning almost essential). Chiriquí Grande is not picturesque but has a number of reasonable hotels.

BOCAS DEL TORO

The most northwesterly province, holding many species typical of the Caribbean lowlands of eastern Costa Rica. Note that rainfall here is much heavier than on the Pacific slope, and can occur at any time of year.

Specialities
Ashy-throated Bush-Tanager.

Others
Green Ibis, Ornate and Black Hawk-Eagles, White-collared Swift, Bronzy Hermit, Long-billed Starthroat, Chestnut-coloured and Pale-billed Woodpeckers, Lovely and Snowy Cotingas, Torrent Tyrannulet, Brown Jay, Band-backed, Stripe-breasted and Black-throated Wrens, Black-headed Nightingale-Thrush, Buff-rumped Warbler, Olive-crowned Yellowthroat, Olive-backed Euphonia, Crimson-collared Tanager, White-collared Seedeater, Montezuma Oropendola.

Access
The town of Chiriquí Grande lies at the northern end of the Trans-Isthmian road. Proceed north from the town of Chiriquí, which is about 12 km east of David (for sections on the Pacific drainage see the Western Chiriquí Highlands). With the exception of Finca La Suiza, there is nowhere to stay except in Chiriquí Grande, which has several reasonable hotels and restaurants. As an early start is essential, it is assumed that Chiriquí Grande is used as a base. Several profitable birding locations are accessible from the latter, along the road leading south to Chiriquí and the Pan-American Highway.

Chiriquí Grande Marshes The road between Chiriquí Grande and Rambala passes through flat marshy country with cattle pasture. Species seen along this road include Bronzy Hermit (*Heliconia* patches), Olive-crowned Yellowthroat and Montezuma Oropendola.

Two Tanks Road About 5 km from Chiriquí Grande two storage tanks are visible on a wooded hillside to the east. The access road forks after 400 m. After about 2 km the right fork offers an overview of Chiriquí Lagoon. The left fork, after about 2.3 km, reaches a locked barrier and about 50 m beyond here is a dyke encircling a marsh. Green Ibis occurs here, as well as Chestnut-coloured and Pale-billed Woodpeckers, Lovely Cotinga, Band-backed Wren, Olive-backed Euphonia and Crimson-collared Tanager.

Rambala Road This road, east of the airstrip, continues for several km, ascending gently. Species seen are similar to those on Two Tanks Road.

Guarumo River Bridge Approximately 20 km from Chiriquí Grande. Beyond the bridge the road climbs slowly. Snowy Cotinga has been seen along here.

Trema Forest 8.5 km beyond Guarumo River Bridge the road enters an area of second growth with berry trees.

Natural Bridge Ten km from Guarumo River Bridge the road crosses a stream. Walk along this to a natural bridge and waterfall. White-collared Swift nests under the waterfall; Torrent Tyrannulet and Buff-rumped Warbler also occur.

Further along the road, stop wherever forest remains. About 2 km past the Natural Bridge there is a driveway to the right. The altitude here is about 800 m. Black-headed Nightingale-Thrush and Ornate Hawk-Eagle occur, and 2.8 km beyond here is the Continental Divide, at about 1050 m. Six km below the Continental Divide, towards Chiriquí Grande, is the Willie Mazu Ecological Ranch, which has a camping site. Details can be obtained via the web page: www-natur.com.

BOQUETE

A pleasant small town in the foothills, at an altitude of about 1000 m, which gives access to several excellent areas for higher altitude species.

Access

Turn right (north) off the Pan-American Highway 438 km from Panama City at a four-way traffic light on the eastern edge of David. Continue for 40 km to the plaza in central Boquete, having taken a right fork about 15 km north of David. Boquete essentially has three main attractions.

Lower areas near the town hold some foothill species such as Blue-hooded Euphonia. Across the road from the fairground, which is on the left side of the road immediately after the bridge, are some woods. Two roads go right beyond the fairground, one to Alto Jaramillo and the other to Palo Alto. Although most forest along these roads has been destroyed, the remnants can be worthwhile.

Finca Lerida, approximately 15 km northwest of Boquete, lies at 1600–2100 m. It is a beautiful area of upland forest preserved by the owners, Fritz and Inga Collins, who also own one of the better hotels in Boquete, the Panamonte, and from whom permission to visit should be sought. 4WD is necessary to reach the Finca. Apart from quetzals, Silvery-fronted Tapaculo, Prong-billed Barbet and several species of highland furnariids can be found. 4WD vehicles can be hired in David.

The third area is **Volcán Barú**, which is accessible via a steep road to the radio towers. To find this road to the summit turn left on the second street beyond the junction of Avenidas Fundadores and A Este (Calle 2a N). If you see a sign to the Panamonte you have gone one block too far north. A paved road goes west out of town, at 7.5 km fork left (the right fork goes to Finca Lerida). Keep straight on the gravel road, ignoring the paved road to the left 600 m beyond the Finca Lerida turn-off. This road reaches to over 3400 m, the National Park boundary being at about 1750 m. At the boundary there is a checkpoint where a permit may be required. This must be obtained in person at the INRENARE office, then at the PDF headquarters located on Avenida 3 de Nov. en route to David airport. These keep government office hours. The road to the summit passes through a great variety of forest types, from oak to bamboo, with elfin forest and high-altitude brush near the top. The upper levels are the only location in Panama for Volcano Junco and Timberline Wren; other species found here are Black Guan*, Black-and-yellow Silky Flycatcher and Slaty Flowerpiercer while Peg-billed Finch, formerly considered a Costa Rican endemic, has also recently been seen here. Although the road is in good condition, some parts are very steep and may require a vehicle with a low-gear range. The steepest sections are above about 2500 m, which still gives access to much good habitat should you have a suitable vehicle.

Accommodation: there are several pleasant and reasonable hotels, and restaurants, in Boquete.

WESTERN CHIRIQUÍ HIGHLANDS

The highest area in Panama, where the Cordillera de Talamanca enters from Costa Rica, bringing with it many highland specialties and shared endemics. A large portion of the area is now protected as part of the cross-border La Amistad National Park and Volcán Barú National Park. There are several access points, which are dealt with individually below.

Specialities
Black Guan*, Resplendent Quetzal*, Timberline Wren, Black-and-yellow and Long-tailed Silky-Flycatchers, Wrenthrush, Yellow-winged Vireo, Volcano Junco.

Others
Scintillant and Volcano Hummingbirds, Prong-billed Barbet, Ochraceous Wren, Black-billed Nightingale-Thrush, Sooty Robin, Slaty Flowerpiercer, Black-cheeked Warbler, Yellow-thighed Finch, Large-footed Sparrow.

Other Wildlife
Jaguar, Tapir.

Access
David is about 450 km west of Panama City on the Pan-American Highway: 25 km west of David turn right in the town of Concepción at signs for the Bambito Hotel, and 23 km from the Pan-American the road reaches the Guardia station at Volcán. There are several possibilities at this point.

The road to the Boquete trail and Volcán Barú Turn right at the Guardia station, passing the Hotel Bambito after 6.6 km and Audubon Cabin at 11.3 km. Head through Cerro Punta; after crossing a small bridge the road makes a gentle right. The paved road finishes at the park boundary. With 4WD it is possible to reach a further 2.4 km and a ridge at about 2500 m. The best birding is along this road and trails leading off it. This is a favoured location for quetzals. Before the Hotel Bambito are some coffee plantations; these and the hotel surrounds can be worthwhile. 200 m after the Audubon Cabin a dirt road to the left parallels the river; this is a good location for American Dipper and Torrent Tyrannulet. Further along here is some bamboo, which has produced Blue Seedeater. 900 m beyond the cabin another dirt road to the left reaches the river, ending in a church camp. This road and the camp surrounds can be rewarding. There are cabins within good habitat at Los Quetzales, which is reached by following the road from Volcán through Cerro Punta and the Haras horse farm, and forking left after a small bridge to the small town of Guadalupe. Go right in the town and look for the sign to Los Quetzales. Telephone 771-2182, fax 771-2226.

Volcán Lagunas Take the left-hand turn at the Guardia station in Volcán towards Río Sereno. Turn left on the fifth street (Calle el Valle), marked by a sign for Volcán Airport (Pista). Turn right at another 'Pista' sign, turn left one block later and fork left after a further 300 m (the right fork goes to the airport). The Lagunas are 2.5 km down a rough road. This road passes through good woodland; take the second fork on the left.

Road to Río Sereno Take the left turn at the Guardia station and continue past Calle el Valle. On the left is the Dos Ríos Hotel; the Costa Rican border is another 38 km along this road. 20.4 km past the Dos Ríos, the Santa Clara woods road leads off to the left, leaving the Río Sereno road at 1200 m and descending, over 1.5 km, to 1050 m, with access to good forest. 3.5 km beyond the Santa Clara woods road is a side road on the right. Beyond the last house a gravel road leads within 1.1 km to the finca of Rativor Hartmann. Here you should ask permission to visit the forest of Ojo de Agua, at 1500 m. This has White-crested Coquette, Fiery-billed Araçari and Smoky-brown Woodpecker.

The National Park office (Amisconde) in Cerro Punta (tel. 771-2171), open Mondays to Fridays 8am–5pm, is a good source of detailed and recent information on trails within the park.

CHANGUINOLA

An area of extreme northwestern Panama that is more readily accessible from Costa Rica but it is possible to fly to Changuinola from Panama City. The area makes a good location to find many of the western lowland Panama specialties.

Accessible by road from Costa Rica via Limón, and by air from Panama City, it is now also possible to drive to Changuinola, via Almirante, from Chiriquí Grande; apparently the birding is quite good in the remnant forest along the road. Cars can be hired in Changuinola (Bocas Rent-a-Car and Ramiro Car Rental). There is public transport from Almirante in the form of a bus with a picture of Jesus which illuminates when the brakes are applied. No further comment is required.

Specialities
Paint-billed Crake, Bare-crowned Antbird, Canebrake and Black-throated Wrens, Almirante (Golden-collared) Manakin.

Others
Red-billed Tropicbird, Brown Booby, White-crowned Pigeon, Crimson-fronted and Olive-throated Parakeets, White-crowned Parrot, Grey-rumped Swift, Rufous-tailed Jacamar, Northern Bentbill, White-collared Manakin, Band-backed Wren, Olive-crowned Yellowthroat, Olive-backed Euphonia, White-collared Seedeater, Black-cowled Oriole, Montezuma Oropendola.

Access
There are three worthwhile areas near the town and an offshore island.

Rice fields Take a dirt road that leaves, at right angles, the road skirting the golf course. This passes through banana plantations. Take two left turns and one right, leading to a road which ultimately forks, one fork returning to Changuinola and the other going to Guabito. Beside this road is an A frame near a bridge. A minor road leads to the left, where Paint-billed Crake is most easily seen just before dusk. Canebrake Wren also occurs here.

Fairground woods Head past the fairgrounds to a marshy area and take a trail through woodland opposite this. Species here include Band-backed and Black-throated Wrens, Bare-crowned Antbird and Olive-backed Euphonia.

Almirante Road Cross the Río Changuinola towards Almirante, which is about 20 km away. Stop wherever you find good habitat. Species seen along here include White-crowned Parrot, Rufous-tailed Jacamar, Snowy Cotinga, Almirante (Golden-collared) Manakin and Northern Bentbill.

Swan Key Boats can be found by enquiring at the Hotel Carol, and pass through interesting areas of the Río Changuinola and canals before crossing the Boca del Drago. Red-billed Tropicbird and Brown Booby nest from September onwards on the key. White-crowned Pigeon also occurs here and on Isla Colón.

Accommodation in Changuinola includes the Hotel Carol (with some truly remarkable circular beds, don't ask questions) and the more expensive Chale Suizo Suites. There are several places to eat in Changuinola. There is very good scuba diving in the area.

EL CHOROGO

An area of the Burica Peninsula, which is divided between Costa Rica and Panama and supports a number of specialties. Rarely visited, it is certainly capable of harbouring surprises.

Specialities
Fiery-billed Araçari, Yellow-billed Cotinga*, White-throated Shrike-Tanager.

Others
Laughing Falcon, Great Curassow*, Blue-throated Goldentail, Blue-chested and Violet-headed Hummingbirds, Baird's Trogon*, Golden-naped and Pale-billed Woodpeckers, Tawny-winged Woodcreeper, Slaty Antwren, Black-hooded Antshrike, White-ruffed Manakin, Three-wattled Bellbird*, Rose-throated Becard, Northern Bentbill, Riverside Wren, Spot-crowned Euphonia.

Quite common in parts of Panama, the elegant White-ruffed Manakin is found in foothills forest

Access

4WD is essential; even with such a vehicle the road is usually passable only at the end of the dry season (around Easter). It's best to enquire about current conditions at AFFABA (a local non-governmental organisation) at Puerto Armuelles, or at the Audubon office in Panama City. Leave the Pan-American Highway just before the Costa Rican border, at Paso Canoa, by taking a sharp left (south) towards Puerto Armuelles (34 km via a paved road). Approximately 3 km before entering Puerto Armuelles cross the Río San Bartolo and about 2 km beyond this bridge, before entering Puerto Armuelles proper, is a large schoolhouse. Turn sharply right immediately past the school, from which distances are quoted. At 4.1 km the road crosses a river via a railway bridge; bear left off the tracks at 4.3 km and continue to bear left at a blue house, leaving the tracks. At 4.8 km keep left, at 5.1 km keep right, going uphill, at 5.3 km sharp left, and at 5.9 km left again. Ford the river at km 6.8; for the next 8 km there are many fords. After about 15 km the road begins to climb for about 6 km further. Bear right at 17.1 km and pass a schoolhouse at km 19. At km 20.4 there is a barbed-wire gate and at km 21 the road forks, shortly afterwards becoming impassable. Take the left fork and walk about 2 km through cattle pasture, initially downhill then climbing steeply to the crest of the hill. The forest starts near the crest of the next ridge (which is the Costa Rican border). By keeping on the road you enter the forest; the road ultimately levels off. The border between Panama and Costa Rica is marked by a well-maintained trail with concrete markers; it climbs to about 690 m and can be followed for several km through good forest (much more virgin on the Costa Rican side).

Accommodation and food are available in Puerto Armuelles; otherwise all food and water must be brought in. With permission from local farmers, there are many places to camp.

ISLA COIBA

A large island off the south coast of Panama, which until recently was largely inaccessible to the general public as it was the site of a penal colony that ironically had the effect of preserving much of the island from deforestation. It is the only site for the endemic Coiba Spinetail* and a good area for the Panama endemic Brown-backed Dove*.

Access

The Autoridad Nacional del Ambiente (ANAM) maintains a field station on the island. At the time of writing they are constructing a web site with information for potential visitors at www.anam.gob.pa which should be consulted for current details.

ISLA ESCUDO DE VERAGUAS

A small, very beautiful and rarely visited island off the north coast of Bocas del Toro, which is the only location for the endemic 'Escudo'

Hummingbird*, a potential future 'split' from Rufous-tailed Hummingbird, as well as an endemic race of the Bay Wren.

Access
Requires time and some money. It is possible to hire a boat in the town
of Bocas del Toro. Recommended is Jeff Smith (tel. 626-7182), whose
first language is Ngöbe, was born in Cricamola and is thoroughly experienced in the area. The trip from Bocas takes about 2.5 hours at about
20 knots and costs $300 for a day; his boat comfortably accommodates
eight passengers to split costs. Only about two families permanently live
on the island, though some temporary residents fish there. The hummingbird is readily found feeding on Noni flowers planted in the understorey near beaches. Other species include nesting Brown Boobies on
the islets at the north end of the main island, while White-crowned
Pigeon is resident. During a visit in mid-May, migrant warblers, a Grey-
cheeked Thrush, Black Terns and an Audubon's Shearwater were also
seen. A day trip permits little time for exploration, but Jeff will transport
people who wish to stay for several days; obviously a price should be
negotiated beforehand. There are several trails leading into forest worthy of extended attention. Those staying on the island would need to
camp and bring all supplies including drinking water. In addition to
birds, superb tropical fish are readily seen in the tiny channels among
the islets at the north end.

ADDITIONAL INFORMATION

Addresses
Panama Audubon Society, Box 2026, Balboa, Republic of Panama. Tel.
(507) 224-9371, fax.224-4740, e-mail audubon@pananet.com; web
pages www.pananet.com/audubon/ and www.panamaaudubon.com.
The society publishes a regular newsletter, El Tucán, which includes
details of recent bird sightings.
Darién Montañez maintains a rare bird alert web page at www.geocities.
com/xenornis.

Books
A Guide to the Birds of Panama, Ridgely, R. S. and Gwynne, J. A. Second edition 1995. Princeton UP. (An excellent field guide.)
The Birds of the Republic of Panama, Wetmore, A. 1965–1984. Four volumes, Smithsonian Institution Press, Washington DC. (A comprehensive handbook, but not a field guide.)

PANAMA ENDEMICS (9)

Brown-backed Dove*	Pacific slope from south Veraguas to western Herrera; Isla Coiba
Veraguan Mango	Chiriquí to south Coclé
Glow-throated Hummingbird*	Highlands of eastern Chiriquí
Stripe-cheeked Woodpecker	Veraguas east to Darién
Coiba Spinetail*	Isla Coiba
Beautiful Treerunner*	Highlands of eastern Darién
Yellow-green Tyrannulet	Canal zone to western Darién
Pirre Bush-Tanager	Foothills and highlands of eastern

	Darién
Yellow-green Finch*	Western Panama, from eastern Chiriquí to Veraguas

NEAR-ENDEMICS

For near-endemics shared by Costa Rica, see that country account. All of the species listed below also occur in adjacent Colombia.

Cinnamon-tailed Sparrow*	Eastern Darién
Tacarcuna Wood-Quail*	Eastern Panama province to Darién
Russet-crowned Quail-Dove*	Colón province to Darién
Violet-capped Hummingbird	Eastern Darién
Pirre Hummingbird*	Lowlands of eastern Darién
Dusky-backed Jacamar	Panamá and Darién provinces
Black Antshrike	San Blas and Darién
Speckled Antshrike*	Highlands of eastern Darién
Pale-throated Tapaculo*	Eastern Darién
Choco Tapaculo	Foothills of eastern Darién
Black-billed Flycatcher*	Lowlands and foothills of eastern Panamá and Darién
Varied Solitaire	Highlands of eastern Darién
Pirre Warbler*	Cerro Pirre and Cerro Tacarcuna, Darién
Viridian Dacnis*	Darién
Green-naped Tanager*	Highlands of eastern Darién
Tacarcuna Bush-Tanager	Panamá province to Darién

Specific status has been proposed for the following forms, but these are currently not recognised as species: Azuero (Painted) Parakeet *Pyrrhura (picta) eisenmanni* (Cerro Hoya) and Escudo* (Rufous-tailed) Hummingbird *Amazilia (tzacatl) handleyi* (Isla Escudo de Veraguas).

ANGUILLA

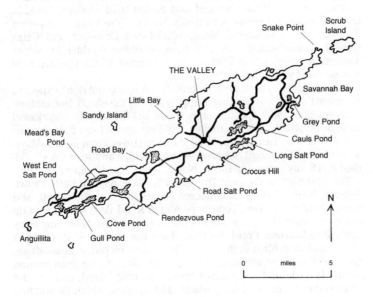

This small, low-lying Leeward Island, in the northern Lesser Antilles, is a great place to look for seabirds, especially in April–May. There are few landbirds but these do include two hummingbirds endemic to the Caribbean.

Anguilla is 25 km long and up to 5 km wide, and covers 91 km². It is accessible via local air services, mainly from St.-Martin, and the airport is close to the capital of this UK Dependent Territory, The Valley, which is in the centre of the island. It is possible to get around using taxis, though these may work out as expensive as hiring a jeep. There is a regular ferry service to St.-Martin (p. 393), which is just 8 km away. Accommodation is mostly restricted to small and expensive hotels and resorts, but there are also some apartments, guesthouses and villas. Low season prices apply in May–November. The official language is English and this is one of the friendliest and safest islands in the Caribbean. The best time to visit is in April–May when the seabirds are breeding. Most rain falls in September–December, usually during early morning.

Anguilla is a low-lying raised coral reef that reaches just 65 m at Crocus Hill. About one-third is bare rock, but inland there are also some corn and pea fields, worn pastures, gardens, areas of low scrub and salt ponds. Lovely white beaches adorn the coastline and there are also some shallow bays and fishing harbours with beds of seagrass. No threatened or near-threatened species are present on the island, though Bridled Quail-Dove has been recorded in the past and due to severe development pressure there is an urgent need for more protected areas and new legislation if the island's birdlife is to remain intact.

No species are endemic to Anguilla and only three of the 51 endemic Caribbean species, not confined to single countries, islands or archipelagos, occur. They are Green-throated Carib, Antillean Crested Hummingbird and Lesser Antillean Bullfinch. Half of the 18 Caribbean near-endemics occur: White-crowned and Scaly-naped Pigeons, Zenaida Dove, Caribbean Elaenia, Caribbean Martin (Feb–Aug), Pearly-eyed Thrasher, Black-whiskered Vireo, Black-faced Grassquit and Carib Grackle. In addition, the *petechia* group of Yellow Warbler, known as 'Golden Warbler', which is also almost endemic to the Caribbean, is represented by the *bartholemica* race.

Over 130 species have been recorded on Anguilla but don't expect to see more than 40, even during a lengthy stay on the island. Non-endemic specialities and spectacular species not previously mentioned include Red-billed (breeds mainly Jan–Jun) and White-tailed (breeds mainly Mar–Jul) Tropicbirds, Masked Booby (breeds mainly Mar–May), Magnificent Frigatebird, White-cheeked Pintail, Caribbean Coot*, Bridled and Sooty Terns, and Brown Noddy (terns breed mainly Apr–Aug).

The best birding site near The Valley is **Little Bay**. Look for Brown Pelican, Brown Booby, Magnificent Frigatebird, Laughing Gull, and Royal, Least and Bridled Terns here, and in **Road Bay**, further west on the north coast. All of the island's salt ponds are worth birding, especially **Rendezvous Pond**, south of Road Bay, where White-cheeked Pintail and shorebirds such as Willet have been recorded. Seabirds are possible anywhere offshore but are most likely to be seen around **Scrub Island**, off the northeast tip of the main island, and on and around the uninhabited **Dog Island** and its islets, which lie within a Marine Park northwest of the main island, and support breeding species such as Masked Booby. Better still is **Sombrero Island**, 56 km northwest of Anguilla, where Red-billed Tropicbird, Masked and Brown Boobies, and Roseate and Least Terns all breed, though the future of this important mixed colony of seabirds was briefly placed at risk, in 1999, by a proposal to build a rocket launch site on the island.

ADDITIONAL INFORMATION

Addresses

Anguilla National Trust, PO Box 1234, Museum Building, The Valley, Anguilla, British West Indies (tel. 497 5297, fax. 497 5571, e-mail: axanat@candw.com.ai).

Anguilla Tourist Board, PO Box 1388, Old Factory Plaza, The Valley, Anguilla, British West Indies (tel. 497 2759, fax. 497 2710, e-mail: atbtour@anguillanet.com; web site: www.anguilla-vacation.com).

Books

A Field Guide to Anguilla's Wetlands. Anguilla National Trust.

ANTIGUA

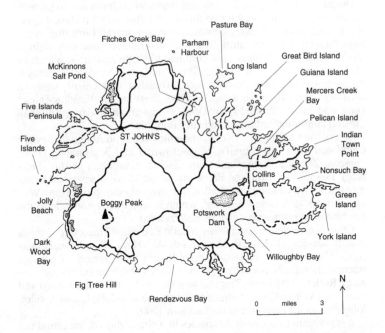

Pasture Bay
Fitches Creek Bay
Parham
Harbour
McKinnons
Salt Pond
Long Island
Great Bird Island
Guiana Island
Mercers Creek
Bay
Five Islands
Peninsula
Pelican Island
Five
Islands
ST JOHN'S
Indian
Town
Point
Collins
Dam
Nonsuch Bay
Jolly
Beach
Boggy Peak
Green
Island
Potswork
Dam
Dark
Wood
Bay
York Island
Willoughby Bay
Fig Tree Hill
N
Rendezvous Bay
0   miles   3

This small island of rolling limestone hills in the Leeward Islands, within the northern Lesser Antilles, supports a fairly diverse avifauna, including some seabirds and several widespread Caribbean endemics. The island has a 130 km-long coastline and covers 280 km^2. Antigua has an international airport about 7 km from the capital, St. John's. All major destinations on the island are signed from here and it is possible to reach them in hired vehicles, buses or taxis. The roads are narrow and in need of repair in remoter areas. A broad range of accommodation is available, but camping is prohibited. Local dishes include chicken with rice, conch, goat stew and saltfish, and can be washed down with beer and rum. Antigua is friendly but it is wise to avoid remote beaches, especially if alone and at night. The official language of this UK Commonwealth State is English.

The best times to visit are in April–May when the seabirds are breeding, and during autumn when numerous shorebirds pass through on migration. The climate is basically hot and dry, although short showers do occur in September–November. Apart from the 4.5 km-wide coastal plain in the northwest, Antigua is an island of rolling limestone hills that terminate abruptly at a steep escarpment inland of Willoughby Bay on the southeast coast. The highest point, Boggy Peak, which reaches 405 m in the southwest, is one of three 305 m plus peaks on Antigua, but there is no forest on this semi-arid island and the 20% of land which is not farmed is dominated by cactus scrub. Other inland habitats include a tiny area of dry woodland in the east and several freshwater reservoirs. Lagoons and salt ponds are dotted along the west coast, and around Guiana Island, on the east coast, is one of the largest remaining expanses of mangrove within the Lesser Antilles.

Despite continuing habitat loss and degradation there are no protected areas on Antigua, so the two threatened and near-threatened species, as well as the relatively common and widespread birds that occur here, face an uncertain future. There are no endemics and only eight of the 51 Caribbean endemics not confined to single countries, islands or archipelagos occur on the island. Three are Lesser Antillean endemics: Purple-throated Carib, Scaly-breasted Thrasher and Lesser Antillean Bullfinch; and five are more widespread: West Indian Whistling-Duck* (rare and local), Bridled Quail-Dove, Green-throated Carib, Antillean Crested Hummingbird and Antillean Euphonia.

Ten of the Caribbean's 18 near-endemics occur on Antigua. They are Caribbean Coot* (has bred), White-crowned and Scaly-naped (rare) Pigeons, Zenaida Dove, Caribbean Elaenia, Caribbean Martin (Feb–Aug), Pearly-eyed Thrasher, Black-whiskered Vireo, Black-faced Grassquit and Carib Grackle. In addition, the *petechia* group of Yellow Warbler, known as 'Golden Warbler', which is also nearly endemic to the Caribbean, is represented by the *bartholemica* race.

Other non-endemic specialities include Red-billed Tropicbird (breeds mainly Jan–Jun), Masked Booby (breeds Mar–May), Magnificent Frigatebird, White-cheeked Pintail, Clapper Rail, a wide variety of passage migrant shorebirds, Sooty Tern, Brown Noddy (both breed mainly Apr–Aug), Ruddy Quail-Dove, Tropical Mockingbird (on Guiana Island) and Grassland Yellow-Finch (believed to have colonised the Lesser Antilles, following its introduction to Barbados in 1900).

It is possible to see over 40 species in a single day on the island but don't expect to see many more than 50 species during a single trip, however long the stay. Regular landbirds include Broad-winged Hawk, White-crowned Pigeon, Zenaida Dove, Green-throated Carib, Antillean Crested Hummingbird, Caribbean Elaenia, Grey Kingbird, Caribbean Martin, Yellow Warbler, Bananaquit, Black-faced Grassquit, Lesser Antillean Bullfinch and Carib Grackle. More localized landbirds, including Scaly-naped Pigeon and Pearly-eyed Thrasher, occur in **Christian Valley**, a few km from St. John's. Other species recorded in the dry scrub here include Bridled Quail-Dove and Scaly-breasted Thrasher. The only other site worth checking carefully for scarce landbirds is the woodland around the tiny **Wallings Dam**, accessible via the lay-by at the top of Fig Tree Road.

Common waterbirds include Brown Pelican, Magnificent Frigatebird, White-cheeked Pintail, and Royal and Least Terns. One of the best places for egrets, herons and shorebirds is **McKinnons Salt Pond**, a few km north of St. John's. This pond, which is about 2 km long and 0.75 km wide, is best viewed from its western shore in the evening when the light is at its most favourable. During August, at least, McKinnons may hold in excess of 4,000 shorebirds and autumn counts have included over 1,000 Lesser Yellowlegs, and over 850 Semipalmated, 180 Stilt, 80 Least, 50 White-rumped and 25 Western Sandpipers, as well as over 250 Black-necked Stilts. Egrets and herons, including Yellow-crowned Night-Heron, are also usually present in impressive numbers and many of these roost in the trees ahead of the T-junction with the road to St. John's at the south end of the pond.

Other sites worth checking for shorebirds include the ponds on **Five Islands Peninsula**, west of St. John's; the ponds inland of **Jolly Beach** on the southwest coast; and the beach and ponds south of here at **Dark Wood Bay** (where Clapper Rail has been recorded). Also in the southwest, Masked Booby breeds on **Five Islands** off Pearns Point.

Sites to concentrate on in the east of the island include **Fitches Creek Bay** (Clapper Rail); **Parham Harbour**, **Collins Dam** (Caribbean Coot*); and **Potswork Dam**, the island's largest freshwater reservoir. Off the northeast coast, West Indian Whistling-Duck* and Tropical Mockingbird occur on **Guiana Island**, which lies among one of the most extensive remaining mangroves in the Lesser Antilles. Red-billed Tropicbird breeds on **Great Bird Island**, while hawksbill sea-turtles lay their eggs in the beaches at Pasture Bay on **Long Island** in Jun–Dec, and fairly large numbers of Brown Noddy breed on the islets in this area, south to Mercers Creek Bay at least. About 50 km west of Antigua, Masked Booby breeds on the uninhabited rocky islet of **Redonda**.

ADDITIONAL INFORMATION

Addresses
Antigua Tourist Office, PO Box 363, Thames Street, St. John's, Antigua, West Indies (tel. 462 0480, fax. 462 2483).

Books and papers
A Guide to the Birds of Antigua. Spencer, W., 1981. Benji's Printery, St. John's.
Observations on the birds of Antigua, Holland, C. S. and Williams, J. M. 1978. *Amer. Birds* 32: 1095–1105.

BAHAMAS

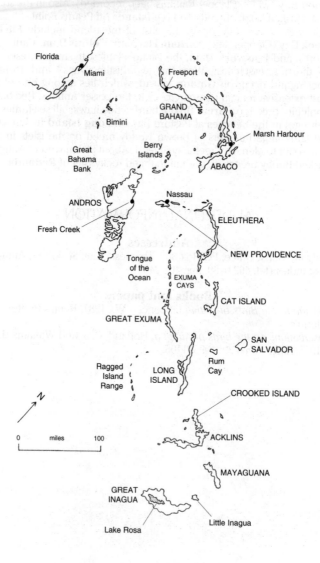

INTRODUCTION

Summary

The Bahamas lie less than 80 km from the east coast of Florida at their nearest point and yet they support about 25 species rarely or never recorded in the USA. These include 16 Caribbean endemics, three of which—a hummingbird, a swallow and a yellowthroat—are endemic

244

or virtually endemic to this lovely 960 km-long archipelago. Additional summertime attractions include seabirds such as White-tailed Tropicbird, while during winter and passage periods there are many New World warblers, including the rare Kirtland's Warbler*, which, outside its breeding season, occurs nowhere else on earth except the Turks & Caicos Islands. Although there are numerous islands in this extensive archipelago it is necessary only to visit Abaco and Andros to see all of the specialities.

Size
The islands of the Bahamas, which amount to 13,857 km^2 of land, are spread across about 960 km of the Atlantic Ocean, from Bimini in the north, which is just 80 km east of Florida, to Great Inagua in the south, which is only 80 km north of Haiti.

Getting Around
The hub of the inter-island air network is Nassau, the capital of the Bahamas, which is situated on the island of New Providence in the north of the archipelago between Abaco and Andros. Airpasses designed to cater for visitors who intend to island-hop are available from airlines such as Bahamasair. It is also possible to travel between islands by sea, on mail boats, most of which are equipped to carry passengers. For more details contact the Dock Master's Office on Potter's Cay, Nassau (tel. 393 1064). Once on *terra firma* it is almost essential for birders with little time to hire a vehicle in order to visit the majority of the best sites, although it is possible to reach most of those on Andros, Grand Bahama and New Providence using local minibuses, known as Jitneys, and land and water taxis operate on and around these, as well as the other major islands. Other modes of transport, from bicycles to golf carts, can be hired to get around these islands and those without motorized vehicles. Some roads are rather poor and driving standards not much better. The Bahamas are a Commonwealth Nation and the official, widely spoken, language is English.

Accommodation and Food
A full range of accommodation is available, but, unfortunately, whether it's a luxurious resort or a self-catering apartment, all types of accommodation as well as places to eat out are exceptionally expensive. The numerous restaurants serve a cosmopolitan selection, but most local dishes are based on conch and fruit, although 'peas 'n' rice' is also popular with the locals who like to wash their food down with beer, rum (here in the form of Bacardi), or rum cocktails.

Health and Safety
Vaccinations against hepatitis A, polio, tetanus, typhoid and yellow fever (if arriving from an infected area) are recommended.

Climate and Timing
The best time to visit is during the second half of April when lingering Kirtland's Warblers*, northbound passage migrants and breeding seabirds such as White-tailed Tropicbird are present. Autumn and winter are also excellent but there is less chance of seeing seabirds at these times. The climate is pleasant year-round, though it is less humid in winter so from December to May high-season prices apply. During this per-

iod cold fronts from the north can produce spells of heavy rain, strong winds and lower temperatures. The summer months of May–July are usually the hottest and most humid, and frequent thunderstorms occur during this period, especially in June. The hurricane season usually lasts from June to October and when the big ones hit, such as Andrew in 1992, they can cause considerable damage.

Habitats

This subtropical coral archipelago consists of about 700 low-lying islands and 2000 or so cays. Most islands, 29 of which are inhabited, rise to just 30 m, although the hills on Cat Island reach 63 m at Mount Alvernia, the highest point in the Bahamas. There are no major watercourses and very little fertile soil, hence only about 1% of the land is cultivated and over 30% is forested, mainly with Caribbean pine. The major wooded areas are confined to the northern islands of Abaco, Andros, Grand Bahama and New Providence, where they are often extensive. In the midst of the islands the seabed drops a sheer 1829 m, and the 225 km-long wall of this underwater fissure forms the third longest barrier reef on the planet, renowned for its blue holes (circular depressions within the limestone) and stunningly varied marine life. Back on land there are 90 species of butterfly, but only 13 mammals, 12 of which are bats.

Conservation

The tourist brochures carefully avoid the fact that vast areas of the natural vegetation cover of the islands, including the Caribbean pine forests, have been degraded or destroyed, and that the near absence of insectivorous birds on New Providence, for example, may be due to the intensive spraying used in mosquito control. There are 12 National Parks but greater efforts need to be made in order to protect the five threatened and near-threatened species, as well as the relatively common and widespread birds, which occur on the Bahamas.

Endemics

Two species are endemic to the Bahamas:

Bahama Swallow*	a relatively common resident on Abaco, Andros and Grand Bahama; outside the breeding season it may be seen on other islands, including New Providence where it has also bred.
Bahama Yellowthroat	a relatively common resident on Abaco, Grand Bahama, Eleuthera and Cat Island; uncommon on Andros and rare on New Providence.

Other Caribbean Endemics

A total of 14 of the 51 Caribbean endemics not confined to single countries, islands or archipelagos, occur on the Bahamas. They are: one species, Bahama Woodstar, which otherwise occurs only on the Turks & Caicos Islands; four species that occur only in the Bahamas and on Cuba: Great Lizard-Cuckoo (Andros, New Providence and Eleuthera), Cuban Emerald (Abaco, Andros and Grand Bahama), Cuban Pewee (northern islands) and Olive-capped Warbler (Abaco and Grand Bahama); three species that occur only in the Bahamas, Cuba and Cayman Islands: Cuban Parrot* (Abaco and Great Inagua), West Indian

Woodpecker (Abaco and San Salvador) and La Sagra's Flycatcher; two species that occur only on the Bahamas and Greater Antilles: Key West Quail-Dove and Greater Antillean Bullfinch; and four more widespread species: West Indian Whistling-Duck*, Loggerhead Kingbird (northern islands), Bahama Mockingbird and Red-legged Thrush (northern islands).

Caribbean Near-endemics

Nine of the 18 species nearly endemic to the Caribbean occur on the Bahamas. They are White-crowned Pigeon, Zenaida Dove, Antillean Nighthawk (mainly May–Aug), Pearly-eyed Thrasher (central and southern islands), Thick-billed and Black-whiskered (Feb–Aug) Vireos, Kirtland's Warbler* (the entire world population of this species—a record 905 singing males in the USA in 1999—winters in the Bahamas and Turks & Caicos Islands, in Sep–Apr), Northern Stripe-headed Tanager and Black-faced Grassquit. In addition, the *petechia* group of Yellow Warbler, known as 'Golden Warbler', which is nearly endemic to the Caribbean, is represented by the *gundlachi* race.

Bird Species

Approximately 320 species have been recorded on the Bahamas. Non-endemic specialities and spectacular species not previously mentioned include Audubon's Shearwater (breeds Mar–Jul), White-tailed Tropicbird (breeds mainly Mar–Jun), Magnificent Frigatebird, Reddish Egret, Greater Flamingo, White-cheeked Pintail, Limpkin, Piping Plover*, Bridled and Sooty Terns, Brown Noddy (all terns breed mainly Apr–Aug), Burrowing Owl, Hairy Woodpecker, Grey Kingbird (most Apr–Oct), Blue-grey Gnatcatcher, Brown–headed Nuthatch (the endemic *insularis* race occurs on Grand Bahama only, where it is very rare), Yellow-throated (including the resident endemic *flavescens* race) and Pine (resident *achrustera* race) Warblers, passage migrant and wintering New World Warblers such as Magnolia, Cape May, Black-throated Blue, Prairie, Palm, Blackpoll and Worm-eating Warblers, and Black-cowled Oriole.

Introduced species include Northern Bobwhite, Ring-necked Pheasant, Indian Peafowl, Eurasian Collared-Dove, Caribbean Dove (New Providence), Northern Mockingbird, European Starling, House Sparrow and Cuban Grassquit (New Providence).

Other Wildlife

The Bahamas are one of the best places on earth to swim with dolphins and sharks. In May–Aug regular boat trips run from Grand Bahama and North Bimini to Little Bahama Bank, which supports a large population of Atlantic spotted dolphins and there are also boat trips to the southern shore of Grand Bahama where small numbers of Atlantic bottlenose dolphins are usually present in summer. Off Grand Bahama divers can also watch lemon, nurse and reef sharks being fed underwater.

Expectations

It is possible to see over 100 species during a short trip, especially in spring and autumn, and even during the winter when, for example, on Abaco such a total may include Bahama Woodstar, Bahama Swallow*, Bahama Yellowthroat and 20 or so other New World warblers.

*The brilliant Bahama Woodstar is a resident endemic on the Bahamas,
and some of the Turks & Caicos Islands*

ABACO

This narrow twin-island, which consists of the 180 km-long Great Abaco
and the 32 km-long Little Abaco to the north, supports more specialities
than any other island in the Bahamas, including Cuban Parrot*, West
Indian Woodpecker and Olive-capped Warbler. The excellent mix of
habitats, which include extensive, but mainly secondary, Caribbean
pine forests, mangroves and mudflats along the west coast, and many
cays and rocky islets to the east, also supports such star birds as White-
tailed Tropicbird and Bahama Yellowthroat.

Bahamian Endemics
Bahama Swallow*, Bahama Yellowthroat.

Localised Caribbean Endemics
Bahama Woodstar, Bahama Mockingbird, Olive-capped Warbler.

Other Caribbean Endemics
Key West Quail-Dove, Cuban Parrot*, Cuban Emerald, West Indian
Woodpecker, Cuban Pewee, La Sagra's Flycatcher, Loggerhead King-
bird, Red-legged Thrush, Greater Antillean Bullfinch.

Caribbean Near-endemics
White-crowned Pigeon, Zenaida Dove, Antillean Nighthawk (mainly
May–Aug), Thick-billed Vireo, Northern Stripe-headed Tanager, Black-
faced Grassquit.

Passage Migrants and Winter Visitors
White-eyed and Yellow-throated Vireos, Northern Parula, Magnolia,
Cape May, Black-throated Blue, Yellow-rumped, Prairie, Palm and Black-
and-white Warblers, American Redstart, Worm-eating Warbler, Ovenbird, Northern Waterthrush, Common Yellowthroat, Blue Grosbeak, Indigo and Painted Buntings.

Others

Least Grebe, White-tailed Tropicbird (mainly Mar–Jun), Brown Pelican, Magnificent Frigatebird, Least Bittern, White-cheeked Pintail, Red-tailed Hawk, Piping Plover*, Roseate (mainly Apr–Aug), Bridled (mainly Apr–Aug) and Sooty (mainly Apr–Aug) Terns, Brown Noddy (mainly Apr–Aug), Smooth-billed Ani, Chuck-will's-widow (Sep–May), Hairy Woodpecker, Blue-grey Gnatcatcher, Black-whiskered Vireo (Feb–Aug), Yellow, Yellow-throated (resident *flavescens*, wintering *dominica*) and Pine Warblers, Red-winged Blackbird.

(Other species recorded include Audubon's Shearwater (mainly Mar–Jul), West Indian Whistling-Duck*, Mangrove Cuckoo, Ruby-throated Hummingbird (Nov–Apr); passage migrant and wintering Blue-winged, Nashville, Black-throated Green and Kirtland's* Warblers, Summer Tanager, and Chipping, Savannah and Lincoln's Sparrows; and Shiny Cowbird. Introduced species include Northern Bobwhite).

Many of the birds listed above can be seen in and around **Marsh Harbour**, the largest town on the island. The grounds of the Great Abaco Beach Hotel are a good starting point and, with a walk from Conch Inn to Albury's Ferry Landing, it shouldn't be too difficult to find Bahama Woodstar, Red-legged Thrush, Thick-billed Vireo and Northern Stripe-headed Tanager. More localized species including a few Caribbean pine specialists occur south of **Dundas Town Road** which is west of Marsh Harbour. Bird along the tracks leading through the pine woods where Bahama Swallow*, Bahama Mockingbird, Olive-capped Warbler and Bahama Yellowthroat occur. The area around the pond and rubbish dump, south of town, attracts masses of wintering Palm Warblers (over 250 in January 1999), as well as sparrows and Red-winged Blackbirds (which are worth checking for Shiny Cowbird). To reach here head south from town then turn west at Abaco Wholesale on to the Scherlin Bootle Highway. The pond is on the north side of this road after about 0.75 km and the dump is on the south side after another 0.75 km or so.

The best place to look for Key West Quail-Dove is on **Elbow Cay**, accessible via several daily ferries (20 minutes) from Albury's Ferry Landing. Bicycles and golf carts can be hired in Hope Town, from where head south to the pine woods alongside the road from Nigh Creek to the next junction. The area behind the rubbish dump (alive with passerines in winter) has been particularly productive in the past, and Bahama Mockingbird has also been seen here.

From May to August it is possible to see White-tailed Tropicbird, Bridled and Sooty Terns, and Brown Noddy on boat trips to the cays and rocky islets in **Abaco Sound**, some of which lie within Pelican Cays Land and Sea Park. White-tailed Tropicbird breeds on Tilloo Cay and at the entrance to Little Harbour, as well as on Great Guana Cay which is north of Marsh Harbour and accessible by ferry from there.

One of the best places for White-cheeked Pintail on Abaco is the large, enclosed pond at **Different of Abaco**, a lodge reached by turning east off the Great Abaco Highway south of Marsh Harbour. Antillean Nighthawk (mainly May–Aug) and Bahama Swallow* also occur here, but the Greater Flamingos are feral.

It is usually necessary to continue further south in order to find Cuban Parrot* and the extensive pine woods alongside the 10.5 km stretch of the Great Abaco Highway between Crossing Rock and the junction

SOUTHERN ABACO

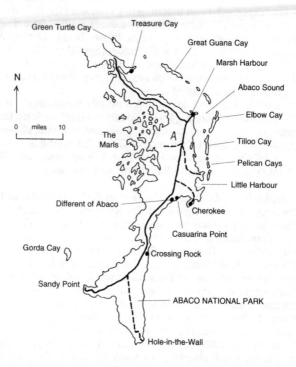

where the highway swings right to Sandy Point and the track south to Hole-in-the-Wall begins, are as good as any for this species, as are those alongside the first couple of km of the Hole-in-the-Wall track. Some of these woods lie in the 83 km² **Abaco National Park** and they also support Bahama Woodstar, Olive-capped Warbler and Bahama Yellowthroat. The 24 km-long track to Hole-in-the-Wall is much rougher at its southern end and a high-clearance 4WD vehicle may be needed to reach the lighthouse, which is a good sea-watching site. The mangroves at **Sandy Point** support Yellow Warbler, while shorebirds such as Piping Plover* occur on the shore at the very tip of the point, reached by walking east from the end of the road at Sandy Point settlement. North of Marsh Harbour White-cheeked Pintail has been recorded on the pond by the 11th hole on the golf course en route to **Treasure Cay**, along with Least Grebe and Least Bittern. Large numbers of warblers winter around Treasure Cay, from where it is possible to catch a ferry to Green Turtle Cay, where Key West Quail-Dove and Mangrove Cuckoo have been recorded.

ANDROS

Andros is composed of several main islands, separated by a maze of shallow mangrove-lined bays and creeks, which together cover 3700 km^2 and therefore form the largest 'island' in the Bahamas. It is 167 km from the north end of these islands to the south and up to 64 km from west to east, and the remnant, secondary and planted pine woods, together with the mangroves and dense scrub support many birds, including West Indian Whistling-Duck*, Great Lizard-Cuckoo and the endemic 'Northrop's' race of Black-cowled Oriole.

Bahamian Endemics
Bahama Swallow*, Bahama Yellowthroat.

Localised Caribbean Endemics
West Indian Whistling-Duck*, Bahama Woodstar, Bahama Mockingbird.

Other Caribbean Endemics
Key West Quail-Dove, Great Lizard-Cuckoo, Cuban Emerald, Cuban Pewee, La Sagra's Flycatcher, Loggerhead Kingbird, Red-legged Thrush, Greater Antillean Bullfinch.

Caribbean Near-endemics
White-crowned Pigeon, Zenaida Dove, Antillean Nighthawk (mainly May–Aug), Thick-billed Vireo, Northern Stripe-headed Tanager, Black-faced Grassquit.

Passage Migrants and Winter Visitors
A wide variety of New World warblers.

Others
Reddish Egret, Yellow-crowned Night-Heron, Greater Flamingo, Red-tailed Hawk, Limpkin, Clapper Rail, Willet, Gull-billed Tern, Mangrove Cuckoo, Smooth-billed Ani, Chuck-will's-widow (Sep–May), Hairy Woodpecker, Blue-grey Gnatcatcher, Black-whiskered Vireo (Feb–Aug), Yellow and Pine Warblers, Red-winged Blackbird, Shiny Cowbird, Black-cowled Oriole (*northropi*).
(Other species recorded include Audubon's Shearwater (mainly Mar–Jun), White-tailed Tropicbird (mainly Mar–Jul), White-cheeked Pintail, and passage migrant and wintering species such as Kirtland's* and Blackpoll Warblers, Northern Waterthrush, Connecticut Warbler, Common Yellowthroat and Bobolink).

Other Wildlife
Butterflies include Bahamian, DeVillier's and Schaus's Swallowtails.

The area around Nicholl's Town and **Lowe Sound** at the northern tip of the main island supports Reddish Egret, White-crowned Pigeon (look for these flying over at dawn), Key West Quail-Dove, Mangrove Cuckoo, Great Lizard-Cuckoo, Antillean Nighthawk, Chuck-will's-widow, Cuban Emerald, Bahama Woodstar, La Sagra's Flycatcher, Bahama Swallow* (San Andros Airport Pond is a good place), Bahama Mockingbird, Red-legged Thrush, Thick-billed Vireo and Bahama Yellowthroat. To the south West Indian Whistling-Duck*, Clapper Rail, Great Lizard-Cuckoo, Yellow Warbler and Black-cowled Oriole occur around Small Hope Bay Lodge, just north of **Fresh Creek**. The west side of the main island and those islands to the south are best for Greater Flamingo. **Green Cay**, one of the many small islands off Andros, which lies 32 km east of Deep

Creek, supports what is reputed to be the world's second largest population of White-crowned Pigeon.

Andros is just 1.5 km from the **Tongue of the Ocean**, where the seabed drops almost vertically for 1829 m, and the 225 km-long wall of this underwater fissure forms the third longest barrier reef on the planet. It is renowned for its spectacular marine life.

Accommodation: Small Hope Bay Lodge, which consists of about 20 cottages set among palm trees at the top of the beach, is situated just north of Fresh Creek about five minutes by road from the airport.

NEW PROVIDENCE

Two-thirds of the human population of the Bahamas live within the sprawling suburbia of Nassau on this small, low-lying island which is 39 km long and up to 11 km wide, but the remaining pine woods, scrub, lakes and mangroves support several Caribbean endemics, including Great Lizard-Cuckoo.

Bahamian Endemics
Bahama Swallow*.

Localised Caribbean Endemics
Bahama Woodstar, Bahama Mockingbird.

Other Caribbean Endemics
Key West Quail-Dove, Great Lizard-Cuckoo, Cuban Pewee, La Sagra's Flycatcher, Loggerhead Kingbird, Red-legged Thrush, Greater Antillean Bullfinch.

Caribbean Near-endemics
Zenaida Dove, Antillean Nighthawk (mainly May–Aug), Thick-billed Vireo, Northern Stripe-headed Tanager, Black-faced Grassquit.

Passage Migrants and Winter Visitors
Least Bittern, Blue-winged Teal, Lesser Scaup, Sora, Least Sandpiper, Grey Catbird, White-eyed Vireo, Northern Parula, Magnolia, Cape May, Black-throated Blue, Yellow-rumped, Black-throated Green, Prairie, Palm and Black-and-white Warblers, American Redstart, Worm-eating Warbler, Ovenbird, Northern Waterthrush, Common Yellowthroat, Indigo and Painted Buntings.

Others
Least Grebe, Yellow-crowned Night-Heron, Least Bittern, White and Glossy Ibises, White-cheeked Pintail, Osprey, Limpkin, Bridled Tern (mainly Apr–Aug), White-crowned Pigeon, Mangrove Cuckoo, Smooth-billed Ani, Belted Kingfisher, Hairy Woodpecker, Black-whiskered Vireo (Feb–Aug), Yellow, Yellow-throated (resident *flavescens* and wintering *dominica*) and Pine Warblers, Red–winged Blackbird.

(Other species recorded include White-tailed Tropicbird (mainly Mar–Jul), West Indian Whistling-Duck*, Hooded Merganser (Nov–Feb), Wilson's Plover, Burrowing Owl, Bahama Yellowthroat (rare) and passage migrants and winter visitors including Kirtland's* and Blackpoll Warblers, Louisiana Waterthrush, Hooded Warbler and Blue Grosbeak. Introduced species include Caribbean Dove and Cuban Grassquit).

For the latest information on site access and birding hot-spots visit the Bahamas National Trust HQ at **The Retreat** on the east side of Village Road in Nassau. The grounds here are worth checking for Cuban Pewee and Yellow Warbler, while La Sagra's Flycatcher, Northern Stripe-headed Tanager and Painted Bunting have been recorded in the grounds of **St. Augustine's Monastery** in the southeast outskirts of Nassau. The golf course on **Paradise Island** north of Nassau supports Yellow-crowned Night-Heron, Least Bittern, White-cheeked Pintail and Antillean Nighthawk. The best area is around the ponds by Lakeside Drive. The **Botanical Gardens**, off West Bay Street close to the cricket ground at Fort Charlotte in the northwestern suburbs of Nassau, is one of the best sites on the island for wintering warblers and Painted Bunting.

Slightly further afield, large numbers of egrets and herons (evening roost counts have exceeded 500), as well as Sora, passage migrant and wintering shorebirds, White-crowned Pigeon, Bahama Mockingbird, Red-legged Thrush and Red-winged Blackbird all occur on and around **Wilson's and Harold Ponds**, which are accessible from the Milo Butler Highway southwest of Nassau. Mangrove Cuckoo, Cuban Pewee and La Sagra's Flycatcher have been recorded along **Skyline Drive**, which runs west from Nassau along Cable Beach, where the ponds and their surrounds support White-cheeked Pintail and warblers such as Yellow-throated. **Lake Cunningham**, to the south, is also worth checking for waterbirds, but **Lake Killarney**, to the southwest, is often more productive. To bird the surrounds of this lake it is usually necessary to don a pair of waterproof boots, although the north shore (a good area for Limpkin) may be accessible via South Westridge, a development either side of John F. Kennedy Drive about 1.5 km east of the airport. If Bahama Swallow* remains elusive cruise along **Coral Harbour Road**, which

NEW PROVIDENCE

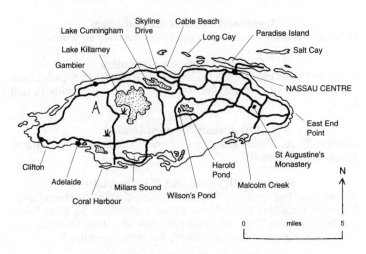

runs north–south between the airport and the south coast through the west of the island.

Accommodation: Orange Hill Beach Inn, at the less crowded and built-up western end of the island near the airport.

Northern Stripe-headed Tanager. The only 'stripe-headed tanagers' with black backs occur on the Bahamas

GRAND BAHAMA

The pine woods and scrub on this mostly flat 154 km-long and up to 27 km-wide island, the northernmost in the archipelago, support a wide range of specialities including Olive-capped Warbler.

Bahamian Endemics
Bahama Swallow*, Bahama Yellowthroat.

Localised Caribbean Endemics
Bahama Woodstar, Bahama Mockingbird, Olive-capped Warbler.

Other Caribbean Endemics
Key West Quail-Dove, Cuban Emerald, Cuban Pewee, La Sagra's Flycatcher, Loggerhead Kingbird, Red-legged Thrush, Greater Antillean Bullfinch.

Caribbean Near-endemics
Zenaida Dove, Thick-billed Vireo, Northern Stripe-headed Tanager, Black-faced Grassquit.

Passage Migrants and Winter Visitors
Blue-winged Teal, Yellow-billed Cuckoo, Grey Catbird, Northern Parula, Magnolia, Cape May, Black-throated Blue, Yellow-rumped, Black-throated Green, Prairie, Palm and Black-and-white Warblers, American Redstart, Worm-eating Warbler, Ovenbird, Northern Waterthrush.

Others

Least Grebe, Magnificent Frigatebird, Osprey, Red-tailed Hawk, Piping Plover*, Willet, Royal Tern, White-crowned Pigeon, Smooth-billed Ani, Chuck-will's-widow (mainly Sep–May), Belted Kingfisher, Hairy Woodpecker, Blue-grey Gnatcatcher, Yellow-throated (resident *flavescens* and wintering *dominica*) and Pine Warblers, Red-winged Blackbird.

(Other species recorded include Sooty and Audubon's (mainly Mar–Jun) Shearwaters, White-cheeked Pintail, Bridled and Sooty Terns (both mainly Apr–Aug), and the very rare and localised endemic *insularis* race of Brown-headed Nuthatch (try the Emlen Tract).)

Other Wildlife

Atlantic bottlenose (May–Sep) and Atlantic spotted (May–Sep) dolphins, lemon, nurse and reef sharks.

For the latest information on birding on Grand Bahama contact the **Rand Nature Centre**, PO Box F-43441, Freeport, Bahamas (tel. 352 5438), off East Settlers Way 3 km east of Freeport (open 9am–4pm, Monday to Friday). The pine woods surrounding the centre are a good place to search for Olive-capped Warbler. One of the best sites on the island for Bahama Woodstar is the **Garden of the Groves**, a popular tourist attraction complete with artificial streams and waterfalls, where Cuban Emerald also occurs. It is best to bird the gardens early before the tourist buses turn up, usually around 10am.

One of the best sites in the archipelago for Bahama Swallow* and Bahama Yellowthroat is the 17 ha **Lucaya National Park**, which is south of the Grand Bahama Highway about 24 km east of Freeport. The yellowthroat occurs around Ben's Cave, across the road from which there is a trail and boardwalk through mangroves to the secluded Gold Rock Beach where the coastal scrub is also worth birding. Other species recorded here include Greater Antillean Bullfinch.

The Emerald golf course, one of two attached to the **Bahama Princess** holiday complex, which is south of the West Sunrise Highway just west of the International Bazaar and accessible via Santa Maria Avenue, is a good place for Bahama Mockingbird (most likely along the north side of the 3rd fairway), warblers (especially between the 4th and 7th fairways) and Northern Stripe-headed Tanager. West of **West End**, a settlement in the extreme northwest of the island, 32 km from Freeport, the road reaches the grounds of a holiday complex, complete with a golf course known as Jack Tar. The security guards at the gate usually permit birders to enter the area which supports Piping Plover*, Cuban Emerald, Yellow-throated Warbler and Red-winged Blackbird.

In May–Aug it is possible to join organised boat trips out of West End in order to see and even swim with Atlantic spotted dolphins at **Little Bahama Bank** (which is also accessible from North Bimini, see below). Atlantic bottlenose dolphins are also occasionally seen here but the best method to see this species is to join the organised boat trips which run along the south shore of the island to **Sanctuary Bay**, where a small population is usually present in summer. Off Grand Bahama divers can also watch lemon, nurse and reef sharks being fed underwater, and on pelagic trips 8 km south of the island Sooty and Audubon's Shearwaters, and Bridled and Sooty Terns have been seen.

Accommodation: several expensive places to choose from.

The **Bimini Islands** are the big-game fishing capital of the world, but not so good for birds. The gardens, *Casuarina* stands and coconut palm groves that have replaced virtually all of the natural vegetation on **North Bimini**, which is 20 minutes by air from Miami, support few notable birds, but the island of **South Bimini**, reached from North Bimini via a short ferry ride, where there is more natural vegetation and far fewer human inhabitants, is better and supports species such as Thick-billed Vireo. However, the most abundant bird on Bimini is the introduced Eurasian Collared-Dove.

South of the main northern islands the Kinley and Schooner Cays, off the west coast of the narrow, 177 km-long island of Eleuthera, support large numbers of White-crowned Pigeons, and Sooty Tern and Brown Noddy occur on Finlay Cay, mainly in Apr–Aug. Other species recorded on Eleuthera include White-tailed Tropicbird (mainly Mar–Jul), White-cheeked Pintail, Bridled Tern (mainly Apr–Aug), Great Lizard-Cuckoo, Bahama Woodstar and Bahama Yellowthroat. The 80 km-long Cat Island, to the south, where the rolling hills reach 63 m at Mount Alvernia, the highest point in the Bahamas, also supports Bahama Yellowthroat. Some of the **Exuma Cays**, a 144 km-long chain of 365 cays west of Cat Island, lie within the Bahamas National Trust's 283 km^2 Exuma Cays Land and Sea Park, which supports Audubon's Shearwater (mainly Mar–Jun), White-tailed Tropicbird (mainly Mar–Jul) and Greater Flamingo, as well as Atlantic bottlenose dolphin and loggerhead sea-turtle. The first confirmed breeding record of Red-footed Booby in the Bahamas during the 20th Century involved a pair on a small cay off the island of **San Salvador** in April 1995. In June 1998 there were two pairs of this species, as well as a pair of Masked Boobies and many more pairs of Brown Boobies, breeding on White Cay, off Graham's Harbour at the north end of the island, and there are many birds on nearby Green Cay. **Long Island**, west of San Salvador, is the best in the Bahamas for West Indian Whistling-Duck*. South of here Greater Flamingo occurs on **Crooked Island** and the islands of **Acklins** and **Mayaguana**, but numbers are very small compared to those on **Great Inagua**, at the southern end of the Bahamas, which supports the largest breeding colony of flamingos in the West Indies. About 60,000 birds usually breed (Mar–Jul) on the 19 km-long **Lake Rosa**, part of which lies within the 178 km^2 Bahamas National Trust Park, access to which is restricted. To visit the lake contact the trust which has a basic camp on the western shore, accessible only by 4WD, 37 km from Matthew Town. The island also supports Cuban Parrot*, while Reddish Egret is one of many waterbirds which occur in mangroves along the east coast and this area of the island is also a good place to look for White-tailed Tropicbird. In addition, the Bahamas National Trust's camp at **Union Creek** on the northwest side of the island is situated near a breeding area of green and hawksbill sea-turtles.

ADDITIONAL INFORMATION

Addresses

Bahamas Ministry of Tourism, Market Plaza, Bay Street, PO Box N-3701, Nassau, Bahamas (tel. 322 7500, fax. 325 5835, web site: www. interknowledge.com/bahamas).

Bahamas National Trust, PO Box N-4105, Nassau, Bahamas (tel. 362 1574, fax 362 2044).

Conservation Unit, Department of Agriculture, PO Box N-3704, Nassau, Bahamas (tel. 325 0430, fax. 328 5874).

Books

A Birder's Guide to the Bahama Islands (including Turks and Caicos), White, A. W. 1998. ABA.

The Birds of New Providence and the Bahama Islands, Brudenell-Bruce, P. G. C. 1975. Collins.

Birds of the Southern Bahamas: An Annotated Checklist, Buden, D. W. 1987. BOU.

Bah Mar the Shallow Seas: An Underwater Guide to the Bahamas, Palmer, R. 1995. Immel.

BARBADOS

Cluff's Bay North Point

Greenidge

St Nicholas Abbey

Long Pond

Speightstown

Welchman Hall Gully

Horse Hill

Turners Hall
Woods

Bathsheba

Gibbes Bay

Andromeda Gardens

Bath

Mount
Hillaby

East Point

Holetown

Hackleston
Cliff

Ragged
Point

Welchman
Hall

Fresh Water
Bay

Six Cross
Roads

Marley Vale

Graeme
Hall Swamp

Bridgetown

Robinsons

N

Hastings

A

Worthing

Oistins

Chancery
Lane Swamp

0   miles   5

INTRODUCTION

Summary
In contrast to virtually all other islands in the Lesser Antilles this small coral island, which is about 160 km east of that chain, has no forested mountains and, consequently, is devoid of endemic birds. It does support two endemic Caribbean hummingbirds and a distinctive aberrant race of Lesser Antillean Bullfinch, but Barbados is more renowned for the regular arrival of transatlantic vagrants, especially egrets, herons and shorebirds.

Size
At 34 km long and up to 22.5 km wide, Barbados covers 430 km².

258

Getting Around

The cheapest method of travel is on the fairly efficient but crowded bus network or in ZR taxis. Private taxis are more expensive and hire vehicles even more so. Visitors who do hire a vehicle are advised to carry a large-scale map for there are few road signs, especially inland. The official language of this Commonwealth State is English.

Accommodation and Food

Barbados boasts one of the best tourist infrastructures in the Caribbean, including a broad range of accommodation, from luxurious hotels to a youth hostel (in Bridgetown), and many bars and restaurants, which, apart from local diners, Chinese restaurants and pizza places, are rather expensive. One of the favourite local dishes is flying-fish with a green vegetable known as christophenes. Beer is much cheaper away from tourist hot-spots and supermarket rum is good value. A well-known local tipple is Malibu (rum and coconut).

Health and Safety

The laid-back locals are among the friendliest people on the planet but, as is the case almost everywhere else in the westernized world, petty theft occurs in the major tourist areas.

Climate and Timing

The best time to visit is arguably in Apr–May, when some seabirds are possible, hurricanes are very unlikely (the season usually lasts Jun–Nov) and the guns fall silent over the island's wetlands (the shooting season lasts from July to mid-Oct). Seabirds are actually very rare around Barbados so anytime in Dec–May could be just as productive.

Habitats

Barbados has evolved from a coral reef rather than volcanic eruptions, so it has no mountainous terrain and no rain forest. The southern and western Caribbean coasts are low lying, but inland pastures and extensive sugarcane plantations have been established on the rolling hills that rise to 340 m at Mount Hillaby in the centre of the island. The northern and eastern Atlantic coasts are rather rugged, and inland of these several steep cliffs (former shorelines) run parallel to the coast. What decent habitat for birds exists is in small pockets, mainly in the form of seasonal shooting ponds and wooded gullies.

Conservation

The natural vegetation of Barbados was largely destroyed within forty years of the island being settled by the English in 1627. Over 40,000 white settlers were present on the island by the 1640s and they quickly cleared the land to make way for agriculture. Most of the island is still densely populated (1596 people per 1.6 km^2 in 1997) and intensively cultivated, with the landscape dominated by sugarcane plantations, hence the birdlife, further limited through predation by introduced species such as the green vervet monkey, could do without the unwanted attention of the island's large shooting fraternity. Although those with the guns will argue that many of the ponds they have constructed are good for birds, what is the point of providing the birds with good habitat if they then get shot? It would be better if the government outlawed shooting, managed the ponds only for nature conservation purposes and constructed more, preferably with hides so that local people and visitors can watch and enjoy birds rather than kill them. The government have introduced a Wild Birds Protection Act but it covers too few species and is rarely enforced, so the two threatened and near-threatened species, as well as the relatively common and widespread birds, which occur on Barbados, need much more protection if the island's avifauna is to be conserved for future generations, who will doubtless look back in amazement on the fact that their ancestors were still shooting birds for fun at the beginning of the 21st Century.

Caribbean Endemics
There are no endemics on Barbados and only three of the 51 Caribbean endemics not confined to single countries, islands or archipelagos occur. One is a Lesser Antillean endemic: Lesser Antillean Bullfinch (in this race both sexes of this bird, the most abundant on the island, exhibit female plumage), and two are more widespread, Green-throated Carib and Antillean Crested Hummingbird. Another Lesser Antilles endemic, Scaly-breasted Thrasher, was possibly extinct by the end of the 20th Century.

Caribbean Near-Endemics
Seven of the 18 species almost endemic to the Caribbean occur on Barbados. They are Scaly-naped Pigeon, Zenaida Dove, Caribbean Elaenia, Caribbean Martin (Feb–Aug), Black-whiskered Vireo, Black-faced Grassquit and Carib Grackle. In addition, the *petechia* group of Yellow Warbler, known as 'Golden Warbler', which is also nearly endemic to the Caribbean, is represented by the *petechia* race.

Bird species
Approximately 150 species have been recorded on Barbados. Non-endemic specialities and spectacular species not mentioned above include Audubon's Shearwater (mainly late autumn to early summer), Magnificent Frigatebird, Masked Duck, Bridled (mainly Apr–Aug) and Sooty (mainly Apr–Aug) Terns, and Eared Dove (very local). Introduced species include Grassland Yellow-Finch (local in open farmland, mainly in the east and north).

Barbados is the Caribbean counterpart of the Isles of Scilly, in Europe, in that it has hosted an amazing number of vagrants that have presumably flown the Atlantic Ocean. The remarkable roll-call includes Grey and Purple Herons, Little Egret (which bred here, for the first time on the west side of the Atlantic, in 1995, and by the end of the 1990s there were up to 80 birds, including 20 breeding pairs), the *gularis* race of Little Egret, known as 'Western Reef-Egret' (due to the presence of these three species it was possible to see ten species of egret and heron in just a couple of hours on Barbados in early 1999), Collared Pratincole, Northern Lapwing, Pacific Golden-Plover, Jack Snipe, Spotted Redshank, Wood Sandpiper, Ruff, Great Black-backed Gull, Whiskered Tern, Common Cuckoo, Alpine Swift and Northern Wheatear! North American shorebirds which have turned up include Hudsonian Godwit, and Upland and Buff-breasted Sandpipers, while as late as the 1950s Eskimo Curlew* was a regular migrant (the last record was in 1963).

Expectations
Don't expect to see many more than 40 species, even on a long trip.

The best birding sites are discussed in a clockwise direction from the International Airport in the south of the island. There are many ponds on Barbados, most of which have been created in order to attract birds which are shot between July and mid-October when there is absolutely no access to such ponds. Outside of the shooting season there is usually no problem in accessing these complexes, most of which comprise several small ponds around a large hut, in which the shooters hide. Unfortunately these ponds hold few shorebirds outside of the shooting season, but are always worth checking for transatlantic vagrants, including other waterbirds, and more regular passage migrant and wintering shorebirds such as Killdeer, Greater and Lesser Yellowlegs, and Solitary, Semipalmated, Western, Least and Stilt Sandpipers. In the past Eskimo Curlew* was regularly recorded, mainly in the company of American Golden-Plovers, but the last documented record involved one shot in 1963.

The closest complex to the airport is **Chancery Lane Swamp**, which is accessible via Silversands. Follow the coast road from here for about 2.5 km until reaching the 'Private Shooting—Keep Out' signpost, then continue on foot to an area of open water, visible from the top of the 'cliff' at the end of the no-through road. Rarities recorded here include Grey Heron.

One of the best places on the island to look for Magnificent Frigatebird is **Oistins Bay**, where a few are occasionally attracted to the fish guts discarded from the fish market. Park to the west of the market by the beached boats and scan. Other species recorded include Great Black-backed Gull (a transatlantic rarity) and Royal Tern (a rare winter visitor).

The best birding site on Barbados is arguably **Graeme Hall Swamp**, about 30 ha of mangroves and pools north of St. Lawrence and Worthing on the southwest coast. There is a large egret and heron roost here, which is worth checking carefully for Little Egret and rarities, which have included Purple Heron. Other species to be seen here include Blue-winged Teal (mainly winter), Osprey, Sora (rare winter visitor), Caribbean Coot*, Solitary Sandpiper (mainly winter), Green-throated Carib, Antillean Crested Hummingbird, Belted Kingfisher, Caribbean Elaenia, Yellow and Prothonotary (scarce in winter) Warblers, Northern Waterthrush (mainly winter) and Black-faced Grassquit. Most of the area, which was formerly much more extensive, is privately owned and at the end of the 1990s a security fence was erected and a boardwalk installed through the mangroves.

The occasional seabird, such as Brown Booby, Magnificent Frigatebird and Bridled Tern, may be seen off the southwest coast, from places such as **Rockley Beach, Hastings**, although the best place to look for Bridled Tern off the southwest coast is from **Bridgetown** (where they have been seen roosting on the end of the fishing harbour breakwater) northwards. Scaly-naped Pigeon can be found in leafier areas of Bridgetown. The botanical gardens in **Welchman Hall Gully**, in the centre of the island, support Caribbean Elaenia and attract occasional wintering New World warblers such as American Redstart. The gardens, open 9am–5pm daily, are well signed. Scaly-naped Pigeon, Caribbean Elaenia and Black-whiskered Vireo occur in the only remaining area of native woodland on the island, the 18 ha of **Turners Hall Woods**, north of Welchman Hall.

Another good place to look for Magnificent Frigatebird is **Speightstown** on the northwest coast, where they are again attracted to discarded fish guts. The island's only known breeding colony of Audubon's Shearwaters (about 25 pairs) is on a tiny islet about 100 m offshore from the north end of **Cluff's Bay** at the extreme northern tip of the island. When present, between late autumn and early summer, they return to their burrows after dark, usually between 7.30pm and 8pm, and can be seen with the aid of a telescope and very powerful spotlight. However, to reach the best viewing point it is necessary to climb down a set of steep rock steps, clamber over some slippery rocks at the cliff edge, virtually crawl through the undergrowth up a steep bank and then cling to a sharp coral outcrop, all with the aforementioned equipment, so it may be wise to enlist the help of local birders before attempting such bravado. Alternatively, dig deep into your wallet, dine at the ridiculously expensive Carambola beach-side restaurant a couple of km south of Holetown, on the mid-west coast of the island, and hope a shearwater is attracted to the lights as they have been before. Other seabirds, including Brown Booby and Bridled Tern, have been recorded off **North Point**, where the nearby shooting ponds are worth checking for shorebirds (the first Collared Pratincole for the New World was present here in January 1997). The shooting ponds at **Alaska** near Cluff's Bay are also worth a quick scan and the fields opposite the chicken farm on the south side of nearby **Connell Town** occasionally attract Grassland Yellow-Finch.

At the northeast end of the island Caribbean Elaenia occurs along the entrance road to **St. Nicholas Abbey**, which is signed south of Boscobelle. Birds recorded at the **Long Pond** shooting ponds, next to the beach at Long Pond on the northeast coast, include Osprey and a variety of shorebirds. The steep, rocky, former sea-cliff that runs parallel to the Atlantic coast for about 4.5 km, a mile inland from Bathsheba, is known as **Hackleston Cliff**. To reach the woodland at its base, where hummingbirds, Caribbean Elaenia, Black-whiskered Vireo and the occasional New World warbler such as Black-and-white Warbler and American Redstart occur, head northeast from Horse Hill on a steeply descending road, then turn right a few hundred metres beyond the sign for Cotton Tower onto a track to a government forestry area (marked by an old green sign). It is best to continue along this track on foot to reach the network of trails that run through the woodland. The two species of hummingbird, which enliven the island's avifauna, also occur in **Andromeda Gardens**, south of Tent Bay near the east coast. **Coles Pasture** shooting ponds near Marley Vale at the extreme east end of the island are worth checking for shorebirds and Masked Duck is an outside possibility here.

One of the best sites for the highly localised Eared Dove is around the farm at **Jezreel**, north of Highway 5 between Robinsons and Six Cross Roads. At Jezreel turn north onto a farm road lined with *Casuarinas* then turn right to reach the farm where the doves occur around the buildings, especially when the chickens are fed at about 4pm. Grassland Yellow-Finch occurs in nearby fields. Make sure the people living and working at the farm are fully aware of what you are doing. Southwest of Jezreel, along Highway 5, look out for **Congo Road** shooting ponds to the north of the road. Shorebirds such as Greater and Lesser Yellowlegs occur here and rarities have included Ruff. A few km southwest of Six Cross Roads (a couple of km north of the airport) turn north off Highway 6 in response to the 'Packers' signpost to reach **Packers** shooting ponds where Masked Duck has been recorded.

ADDITIONAL INFORMATION

Addresses

Barbados National Trust, Wildey House, Wildey, Barbados, West Indies (tel. 436 9033).

Barbados Tourism Authority, PO Box 242, Harbour Road, Bridgetown, Barbados, West Indies (tel. 427 2623/4, fax. 426 4080; web site: www. barbados.org).

Papers

New and rare species of Nearctic landbird migrants during autumn for Barbados and the Lesser Antilles, Frost, M., 1999. *Caribbean J. Sci.* 1–2: 46–53.

BARBUDA

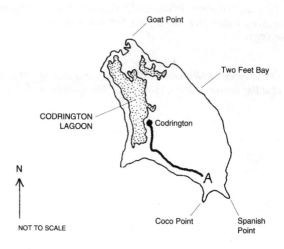

Goat Point

Two Feet Bay

CODRINGTON LAGOON

Codrington

N

A

Coco Point

Spanish Point

NOT TO SCALE

Barbuda, a small island at the northern end of the Lesser Antilles, does not support any endemic species, but it does support several breeding seabirds, including the largest breeding colony of Magnificent Frigatebird in the Caribbean. This 176 km² Leeward Island is accessible by air via Antigua (p. 241), which is about 45 km to the south. There is just the one road, from the airstrip near Coco Point to the island's only settlement, Codrington, although some other parts of the island are accessible via 4WD-only dirt tracks. Accommodation is limited to a couple of very expensive hotels and a few guest houses, and there are only a few poorly stocked food shops in Codrington. The official language of this UK Commonwealth State is English. The best times to visit are when most of the seabirds are breeding (Apr–Jun) or when the Magnificent Frigatebird colony is usually occupied (Aug–Dec). The climate is basically hot and dry, although some short rain showers normally occur in Sep–Nov.

Barbuda is a low-lying coral island, most of which is covered by impenetrable scrub, although a very large mangrove-fringed lagoon dominates the western half of the island. Protection of this very important lagoon as well as some other parts of the island is required to conserve the two threatened and near-threatened species, as well as the relatively common and widespread birds, which occur on Barbuda.

No species are endemic to Barbuda and only nine of the 51 Caribbean endemics not confined to single countries, islands or archipelagos have been recorded here. Three are Lesser Antillean endemics: Lesser Antillean Flycatcher (rare), Scaly-breasted Thrasher (possibly extinct) and Lesser Antillean Bullfinch, and six are more widespread, namely West Indian Whistling-Duck* (rare), Bridled Quail-Dove (rare), Green-throated Carib, Antillean Crested Hummingbird (rare), Adelaide's Warbler (possibly extinct) and Antillean Euphonia (possibly extinct).

Eight of the 18 species almost endemic to the Caribbean occur on Barbuda. They are Scaly-naped Pigeon (rare), Zenaida Dove, Caribbean Elaenia, Caribbean Martin (Feb–Aug), Pearly-eyed Thrasher, Black-whiskered Vireo, Black-faced Grassquit and Carib Grackle. In addition, the *petechia* group of Yellow Warbler, known as 'Golden Warbler', which is also nearly endemic to the Caribbean, is represented by the *bartholemica* race.

Non-endemic specialities and spectacular species not mentioned above which also occur include Red-billed Tropicbird (breeds mainly Jan–Jun), White-cheeked Pintail, Clapper Rail, Sooty Tern (breeds Apr–Aug), Brown Noddy (breeds Apr–Aug) and Ruddy Quail-Dove. Barbuda's breeding colony of 2000–3000 pairs of Magnificent Frigate-bird is the largest in the Caribbean. They nest in Aug–Dec on Man-of-War Island in the mangroves of the large **Codrington Lagoon** at its west end, and it is possible to visit the colony using local boats. Other sites worth visiting on the island include Bull Hole, River Beach, Two Feet Bay, Coco Point and Spanish Point.

Barbuda supports the largest breeding colony of Magnificent Frigatebirds, the supreme flying pirates, in the Caribbean

CAYMAN ISLANDS

INTRODUCTION

Summary
The three Cayman Islands, which lie south of Cuba and west of Jamaica, support extensive areas of mangrove, complete with the largest colony of Red-footed Boobies in the West Indies, and dry limestone woodlands, where it is possible to see such localized landbirds as Vitelline Warbler*, which otherwise occurs only on the Swan Islands off northern Honduras. With a surprisingly wide variety of other notable species, from White-tailed Tropicbird to Cuban Parrot*, these typically tropical islands make an ideal destination for birders who dream of a relatively relaxed but rewarding break, either from more intense birding trips or the drudgery of daily life.

Size
The total land area of the Cayman Islands is about 259 km². Grand Cayman is situated about 135 km southwest of Little Cayman, which is about 8 km west of Cayman Brac.

Getting Around
The two international airports are situated on Grand Cayman (just a couple of km from the capital, George Town) and Cayman Brac, and all three islands are connected by the inter-island air network. Hiring a vehicle is relatively cheap, but it is also possible to use public transport. Many stretches of road, especially on Cayman Brac and Little Cayman, are rather poor. The official language of this UK Dependent Territory is English.

Accommodation and Food
Virtually all types of accommodation, which range from luxurious resorts through self-catering villas to small guest houses, are expensive, but it is possible to camp and, fortunately, the best time to visit the islands, between mid-April and June, falls within the mid-April to November low season, when it may be possible to negotiate substantial price reductions. During the December to mid-April high season it is wise to book any accommodation well in advance. The wide range of food available includes Cayman Island specialities such as sauteed fish, but eating out will probably prove much more expensive than self-catering.

Health and Safety
The only problem anyone is likely to encounter on these friendly islands is from the mosquitoes, although, fortunately, the local bloodsuckers rarely carry malaria (check the recent situation before departure).

Climate and Timing
The best time to visit the Cayman Islands is April–June when seabirds such as White-tailed Tropicbird and Red-footed Booby are breeding. Most rain, in the form of short, sharp showers, falls in May–October.

Habitats

The Cayman Islands support extensive mangroves, including the largest single stand in the Caribbean (on Grand Cayman), as well as dry limestone woodlands and scrub, a few salt ponds, and, along or near the coasts, there are low cliffs and coral reefs.

Conservation

A rapidly increasing resident human population, which almost doubled from 18,000 in 1984 to 33,000 in 1995, and an ever-expanding tourist industry is placing severe pressure on the fragile habitats of the Cayman Islands. For example, if the airport on Little Cayman is expanded it could destroy the adjacent mangroves and the Red-footed Booby colony they support. Between them the Department of Environment and Cayman Islands National Trust have managed to 'protect' 5% of the land and they are investigating the potential for implementing environmental taxes, which could be used to purchase and manage land for nature conservation, but more habitat needs protecting now in order to conserve the three threatened and near-threatened species, as well as the relatively common and widespread birds, which occur on these islands.

Endemics

There are no birds endemic to the Cayman Islands. The endemic Grand Cayman Thrush was last reported in 1938, in dense woodland at the eastern end of the island.

Caribbean Endemics

Nine of the 51 Caribbean endemics not confined to single countries, islands or archipelagos occur on the Cayman Islands. They are Vitelline Warbler*, which otherwise occurs only on the Swan Islands off northern Honduras; Cuban Bullfinch (Grand Cayman), which otherwise occurs only on Cuba; three species confined to the Cayman Islands, Cuba and the Bahamas, namely Cuban Parrot* (Grand Cayman and Cayman Brac), West Indian Woodpecker (Grand Cayman) and La Sagra's Flycatcher (Grand Cayman); and four more widespread species, West Indian Whistling-Duck*, Loggerhead Kingbird, Red-legged Thrush (Cayman Brac) and Greater Antillean Grackle. The *bairdi* race of Jamaican Oriole, which was endemic to Grand Cayman, has not been recorded since 1967.

Caribbean Near-endemics

Nine of the 18 species almost endemic to the Caribbean occur on the Cayman Islands. They are White-crowned Pigeon, Zenaida and Caribbean (Grand Cayman, rare on Cayman Brac) Doves, Antillean Nighthawk (mainly May–Aug), Caribbean Elaenia, Thick-billed (Grand Cayman and Cayman Brac), Black-whiskered (Little Cayman and Cayman Brac, Feb–Aug) and Yucatan (Grand Cayman) Vireos, and Northern Stripe-headed Tanager (Grand Cayman). In addition, the *petechia* group of Yellow Warbler, known as 'Golden Warbler', which is also nearly endemic to the Caribbean, is represented by the *eoa* race.

Bird species

Approximately 180 species have been recorded on and around the Cayman Islands, of which at least 45 have bred. Non-endemic specialities and spectacular species not mentioned above include White-tailed

Tropicbird (breeds mainly Mar–Jul), Red-footed Booby (breeds mainly Apr–Jun), Magnificent Frigatebird, Northern Flicker (the *chrysocaulosus* race which is confined to Grand Cayman and Cuba), passage migrant and wintering New World warblers such as Cape May, Black-throated Blue, Yellow-throated and Prairie Warblers, and Yellow-faced Grassquit.

Expectations

It is possible to see over 40 species in a single day on Grand Cayman, and more on a prolonged visit to all three islands, especially during the winter.

GRAND CAYMAN

Almost half of this small, low-lying island, which is about 35 km long and about 6.5 km wide, is composed of mangrove wetlands and the 24 km² shallow bay known as North Sound supports the largest remaining single area of mangrove in the Caribbean. These extensive wetlands support birds such as West Indian Whistling-Duck* (over 360 in 1995), while the dry, often dense, limestone woodland, much of which lies at the east end of the island, supports such species as Cuban Parrot* (about 1900 in 1995), Yucatan Vireo and Vitelline Warbler*.

Localised Caribbean Endemics
West Indian Whistling-Duck*, Vitelline Warbler*, Cuban Bullfinch.

Other Caribbean Endemics
Cuban Parrot*, West Indian Woodpecker, La Sagra's Flycatcher, Loggerhead Kingbird, Greater Antillean Grackle.

Localised Caribbean Near-endemics
Caribbean Dove, Thick-billed and Yucatan Vireos.

GRAND CAYMAN

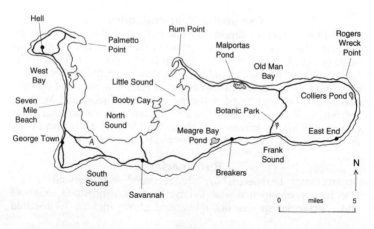

Other Caribbean Near-endemics
White-crowned Pigeon, Antillean Nighthawk (mainly May–Aug), Caribbean Elaenia, Northern Stripe-headed Tanager.

Others
Tricoloured and Green Herons, Osprey, White-winged Dove, Northern Flicker, Grey Kingbird (mainly Apr–Oct), Yellow Warbler, Yellow-faced Grassquit.

Most of the development associated with the tourist industry has taken place along Seven Mile Beach in the west so it is to the east that birders should head: to **North Sound** for West Indian Whistling-Duck* and other waterbirds; **South Sound Swamp** for Yucatan Vireo; the 97 ha of dry limestone woodland in the **Mastic Reserve**, in the centre of the island, where Cuban Parrot*, West Indian Woodpecker, La Sagra's Flycatcher, Vitelline Warbler* and Cuban Bullfinch occur; **Meagre Bay Pond** on the south coast; **Malportas Pond** on the north coast; the 1.5 km-long trail in the **Botanic Park**, off Frank Sound Road; and to **Willie's Pig Farm** where the owner feeds hundreds of wild West Indian Whistling Ducks*.

LITTLE CAYMAN

The extensive areas of primarily mangrove wetlands on this thinly populated, low-lying island, which is about 16 km long and 1.5 km wide, support the largest colony of Red-footed Boobies in the Caribbean. About 5,000 pairs breed here, usually in Apr–Jun, along with 120–150 pairs of Magnificent Frigatebird.

Localised Caribbean Endemics
West Indian Whistling-Duck*, Vitelline Warbler*.

Other Caribbean Endemics
Loggerhead Kingbird.

Caribbean Near-endemics
White-crowned Pigeon, Caribbean Elaenia, Northern Stripe-headed Tanager.

Others
Red-footed Booby, Magnificent Frigatebird, Tricoloured and Green Herons, Yellow-crowned Night-Heron, Wilson's Plover, White-winged Dove, Grey Kingbird (mainly Apr–Oct), Yellow Warbler, Yellow-faced Grassquit.

It is possible to visit the booby and frigatebird colony during a day trip to Little Cayman from one of the other islands, by boat from Cayman Brac and by plane from Grand Cayman, since the sanctuary is just east of the airport at the west end of the island. Part of the mangroves, as well as their adjacent wetlands and some evergreen thicket lie within the **Booby Pond Sanctuary**, but the rest of the area, which also supports the only breeding colony of Magnificent Frigatebird in the Cay-

LITTLE CAYMAN

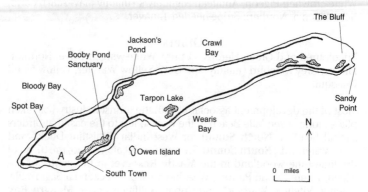

man Islands and West Indian Whistling-Duck*, and is important for wintering herons and migrant shorebirds, is under threat of development. Other areas worth including on a short visit include **Tarpon Lake** and nearby **Wearis Bay**.

CAYMAN BRAC

This island, which is about 16 km long and 1.5 km wide, is a limestone bluff which rises from sea-level in the west, where the airport is situated, to 43 m in the east, where the cliffs support breeding White-tailed Tropicbird.

Localised Caribbean Endemics
Vitelline Warbler*.

Other Caribbean Endemics
Cuban Parrot*, Loggerhead Kingbird, Red-legged Thrush (mainly Apr–Aug).

Localised Caribbean Near-endemics
Thick-billed Vireo.

Other Caribbean Near-endemics
White-crowned Pigeon, Antillean Nighthawk (mainly May–Aug), Caribbean Elaenia, Northern Stripe-headed Tanager.

Others
White-tailed Tropicbird (mainly Mar–Jul), Brown Booby, Magnificent Frigatebird, Tricoloured and Green Herons, Yellow-crowned Night-Heron, Purple Gallinule, Willet, Mangrove Cuckoo, Grey Kingbird (mainly Apr–Oct), Yellow Warbler, Yellow-faced Grassquit. (Other species recorded here include Caribbean Dove and Greater Antillean Grackle).

This island is about 30 minutes by air from Grand Cayman. Most White-tailed Tropicbirds breed in the inland cliff, which runs parallel to the

CAYMAN BRAC

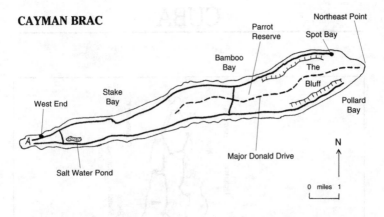

northeast coast and a good place to look for them is along the cliff overlooking the settlement at **Spot Bay**. Antillean Nighthawk and Red-
legged Thrush also occur here, and Brown Booby breeds on the cliffs
around here and **Pollard Bay**. Five of the Cayman Island's eight endemic subspecies are relatively easy to see on Cayman Brac: Caribbean
Elaenia, Loggerhead Kingbird, Red-legged Thrush, Vitelline Warbler*
and Bananaquit, but the remaining three, Caribbean Dove, Cuban Parrot* and Greater Antillean Grackle, are all difficult. The best place for
most of the landbirds, including the parrot, the vireo and the warbler is
the 73 ha **Parrot Reserve** along Major Donald Drive. From the lighthouse at Northeast Point at the end of Major Donald Drive it is possible
to walk west in search of tropicbirds.

ADDITIONAL INFORMATION

Addresses

Cayman Islands Department of Tourism, The Pavilion, Cricket Square,
Elgin Avenue, George Town, Grand Cayman, British West Indies (tel.
949 0623, fax. 949 4053, web site: www.caymanislands.ky).
Cayman Islands National Trust (tel. 949 0121; e-mail: ntrust@candw.ky).

Books

The Birds of the Cayman Islands, Bradley, P. E. 2000. BOU.

CUBA

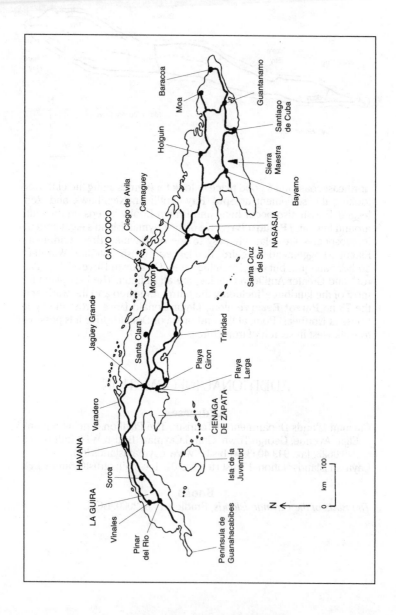

INTRODUCTION

Summary

Cuba supports 24 endemic species and several more with very limited ranges. However, quality arguably outweighs quantity in this corner of

272

the Caribbean thanks to the presence of four of the region's six quail-doves, the brilliant Bee Hummingbird* (the smallest bird on earth), a beautiful endemic trogon, an equally exotic tody, and three endemic New World warblers, which are joined during passage and winter periods by a wonderful range of warblers that breed in North America. Cuba is a costly country to visit, as the quickest and easiest way to cover the 2500 km or so necessary to see the vast majority of endemics and near-endemics is by hire car, but virtually all of the specialities should be fairly easy to find in little more than a week.

Size

At 114,525 km² Cuba is the largest island in the Caribbean. It measures 1250 km from west to east and up to 191 km north to south.

Getting Around

Travel to Cuba by US citizens must be approved by the office of Foreign Assets Control and permission is usually given only to those visiting family members or on official government business, or, in some circumstances, to those such as journalists, scientists and writers visiting in a professional capacity. Many of the US birders who have made it, once permission has been granted, have done so on trips organised by the joint Canadian–Cuban ringing programme, coordinated by Long Point Bird Observatory, Ontario (see Additional Information, p. 293). Even then it is necessary to travel to Cuba from outside the USA, with Canada being the most convenient country from which to fly. For further advice on obtaining a visa to visit Cuba, US citizens should contact the Cuban Interests Section, Cuban Government, 2630 16th Street NW, Washington DC 20009, USA (tel. (202) 797 8518).

The public transport system on Cuba is poor, hence it is almost essential to hire a vehicle and cover something in the region of 2500 km in order to see the highest possible percentage of the endemic and other restricted-range birds. Travel by car is fairly easy and although the main autopista resembles a disused airfield along much of its length the roads are, on the whole, relatively good and largely devoid of other vehicles. However, there are plenty of cattle, bicycle riders, hitchhikers and potholes so it is wise to keep a sharp lookout for these, especially if driving at night. Unfortunately, hiring a vehicle is very expensive so budget birders may wish to use the reasonably priced internal air network (which connects places such as Camagüey and Cayo Coco, two important destinations), the skeletal bus and rail services (both of which are usually booked solid well in advance), taxis and/or by hitchhiking. The majority of Cubans travel by hitchhiking and since most empty trucks stop to pick up passengers this is an extremely cheap way of covering long distances. One reason why there are so few buses and trains is because fuel remains a scarce commodity and tourists are only permitted to fill up at designated petrol stations, which are few and far between, so watch the fuel gauge very carefully and at each major base find out where the filling station that accepts dollars is situated. A basic grasp of Spanish will help in getting around, as Cubans are always willing to help with directions.

Accommodation and Food

All of Cuba's hotels are owned by the government, either solely or in joint ventures with foreign partners, and tourists are officially expected to stay in these expensive, but often basic, establishments. However, foreign visitors who venture away from the package-holiday resorts and travel around the island independently will also be offered cheaper accommodation in private houses, known as casa particulares, licensed by the government to rent rooms and provide food for their guests. Upon arriving in a town or village it doesn't usually take long to find a casa particulare or for the Cubans who run them to find you. There some campsites but camping elsewhere is officially forbidden.

The US embargo on Cuba, in place since the early 1960s, sanctions the export of food (and medicines) and though Canadian and European exporters do supply the country with some foodstuffs most independent travellers leave Cuba wondering what the people eat, and where and when they get whatever it is they eat from, as the only shops that appear to sell food are the few which accept dollars only. Many people in rural areas grow their own food and the favourite dish is, apparently, rice with black beans (congris), though fish followed by fresh fruit is served just as often in the casa particulares or paladares, which are private homes licensed to serve food.

Health and Safety
Vaccination against hepatitis, polio, tetanus, typhoid and yellow fever (compulsory if arriving from an infected country) is recommended. Though malaria has been eradicated there are still plenty of mosquitoes, hence it is wise to take sufficient repellent. Cuba is an extremely safe, friendly and relaxed country where petty and violent crimes are virtually non-existent, and it may well be the safest country in the world to visit.

Climate and Timing
The best time to visit is during March, at the end of the dry season, by which time a few early Antillean Nighthawks may be present, male Bee Hummingbirds* are in their full splendour, Cuban Martin has returned from its unknown winter quarters, most wintering New World warblers are still present and others, along with shorebirds, are passing through, and water levels in Zapata Swamp, where Zapata Wren* occurs, are usually low enough for visitors to get away with having to wade through thigh-high water in order to reach the best areas for this highly localised endemic.

This is a hot, humid country, and it is especially hot during July–August, although northeast trade winds moderate temperatures at this time. Most rain falls in May–October when heavy downpours often dominate the afternoons, and the hurricane season is usually July/August–October/November, with rainfall and humidity peaking at the end of this period. It is relatively cooler and drier in December–March when it can be quite chilly at night during periods when cool air spreads from the north.

Habitats
The predominantly flat and rolling island of Cuba is situated in the Caribbean Sea 145 km south of Florida and 210 km east of Mexico's Yucatán Peninsula. Approximately a quarter of this relatively sparsely populated island is mountainous and there are three main ranges: the Cordillera de Guaniguanico in the west, which is subdivided into the narrow Sierra de los Organos in the west, rising to 750 m, and the Sier-

ra del Rosario in the east; the Sierra del Escambray in the centre, which rises to 1140 m at Pico San Juan; and the Sierra Maestra in the east, which rises to 1974 m at Pico Turquino, the highest peak on the island. About 24% of Cuba is still 'forested', mainly with montane mahogany and Caribbean pine, although original tree cover is mainly confined, in the form of dry, lowland, coastal woodland, to the Zapata area in the west, and, montane Caribbean pine forest, to the steepest slopes of the extreme southeast. Over 30% of the island is cultivated—the moderate climate, excellent soils and ample rainfall constitute ideal growing conditions and much of the island is covered in citrus orchards and great swathes of sugarcane, together with coffee and tobacco plantations, all intermixed with stands of royal palm. A further 27% of the land is used for pasture and about 4% is classified as swamp. The northern coast is slowly rising, forcing offshore coral reefs to the surface and forming a coastline of beaches, limestone cliffs and offshore cays. The southern coast is slowly sinking, hence there are many wetlands there, mainly in the form of mangrove-lined mudflats.

As well as the world's smallest bird Cuba supports the world's smallest mammal (the shrew-like almiquí), smallest bat (the butterfly/moth bat) and smallest frog (the 12 mm-long Cuban pygmy frog). The smallest bird in the world is the Bee Hummingbird*, males of which measure 57 mm, although half of this is bill and tail, leaving a body measuring just 29 mm! The smallest European bird, the Goldcrest, measures 90 mm and weighs 4.2 g, but the Bee Hummingbird* weighs just 1.6 g making it is less than half the weight of a Goldcrest and lighter than a privet hawk-moth!

Conservation

Between the late 15th Century, when the Spanish arrived, and the end of the 20th Century forested land on Cuba was reduced from what was believed to be over 90% to less than 30%. The clearance of large areas of native Caribbean pine forest together with the draining of wetlands for the conversion of land to sugarcane production (Cuba was producing about a third of the world's sugar by the mid-1800s) are probably key reasons why Ivory-billed Woodpecker* and Bachman's Warbler* have almost certainly become extinct, though the warbler was formerly only a winter visitor from North America. A total of 20 threatened or near-threatened species, including 11 endemics, occur on the island. The conservation of their habitats, as well as those of the relatively common and widespread species, is of paramount importance, but while the Cuban government has accorded 10% of the island some form of 'protection', even in areas such as National Parks uncontrolled charcoal production, due to the fuel shortage, and other damaging activities continue apace, so much more must be done to conserve Cuba's exciting and unique avifauna.

Endemics

A total of 24 species are endemic to Cuba and one, Cuban Martin, is a breeding endemic.

Gundlach's Hawk*	Very rare and localised: most likely to be seen in the Zapata area, although also recorded elsewhere, including Cayo Coco and La Güira.

	There are three main population centres for the western and central *gundlachii* race, and two for the eastern *wileyi* race
Zapata Rail*	Very rare and localised; known only from a handful of sites in Zapata, where it is often heard by visiting birders but very rarely seen
Blue-headed Quail-Dove*	Fairly rare and localised; most likely to be seen in Zapata, though also recorded regularly at La Güira (May–Jun) and on Península de Guanaha-cabibes
Cuban Parakeet*	Fairly rare and localised; most likely to be seen in the Najasa area near Camagüey, although it also occurs in the Zapata area, and south of Moa and around La Melba in the east of the island
Cuban Screech-Owl (Bare-legged Owl)	Locally fairly common; most likely to be seen in Zapata where local guides usually know where birds are roosting
Cuban Pygmy-Owl	Common and widespread, and usually easy to find in Zapata
Cuban Nightjar (Greater Antillean)	Widespread, but easiest to locate in the Zapata area
Bee Hummingbird*	Rare and localised; most likely to be seen in Zapata, where local guides usually know a favoured locality
Cuban Trogon	Fairly common and widespread
Cuban Tody	Common and widespread
Cuban Woodpecker	Fairly common and widespread
Fernandina's Flicker*	Very rare and localised: most likely to be found in Zapata (where 60% of the world population of 120 pairs occurs). Also recorded around Soroa and the central provinces east to Holguín
Giant Kingbird*	Endemic to Cuba following its extirpation from Great Inagua and the Caicos Islands. Rare and localised; known from few localities in the late 1990s, and only likely to be seen in the Najasa area near Camagüey, or around Moa in the east of the island
Zapata Wren*	Very rare and localised; confined to Zapata where it is only likely to be seen with the assistance of local guides
Cuban Solitaire*	Locally fairly common, especially at La Güira, the Sierra de los Organos and the Sierra del Rosario in the

	west, and more widely in the east
Cuban Gnatcatcher	Fairly common on larger cays off the north-central coast; usually fairly easy to find on Cayo Coco, and in eastern Cuba, especially in coastal areas
Cuban Palm Crow*	Confined to the northwestern Sierra de los Organos in Pinar del Río Province and Camagüey Province where it is easiest to locate (in the Najasa area)
Cuban Vireo	Common and widespread
Yellow-headed Warbler	Fairly common and widespread in western Cuba.
Oriente Warbler	Locally common in eastern Cuba, west to Villa Clara Province
Cuban Grassquit	Widespread and common in the east, but scarce and increasingly difficult to locate in the Zapata and Najasa areas
Zapata Sparrow*	Rare and localised: three races occur, in the Zapata area (*inexpectata*), where usually seen with the aid of local guides, on Cayo Coco (*varonai*), where regularly recorded by visiting birders, and on the far southeast coast, east of Guantánamo Bay (*sigmani*)
Red-shouldered Blackbird	Locally fairly common in western Cuba, where most likely to be seen in the Zapata area, although it can be difficult to locate
Cuban Blackbird	Common and widespread

Some taxonomists believe the following races of species, endemic to Cuba, should be treated as a full species: Hook-billed Kite (*wilsonii*), Common Black-Hawk (*gundlachii*) and Grey-headed Quail (*caniceps*). In addition, the Cuban Poorwill (*siphonorhis daiquiri*), known only from fossils, could still exist where xerophytic scrub remains, such as along the coast of Guantánamo province.

One species breeds only on Cuba:

Cuban Martin	Fairly common and widespread in Feb–Aug; probably winters in South America.

Other Caribbean Endemics
A total of 19 of the 51 Caribbean endemics not confined to single countries, islands or archipelagos occur on Cuba. They are: four species which occur only on Cuba and the Bahamas, namely Great Lizard-Cuckoo, Cuban Emerald, Cuban Pewee and Olive-capped Warbler; three species confined to Cuba, the Bahamas and the Cayman Islands, Cuban Parrot*, West Indian Woodpecker and La Sagra's Flycatcher; one con-

fined to Cuba and Cayman Islands, Cuban Bullfinch; one restricted to Cuba and the Turks & Caicos Islands, Cuban Crow; one confined to Cuba and Haiti, Tawny-shouldered Blackbird; one solely found in Cuba and the Dominican Republic, Grey-headed Quail-Dove*; and eight more widespread species, West Indian Whistling-Duck*, Plain Pigeon*, Key West Quail-Dove, Antillean Palm-Swift, Loggerhead Kingbird, Bahama Mockingbird (cays off the north coast), Red-legged Thrush and Greater Antillean Grackle.

Caribbean Near-endemics

Eight of the 18 species nearly endemic to the Caribbean occur on Cuba. They are White-crowned and Scaly-naped Pigeons, Zenaida Dove, Antillean Nighthawk (mainly May–Aug), Thick-billed (principally one cay off north coast) and Black-whiskered (Feb–Aug) Vireos, Northern Stripe-headed Tanager and Black-faced Grassquit (rare). In addition the *petechia* group of Yellow Warbler, known as 'Golden Warbler', which is also nearly endemic to the Caribbean, is represented by the *gundlachi* race.

The above lists do not include Black-capped Petrel*, which was recorded in the Valle de Yaguanabo, Alturas de Trinidad, in 1976–1990 at least; Ivory-billed Woodpecker*, the last sight record of which was of two in April 1986 at Ojito de Agua in the east of the island (two extensive expeditions in 1991 and 1993 failed to find any but the species may have been heard in the late 1990s); and Bachman's Warbler*, the last widely accepted record for Cuba being in 1964 and the last certain record for North America being of a singing male near Charleston, South Carolina, in 1962.

Bird species

Over 350 species have been recorded in Cuba. Non-endemic specialities and spectacular species not already mentioned include Magnificent Frigatebird, Reddish Egret, Greater Flamingo, White-cheeked Pintail, Masked Duck, Snail Kite, Sandhill Crane (endemic *nesiotes* race), Limpkin, Yellow-breasted Crake, Spotted Rail, Northern Jacana, Ruddy Quail-Dove, Stygian Owl (endemic *siguapa* race), White-collared Swift, Blue-grey Gnatcatcher, a whole host of passage migrant and wintering New World warblers including Cape May, Black-throated Blue and Prairie Warblers, Red-legged Honeycreeper, Yellow-faced Grassquit and Black-cowled Oriole.

Expectations

It is possible to see 140–180 species on a two-week trip in November–April, including most, if not all, of the endemics (Zapata Rail* is only very rarely seen, even by the local birders) and near-endemics, as well as 20 New World warblers.

Few birds occur in central Havana but they include numerous pairs of Cuban Martin (Feb–Aug), as well as Antillean Palm-Swift. **Parque Lenin**, a large park on the southern outskirts of the capital with remnant forest (best near the Motel La Herradura), large areas of open grassland and a shallow lake known as Embalse Paso Sequito, supports Great Lizard-Cuckoo, Cuban Emerald, La Sagra's Flycatcher and Red-legged Thrush, as well as Least Grebe, Osprey, Purple Gallinule, Killdeer, Black Skimmer (rare), Belted Kingfisher, Yellow-bellied Sapsucker (Oct–Apr), and passage and wintering New World vireos (including Yellow-throated) and warblers (including Magnolia, Prairie and the very occasional Blue-winged).

The 20 km-long sandspit known as **Península de Hicacos**, on which Varadero, Cuba's premier beach resort, is situated, 144 km east of Havana, supports few birds but they do include Magnificent Frigatebird, passage migrant and wintering shorebirds such as Wilson's and Piping* Plovers, Short-billed Dowitcher and Willet, Royal Tern and Cuban Emerald, and Cayo Mono, about 10 km northeast of Punta de Morlas, has breeding seabirds such as Bridled and Sooty Terns, and Brown Noddy, mainly in April–August.

The forest around Villa Soroa (tel. 85 2122), an expensive inland spa resort in the Sierra del Rosario about 80 km southwest of Havana (signed off the autopista), supports Scaly-naped Pigeon, Ruddy and Blue-headed* Quail-Doves, Cuban Screech-Owl (around Bar Eden is a good place to look for this species), Cuban Solitaire*, Yellow-headed Warbler, passage migrant and wintering New World warblers, Northern Stripe-headed Tanager and Red-legged Honeycreeper. In addition, rarities such as Gundlach's Hawk* and Fernandina's Flicker* have been recorded here. From the resort bird the track that ascends a limestone knoll to the viewpoint (El Mirador).

The vast irrigated fields of black beans and tomatoes, together with the nearby mangrove-lined mudflats around **Maspoton** in southwest Cuba, support a wide range of waterbirds, including Anhinga, Fulvous Whistling-Duck, Wood and Masked Ducks, Sandhill Crane, King Rail, Sora (Oct–Apr) and Northern Jacana, as well as Crested Caracara, Yellow Warbler and Red-shouldered Blackbird. To reach there take the turning off the autopista (heading towards Pinar del Río) to Los Palacios, cross the railway line at the east end of town and continue to the small village of Sierra Maestra. The basic cabins, used by hunters, at Maspoton are 9 km further. To look for Masked Duck stop at roadside ditches and wait for them to slowly resurface, often with just their heads above water, having dived on your approach. The mangrove-lined mudflats at Los Ramplacos, 3 km to the south, are important for shorebirds (over 500 Stilt Sandpipers in Feb 1991 for example), and best explored with a local guide.

PARQUE NACIONAL DE LA GÜIRA

The semi-evergreen broadleaf and Caribbean pine forests on the limestone hills of the Cordillera de Guaniguanico, which rises to 750 m just two hours by road southwest of Havana, support two localized species, the endemic Cuban Solitaire* and near-endemic Olive-capped Warbler, which, along with Scaly-naped Pigeon, are best looked for here.

Localised Cuban Endemics
Cuban Solitaire*.

Other Cuban Endemics
Cuban Trogon, Cuban Tody, Cuban Woodpecker, Cuban Vireo, Yellow-headed Warbler, Cuban Blackbird.

Localised Caribbean Endemics
Olive-capped Warbler, Cuban Bullfinch, Tawny-shouldered Blackbird.

Other Caribbean Endemics
Great Lizard-Cuckoo, Antillean Palm-Swift, Cuban Emerald, West Indian Woodpecker, Cuban Pewee, La Sagra's Flycatcher, Loggerhead Kingbird, Red-legged Thrush, Greater Antillean Grackle.

Caribbean Near-endemics
Scaly-naped Pigeon, Zenaida Dove, Antillean Nighthawk (mainly May–Aug), Cuban Martin (Feb–Aug), Northern Stripe-headed Tanager.

Non-endemic Specialities
Stygian Owl.

Passage Migrants and Winter Visitors
Yellow-bellied Sapsucker, Grey Catbird, White-eyed Vireo, Northern Parula, Magnolia, Cape May, Black-throated Blue, Black-throated Green, Yellow-throated, Prairie, Palm and Black-and-white Warblers, American Redstart, Worm-eating Warbler (scarce), Ovenbird, Hooded Warbler (scarce).

PARQUE NACIONAL DE LA GÜIRA

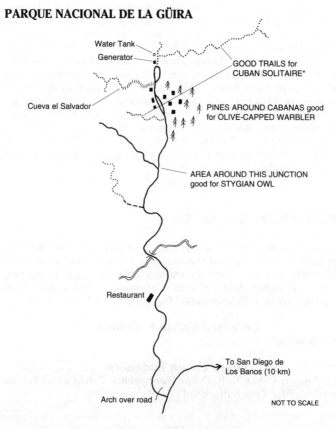

Others

Sharp-shinned, Red-tailed and Broad-winged Hawks, Northern Bob-white, Ruddy Quail-Dove, Smooth-billed Ani, Grey Kingbird (mainly Apr–Oct), Cave Swallow (mainly Mar–Oct), Blue-grey Gnatcatcher, Red-legged Honeycreeper, Yellow-faced Grassquit, Black-cowled Oriole.

(Other species recorded here include Gundlach's Hawk*, Plain Pigeon*, Grey-headed*, Key West and Blue-headed* Quail-Doves, Cuban Pygmy-Owl, Northern Flicker and Cedar Waxwing (Oct–Apr).)

To reach the park from Havana head southwest on the A4 autopista towards Pinar del Rio and turn north at km 103 to the small town of San Diego de Los Baños. Continue through here for 10 km to the park entrance, which is marked by a stone archway. Head through the archway for 5 km or so, then turn right to reach the Cabañas Los Pinos at the end of the road. The cabins are rundown wooden 'tree houses', built in a bold but alas unsuccessful attempt to start a hill-top resort. They are surrounded by excellent pine forest, which supports Olive-capped Warbler, and when the palm trees alongside the road are fruiting they attract a variety of species including Cuban Trogon, Black-throated Blue and Yellow-throated Warblers, Northern Stripe-headed Tanager and Red-legged Honeycreeper. Also bird along the trail above the cabins, which starts opposite the water tank, and along the trail below the cabins, which starts opposite the lowest cabin. These trails run through excellent forest where Cuban Solitaire* is quite common, along with the stunning Cuban Tody and many other birds. Stygian Owl occurs at the road junction a couple of km below the cabins.

Accommodation: San Diego de Los Baños—Motel Mirador.

The large town of Pinar del Río, 174 km west of Havana, is the gateway to a scenic valley near **Viñales** in the Sierra de los Organos to the north, where Cuban Solitaire*, Olive-capped Warbler and Cuban Grassquit

The endemic Cuban Trogon, known locally as 'tocoloro' because of its familiar call, is one of the world's most beautiful trogons

occur and where rarities such as Gundlach's Hawk* and Fernandina's Flicker* have also been recorded. To reach the valley ask for directions in the small town of Viñales, which is about 25 km north of Pinar del Río. The road leads to a sheer limestone cliff, one of the many in this area of steep-sided limestone hills (known as Mogotes) which rise from the flat, fertile valley bottom. At the base of the cliff there is a restaurant. The large reservoir near La Ermita Motel is also worth checking as it supports Masked Duck, wintering waterfowl such as Lesser Scaup, Snail Kite, and passage and wintering shorebirds.

A broad range of waterbirds, including Masked Duck, Snail Kite, King Rail, Sora (Oct–Apr), Yellow-breasted Crake (Playa Colorada), Northern Jacana and Black Skimmer (Playa Colorada), as well as Ruby-throated Hummingbird (very scarce, Nov–Apr) and Cuban Grassquit have been recorded at **Laguna Grande** and **Playa Colorada**. To reach these sites take the main road west from Pinar del Río to San Juan Martínez and Isabel Rubio, then continue straight on for about 10 km and turn right, opposite a military base. Near the village of Simon Bolívar turn left at the crossroads and Laguna Grande is 3 km further. The brackish lagoon at Playa Colorada is 15 km beyond Simon Bolívar.

The sparsely populated **Península de Guanahacabibes**, a 1175 km^2 Biosphere Reserve in extreme western Cuba, is accessible only with a permit, which can be obtained, often with difficulty, from the tourist office in Pinar del Río. To reach here head west towards Sandino, then La Fé and on to El Cayuco where a right turn leads to the barrier at La Bajada, where it is necessary to show the permit in order to continue. About 150 species have been recorded, including nine Cuban endemics. The grasslands and forests west of La Fé and the dense scrub, forest and mangrove (on the north coast) of the peninsula itself support Plain Pigeon*, Blue-headed Quail-Dove*, Cuban Parrot*, Cuban Crow, Yellow-headed Warbler, passage and wintering New World warblers, and Red-legged Honeycreeper. There is a small tourist development with beach huts and a restaurant.

CIÉNAGA DE ZAPATA

The 7500 km^2, 130 km-long Ciénaga de Zapata peninsula, nearly half of which lies within the 3278 km^2 National Park, is situated alongside the Bahía de Cochinos (Bay of Pigs) on Cuba's south coast, 157 km and 2.5 hours by road southeast of Havana. The peninsula is bordered to the south by mangrove-lined mudflats and saline lagoons/salinas that support numerous waterbirds. Inland there is a 1–2 km-broad strip of dry coastal forest with a low floral diversity, few palms and a maximum tree height of 7 m. This gives way to another 1–2 km-wide belt of dry forest with higher floral diversity, more palms and a maximum tree height of 10 m, known as the *costanera*. Inland of this are vast expanses of seasonally flooded swamps with 2.4 m-high sawgrass and buttonwood bushes. This rare combination of rich habitats which extends east of the peninsula supports two birds which occur only in this part of Cuba: the very rarely seen Zapata Rail* and the extremely rare, but frequently observed, Zapata Wren*; three highly local endemics, the very rare but frequently observed Gundlach's Hawk*, the very rare and increasingly difficult to find Fernandina's Flicker*, and the rare *inexpectata* race of Zapata Sparrow*; as well as 'Pájaro mosca', the local name for Bee Hummingbird*.

In all, 19 of the 24 Cuban endemics occur in the area and the presence of these, together with a wide variety of other Caribbean endemics and many widespread Nearctic species, including a host of passage and wintering New World warblers, makes Zapata one of, if not, *the* richest area for birds in the entire Caribbean. Over 200 species have been recorded in total and in a few days between November and March it is possible to see well over 130 species, including over 75 in a single day.

Localised Cuban Endemics
Gundlach's Hawk*, Zapata Rail*, Blue-headed Quail-Dove*, Cuban Parakeet*, Cuban Screech-Owl, Bee Hummingbird*, Fernandina's Flicker*, Zapata Wren*, Cuban Grassquit, Zapata Sparrow*, Red-shouldered Blackbird.

Other Cuban Endemics
Cuban Pygmy-Owl, Cuban Nightjar, Cuban Trogon, Cuban Tody, Cuban Woodpecker, Cuban Vireo, Yellow-headed Warbler, Cuban Blackbird.

Localised Caribbean Endemics
Grey-headed Quail-Dove*, Cuban Crow, Cuban Bullfinch, Tawny-shouldered Blackbird.

Other Caribbean Endemics
Key West Quail-Dove, Cuban Parrot*, Great Lizard-Cuckoo, Cuban Emerald, Antillean Palm-Swift, West Indian Woodpecker, Cuban Pewee, La Sagra's Flycatcher, Loggerhead Kingbird, Red-legged Thrush, Greater Antillean Grackle.

Caribbean Near-endemics
White-crowned Pigeon, Zenaida Dove, Antillean Nighthawk (mainly May–Aug), Cuban Martin (Feb–Aug), Northern Stripe-headed Tanager (scarce).

Non-endemic Specialities
Common Black-Hawk, Sandhill Crane, Stygian Owl.

Passage Migrants and Winter Visitors
Blue-winged Teal, Sora, Short-billed Dowitcher, Least, Pectoral and Stilt Sandpipers, Yellow-bellied Sapsucker, Grey Catbird, White-eyed and Yellow-throated Vireos, Northern Parula, Magnolia, Cape May, Black-throated Blue, Black-throated Green, Yellow-throated, Prairie, Palm and Black-and-white Warblers, American Redstart, Worm-eating Warbler (scarce), Ovenbird, Northern and Louisiana Waterthrushes, Common Yellowthroat, Indigo Bunting (scarce).

Others
Least Grebe, Brown Pelican, Anhinga, Reddish Egret, Yellow-crowned Night-Heron, Least Bittern, Wood Stork, White and Glossy Ibises, Roseate Spoonbill, Greater Flamingo, Fulvous Whistling-Duck, Osprey, Snail Kite (scarce), Sharp-shinned Hawk, Crested Caracara (scarce), Northern Bobwhite, Limpkin, Clapper and King Rails, Purple Gallinule,

Northern Jacana, Wilson's Plover, Caspian and Royal Terns, White-winged Dove (local), Ruddy Quail-Dove, Smooth-billed Ani, Belted Kingfisher, Northern Flicker, Grey Kingbird (mainly Apr–Oct), Cave Swallow (mainly Mar–Oct), Blue-grey Gnatcatcher, Yellow Warbler, Red-legged Honeycreeper, Yellow-faced Grassquit, Shiny Cowbird, Black-cowled Oriole.

(Other species recorded include Magnificent Frigatebird, West Indian Whistling-Duck*, Wood and Masked Ducks, Yellow-breasted Crake, Spotted Rail, Black Skimmer, Chuck-will's-widow (Sep–May), passage migrant and wintering Blue-winged, Golden-winged, Yellow-rumped and Swainson's Warblers, Savannah Sparrow and Orchard Oriole).

Other Wildlife
Cuban crocodile, white-tailed deer, hutia, manatee, powo (a black-and-white snake).

To reach Playa Larga, the main base for birding the Zapata area, head southeast on the A1 autopista towards Santa Clara, then turn south at Jagüey Grande, about 120 km from Havana. It is a 90 km round trip to some of the important sites from Playa Larga and the bus service is poor, thus a vehicle is more or less essential. If using a vehicle try to use as little fuel as possible because this is not always available in the Playa Larga area and it may be necessary to drive to Australia, near Jagüey Grande, to fill up.

In order to search for the rail, wren and sparrow, as well as a number of other species if required, you should contact Orestes Martínez García, alias 'El Chino', by writing or telephoning him in advance, or by asking at Villa Playa Larga or a casa particulare on arrival. He and his brother, Angel, who often accompanies El Chino in the field, can be contacted as follows: Orestes Martínez García (El Chino), Centre de Interpretación, Ambiental, Km 26 Carretera en Playa Larga, Ciénaga de Zapata, CP 43000, Matanzas, Cuba (tel. 59 5670); Angel Martínez García, EMA 'Victoria de Girón', Ciénaga de Zapata, Matanzas (tel. 59 7249). Alternatively you may hire one of the other excellent local guides that work in the National Park, at the EFI office near Playa Larga (see below). All are very knowledgeable, speak some English and carry tape recorders. Once a date has been set to visit the swamp where the 'big three' reside it is necessary to obtain a permit from the Empresa Florestal Integral (EFI) office in Buenaventura, 1 km northwest of Playa Larga by the main road, although El Chino or Angel may deal with this and thus save a considerable amount of time. Permits are also needed to visit Las Salinas, which is within the National Park too. There is a check-point at the park entrance, a km or so west of the EFI office, so anyone attempting to avoid obtaining permits or using guides, is very unlikely to get in, let alone see any of the top birds.

The rail, wren and sparrow inhabit swampy areas near **Santo Tomás**, El Chino's home village, which is about 30 km northwest of Playa Larga. Looking for these involves a short trip in a punt, then, during the wet season (Nov–Feb) there is no choice but to wade in up to your knees and start off through the swamp, complete with biting beetles, sawgrass and, worst of all, invisible limestone sink-holes where the water is considerably deeper. By March it is usually possible, with waterproof boots, to reach far enough into the swamp without getting wet. Once in the swamp it is usually Angel who starts playing the tape of Zapata Wren*, at full blast from a hand-held speaker, but it still usually takes about 40 minutes for the birds to arrive. While waiting it is possible to see Zapata Sparrow* and hear Zapata Rail*, but the chances of seeing the latter are virtually nil, due to the dense vegetation they inhabit. It is best to arrange to be at Santo Tomás by dawn in order to stand a chance of seeing the wren, and if driving to meet El Chino at this time it is worth looking for Cuban Nightjars on the track between the park entrance and Santo Tomás. Other species present around the village include Sandhill Crane, Grey-headed Quail-Dove*, Bee Hummingbird* and Red-shouldered Blackbird*, all of which are most likely to be seen with El Chino's assistance.

The brilliant Bee Hummingbird*, the smallest bird on earth, is endemic to Cuba

The abandoned salt pans, mangroves and mudflats at **Las Salinas**, 21 km south of the park entrance, support Cuban Martin (which breeds in dead snags), as well as arguably the most flamboyant flamingos on earth (they are a deep salmon-pink colour), Reddish Egret, Clapper Rail, Wilson's Plover, Short-billed Dowitcher and, very occasionally, Black Skimmer.

Zapata Sparrow* and Red-shouldered Blackbird can also been seen at **Turba**, although access to this site was restricted at the time of writing (March 2001). To reach here turn west off the road between Playa Larga and the autopista at Jagüey Grande a few hundred metres south of the old entrance to the National Park, marked by an arch over the road 30 minutes drive north of Playa Larga. About 5–6 km along the broad dirt track turn south and cross a wide canal to reach a marshy area, after a km or so, where the sparrow and blackbird frequent the surrounding bushes. Other species recorded here include Least Bittern, Snail Kite, Gundlach's Hawk*, King Rail, Sora, Yellow-breasted Crake, Zapata* and Spotted Rails, and Purple Gallinule.

Cuban Parrot* and Bee Hummingbird* have been recorded at **La Boca**, 11 km north of Playa Larga, where it is possible to travel by boat to Villa Guamá, a replica Indian village and hotel on a small island near the far shore of Laguna del Tesoro. The roadside marshes south of La

Boca (500 m north of Pálpite) support Northern Jacana and other water-birds.

In April 1961 a bunch of Cuban exiles, spurred on by the CIA, attempted to invade Cuba and seize power from Fidel Castro. They attacked from the Bahía de Cochinos but were easily defeated, albeit with much loss of life (military graves can be seen alongside roads in the area) and the final battle took place at **Playa Larga** where there is now a quiet resort with a large accommodation complex known as Villa Playa Larga. Birders staying at this complex often awake to the sound of 'parrot-like squawks and guttural jabbering', which may just be another overtired birder talking in their sleep, but is more likely to be, as James Bond so aptly described it in *Birds of the West Indies*, the call of Cuban Crows, which often appear in the surrounding trees at dawn. The grounds are also the best place in the area to look for Cape May and Yellow-throated Warblers, which visit fruiting palm trees, and Stygian Owl is always worth searching for here.

CIÉNAGA DE ZAPATA AREA

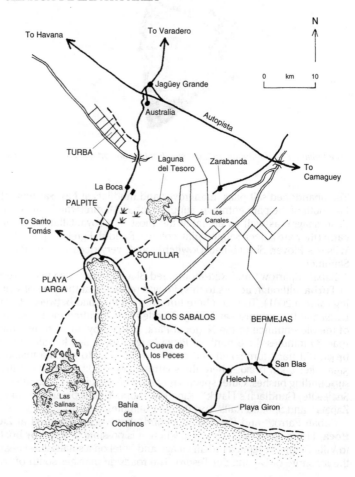

After Santo Tomás the second main area to concentrate on near Playa Larga is alongside the track (and its side tracks) between **Pálpite, Soplillar** and **Los Sabalos** to the east, where the poor-looking remnant forest patches actually deserve considerable attention, because they support Gundlach's Hawk*, the unobtrusive Key West and Blue-head-ed* Quail-Doves, Cuban Nightjar, Bee Hummingbird* (listen for them singing from treetops and check flowering climbers for feeding birds), Cuban Trogon, Cuban Tody and Fernandina's Flicker* (check stumps of broken palm trees). Inland of here the abandoned rice lagoons in and around the series of canals known as **Los Canales**, which drain the freshwater Laguna del Tesoro, support West Indian Whistling-Duck* and Red-shouldered Blackbird, while other species include Snail Kite, King Rail, Sora, Least and Stilt Sandpipers, Savannah Sparrow and Indi-go Bunting. During the wet season (Nov–Feb) the access track from Los Sabalos may be passable only using 4WD, but the area is usually acces-sible with a 2WD during this period from the north, via the autopista and Zarabanda.

About 15 km south of Playa Larga, along the main coast road, Key West Quail-Dove (on the rubbish tip, usually guarded by two dogs, beyond the toilet block, early morning perhaps best) and Blue-headed Quail-Dove* (around the restaurant from 3pm onward) occur around the pool at Cueva de los Peces.

The bejeweled Blue-headed Quail-Dove* is one of Cuba's several superb endemics

The third major birding area near Playa Larga is the excellent forest northwest of **Bermejas**, a small village 8 km north of Playa Girón, anoth-er resort to the southeast of Playa Larga. All four quail-doves, Cuban Screech-Owl, Bee Hummingbird* and Cuban Grassquit occur here, plus many passage and wintering New World warblers. An apparently unique colony of about 20 Fernandina's Flickers* used to breed here, but the dead palms they used were blown down by Hurricane Lillie, in September 1996, and the species is now both extremely elusive and depressingly rare in this area. East and north of Bermejas the road leads through degraded forest and pools where Spotted Rail, Cuban Para-keet*, Fernandina's Flicker* and Cuban Grassquit have been recorded.

Accommodation: Villa Playa Larga (tel. 59 7219), a large complex of 50 or so cabins, a shop, a restaurant, a bar and good birding in the quiet grounds (A); Villa Playa Girón (tel. 59 4118), another large complex with over 290 rooms, busier and slightly more expensive than Playa Larga; and Villa Guamá (more expensive). All three are operated by Horizontes Hoteles, Calle 23 no. 156e/N y O, Vedado, Ciudad de La Habana 4, Cuba (tel. 7 33 4042, fax. 7 33 3722). There are also several casa particulares in Playa Larga and Playa Girón villages, but it may be necessary to visit the villages in order to find one of these rather than wait for one of the locals to find you, as they may assume tourists in the area are staying at one of the villa complexes.

CAYO COCO

This low-lying coral island off the north coast of Cuba is surrounded by beautiful beaches and mangrove-lined mudflats. It is the inland habitats of xerophytic thorn-scrub and dwarf semi-deciduous forest though where the *varonai* race of the endemic Zapata Sparrow* occurs, along with two other endemics confined to eastern Cuba, Cuban Gnatcatcher and Oriente Warbler. In addition, two of the adjacent cays support Bahama Mockingbird and Thick-billed Vireo, both of which, in Cuba, are usually only seen here.

Localised Cuban Endemics
Cuban Gnatcatcher, Zapata Sparrow*.

Other Cuban Endemics
Cuban Nightjar, Cuban Tody, Cuban Woodpecker, Cuban Vireo, Oriente Warbler.

Localised Caribbean Endemics
Bahama Mockingbird, Cuban Bullfinch.

Other Caribbean Endemics
Key West Quail-Dove, Great Lizard-Cuckoo, Cuban Emerald, Cuban Pewee, La Sagra's Flycatcher, Loggerhead Kingbird, Red-legged Thrush, Greater Antillean Grackle.

Localised Caribbean Near-endemics
Thick-billed Vireo.

Other Caribbean Near-endemics
White-crowned Pigeon, Northern Stripe-headed Tanager.

Non-endemic Specialities
Common Black-Hawk.

Passage Migrants and Winter Visitors
Red-breasted Merganser, Short-billed Dowitcher, Greater and Lesser Yellowlegs, Solitary Sandpiper, Willet, Western, Least and Stilt Sandpipers, Grey Catbird, White-eyed Vireo, Northern Parula, Magnolia, Cape May, Black-throated Blue, Prairie, Palm and Black-and-white Warblers,

American Redstart, Worm-eating Warbler, Ovenbird, Northern Water-thrush, Common Yellowthroat, Summer Tanager (scarce).

Others
Least Grebe, Brown Pelican, Magnificent Frigatebird, Great Blue Heron (including the white phase), Reddish Egret, Yellow-crowned Night-Heron, Wood Stork, White Ibis, Roseate Spoonbill, Greater Flamingo, Osprey, Snail Kite, Crested Caracara, Limpkin, Clapper Rail, Killdeer, Caspian and Royal Terns, Belted Kingfisher, Yellow Warbler, Yellow-faced Grassquit, Black-cowled Oriole.

(Other species recorded include Brown Booby, West Indian Whist-ling-Duck*, Piping Plover*, Black Skimmer, Mangrove Cuckoo and Orchard Oriole. In addition, Snail Kite and Sandhill Crane occur near Morón.)

It is about 500 km from Havana east to Morón, the nearest mainland town to Cayo Coco and the best base for budget birders as there are many places to eat and stay, but only expensive resort hotels on Cayo Coco. The cay is about an hour by road north of Morón via a 27 km-long causeway. On reaching the cay continue north to the major roundabout and turn west. Seven km from here look for a 'E. Agua Cayo Coco' sign-post and a large model of a pig. Turn north here to look for Zapata Spar-row* alongside the 1 km-long entrance track to **Playa Flamenco**, a pleasant place to eat and drink at one end of a long beach. Turn south back at the main road to reach a lagoon, after a couple of km, where West Indian Whistling-Duck* occurs. Back on the main road continue west (looking for Common Black-Hawks) to reach the 13 km^2 offshore islet of Cayo Güillermo where Bahama Mockingbird occurs, along with Cuban Gnatcatcher. Back at the main roundabout on Cayo Coco head north, ignoring signs to the Hotel Tryp, and bird the tracks through the forest and scrub for Cuban Gnatcatcher, Oriente Warbler and Zapata Sparrow* (scarce). To find Thick-billed Vireo it is necessary to head east from Cayo Coco to Cayo Paredón Grande, reached via a short bridge to Cayo Romano and a causeway to Cayo Paredón Grande. The

CAYO COCO

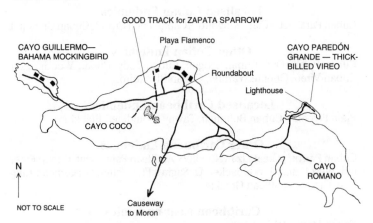

GOOD TRACK for ZAPATA SPARROW*

Playa Flamenco

CAYO GUILLERMO—
BAHAMA MOCKINGBIRD

CAYO PAREDÓN
GRANDE — THICK-
BILLED VIREO

Roundabout

Lighthouse

CAYO COCO

N

CAYO
ROMANO

NOT TO SCALE

Causeway
to Moron

vireo has been recorded along the track southeast of the black-and-yellow lighthouse along with Mangrove Cuckoo, Cuban Gnatcatcher and Oriente Warbler.

Accommodation: Morón—Club de Caza y Pesca (A–B) and many casa particulares; Cayo Coco—several including the Hotel Tryp (A+); Cayo Güillermo—several including the Villa Cojimar (A) and Villa Vigia (A).

The endemic Cuban race of Common Black-Hawk can be seen pouncing on crabs on Cayo Coco

NAJASA

The forested hills, palm groves and fields of the Sierra de Najasa about 75 km southeast of Camagüey in east-central Cuba support the now endemic Giant Kingbird* and Cuban Palm Crow*, as well as Plain Pigeon* and Cuban Parakeet*, all of which are more likely to be seen here than at any of the other well-known birding areas on the island.

Localised Cuban Endemics
Cuban Parakeet*, Giant Kingbird*, Cuban Palm Crow*, Cuban Grassquit.

Other Cuban Endemics
Cuban Pygmy-Owl, Cuban Trogon, Cuban Tody, Cuban Woodpecker, Cuban Vireo, Oriente Warbler, Cuban Blackbird.

Localised Caribbean Endemics
Plain Pigeon*, Cuban Bullfinch, Tawny-shouldered Blackbird.

Other Caribbean Endemics
Cuban Parrot*, Great Lizard-Cuckoo, Antillean Palm-Swift, Cuban Emerald, West Indian Woodpecker, La Sagra's Flycatcher, Loggerhead Kingbird, Greater Antillean Grackle.

Caribbean Near-endemics
Cuban Martin (Feb–Aug).

Passage Migrants and Winter Visitors
Yellow-bellied Sapsucker, Yellow-throated Vireo, Northern Parula, Magnolia, Cape May, Black-throated Blue, Black-throated Green, Yellow-throated, Prairie and Black-and-white Warblers, American Redstart, Ovenbird, Louisiana Waterthrush, Common Yellowthroat.

Others
Purple Gallinule, Northern Jacana, White-winged Dove, Northern Flicker, Cave Swallow (mainly Mar–Oct), Red-legged Honeycreeper, Yellow-faced Grassquit, Eastern Meadowlark. (Other species recorded include Gundlach's Hawk*).

From Camagüey head south towards Santa Cruz del Sur then turn east after 44 km (from the petrol station in the centre of Camagüey) to the small village of Nasasja 22 km away. In the village turn south and proceed for several km. Giant Kingbird* can usually be seen fairly easily in the area, even in trees by the roadside, along with Plain Pigeon*, Cuban Parakeet*, Cuban Palm Crow* and Cuban Grassquit.

Cuban Palm Crow* also occurs along the road to Santa Cruz del Sur from at most 34 km south of Camagüey, and in the large stand of palms alongside the road to Nasasja 1.5 km from the Santa Cruz del Sur road turn-off. There is also another site for the crow, as well as Plain Pigeon*,

CAMAGUEY–NASASJA

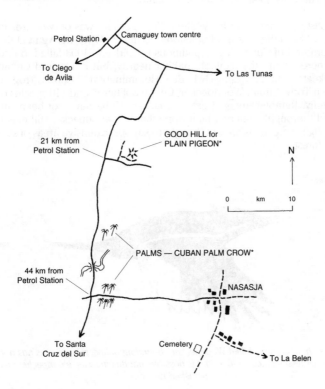

closer to Camagüey. To reach it turn east off the road to Santa Cruz del Sur 21 km south of Camagüey, just beyond two signposts with the words 'Empresa Genetica', then 3.5 km along the minor road turn north onto a track leading north. Turn east after 1 km and park at the farmhouse after 300 m. The crows may be seen around the farm and the pigeon on the wooded hill beyond. A vague trail leads north around the base of the hill, which can also be approached from other angles via the field edges. The crow also occurs 20 km along the road to Vertientes, southwest of Camagüey.

Accommodation: Hotel Camagüey and others (A).

Near the city of **Santiago de Cuba** in eastern Cuba, 970 km and 1.5 hours by air from Havana, it is possible to find Cuban Gnatcatcher, Oriente Warbler, Cuban Grassquit and the *sigmani* race of Zapata Sparrow* in coastal xerophytic thorn scrub, as well as Black (around the peak of Gran Piedra in the Sierra Maestra) and White-collared Swifts, and rarities such as Gundlach's Hawk* (Gran Piedra). Previously productive areas include: (i) next to the Buccanero Hotel (Cuban Gnatcatcher and Oriente Warbler), which is about 30 km southeast of Santiago near the town of Siboney; (ii) around Lake Baconao in Baconao National Park (Cuban Gnatcatcher and Cuban Grassquit), which is about 30 km east of Siboney; and (iii) around the village of Baitiquirí (Cuban Gnatcatcher, Cuban Grassquit and Zapata Sparrow*), which is approximately 45 km east of Guantánamo.

The last sight record of Ivory-billed Woodpecker* was of two birds in April 1986, in the 56 km² of pine-forested hills of **Ojito de Agua** at the eastern end of Cuba. Two expeditions in 1991 and 1993 failed to find any here, or in other suitable habitat nearby, but did record Cuban Parakeet*, Cuban Pygmy-Owl, Bee Hummingbird*, Cuban Trogon, Cuban Tody, Cuban Woodpecker, Cuban Solitaire* and 110 species of butterfly. Remoter areas of extreme eastern Cuba have not been surveyed thoroughly, offering faint hope that the woodpecker still exists, although these areas are not thought to support extensive areas of suitable forest.

The sight of an Ivory-billed Woodpecker bounding between large trees has not been witnessed since 1986, and it is possible that this massive woodpecker has vanished forever*

The **Isla de la Juventud** (also known as the Isle of Youth or Isle of Pines), southwest of Zapata, supports Sandhill Crane (115 were recorded in the north during December 1995) and Cuban Parrot* (1,320 were recorded in the north at the same time).

ADDITIONAL INFORMATION

Addresses

The following officers help run the Canadian–Cuban ringing programme:
Director, Museo Nacional de Historia Natural, Capitolio Nacional, La Habana 2, Ciudad de Habana 10200 (tel/fax. 537620353) or
Laboratorio de Aves Migratorias, Instituto de Ecologia y Sistematica, Ministerio de Ciencia, Carretera de Varona km 3.5, AP 8010, La Habana 8, Ciudad de Habana 10800.
Director, Centro de Investigaciones de Ecosistemas Costeros, Ministerio de Cienca, Cayo Coco, Municipio Moron, Provincia de Ciego de Avila, CP 69400 (tel. 5333301161, fax. 5333301151).
Long Point Bird Observatory, Box 160, Port Rowan, ON N0E 1M0.

Books and papers

Birdwatching in Cuba, Williams I. 1998. Privately published report (covering observations throughout the country at various times between 1987 and 1997), available from specialist booksellers.
Field Guide to the Birds of Cuba, Garrido, O. H. and Kirkconnell, A. 2000. Cornell UP.
Population size of Cuban Parrots Amazona leucocephala *and Sandhill Cranes* Grus canadensis *and community involvement in their conservation in northern Isla de la Juventud, Cuba.* Aguilera, X. G. *et al.* 1999. *Bird Conserv. Intern.* 9: 97–112.
Natural Cuba (in English and Spanish), Silva Lee, A. 1996. Pangaea, USA.
In addition many papers on the distribution and status of Cuban birds are published in the journal of the Neotropical Bird Club, *Cotinga*, and bulletin of the Caribbean Ornithological Society, *El Pitirre*.

DOMINICA

INTRODUCTION

Summary
This small mountainous island in the central Lesser Antilles supports a rather rich avifauna due to the presence of extensive forested areas where two endemic parrots reside, as well as ten of the 14 widespread

Lesser Antillean endemics, including Blue-headed Hummingbird, which is easier to see here than on Martinique, the only other island where this species occurs, and Plumbeous Warbler, which otherwise occurs only on Guadeloupe. Dominica therefore makes an ideal destination for birders hoping to see a broad range of Lesser Antilles endemics without island-hopping through the archipelago, despite its rudimentary tourist infrastructure.

Size
At about 46.5 km long and up to 26 km wide Dominica covers 790 km^2.

Getting Around
There are two airfields, neither of which is sufficiently large to receive direct international flights, making it necessary to fly in from Puerto Rico or one of the other Lesser Antilles. One airstrip is at Melville Hall in the northeast and the other, more conveniently situated, is at Canefield, near the capital, Roseau, in the southwest. Though plenty of cheap minibuses serve the major routes and reach most other parts of the island, it is very difficult to get to some inland sites and back within a day using public transport, and most of the accommodation is on the coast. Therefore, since taxis are expensive birders who are short of time and like a roof over their head at night would be wise to hire a vehicle. Road signs are almost non-existent but the roads and tracks are in fairly good condition and, with the aid of a large-scale map, it is usually possible to reach the best birding sites without a 4WD. Off road there are many well-marked and well-maintained walking trails. The official language of this Commonwealth State is English, but it is a former French colony and local people usually speak a French-based patois among themselves.

To arrange birding with a guide, as well as car hire, accommodation and whale-watching trips, contact Nature Island Destinations, PO Box 1639, Roseau, Dominica, West Indies (tel. 449 6233, fax. 449 7100, e-mail: nid@cwdom.dm, web site: www.natureisland.com).

Accommodation and Food
Dominica is one of the poorest island nations in the Caribbean and the tourist industry has yet to take off, mainly due to the shortage of beaches, so accommodation is limited to small hotels (the largest has 54 rooms), guest houses and apartments, virtually all of which are confined to the west coast. Camping is not encouraged and forbidden within National Parks and other reserves. There are few places to buy food away from the main settlements on the coast, but many places to eat in and around the main towns, especially on the west coast, though it may be difficult to get a large meal after 4pm because the locals prefer to eat their main meal in the middle of the day. Local delicacies include frog's legs, taken from a large native frog (*Leptodactylus fallax*) and called crapaud or 'mountain chicken', but mainstream menu items include spicy shrimps and crayfish, which can be washed down with 'Sea Moss', a drink of seaweed, milk and sugar.

Health and Safety
Some locals have taken to selling their wares to visitors, which can be a hassle at tourist hot-spots, but crime is negligible.

Climate and Timing

The best time to visit Dominica is in April when the chance of spicing a trip list with some seabirds is increased, many trees are in flower, making it easier to find birds such as hummingbirds, and there is a small passage of spring migrants heading to North America for the summer. April also coincides with the end of the driest period of the year, which lasts from January. The main rainy season is in May–October, peaking in July–August, though heavy downpours occur throughout the year in the mountains, where lush forests are sustained by a very high annual rainfall of over 635 cm. Leave a visit until June and there is a risk of birding in hurricanes, which occur between then and November. Although the climate in general is tropical and therefore rather hot and humid, cooling northeast trade winds help take the edge off the temperatures.

Habitats

Dominica is the most mountainous of the Lesser Antilles—almost half of the island is above 305 m and the highest peak, Morne Diablotin, reaches a mighty 1447 m—and due to its rugged interior has largely escaped deforestation, hence large tracts of relatively pristine montane rain forest remain. However, although a remarkable 60% of the island is still forested, not all is free from degradation. Rain forests grow at 305–762 m, above which are montane thickets on sheltered slopes and elfin woods on exposed ridges and higher tops. These diverse montane habitats account for such a small island having a relatively rich avifauna, and over 55 species of butterfly. Flatter areas are limited to a few fertile river valleys and the northeast coastal plain, but over 20% of the island is cultivated and another 3% used for pasture, most of the dry, scrubby, open deciduous woodland that once covered the lowlands having been replaced by banana, citrus and coconut plantations. The coastline consists of steep cliffs, small black or golden sand coves and some estuaries and marshes with a little mangrove.

Conservation

The Dominican Department of Wildlife and Forestry, with help from the RARE Center for Tropical Conservation, have promoted ecotourism, influenced new legislation, especially with regard to shooting and trapping, initiated environmental education programmes, established park patrols, undertaken vital research on such important matters as habitat utilization by the endemic parrots, and designated new protected areas, all of which have helped, thus far, to protect the three threatened and near-threatened species, as well as the commoner and more widespread birds, which occur on the island. However, the main problems facing this government department now are habitat loss and degradation, both of which are primarily caused by agricultural encroachment, a much more difficult issue to tackle, but one that perhaps the enlightened department can overcome. If successful, all they will have to worry about is hurricanes, which can wreak considerable damage to forested areas, although the conservation of sufficient habitat should ensure some areas escape destruction and provide refuge for the forest specialists while devastated areas regenerate.

Endemics

Two species are endemic to Dominica. Red-necked Parrot*: a survey in 1995 estimated a population of 600–1000, mainly in the Northern Forest

Reserve and forests of the northeast, where the highest concentration was between Bense and Marigot Heights. Fewer were present elsewhere, but it has been recorded as far south as the Pont Casse area in the centre of the island. Imperial Parrot*: following Hurricane David in 1979, which destroyed much of the species' preferred habitat in the south, the remainder moved to the northwest where 100–150 were estimated in 1995, mainly above 500 m on the slopes of Morne Diablotin in the Northern Forest Reserve.

Caribbean Endemics

A total of 17 of the 51 Caribbean endemics not confined to single countries, islands or archipelagos occur on Dominica. They include ten of the 14 species restricted to the Lesser Antilles (but present on more than one island): Lesser Antillean Swift, Purple-throated Carib, Blue-headed Hummingbird (which otherwise occurs only on Martinique), Lesser Antillean Flycatcher, Brown Trembler, Scaly-breasted Thrasher, Forest Thrush*, Plumbeous Warbler (which otherwise occurs only on Guadeloupe), Lesser Antillean Bullfinch and Lesser Antillean Saltator; and seven more widespread species, namely Bridled Quail-Dove (very rare in dry forest), Green-throated Carib, Antillean Crested Hummingbird, Lesser Antillean Pewee (*brunneicapillus*), Rufous-throated Solitaire, Red-legged Thrush and Antillean Euphonia.

Near-Endemics

Nine of the 18 species nearly endemic to the Caribbean occur on Dominica. They are Black-capped Petrel*, Scaly-naped Pigeon, Zenaida Dove, Caribbean Elaenia, Caribbean Martin (Feb–Sep), Pearly-eyed Thrasher, Black-whiskered Vireo (mainly Apr–Oct), Black-faced Grassquit and Carib Grackle. In addition the *petechia* group of Yellow Warbler, known as 'Golden Warbler', which is almost endemic to the Caribbean, is represented by the *melanoptera* race.

Bird species

About 170 species have been recorded on Dominica, of which at least 50 have bred. Non-endemic specialities and spectacular species not mentioned above include Red-billed (occasional, Mar–Jun) and White-tailed (breeds mainly Dec–Jun) Tropicbirds, Masked and Red-footed Boobies (both occasional, Oct–May), Magnificent Frigatebird, Bridled and Sooty Terns, Brown Noddy (all three mainly Apr–Aug), Ruddy Quail-Dove (scarce), Black Swift (mainly Mar–Oct), Ringed Kingfisher (on larger rivers such as Layou, Melville Hall or Roseau), House Wren and Bare-eyed Thrush (first recorded in 1993).

Expectations

It is possible to see both Dominican endemics, as well as all ten of the widespread Lesser Antilles endemics that occur on the island in a single day, but it is difficult to see many more than 50 species on a trip lasting a few days or more.

NORTHERN FOREST RESERVE

The upper montane rain forest in and adjacent to this 36 km² reserve on the slopes of Morne Diablotin, which rises to 1447 m, at the north end of the island, is the best area to find the island's two endemic parrots. All ten of the Lesser Antilles endemics not restricted to single islands occurring on Dominica are also present, including Blue-headed Hummingbird, Forest Thrush* and Plumbeous Warbler.

Dominican Endemics
Red-necked* and Imperial* Parrots.

Lesser Antillean Endemics
Lesser Antillean Swift, Purple-throated Carib, Blue-headed Hummingbird, Lesser Antillean Flycatcher, Brown Trembler, Scaly-breasted Thrasher, Forest Thrush*, Plumbeous Warbler, Lesser Antillean Bullfinch, Lesser Antillean Saltator.

Other Caribbean Endemics
Green-throated Carib, Antillean Crested Hummingbird, Lesser Antillean Pewee, Rufous-throated Solitaire, Red-legged Thrush, Antillean Euphonia.

Caribbean Near-endemics
Scaly-naped Pigeon, Zenaida Dove, Caribbean Elaenia, Pearly-eyed Thrasher, Black-faced Grassquit.

Others
Broad-winged Hawk, Ruddy Quail-Dove, Mangrove Cuckoo, Black Swift (mainly Mar–Oct), Grey Kingbird, House Wren, Yellow Warbler.

(Morne Diablotin is named after Black-capped Petrel* ('diablotin' means little devil, a name used for this species in reference to its weird call), which bred here in large numbers until at least the early 19th Century and may still do so, in Nov–Mar; some bold and adventurous birders may wish to arrange to camp here to try to confirm its presence).

From the airfield at Canefield it is about an hour by road to the private **Syndicate Estate**, at 550 m, where there is a short, well-maintained nature trail which is open to the public and enables access to a few rather hair-raising viewpoints over the Picard River Valley; the only places from where Imperial Parrot* is likely to be seen. To reach the estate turn east off the main coast road about 10 km south of Portsmouth, in response to the sign, and follow the track through banana plantations for 6.8 km. Turn left onto the rough track leading through more banana plantations before reaching the start of the trail, a distance of about 1 km from the main track. This last km may be passable only with a 4WD so birders with a 2WD may prefer to walk, which is advisable because Red-necked Parrot*, or Jacquot as it is known locally, frequents the forest edge close to cultivation and often flies over this stretch. Imperial Parrot*, or Sisserou as it is known locally, favours the upper reaches of deep forested valleys and is most likely to be seen from the viewpoints (the second one is usually best) along the trail, as the birds fly to and from their roosts, or feed in nearby fruiting trees. This species is also easier to see during the breeding season (Apr–early May), and both parrots are most active between dawn and 10am, and then between 4pm and dusk. There is virtually no chance of seeing parrots inside the forest but many of the other species listed above, including Blue-headed Hummingbird and Forest Thrush*, occur in dense forest along the steep and muddy trail to the summit of Morne Diablotin, which starts 0.4 km from the main track.

Birders who wish to improve their chances of seeing the parrots and other birds can hire a guide from the Department of Wildlife and Forestry (tel. 448 2401), and Bertrand Baptiste (tel. 446 6358) is one forestry officer who has been recommended. He or any other guides may also be able to help with visiting alternative sites for the parrots, such as Dyer Estate (adjacent to Picard River Valley—walk towards Colihaut), Colihaut Heights, Morne Plaisance, Bense Heights (scan from the Ti Branches Viewing Point), Simpa Heights (above Woodford Hill village) and Palmiste Ridge (above Governor Estate and Melville Hall River).

Accommodation: Portsmouth.

An isolated population of the striking Red-legged Thrush survives on Dominica

From the river bridge just south of Portsmouth it is possible to take two-hour boat trips on the mangrove-lined **Indian River** where Ringed Kingfisher, as well as Green Heron, Scaly-naped Pigeon, Red-necked Parrot*, Antillean Crested Hummingbird, Brown Trembler, and Yellow and Plumbeous Warblers occur. To organise such a trip contact Cobra's Indian River and Sightseeing Tours, Glanvillia, Portsmouth, Dominica, West Indies (tel. 445 4826, fax. 445 4453) and ask to be taken during early morning when the majority of birds present are easier to find. Bridled Quail-Dove is rare on Dominica but it has been recorded in the dry, open woodland and scrub on the 5 km² **Cabrits Peninsula** a couple of km northwest of Portsmouth, along with Scaly-naped Pigeon, Mangrove Cuckoo, Plumbeous Warbler and Lesser Antillean Saltator. Most people visit this National Park to view the remains of Fort Shirley but there are several trails around the fort and through the woods worth birding, including one ascending the 171 m peak of West Cabrit. The **Cabrits Marshes**, which separate the rocky Cabrits Peninsula from the mainland, together with the Glanvillia Marshes, adjacent to Portsmouth, hold Caribbean Coot* and Belted Kingfisher, attract the odd Least Bittern and Sora during winter, and act as an important stopover for passage shorebirds, especially in Aug–Oct when regular Semipalmated and Least Sandpipers are worth scouring for less frequently observed species such as Short-billed Dowitcher, and Western and Pectoral Sand-pipers. In far northwestern Dominica White-tailed Tropicbird breeds (mainly Dec–Jun) on the cliffs around **Toucari Bay**.

Between Portsmouth and Roseau on the west coast of Dominica, Mangrove Cuckoo occurs in coastal scrub just north of **Coulibistrie**. Ringed Kingfisher occurs at the mouth of the **River Layou**, and a few pairs of White-tailed Tropicbird breed (mainly Dec–Jun) on cliffs around **Tarou Point**. The **Botanical Gardens** in Roseau, south of the River Roseau on the east side of town, support Green Heron, Smooth-billed Ani, Purple-throated and Green-throated Caribs, Antillean Crested Hummingbird, Caribbean Elaenia, Lesser Antillean Pewee, Scaly-breasted Thrasher, Yellow and Plumbeous Warblers, Black-faced Grassquit, Lesser Antillean Bullfinch and Carib Grackle.

MORNE TROIS PITONS NATIONAL PARK

This 69 km^2 World Heritage Site northeast of Roseau encompasses Morne Trois Pitons, which rises to 1,432 m, and the second largest boiling lake on earth, parts of which simmer at 92ºC, along with other features associated with the four volcanoes present, such as hot springs and fumaroles. There is also plenty of montane rain forest in and around the park, which supports Blue-headed Hummingbird, Forest Thrush* and Plumbeous Warbler.

Lesser Antillean Endemics
Purple-throated Carib, Blue-headed Hummingbird, Lesser Antillean Flycatcher, Brown Trembler, Forest Thrush*, Plumbeous Warbler, Lesser Antillean Bullfinch, Lesser Antillean Saltator.

Caribbean Endemics
Green-throated Carib, Antillean Crested Hummingbird, Lesser Antillean Pewee, Rufous-throated Solitaire, Antillean Euphonia.

Caribbean Near-endemics
Scaly-naped Pigeon, Zenaida Dove, Caribbean Elaenia, Pearly-eyed Thrasher, Black-faced Grassquit.

Others
Broad-winged Hawk, Mangrove Cuckoo, House Wren. (Other species recorded here include American Coot, and Red-necked* and Imperial* Parrots).

There are several places worth birding in and around the park, including: (i) the **Emerald Pool** area, which is a 15 minute walk from the road between Pont Casse and Castle Bruce. This is particularly good for Forest Thrush*, but it is best to look for this shy species during the early morning before the crowds arrive. There is also a chance of seeing either parrot here, or at Castle Bruce Heights to the northeast; (ii) the trail to the top of **Morne Trois Pitons**, which is signed on the right-hand side of the road east from the roundabout at Pont Casse. Allow three hours for the hike, along which both parrots have also been recorded; (iii) the intertwined **Middleham Trails**, which are accessible from Cochrane and Sylvania and traverse the forest on the northwest border of the park. Cochrane can be reached via the road from the Old Mill Cultural Centre in Canefield. It is a couple of hours walk from the other side of this village to Middleham Falls (a good spot for Blue-headed Hummingbird and Rufous-throated Solitaire), beyond which the trail connects with the Laudat Road. To reach the Middleham Trails via Springfield Estate and Middleham Estates (best with a 4WD) turn east about 5 km north of Roseau (at the middle of the Canefield airfield). After 4–5 km there is a sharp left turn and a signpost announcing Springfield Estate. Bird around the parking area, do a U turn and drive back about 300 m to where there is a steep track on the left. About 1 km along the track, in the vicinity of some houses and plantations, take the second left and drive, if you dare, as far as the hairpin bend, about 2 km from the main road. Park and walk through the orange groves to the start of the trail to the falls; (iv) alongside the track from the ridge-top village of Laudat to **Freshwater Lake** (where American Coot has been recorded), Boeri Lake and beyond, on the eastern slopes of **Morne Macaque** at 762 m. Though some of the forest here is not pristine—much of it was just 20 years-old in the year 2000 because Hurricane David destroyed large areas of forest around Morne Trois Pitons in 1979—it is a good area for Rufous-throated Solitaire and Forest Thrush*. Laudat can be reached by heading east on the road just north of the River Roseau and keeping left at all major intersections. The road may be rough in places and beyond Laudat the track may be passable in a 4WD only.

Accommodation: Laudat—Roxy's Mountain Lodge (tel. 448 4845).

South of Roseau, White-tailed Tropicbird breeds (mainly Dec–Jun) on **Pointe Michel**, south of Loubiere. One of the best places to look for other seabirds from mainland Dominica is **Scotts Head**, at the southern tip of the island, although birds such as Brown Booby (mainly Dec–May), Magnificent Frigatebird and Brown Noddy (mainly Apr–Aug), which have been seen from here, are rare in the shallow inshore waters and much more likely to be seen on organised whale-watching trips to the deeper waters west of Roseau, when other species such as Audubon's Shearwater (mainly Mar–Jul), White-tailed Tropicbird (mainly Dec–Jun), Masked Booby (mainly Oct–May), Pomarine and Long-tailed Skuas (both mainly Aug–May), and Royal and Sooty (mainly Apr–Aug) Terns enter the equation. Boat trips usually take place throughout the year when small numbers of great sperm whales (most likely in winter), as well as false killer, pilot and pygmy sperm whales, and Atlantic spotted and spinner dolphins may also be seen. Other, rarer, species which have been recorded include killer and melon-headed whales, and Atlantic bottlenose, Fraser's and Risso's dolphins. These trips can be arranged at: (i) the Anchorage Hotel (Anchorage Dives), PO Box 34 (tel. 448 2638, fax. 448 5680, e-mail: anchorage@tod.dm), which is at Castle Comfort about 1.5 km south of Roseau; (ii) the nearby Castle Comfort Lodge (Dive Dominica), PO Box 2253 (tel. 448 2188; fax. 448 6088, e-mail: dive@tod.dm, web site: www.dive-dominica.com); or (iii) Dive Castaways, at Mero. Other birds recorded on Scotts Head itself include Broad-winged Hawk, Mangrove Cuckoo, Caribbean Martin (Mar–Oct), House Wren, Plumbeous Warbler and Lesser Antillean Saltator.

In Apr–Aug large numbers of Bridled and Sooty Terns, and Brown Noddy, breed in colonies along the **Atlantic Coast** (e.g. at Pointe des

Fous in the extreme southeast) and, together with Magnificent Frigate-bird, on islets offshore, such as L'Illet and Mastle Rock, both of which also attract Brown (Dec–May) and occasional Masked (mainly Oct–May) Boobies. Along the southeast coast small numbers of Black-capped Petrels* have been observed flying inland from the sea at dusk and these may be breeding on coastal hills such as Morne Fou (a former breeding site) in Nov–Mar.

Seabirds also breed on **Aves Island**, to the west of Dominica, where there may be as many as 10,000–20,000 pairs of Sooty Tern.

ADDITIONAL INFORMATION

Addresses

Dominican Conservation Association, PO Box 71, Roseau, Dominica, West Indies.

The Department of Wildlife and Forestry, Botanical Gardens, Roseau, Dominica, West Indies (tel. 448 2401/7999), stocks a wide range of park guides, trail maps etc.

Dominica Division of Tourism, National Development Corporation, PO Box 293, Valley Road, Roseau, Dominica, West Indies (tel. 448 2045, fax. 448 5840).

Books and papers

A *Guide to Birdwatching* (in Dominica), Evans, P. and James, A. 1997. Dominica Nature Island of the Caribbean Series No. 3. Ecosystems Ltd.

Guide to Nature Sites (in Dominica), Evans, P. and James, A. 1997. Dominica Nature Island of the Caribbean Series No. 7. Ecosystems Ltd.

Nature Map of Dominica, Evans, P. and James, A. 1997. Dominica Nature Island of the Caribbean Series No. 8. Ecosystems Ltd.

Wildlife Checklists (of Dominica), Evans, P. and James, A. 1997. Dominica Nature Island of the Caribbean Series No. 2. Ecosystems Ltd.

Parrots on Dominica, Evans, P. 1991. *Bird Conserv. Intern.* 1: 11–32.

DOMINICAN REPUBLIC

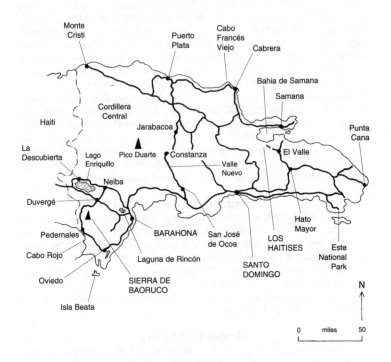

INTRODUCTION

Summary

The Dominican Republic occupies about two-thirds of the island of Hispaniola (the other third is Haiti), enough to support virtually all of the island's 28 endemic species, including Palmchat, the sole member of a family endemic to Hispaniola, two of the Caribbean's endemic tody family and a trogon, as well as many other goodies, including the likes of White-tailed Tropicbird, Northern Potoo and Golden Swallow*. Virtually all of the country's top birds occur in the mountainous southwest and it is possible to see the lot within a few days, hence many birders combine a trip to this popular package holiday destination with Puerto Rico, two of the best connected islands in the Caribbean.

Size

The Dominican Republic covers 48,440 km^2.

Getting Around

As Puerto Plata, on the north coast, is a long way from the southwest where virtually all of the endemics occur, the best arrival point is the international airport at Santo Domingo on the south coast. From here it

303

is four hours on a good road to Barahona, the gateway to this part of the country. The good road network enables fairly easy access to the best birding sites, although a 4WD with high clearance may be needed to reach some of the higher reaches of the Sierra de Baoruco in the southwest, where a few highly localised endemics occur, and Los Haïtises National Park, the most reliable site for the endemic Ridgway's Hawk*. Hiring a vehicle is expensive but is the most efficient way to get around, especially if time is short, although cheap minibuses and pick-ups cover much of the country. A good map is essential for there are few roadsigns.

Kate Wallace, a member of the Club de Observadores de Aves Annabelle Dod., acts as a professional local guide, and can be contacted via Calle Luperon 52 A, Zona Colonial, Santo Domingo, Dominican Republic, West Indies (tel. 238 5347; e-mail: wallacekate@hotmail.com). Officially, permits are required in advance from the Dominican Republic National Parks Office (DNP), in Santo Domingo, to visit the main parks and reserves, but these are not essential. A basic grasp of Spanish is useful, especially for conversing with the police and soldiers at the road checkpoints in the southwest near the border with Haiti.

Accommodation and Food

There are many package holiday resorts in the Dominican Republic but these are not near the best birding sites, so birders who like a bed to sleep in after a long, hard day in the field will be better off using the hotels and guest houses, which are also reasonably priced. Local dishes, washed down with beer ('El Presidente' is the most popular), rum and/or rum cocktails, include bandera dominicana (meat with avocado, beans, platano/yuca and rice), seafood, soups and stews, most of which have a Spanish flavour.

Health and Safety

Vaccinations against hepatitis A, polio, tetanus and typhoid are recommended, as are precautions against malaria. On long birding days in the southwest take plenty of food and water (don't drink the tap water anywhere), for both are difficult to obtain beyond Barahona. In the major tourist areas prepare for usual hassles, which in the Dominican Republic could involve dealing with people insistent on selling anything from a bottle of rum to sex.

Climate and Timing

Birders who are keen to see as many endemics as possible and simultaneously bolster their trip list with a wide range of wintering and/or passage New World warblers should visit the Dominican Republic between mid-March and mid-April, for many endemics start breeding during this period and many warblers are still in their winter quarters or passing north. However, some endemics, including La Selle Thrush* and Eastern Chat-Tanager*, are not thought to begin breeding until May so birders who are primarily interested in seeing such species may be better off visiting at the end of the spring rainy season, in June–July, when such species are more active and probably easier to locate. Those birders who decide to visit during summer will also have a better chance of seeing White-tailed Tropicbirds, as they normally frequent their breeding cliffs in May–August. A second rainy season usually lasts from August to September–November, after which the heat and humidity reach their lowest in December.

Habitats

The country occupies the eastern two-thirds of Hispaniola, the highest island in the Caribbean, rising to 3175 m at Pico Duarte in the Cordillera Central of the Dominican Republic. The terrain is very mountainous and the slopes of the steepest mountain support deciduous, semi-evergreen, montane rain and Caribbean pine forests, which combined account for about 12% of the land and host a relatively rich avifauna compared to the rather less bountiful expanses of pasture (over 43% of the land), and coffee, fruit and sugar plantations (over 30%). The major remaining terrestrial habitats; deciduous arid thorn woods, cactus scrub and deserts are productive for birds, and the same can be said for the coastline, which has everything, from beautiful beaches and impressive high cliffs to mangrove-lined mudflats. The greatest diversity of habitats, including, most importantly, montane rain forest, is in the southwest, which is the best birding area.

Conservation

Approximately two-thirds of the forests that once covered much of the Dominican Republic have been cleared since the first Europeans arrived in the late 15th Century, making contemporary conservation problems the more critical. These include agricultural encroachment, illegal logging, charcoal burning, the lack of adequate legislation or the will to oversee that which exists (hunting and trapping is illegal but widespread), and chaotic urban development, all of which require swift control if the 21 threatened and near-threatened species are to survive. The government has established 16 National Parks, six Scientific Reserves and several sanctuaries, but the lack of environmental awareness or concern among the populace makes it easy for the country's controllers to get away with as little as possible, leaving the non-governmental organisations to do the best they can with limited resources.

Endemics

No birds are endemic to the Dominican Republic but it does support 27–28 of the 28 species confined to Hispaniola.

Ridgway's Hawk*	Very rare and only likely to be seen in the remote Los Haïtises National Park, accessible by 4WD only
Hispaniolan Parakeet*	Locally common, especially in the Sierra de Baoruco and Sierra de Neiba, at 900–1800 m
Hispaniolan Parrot*	Locally common in areas such as the Sierra de Baoruco
Hispaniolan Lizard-Cuckoo	Relatively common throughout
Bay-breasted Cuckoo*	Rare and localised, even in the Sierra de Baoruco
Ashy-faced Owl	Widespread but uncommon. Most likely to be seen at Los Haïtises National Park, the Barahona Peninsula and the southeast
Least Poorwill*	Fairly common in thorn scrub in the southwest, especially in the Sierra de Baoruco area
Hispaniolan Nightjar	Fairly common in the west

Hispaniolan Emerald	Relatively common in the mountains
Hispaniolan Trogon*	Locally common in the Cordillera Central, Cordillera Septentrional, Sierra de Baoruco, Sierra de Neiba, and, outside the breeding season (Aug–Feb), at lower elevations such as Ebano Verde and Las Cruces de Puerto Escondido.
Broad-billed Tody	Relatively common in the lowlands
Narrow-billed Tody	Relatively common in the highlands and local in the lowlands
Antillean Piculet	Relatively common throughout
Hispaniolan Woodpecker	Common throughout
Hispaniolan Pewee	Relatively common throughout
Palmchat	Relatively common in the lowlands to mid-altitudes.
La Selle Thrush*	Rare in the Cordillera Central, Sierra de Baoruco and Sierra de Neiba
Hispaniolan Palm Crow*	Relatively common in the Cordillera Central and Sierra de Neiba, and also in some lowland areas such as Lago Enriquillo in the southwest
White-necked Crow*	Rare but locally rather common
Flat-billed Vireo	Local and uncommon in semi-arid lowlands and moist hills
Antillean Siskin	Relatively common in the montane west
Green-tailed Warbler	Local and rather common, but declining
White-winged Warbler*	Uncommon in the Cordillera Central and Sierra de Baoruco, and very localised in the Sierra de Neiba
Black-crowned Palm-Tanager	Relatively common, especially in the lowlands
Western Chat-Tanager*	Very rare in the extreme southwest
Eastern Chat-Tanager*	Local and uncommon; most likely to be seen in the Cordillera Central and Sierra de Baoruco
Hispaniolan Stripe-headed Tanager	Relatively common in highlands, but scarcer in the lowlands

The other Hispaniolan endemic, Grey-crowned Palm-Tanager, has been reported occasionally in the Sierra de Baoruco and is described as rare down to 1100 m there by Raffaele, H. *et al.*, *Birds of the West Indies*, 1998, but some observers believe there have been no reliable reports of this extremely difficult to identify species in this area and some taxonomists even dispute its validity as a species!

The following race, endemic to Hispaniola, is treated as a full species by some taxonomists:

Hispaniolan Crossbill*	the *megaplaga* race of Two-barred Crossbill is local and uncommon in the highest mountains, including the Sierra de Baoruco

Caribbean Endemics

A total of 16 of the 51 Caribbean endemics not confined to single countries, islands or archipelagos also occur in the Dominican Republic. They are: Grey-headed Quail-Dove*, which is otherwise confined to Cuba (the race present here may be a full species); four species that occur only on Hispaniola and Jamaica, namely Vervain Hummingbird, Greater Antillean Elaenia, Stolid Flycatcher and Golden Swallow* (which may now be endemic to Hispaniola, as it has not been reliably reported from Jamaica since the 1980s); and 11 more widespread species, West Indian Whistling-Duck* (six known populations, four coastal), Plain Pigeon*, Key West Quail-Dove, Antillean Palm-Swift, Antillean Mango, Loggerhead Kingbird, Rufous-throated Solitaire, Red-legged Thrush, Antillean Euphonia, Greater Antillean Bullfinch and Greater Antillean Grackle.

Near-Endemics

Nine of the 18 species nearly endemic to the Caribbean occur in the Dominican Republic. They are Black-capped Petrel* (a few breed in the Sierra de Baoruco, in early Nov to mid-May), Caribbean Coot*, White-crowned and Scaly-naped Pigeons, Zenaida Dove, Antillean Nighthawk (mainly Apr–Aug), Caribbean Martin (Feb–Aug), Black-whiskered Vireo and Black-faced Grassquit. In addition, Pearly-eyed Thrasher occurs on Isla Beata, off the southwest coast, and the *petechia* group of Yellow Warbler, known as 'Golden Warbler', also nearly endemic to the Caribbean, is represented by the *albicollis* race.

Bird species

About 245 species have been recorded in the Dominican Republic. Non-endemic specialities and spectacular species not already mentioned include White-tailed Tropicbird (mainly May–Aug), Magnificent Frigatebird, Greater Flamingo, White-cheeked Pintail, Northern Jacana, Double-striped Thick-knee (the *dominicensis* race endemic to Hispaniola is local and uncommon, and rarely seen by visiting birders), Ruddy Quail-Dove, Burrowing and Stygian Owls, Northern Potoo (the *abbotti* race endemic to Hispaniola is regularly seen by visiting birders), Chuck-will's-widow (Sep–May), Black and White-collared Swifts, Cave Swallow, Bicknell's Thrush* (Oct–Apr), Pine Warbler (resident *chrysoleuca* race), passage and wintering New World warblers such as Cape May, Black-throated Blue and Prairie Warblers, Yellow-faced Grassquit, Grasshopper and Rufous-collared (the isolated *antillarum* race endemic to the Dominican Republic occurs only in the Cordillera Central and Sierra de Neiba) Sparrows, and Black-cowled Oriole.

Expectations

On a two-week trip that combines the Dominican Republic with Puerto Rico it is possible to see about 130 species. Birders confined to the Dominican Republic may still breach 100 if they manage to catch up with plenty of waterbirds.

In the Dominican Republic it is possible to begin or end a birding trip in style with the wonderful White-tailed Tropicbird, several pairs of which breed near the Acuário Nacional, Avenida España, on the coast east of **Santo Domingo** city centre, usually in May–Aug. The extensive National Botanical Gardens, which cover about 240 ha and encompass a forested canyon within Santo Domingo city, support several wide-spread Hispaniolan endemics, including Hispaniolan Woodpecker, Palmchat and Black-crowned Palm-Tanager, as well as Antillean Palm-Swift, Antillean Mango, Vervain Hummingbird and Red-legged Thrush, and scarcer species recorded here have included Hispaniolan Parrot*, Hispaniolan Lizard-Cuckoo, Ashy-faced Owl and Broad-billed Tody. To see Hispaniolan Parakeet* in Santo Domingo head for the Hotel Embajador where over 100 have been recorded roosting in the palm trees just outside the hotel. Other possibilities here include Antillean Nighthawk (mainly May–Aug) and the introduced Olive-throated Parakeet.

The noisy and gregarious Palmchat, the sole member of its family, is widespread and conspicuous on Hispaniola, the only island in the world on which it occurs

The beach resort of **Barahona** on the southwest coast 193 km (four hours by road) west of Santo Domingo is the gateway to, and the best base for birding, the Sierra de Baoruco and the rest of the southwest as there is no accommodation and few places to eat beyond there. Recommended accommodation in Barahona includes the Hotel Guarocuya. Ashy-faced Owl is most regularly seen in coastal forests near limestone cliffs (in which it breeds) south of Barahona. To reach one good area for this member of the Barn Owl family head south from Barahona on the coast road for 4.3 km (from the Hotel Caribe), turn west and start birding a couple of km inland from the turning. Northern Potoo and Least Poorwill* also occur along this road, and the potoo, as well as the owl, can also be found in the valley reached by turning west off the coast road 7.2 km south of the Hotel Caribe. Walk the track behind the house with the bee hives, near the coast road. This valley also has Key West and Ruddy Quail-Doves.

The **Laguna de Rincón** Scientific Reserve complete with visitor centre, northwest of Barahona, is a good place for waterbirds including Roseate Spoonbill, Greater Flamingo, White-cheeked Pintail, American and Caribbean* Coots, and Wilson's Plover. Other, scarcer species recorded here include Northern Jacana, while Masked Duck occurs on freshwater lagoons in the area. About an hour by road northwest of Barahona, between there and Duvergé, lies Mella, about half a mile west of which the roadside scrub is worth checking for the likes of Least

Poorwill*, as well as Mangrove Cuckoo, Antillean Mango, Broad-billed Tody and Stolid Flycatcher.

At 90 km long and up to 13 km wide **Lago Enriquillo**, north of the road between Duvergé (fill up with fuel here) and Jimani, is the largest in the West Indies. It lies up to 40 m below sea level between the Sierra de Neiba to the north and Sierra de Baoruco to the south within an ancient 193 km-long sea channel. This is one of the hottest places in the Caribbean and the lake is highly saline but still attracts small numbers of waterbirds, including Greater Flamingo, shorebirds such as Willet, and terns such as Caspian and Royal. However, the principal avian interest in this exceptionally arid area concerns Hispaniolan Palm* and White-necked* Crows, both of which occur in the bizarre low cactus scrub and palm stands around the lake. Hispaniolan Palm Crow* is fairly common and especially easy to see along the main road out of Duvergé early in the morning. The nearest area of tall palms, the most suitable habitat for White-necked Crow*, is 8.2 km west of the plaza in Duvergé. Other species recorded here include Plain Pigeon*, Hispaniolan Lizard-Cuckoo, Burrowing Owl, Antillean Nighthawk (mainly Apr–Aug), Antillean Mango, Antillean Piculet, Stolid Flycatcher, Palmchat and Shiny Cowbird, as well as American crocodile and rhinoceros iguana. One place where some decent food can be obtained beyond Barahona is at the cafe near the plaza in La Descubierta, a village surrounded by coconut and date palms at the northwest end of the lake.

The **Sierra de Neiba** north of Lago Enriquillo supports Hispaniolan Parakeet*, Hispaniolan Trogon*, Golden Swallow*, La Selle Thrush* and White-winged Warbler* (very local), as well as Grey-headed Quail-Dove*, Hispaniolan Nightjar, Bicknell's Thrush* (in montane rain forest at Vuelta de Quince and the Monte Bonito area above Apolinario, in Oct–Apr), Hispaniolan Palm Crow* and Rufous-collared Sparrow. However, finding such birds may take some time because the best forest in this largely degraded mountain range is often far from roadsides.

The Hispaniolan Lizard-Cuckoo is one of four members of the Saurothera genus, which is unique to the Caribbean

SIERRA DE BAORUCO

The arid rain shadow deciduous thorn woods and mesquite at the foot of this rugged mountain range, which rises above 2134 m about 60 km west of Barahona, together with the epiphyte-enlivened montane rain forest and extensive areas of Caribbean pine forest on the high tops support the greatest diversity of birds in the Dominican Republic. Virtually all of the Hispaniolan endemics are recorded here on a regular basis, as well as Golden Swallow*, which may now be endemic to Hispaniola, and many other species including the endemic *megaplaga* race of Two-barred Crossbill.

Localised Hispaniolan Endemics

Hispaniolan Parakeet*, Bay-breasted Cuckoo*, Least Poorwill*, Hispaniolan Emerald, Hispaniolan Trogon*, Narrow-billed Tody, Antillean Piculet, Hispaniolan Pewee, La Selle Thrush*, Hispaniolan Palm Crow*, White-necked Crow*, Flat-billed Vireo, Antillean Siskin, Green-tailed and White-winged* Warblers, Eastern Chat-Tanager*.

Other Hispaniolan Endemics

Hispaniolan Parrot*, Hispaniolan Lizard-Cuckoo, Hispaniolan Nightjar, Broad-billed Tody, Hispaniolan Woodpecker, Palmchat, Black-crowned Palm-Tanager, Hispaniolan Stripe-headed Tanager.

Localised Caribbean Endemics

Grey-headed Quail-Dove*, Antillean Mango, Vervain Hummingbird, Greater Antillean Elaenia, Stolid Flycatcher, Golden Swallow*.

Other Caribbean Endemics

Plain Pigeon*, Key West Quail-Dove, Antillean Palm-Swift, Loggerhead Kingbird, Rufous-throated Solitaire, Red-legged Thrush, Antillean Euphonia, Greater Antillean Bullfinch, Greater Antillean Grackle.

Caribbean Near-endemics

White-crowned and Scaly-naped Pigeons, Zenaida Dove, Antillean Nighthawk (mainly Apr–Aug), Caribbean Martin (Feb–Aug), Black-faced Grassquit.

Passage Migrants and Winter Visitors

Bicknell's Thrush*, Northern Parula, Magnolia, Cape May, Black-throated Blue, Black-throated Green, Prairie, Palm and Black-and-white Warblers, American Redstart, Worm-eating Warbler, Ovenbird, Common Yellowthroat.

Others

Sharp-shinned and Red-tailed Hawks, White-winged Dove, Ruddy Quail-Dove, Mangrove Cuckoo, Burrowing Owl, White-collared Swift, Grey Kingbird, Two-barred Crossbill (endemic *megaplaga* race), Pine Warbler, Yellow-faced Grassquit, Black-cowled Oriole.

(Other species recorded here include Black-capped Petrel* (a few pairs breed from early Nov to mid-May in a small colony on the rocky, partially forested, slopes of Loma de Toro, above El Aguacate, at about 2250 m, just above the densest areas of pine forest, and there may be other colonies in the sierra), Ridgway's Hawk* (rare) and Grey-crowned

Palm-Tanager, as well as Ashy-faced and Stygian Owls, Northern Potoo, and Blue-winged and Wilson's Warblers, and Rose-breasted Grosbeak (all very rare winter visitors). Introduced species include Olive-throated Parakeet).

A 4WD with high clearance may be needed to cover this area thoroughly. To reach the sierra from the north turn south at the first street west of the tiny telecommunications office in Duvergé. From here the road climbs steeply for 8 km through arid thorn scrub, which supports Least Poorwill*, Antillean Piculet and Flat-billed Vireo, as well as Burrowing Owl and Antillean Nighthawk, to the National Park gate at the village of **Puerto Escondido**, where it is necessary to pay a small entrance fee.

The rough track above Puerto Escondido ascends Loma de Toro and passes through what is arguably the best birding area in the Dominican Republic. The dry thorn woods of the lower canyon 8–11 km above Puerto Escondido support Plain Pigeon*, Key West Quail-Dove, Bay-breasted Cuckoo* (in low thorn scrub where the track starts to rise into the foothills, about 12 km from Puerto Escondido, where there is a small

SIERRA DE BAORUCO

side track into the thorn scrub by a yellow 'Sierra Baoruco' signpost), Hispaniolan Trogon*, Narrow-billed Tody, Hispaniolan Pewee, White-necked Crow* (in palms lining the irrigation ditches just beyond the village) and Flat-billed Vireo. Above the lower canyon the track climbs out of the rain shadow into more humid foothill forest, with Hispaniolan Parakeet* and Hispaniolan Parrot*, before reaching **El Aguacate**, which is situated at the head of a long canyon near the border with Haiti, at 1097 m. There is a military camp and a checkpoint here where it is necessary to ask the commanding officer for permission to proceed, which is usually granted without a problem. Birds showing characteristics of Grey-crowned Palm-Tanager, which is extremely difficult to separate from Black-crowned Palm-Tanager, have been seen in the gulley below El Aguacate. A further 4–5 km beyond El Aguacate, at over 1524 m, lies the area known as **Zapotén** (about 30 km from Duvergé), on the south side of Loma de Toro, where the three high-altitude forest specialities; La Selle Thrush*, White-winged Warbler* and Eastern Chat-Tanager*, occur in the steep barrancas (large canyons) below, along with Hispaniolan Trogon*, Narrow-billed Tody, Golden Swallow* and Rufous-throated Solitaire. In addition, the Caribbean pine forest above here supports Two-barred Crossbill and Antillean Siskin. A flat, grassy clearing on the right, just before the remains of a rusty old bulldozer (from where the area takes its unofficial name), marks the spot to start birding. La Selle Thrush* and Eastern Chat-Tanager* are usually the most difficult endemics to get to grips with here. To start searching for them walk downhill, scouring the undergrowth by the main track for the tanager and listening for the thrush, which is most vocal at dawn and dusk.

SOUTHWEST DOMINICAN REPUBLIC

All of the species that occur between Duvergé and Zapotén, except Rufous-throated Solitaire and La Selle Thrush* can also be seen along the 15 km or so stretch of road south of the National Park gate at **Pedernales**, which is about 55 km northwest of Oviedo. The area around the small, artificial pool, on the right-hand side of the Las Mercedes road, is particularly good, with birds such as Hispaniolan Parakeet*, Golden Swallow* (which breeds in the abandoned bauxite quarry above here) and Two-barred Crossbill often present.

Accommodation: it is possible to make daily excursions to the sierra from Barahona, but to ensure being on site at Zapotén at dawn it may be best to camp for at least one night in the mountains.

White-tailed Tropicbird breeds (mainly Apr–Aug) on suitable cliffs and offshore islands along the extreme southwest coast of the Dominican Republic from Cabo Rojo to Bahía de Las Aguilas and Bucan de Base. Some nest on the small islands off the southern side of **Cabo Rojo**, the cape south of Pedernales, but, unfortunately, this is a private, fenced-off, area to which birders are unlikely to gain entry, even those who speak fluent Spanish with a silver tongue, for the guards are very dutiful. However, it may be possible to see the tropicbirds from a distance by scanning from the shore near the fence or by hiring a fishing boat from Pedernales. Alternatively, try sea-watching from the headlands on the other side of the Cabo Rojo peninsula. The mangrove-fringed pools outside the fence attract West Indian Whistling-Duck* and a variety of shorebirds, along with Brown Pelican, Magnificent Frigatebird, Royal Tern, Antillean Nighthawk (mainly Apr–Aug), Antillean Mango, Caribbean Martin (Feb–Aug) and Yellow Warbler. **Jaragua National Park** east of Cabo Rojo, supports White-crowned Pigeon, Hispaniolan Parrot*, Least Poorwill*, Flat-billed Vireo and Green-tailed Ground-Warbler. At **Laguna Oviedo** it is possible to see Greater Flamingo and White-necked Crow*.

Black-capped Petrels* are very rarely seen at sea in the Caribbean, but there may be a slim chance of spotting some off the southwestern coasts of the Dominican Republic, for a few pairs breed inland of there, in the Sierra de Baoruco

In the southeast corner of the Dominican Republic, east of Santo Domingo, Hispaniolan Parrot* occurs in **Este National Park**, accessible via San Rafael del Yuma. Sea-turtles breed on the remote beaches in this park and the inshore waters support manatee. Ridgway's Hawk* has been recorded nearby but the most reliable place to see this rare raptor is in **Los Haïtises National Park**, accessible only by 4WD. Head for the ranger station at Trepada Alta, which is about 16 km northwest of El Valle, 2–3 hours by road northeast of Santo Domingo. This is a difficult place to find so ask locally for directions in El Valle and once there seek a ranger known as Aquiles, who is usually happy to help visitors look for the hawk. The chances of seeing this rare endemic are about one in five, but species such as Hispaniolan Parrot*, Ashy-faced Owl, Narrow-billed Tody (here at one of its few lowland sites) and White-necked Crow*, some of the other endemics present in the park, may be easier to find.

In Dec–Mar humpback whales occur in the **Bahía de Samaná**, north of Los Haïtises, and they can be looked for on organised boat trips out of Samaná, which is situated on the Samaná Peninsula on the north side of the bay. Other possibilities on these trips, which last 2–4 hours, include Atlantic spotted dolphin and pilot whale, and these as well as humpback whale can also be seen from Cabo Samaná or Punta Balandra at the east end of the peninsula. On the north coast about 20 pairs of White-tailed Tropicbird breed (mainly May–Aug) at Cabo Cabrón and Punta Tibice but these headlands are accessible only by boat, from the small town of Las Galeras.

The broadleaf and pine forests of **Valle Nuevo**, a Scientific Reserve traversed by a 4WD-only stretch of road between San José de Ocoa and Constanza in the central Dominican Republic, support Antillean Siskin, Hispaniolan Stripe-headed Tanager and Rufous-collared Sparrow. To the northwest of Constanza the **Cordillera Central**, which rises to 3175 m at Pico Duarte, the highest peak in the Caribbean, supports Stygian Owl, Hispaniolan Trogon*, Antillean Piculet, Golden Swallow*, La Selle Thrush* (confined to the Alto Bandera area), Hispaniolan Palm Crow*, White-winged Warbler* and Eastern Chat-Tanager*, as well as Grey-headed Quail-Dove* and Rufous-collared Sparrow (Constanza to Manabao). The only remaining areas of extensive forest in this range are in the José Armando Bermudez and adjacent José del Carmen Ramírez National Parks, both of which lie within a large and relatively remote area which is only likely to prove productive on an extended camping excursion. The best starting point may be the information hut 4 km from La Ciénaga, which is accessible by road from Jarabacoa.

Hispaniolan Trogon* also occurs at **Ebano Verde**, a Scientific Reserve near Jarabacoa established to protect remnant cloud forest and managed by Fundación Progreso (tel. 565 1422, fax. 549 3900).

In Feb–Mar there are regular organised boat trips to about 80 km north of Puerto Plata (where Palmchat is common) on the north coast in order to look for, and possibly swim with, humpback whales. At this time of year 1000s of hyperactive humpbacks from as far afield as Iceland and Greenland gather between the Dominican Republic and the Turks & Caicos Islands, in an area known as the **Silver Bank** (Banco de la Plata). This is believed to be the principal mating and calving area for the species in the North Atlantic and it is possible to see 100s in a day, including large groups of males breaching, flipper-slapping, lob-tailing and slamming, as well as Atlantic bottlenose, Atlantic spotted and spinner dolphins, and Bryde's and other whales. For details of boat trips, which last all day, contact the DNP (address below). It is also possible to see some whales and dolphins from land on the north coast of the Dominican Republic, especially at Cabo Francès Viejo National Park, near Cabrera, east of Puerto Plata.

Birds recorded in and around the **Monte Cristí National Park** in the country's extreme northwest corner include Hispaniolan Parakeet*, Hispaniolan Lizard-Cuckoo, Broad-billed Tody and Palmchat, as well as Brown Pelican, Osprey, Clapper Rail, Wilson's Plover, Royal Tern, Antillean Mango, Vervain Hummingbird, Belted Kingfisher, Caribbean Martin (Feb–Aug), Yellow Warbler, Black-crowned Palm-Tanager, Yellow-faced Grassquit, Greater Antillean Bullfinch and Black-cowled Oriole. Also in this area, West Indian Whistling-Duck* occurs at **Laguna del Salodillo**.

ADDITIONAL INFORMATION

Addresses

Dirección Nacional de Parques (Dominican Republic National Parks Office—DNP), Aptdo. Postal 2487, Avenida Independencia 539 Esquina Cervantes, Santo Domingo, Dominican Republic, West Indies (tel. 221 5340, ecotourism office tel. 472 3717/4204).

Secretaria de Estado de Turismo (Tourist Office), Edificio de Oficinas Gubernamentales, PO Box 497, Avenida Mexico 30 Esquina de Marzo, Ala 'D', Santo Domingo, Dominican Republic, West Indies (tel. 221 4660/1, fax. 682 3806, e-mail: sectur@codetel.net.do).

Ecoturisa, Santiago 203 B, Santo Domingo, Dominican Republic, West Indies (tel. 221 4104/6, fax. 685 1544).

Books

Aves de la República Dominicana, Dod, A. S. 1987. Museo Nacional de Historia Natural.

The Birds of Haiti and the Dominican Republic, Wetmore, A. and Swales, B. H. 1931. US National Mus. Bull. 155.

Annotated Checklist of the Birds of Hispaniola, Keith, A. R. in prep. BOU.

Recent Ornithological Research in the Dominican Republic, Latta, S. C. 1998. Ediciones Tinglar.

The history and taxonomic status of the Hispaniolan Crossbill Loxia megaplaga, Smith, P. W. 1997. *Bull. Brit. Orn. Club* 117: 264–271.

The Dominican Republic. A Country between Rain Forest and Desert: Contributions to the Ecology of a Caribbean Island, Bolay, E. 1997.

GRENADA

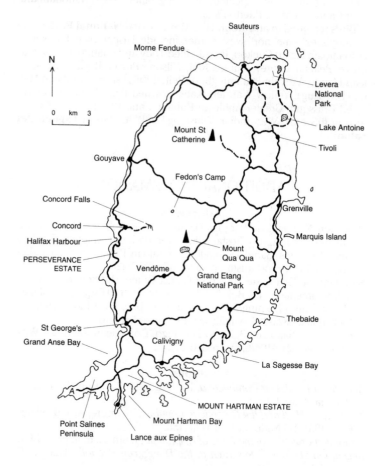

N

0   km   3

Sauteurs
Morne Fendue
Levera National Park
Lake Antoine
Mount St Catherine
Tivoli
Gouyave
Fedon's Camp
Concord Falls
Grenville
Concord
Halifax Harbour
Marquis Island
PERSEVERANCE ESTATE
Mount Qua Qua
Vendôme
Grand Etang National Park
St George's
Thebaide
Grand Anse Bay
Calivigny
La Sagesse Bay
MOUNT HARTMAN ESTATE
Point Salines Peninsula
Mount Hartman Bay
Lance aux Epines

INTRODUCTION

This rather rugged and mountainous small island, the most southerly of the Lesser Antilles, supports the very rare endemic Grenada Dove*, several Lesser Antillean endemics, an endemic race of Hook-billed Kite and a handful of species that are much more common in nearby South America, including Rufous-breasted Hermit.

At approximately 34 km long and up to 20 km wide Grenada covers 345 km². It is possible to reach most parts of the island in taxis or minibuses. Vehicles are available for hire but drivers will need to be very alert at all times, for the roads do not match western standards, there are few roadsigns and the minibuses hurtle around the island at breakneck speed. The official language of this Commonwealth State is English, though the local people also speak a French patois. The majority of hotels and guest houses, as well as apartments and villas, are concentrated in the southwest of the island, especially in and around the capital, St. George's, and by Grand Anse Bay to the south. Most of the international restaurants are also here. They serve a wide variety of dishes, including local specialities such as callaloo soup, conch, pumpkin pie and seafood, most of which are spiced with nutmeg. The most popular local drinks are beer, rum and 'sea moss', which is made from algae, milk and vanilla. Grenada is, on the whole, a safe place though petty crime is a problem in the main tourist areas. The best time to visit is during the breeding season of Grenada Dove*, when these shy and elusive birds are calling and therefore easier to locate. However, though they usually breed in December–February, their timing appears to vary according to local conditions such as rainfall, and occupied nests have even been found in July. Fortunately, the most pleasant time of year to be on this hot tropical island, when the heat and humidity are at their least debilitating, coincides with the dove's normal breeding season, though high-season prices for accommodation apply from mid-December until mid-April. The wet season is normally June–November, although it can rain anytime during the year on the high tops, which receive 381 cm of rainfall per annum.

The mountainous interior rises to 840 m at Mount St. Catherine in the north. Only 9% of the island is forested, with most of the fertile lowlands and slopes having been turned over to agriculture and 35% of the island is now intensively cultivated with bananas and spices, especially cloves and nutmeg (Grenada produces about 30% of the world's nutmeg). The island's richest habitats for birds, montane rain forest and elfin woods, are now largely restricted to the steepest slopes and highest ridges, and in the lowlands there are only a few remaining areas of mature dry scrub forest which Grenada Dove* inhabits. Around the rather rugged coastline there are some small areas of mangrove, white sand beaches, and offshore islands and reefs.

Although there are some 'protected' areas and a special effort is being made to conserve Grenada Dove*, continuing habitat loss and degradation, poor legislation and its enforcement, poaching, shooting, and the problems caused by introduced species such as green vervet and mona monkeys, all require swift resolution if the dove, the only threatened species to occur on the island, as well as the relatively common and widespread birds of Grenada, are to survive.

Grenada Endemics and Other Bird Species

One species is endemic to Grenada; the Grenada Dove*, which is very rare and restricted to the southwest where it is most likely to be seen near Halifax Harbour and at Mount Hartman Estate. The population declined by about 50% between 1987 and 1997, when there were possibly fewer than 70 of these birds left on the planet.

Nine of the 51 Caribbean endemics not confined to single islands or archipelagos occur on Grenada. They are six of the 14 Lesser Antillean endemics not confined to single islands: Purple-throated Carib, Grenada Flycatcher (which otherwise occurs only on the Grenadines and St. Vincent), Brown Trembler (rare), Scaly-breasted Thrasher (rare), Lesser Antillean Tanager (which otherwise occurs only on St. Vincent) and Lesser Antillean Bullfinch; and three more widespread species, namely Green-throated Carib, Antillean Crested Hummingbird and Antillean Euphonia.

Seven of the 18 species nearly endemic to the Caribbean occur. They are Scaly-naped Pigeon, Zenaida Dove, Caribbean Elaenia, Caribbean Martin (Jan–Sep), Black-whiskered Vireo, Black-faced Grassquit and Carib Grackle. In addition, members of the *petechia* group of Yellow Warbler, known as 'Golden Warbler', which is also nearly endemic to the Caribbean, occur in the non-breeding season (Sep–Feb).

About 120 species have been recorded on the island. Non-endemic specialities and spectacular species not otherwise mentioned include Magnificent Frigatebird, Hook-billed Kite (the endemic race is very rare in the southwest and northeast, with just 15–35 individuals believed present in 1987, though more recent surveys indicate that the population may be larger than realized), Collared Plover (rare to uncommon breeding resident), Bridled and Sooty Terns, Brown Noddy (all three mainly Apr–Aug), Eared Dove, Ruddy Quail-Dove, Grey-rumped Swift (probably only a summer visitor, Mar–May), Rufous-breasted Hermit, Yellow-bellied Elaenia, Fork-tailed Flycatcher (very rare migrant, mainly around the airport in the southwest in Jul–Aug, when thought to overshoot its breeding grounds in northern South America), House Wren, Tropical Mockingbird, Cocoa and Bare-eyed Thrushes, Blue-black Grassquit (mainly Jun–Sep) and Yellow-bellied Seedeater (uncommon, Mar–Nov). The endemic *johnstonei* race of Euler's Flycatcher which was formerly a rare resident near Grand Étang has not been recorded since 1950. It is possible to see over 35 species in a single day on the island, but don't expect too many more than that, even on a prolonged trip.

MOUNT HARTMAN ESTATE

The 480 ha of dry scrub forest on the hillsides above the Government Farm in this Reserve in the southwest of the island supports 75% of the 70 or so surviving Grenada Doves*. This is a difficult species to find, but the endemic race of Hook-billed Kite, which also occurs here, is seen even less frequently.

Grenada Endemics
Grenada Dove*.

Grenada and St. Vincent Endemics
Grenada Flycatcher.

Lesser Antillean Endemics
Lesser Antillean Tanager, Lesser Antillean Bullfinch.

Caribbean Near-endemics
Zenaida Dove, Black-faced Grassquit, Carib Grackle.

Others
Broad-winged Hawk, Eared Dove, Mangrove Cuckoo, Smooth-billed Ani, Yellow-bellied Elaenia, Grey Kingbird, Bare-eyed Thrush, Blue-black Grassquit (mainly Jun–Sep). (Other species recorded here include Hook-billed Kite and Fork-tailed Flycatcher [mainly Jul–Aug]).

To reach the west side of Mount Hartman head east from the main north–south highway at the second roundabout north of the international airport on Point Salines Peninsula. About 300 m from the highway take the obscure right-hand turn, continue along here and scour any dense thorn scrub for the dove. To reach the east side of Mount Hartman from the north–south highway turn southeast 1 km north of the above-mentioned roundabout. It may be necessary to cover a considerable amount of ground in the thorny scrub before coming across a shy and elusive Grenada Dove*, so it is wise to wear suitable clothing and beware of chiggers. For more information on the best places to look and the possibility of arranging help from a local guide contact the Government Forestry Unit (tel. 440 6197), the Parks Unit (tel. 440 0366) and/or the La Sagesse Nature Centre (tel. 444 6458).

Accommodation: No Problem Motel, ten minutes from the airport and a few km from the Government Farm.

Wet areas on the **Point Salines Peninsula** and around **Calivigny**, northeast of Mount Hartman, are worth checking for waterbirds, especially shorebirds. In Dec–Apr it is possible to see migrating humpback whales, as well as dolphins and pilot whales, on boat trips from **St. George's**. House Wren, Tropical Mockingbird and Bare-eyed Thrush are widespread and can be seen beside the coast road north from St. George's to **Perseverance Estate**, near Halifax Harbour, where there are even fewer Grenada Doves* than at Mount Hartman Estate, but where the species is arguably easier to find. To reach there proceed through the Sendahl Tunnel (the only tunnel just north of St. George's), pass the River Road (which heads inland into the mountains) and opposite the green shed on the left-hand side of the road at the southern edge of the rubbish dump (due to be closed in 2000), along the main coast road several km further north, look for a small trail into the thorn scrub at the southern end of a wide bowl of hills. The dove occurs along here, as well as Grenada Flycatcher and Lesser Antillean Bullfinch.

Grand Étang, a volcanic crater lake at 530 m, is set within the 15 km^2 **Grand Étang National Park**, with a visitor centre overlooking the lake and network of trails, about 13 km northeast of St. George's via River Road. The lake is surrounded by secondary montane rain forest, consisting mostly of blue mahoe trees replanted after Hurricane Janet laid waste to those already present in September 1955, as well as palm brakes and elfin woods, that support Grey-rumped Swift (mainly Mar–May), Rufous-breasted Hermit, Purple-throated and Green-throated Caribs, Antillean Crested Hummingbird, Cocoa Thrush and Lesser Antillean Tanager, as well as the introduced mona monkey. Some of these may be seen around the visitor centre but the best chance of seeing Cocoa Thrush is probably to walk the Shoreline Trail to the south end of the lake early in the morning, although it has also been recorded at the Forest Nursery. It takes about 1.5 hours to walk the entire Shoreline Trail, which circles the lake. Other trails, which are particularly wet and muddy during and after rain, include that ascending Mount Qua Qua, along which it takes about 1.5 hours to reach the summit and a further three hours downhill to reach Concord Falls (with a 30 minute detour to Fedon's Camp at 765 m if preferred). From Concord Falls it is 25 minutes to the road where it is possible to catch a bus back to St. George's. Most visitors who stay near the park do so at Lake House (tel. 442 7425) though it may be possible to camp in the park (ask at the visitor centre).

The other major birding site on Grenada is **Levera National Park** in the far northeast of the island. The large brackish lake, dry littoral woods, cactus scrub, mangroves, white-sand beaches, and offshore islands and reefs within the park support waterbirds, Hook-billed Kite and breeding leatherback sea-turtles (Apr–Jun). There are a few trails here and guides are available. To the south it is worth checking **Lake Antoine** for water-birds. Elsewhere along the rugged east coast seabirds breed on offshore islets such as **La Baye Rock**, which is off Marquis Island and has a Brown Booby colony (Mar–Oct).

ADDITIONAL INFORMATION

Addresses

Grenada Board of Tourism, Burn's Point, PO Box 293, St. George's, Grenada, West Indies (tel. 440 2279, fax. 440 6637, e-mail: gbt@caribsurf.com; web site: interknowledge.com/grenada). For more information on the parks and reserves contact the Forestry Department, Ministry of Agriculture, Archibald Avenue, St. George's, Grenada, West Indies.

Books and Papers

Birds of Grenada, St. Vincent and the Grenadines, Devas, R. P. 1970. Carenage Press.

Population declines of the endangered endemic birds on Grenada, West Indies, Blockstein, D. E. 1991. *Bird Conserv. Intern.* 1: 83–91.

*Grenada Hook-billed Kite (*Chondrohierax uncinatus mirus*) surveys and nesting activity.* Thorstrom, R. *et al.* 2000. *El Pitire* 13: 92.

GRENADINES

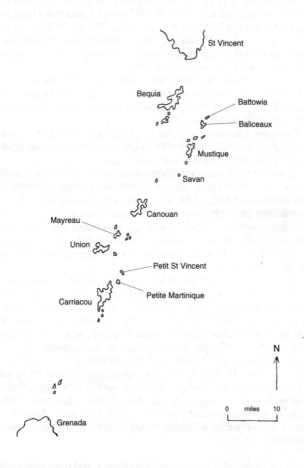

There is little to tempt anyone interested in birds to this archipelago in the southern Lesser Antilles apart from a few seabirds and Caribbean endemics, but any birder with a yacht and/or limitless amounts of money may find these delightful islands the ideal place to unwind during a long stay in the region. The 100 or so rocky islands and cays that comprise the Grenadines cover just 80 km² and Mustique and Union, two of the larger islands, for example, are just 5 km long and 1.5–3 km miles wide, while the largest, Carriacou, is just 21 km² in extent. Most of these, as well as the other islands, are off the beaten tourist track but some of the larger ones are connected by cheap, if rather unreliable, internal air and ferry networks, and airpasses to visit three islands from St. Vincent may be available. On the main islands it is possible to hire vehicles or get around by bus and truck-taxi. English is the official language of this Commonwealth State, where the northern islands, which include Bequia, Mustique and Union, are administered by St. Vincent, and the southern islands of Carriacou and Petite Martinique by Grenada.

The Grenadines cater primarily for rich people and virtually all of the accommodation is priced well beyond the range acceptable to most birders. It's a good job there are no beautiful endemics here for camping is discouraged, except on Carriacou. The wide range of food includes anything from fish-and-chips to lobster pizza, although away from the main resorts menus may be limited to fried fish with breadfruit. Beer and rum is widely available however.

The best time to visit the Grenadines, where the hot tropical climate is tempered by northeasterly trade winds, is in April–August, when most seabirds are present, though the wet season usually commences in May and lasts until November.

The main islands, which rise to 274 m on Union, have, for the most part, lightly forested hills, fertile valleys and long beaches, and are surrounded by small offshore islets and reefs.

There are no threatened or near-threatened species present but habitat loss and degradation are still a problem for the relatively common and widespread birds of the archipelago. No species are endemic to the Grenadines and only three of the 51 Caribbean endemics not confined to single countries, islands or archipelagos occur here. They are Green-throated Carib, Antillean Crested Hummingbird and Grenada Flycatcher (the only one of the 14 Lesser Antillean endemics not confined to single islands to occur).

Seven of the 18 species almost endemic to the Caribbean occur on the Grenadines. They are Scaly-naped Pigeon, Zenaida Dove, Caribbean Elaenia, Caribbean Martin (Jan–Sep), Black-whiskered Vireo, Black-faced Grassquit and Carib Grackle. In addition, the *petechia* group of Yellow Warbler, known as 'Golden Warbler', which is also nearly endemic to the Caribbean, is represented by the *alsiosa* race.

Non-endemic specialities and spectacular species not mentioned above include Masked Booby (breeds mainly Mar–May), Bridled and Sooty Terns, Brown Noddy (all three, mainly Apr–Aug), Eared Dove, Yellow-bellied Elaenia, Tropical Mockingbird, Bare-eyed Thrush and Yellow-bellied Seedeater (uncommon on Carriacou, Mar–Nov). Introduced species include Rufous-vented Chachalaca (Union) and Crested Bobwhite (Mustique).

Organised boat trips from Hillsborough on **Carriacou** visit seabird sanctuaries and look for humpback (Dec–Apr) and pilot whales, as well as dolphins, in the waters west of the island. Seabirds also breed on Hog Island in Woburn Bay along the north coast of the 11 km² island of Bequia.

For more information contact the St. Vincent and the Grenadines Department of Tourism, Finance Complex, Bay Street, PO Box 834, Kingstown, St. Vincent, West Indies (tel. 457 1502, fax. 456 2610, e-mail: tourism@caribsurf.com, web site: www.stvincentandgrenadines.com).

Books

Birds of Grenada, St. Vincent and the Grenadines, Devas, R. P. 1970. Carenage Press.

GUADELOUPE

- Pointe de la Grande Vigie
- Pointe d'Antigues
- Porte d'Enfer
- Port-Louis
- Grand Cul-de-Sac Marin
- Le Moule
- GRANDE-TERRE
- Maison de la Foret
- Pointe-Noire
- Pointe-a-Pitre
- Mahaut
- D23
- VERNOU
- Pointe des Châteaux
- BASSE-TERRE
- La Soufrière
- St-Claude
- Chutes du Carbet
- Basse-Terre
- Marie Galante
- St-Louis
- Mangles de Folle Anse
- Capesterre
- N
- Grand Bourg
- 0   km   10
- Les Saintes

INTRODUCTION

Summary

This large twin-island in the northern Lesser Antilles, one island of which is well forested, supports a common endemic woodpecker and nine of the 14 Lesser Antillean endemics not confined to single islands, including Brown Trembler, Forest Thrush*, which is arguably easier to locate here than on any other island, and Plumbeous Warbler, which otherwise occurs only on Dominica.

Size

Guadeloupe comprises two roughly equal-sized islands, Basse-Terre and Grande-Terre, which together cover 1780 km^2.

Getting Around

Most roads are in excellent condition and well signed, but this rare treat (for the Caribbean) can be tainted by the crazy local drivers who career around the island at top speed, making driving dangerous in some areas.

It is also possible to use the expensive taxis, or the cheap and extensive, but crowded and slow, bus network. The official language of this Overseas Department of France is French and as very few local people speak good English, even in tourist areas, a basic grasp of this will be useful.

Accommodation and Food
The wide range of accommodation available includes gîtes and a few campsites. Most of the food is a mix of African and French, and favourite local dishes combine fresh local ingredients with exotic seasonings. Such delights can be washed down with beer, rum and wine.

Climate and Timing
The peak time to visit Guadeloupe is in April–May, at the end of the dry season, when the chances of seeing some seabirds as well as the endemic and near-endemic landbirds increase. The climate is tropical with cooling northeast trade winds. The rainy season in the lowlands is in May–November, peaking at the end of this period, though heavy downpours occur throughout the year in the mountains. The hurricane season is in June–November.

Habitats
The western island, the volcanic Basse-Terre, is separated from the ancient coral reef that comprises the eastern island, Grande-Terre, by la Rivière Salée, a very narrow strait with a bridge across it. Nearly 40% of the land is forested and most of this is the extensive remaining rain forest on Basse-Terre, where the 20 km^2 of relatively undisturbed forest surrounding La Soufrière is arguably the largest area of relative wilderness in the whole of the Lesser Antilles. The many fumaroles spewing gas steam are a reminder that La Soufrière volcano, which rises to 1467 m and last erupted in 1976, is still active. Cultivation is mostly restricted to the coastal areas of Basse-Terre, whereas fruit and sugarcane plantations, and pastures, are more widespread on the limestone hills of Grande-Terre, where there are also mangroves on the west coast. About 16% of the total area of land is cultivated and 14% pasture.

Conservation
Although much of the montane rain forest of Basse-Terre is intact, habitat loss due to such activities as clear-felling and the removal of old trees, as well as hunting and pollution must all be stopped in order to conserve the three threatened and near-threatened species, as well as the relatively common and widespread birds, which occur on Guadeloupe.

Endemics
One species is endemic to Guadeloupe, the Guadeloupe Woodpecker*, around 10,000 pairs of which occur below 610 m, especially on the moist east-facing slopes of Basse-Terre.

Other Caribbean Endemics
Fourteen of the 51 Caribbean endemics not confined to single countries, islands or archipelagos occur on Guadeloupe. They are nine of the 14 Lesser Antillean endemics not confined to single islands: Lesser Antillean Swift, Purple-throated Carib, Lesser Antillean Flycatcher (rare), Brown Trembler, Scaly-breasted Thrasher, Forest Thrush*, Plumbeous Warbler (which elsewhere occurs only on Dominica), Lesser Antillean

Bullfinch and Lesser Antillean Saltator; and five more widespread species, namely Bridled Quail-Dove, Green-throated Carib, Antillean Crested Hummingbird, Lesser Antillean Pewee (*brunneicapillus*) and Antillean Euphonia.

Near-Endemics
Ten of the 18 species nearly endemic to the Caribbean occur on Guadeloupe. They are Caribbean Coot* (rare, has bred), White-crowned (rare) and Scaly-naped Pigeons, Zenaida Dove, Caribbean Elaenia, Caribbean Martin (Feb–Aug), Pearly-eyed Thrasher, Black-whiskered Vireo, Black-faced Grassquit and Carib Grackle. In addition the *petechia* group of Yellow Warbler, known as 'Golden Warbler', which is also nearly endemic to the Caribbean, is represented by the *melanoptera* race.

Bird species
Over 190 species have been recorded. Non-endemic specialities and spectacular species not already mentioned include Red-billed Tropicbird (mainly Jan–Jun), Magnificent Frigatebird, Bridled and Sooty Terns, Brown Noddy (all three mainly Apr–Aug), Ruddy Quail-Dove, Black Swift (mainly Apr–Sep) and Ringed Kingfisher (local and uncommon).

Expectations
It is possible to see the endemic woodpecker, as well as all nine widespread Lesser Antillean endemics that occur on the island in a single day, but don't expect to see many more than 50 species during a trip lasting a few days, or even longer.

VERNOU

The small village of Vernou is a good base from which to bird the interior montane rain forests on Basse-Terre, which support Bridled Quail-Dove, the endemic woodpecker and all nine of the Lesser Antillean endemics not confined to single islands that occur on Guadeloupe. These include Forest Thrush*, which is arguably easier to see here than at any other site on the four islands it occurs on.

Guadeloupe Endemics
Guadeloupe Woodpecker*.

Lesser Antillean Endemics
Lesser Antillean Swift, Purple-throated Carib, Lesser Antillean Flycatcher, Brown Trembler, Scaly-breasted Thrasher, Forest Thrush*, Plumbeous Warbler, Lesser Antillean Bullfinch, Lesser Antillean Saltator.

Other Caribbean Endemics
Bridled Quail-Dove, Green-throated Carib, Antillean Crested Hummingbird, Lesser Antillean Pewee.

Caribbean Near-endemics
Scaly-naped Pigeon, Zenaida Dove, Caribbean Elaenia, Caribbean Martin (Feb–Aug), Pearly-eyed Thrasher, Black-faced Grassquit, Carib Grackle.

Others

Ruddy Quail-Dove, Mangrove Cuckoo, Black Swift (mainly Apr–Sep), Grey Kingbird.

Any areas of good forest around Vernou are worth birding, but the best previously productive sites are as follows: (i) the track north from the D23 (Route de la Traversée) 3–4 km west of the intersection with the D1, which is good for Lesser Antillean Flycatcher; (ii) the picnic area at the **Rivière Corossol**, where Brown Trembler and Forest Thrush* may be seen at dawn (can be crowded at weekends). To reach here turn south off the D23 a km or so west of the Rio Corossol, which is 4–5 km west of the D1/D23 intersection, and follow the poor track for a couple of km to its end, where the picnic area is situated next to the river. Plumbeous Warbler occurs beside the access track, about halfway along which there is a trail on the right (when coming from the D23), which ascends into good forest and joins the well-marked trail system of; (iii) the **Maison de la Fôret**, where Bridled and Ruddy Quail-Doves occur, and Forest Thrush* is possible near the Rio Bras David. The forest visitor centre (opens 9.30am) is situated 1–2 km west of the turning to the Rivière Corossol picnic area; and (iv) the **Pris de l'Eau** area. To reach here turn west off the D1 1–2 km north of the D1/D23 intersection, in response to the 'INA—Station de Reserches de Zoologie' signpost. Follow this track for a few km, bearing right at each intersection, then continue on foot for a couple of km. The last occasion House Wren (four singing males) was recorded on Guadeloupe was here, in 1973. If any species remain elusive try any good-looking forest along the D23, between its intersection with the D1 and the west coast.

Accommodation: Vernou - Le Monte Fleuri Guesthouse.

VERNOU AREA

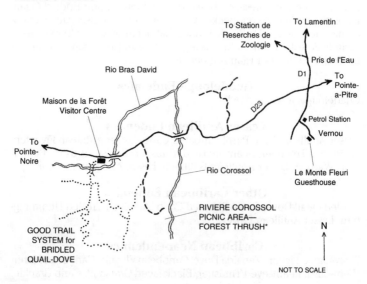

The Vernou area lies within the 300 km² Parc Naturel Regional de la Guadeloupe, which extends south to **La Soufrière** volcano. To reach here take the narrow road northeast out of St-Claude, a village with accommodation at 572 m northeast of the town of Basse-Terre, for about 6 km to the parking area at Savane à Mulets, at 1142 m. The trail to the crater and summit of La Soufrière begins here. Alongside the access road and the summit trail it is possible to see Purple-throated Carib, Brown Trembler, Scaly-breasted Thrasher and Plumbeous Warbler. The summit of La Soufrière is also accessible from the east, along the forest trail known as Trace Michael which begins at the parking area below the Chutes du Carbet waterfall. There is an information centre at Maison du Volcan but for more details in advance contact the Organisation des Guides de Montagne de la Caraïbe (OGMC), Maison Forestiere, 97120 Matouba, Guadeloupe, French West Indies (tel. 800579). This organisation may also be able to provide information on the trails that begin near the northwest coast of Basse-Terre and traverse the forested peaks inland from there where some of the species listed for the Vernou and La Soufrière areas, including Guadeloupe Woodpecker*, Lesser Antillean Pewee and Brown Trembler, as well as Yellow Warbler and American Redstart (Oct–Apr) occur. One such peak is La Couronne where a trail begins at the end of the track leading inland off the main N2 coast road from the southern outskirts of Pointe-Noire and passes through the village of Bellevue.

Most of the mangrove and many small islets in the northern bay between Basse-Terre and Grande-Terre lie within a 37 km² marine nature reserve known as the **Grand Cul-de-Sac Marin**, where seabirds breed. At the northeastern end of the bay the mangrove-lined mudflats and marshes at Pointe d'Antigues, just north of the town of Port-Louis in northern Grande-Terre, support waterbirds such as egrets, herons, and passage and wintering shorebirds. Several rough tracks leading north from the cemetery by the beach at the north end of the town access the area. The rocky headlands of Grande-Terre's north coast between Pointe de la Grande Vigie and Pointe des Gros Cap support small numbers of

The black and maroon Guadeloupe Woodpecker is one of seven surviving woodpeckers that occur only in the Caribbean*

breeding Red-billed Tropicbirds (mainly Jan–Jun). One of the best places to look for this splendid bird is from the cliff-top trail which begins at Porte d'Enfer and leads south. The mangroves around **Le Moule** on the east coast of Grande-Terre are worth a look and the fishing cooperative here organises boat trips in Nov–Apr to look for humpback, pilot and sperm whales, as well as dolphins. At the extreme eastern end of Grande-Terre Caribbean Elaenia occurs by the trail through the stunted littoral limestone woods on the rugged ridge of Pointe des Colibris, a short walk from the parking area at **Pointe des Châteaux**. The lagoons here are worth checking for waterbirds and off the Atlantic shore it is possible to see Sooty Tern (mainly Apr–Aug, on the inshore island of La Roche) and Brown Noddy (mainly Apr–Aug), while other seabirds recorded here include Manx Shearwater (mainly Nov–Mar), tropicbirds (mainly Jan–Jul) and Roseate Tern (mainly Apr–Sep). Some seabirds do breed in this area but there are more on the island of **Marie Galante** (where the wetlands at Mangles de Folle Anse are worth a good look) and the archipelago known as **Les Saintes**, both of which are south of Guadeloupe and accessible by air and sea from the main islands.

ADDITIONAL INFORMATION

Addresses

Union Regionale des Associations du Patrimoine et de l'Environment de Guadeloupe, 97112 Pointe-à-Pitre, Guadeloupe, French West Indies.

Office Departemental du Tourisme de la Guadeloupe, 5 Square de la Banque, 422-97163 Pointe-à-Pitre, Guadeloupe, French West Indies (tel. 820930, fax. 838922).

Books

Oiseaux des Petites Antilles/Birds of the West Indies (or, more accurately, a photographic guide to the birds of Guadeloupe and Martinique, in French and English), Benito-Espinal, E. 1990. Editions du Latanier, Saint-Barthélémy.

HAITI

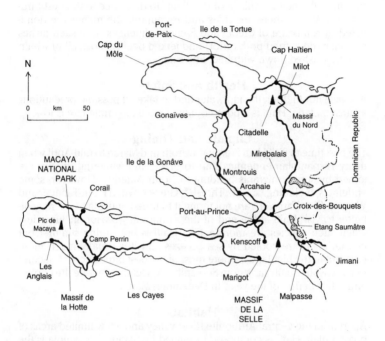

INTRODUCTION

Summary

The presence of all 28 Hispaniolan endemics, including Palmchat, the sole member of its family, which is endemic to Hispaniola, two todies and a trogon also endemic to Hispaniola, as well as many other Caribbean endemics make Haiti sound a terrific birding destination. However, this republic, which shares the island of Hispaniola with the Dominican Republic, is the poorest, most environmentally degraded country in the Caribbean and has the least developed tourist infrastructure, so finding the best birds let alone any decent forest, which many depend on for survival, will be tough and is likely to involve at least a couple of camping expeditions and some long, hot hikes.

Size

Haiti occupies the western third of the island of Hispaniola and covers 27,750 km².

Getting Around

The best birding sites are not easily accessible from the rudimentary road network, hence it will be necessary to walk considerable distances

329

to see the best birds. The main language is Haitian Creole, although some people also speak French.

Accommodation and Food

Most towns have hotels, but it will be necessary to camp (with permission from the nearest village or dwelling) to do justice to the best birding sites. Where there are cafes and restaurants the menus are dominated by a mixture of Creole and French influences, with such dishes as conch, deep-fried pork (griot) and jerked beef (tassot), all of which may be washed down with beer and rum.

Health and Safety

It is wise not to drink the tap water and to take all possible precautions against malaria. Haiti is a poor country, hence the crime rate is low.

Climate and Timing

The best time to visit Haiti is arguably from mid-March to mid-April when many Hispaniolan endemics start to breed and wintering species are joined by spring migrants heading to North America. However, some endemics, including La Selle Thrush*, Grey-crowned Palm-Tanager and Western Chat-Tanager* are not thought to breed until May, so it may be better to visit Haiti at the end of the spring rainy season in June–July when such species are more active. Haiti is hot during summer but coastal areas are cooled by sea breezes and it is usually much more pleasant in the highlands, where most of the best birds occur. A second rainy season usually lasts from September to October, before the coolest and driest period of the year, in December–March.

Habitats

Apart from the central Artibonite River valley and a few limited areas of coastal plain Haiti is composed of rugged highlands. Hispaniola is the most mountainous island in the Caribbean and although nowhere in Haiti exceeds 3000 m, unlike the neighbouring Dominican Republic, the highest peak, Pic La Selle, rises to 2674 m in the southeast. The mountains were once completely cloaked in montane rain forest but by the end of the 20th Century less than 5% of the country was forested, virtually every slope having been denuded to make way for cultivation and grazing, and yet these two activities account for just 33% and 18% of the land because much of the rest is no longer fit for either.

Conservation

Haiti is an ecological hell-hole where soil erosion and desertification resulting from devastating deforestation and widespread ongoing agricultural encroachment are just two of the most serious problems that require immediate resolution if the 20 threatened and near-threatened species, as well as the relatively common and widespread species, are to survive. The government has designated two National Parks of about 50,000 ha, listed 35 other sites for 'protection', tightened some hunting regulations and established environmental education programmes, but, as usual, this is not nearly enough.

Endemics

One species may be endemic to Haiti, Grey-crowned Palm-Tanager. According to Clements in *Birds of the World: A Checklist*, 2000 this species is restricted to Haiti's southern peninsula and the offshore islands of Île de la Gonâve, Grande Cayemite and Île-à-Vache, but Raffaele H. *et al.* in *Birds of the West Indies* state that it is rare in the Sierra de Baoruco, in the adjacent Dominican Republic, from where this notoriously difficult to identify species has been reported by visiting birders. Others doubt if it is a full species at all, it being extremely similar to the widespread Black-crowned Palm-Tanager. The remaining 27 species endemic to Hispaniola and which occur in Haiti are:

Ridgway's Hawk*	Very rare in the Massif du Nord and on offshore islands
Hispaniolan Parakeet*	Rare in the Massif de la Selle and Massif du Nord (Citadelle area)
Hispaniolan Parrot*	Rare in the highlands
Hispaniolan Lizard-Cuckoo	Relatively common and widespread
Bay-breasted Cuckoo*	Rare in extreme east and on Île de la Gonâve
Ashy-faced Owl	Relatively common and fairly widespread
Least Poorwill*	Locally relatively common between Arcahaie and Montrouis north of Port-au-Prince, and near Pointe-a-Raquette on Île de la Gonâve
Hispaniolan Nightjar	Believed to be fairly common
Hispaniolan Emerald	Relatively common in the highlands, rarer in the lowlands in the non-breeding season (Jul–Mar) and most likely to be seen in the Massif de la Selle and Massif de la Hotte
Hispaniolan Trogon*	Locally relatively common, especially in the Massif de la Hotte
Broad-billed Tody	Relatively common, primarily in the lowlands
Narrow-billed Tody	Locally relatively common, primarily in the highlands
Antillean Piculet	Locally relatively common
Hispaniolan Woodpecker	Relatively common and widespread
Hispaniolan Pewee	Relatively common and widespread
Palmchat	Relatively common and widespread from lowlands to foothills
La Selle Thrush*	Rare above 1400 m in the Massif de la Selle and to the north of there near the border with the Dominican Republic; in the late 1990s it could not be found at four previously known sites in these two areas
Hispaniolan Palm Crow*	Known from Artibonite, Étang Saumâtre, the Massif de la Selle, Mirebalais and other localities
White-necked Crow*	Locally relatively common
Flat-billed Vireo	Local and uncommon
Antillean Siskin	Uncommon in the Massif de la Hotte and very rare in the Massif de la Selle
Green-tailed Warbler	Rather common near sea level in the

	northwest and above 1700 m in the Massif de la Selle
White-winged Warbler*	Very rare in the Massif de la Hotte and possibly extinct in the Massif de la Selle
Black-crowned Palm-Tanager	Fairly common in the lowlands east of Port-au-Prince
Western Chat-Tanager*	Locally fairly common in higher parts of the Massif de la Hotte and Massif de la Selle, including Pic de Macaya and Morne la Viste
Eastern Chat-Tanager*	Formerly fairly common in semi-arid scrub on Île de la Gonâve but not reported in recent years
Hispaniolan Stripe-headed Tanager	Relatively common, especially in the highlands

Some taxonomists believe the following race, endemic to Hispaniola, should be treated as a full species:

Hispaniolan Crossbill*	the *megaplaga* race of Two-barred Crossbill is very uncommon in the highest mountains

Other Caribbean Endemics

A total of 16 of the other 51 Caribbean endemics not confined to single countries, islands or archipelagos also occur. They are: one species confined to Cuba and Haiti, Tawny-shouldered Blackbird (along the Artibonite River); four confined to Jamaica and Hispaniola, Vervain Hummingbird, Greater Antillean Elaenia, Stolid Flycatcher and Golden Swallow* (not reliably reported from Jamaica since the 1980s and therefore perhaps now endemic to Hispaniola); and 11 more widespread species, West Indian Whistling-Duck*, Plain Pigeon*, Key West Quail-Dove, Antillean Mango, Antillean Palm-Swift, Loggerhead Kingbird, Rufous-throated Solitaire, Red-legged Thrush, Antillean Euphonia, Greater Antillean Bullfinch and Greater Antillean Grackle.

Near-Endemics

Nine of the 18 species nearly endemic to the Caribbean occur in Haiti. They are Black-capped Petrel*, Caribbean Coot*, White-crowned and Scaly-naped Pigeons, Zenaida Dove, Antillean Nighthawk (mainly May–Aug), Caribbean Martin (Feb–Aug), Black-whiskered Vireo, Black faced Grassquit. In addition, Thick-billed Vireo occurs on Île de la Tortue off the north coast, and the *petechia* group of Yellow Warbler, known as 'Golden Warbler', is represented by the *albicollis* race.

Bird species

Over 240 species have been recorded in Haiti. Non-endemic specialities and spectacular species not mentioned above include White-tailed Tropicbird (mainly Apr–Aug), Magnificent Frigatebird, Greater Flamingo, Northern Jacana, Double-striped Thick-knee (the *dominicensis* race endemic to Hispaniola is local and uncommon), Bridled and Sooty Terns, Brown Noddy (all three mainly Apr–Aug), Ruddy Quail-Dove, Burrowing and Stygian Owls, Northern Potoo (*abbotti* is endemic to Hispaniola), Chuck-will's-widow (mainly Sep–May), Black and White-collared Swifts, Cave Swallow, Bicknell's Thrush* (Oct–Apr), Pine Warbler (resident *chrysoleuca* race), passage migrant and wintering New World warblers such as Cape May, Black-throated Blue and Prairie Warblers, Yellow-faced Grassquit and Black-cowled Oriole.

The only known significant breeding populations of Black-capped Petrel* on earth are restricted to the **Massif de la Selle** (11 known small colonies) and **Massif de la Hotte** (one colony) in southern Haiti, where the montane rain and Caribbean pine forests support a similar avifauna to that in the Sierra de Baoruco within the adjacent Dominican Republic (p. 310). In the Massif de la Selle about 80 species, including Black-capped Petrel*, have been recorded in **Parc National La Visite**, accessible via a trail from the hill resort of Kenscoff, which is situated at about 1500 m, 45 minutes by road southeast of Port-au-Prince. The trail starts on the ridge east of the radio mast above Kenscoff and leads to the village of Seguin, from where it is a five-hour hike to Marigot on the south coast. From here it is possible to return to Port-au-Prince via a four-hour bus journey.

In and around **Macaya National Park**, where one of the last remnants of untouched rain forest in Haiti is present, in the Massif de la Hotte, about 65 species have been recorded, including Western Chat-Tanager*, as well as Black-capped Petrel*, Hispaniolan Trogon* and Grey-crowned Palm-Tanager. To reach the park from Les Cayes, 196 km west of Port-au-Prince via Route 2, take the coast road southwest, then, just beyond Torbeck, head inland via Ducis to the village of Dubreuil. From there it is a 2–3 hour-hike to the Fortresse des Platons, then another couple of hours, via Formond, to Plaine Durand at the edge of the park, where the University of Florida research station, with basic camping facilities, is situated. From here it is a tough two-day climb (best attempted with local guides) to the 2347 m Pic de Macaya where Western Chat-Tanager* occurs.

East of Port-au-Prince over 100 species, including Greater Flamingo and Hispaniolan Palm Crow*, have been recorded on and around the **Étang Saumâtre**, which is situated in the 193 km-long ancient sea channel that once separated the southern peninsula of Haiti from the main island of Hispaniola and lies to the west of the more brackish Lago Enriquillo, across the border in the Dominican Republic. Étang Saumâtre is best viewed from its northern end, reached by heading northeast from Port-au-Prince on Route 3 towards Mirebalais. Take the right fork at Thomazeau along here and then turn to the lakeside villages of Manneville and Fond Pite, about 90 minutes by road from Port-au-Prince. The road from Croix-des-Bouquets to the border at Malpasse runs along parts of the southern shore. In northern Haiti, Ridgway's Hawk* and Hispaniolan Parakeet* (most likely around Citadelle) have been recorded in the **Massif du Nord**.

ADDITIONAL INFORMATION

Addresses

Haiti Tourist Office, Département du Commerce et de l'Industrie, 8 rue Légitime, Port-au-Prince, Haiti, West Indies (tel. 68 6150).

Books and Papers

The Birds of Haiti and the Dominican Republic, Wetmore, A. and Swales, B. H. 1931. US National Mus. Bull. 155.

Annotated Checklist of the Birds of Hispaniola, Keith, A. R. in prep. BOU.

Parc National La Visite, Haiti: a last refuge for the country's montane birds, Dávalos, L. M. and Brooks, T. in press. *Cotinga* 16.

The threatened and endangered birds of Haiti: lost horizons and new hopes, Woods, C. A. 1987. Pp. 385–429 in *Proc. 1987 Jean Delacour/ IFCB Symposium on Breeding Birds in Captivity*. International Foundation for the Conservation of Birds.

JAMAICA

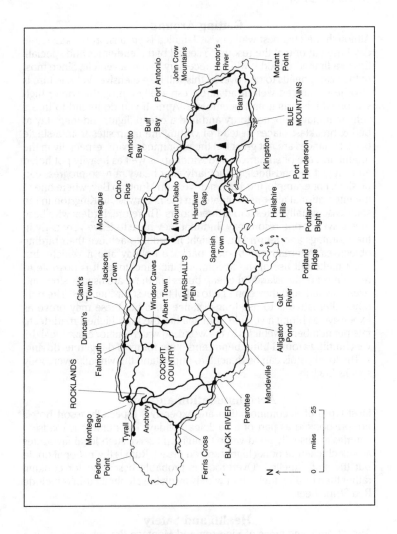

INTRODUCTION

Summary

The tropical island of Jamaica supports a staggering 28 endemics, many of which are widespread, including two parrots, three hummingbirds, two of which are stunning streamertails, a tody and two thrushes. Add to this a near-endemic oriole and there are more unique birds on this island than on any other in the Caribbean, all of which may be seen at just three main sites during a short trip. With birds such as White-tailed Tropicbird also possible Jamaica is without doubt one of the best birding destinations in the region.

Size

Jamaica is 234 km from west to east and up to 80 km north to south, and covers 11,425 km².

Getting Around

Although the cheapest way to visit Jamaica is via a short package holiday based at one of the resorts, to see all of the endemics and specialities in a limited period it will be necessary to hire a vehicle. Since most of the island needs to be covered this will be expensive. Vehicle hire is also best arranged well in advance, especially during the winter high season which lasts from December to April. If you do intend to hire a vehicle it may be better to try and find a cheap flight, and then stay at bed & breakfast places instead of visiting the main sites from a single base. Distances are not great but the poor minor roads, especially in the mountains, are often narrow and winding, as well as heavily pot holed and subject to landslides, particularly after heavy rain, so progress can be slow. For example, the 188 km-drive from Montego Bay, where one of the international airports is situated in the northwest, to Kingston in the southeast, usually takes about three hours. Therefore, birders who base themselves at one resort may find that they have to leave very early in the mornings and return late at night in order to achieve their birding objectives. Alternatively, book a package holiday and a vehicle, but don't make full use of the accommodation included. It is possible to reach most of the island on cheap buses but these are usually slow and overcrowded, and they don't go to all of the best birding sites. The only other alternative is to use long-distance taxis but these may prove as expensive as hiring a vehicle. Jamaica has the third highest road death rate per number of vehicles in the world, so watch out for crazy local drivers hurtling around blind bends and other forms of dangerous driving.

The local patois can be difficult to understand but virtually everybody speaks English.

Accommodation and Food

Most types of accommodation are expensive, especially resort hotels not pre-booked as part of a package holiday. The numerous roadside eateries are usually good value though and serve such local favourites as jerk chicken or pork (highly spiced meat). Rum is the national tipple but the stuff labelled 'Overproof' is probably best used for cooking rather than birding fuel. Other widely available alcoholic drinks include Red Stripe beer.

Health and Safety

Away from some areas of Kingston and Montego Bay where crime is a major problem—if driving through Kingston keep vehicle doors locked and windows shut—Jamaica is a very friendly and safe place to visit, though hassle from people selling ganja etc. at the major tourist areas can be annoying. Malaria has been eradicated but there are still many mosquitoes.

Climate and Timing

The best time of the year for birding in Jamaica is late March–early May, when the majority of resident endemics are breeding, and wintering and passage species can be seen before they head north. It is relatively cool and dry in December–April, but the temperature starts to rise in

May before peaking in July–August. Trade winds take the edge off the heat and it can be chilly and damp at high altitude throughout the year, especially December–April, so it is wise to take a warm jumper and a light waterproof jacket when birding in the mountains, where cloudy, damp mornings are the norm. The wettest months are May and October, and the hurricane season is in June–November.

Habitats

Inland of the palm-fringed white beaches, rocky headlands and small areas of mangrove around the Jamaican coast there are dry limestone woods, sugar plantations and mist-enshrouded mountains with terraced coffee plantations, and remnant wet limestone and montane rain forests. Over half of the island is above 305 m and Blue Mountain Peak, the highest on the island, rises to 2256 m. These highlands were once almost entirely forested, but by the end of the 20th Century just 17% of the island was tree covered and only about 6% of this was relatively untouched forest. Nevertheless, the avifauna is still rich for such a small island, which also supports a fishing bat and some spectacular butterflies, including the threatened endemic, giant swallowtail (*Papilio homerus*), which at 15 cm across is the largest butterfly in the Americas and one of the largest on earth.

Conservation

In the mid-1990s the deforestation rate of 5.3% per annum was one of the highest in the world, and this depressing fact together with other major problems, including predation by introduced species such as the small Indian mongoose (which may have played at least a small part in the presumed extinction of the endemic *caribbaea* race of Black-capped Petrel*, as well as Jamaican Poorwill*), brood parasitism by Shiny Cowbird, a government far from committed to the conservation of its natural resources, and poorly resourced non-governmental conservation organisations, means the future survival of the 13 threatened and near-threatened species, as well as the relatively common and widespread birds, which occur on Jamaica, is uncertain.

Endemics

A total of 28 species are endemic to Jamaica. They are as follows:

Ring-tailed Pigeon*	Rare and local; most likely to be seen in Cockpit Country and the Blue and John Crow Mountains
Crested Quail-Dove*	Uncommon and local; most likely in Cockpit Country and the Blue Mountains
Yellow-billed Parrot*	Widespread and locally fairly common, particularly in Cockpit Country, the John Crow Mountains, and the Mount Diablo area
Black-billed Parrot*	Localised; most likely to be seen in Cockpit Country and the Mount Diablo area
Jamaican Lizard-Cuckoo	Widespread and fairly common
Chestnut-bellied Cuckoo	Widespread and relatively common
Jamaican Owl	Widespread and fairly common, but

	only likely to be seen at Marshall's Pen or Windsor Caves
Jamaican Mango	Widespread and relatively common, especially in the lowlands
Red-billed Streamertail	The most widespread and abundant resident bird
Black-billed Streamertail	Relatively common in the extreme east
Jamaican Tody	Widespread and relatively common
Jamaican Woodpecker	Widespread and relatively common
Jamaican Elaenia	Widespread but uncommon and most likely to be seen in mid-altitude wet forests
Jamaican Pewee	Widespread and relatively common from foothills upwards
Sad Flycatcher	Widespread and relatively common
Rufous-tailed Flycatcher	Widespread but less common than Sad Flycatcher
Jamaican Becard	Widespread and locally common, especially at woodland edges
White-eyed Thrush	Fairly common in the mountains
White-chinned Thrush	Widespread and relatively common
Jamaican Crow	Locally rather common, particularly in Cockpit Country, the John Crow Mountains and hills around Moneague (between Kingston and Ocho Rios)
Jamaican Vireo	Widespread and relatively common
Blue Mountain Vireo*	Locally common and most frequent in Cockpit Country, the Blue and John Crow Mountains, and the Mount Diablo area
Arrow-headed Warbler	Locally common, particularly in mid- to high-altitude woodlands and forests
Jamaican Stripe-headed Tanager	Widespread and relatively common
Jamaican Euphonia	Widespread and relatively common
Yellow-shouldered Grassquit	Widespread and fairly common
Orangequit	Locally rather common
Jamaican Blackbird*	Rare at high altitude, and most likely to be seen in the Blue Mountains

The endemic Jamaican Poorwill* is believed extinct. It is known from just four specimens, the last of which was collected in 1866, but a small population may persist in remote dry limestone regions, in parts of Cockpit Country and the Hellshire Hills for example.

The endemic *caribbaea* race of Black-capped Petrel*, known as 'Jamaican Petrel' and considered a distinct species by some taxonomists, is also presumed extinct. It is believed to have been a common breeding bird (Oct–May) in the Blue and John Crow Mountains 200 years ago, but the most recent possible record was in 1965 when there was a report of 'noisy birds flying overhead from the ocean to the high mountains'. Some parts of the John Crow Mountains are rather remote so there is a slim possibility that it may still breed there, but recent searches have failed to discover it.

Other Caribbean Endemics

Twelve of the 51 Caribbean endemics not confined to single countries, islands or archipelagos also occur on Jamaica. They are: one species confined to Jamaica and the remote island of San Andrés, Jamaican Oriole, which is relatively common throughout the island (the *bairdi* race endemic to the Cayman Islands has not been reported since 1967); three confined Jamaica and Hispaniola, Vervain Hummingbird, Greater Antillean Elaenia and Stolid Flycatcher (Golden Swallow* has not been recorded since the 1980s); and eight more widespread species, West Indian Whistling-Duck* (rare), Plain Pigeon* (rare), Antillean Palm-Swift, Loggerhead Kingbird, Bahama Mockingbird (Hellshire Hills and Portland Ridge areas in the south), Rufous-throated Solitaire, Greater Antillean Bullfinch and Greater Antillean Grackle.

Near-Endemics

Eight of the 18 species nearly endemic to the Caribbean occur on Jamaica. They are Caribbean Coot* (rare), White-crowned Pigeon, Zenaida and Caribbean Doves, Antillean Nighthawk (mainly May–Aug), Caribbean Martin (Feb–Aug), Black-whiskered Vireo (Feb–Aug) and Black-faced Grassquit. In addition, the *petechia* group of Yellow Warbler, known as 'Golden Warbler', also nearly endemic to the Caribbean, is represented by the *eoa* race.

Bird species

About 265 species have been recorded on Jamaica. Non-endemic specialities and spectacular species not already mentioned include White-tailed Tropicbird (mainly Jan–Mar), Masked Booby (breeds, mainly Mar–May, on Pedro and Serranilla Cays), Magnificent Frigatebird, Masked Duck, Limpkin, Northern Jacana, Sooty Tern, Brown Noddy (both breed, mainly Apr–Aug, on Pedro and Morant Cays, and Brown Noddy also on Portland Bight Cays), Ruddy Quail-Dove, Olive-throated Parakeet (endemic *nana* race), Northern Potoo (endemic *jamaicensis* race),

Red-billed Streamertail is not only one of Jamaica's most stunning birds it is also one of the most widespread and abundant on the island

Black and White-collared Swifts, passage and wintering New World warblers such as Cape May, Black-throated Blue and Prairie Warblers, and Yellow-faced Grassquit. Introduced species include Green-rumped Parrotlet, European Starling, Yellow-crowned Bishop, Chestnut Munia and Saffron Finch.

Expectations

It is possible to see 100–120 species, including all 28 endemics, in 1–2 weeks, and perhaps up to 150 species during a longer and more extensive visit.

ROCKLANDS

Some of Jamaica's most beautiful birds can be seen easily and at very close range at the late Lisa Salmon's remarkable Rocklands feeding station near Montego Bay on the northwest coast, including Jamaican Mango and Red-billed Streamertail, both of which perch on visitor's fingers to feed from tiny hand-held bottles of sugared water! In addition, the adjacent dry woodland supports nearly 20 widespread endemics.

Jamaican Endemics

Jamaican Lizard-Cuckoo, Chestnut-bellied Cuckoo, Jamaican Mango, Red-billed Streamertail, Jamaican Tody, Jamaican Woodpecker, Jamaican Elaenia, Jamaican Pewee, Sad and Rufous-tailed Flycatchers, Jamaican Becard, White-cheeked Thrush, Jamaican Vireo, Arrow-headed Warbler, Jamaican Stripe-headed Tanager, Jamaican Euphonia, Yellow-shouldered Grassquit, Orangequit.

Localised Caribbean Endemics

Vervain Hummingbird, Stolid Flycatcher, Jamaican Oriole.

Other Caribbean Endemics

Antillean Palm-Swift, Loggerhead Kingbird, Greater Antillean Bullfinch.

Localised Caribbean Near-endemics

Caribbean Dove.

Other Caribbean Near-endemics

White-crowned Pigeon, Zenaida Dove, Black-faced Grassquit.

Passage Migrants and Winter Visitors

Northern Parula, Black-throated Blue and Black-and-white Warblers, American Redstart.

Others

White-winged Dove, Ruddy Quail-Dove, Olive-throated Parakeet, Mangrove Cuckoo, Yellow-faced Grassquit. (Introduced species include Green-rumped Parrotlet and Saffron Finch.)

To reach Rocklands head southwest from Montego Bay towards Reading then turn south towards Anchovy. About 1.25 km before the railway crossing, just north of Anchovy, turn east. The house at the feeding station is about 1 km further on and the trail through the woods just past there, on the same side of the road. The feeding station is open 2–4pm daily and other species attracted to the feeders apart from humming-birds include warblers, Orangequit and Jamaican Oriole.

Accommodation: Orange River Lodge, about 30 minutes by road from Montego Bay and an hour by road from Rocklands, is situated in forest-ed foothills and alongside the access road it is possible to see White-crowned Pigeon, Jamaican Mango, Vervain Hummingbird, Jamaican Tody, Jamaican Elaenia, Jamaican Becard and Jamaican Crow. To get there head south on the A1 from the airport at Montego Bay, then turn left onto the road signed to 'Adelphi' just before reaching the Westgate Shopping Centre (which is on the left just before Montego River). After a couple of km ignore the right fork, instead following signs for the lodge. To book and obtain more detailed directions in advance contact the Orange River Lodge, PO Box 822, Montego Bay, POI St. James, Jam-aica, West Indies (tel. 979 3294/5) (A+).

Between Montego Bay and Cockpit Country it may be worth spending a couple of hours in the mangroves at **Martha Brae** accessible via tracks running inland of the bridge over the Martha Brae River a few km east of Falmouth, or from the track running towards the sea just east of Phosphorescent Lagoon. Species here include Least Bittern, Caribbean Coot*, Stilt Sandpiper and Palm Warbler.

COCKPIT COUNTRY

This sparsely populated 232 km^2 rugged region of central Jamaica takes its name from the huge sheer-sided sinkholes within the rounded lime-stone hills, which resemble old cock-fighting pits. It is due to the tricky terrain that large areas of the wet forest here have survived and these relatively extensive areas of excellent habitat support most of the is-land's endemics, including the rare Crested Quail-Dove*, one of ten species of pigeons and doves present, and both parrots.

Localised Jamaican Endemics

Ring-tailed Pigeon*, Crested Quail-Dove*, Jamaican Owl, Yellow-billed* and Black-billed* Parrots, Jamaican Crow, Blue Mountain Vireo*, Jam-aican Blackbird*.

Other Jamaican Endemics

Jamaican Lizard-Cuckoo, Chestnut-bellied Cuckoo, Jamaican Mango, Red-billed Streamertail, Jamaican Tody, Jamaican Woodpecker, Jam-aican Elaenia, Jamaican Pewee, Sad and Rufous-tailed Flycatchers, Jamaican Becard, White-eyed and White-chinned Thrushes, Jamaican Vireo, Arrow-headed Warbler, Jamaican Stripe-headed Tanager, Jam-aican Euphonia, Yellow-shouldered Grassquit, Orangequit.

Localised Caribbean Endemics

Vervain Hummingbird, Greater Antillean Elaenia, Stolid Flycatcher, Jamaican Oriole.

Other Caribbean Endemics
Antillean Palm-Swift, Loggerhead Kingbird, Greater Antillean Bullfinch, Greater Antillean Grackle.

Localised Caribbean Near-endemics
Caribbean Dove.

Other Caribbean Near-endemics
White-crowned Pigeon, Zenaida Dove, Black-faced Grassquit.

Passage Migrants and Winter Visitors
Northern Parula, Black-throated Blue Warbler, American Redstart, Worm-eating and Swainson's Warblers.

Others
Limpkin, White-winged Dove, Ruddy Quail-Dove, Olive-throated Parakeet, Smooth-billed Ani, Black and White-collared Swifts, Cave Swallow, Yellow-faced Grassquit.

(Other species recorded here include Masked Duck, Plain Pigeon* and Golden Swallow* (not recorded since the 1980s). Introduced species include Green-rumped Parrotlet).

The best birding area in Cockpit Country is Barbecue Bottom Road between Albert Town and Clark's Town, especially at the Albert Town end. The road here is also usually negotiable in a 2WD, hence it may be best to approach the area from Marshall's Pen in the south, as some stretches of the roads and tracks may be in poor condition, and it may not be possible to reach Albert Town from Montego Bay in the north without a 4WD. Other sites worth visiting include the roadside north of Ulster Springs (which is northeast of Albert Town), where it crosses a ridge and descends into a broad forested valley; the small pond on the east side of Clark's Town, where Masked Duck has been recorded; and Windsor Caves, where the dusk departure of the many bats that roost in these caves can be spectacular. The best area for birds here is around the junction of the trails to the caves and Troy. Prepare for many mosquitoes in this part of the island.

The Jamaican Tody is one of the five brilliant members of the tody family, which is endemic to the Greater Antilles in the Caribbean

Accommodation: most birders use Marshall's Pen to the south or Falmouth on the north coast as their base, but it is possible to stay in more basic accommodation at Windsor Caves (B).

BLACK RIVER MORASS

The shallow estuary, mangroves, marshes and lagoons of Jamaica's most extensive wetland, which covers about 200 km^2 at the mouth of the island's longest river, on the southwest coast, support a broad range of waterbirds, from the rare West Indian Whistling-Duck* to Northern Jacana.

Localised Caribbean Endemics
West Indian Whistling-Duck*, Vervain Hummingbird.

Caribbean Near-endemics
Caribbean Coot*, White-crowned Pigeon, Caribbean Martin (Feb–Aug).

Passage Migrants and Winter Visitors
Lesser Scaup, Short-billed Dowitcher, American Redstart.

Others
Least Grebe, Brown Pelican, Magnificent Frigatebird, Great Egret, Black-crowned Night-Heron, Least Bittern, Glossy Ibis, Osprey, Limpkin, Purple Gallinule, Northern Jacana, Royal Tern, Mangrove Cuckoo, Belted Kingfisher, Yellow Warbler, Yellow-faced Grassquit, Grasshopper Sparrow. (Other species recorded here include Masked Duck, Yellow-breasted Crake, Spotted Rail (three records only, from the Upper Morass, but a small population may be present) and Jamaican Oriole).

Other Wildlife
American crocodile, tarpon.

The marshes upstream of the town of Black River are accessible only by boat. Fortunately, local people have realized that the wetlands are a valuable natural resource and run boat trips to look for birds and other wildlife from the bridge at the east end of town. The 9am and 3.30pm departures are best for birds, with the latter timed to coincide with the egrets and herons going to roost. Ask to be taken to the Lower Morass, which is usually best for Least Bittern, Yellow-breasted Crake and American crocodile, and the Upper Morass, which is best for West Indian Whistling-Duck* (284 were present here in April 2000, a record recent count for Jamaica), large numbers of Great Egrets (up to 500 have been recorded here) and Northern Jacana. Many trips, which last about two hours, concentrate on feeding the crocodiles because this is what appeals to the majority of visitors, and on such trips few birds are seen, so birders keen to see West Indian Whistling-Duck* and Yellow-breasted Crake would be wise to block-book a boat run by someone who knows about birds, and ensure, before departure, that the trip will concentrate on looking for them.

Accommodation: Invercauld Great House and Hotel, on the seafront.

The mudflats, mangroves and large saline lagoons at **Parottee**, 6.5 km southeast of Black River, are one of the best places on Jamaica to look for passage, wintering and resident shorebirds such as Black-necked Stilt, Wilson's Plover, Short-billed Dowitcher, Greater and Lesser Yellow-legs, Willet, and Least and Stilt Sandpipers, and in the general area it is also possible to find Least Grebe, Brown Pelican, Magnificent Frigate-bird, egrets and herons, West Indian Whistling-Duck*, Osprey, Caspian and Royal Terns, Belted Kingfisher, Mangrove Cuckoo, Loggerhead Kingbird, Caribbean Martin (Feb–Aug), Yellow Warbler and passage and wintering New World warblers such as Magnolia, Cape May and Prairie Warblers. To reach here turn south off the road to Mountainside 3 km east of the bridge the boats to the Black River Morass depart from.

MARSHALL'S PEN

The lightly wooded rolling pastures of this delightful private ranch, situated at about 610 m near Mandeville in south-central Jamaica, support many birds, including an array of endemics. Over 50 species have bred here and it is the best place on the island to look for the endemic Jamaican Owl and endemic race of Northern Potoo.

Localised Jamaican Endemics
Jamaican Owl.

Other Jamaican Endemics
Jamaican Lizard-Cuckoo, Chestnut-bellied Cuckoo, Jamaican Mango, Red-billed Streamertail, Jamaican Tody, Jamaican Woodpecker, Jamaican Elaenia, Jamaican Pewee, Sad and Rufous-tailed Flycatchers, Jamaican Becard, White-eyed and White-chinned Thrushes, Jamaican Vireo, Arrow-headed Warbler, Jamaican Stripe-headed Tanager, Jamaican Euphonia, Yellow-shouldered Grassquit, Orangequit.

Localised Caribbean Endemics
Vervain Hummingbird, Greater Antillean Elaenia, Stolid Flycatcher, Jamaican Oriole.

Other Caribbean Endemics
Antillean Palm-Swift, Loggerhead Kingbird, Rufous-throated Solitaire (Nov–Mar), Greater Antillean Bullfinch.

Localised Caribbean Near-endemics
Caribbean Dove.

Other Caribbean Near-endemics
White-crowned Pigeon, Zenaida Dove, Antillean Nighthawk (mainly May–Aug), Black-faced Grassquit.

Other Localised Specialities
Northern Potoo.

Passage Migrants and Winter Visitors
Northern Parula, Black-throated Blue, Black-throated Green, Yellow-

throated, Prairie and Black-and-white Warblers, American Redstart, Worm-eating Warbler, Ovenbird, Common Yellowthroat.

Others

Least Grebe, Red-tailed Hawk, White-winged Dove, Ruddy Quail-Dove, Olive-throated Parakeet, Black and White-collared Swifts, Grey Kingbird (mainly Apr–Oct), Cave Swallow, Yellow-faced Grassquit, Grasshopper Sparrow. (Other species recorded here include Crested Quail-Dove*, Barn Owl and Jamaican Crow. Introduced species include Saffron Finch).

Jamaican Owl and Northern Potoo are often seen in the very birdy grounds of the main house at Marshall's Pen, where Robert Sutton, co-author of *Jamaica: A Photographic Field Guide*, and his wife Ann live. They are always pleased to welcome visiting birders to their farm but please respect their privacy and contact them well in advance to arrange any intended visit, at Marshall's Pen, PO Box 58, Mandeville, Jamaica, West Indies (tel. 904 5454, fax. 964 6383). It is usually possible to stay in self-catering accommodation at the farm, which makes a good base for visiting Cockpit Country, Black River Morass and the Portland Ridge area. Marshall's Pen is about 5 km northwest of Mandeville, which is about 55 miles west of Kingston via the A2. Turn west off the Mandeville by-pass at the bottom of a hill beside a concrete bus shelter with a large painted sign that reads 'A project of Mike Town Community Centre'. Once off the main road pass two sub-division street signs ('Nightingale' and 'Elaenia'), go up a little rise, and take the right fork. Pass the long concrete wall on the right, go round a sharp right bend and look for two stone gate-posts on the right (opposite a small shop) about 1 km from the by-pass. Turn at the gate-posts and Robert and Ann Sutton's house is the second one about 1 km along the track.

LOCATION OF
MARSHALL'S PEN

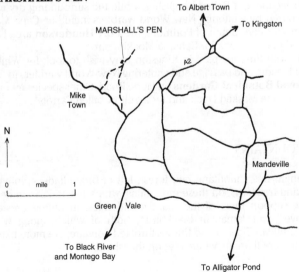

Accommodation: Mandeville. Marshall's Pen (A+).

Birders keen to look for West Indian Whistling-Duck*, as well as other waterbirds, should ask at Marshall's Pen for directions to the pumping station in the nearby Black River Upper Morass. The duck is certainly not guaranteed but species occurring on a regular basis include Least Bittern, Glossy Ibis, Purple Gallinule, Caribbean Coot*, Northern Jacana, Mangrove Cuckoo, Caribbean Martin (Feb–Aug) and Yellow Warbler, while there are also a few records of Masked Duck, Yellow-breasted Crake and Spotted Rail. South of Mandeville it is possible to see West Indian manatee, as well as American crocodile, on boat trips from the Manatee Centre at **Alligator Hole**, along the new road west of Milk River Bath.

Some of the best remaining stands of dry limestone scrub on Jamaica lie beside the road which traverses **Portland Ridge**, the island's most southerly point, and this arid terrain supports Bahama Mockingbird, as well as White-winged and Caribbean Doves, Mangrove Cuckoo, Jamaican Mango, Stolid Flycatcher, Loggerhead Kingbird, Yellow Warbler and Jamaican Oriole, while Clapper Rail inhabits the nearby mangroves. Head for Portland Cottage and ask there for the track to the lighthouse, one of many tracks in the area alongside which most of the aforementioned species can be seen. In the fishing village of Portland it is possible to organise boat trips to **Portland Bight** where several sand cays support Yellow-crowned Night-Heron, Willet, Royal and Roseate Terns, Brown Noddy (all three terns are mainly present Apr–Aug), Mangrove Cuckoo, Yellow Warbler and a large colony of Magnificent Frigatebird, which can be observed at close quarters during the breeding season (usually Aug–Apr, although many young birds are usually ready to fledge by late February).

Caymanas Dyke Ponds, just north of the main road between Spanish Town and Kingston, to the west of the turning to Portmore, attract waterbirds such as Least Bittern, large numbers of coots (especially in Oct–Mar when both American and Caribbean* are apparently present), Northern Jacana and Belted Kingfisher, while the surrounding dry forest is favoured by wintering New World warblers including Cape May and Palm Warblers. South of Portmore, the **Port Henderson** area is a fairly good place to look for Bahama Mockingbird.

Birders with time to spare in Kingston may wish to look for White-crowned Pigeon, and passage and wintering New World warblers in the **Hope Royal Botanical Gardens** on Hope Road. Other species recorded here include Masked Duck and feral Yellow-billed Parrots*.

BLUE MOUNTAINS

The remnant misty montane rain forest, full of bromeliads, epiphytic orchids and tree-ferns, on these mountains, which rise to 2256 m near Kingston, support most of the island's endemics, including Crested Quail-Dove* and Jamaican Blackbird*, both of which, along with Greater Antillean Elaenia and Rufous-throated Solitaire, are more likely to be seen here than anywhere else on the island.

Localised Jamaican Endemics

Ring-tailed Pigeon*, Crested Quail-Dove*, Blue Mountain Vireo*, Jamaican Blackbird*.

Other Jamaican Endemics

Jamaican Lizard-Cuckoo, Chestnut-bellied Cuckoo, Red-billed Stream-ertail, Jamaican Tody, Jamaican Woodpecker, Jamaican Elaenia, Jamaican Pewee, Sad and Rufous-tailed Flycatchers, Jamaican Becard, White-eyed and White-chinned Thrushes, Jamaican Vireo, Arrow-headed Warbler, Jamaican Stripe-headed Tanager, Jamaican Euphonia, Yellow-shouldered Grassquit, Orangequit.

Localised Caribbean Endemics

Vervain Hummingbird, Greater Antillean Elaenia, Jamaican Oriole.

Other Caribbean Endemics

Antillean Palm-Swift, Loggerhead Kingbird, Rufous-throated Solitaire, Greater Antillean Bullfinch.

Localised Caribbean Near-endemics

Caribbean Dove.

Other Caribbean Near-endemics

Black-faced Grassquit.

Passage Migrants and Winter Visitors

Northern Parula, Cape May, Black-throated Blue, Prairie, Palm and Black-and-white Warblers, American Redstart, Ovenbird, Common Yellowthroat.

Others

Red-tailed Hawk, Ruddy Quail-Dove, Black and White-collared Swifts, Grey Kingbird (mainly Apr–Oct), Cave Swallow. (Other species recorded in winter (Oct–Apr) include Bicknell's Thrush*).

To reach the best area head northeast from Kingston on the narrow and winding B1, which runs between Kingston on the south coast and Buff Bay on the north coast, and traverses the western edge of the Blue Mountains. Just below Gordon Town look for the unsigned left turn to Newcastle. Good forest starts about halfway up to Newcastle from this turn, above the 16 km marker, but it is probably best to start birding along the road from just below Newcastle, a couple of km further up. Bird from there to **Hardwar Gap**, a natural pass at 1219 m.

The best chance of seeing Crested Quail-Dove* is at dawn on: (i) the stretch of main road above Newcastle, from 5.30am until the road becomes too busy. Try to be the first vehicle along the road to Woodside Drive, and especially between there and Hardwar Gap; and (ii) the Woodside Drive track itself. The stretch of the road above Newcastle is also the best area for Jamaican Blackbird*. Look for these birds tearing bromeliads apart (usually at the base of tree-fern fronds in the largest trees) in search of bromeliad crabs. They may also be seen along the Waterfall Trail, which is below Hardwar Gap near the Gap Café, where they may even be seen, along with Red-billed Streamertails, at close quarters while drinking the local coffee. Birders with time may also

BLUE MOUNTAINS

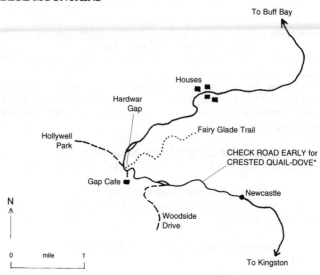

wish to walk other mountain trails in the area, which radiate from New-castle, Hollywell Park and, further east, Mavis Bank, though the previously popular Fairy Glade Trail near Hollywell Park was closed to the public in early 1999.

Accommodation: the situation in the Blue Mountains changes frequently but when open the basic Greenhills Guesthouse, signed on the left-hand side of the road just north of Hardwar Gap, is perhaps the most popular place to stay, though some birders prefer to camp at Hollywell Park. In early 1999 it was also possible to stay in a cabin just beyond the Gap Café, although this may now be possible only with prior permission from the Jamaica Conservation and Development Trust (JCDT). There are several other relatively inexpensive guest houses in the area.

West of Buff Bay and Annotto Bay on the northeast coast Yellow-breasted Crake has been recorded in and around the farm ponds, streams and wet meadows of **Strawberry Fields**. Further west along the north coast, roadside forest uphill from the resort of **Ocho Rios** and the near-by **Shaw Park Gardens** support endemics such as Chestnut-bellied Cuckoo, Jamaican Mango, Red-billed Streamertail, Jamaican Tody, Jamaican Crow, Jamaican Stripe-headed Tanager, Jamaican Euphonia and Yellow-shouldered Grassquit, while the area as a whole supports Magnificent Frigatebird, Yellow-crowned Night-Heron, Royal Tern, White-crowned Pigeon, Caribbean Dove, Antillean Nighthawk (mainly May–Aug), Antillean Palm-Swift, White-collared Swift, Vervain Hummingbird, Caribbean Martin (mainly Feb–Aug), Cave Swallow, wintering and passage New World warblers such as Black-throated Blue and Prairie, and Jamaican Oriole.

The endemic Black-billed Streamertail is best looked for in the grounds of resorts and hotels east of Buff Bay on the northeast coast and southeast from there to **Bath**. For example, try: (i) the lovely gardens at

The lovely Black-throated Blue Warbler is one of several New World warblers which breed in North America and spend the winter on Caribbean islands such as Jamaica

Crystal Springs, just east of Buff Bay; (ii) around **San San**, east of Port Antonio (try the Dragon Bay Villas for starters); (iii) at **Reach Falls**, which are signed from the main coast road in Manchioneal (Worm-eating and Swainson's Warblers have also been recorded here); and (iv) **Bath Springs**, where the beauty adorns the grounds of the Bath Fountains Hotel, as well as the flowering shrubs at the entrance to the hot springs and mineral baths (where Louisiana Waterthrush occurs along the streams flowing from the springs), and the botanical gardens. Species occurring in the **John Crow Mountains** between Port Antonio and Bath include Ring-tailed Pigeon*, Yellow-billed* and Black-billed* Parrots, Jamaican Crow, Blue Mountain Vireo* and Jamaican Blackbird*, as well as Black and White-collared Swifts, and passage and wintering passerines such as Northern Parula, Black-throated Blue and Palm Warblers, American Redstart, Swainson's Warbler, Ovenbird and Louisiana Waterthrush, but this is a difficult area to access and the endemics at least may take considerable time to track down. To complete a jaunt to Jamaica in style head to **Hector's River** in the extreme east of the island, where White-tailed Tropicbird breeds, mainly in Jan–Mar. The sea can be viewed from several places along the road north and south of the small village, though one of the most reliable viewpoints for the tropicbird is the one south of the village where the road starts to head inland.

ADDITIONAL INFORMATION

Addresses

For advice on birding in Jamaica contact Robert and Ann Sutton, Marshall's Pen, PO Box 58, Mandeville, Jamaica, West Indies (tel. 904 5454, fax. 964 6383).

Jamaica Conservation and Development Trust (JCDT), 95 Dumbarton Avenue, Kingston 10, Jamaica, West Indies (e-mail: JCDT@kasnet. com).

Jamaican Tourist Office, ICWI Building, PO Box 360, 2 St. Lucia Avenue, Kingston 5, Jamaica, West Indies (helpline: (0888) 995 9999/4400, tel. 929 9200/19, fax. 929 9375, e-mail: JAMAICATRV@aol.com, web site: www.jamaica-travel.com).

BirdLife Jamaica, c/o 2 Starlight Avenue, Kingston 6, Jamaica, West Indies (tel. 927 1864, email: gosse@infochan.com).

Books

Birds of Jamaica: A Photographic Field Guide, Downer, A. and Sutton, R. 1990. Cambridge UP.

Birds of Jamaica, Bernal, F. 1990. Bernal.

A Birder's Field Checklist of the Birds of Jamaica, Levy, C. and Loftin, H. 1994. Privately published.

MARTINIQUE

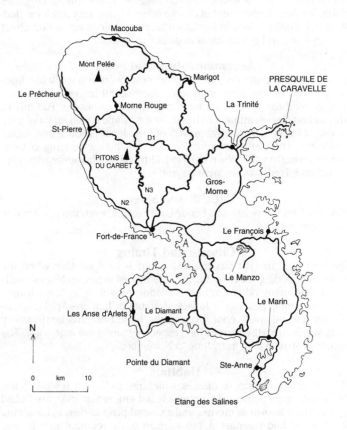

Macouba

Mont Pelée

Marigot

PRESQU'ILE DE
LA CARAVELLE

Le Prêcheur

Morne Rouge

La Trinité

St-Pierre

D1

PITONS
DU CARBET

Gros-
Morne

N3

N2

Fort-de-France

Le François

Le Manzo

Le Marin

Les Anse d'Arlets

Le Diamant

N

0   km   10

Pointe du Diamant

Ste-Anne

Etang des Salines

INTRODUCTION

Summary

This mountainous island in the central Lesser Antilles supports a lovely endemic oriole, as well as ten of the 14 Lesser Antilles endemics not confined to single islands, including White-breasted Thrasher*, which is much easier to find here than on St. Lucia, the only other island where this striking bird occurs.

Size

Martinique is about 65 km long and up to 40 km wide, and it covers 1079 km².

Getting Around

Most roads are excellent and there are plenty of road signs, but these rare pluses (for the West Indies) are offset by busy main roads and aggressive local drivers who tear around the island. There is a fairly good bus service around the capital, Fort-de-France, but to reach the best birding sites without hiring a vehicle it will be necessary to use the taxi collectif, a mix of estate cars and minibuses. The official language of this Overseas Department of France is French and very few local people speak English, even in tourist areas, so a basic grasp of French, at the very least, will greatly assist in getting around.

Accommodation and Food
A wide range of primarily expensive accommodation is available, from fancy resorts to gîtes and family-run auberges, but budget birders may wish to head for the few, sometimes crowded, campsites. The mix of African and French influences has produced some excellent local dishes, most of which are a combination of fresh local produce and exotic seasonings. There are numerous places to eat and a wide range of beer, rum and wine to wash down the food, although the favourite island tipple is rum mixed with sugarcane syrup.

Health and Safety
Watch out for the poisonous Fer-de-Lance snake, even though it is rare and nocturnal.

Climate and Timing
The best time to visit this tropical island is in April–May when the chances of adding some seabirds to the trip list increase. Martinique is wetter than many other Caribbean islands, especially in May–November, with rainfall peaking in July–August, but in January–April it is usually dry and relatively cool. Even in the hottest months northeasterly trade winds keep the heat at bay, especially along the east coast. The hurricane season lasts from June to November.

Habitats
Martinique's mountainous massifs, which rise to 1397 m at Mont Pelée, the island's only active volcano which last erupted in 1902, are linked by small hills known as mornes and a central plain known as Lamentin. The highest and steepest slopes support some remnant rain forests, especially in the north, but banana and pineapple plantations cover most other hill and mountain sides, and in the south great expanses are covered with sugarcane plantations. The northern and eastern coasts are a mix of steep cliffs and black-sand coves, whereas in the south and west there are long grey- or white-sand beaches frequented by rich French sun seekers.

Conservation
The three threatened and near-threatened species, as well as the relatively common and widespread birds, which occur on Martinique face an uncertain future due to habitat loss, hunting (there are few doves, pigeons etc. on the island) and pollution.

Endemics
The island's single endemic, Martinique Oriole*, is uncommon and most likely to be seen in the semi-arid hills of the south and east or, possibly, in the moist forests in the north of the island.

Other Caribbean Endemics

A total of 16 of the 51 Caribbean endemics not confined to single countries, islands or archipelagos occur. They are ten of the 14 species confined to the Lesser Antilles, but present on more than one island: Lesser Antillean Swift, Purple-throated Carib, Blue-headed Hummingbird (which usually occurs at 500–1200 m and is otherwise confined to Dominica), Lesser Antillean Flycatcher, White-breasted Thrasher* (a rarity that occurs on the peninsula known as Presqu'île de la Caravelle, and is otherwise confined to St. Lucia), Grey Trembler (which elsewhere occurs only on St. Lucia), Brown Trembler (rare), Scaly-breasted Thrasher, Lesser Antillean Bullfinch and Lesser Antillean Saltator; and six more widespread species, namely Bridled Quail-Dove, Green-throated Carib, Antillean Crested Hummingbird, Lesser Antillean Pewee (*brunneicapillus*), Rufous-throated Solitaire and Antillean Euphonia.

Near-Endemics

Nine of the 18 species nearly endemic to the Caribbean occur on Martinique. They are Caribbean Coot* (rare but has bred), Scaly-naped Pigeon, Zenaida Dove, Caribbean Elaenia, Caribbean Martin (Feb–Aug), Pearly-eyed Thrasher (uncommon), Black-whiskered Vireo, Black-faced Grassquit and Carib Grackle. In addition, the *petechia* group of Yellow Warbler, known as 'Golden Warbler', also nearly endemic to the Caribbean, is represented by the *ruficapilla* race.

Bird species

Over 185 species have been recorded on Martinique. Non-endemic specialities and spectacular species not already mentioned include Red-billed Tropicbird (mainly Jan–Jun), Magnificent Frigatebird, Masked Duck, Bridled and Sooty Terns, Brown Noddy (all three, mainly Apr–Aug), Ruddy Quail-Dove, White-tailed Nightjar (this species is widespread from Costa Rica to northern South America, but Martinique is the only Caribbean island on which it occurs. However, the disjunct population of the endemic *manati* race is very rare and local, occurring only on the peninsula known as Presqu'île de la Caravelle and in the south of the island, with only a few records since 1980), Black Swift (mainly Apr–Sep), Ringed Kingfisher and Bare-eyed Thrush.

Expectations

It is possible to see the endemic oriole and most of the ten Lesser Antillean endemics not confined to single islands within a couple of days, but don't expect to see many more than 50 species even on a long trip.

Birders with time to spare in the capital, **Fort-de-France**, may wish to visit the Jardin Balata where Purple-throated Carib, Lesser Antillean Swift and Lesser Antillean Saltator occur.

PRESQU'ÎLE DE LA CARAVELLE

This 10 km-long peninsula on the east coast, the outer half of which is a reserve, is the best place on earth to see the very rare White-breasted Thrasher*. This species is more numerous on St. Lucia but is restricted to remote parts of that island, so, while there are only about 40 pairs on the Presqu'île de la Caravelle, there is a much greater chance of seeing the species here. This is also one of the best sites on the island for the endemic oriole, and the dry littoral woods, scrubby headlands, mangroves, sea cliffs and surrounding waters of the peninsula support a good selection of other birds, including seabirds such as Red-billed Tropicbird.

Martinique Endemics
Martinique Oriole*.

Martinique and St. Lucia Endemics
White-breasted Thrasher*.

Other Lesser Antillean Endemics
Purple throated Carib, Scaly-breasted Thrasher, Lesser Antillean Bullfinch, Lesser Antillean Saltator.

Other Caribbean Endemics
Green-throated Carib, Antillean Crested Hummingbird.

Caribbean Near-endemics
Zenaida Dove, Caribbean Elaenia, Caribbean Martin (mainly Feb–Aug), Black-faced Grassquit, Carib Grackle.

Others
Red-billed Tropicbird (mainly Jan–Jun), Magnificent Frigatebird, Roseate (mainly Apr–Sep) and Bridled (mainly Apr–Aug) Terns, Ruddy Quail-Dove, Mangrove Cuckoo, Grey Kingbird, Bare-eyed Thrush, Yellow Warbler.

(Other species recorded here include Sooty Tern (mainly Apr–Aug), Scaly-naped Pigeon, White-tailed Nightjar, Lesser Antillean Flycatcher and Pearly-eyed Thrasher).

The peninsula is about 45 minutes by road northeast from Fort-de-France. The thrasher is highly localised, even within this small area, and appears to be confined to the bottom of wooded ravines with an open understorey, where it feeds among the leaf litter. The best place to start looking for it is along the trails just east of the **Ruines du Château Dubuc**. To reach this head for the last small parking area at the end of the access track, where the entrance to the ruins and the start of the trail system are situated. The short circular trail is as good as any. The oriole may be seen along these trails or even in the trees around the information board, complete with a handy illustration of the bird! The trails are best visited in early morning (6.30–9am) before tourists start to arrive *en masse*. To look for seabirds continue around the coast where Red-billed Tropicbirds breed in the cliffs at the southeast end of the peninsula and there is a Bridled Tern colony on **Ilet Lapin**, just offshore from the meteorological station at the northeast end. It takes a few hours to walk the circuit from the ruins, around the coast, and back via the meteorological station access road, in often very hot conditions, so take plenty of water.

The world population of White-breasted Thrasher*, which is confined to the islands of Martinique and St. Lucia, may number less than 150 pairs

PITONS DU CARBET

The montane rain forest in the north-central highlands of Martinique, which rise over to 1113 m at Pitons du Carbet, is the best place on the island to look for Blue-headed Hummingbird and Grey Trembler, while the endemic oriole also occurs in the area.

Martinique Endemics
Martinique Oriole*.

Martinique and Dominica Endemics
Blue-headed Hummingbird.

Martinique and St. Lucia Endemics
Grey Trembler.

Other Lesser Antillean Endemics
Lesser Antillean Swift, Purple-throated Carib, Lesser Antillean Bullfinch, Lesser Antillean Saltator.

Other Caribbean Endemics
Antillean Crested Hummingbird, Rufous-throated Solitaire.

Caribbean Near-endemics
Caribbean Elaenia, Black-faced Grassquit, Carib Grackle.

Others
Ruddy Quail-Dove, Bare-eyed Thrush, Yellow Warbler. (Other species recorded here include Scaly-breasted Thrasher).

Head for the picnic area, which is about 10 km north of Fort-de-France on the west side of the Route de la Trace (N3). Bird around the picnic area, along the steep trail to the summit of **Pitons du Carbet**, which starts here (it takes about an hour to reach the summit but it is not usually necessary to walk the whole trail to see most of the birds), and along the other forest trails which also start here. Alternatively or in addition, try the forest just beyond the village of Treu Matelots between St-Pierre and Gros-Morne, where the road passes through one of the scattered parts of the **Parc Naturel Regional de la Martinique**. Stop just south of the D1/N3 junction and walk down the road where Blue-headed Hummingbird, Scaly-breasted Thrasher, Rufous-throated Solitaire and Martinique Oriole* have been recorded.

On boat trips out of **St-Pierre** on the northwest coast it is possible to see Brown Noddy (perhaps more likely off **Le Prêcheur** further north, mainly Apr–Aug), as well as humpback and sperm whales, and spinner and Atlantic spotted dolphins. North of St-Pierre, Rufous-throated Solitaire occurs on **Mont Pelée**, which can be reached from Morne Rouge on the N3. From here head for the highest parking area, which is just above some elfin woodland.

South from St-Pierre, a short distance north of Fort-de-France, turn inland off the N2 to reach a small area of degraded mid-altitude forest 1 km or so beyond the recreation area known as **La Demarche**, where Blue-headed Hummingbird and Martinique Oriole* occur, albeit sparingly. Park at the end of the access road, head up the trail that leads north for 30 minutes or so, then bird the forested ridge. Other species recorded here include Ruddy Quail-Dove, Mangrove Cuckoo, Purple-throated Carib, Antillean Crested Hummingbird, Caribbean Elaenia, Lesser Antillean Pewee, Scaly-breasted Thrasher, Rufous-throated Solitaire, Bare-eyed Thrush, Lesser Antillean Bullfinch and Lesser Antillean Saltator.

American and Caribbean* Coots are rare visitors to the reservoir of **Le Manzo**, which is situated about 15 km east of Fort-de-France and can be viewed from the N6 road to Le François. Other species here include Caribbean Martin (mainly Feb–Aug) and Scaly-breasted Thrasher.

At the southwest end of the island the creek below the road west of Le Diamant is worth checking for Bare-eyed Thrush, while birds recorded at **Pointe du Diamant** and around **Les Anses d'Arlets** to the west of Le Diamant include Red-billed Tropicbird (mainly Jan–Jun), White-tailed Nightjar and Martinique Oriole*, as well as Brown Booby, Antillean Crested Hummingbird, Caribbean Elaenia, Lesser Antillean Flycatcher, Yellow Warbler, Black-faced Grassquit, Lesser Antillean Bullfinch and Lesser Antillean Saltator. At the southeast end of the island the wetlands around **Ste-Anne** and the Étang des Salines to the south of there are worth checking for waterbirds.

Large numbers of seabirds breed around Martinique, including Audubon's Shearwater (one of the largest colonies of this species in the Lesser Antilles used to be on **Hardy Island**, where there were over 500 pairs in the 1950s, breeding mainly Apr–Jul) and Sooty Tern (about 50,000 pairs have bred (mainly Apr–Jul) on **Ilet Poirier** near Baie des Anglais).

ADDITIONAL INFORMATION

Addresses
Parc Naturel Regional de la Martinique, 9 Boulevard General-de-Gaulle, Fort-de-France, Martinique, French West Indies (tel. 731930).

Union Regionale des Associations du Patrimoine et de l'Environment de Martinique, Centre du PNRM, Caserne Bouille, Rue Redoute de Matouba, Fort-de-France 97200, Martinique, French West Indies.

Office Departemental du Tourisme de la Martinique, BP 250, Fort-de-France 97206, Martinique, French West Indies (tel. 602773/795, fax. 736693).

Books and papers

Oiseaux des Petites Antilles/Birds of the West Indies (or, more accurately, a photographic guide to the birds of Guadeloupe and Martinique, in French and English), Benito-Espinal, E. 1990. Editions du Latanier, Saint-Barthélémy.

Premiers resultáts sur un suivi de l'avifaune de la presqu'île de la Caravelle (An ornithological survey of the Reserve Naturelle de la Caravelle), Bulens, P. 1994. Association pour l'Étude et la protection des Vertebres des petites Antilles.

Report of the 1986 University of East Anglia Martinique Oriole Expedition, Robertson, P. R. *et al.* 1986. ICBP Study Report No. 23. ICBP (BirdLife International).

MONTSERRAT

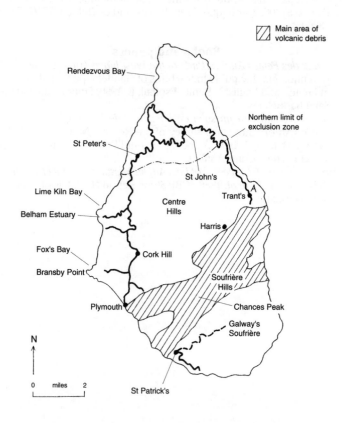

Main area of volcanic debris

Rendezvous Bay

Northern limit of exclusion zone

St Peter's

St John's

Lime Kiln Bay

Trant's

Centre Hills

Belham Estuary

Harris

Fox's Bay

Cork Hill

Bransby Point

Soufrière Hills

Plymouth

Chances Peak

Galway's Soufrière

N

0   miles   2

St Patrick's

This small island in the northern Lesser Antilles was devastated in late June 1997 when the volcano, Chances Peak, erupted. Massive billowing clouds of ash and rivers of red hot lava poured from the volcano, smothering most of the southern half of the island with ash and burning much of the capital, Plymouth, to the ground. Fortunately, most of the population who had their homes destroyed were evacuated in time and moved to the north of the island, though many had to depart the island altogether. In late 2000 the southern two-thirds of the island was still classified as an Exclusion Zone so, getting around, and finding accommodation and the birds, which include an endemic oriole, Forest Thrush* and two tropicbirds, was still virtually impossible.

Before the eruption it was possible to travel around this 19 km-long and up to 11 km-wide island in taxis, minibuses and hire vehicles, on the narrow but relatively good roads. Many visiting birders merely flew in from Antigua (where the nearest international airport is situated, about 48 km to the north), grabbed a taxi and headed for one of the forested gullies, known locally as ghauts, on the northern flanks of the Soufrière Hills in the south of the island, to look for the oriole, but many of these are now full of solidified lava, molten rock and ash. The pyroclastic flows reached the southern edge of the runway at the main airport, near Trant's on the east coast, but the airport just escaped destruction so once it is possible to fly in again and grab a taxi the best place to head for will be the Centre Hills where a 1998–99 survey found a reasonable population of orioles was still present. The island is a UK Crown Colony and the official language is English.

The peak time to visit Montserrat is April–May when the oriole is breeding and chances of seeing some seabirds increase. January–April is the driest period, with the rainy season in the lowlands in May–August. However, heavy rain can occur throughout the year in the mountains. The climate is tropical with relatively low humidity and cooling northeast trade winds. The hurricane season is in June–November.

Prior to 1997 the fertile foothills of Montserrat were intensively cultivated, but on the steepest and highest slopes and ridges there were remnant montane rain forests and elfin woods, below the peaks which rose, before it erupted, to 915 m at Chances Peak. By December 1997 this volcano's dome had collapsed and left a 600 m-wide amphitheatre around Galway's Soufrière, formerly a good birding area. Relatively flat lowlands are restricted to the coast where, on the dry, windward, Atlantic side, *Acacia*, cacti and sage grow. Around the coast the volcanic beaches are composed of black sand.

Five Forest Reserves formerly covered all slopes above 457 m, nearly 20% of the island, but not all were completely forested and in some reserves agricultural encroachment and development continued to eat away the remaining forest and elfin woods. These problems together with the recent and ongoing volcanic activity mean that the future survival of the two threatened species, as well as the relatively common and widespread birds, which occur on Montserrat, remains uncertain.

The single species endemic to the island is the black-and-yellow Montserrat Oriole*. Before the eruption, it occurred in montane rain forest above 800 m in the Soufrière Hills in the south of the island (where Chances Peak is situated) and in the Centre Hills, which being to the north, survived major devastation. Before 1997 there were believed to be about 1000 orioles in the Soufrière Hills and that was the best place to see the bird, but large areas of forest were destroyed by ash and lava which spewed from the volcano there, so the best chance of seeing this bird now is to visit the **Centre Hills**, where a survey in 1998–99 revealed that a reasonable population of about 4000 was present.

Eight of the 51 Caribbean endemics not confined to single countries, islands or archipelagos occur on Montserrat. They are five of the 14 species confined to the Lesser Antilles, but not to single islands: Purple-throated Carib, Brown Trembler, Scaly-breasted Thrasher, Forest Thrush* and Lesser Antillean Bullfinch; and three more widespread species, Bridled Quail-Dove, Green-throated Carib and Antillean Crested Hummingbird.

Eight of the 18 species nearly endemic to the Caribbean occur. They are Scaly-naped Pigeon, Zenaida Dove, Caribbean Elaenia, Caribbean Martin (mainly Feb–Aug), Pearly-eyed Thrasher, Black-whiskered Vireo, Black-faced Grassquit and Carib Grackle. In addition, the *petechia* group of Yellow Warbler, known as 'Golden Warbler', also nearly endemic to the Caribbean, is represented by the *bartholemica* race.

Non-endemic specialities and spectacular species not already mentioned include Red-billed (mainly Jan–Jun) and White-tailed (mainly

Mar–Jul) Tropicbirds, Magnificent Frigatebird and Brown Noddy (mainly Apr–Aug).

The long, narrow beach, which runs for over 1 km north of Bransby Point, together with the shallow, saline pond and mangroves in the nearby bird sanctuary at **Fox's Bay**, 3 km north of Plymouth on the west coast, support Pearly-eyed Thrasher, passage and wintering New World warblers such as Northern Parula and Northern Waterthrush, and Yellow Warbler. Another wetland area worth visiting is the Belham Estuary, north of Fox's Bay, while the coast north of there, between Lime Kiln Bay and Rendezvous Bay, is the best for seabirds.

ADDITIONAL INFORMATION

Addresses

For the latest information on the state of volcanic activity and visiting arrangements try the web site, www.geo.mtu.edu/volcanoes/west.indies/Soufrière/govt.

Books and Papers

Effects of the 1997 eruption on Montserrat's forest birds and their habitats, Arendt, W. J. 1998. *El Pitirre* 11: 57–58.

Fire From The Mountain: The Story of The Montserrat Volcano. Pattullo, P., 2000. Constable.

Effects of Hurricane Hugo on Montserrat's forest birds and their habitats, Arendt, W. J. 1994. *El Pitirre* 7: 5.

Birds of Montserrat, Siegel, A. 1983. Montserrat National Trust.

PUERTO RICO

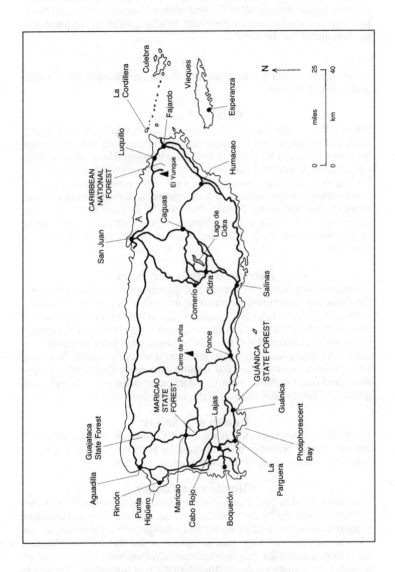

INTRODUCTION

Summary

Puerto Rico may have fewer endemics than the other Greater Antilles, but the 13 that are present include a tody and the superb Elfin-woods Warbler*, and two other species otherwise occur only sparingly on the Virgin Islands. With White-tailed Tropicbird and Adelaide's Warbler (recently treated as three species by the AOU) also on the agenda it is

361

hardly surprising that Puerto Rico is one of the most popular birding destinations in the region, especially when taking into account that it is possible to see virtually all of the best birds within a few days and therefore also visit the Dominican Republic, to which there are frequent connecting flights, on the same trip.

Size
Puerto Rico is about 160 km from west to east and 55 km north to south, and covers 8960 km².

Getting Around
It is possible to reach most parts of the island in minibuses and shared taxis, but public transport is slow and limited, making vehicle hire the preferred option of birders with little time to spare. The road network is excellent by Caribbean standards and enables easy access to the top birding sites, although there are few road signs, especially in the interior where some roads are narrow and winding, so a decent map will help pinpoint the best spots. Though Puerto Rico is a self-governing commonwealth of the USA, the main language is Spanish and a basic grasp of this will be useful if more detailed directions and other help are required.

Accommodation and Food
There are many hotels, haciendas and guesthouses (paradores) around the coast but accommodation can be difficult to find in smaller towns, especially inland. Most such accommodation is cheaper during the low season (mid-April to mid-December). There are also a few campsites, some with cabins, and it is possible to camp, with prior permission, at the main birding sites. American fast food is widely available, but those who prefer to savour the local cuisine can enjoy Creole-type dishes, stews and other national favourites such as mashed plantain with fruit, garlic and rice, washed down, perhaps, with beer or rum.

Health and Safety
Puerto Rico is not the safest place in the Caribbean, though most visiting birders will probably be unaffected by petty crime, which is rife in San Juan and on many of the most popular beaches.

Climate and Timing
The best period to bird Puerto Rico is March–April, when White-tailed Tropicbird and the hardest endemics to see are breeding and therefore at their most active, and wintering and passage migrant New World warblers are still present. May–June is equally productive for the tropicbird and endemics, but the rainy season normally lasts from May to October, though the southwest is much drier than the east throughout the year as it lies within the rainshadow of the Cordillera Central. It is hot and humid year-round, but the north coast is cooled by northeasterly trade winds.

Habitats
A coastal plain encircles almost the entire island, but inland the mountains reach 1338 m at Cerro de Punta in the Cordillera Central. The highest and steepest slopes support deciduous, semi-evergreen and evergreen rain forests, and elfin woods, but only 16.5% of the island is 'forested' and less than 1% of that is pristine. Over 26% of the land is used

for pasture but only 9% is cultivated, due to the many small but steep infertile limestone hills, known as mogotes, to the north of the Cordillera Central, and the aridity of the lowlands, particularly in the southwest where there is much thorn scrub. There are several large inland lakes but the best wetlands are coastal, in the form of saline lagoons and mangrove-lined mudflats. There are many beaches and cliffs on the coast, and these complete a wide diversity of habitats which supports a surprisingly rich avifauna for an island of this size. There are few mammals but these include a fishing bat.

Conservation

The government has established several reserves, and current conservation initiatives include a Shiny Cowbird control programme (this brood parasite is believed to be partially responsible for the decline of Puerto Rican Vireo and considered likely to pose a considerable threat to the continued survival of Yellow-shouldered Blackbird*), and a Puerto Rican Parrot* recovery programme. However, in order to conserve the ten threatened and near-threatened species, as well as the relatively common and widespread birds, measures to halt further habitat loss and degradation (predominantly due to agricultural encroachment, development, wetland drainage and the switch from shade- to sun-coffee plantations), control feral cats and rats (which infest areas such as the Caribbean National Forest), act upon and improve existing legislation, and establish a serious environmental education programme are required. There is little anyone can do about hurricanes (in September 1989, Hurricane Hugo felled or damaged 15% of the Caribbean National Forest and reduced the Puerto Rican Parrot* population from 46 or 47 to 22) but conservation, restoration and appropriate management of sufficient habitat should ensure that there are not only enough birds to survive a worse hurricane than Hugo, but also sufficient habitat in which they can find sanctuary and replenish their populations.

Endemics

The 13 species endemic to Puerto Rico are:

Puerto Rican Parrot*	One of the rarest birds on earth, with just 44 in the wild in Aug 1996 (there were only 13 in 1975), most in the mid-altitude wet forests of the Sierra de Luquillo in the northeast of the island, where the Caribbean National Forest is the best place to look, although the part of the reserve where they are most frequently seen is usually closed to the public, for obvious reasons
Puerto Rican Lizard-Cuckoo	Widespread and fairly common
Puerto Rican Nightjar*	Restricted to the southwest of the island where it is most often seen in and around Guánica State Forest; the population was considered to number 1400–2000 birds in the late 1990s
Green Mango	Relatively common in the western and central mountains, but scarce

	in the Sierra de Luquillo in the northeast
Puerto Rican Emerald	Relatively common in the mountains
Puerto Rican Tody	Widespread and relatively common
Puerto Rican Woodpecker	Widespread and relatively common
Puerto Rican Vireo	Restricted to the west where it is relatively common and occurs in both Guánica and Maricao State Forests
Elfin-woods Warbler*	Rare and local, and most frequently seen at high altitude in Maricao State Forest, or, less reliably, in the Caribbean National Forest in the Sierra de Luquillo. Only 600 or so birds were believed extant in the 1990s
Puerto Rican Tanager	Relatively common in the mountains
Puerto Rican Stripe-headed Tanager	Widespread and relatively common
Puerto Rican Bullfinch	Widespread and relatively common
Yellow-shouldered Blackbird*	Only fairly common on the southwest coast and on Mona Island, where it is estimated that about 1250 survive; usually easy to find at La Parguera, near Guánica State Forest

Some taxonomists believe the following race, which is endemic to Puerto Rico, should be treated as a full species:

Puerto Rican Pewee	the *blancoi* race of Lesser Antillean Pewee is fairly common, especially in the west

Other Caribbean Endemics

Fifteen of the 51 Caribbean endemics not confined to single countries, islands or archipelagos occur on Puerto Rico. They are: two species confined to Puerto Rico and the Virgin Islands, Puerto Rican Screech-Owl (very rare on the Virgin Islands) and Puerto Rican Flycatcher; one confined to Puerto Rico, Hispaniola and the Virgin Islands, Antillean Mango; one confined to Puerto Rico, Barbuda and St Lucia, Adelaide's Warbler (recently regarded as three species by the AOU); four restricted to Puerto Rico and the Lesser Antilles, Bridled Quail-Dove (very rare), Green-throated Carib (confined to the east/northeast), Antillean Crested Hummingbird (confined to the east/northeast) and Lesser Antillean Pewee (*blancoi*); and seven more widespread species, namely West Indian Whistling-Duck* (rare), Plain Pigeon*, Key West Quail-Dove, Loggerhead Kingbird, Red-legged Thrush, Antillean Euphonia and Greater Antillean Grackle.

Caribbean Near-Endemics

Ten of the 15 species nearly endemic to the Caribbean occur on Puerto Rico, namely Caribbean Coot*, White-crowned and Scaly-naped Pigeons, Zenaida Dove, Antillean Nighthawk (mainly May–Aug), Caribbean Elaenia, Caribbean Martin (mainly Feb–Aug), Pearly-eyed Thrasher, Black-whiskered Vireo (mainly Feb–Aug) and Black-faced Grassquit.

In addition, the *petechia* group of Yellow Warbler, known as 'Golden Warbler', which is also nearly endemic to the Caribbean, is represented by the *cruciana* race.

Other Birds

About 250 species have been recorded on Puerto Rico, which has the greatest number of breeding landbirds in the Caribbean. Non-endemic specialities and spectacular species not already mentioned include White-tailed Tropicbird (mainly Feb–Jul), Magnificent Frigatebird, White-cheeked Pintail, Yellow-breasted Crake, Bridled and Sooty Terns, Brown Noddy (all three mainly Apr–Aug), Ruddy Quail-Dove, passage migrant and wintering New World warblers, Yellow-faced Grassquit, Grasshopper Sparrow and Black-cowled Oriole.

Puerto Rico also has the dubious distinction of supporting more introduced species than any other island in the Caribbean. These include Hispaniolan*, Orange-fronted, Nanday, Monk and Canary-winged Parakeets, Hispaniolan*, Red-crowned, Yellow-headed and Orange-winged Parrots, Common Hill Myna, House Sparrow, Yellow-crowned and Orange Bishops, Orange-cheeked and Black-rumped Waxbills, Red Avadavat, White-throated Munia, Bronze Mannikin, Nutmeg and Chestnut Munias, Java Sparrow, Pin-tailed Whydah, Red Siskin, Saffron Finch and Troupial.

Expectations

On a two-week trip combining Puerto Rico with the Dominican Republic it is possible to see around 130 species. Birders confined to Puerto Rico, however, may find it difficult to find anywhere near 100 species, even during a prolonged trip.

CARIBBEAN NATIONAL FOREST

The largest remaining area of relatively untouched montane rain forest, 75% of that left on Puerto Rico, is situated on the slopes of the Sierra de Luquillo less than an hour by road from the international airport at San Juan. It was here, in 1971, that Elfin-woods Warbler* was discovered, in the gnarled elfin woods of the exposed high ridges and peaks, which rise to 1067 m at El Yunque. The forest, which is full of tree ferns, also supports the only remaining wild population of Puerto Rican Parrot*, but both this species and the warbler are very difficult to find in this 113 km² reserve due to access restrictions. The endemic Green Mango can also be difficult to find here, but seven endemics and the near-endemic Puerto Rican Screech-Owl are comparatively easy to track down.

For possible access to restricted areas, where there is a parrot observation platform, and to discover which trails are open, contact, well in advance, the Caribbean National Forest, PO Box 490, Palmer, PR 00721, West Indies, the US Forest Service (tel. 888 1880), or the reserve visitor centre (tel. 776 5335, 887 2875).

Localised Puerto Rican Endemics

Puerto Rican Parrot* (scarce), Green Mango (scarce), Elfin-woods Warbler* (scarce).

Other Puerto Rican Endemics
Puerto Rican Lizard-Cuckoo, Puerto Rican Emerald, Puerto Rican Tody, Puerto Rican Woodpecker, Puerto Rican Tanager, Puerto Rican Stripe-headed Tanager, Puerto Rican Bullfinch.

Puerto Rican and Virgin Islands Endemics
Puerto Rican Screech-Owl.

Other Caribbean Endemics
Red-legged Thrush.

Caribbean Near-Endemics
Scaly-naped Pigeon, Caribbean Martin (mainly Feb–Aug), Pearly-eyed Thrasher.

Passage Migrants and Winter Visitors
Black-and-white Warbler, American Redstart.

Others
Sharp-shinned, Broad-winged and Red-tailed Hawks, Black Swift (mainly Apr–Sep), Yellow-faced Grassquit, Black-cowled Oriole.

Head east from San Juan on Highway 3 towards Fajardo then turn south in response to the 'El Yunque' sign, between Rio Grande and Luquillo, onto Route 191. Although this road traverses the reserve, the access gate at La Coca Falls is usually closed between 6pm and 7.30am, and a second gate 5 km further is usually permanently closed. About 3.5 km beyond La Coca Falls bird around the Palma de Sierra Visitor Centre and Picnic Area, where, especially at dawn, it is possible to see Puerto Rican Screech-Owl, as well as Green Mango and the endemic lizard-cuckoo,

CARIBBEAN NATIONAL FOREST

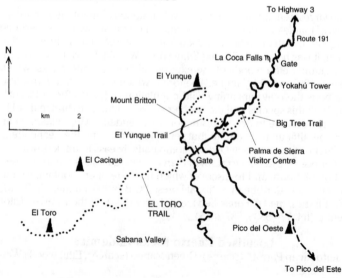

emerald, tody, woodpecker, tanagers and bullfinch. There is a slim chance of seeing Puerto Rican Parrot* here, at dawn and dusk, when they fly to or from their roosts, and they have also been seen feeding in trees across the ravine behind the restaurant, but the parrots normally only frequent a closed area of the reserve and in the late 1990s rarely crossed the ridge separating that area from the area open to the public.

The upper ridges below the peak of El Toro, where the hyperactive Elfin-woods Warbler* occurs, may be accessible via the El Toro Trail which begins on the right-hand side of Highway 191 about 300 m beyond the second gate. However, this and other trails are often closed to the public due to fallen trees.

Accommodation: for permission to camp (no facilities) in the reserve contact the Caribbean National Forest office, the US Forest Service or the reserve visitor centre.

On Puerto Rico, Green-throated Carib and Antillean Crested Humming-bird are confined to the east and northeast coasts, where they can be seen in flowering trees and shrubs along the beach at **Playa de Fajardo**. Other birds in this area include Brown Booby, Magnificent Frigate-bird, Yellow-crowned Night-Heron, Puerto Rican Lizard-Cuckoo, Puerto Rican Woodpecker, Pearly-eyed Thrasher and Red-legged Thrush. The hummingbirds also occur at **Humacao National Wildlife Refuge**, south of Fajardo, along with Magnificent Frigatebird, Least Bittern, West Indian Whistling-Duck*, White-cheeked Pintail, American and Carib-bean* Coots, Mangrove Cuckoo, Loggerhead Kingbird and Pearly-eyed Thrasher. To reach here turn east off Highway 3 at the first exit northeast of Humacao, from where it is a few km to the reserve entrance. Continue past here and park on the right-hand side of the road beyond a small canal. Walk the narrow trail, which runs parallel to the canal, until you reach a dirt track. Turn left, cross the wooden bridge and head to a lake on the left. West Indian Whistling-Duck* has been recorded on the

The black, white and red Puerto Rican Woodpecker occurs throughout the island, from coastal plantations to montane forests

canal at the end of this lake and on the lake reached by continuing along the dyke.

There were believed to be fewer than 300 Plain Pigeons* in the wild on Puerto Rico in 1993, but over 100 have since been raised as part of a captive-breeding programme and some have been released into the wild. One of the best places to look is around **Lago de Cidra**, where up to 18 were seen in December 1996. This lake is west of Highway 52 near Cidra. To the west of here, near **Comerío**, Plain Pigeon* and Scaly-naped Pigeon, may also be seen in the large trees behind the school about 1.5 km south of the intersection between Highways 156 and 172.

GUÁNICA STATE FOREST

The thorn scrub, dry woodland, and semi-evergreen and montane deciduous forests in this 655 ha Biosphere Reserve, about 140 km southwest of San Juan, support most of the arid country specialities, including Puerto Rican Nightjar*, Antillean Mango and Adelaide's Warbler. This is a much richer area for birds than the Caribbean National Forest with species diversity and populations over three times higher, but be sure to be in the field at dawn.

Localised Puerto Rican Endemics
Puerto Rican Nightjar*, Puerto Rican Vireo.

Other Puerto Rican Endemics
Puerto Rican Lizard-Cuckoo, Puerto Rican Tody, Puerto Rican Woodpecker, Puerto Rican Bullfinch.

Puerto Rican and Virgin Islands Endemics
Puerto Rican Screech-Owl, Puerto Rican Flycatcher.

Localised Caribbean Endemics
Antillean Mango, Lesser Antillean Pewee, Adelaide's Warbler.

Other Caribbean Endemics
Loggerhead Kingbird, Red-legged Thrush, Antillean Euphonia, Greater Antillean Grackle.

Caribbean Near-Endemics
Zenaida Dove, Caribbean Elaenia, Caribbean Martin (mainly Feb–Aug), Pearly-eyed Thrasher, Black-faced Grassquit.

Others
Magnificent Frigatebird, White-cheeked Pintail, Red-tailed Hawk, Wilson's Plover, White-winged Dove, Mangrove Cuckoo, Belted Kingfisher, Cave Swallow, Yellow Warbler, Shiny Cowbird.

(Other species recorded here include White-tailed Tropicbird (mainly Feb–Jul), Key West and Bridled Quail-Doves, and Antillean Nighthawk (mainly May–Aug). Introductions include Troupial).

Two dead-end roads penetrate the reserve: (i) Route 334, which provides access to the north side, is reached by turning south off Highway

GUÁNICA STATE FOREST

2 onto Route 116 towards Guánica, and then turning east onto Route 334 which traverses semi-evergreen and montane deciduous forests. Bear left at the two forks along here to reach the barrier at the reserve edge, which is usually closed between 3.30pm and 8.30am. The section between the barrier and the HQ, further on, is best for the owl and nightjar, both of which are most likely to be seen at dawn or dusk. Also bird the network of trails around the HQ, where the endemic lizard-cuckoo and vireo, as well as Antillean Mango and Adelaide's Warbler occur. (ii) Route 333 provides access to the south end and is accessible via Route 116, south of the Route 334 turning. The road follows the coast east for 10 km or so and passes through low, arid thorn scrub before ending at a large parking area near a lagoon where White-cheeked Pintail occurs. Bird the Guitarra Trail north of here and the Meseta Track to the east for Antillean Nighthawk, Puerto Rican Nightjar*, Puerto Rican Flycatcher, and Yellow (in the mangroves) and Adelaide's Warblers. Overhead and offshore look out for White-tailed Tropicbird and Magnificent Frigatebird.

Accommodation: Copamarina Beach Resort (on Route 333). For permission to camp on the reserve contact the Department of Natural Resources.

Some birders stay at the Hotel Villa Parador in **La Parguera** when birding Guánica State Forest because Yellow-shouldered Blackbirds* come to feed on scraps here (and elsewhere in the town) and roost in palms behind the parador. This rare icterid can also be seen along the water's edge by the town, with Caribbean Martin (mainly Feb–Aug) and Yellow Warbler also present. **Phosphorescent Bay**, between Guánica and La Parguera, is named after the luminescent dinoflagellates that light the waters of the bay at night, and it is possible to witness one of nature's strangest spectacles with the help of local fishermen in La Parguera, who are usually willing to take people out. The show is usually at its best on moonlit nights in early Oct.

MARICAO STATE FOREST

The windswept elfin woods of this reserve, about 50 km northwest of Guánica, are the best places to look for the endemic Elfin-woods Warbler*, which is always elusive, but, nevertheless, easier to locate here than in the Caribbean National Forest. It also occasionally ventures into the lush montane forests here, where it joins the very similar Black-and-white Warbler.

Localised Puerto Rican Endemics
Green Mango, Puerto Rican Vireo, Elfin-woods Warbler*.

Other Puerto Rican Endemics
Puerto Rican Lizard-Cuckoo, Puerto Rican Emerald, Puerto Rican Tody, Puerto Rican Woodpecker, Puerto Rican Tanager, Puerto Rican Stripe-headed Tanager, Puerto Rican Bullfinch.

Puerto Rican and Virgin Islands Endemics
Puerto Rican Screech-Owl, Puerto Rican Flycatcher.

Localised Caribbean Endemics
Lesser Antillean Pewee, Adelaide's Warbler.

Other Caribbean Endemics
Key West Quail-Dove, Loggerhead Kingbird, Red-legged Thrush, Antillean Euphonia, Greater Antillean Grackle.

Caribbean Near-Endemics
Scaly-naped Pigeon, Pearly-eyed Thrasher, Black-faced Grassquit.

Passage Migrants and Winter Visitors
Black-and-white Warbler, American Redstart.

Others
Sharp-shinned Hawk, White-winged Dove, Ruddy Quail-Dove, Black Swift (mainly Apr–Sep), Grey Kingbird, Shiny Cowbird, Black-cowled Oriole.

*No trip to Puerto Rico would be complete without seeing the elusive but excellent Elfin-woods Warbler**

The scenic Route 120 runs through the reserve between Sabana Grande and Maricao. Along this road look for Elfin-woods Warbler* around the lay-bys at km 9.1, 9.3 and 14, as well as along any of the tracks which penetrate the hillsides in the area. One of the best areas is around km 16 on the hillsides between the antenna on the east side of the road, just north of the Route 366 turn-off, and the access road to the Forest Service buildings on the west side of the road, as shown on the map below.

MARICAO STATE FOREST

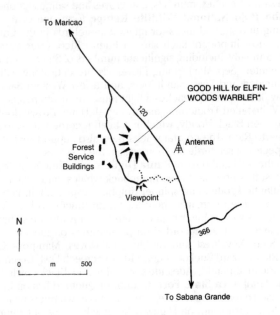

Accommodation: La Hacienda Juanita (A+/tel. 833 2550), which is situated just off Highway 105 at km 23.5 about 0.5 km west of Maricao, is the most popular choice, because the grounds and adjacent forest (bird the Loop Trail) support Puerto Rican Screech-Owl, as well as Scaly-naped Pigeon, Green Mango, Puerto Rican Emerald, Puerto Rican Tody, Lesser Antillean Pewee, Puerto Rican Flycatcher, Loggerhead Kingbird, Puerto Rican Vireo, Puerto Rican Tanager and Black-cowled Oriole, and outside possibilities include Ruddy Quail-Dove and even Elfin-woods Warbler*. For permission to camp at Maricao State Forest contact the Department of Natural Resources.

There are several other sites worth visiting in southwest Puerto Rico. West Indian Whistling-Duck*, and other waterbirds such as Least Bittern, Fulvous Whistling-Duck and Yellow-breasted Crake have been recorded on **Laguna Cartagena**, the finest freshwater marsh on the island, which is within a reserve west of Highway 303 south of Lajas. The **Boquerón National Wildlife Refuge**, which can be reached by taking the signed rough access track west off Highway 301, a km or so south of the 101/301 intersection, is also excellent for waterbirds, including Yellow-breasted Crake, and passage migrant and wintering shorebirds such as Solitary and Stilt Sandpipers, as well as Caribbean Martin (mainly Feb–Aug) and Yellow Warbler. Bird along the access track, the trails which radiate from the HQ and the marshy area by the track about 1 km south of the HQ (Yellow-breasted Crake). To reach an area of mangrove which supports Yellow-shouldered Blackbird* head south from the entrance to Boquerón on Highway 301, then east on Highway 303 and continue for a few km to the end of this road then turn right onto a track which ends at the mangroves after a few more km. Further south on Highway 301 the sandy beaches, mudflats, mangroves and saline lagoons within the **Cabo Rojo National Wildlife Refuge** form one of the largest remaining undisturbed areas for migrant shorebirds in the Caribbean and the most important such site on Puerto Rico. Over 40,000 pass through annually, including significant numbers of Stilt Sandpiper, and during winter (Sep–Mar) Piping Plover* is present, along with many Semipalmated and Least Sandpipers, and a few Western Sandpipers. Highway 301 eventually reaches a lighthouse, from where it is possible to see White-tailed Tropicbird (mainly Feb–Jul) and Brown Booby, and perhaps even Black Noddy, which has been recorded at sea off southwest Puerto Rico. The coastal waters here also support manatee, and three species of sea turtle lay their eggs in the beaches.

From the old lighthouse at **Punta Higüero** near Rincón on the northwest coast it is possible to see humpback whales, and Atlantic bottlenose, Atlantic spotted and spinner dolphins, especially in Feb–Mar. It may be possible to organise boat trips from Rincón to look for these cetaceans, as well as Black-capped Petrel* and Audubon's Shearwater which have also been recorded on pelagic trips off the west coast of Puerto Rico. Key West and Ruddy Quail-Doves, Mangrove Cuckoo, Puerto Rican Lizard-Cuckoo, Puerto Rican Screech-Owl, Green Mango, Puerto Rican Emerald, Adelaide's Warbler and Black-cowled Oriole occur in **Guajataca State Forest**, south of Quebradillas on the northwest coast. To reach the reserve, which is about two hours by road west of San Juan, turn south off Highway 2 a few km west of Quebradillas, onto Route 446 and follow the 'Bosque de Guajataca' signs. A stone pyramid and picnic shelter denote the reserve entrance. Bird the trails to and through the campsites and the trails off Route 446 further on. The **Parador Guajataca**, a viewpoint overlooking the sea north of Quebradillas, is a good place to look for White-tailed Tropicbird (mainly Feb–Jul). This superb seabird can also be seen off the Castillo del Morro in old **San Juan**, where other exotic but less exciting, introduced, species include Monk Parakeet and Java Sparrow. Birders interested in Puerto Rico's varied collection of introductions may also wish to try the Isla Grande Naval Reserve, near Isla Grande Airport in Santurce, old San Juan, where Canary-winged Parakeet, Orange-cheeked Waxbill, Bronze Mannikin, Pin-tailed Whydah and Saffron Finch all occur. Yellow-crowned Bishop, Black-rumped Waxbill, Red Avadavat, and White-throated, Nutmeg and Chestnut Munias occur elsewhere in the coastal lowlands around San Juan.

In Apr–Jul the island of **La Cordillera** and its satellites, just off the northeast tip of Puerto Rico, have supported as many as 2000 pairs of Bridled Tern and 100,000–200,000 pairs of Sooty Tern. Further east the 600 ha National Wildlife Refuge (tel. 742 0115) at **Culebra** island, which includes four areas on the main island as well as 23 offshore islets, supports breeding colonies of Red-billed Tropicbird (mainly Jan–Jun),

Masked (Mar–May) and Red-footed (mainly Apr–Jun) Boobies, Bridled Tern (about 2000 pairs, Apr–Jul) and Sooty Tern (formerly 100,000–200,000 pairs on Punta Flamenco but numbers much lower now, Apr–Jul), as well as sea-turtles (Apr–Aug). In addition, Black Noddy has been recorded offshore. Culebra is accessible by air and ferry from the mainland, and there is plenty of accommodation, including a campsite. The main seabird colonies are situated on the Cayo Luis Peña Peninsula, Flamenco and on offshore islets.

ADDITIONAL INFORMATION

Addresses

Department of Natural Resources, Division of Forest Land Use Permits, PO Box 5887, Puerta de Tierra, San Juan, Puerto Rico 00906, West Indies.

Sociedad Ornitológica Puertorriquena (web site: www.mindspring.com).

Natural History Society of Puerto Rico (Incorporating Netherlands Antilles National Parks Foundation—STINAPA), PO Box 2090, Curaçao, Netherlands Antilles.

Puerto Rican Tourism Company, PO Box 3960, San Juan, Puerto Rico 00902, West Indies.

Books and papers

A Guide to the Birds of Puerto Rico and the Virgin Islands, Raffaele, H. A. 1989. Princeton UP.

Puerto Rico's Birds in Photographs, Oberle, M. W. 2000. Editorial Humanitas (with CD-Rom).

Las Aves de Puerto Rico, Biaggi, V. 1996 (Fourth Edition). Puerto Rico UP.

SABA

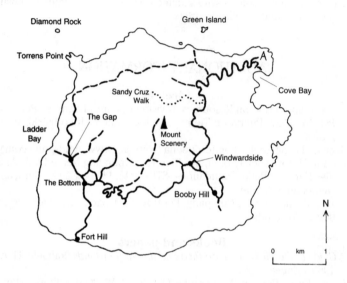

This tiny, mountainous island in the northern Lesser Antilles supports several Caribbean endemics, including Bridled Quail-Dove and Brown Trembler, as well as breeding seabirds such as Red-billed and White-tailed Tropicbirds.

Saba is a circular island with a diameter of about 5 km. Its tiny airstrip is situated between two cliffs on the island's only sizeable level area and is only accessible via a 20-minute flight on small aircraft from St.-Martin (p. 393). Minibus-taxis run from here, via a road that ascends 549 m in just 8 km, to the village of Windwardside in the centre of the island where many visitors stay. There are only about 100 beds for tourists on the island, mainly in small, expensive hotels and guesthouses, though it is also possible to stay in rented cottages. The island is part of the Netherlands Antilles and Dutch is the official language, but almost everyone also speaks English. Take a light waterproof, as it is often cool and damp in the montane interior. Crime is almost non-existent and there are probably few safer places on the planet than Saba. The best time to visit is in April–May when many resident birds are breeding and there are many seabirds present. The wet season usually lasts from September to December, but it can rain in any month in the highest areas.

Though Saba is just 13 km² it rises to 887 m at the extinct volcano of Mount Scenery and the interior slopes support mainly secondary montane rain forest and elfin woods, adorned with epiphytes, mosses and tree ferns. There are no beaches on the coast, only steep cliffs, and the island is surrounded by deep waters frequented by humpback whales

374

in February–April as they migrate south. Conservation problems include continuing habitat loss and predation by introduced predators. The Saba Conservation Foundation is lobbying for the establishment of reserves, predator control and greater environmental education in order to protect the island's flora and fauna.

Over 60 species have been recorded on Saba, including 12 seabirds, 26 breeding species and 24 passage migrants and/or winter visitors. Red-billed (over 750 bred on Saba in 1998) and White-tailed Tropicbirds breed mainly in Jan–May, and one excellent place to look for these lovely birds is along the cliffs of **Cove Bay** at the south end of the airstrip. Numerous steep trails with stone steps link the island's interior villages and the best for landbirds is arguably that with about 1050 steps and several shelters which ascends **Mount Scenery** from Windwardside. It is possible to find Purple-throated and Green-throated Caribs, Caribbean Elaenia, Brown Trembler, Scaly-breasted and Pearly-eyed Thrashers, and Lesser Antillean Bullfinch on this route. Other birds which occur on and around the island include Audubon's Shearwater (breeds on Mount Scenery, Feb–Jul), Brown Booby (breeds on **Diamond Rock** off the northwest coast, Mar–Oct), Magnificent Frigatebird, Bridled Tern (also breeds on Diamond Rock, mainly Apr–Aug), Brown Noddy (breeds on **Green Island**, off the north coast, mainly Apr–Aug), Scaly-naped Pigeon, Zenaida Dove, Chuck-will's-widow (Sep–May), Antillean Crested Hummingbird, Caribbean Martin (mainly Feb–Aug) and Black-faced Grassquit. The road west from Windwardside descends to the village known as The Bottom, which is situated on a plateau at 245 m. Bridled Quail-Dove occurs here but it may be easier to locate this skulker by the long stone path which runs between the road northwest of The Bottom and **Ladder Bay** on the west coast.

ADDITIONAL INFORMATION

Addresses

Saba Conservation Foundation, The Bottom, Saba, Netherlands Antilles, West Indies.

Saba Tourist Board, PO Box 527, Windwardside, Saba, Netherlands Antilles, West Indies (tel. 62231, fax. 62350, web site: www.turq.com/saba).

ST. BARTHÉLÉMY

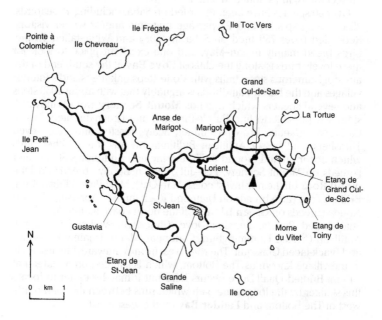

'St. Barts', as it is affectionately known to some, is a tiny, 21 km², luxury-holiday island frequented by the rich and famous, in the Leeward Islands of the northern Lesser Antilles. There is little to entice those with a keen interest in birds, but seabird enthusiasts may enjoy a visit to the island, which also supports several Caribbean endemics, including three hummingbirds.

The tiny airstrip can only receive planes carrying a maximum of 20 passengers, hence the island is only accessible via nearby islands such as Antigua or, further afield, from Puerto Rico. It is a short distance from the airstrip to the hotels, most of which are on the north coast and connected by a minor road network that also accesses some of the remainder of the island. It is possible to hire a vehicle, but there are also minibuses and taxis. The island is administered by France and the principal language is French, but many locals also speak English.

St. Barts' lush volcanic hillsides are surrounded by cliffs, beaches (where sea-turtles nest in April–August), coral reefs and deep waters, where sperm whales can be seen during May on migration. There are also several inland lagoons that support waterbirds such as White-cheeked Pintail. Habitat loss and degradation must be halted if the birds are to be conserved.

Specialities and spectacular species include White-tailed Tropicbird (mainly Mar–Jul), Magnificent Frigatebird, White-cheeked Pintail, Bridled and Sooty Terns, Brown Noddy (all three mainly Apr–Aug), White-crowned and Scaly-naped Pigeons, Zenaida Dove, Bridled Quail-Dove, Purple-throated and Green-throated Caribs, Antillean Crested Hummingbird, Caribbean Elaenia, Caribbean Martin (mainly Feb–Aug), Scaly-breasted and Pearly-eyed Thrashers, Yellow Warbler (*bartholemica*), Black-faced Grassquit, Lesser Antillean Bullfinch and Carib Grackle.

The best time to visit is April–May when the seabirds are around and many landbirds are breeding, and the best birding sites are wetlands such as Étang de St.-Jean, Grande Saline, Anse de Marigot, Étang de Grand Cul-de-Sac and Étang de Toiny, and tree-covered terrain such as that on Morne du Vitet.

ADDITIONAL INFORMATION

Addresses

St. Barthélémy Tourist Office, Quai de Gaulle, Gustavia, St. Barthélémy, French West Indies (tel. 278727, fax. 277447, web site: www.st.barths. com).

ST. EUSTATIUS

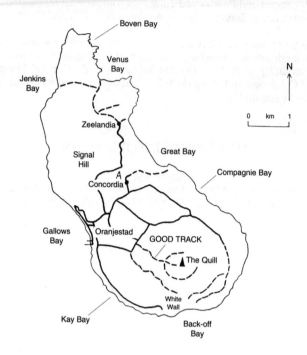

This tiny 30 km² Leeward island in the northern Lesser Antilles supports a few Caribbean endemics, including three hummingbirds, and both Red-billed and White-tailed Tropicbirds.

The island is 20 minutes by air from St.-Martin, where connections with international flights from Europe and the USA are possible. There are only a few, narrow roads on the island. It is possible to hire a vehicle, but this seems unnecessary in such a small place where there are taxis. There are few hotels and just one guesthouse making it wise to book accommodation well in advance. Being one of the Netherlands Antilles, the official language is Dutch but most people also speak English. St. Eustatius is a relatively poor, quiet and friendly Caribbean island with virtually no crime.

The island is dominated by an extinct, forested volcano known as The Quill, which rises to 600 m at its southern end. Most native forest on the volcano and elsewhere has long since been felled for plantations and pastures (many now overgrazed by goats). Though flora and fauna within reserves is 'protected', more areas require conserving and restoring, existing and preferably new legislation needs enforcing, and introduced predators should be controlled, if the birds are to survive.

Approximately 60 bird species have been recorded, including Audubon's Shearwater (mainly Mar–Jul), Red-billed (mainly Jan–Jun) and White-tailed (mainly Mar–Jul) Tropicbirds, Magnificent Frigatebird, Zenaida Dove, Bridled Quail-Dove (rare), Purple-throated and Green-throated Caribs, Antillean Crested Hummingbird, Caribbean Elaenia, Caribbean Martin (mainly Feb–Aug), Scaly-breasted (possibly extinct) and Pearly-eyed Thrashers, Yellow Warbler (*bartholemica*), Black-faced Grassquit and Lesser Antillean Bullfinch.

The best time to visit the island is April–May when the seabirds and most landbirds are breeding. There are several tracks and trails and the one leading from Rosemary Lane to the crater of **The Quill** (allow at least a couple of hours there and back) is arguably best for landbirds. White Wall, on the southern slope of The Quill, supports breeding tropicbirds.

ADDITIONAL INFORMATION

Addresses

St. Eustatius National Parks Association (STENAPA), White Wall Road, St. Eustatius, West Indies (tel./fax. 82661).

St. Eustatius Tourism Development Foundation, Fort Oranjestraat, St. Eustatius, West Indies (tel. 82433, web site: www.turq.com/statia).

ST. KITTS AND NEVIS

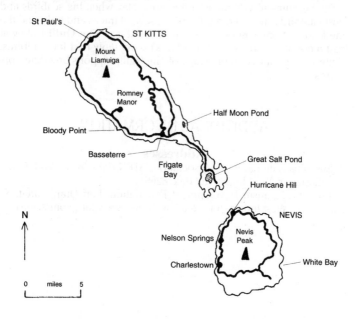

This pair of small but spectacular mountainous Leeward Islands support five of the 14 species that are endemic to the Lesser Antilles but not confined to single islands, though three of these, including Brown Trembler, occur only on Nevis.

A regular passenger ferry, which usually takes 45 minutes, connects the two islands that together cover just 269 km². Public minibuses on both islands do not run strict timetables but are fairly frequent, rather quick and cheap, so birders with little money to spare may wish to avoid using the more expensive taxis or hiring a vehicle. A wide range of accommodation, food and drink is available. The islands are a Commonwealth State of the UK and English is the official language. Vaccination against yellow fever, if arriving from an infected country, is compulsory.

The 176 km² island of St. Kitts is dominated by three groups of volcanic peaks, the highest rising to 1156 m at the dormant Mount Liamuiga. Deep ravines separate the highlands and the only extensive lowlying area is on the island's southeastern arm, where there are several salt ponds. A 3 km-wide channel separates St. Kitts from the smaller, 93 km², Nevis, which rises to 985 m. Remnant rain forest survives on both islands but more land is cultivated, mainly in the form of sugarcane plantations. The three main contemporary conservation problems are continuing habitat loss and degradation (especially due to tourist development on coasts), predation by introduced species such as the small

Indian mongoose and green vervet monkey, and hunting, which is not as rife as it used to be but still takes an unnecessary toll on the birdlife. There is an urgent need to establish protected areas, control predators, enforce current and introduce new legislation, and improve environmental education, in order to protect the two threatened and near-threatened, as well as the more common and widespread, birds.

There are no endemics on St. Kitts and Nevis, and only eight of the 51 Caribbean endemics not confined to single countries, islands or archipelagos occur. They include five of the 14 species confined to the Lesser Antilles, but not to single islands: Purple-throated Carib (Nevis only), Lesser Antillean Flycatcher (Nevis only), Brown Trembler (Nevis only), Scaly-breasted Thrasher and Lesser Antillean Bullfinch; and three more widespread species: Bridled Quail-Dove, Green-throated Carib and Antillean Crested Hummingbird.

Eight of the 18 species almost endemic to the Caribbean occur. They are Scaly-naped Pigeon, Zenaida Dove, Caribbean Elaenia, Caribbean Martin (mainly Feb–Aug), Pearly-eyed Thrasher, Black-whiskered Vireo, Black-faced Grassquit and Carib Grackle. In addition, the *petechia* group of Yellow Warbler, known as 'Golden Warbler', which is also nearly endemic to the Caribbean, is represented by the *bartholemica* race.

The best time to visit St Kitts and Nevis is during the dry season, in November–May, and especially in April–May when the seabirds and most landbirds are breeding. It is possible to see over 30 species in a single day on **St. Kitts**, especially by concentrating on the Frigate Bay area and at least one of the island's several trails, the best of which are arguably the Romney Manor Trail and that ascending the northern slopes of Mount Liamuiga. To reach the latter head for St. Paul's in the north of the island and, just beyond the village entrance sign, take the track leading through farmyards and sugarcane plantations. About 20 minutes along here take the left fork, whereupon the track becomes a trail through forest. The crater at 793 m is a day's hike away, the peak even further and the trail is best tackled with a local guide. Wetlands worth a look on St. Kitts include Greatheeds Pond, Half Moon Pond, Muddy Pond and Great Salt Pond.

On **Nevis** the best place to look for landbirds is, arguably, around Nevis Peak in the centre of the island, and the best places for waterbirds are The Bogs (near Charlestown), Nelson Springs, and the areas behind the beaches at Hurricane Hill and White Bay.

ADDITIONAL INFORMATION

Addresses

St. Kitts Department of Tourism, Pelican Mall, PO Box 132, Basseterre, St. Kitts, West Indies (tel. 465 2620/4040, fax. 465 8794).

Nevis Tourist Office, Main Street, Charlestown, Nevis, West Indies (tel. 469 1042, fax. 469 1066).

Books

The Birds of Nevis, Hilder, P. 1989. The Nevis Historical and Conservation Society.

ST. LUCIA

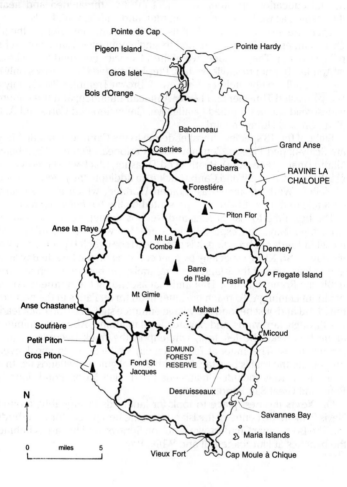

Pointe de Cap
Pigeon Island
Pointe Hardy
Gros Islet
Bois d'Orange
Babonneau
Castries
Grand Anse
Desbarra
RAVINE LA CHALOUPE
Forestiére
Piton Flor
Anse la Raye
Mt La Combe
Dennery
Barre de l'Isle
Fregate Island
Praslin
Mt Gimie
Anse Chastanet
Mahaut
Soufrière
Micoud
Petit Piton
Gros Piton
EDMUND FOREST RESERVE
Fond St Jacques
Desruisseaux
N
Savannes Bay
Maria Islands
0   miles   5
Vieux Fort
Cap Moule à Chique

INTRODUCTION

Summary

This small rugged island in the central Lesser Antilles has the richest avifauna in the chain, including three endemics, ten of the 14 Lesser Antilles endemics not confined to single islands, both Red-billed and White-tailed Tropicbirds, and Adelaide's Warbler, which elsewhere occurs only on Puerto Rico and Barbuda (and has recently been treated as three species by the AOU). St. Lucia is therefore an ideal destination for birders seeking to see a wide range of Lesser Antilles endemics and several other superb birds without island hopping through the archipelago.

Size
St. Lucia is 44 km long and up to 22 km wide, and covers 616 km².

Getting Around
There is no question about it, it is best to hire a high-clearance 4WD vehicle in order to bird St. Lucia thoroughly, as roads and tracks in the montane interior, where the vast majority of the endemics can be found, and in the remote northeast of the island, where the rare White-breasted Thrasher* occurs, are poor. Due to some improvements made in the late 1990s some of these roads are no longer as rough and scary as formerly, but all easily become pot-holed and are subject to frequent landslides. Even on the better roads driving around the island is not a pleasure, as many of the islanders employ driving techniques that would land them in jail in many other parts of the world. There is also a serious lack of road signs, so a detailed map is very useful, though many locals know where the major birding sites are. St. Lucia is a Commonwealth State of the UK and English is the official language, although local people usually speak a French-based patois among themselves. If prepared for some 'leg work' budget birders could probably hire a 2WD vehicle, or even, if time was not a major factor, use public transport, although this could be a traumatic experience based on the antics of local drivers. Buses have no timetables, as one might expect in the care-free Caribbean, but are fairly priced and serve most towns and villages.

It may be necessary to obtain permits and organise (expensive) compulsory guides before visiting the reserves on St. Lucia. Contact the Forestry Department to discover the latest details (tel. 450 2078/2231, fax. 450 2287).

Accommodation and Food
St. Lucia is a major tourist destination, thus there is plenty of accommodation, albeit mostly expensive. The major resort area is on the northwest coast, a couple of hours by road from the main birding sites, making it more convenient to stay elsewhere, in some of the small hotels and guesthouses scattered around the rest of the coast. There are many good places to eat on the west coast but nowhere in remote parts of the interior, although there is usually at least one bar and a shop with basic goods in most inland villages. Clearly, birders planning a full day or overnight excursion, especially in the northeast, will need to take suitable provisions with them.

Climate and Timing
The best time of the year to visit is during April when endemic landbirds such as White-breasted Thrasher* and Grey Trembler, as well as seabirds, including both tropicbirds, are breeding and therefore easier to locate. Any time in April–June may be productive but the lowland rainy season normally commences in May and may hamper birding. The rains usually peak at their end, in July–August, although heavy downpours are possible throughout the year in the mountains. January–April is the driest period when it can be very hot, despite northeasterly trade winds, which tend to cool the island. The hurricane season is June–November.

Habitats
St. Lucia is, in places, a spectacularly rugged island with precipitous

mountains, and the scenery is arguably at its most awesome around Morne Pitons on the southwest coast, where the towering volcanic peaks of Petit Piton and Gros Piton soar straight from the sea. Just a few km inland, Mount Gimie, the island's highest peak, rises to 950 m. Some of the less vertical slopes are still covered in luxuriant forest, but only 13% of the island is now forested because the volcanic soil is extremely fertile, providing nutrients for crops such as almond, avocado and breadfruit, especially in the south. Approximately 30% of land is cultivated, mainly in the wide, fertile valleys, some of which have been carved by the short rivers that rush down the largely inaccessible high reaches of the mountains. In some areas of the lower north of the island and in arid coastal areas there is also dry, open, scrubby woodland, while the coast is a fine mixture of beautiful beaches and bays, and often spectacular headlands, with some offshore islets where seabirds breed. Volcanic activity is ongoing in some areas and near Soufrière in the southwest there are vents from which steam and other gases spew forth.

Conservation

Though much of the original forest has been cleared for agriculture some extensive areas remain due to the rugged terrain and a long-standing conservation policy. However, a growing human population is placing new pressure on the land at the start of the 21st Century, and if St. Lucia is to conserve the six threatened and near-threatened species, as well as relatively common and widespread birds, and thereby continue to support the richest avifauna in the Lesser Antilles, it will need to ensure against further habitat loss and degradation.

Aided by the RARE Center for Tropical Conservation, which helped initiate the 'Promoting Protection Through Pride' campaign in 1990, the government has already educated local people about the value of their natural environment and associated birdlife. It has done such a good job that the island serves as a model for community conservation throughout the world. This is because the amazing recovery of the St. Lucia Parrot* population is at least partially due to a dramatic change in local attitudes, as well as government policy. In 1977 a law was passed making it illegal to shoot parrots or destroy their habitat and this, together with a public education programme launched in 1979 which made the parrot the national bird, helped increase numbers from about 100 in 1976 to as many as 250 in 1986, and 450 or so in 1998. Proof of the value of conserving the environment is available for all to see on St. Lucia, in the form of a healthy population of endemic parrots, and financial proof is provided by the Des Cartier Trail, established with help from the RARE Center, which was visited by 4500 tourists in 1998 and contributed US$247,000 (c.£150,000) to the country's economy. However, only US$30,000 (c.£19,000) is believed to have reached Forestry Department coffers, so even the government of St. Lucia can still improve on its example to the rest of the world!

Endemics

Three species are endemic to St. Lucia:

St. Lucia Parrot*   Local and uncommon, about 450 were present in 1998 but the population is still subject to periodic fluctuations, due, at least in part, to

	tropical storms, one of which, Debbie, in September 1994, flattened many of the dead trees used for nesting and forced many birds to move, temporarily, to the north of the island
St. Lucia Black Finch*	Local and uncommon
St. Lucia Oriole*	Widespread but uncommon

The endemic Semper's Warbler* is possibly extinct. It has been certainly recorded only a handful of times since the 1920s and was last definitely recorded in 1961. Extensive ongoing searches have failed to confirm its presence since, but it was reported in 1989 and 1995, and the largely inaccessible interior may still support a small population. Most records have come from the Barre de l'Isle ridge between Piton Canarie and Piton Flor in the centre of the island, though the 1989 report was from Gros Piton in the southwest.

Some taxonomists believe the following races, which are endemic to St Lucia, should be treated as full species:

St. Lucia Nightjar	the endemic *otiosus* race of Rufous Nightjar, which away from Central and South America occurs only on St. Lucia, is locally common in the northeast, from Grande Anse south to Dennery, and may also still occur around Anse la Raye on the west coast
St. Lucia Pewee	the endemic *latirostris* race of Lesser Antillean Pewee is widespread and fairly common

Other Caribbean Endemics
Seventeen of the 51 Caribbean endemics not confined to single countries, islands or archipelagos occur on St. Lucia. They are: ten of the 14 species confined to the Lesser Antilles, but not restricted to single islands, namely Lesser Antillean Swift, Purple-throated Carib, Lesser Antillean Flycatcher, White-breasted Thrasher* (about 100 survive on St. Lucia, where they are much harder to see than on Martinique, the only other island where it occurs), Grey Trembler (more common than on Martinique, the only other island where it occurs), Brown Trembler, Scaly-breasted Thrasher, Forest Thrush* (possibly extirpated), Lesser Antillean Bullfinch and Lesser Antillean Saltator; one that occurs only on St. Lucia, Puerto Rico and Barbuda, Adelaide's Warbler; one confined to the Lesser Antilles and Puerto Rico, Lesser Antillean Pewee (*latirostris*); and five more widespread species, Bridled Quail-Dove, Green-throated Carib, Antillean Crested Hummingbird, Rufous-throated Solitaire and Antillean Euphonia.

Caribbean Near-Endemics
Eight of the 18 species nearly endemic to the Caribbean occur on St. Lucia: Scaly-naped Pigeon, Zenaida Dove, Caribbean Elaenia, Caribbean Martin (mainly Feb–Aug), Pearly-eyed Thrasher, Black-whiskered Vireo, Black-faced Grassquit and Carib Grackle. In addition, the *pet-*

echia group of Yellow Warbler, known as 'Golden Warbler', which is also nearly endemic to the Caribbean, is represented by the *babad* race.

Other Birds
Over 160 species have been recorded on St. Lucia. Non-endemic specialities and spectacular species not previously mentioned include Red-billed (mainly Jan–Jun) and White-tailed (mainly Mar–Jul) Tropicbirds, Brown Booby, Magnificent Frigatebird, Masked Duck, Bridled and Sooty Terns, Brown Noddy (all three mainly Apr–Aug), Eared Dove, Ruddy Quail-Dove, Rufous Nightjar (endemic *otiosus* race), Black Swift (mainly Apr–Sep), House Wren, Tropical Mockingbird and Bare-eyed Thrush.

Expectations
It is possible to see all three known surviving endemics, all nine of the known extant widespread Lesser Antilles endemics which occur on the island and Adelaide's Warbler within a few days, but don't expect many more than 50 species even during a long trip.

The black-and-orange St. Lucia Oriole* is widespread on the island

From Cap Moule à Chique, the spectacular headland near the Hewanorra international airport at the southeast end of St. Lucia, it is possible, with a telescope, to see Red-billed (mainly Jan–Jun) and the occasional White-tailed (mainly Mar–Jul) Tropicbirds, and Bridled and Sooty Terns (both mainly Apr–Aug) around the **Maria Islands**, which are just offshore. The main seabird breeding season is May–July, when access to the islands is restricted but expensive boat trips are organised by the St. Lucia National Trust (tel. 452 5005/453 2479) and the Eastern Caribbean Natural Areas Management Programme (ECNAMP), and they can be arranged at Anse de Sables visitor centre on the mainland. Other possibilities include Audubon's Shearwater (mainly Mar–Jul), Brown Booby and Magnificent Frigatebird, but most seabirds are potentially more likely to be seen on boat trips organised by the St. Lucia Whale and Dolphin Watching Association, PO Box 1114, Castries, St. Lucia, West Indies (tel. 452 9350, fax. 452 9806). These trips primarily search for sperm whales and dolphins, though Bryde's, humpback, killer and pilot whales have also been recorded in the island's offshore waters.

North of Cap Moule à Chique, the large, mangrove-fringed **Savannes Bay**, part of which is a nature reserve, together with Eau Piquant Lagoon and the surrounding fields at the bay's southern end, attract a variety of waterbirds including passage and wintering shorebirds such as Short-billed Dowitcher, Willet, and Semipalmated, Western, Least and Stilt Sandpipers, as well as Belted Kingfisher. The beach café area at **Point Sable** (look for Red-billed Tropicbird offshore, mainly Jan–Jun) is a good place to see the localised Eared Dove, and the area around the airport and Vie Fort is the best on the island for Shiny Cowbird and the introduced Grassland Yellow-Finch.

EDMUND FOREST RESERVE

The montane forest above 500 m in this reserve in south central St. Lucia supports all three known extant endemics and seven widespread Lesser Antilles endemics, including Grey Trembler, as well as Rufous-throated Solitaire and Adelaide's Warbler.

St. Lucian Endemics
St. Lucia Parrot*, St. Lucia Black Finch*, St. Lucia Oriole*.

St. Lucian and Martinique Endemics
Grey Trembler.

Other Lesser Antillean Endemics
Lesser Antillean Swift, Purple-throated Carib, Lesser Antillean Flycatcher, Scaly-breasted Thrasher, Lesser Antillean Bullfinch, Lesser Antillean Saltator.

Localised Caribbean Endemics
Lesser Antillean Pewee, Adelaide's Warbler.

Other Caribbean Endemics
Green-throated Carib, Antillean Crested Hummingbird, Rufous-throated Solitaire.

Caribbean Near-Endemics
Scaly-naped Pigeon, Zenaida Dove, Caribbean Elaenia, Pearly-eyed Thrasher, Black-faced Grassquit.

Others
Broad-winged Hawk, Ruddy Quail-Dove, Mangrove Cuckoo, Grey Kingbird, Shiny Cowbird. (Other species recorded here include Black Swift (mainly Apr–Sep), Bare-eyed Thrush and Antillean Euphonia).

The more convenient western approach from near Soufrière was blocked by a landslide in the late 1990s, but by April 2000 it was again possible to reach the reserve from here, albeit via a badly pot-holed road perhaps difficult without a high-clearance 4WD. Using this approach it will take about two hours to reach the reserve from Castries at the northwest end of the island. East of Soufrière take the road from Fond St. Jacques to the hamlet of Morne Fond St. Jacques and continue until you reach a parking area where a broad, well-maintained trail through the reserve begins. St. Lucia Parrots* may fly over the approach road but are more likely to be seen over clearings along the trail, several of which are present in the first km. St. Lucia Oriole* can also be seen along the approach road, in the orchards a short distance before from the parking area, but again should be encountered in the forest. The trail continues through the reserve to the adjacent **Quilesse Forest Reserve** and what is known as the Transinsular Rainforest Walk eventually reaches Mahaut, accessible by road from the east coast.

To reach the reserves from the east turn west near Micoud in response to the small 'Nature Reserve Trail' sign, park after 10.5 km and bird on foot. Alternatively, turn west 3.7 km south of the 'Nature Reserve Trail' sign at the junction with bus shelters on both sides of the road, and after 2.7 km bear right towards Desruisseaux, then after a further 4.2 km bear left off the paved road and head through banana plantations. Continue straight on after a further 1.1 km, then turn left after a further 0.9 km where there should be a sign 'Nature Trail'. Turn right after 0.5 km and continue 0.9 km to the end of the track, a parking area and picnic shelter. From here head left on the rough figure-of-eight trail system, turning left again at the central crossroads, to reach the observation platform at about 378 m, from where it is possible to see St. Lucia Parrot*. By walking most trails it should also be possible to see many of the other birds listed above, including Grey Trembler, St. Lucia Black Finch* (most likely in dense understorey) and St. Lucia Oriole*.

Accommodation: it may be possible to stay in the basic cabins at the reserve with prior permission from the Forestry Department (tel. 450 2078/2231, fax. 450 2287).

So called because of its habit of drooping and shaking its wings when agitated, the Grey Trembler enlivens the avifaunas of St. Lucia and Martinique

Species recorded in the **Anse Chastanet** area just northwest of Soufrière on the west coast include White-tailed Tropicbird (mainly Mar–Jul), Mangrove Cuckoo, Green-throated Carib, Belted Kingfisher, Caribbean Elaenia, Lesser Antillean Pewee, Lesser Antillean Flycatcher, Grey Trembler, Scaly-breasted Thrasher, Bare-eyed Thrush, Adelaide's Warbler,

Lesser Antillean Saltator and St. Lucia Oriole*. The endemic race of Rufous Nightjar has been recorded around the town of **Anse la Raye** further north on the west coast, though it became very difficult to locate here in the 1990s. Try the tracks in the dry, open scrubby woodland on the hillside south of the town, especially in Feb–Jul when the species is most likely to be calling.

Scaly-naped Pigeon, Ruddy Quail-Dove, Mangrove Cuckoo, Lesser Antillean Pewee, Lesser Antillean Flycatcher, Grey Trembler, Adelaide's Warbler, Antillean Euphonia, St. Lucia Black Finch* and St. Lucia Oriole* have all been recorded on the forested slopes of **Piton Flor**, which rises to 570 m in the centre of the island. From Castries head southeast to the village of Forestière, which is about 30 minutes by road. This route is passable in a 2WD, except the last few hundred metres, which are too steep and rough, and ends at a visitor centre, from where a trail ascends the mountain for about 2.4 km.

Most of the few records of the possibly extinct Semper's Warbler* come from the montane forest around 550 m on the **Barre de l'Isle**, the island's central ridge, south of Piton Flor, and birders with the time, energy and passion to spare should not miss the opportunity, albeit slim, to try and track down this species, which has not definitely been recorded since 1961 and is so little known that its song and nest remain undescribed. The Barre de l'Isle is traversed by the main cross-island road between Castries and Dennery, so it may be worth exploring from there, perhaps with a local guide along the Barre de l'Isle Rainforest Walk which starts at the high point of the road and leads south to Mount La Combe. To arrange a guide contact the Forestry Department (tel. 450 2078/2231, fax. 450 2287).

From the peninsula known as **Pigeon Island**, an Historic and National Park, at the northwest tip of St. Lucia, it is possible, with a telescope, to see the Brown Booby colony (Mar–Oct) on the **Burgot Rocks** to the north. They are occasionally joined by Red-footed Boobies, while other species possible offshore here include Royal Tern, and the coastal scrub and grassland between Pigeon Island and the town of Gros Islet, just to the south, support Mangrove Cuckoo, Yellow Warbler and the introduced Grassland Yellow-Finch. Other places at the north end of the island worth looking for seabirds from include Pointe de Cap and Pointe Hardy, while species recorded at **La Sport**, just north of Cap Estate, include Mangrove Cuckoo, Caribbean Elaenia, Brown Trembler, Bare-eyed Thrush, Adelaide's Warbler and Lesser Antillean Saltator.

RAVINE LA CHALOUPE

On St. Lucia the rare White-breasted Thrasher* is restricted to dry, wooded ravines along the northeast coast and Fregate Island, and the best place to look for this excellent bird is in the remote Ravine La Chaloupe near Grande Anse, the island's longest beach. This is also the best area on the island for the endemic race of Rufous Nightjar, and other species here include Adelaide's Warbler and St. Lucia Black Finch*.

This part of the island is accessible only via very rough tracks, so birders without a 4WD with high clearance may have to walk several km to reach the best habitat. It is also easy to get lost here so take a detailed map and plenty of food and water. Better still enlist some local help.

Moses Wilford, a Forestry Officer who lives in Desbarra, the gateway to the area, has been recommended and can be contacted at work (tel. 450 2078/2231) or home (tel. 450 6080).

St. Lucian Endemics
St. Lucia Black Finch*, St. Lucia Oriole*.

St. Lucian and Martinique Endemics
White-breasted Thrasher*.

Other Lesser Antillean Endemics
Lesser Antillean Flycatcher, Brown Trembler, Scaly-breasted Thrasher, Lesser Antillean Saltator.

Localised Caribbean Endemics
Bridled Quail-Dove, Lesser Antillean Pewee, Adelaide's Warbler.

Caribbean Near-Endemics
Scaly-naped Pigeon, Caribbean Martin (mainly Feb–Aug), Black-faced Grassquit.

Localised Specialities
Rufous Nightjar.

Others
Brown Booby, Roseate, Bridled and Sooty Terns, Brown Noddy (all four mainly Apr–Aug), Ruddy Quail-Dove, Mangrove Cuckoo, House Wren, Bare-eyed Thrush. (Other species recorded here include Red-billed Tropicbird (mainly Jan–Jun), Yellow-crowned Night-Heron, Masked Duck and Yellow Warbler).

Other Wildlife
Fer-de-lance (introduced), green, hawksbill and leatherback sea-turtles (all three mainly Mar–Sep).

Head east from Castries to Babonneau and Desbarra. The track becomes passable only with a 4WD beyond Desbarra so birders with 2WDs or who have used a bus to get this far will have to walk the remaining few km to the ravine. After fording La Sorcière stream (dangerous after recent rain) walk east from the small farm buildings in the old village of Caille Des along the northern stream in the **Ravine La Chaloupe**, known as D'hers, to a boulder beach, then head south to the mouth of the southern stream in the ravine and head inland to search for the thrasher, which can be quite confiding as it feeds among the leaf litter.

The thrasher also occurs in the **Ravine La Petite Anse**, east of Boquis, which is north of Desbarra, and it and Rufous Nightjar have also been recorded as far south, along the northeast coast, as Dennery. The best place to look for the nightjar, which calls mostly in Feb–Jul, in this area, is in the dry scrub east of Desbarra. Masked Duck has been recorded on a small lake south of the old airstrip inland of **Grande Anse** beach, which is in the valley north of Ravine La Chaloupe and can be reached from there or by turning left at the Desbarra town sign onto the track to the old airstrip. Brown Noddy breeds on cliffs by this beach and the St. Lucia Naturalists Society, together with the Fisheries Division (tel.

**RAVINE LA CHALOUPE AND
GRANDE ANSE AREA**

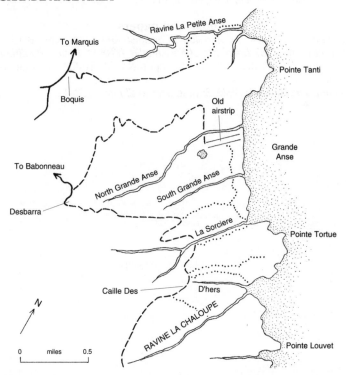

452 2611), organise boat trips to look for sea-turtles, which lay their eggs in the beach. Beware of the dangerous riptide if swimming at Grande Anse, and of the poisonous fer-de-lance snake and chiggers throughout the area.

In addition to White-breasted Thrasher*, **Fregate Island**, a nature reserve off the east coast, also supports a colony of Magnificent Frigatebird and the boa constrictor (*Constrictor orophias*) known locally as tête chien. The island, where Red-billed Tropicbird has also been recorded, may be accessible by boat from Praslin, but is closed to visitors in May–Jul when the frigatebirds nest.

ADDITIONAL INFORMATION

Addresses
Donald Anthony, a Forestry Department Wildlife Officer (home tel. 452 1799, office tel. 450 2078/2231, e-mail: anthonydonald@hotmail.com), is happy to help birders plan their trip and guide them once there.
St. Lucia Naturalists Society, PO Box 783, Castries, St. Lucia, West Indies.
St. Lucia National Trust, PO Box 525, Castries, St. Lucia, West Indies.

St. Lucia Tourist Board, Pointe Seraphine, PO Box 221, Castries, St. Lucia, West Indies (tel. 452 5968, fax. 453 1121).

Books and papers

The Birds of St Lucia: An Annotated Checklist, Keith, A. R. 1997. BOU.

Report of the 1987 University of East Anglia–ICBP St. Lucia Expedition, Babbs, S. *et al.* 1988. ICBP Study Report No. 33 (BirdLife International).

Saint Lucia, Butler, P. 1989. Supplement to *El Pitirre* 2: 7–11.

ST.-MARTIN

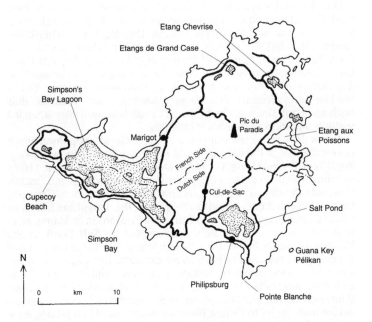

This small, hilly Leeward Island in the northern Lesser Antilles supports a few Caribbean endemics, but it is more renowned for its bays and lagoons, which attract many passage shorebirds, and its offshore islets and cays which support breeding seabirds.

International flights land in the south of the island, which is part of the Netherlands Antilles and known as Sint Maarten. The northern half is part of the French West Indies and known as St.-Martin, but there are no customs posts so visitors are free to travel between the two without hassle from the authorities, in hired vehicles, taxis and buses. Over 1 million people visit the small 89 km² island each year, so it can be rather crowded, especially in November–April, and the predominantly poor roads are usually very busy even in the low season. Nearly everyone speaks English in the Dutch half but few do so in the French part. Due to hurricane damage, building works continue apace, but there is usually a wide variety of accommodation available, as well as plenty of places to eat, both of which are more expensive in the French zone. The hurricane season is June–November.

The south of the island is relatively flat compared to the north, where the land rises to 424 m at Pic du Paradis. Inland, there are remnant dry woodlands where the trees have not been cleared to make way for cultivation, and several lakes and lagoons, one of which, Simpson's Bay Lagoon, occupies much of the western arm of the island. The coast is a splendid mixture of beautiful bays and white-sand beaches. Contemporary conservation problems include continuing habitat loss, pollution, outdated legislation and hurricanes (Hurricane Luis wreaked considerable damage in the south in September 1995), thus, in order to conserve the flora and fauna there is an urgent need for protected areas and updated planning legislation.

Over 100 bird species have been recorded, of which about 40 have bred. Specialities and spectacular species include Audubon's Shearwater (mainly Mar-Jul), Red-billed (mainly Dec–May) and White-tailed (mainly Mar–Jul) Tropicbirds, Magnificent Frigatebird, Bridled and Sooty Terns, Brown Noddy (all three mainly Apr–Aug), Zenaida Dove, Green-throated Carib, Antillean Crested Hummingbird, Caribbean Elaenia, Caribbean Martin (mainly Feb–Aug), Pearly-eyed Thrasher, Yellow Warbler (*bartholemica*), Black-faced Grassquit, Lesser Antillean Bullfinch and Carib Grackle. The best time to visit is in April–May when the seabirds and most landbirds are breeding.

A slow drive with a few stops on the N7, the **Great Loop Road** which covers the east of the island, should reveal the likes of Brown Booby, Royal Tern, Zenaida Dove, Green-throated Carib, Antillean Crested Hummingbird, Caribbean Elaenia, Grey Kingbird, Caribbean Martin (mainly Feb–Aug), Pearly-eyed Thrasher, Yellow Warbler, Black-faced Grassquit, Lesser Antillean Bullfinch and Carib Grackle. The road passes Étangs de Grand Case, Étang Chevrise and Étang aux Poissons in St.-Martin, all of which are worth scanning for shorebirds, but the **Salt Pond**, in Sint Maarten, is usually better, even though it is slowly being drained and developed as the town of Philipsburg expands. This large lagoon has attracted a wide range of passage and some wintering shorebirds, including Short-billed Dowitcher, and Semipalmated, Western, Least, White-rumped and Stilt Sandpipers. In Sint Maarten it is worth making a detour from the N7 to **Pointe Blanche**, southeast of Philipsburg, especially in Dec–May, when Red-billed Tropicbirds usually breed in the cliffs. Other sites worth visiting in the south of the island include the hillside park in the **Cul-de-Sac** area northwest of the Salt Pond, and the marine park, which includes the adjacent coastline, between Oyster Bay and **Cupecoy Beach** on the south coast of the western arm, both of which are managed by the local Nature Foundation (tel. 20267, fax. 20268).

It may be possible to charter a boat to visit the cays between the island and St Barthélémy, about 20 km to the southeast, where breeding seabirds include Red-billed (mainly Dec–May) and White-tailed (mainly Mar–Jul) Tropicbirds, Gull-billed, Roseate, Least, Bridled and Sooty Terns, and Brown Noddy (all mainly Apr–Aug).

ADDITIONAL INFORMATION

Addresses

Sint Maarten Tourist Office, 3rd Floor, Imperial Building, 23 Walter Nisbeth Road, Philipsburg, Sint Maarten, West Indies (tel. 22337, fax. 22734; web site: www.st-maarten.com).

St.-Martin Tourist Office, Port de Marigot, 97150 St.-Martin, West Indies (tel. 875721/3, fax. 875643, e-mail: stmartin@megatropic.com; web site: www.st-martin.org).

ST. VINCENT

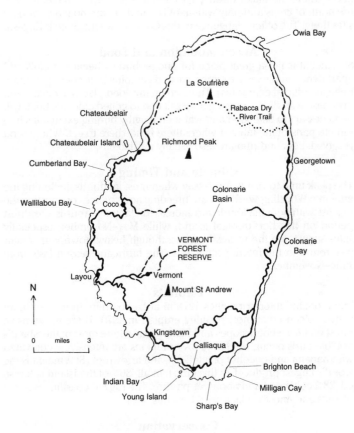

INTRODUCTION

Summary

This well-forested, mountainous small island in the southern Lesser Antilles supports an endemic parrot and warbler, as well as half of the 14 Lesser Antillean endemics not confined to single islands, including Grenada Flycatcher and Lesser Antillean Tanager, which otherwise occur only on Grenada and the Grenadines.

Size

At about 30 km long and up to 18 km wide St. Vincent covers 345 km².

Getting Around

Driving around St. Vincent can be dangerous because the narrow roads, most of which are confined to the coast, are busy with taxis and minibuses which zap around the island at high speed and with little regard for the safety of their passengers, let alone other road-users. There are very few road signs making a detailed map useful, though most locals know where the major birding sites are. It is possible to travel around the north of the island only with a 4WD, but there are no major birding sites there. The official language of this Commonwealth State is English.

Accommodation and Food

St. Vincent is not a great place for budget birders because hotels and apartment complexes are expensive and camping is discouraged (there being no official campsites). There are many good places to eat around the coast, with dishes ranging from salt cod to grilled chicken, but it will be necessary to take food and water on lengthy birding excursions into remote parts of the interior where there is nowhere to eat. Where food is served, beer and rum are also usually available.

Climate and Timing

The peak time to visit is April–May when most landbirds, including the endemic Whistling Warbler*, are breeding and chances of boosting the trip list with some seabirds are increased. January–April is the driest period on this hot, tropical island, while May–November, especially July–August, are the wettest months, though heavy downpours occur year-round in the interior highlands. The hurricane season lasts from June–November.

Habitats

The montane interior reaches 1272 m at La Soufrière in the north, an active volcano that most recently erupted in 1979. There is extensive forest on the steepest slopes and high ridges, where most of the island's notable birds occur, but fertile lower regions are intensively cultivated with banana and coconut plantations, and arrowroot (St. Vincent is the world's largest producer of this crop). In all, 36% of the island is forested, 28% cultivated and about 5% pasture. The rugged coastline is a mix of cliffs and, mostly, black-sand beaches.

Conservation

The major problems that need to be overcome if the two threatened species, as well as the relatively common and widespread birds, are to survive, include habitat loss and degradation, inadequate legislation, hunting, egg collecting and a lack of environmental awareness.

Endemics

Two species are endemic to St Vincent:

St Vincent Parrot*	Uncommon and primarily restricted to the upper Buccament Valley (where it is usually easy to see at Vermont Forest Reserve), and the Wallilabou and Cumberland Valleys; at least 500 were present in 1990
Whistling Warbler*	Rare and primarily restricted to the Buccament Valley (where it is usually easy to see at Vermont Forest Reserve), and the Colonarie and

Perserence Valleys, as well as the
Richmond Peak area

Other Endemics

Eleven of the 51 Caribbean endemics not confined to single countries,
islands or archipelagos occur on St. Vincent. They are: seven of the 14
species confined to the Lesser Antilles, which occur on more than one
island, namely Lesser Antillean Swift, Purple-throated Carib, Grenada
Flycatcher (which otherwise occurs only on Grenada and the Grenadines), Brown Trembler, Scaly-breasted Thrasher, Lesser Antillean Tanager (which otherwise occurs only on Grenada) and Lesser Antillean
Bullfinch; and four more widespread species, Green-throated Carib,
Antillean Crested Hummingbird, Rufous-throated Solitaire and Antillean Euphonia.

Caribbean Near-Endemics

Seven of the 18 species nearly endemic to the Caribbean occur on St.
Vincent: Scaly-naped Pigeon, Zenaida Dove, Caribbean Elaenia, Carib-
bean Martin (mainly Feb–Aug), Black-whiskered Vireo, Black-faced
Grassquit and Carib Grackle. In addition, the *petechia* group of Yellow
Warbler, known as 'Golden Warbler', which is also nearly endemic to
the Caribbean, occurs outside the breeding season (Sep–Feb).

Other Birds

Over 110 species have been recorded on St. Vincent. Non-endemic specialities and spectacular species not mentioned above include Magnificent Frigatebird, Common Black-Hawk, Bridled and Sooty Terns, Brown
Noddy (all three mainly Apr–Aug), Eared Dove, Ruddy Quail-Dove,
Black (mainly Apr–Sep) and Short-tailed (mainly Mar–Sep) Swifts, Yellow-bellied Elaenia, House Wren, Tropical Mockingbird, and Cocoa
and Bare-eyed Thrushes.

Expectations

It is possible to see both endemics, as well as all seven of the widespread Lesser Antillean endemics that occur on the island, in a single
day, but don't expect to see many more than 50 species during a trip of
a few days, or even longer.

The 8 ha **Kingstown Botanical Gardens** on the western outskirts of the
island's capital, which can be reached by turning east off Leeward Highway just as it begins to climb north out of town, support Smooth-billed
Ani, Green-throated Carib, Antillean Crested Hummingbird, Short-tailed
Swift (mainly Mar–Sep), Yellow-bellied Elaenia, House Wren, Bare-
eyed Thrush, Black-faced Grassquit and Carib Grackle, as well as the all-
black form of Bananaquit, which dominates the population of this species on St. Vincent (and Grenada).

VERMONT FOREST RESERVE

The extensive montane forest in this reserve is the best on the island in
which to look for the endemic parrot and warbler, and all seven of the
widespread Lesser Antillean endemics that occur on the island.

St. Vincent Endemics
St. Vincent Parrot*, Whistling Warbler*.

Localised Lesser Antillean Endemics
Grenada Flycatcher, Lesser Antillean Tanager.

Other Lesser Antillean Endemics
Lesser Antillean Swift, Purple-throated Carib, Brown Trembler, Scaly-breasted Thrasher, Lesser Antillean Bullfinch.

Other Caribbean Endemics
Antillean Crested Hummingbird, Antillean Euphonia.

Caribbean Near-Endemics
Scaly-naped Pigeon, Caribbean Elaenia, Black-faced Grassquit.

Others
Common Black-Hawk, Broad-winged Hawk, Ruddy Quail-Dove, Black Swift (mainly Apr–Sep), Yellow-bellied Elaenia, House Wren, Cocoa Thrush, Bananaquit.

To reach the reserve head northwest from Kingstown on the Leeward Highway for about 8 km then, 200 m north of a river bridge, turn northeast onto the road that ascends Buccament Valley and follow signs for 'Vermont Nature Centre'. After about 7 km turn left in the village of Vermont and continue to the poorly signed right-hand turning, by a house, which leads to the small parking area where the main trails begin, at the top of a set of steps. Head uphill on the Loop Trail to the observation platform at 442 m, from where parrots can be seen. Continue on the Loop Trail to look for Whistling Warbler* and most other forest specialists. Another good place to look for parrots can be reached by continuing straight at the house by the poorly signed right-hand turning, on a very steep, narrow road which eventually ends at a turning circle. From here there is a superb view across a large expanse of forest, which parrots frequently fly over. Common Black-Hawks, which feed on yellow crabs that inhabit the mountain streams, can also be seen soaring above the forest here, and from the observation platform on the Loop Trail. Some species, including Caribbean Elaenia and Lesser Antillean Tanager, also occur in second growth and may be easier to find alongside the road below the reserve. Beware of chiggers, mosquitoes and wet weather throughout the Vermont area.

Most of the species listed for Vermont Forest Reserve, but probably not St. Vincent Parrot*, may also be seen around **Mount St. Andrew**, which rises to 736 m north of Kingstown. To reach here turn northeast off the Leeward Highway a little way northwest of Kingstown on the track which leads to the radio mast at the summit.
Large schools of Atlantic spotted and spinner dolphins occur in the waters west of St. Vincent and are occasionally joined by Atlantic bottlenose dolphins, as well as humpback and pilot whales. It is possible to look for these cetaceans on boat trips from Calliaqua, southeast of Kingstown; such trips are usually most successful in Apr–Sep. Brown Booby and Magnificent Frigatebird may be the avian highlights of such trips, as both occur in **Indian Bay**, especially around Young Island, not

The aptly named Whistling Warbler is endemic to St. Vincent, where it
is locally fairly common but usually shy and secretive*

far from Calliaqua. A wider variety of seabirds may be seen off the southern or southeast coasts, notably in the **Milligan Cay** area where some
species breed. The cay is situated off the south end of Brighton Beach
where the dry scrub supports Mangrove Cuckoo. Seabirds also breed on
the cliffs near **Chateaubelair** on the northwest coast. At the north end
of the island it is possible to hike to the rim of the 1.6 km-wide, 213 m
deep, crater of **La Soufrière** in a couple of hours, via the Rabacca Dry
River Trail, which is best tackled with a local guide from its northeast
end.

ADDITIONAL INFORMATION

Addresses

St. Vincent and the Grenadines Department of Tourism, Finance Complex, Bay Street, PO Box 834, Kingstown, St. Vincent, West Indies (tel.
457 1502, fax. 456 2610, e-mail: tourism@caribsurf.com; web site: www.
stvincentandgrenadines.com).

Books

Birds of Grenada, St. Vincent and the Grenadines, Devas, R. P. 1970. Carenage Press.

TURKS & CAICOS ISLANDS

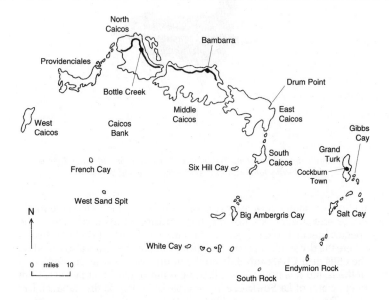

This small archipelago at the southern end of the Bahamas supports a few Caribbean endemics, including Bahama Woodstar and Cuban Crow, seabirds such as White-tailed Tropicbird and, during the winter months, the rare Kirtland's Warbler*.

The capital, Cockburn Town, is situated on Grand Turk, a tiny island at the east end of the archipelago, but the major international airport is on Providenciales, another small island, in the west of the island group. From here it is possible to reach the other major islands and cays via the internal air network. Once on the ground, on the major islands it is only possible to hire vehicles or taxis, as there is no public bus service. Where roads exist they are in fairly good condition, especially on Providenciales. The islands are a UK Dependent Territory and most people speak English. Many of the hotels are expensive, especially on Providenciales, but budget birders may be able to camp on beaches, albeit without any facilities. Locally available foods include conch and lobster, but most other dishes, except seafood and 'peas 'n' rice', are composed of at least some imported ingredients and are therefore expensive. Drinks include beer, rum and rum cocktails.

The best time to visit the Turks & Caicos Islands is in April, when northbound migrants join lingering winter visitors, including Kirtland's Warbler*, and seabirds such as White-tailed Tropicbird are breeding. Birders primarily interested in looking for Kirtland's Warbler* should visit in October–April, while those more concerned about seabirds should concentrate on April–July, although the hurricane season (and hottest period) begins in June, lasting until October. Cool northeast trade winds take the edge off the heat at this time, making for a pleasant year-round climate, with no rainy season as such.

This subtropical coral archipelago consists of 40 or so small, low-lying islands and cays, which cover 430 km², surrounded by one of the longest coral reefs on earth. There are two main island groups: the larger Caicos to the northwest and much smaller Turks to the southeast, separated by a 35 km-wide channel, known as the Turks Island Passage, which reaches a depth of 2134 m. Generally, the windward or Atlantic sides of the islands are composed of limestone cliffs and sand dunes, whereas leeward areas support scrub and mangrove-lined mudflats. There are also salt ponds on most of the larger islands. The 33 protected areas, which include 11 National Parks, ten Nature Reserves and four Sanctuaries, as well as an environmental tax, designed to fund these areas and possibly acquire more protected land, help to conserve the birds and other wildlife.

No birds are endemic to the Turks & Caicos but six of the 51 Caribbean endemics not confined to single countries, islands or archipelagos occur: West Indian Whistling-Duck*, Key West Quail-Dove, Bahama Woodstar (which otherwise occurs only in the Bahamas), Bahama Mockingbird, Cuban Crow (which occurs on North and Middle Caicos, and rarely on Providenciales, and otherwise only on Cuba) and Greater Antillean Bullfinch.

Nine of the 18 species nearly endemic to the Caribbean occur on the islands: White-crowned Pigeon, Zenaida Dove, Antillean Nighthawk (mainly May–Aug), Pearly-eyed Thrasher, Thick-billed and Black-whiskered Vireos, Kirtland's Warbler* (Oct–Apr), Northern Stripe-headed Tanager and Black-faced Grassquit. In addition, the *petechia* group of Yellow Warbler, known as 'Golden Warbler', which is also nearly endemic to the Caribbean, is represented by the *gundlachi* race.

About 190 species have been recorded in the Turks & Caicos. Non-endemic specialities and spectacular species not already mentioned include Audubon's Shearwater, White-tailed Tropicbird (mainly Mar–Jul), Brown Booby, Magnificent Frigatebird, Greater Flamingo, White-cheeked Pintail, Bridled and Sooty Terns, Brown Noddy (all three mainly Apr–Aug), Blue-grey Gnatcatcher and passage and wintering New World warblers such as Cape May, Black-throated Blue and Prairie Warblers.

The tidal mudflats and saline lagoons of the southern coasts of the Caicos Islands, together with **Caicos Bank** to the south, lie within a 450 km² wetland of international importance. A small population of Greater Flamingo frequents this area and breeds, usually in Mar–Jul, on the nature reserve at Lake Catherine, which is situated on the rugged, uninhabited island of **West Caicos**. Good birding sites on **North Caicos** include the reserves at Dick Hill Creek and Bellefield Landing Pond, Cottage Pond, Pumpkin Bluff Pond, Three Mary's Cays and Flamingo Pond (best at high tide), all of which are worth checking for Greater Flamingo, West Indian Whistling-Duck* and White-cheeked Pintail. On **Middle Caicos** head for the sand bar connecting Pelican Cay to the island, as this is a good place for shorebirds, especially at low tide. Cuban Crow occurs on both North and Middle Caicos. The mangroves and mudflats around uninhabited **East Caicos**, and the saline lagoons of **South Caicos** would also doubtless repay investigation. One of the best places for breeding seabirds, including Magnificent Frigatebird, is **French Cay** at the southern edge of Caicos Bank.

At Leeward Marina on the northeast tip of **Providenciales** it is possible to charter boats in order to look for humpback whales and dolphins such as Atlantic bottlenose, Atlantic spotted and spinner. Large numbers of humpback whales migrate south through the islands, especially through the **Turks Island Passage**, in Jan–Mar, en route to their breeding waters at Silver Bank, north of the Dominican Republic, and they may also be seen off the west coasts of the Turks Islands, including **Salt Cay**, south of Grand Turk. There are many seabirds in these waters too and southeast of **Grand Turk** Magnificent Frigatebird breeds on Penniston Cay, usually in Aug–Apr, and Sooty Tern and Brown Noddy breed on Gibbs Cay, normally in Apr–Aug.

Although widespread and locally common in the Caribbean, pelagic Brown Noddies are difficult to find away from their breeding colonies

ADDITIONAL INFORMATION

Addresses
The Turks and Caicos National Trust main office is at PO Box 261, Grand Turk, Turks & Caicos Islands. The trust also has an office on Providenciales (tel. 941 5710).
Turks and Caicos Islands Tourist Board, PO Box 128, Pond Street, Grand Turk, Turks & Caicos Islands (tel. 946 2321/2322 or 800 241 0824, fax. 946 2733, e-mail: tci.tourism@carib_surf.com, web site: www.turksandcaicostourism.com).

Books
A Birder's Guide to the Bahama Islands (including Turks and Caicos), White, A. W. 1998. ABA.
The Birds of the Turks and Caicos Islands—The Official Checklist, Bradley, P. W. 1994. NTTCI.
Birds of the Southern Bahamas: An Annotated Checklist, Buden, D. W. 1987. BOU (includes the Turks and Caicos).

VIRGIN ISLANDS

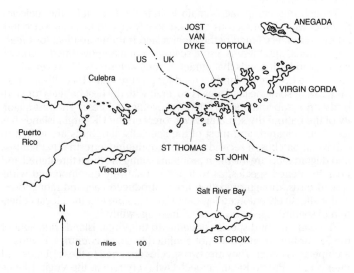

INTRODUCTION

This archipelago to the east of Puerto Rico supports several Caribbean endemics, including Bridled Quail-Dove, which is probably easier to see on the island of St. John than on any other island in the region, but the principal avian appeal is provided by the large numbers of breeding seabirds, which include both Red-billed and White-tailed Tropicbirds.

The Virgin Islands cover 498 km², 345 km² of which are an External Territory of the USA, and 153 km² of which are a UK Dependent Territory. There are three main islands within the 68 islands and cays of the US Virgin Islands, the larger, more developed, western part of the archipelago: St. Thomas, St. John and St. Croix; and four main islands in the 50 islands and cays of the UK Virgin Islands: Jost Van Dyke, Tortola, Virgin Gorda and Anegada. Most are connected by the inter-island air networks and there are ferries between St. Thomas and St. John (5 km) and St. Thomas and St. Croix (64 km) in the US Virgin Islands, and Tortola and Virgin Gorda in the UK Virgin Islands. There are local buses and taxis on Tortola, but elsewhere it is necessary to hire a vehicle to get around. The widely spoken language is English. There is a wide range of accommodation on the US Virgin Islands, including campsites, but a more limited selection in the UK Virgin Islands. Virtually all types of accommodation are more expensive during the high season (mid-December to mid-April). Fortunately the best time to visit the Virgin

Islands is at the beginning of the low season through to July, when most seabirds are breeding, but late April and May is the peak time because many of the resident landbirds are breeding, and some wintering and spring passage New World warblers may be present. The climate is hot most of the year although northeasterly trade winds help alleviate the heat and humidity.

Though the archipelago's main islands are fairly lofty the majority, together with the numerous cays, are low lying and most are surrounded by coral reefs. Much of the archipelago is therefore ideal for breeding seabirds, and there is also a scattering of mangrove-lined mudflats, lagoons and salt ponds that attract various waterbirds. However, about 75% of the US Virgin Islands is used for pasture and 11% cultivation, so only 10% or so of the land area is covered with the best habitats for landbirds; dry scrub and both dry and wet evergreen forests. The vast majority of the natural dry scrub and wet forest on the UK Virgin Islands has also been cleared, and most of the specialist landbirds are forced to survive in patches of second growth. Continuing terrestrial habitat loss and degradation are the main problems facing the three threatened and near-threatened species, as well as the relatively common and widespread birds, though predation from introduced cats and mongooses, and ineffectively enforced legislation (e.g., to prevent the illegal collection of seabird eggs) also need addressing swiftly.

There are no bird species endemic to the Virgin Islands but eight of the 51 Caribbean endemics not confined to single countries, islands or archipelagos occur. They are: two species confined to these islands and Puerto Rico, Puerto Rican Screech-Owl (very rare in the Virgin Islands where it has been recorded from St. Thomas, St. John, St. Croix, Tortola and Virgin Gorda, and possibly Guana), and Puerto Rican Flycatcher (fairly common on St. John, but rare on St. Thomas, Tortola and Virgin Gorda); and six more widespread species, namely West Indian Whistling-Duck* (rare), Bridled Quail-Dove, Antillean Mango (rare), Greenthroated Carib, Antillean Crested Hummingbird and Lesser Antillean Bullfinch (St. John and St. Croix).

Ten of the 18 species nearly endemic to the Caribbean occur on the Virgin Islands: Caribbean Coot* (rare), White-crowned and Scaly-naped Pigeons, Zenaida Dove, Antillean Nighthawk (mainly May–Aug), Caribbean Elaenia, Caribbean Martin (mainly Feb–Aug), Pearly-eyed Thrasher, Black-whiskered Vireo and Black-faced Grassquit. In addition, the *petechia* group of Yellow Warbler, known as 'Golden Warbler', which is also nearly endemic to the Caribbean, is represented by the *cruciana* race.

About 180 species have been recorded on the US Virgin Islands and around 140 on the UK Virgin Islands. Non-endemic specialities and spectacular species not mentioned above include Red-billed (mainly Nov–Apr) and White-tailed (mainly Mar–Jul) Tropicbirds, Magnificent Frigatebird, Red-footed (mainly Apr–Jun), Masked (mainly Mar–May) and Brown Boobies, White-cheeked Pintail, Bridled (c.2000 pairs, mainly Apr–Jul) and Sooty (100,000–200,000 pairs, mainly Apr–Jul) Terns, and Brown Noddy (2000–4000 pairs, mainly Apr–Jul).

US VIRGIN ISLANDS

The 51 km² island of **St. Thomas**, which reaches 472 m, is densely populated but the remnant wet forests do support some wintering New World warblers, including Black-throated Blue, Black-throated Green, Black-and-white and Worm-eating Warblers, and Ovenbird, while wetlands worth checking for shorebirds include Mangrove Lagoon and Benner Bay, Perseverence Bay Pond, and Magen's Bay. There are also breeding colonies of seabirds on several cays and islets around St. Thomas, including Cockroach (Masked Booby, mainly Mar–May), Saba, Flat, Dutchcap (Red-footed Booby, mainly Apr–Jun), Frenchcap, Little Cap, Dog and Shark. In winter (Oct–Feb) 60–100 humpback whales, as well as spinner and other dolphins, occur north of both the US and UK Virgin Islands and it may be possible to charter a boat to look for these, especially from Ramada Yacht Haven Marina on St. Thomas.

ST. JOHN

The pastures, dry scrub and evergreen forests of this 26 km² mountainous island support 21 breeding species and one, Bridled Quail-Dove, is more numerous here than on any other Caribbean island. A further 17 species have been recorded in winter or on passage, including several New World warblers.

Localised Caribbean Endemics
Bridled Quail-Dove, Puerto Rican Flycatcher.

Other Caribbean Endemics
Green-throated Carib, Antillean Crested Hummingbird, Lesser Antillean Bullfinch.

Caribbean Near-Endemics
White-crowned and Scaly-naped Pigeons, Zenaida Dove, Caribbean Elaenia, Caribbean Martin (mainly Feb–Aug), Pearly-eyed Thrasher, Black-faced Grassquit.

Passage Migrants and Winter Visitors
Yellow-throated Vireo, Northern Parula, Magnolia, Cape May, Prairie, Blackpoll and Black-and-white Warblers, American Redstart, Worm-eating Warbler, Ovenbird, Northern Waterthrush.

Others
Red-tailed Hawk, Mangrove Cuckoo, Grey Kingbird, Yellow Warbler.

The Virgin Islands National Park, which covers over 65% of the island, is probably the easiest place in the Caribbean to see Bridled Quail-Dove. There are over 20 marked trails within the park, but the 4 km-long **Reef Trail**, which starts on Centerline Road and traverses both dry and moist evergreen forests before reaching the remote Reef Bay, is arguably best for this particularly shy species, as well as Puerto Rican Flycatcher. Less likely here is Lesser Antillean Bullfinch, a species more regularly recorded along the **Lynn Point Trail** which starts just behind the visitor centre at Cruz Bay. This centre is on the north side of the harbour and is open daily from 8am to 4.30pm (tel. 776 6201). Bridled Quail-Dove also occurs at **Cinnamon Bay** on the northwest coast. Many interior roads on the island are rocky and steep, and if hiring a vehicle a 4WD would be best.

ST. CROIX

This isolated 135 km² island, which is high, wet and forested at its western end, but arid and rocky in the east, supports over 30 breeding species, and during autumn and winter it is possible to see over 75 species in a day due to the presence of a wide variety of shorebirds and New World warblers.

Localised Caribbean Endemics
West Indian Whistling-Duck*.

Other Caribbean Endemics
Green-throated Carib, Antillean Crested Hummingbird.

Caribbean Near-Endemics
White-crowned and Scaly-naped Pigeons, Zenaida Dove, Antillean Nighthawk (mainly May–Aug), Caribbean Elaenia, Pearly-eyed Thrasher, Black-faced Grassquit.

Passage Migrants and Winter Visitors
Piping Plover*, Short-billed Dowitcher, Stilt Sandpiper, Wilson's Phalarope, Yellow-billed Cuckoo, Yellow-throated Vireo, Northern Parula, Magnolia, Cape May, Prairie, Blackpoll (autumn) and Black-and-white Warblers, American Redstart, Worm-eating Warbler, Ovenbird, Northern Waterthrush, Common Yellowthroat.

Others
Brown Pelican, Yellow-crowned Night-Heron, White-cheeked Pintail, Osprey, Red-tailed Hawk, Clapper Rail, Willet, Royal, Roseate (mainly Apr–Sep) and Least (mainly May–Aug) Terns, Mangrove Cuckoo, Smooth-billed Ani, Grey Kingbird, Yellow Warbler, Shiny Cowbird. (Other species recorded here include Bridled Quail-Dove, and Blue-winged and Hooded Warblers).

Other Wildlife
Green, hawksbill and leatherback sea-turtles, humpback whale (Feb–Apr).

The salt pond, freshwater marshes, mangrove-lined mudflats and coral reefs around **Salt River Bay** on the north coast of the island form one of the most extensive wetlands in the Virgin Islands. Fortunately, the area has been declared a National Park and still supports a wide range of waterbirds, including West Indian Whistling-Duck*, shorebirds such as Piping Plover* (mainly Sep–Mar), and many passage migrant and wintering New World warblers, as well as three species of sea-turtle. The entire island acts as an important resting and refuelling site for passage shorebirds, with numbers peaking at several thousand in Sep, and other particularly good places to look, apart from Salt River Bay, include Westend Salt Pond, Great Pond, Manning Bay, Altona and Krause Lagoons, Southgate, Coakley Bay and Vessup Bay Ponds, and elsewhere on the south coast. Bridled Quail-Dove has been recorded at Salt River Bay but before Hurricane Hugo hit in 1989 was easier to find in the **Caledonia Valley** in the northwest of the island. However, it could not be found there after the hurricane up until early 1993 at least. For the latest information on birding St. Croix visit the National Parks Service Office in the old customs building on the waterfront in Christiansted. For details of boat trips and guided walks to see leatherback sea-turtles coming ashore to lay their eggs at Sandy Point (Mar–May) contact the Environmental Association, PO Box 3839, Apothecary Hall Courtyard, Company Street, Christiansted, St. Croix, US Virgin Islands 00822, USA (tel. 773 1989, 773 7545). One place where it is possible to see sea-turtles (hawksbill) in their element is on one of the underwater snorkelling trails at **Buck Island**, a National Park off the northeast coast, which also supports breeding seabirds. There is also a seabird colony on Cassava Garden.

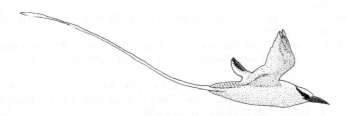

The superb Red-billed Tropicbird may grace any coast from Puerto Rico east and south through the Lesser Antilles, but in the Caribbean it is most common in the Virgin Islands

UK VIRGIN ISLANDS

The 40 km² island of **Tortola** supports Red-tailed Hawk, Scaly-naped Pigeon, Zenaida Dove, Green-throated Carib, Antillean Crested Hummingbird, Pearly-eyed Thrasher, Caribbean Martin (mainly Feb–Aug) and passage New World warblers such as Blackpoll Warbler, over 100 of which were recorded on a single day in mid-October 1998, on Mount Sage. Apart from the Sage Mountain Trail, within the 37 ha Sage Mountain National Park, which leads through remnant wet forest to the island's highest peak at 543 m, it is worth birding the Botanical Gardens in Road Town, the wetlands at Josiah's Bay on the north coast, and the western end of Beef Island.

On the 13 km² island of **Virgin Gorda**, which rises to 418 m, it is worth birding the 67 ha Gorda Peak National Park and South Sound. In 1994, four wild Greater Flamingos joined the 20 released on the 21 km² coral island of **Anegada** in 1992, and in 1995 the colony produced five young. These birds can usually be seen from the bridge over the creek on the road between the airport turn-off and Anegada Reef Hotel, and at the Flamingo Pond Bird Sanctuary. Elsewhere on the island check East End Pond. The best place for waterbirds on the tiny island of **Jost Van Dyke** is East End Harbour. West of this island there is a seabird colony on Tobago Island.

The smaller islands and cays of the UK Virgin Islands support 13 species of breeding seabirds: Red-billed (mainly Nov–Apr) and White-tailed (mainly Mar–Jul) Tropicbirds, Brown Pelican, Brown Booby (mainly Mar–Oct), Magnificent Frigatebird (mainly Aug–Apr), Laughing Gull (mainly May–Jul), Gull-billed, Royal, Roseate, Least, Bridled and Sooty Terns, and Brown Noddy (all terns, mainly Apr–Aug).

ADDITIONAL INFORMATION

Addresses

The Island Resources Foundation, 1718 P St. NW, Suite T4, Washington DC 20036, USA (tel. 265 9712) or Red Hook, St. Thomas, US Virgin Islands, USA (tel. 775 6225), deals with 'serious' wildlife enquiries.

National Parks Service HQ, Red Hook, St. Thomas, US Virgin Islands, USA.

Virgin Islands Conservation Society, PO Box 12379, St. Thomas, US Virgin Islands 00810, USA.

British Virgin Islands National Parks Trust, c/o Ministry of Natural Resources, Road Town, Tortola, British Virgin Islands, West Indies (tel. 494 3904).

British Virgin Islands Tourist Board Office, PO Box 134, Social Security Building, Wickhams Cay, Road Town, Tortola, British Virgin Islands, West Indies (tel. 494 3134, fax. 494 3866).

Books and papers

A Guide to the Birds of Puerto Rico and the Virgin Islands, Raffaele, H. A. 1989. Princeton UP.

The effect of Hurricane Hugo on bird populations on St Croix, US Virgin Islands, Wauer, R. H. and Wunderle, J. M. 1992. *Wilson Bull.* 104: 656–673.

Virgin Islands Birdlife, Wauer, R. H. 1988. Cooperative Extension Service, St. Croix University.

Observations on the birds of St. John, Virgin Islands, Robertson, W. B. 1962. *Auk* 79: 44–76.

Natural History Atlas to the Cays of the US Virgin Islands, Nellis, D. and Damman, A. 1992. Pineapple Press.

A Guide to the Natural History of St. John, Jadan, D., 1985. Environmental Studies Program, Inc. St. Thomas Graphics.

ISLAS DE PROVIDENCIA AND SAN ANDRÉS

These small islands, off the east coast of Nicaragua, support an endemic vireo, which is perhaps still fairly common in the southern third of the 52 km² San Andrés, a densely populated island popular with tourists. However, the future existence of this threatened species is in doubt because the scrubby pastures and mangroves it inhabits are being replaced with coconut palms and new-built developments. The islands are administered by Colombia and the responsibility for the conservation of this bird and the rest of the wildlife on the islands lies there.

Only one of the 51 Caribbean endemics not confined to single countries, islands and archipelagos is present: Jamaican Oriole (which otherwise occurs only on Jamaica), and it too is confined to San Andrés, where it is also fairly common. Of the six species of 18 nearly endemic to the Caribbean known to occur on the islands Caribbean Dove is also restricted to San Andrés. Another species, Thick-billed Vireo, is confined to Providencia, and the *approximans* race recorded there may, in fact, be a race of Mangrove Vireo. The remaining four Caribbean near-endemics are White-crowned Pigeon, Caribbean Elaenia (rare on both islands), Black-whiskered Vireo and Black-faced Grassquit, all of which occur on both islands. In addition, the *petechia* group of Yellow Warbler, known as 'Golden Warbler', which is also nearly endemic to the Caribbean, is represented by the rare *armouri* race on Providencia and the *flavida* race on San Andrés.

Other birds that occur on both islands include Little Blue and Green Herons, Yellow-crowned Night-Heron, White-winged Dove, Green-breasted Mango (which otherwise occurs from Mexico south to Venezuela), Belted Kingfisher, and passage and wintering New World warblers such as Northern Parula, Magnolia, Cape May, Black-throated Blue, Palm, Black-and-white and Worm-eating Warblers, American Redstart, Ovenbird, Northern Waterthrush and Common Yellowthroat. Other species apparently confined to San Andrés include Magnificent Frigatebird, Tricoloured Heron, Purple Gallinule, Royal Tern, Mangrove Cuckoo (rare), Smooth-billed Ani (rare) and Tropical Mockingbird. For birders primarily interested in seeing the endemic San Andrés Vireo* the best time to visit is May–July, during its breeding season.

REQUEST

This book is intended to be a first edition. The authors welcome contributions to the second edition and will be grateful to receive details of any errors, changes, updates and new sites you feel deserve inclusion. It would be very helpful if information could be submitted in the following format to David Brewer (Central America) and Nigel Wheatley (Caribbean), c/o A. & C. Black (Publishers) Limited, 37 Soho Square, London W1D 3QZ, UK.

A summary of the site's position (in relation to the nearest city, town or village), altitude, habitats, number of species recorded (if known), best birds, its richness compared with other localities and the best times to visit.

A species list, preferably following the taxonomic order and nomenclature in *Birds of the World: A Check List* by James Clements (Fifth Edition, 2000) and details of how to get to the site and where to look for the best birds once there, with information on trails, permits etc.

A map complete with scale and compass point and, finally, details of any recommended places to stay.

Information on where to look for the following species would also be very useful:

Central America

Rufous-bellied Chachalaca, Tamaulipas Pygmy-Owl, Tawny-collared and Spot-tailed Nightjars, Short-crested Coquette, Honduran Emerald, White-tailed and Blue-capped Hummingbirds, Veraguan Mango, Coiba Spinetail, White-throated Jay, Cozumel Thrasher (recent information), Altamira and Black-polled Yellowthroats, Bridled Sparrow (DB found an excellent area where this endemic is abundant, somewhere near Tehuacán, Puebla, but has forgotten where it was!), Black-chested, Worthen's and Sierra Madre Sparrows (additional sites), and, of course, Alfaro's Hummingbird and the mystery white-naped swift of Honduras!

Caribbean

Black-capped Petrel*, West Indian Whistling-Duck*, Masked Duck, Hook-billed Kite, Gundlach's* and Ridgway's* Hawks, Sandhill Crane, Yellow-breasted Crake, Spotted Rail, Double-striped Thick-knee, Piping Plover*, Bridled and Sooty Terns, Black and Brown Noddies, Plain Pigeon*, Jamaican Owl, Northern Potoo, White-tailed Nightjar, Fernandina's Flicker*, Giant Kingbird*, Golden Swallow*, Bicknell's Thrush*, Grey-crowned Palm-Tanager, Western and Eastern Chat-Tanagers*, Rufous-collared Sparrow, Jamaican Blackbird* and Montserrat Oriole*.

Finally, we would be extremely grateful if you could also include a statement outlining your permission to use your information in the next edition, and, finally, your name and address, so that you can be acknowledged appropriately.

CALENDAR

The following is a brief summary of the best countries, islands and archipelagos to visit according to the time of the year.

January: Bahamas, Costa Rica, Cuba, Dominican Republic, El Salvador, Grenada, Guatemala, Haiti, Honduras, Jamaica, Mexico, Nicaragua, Panama, Puerto Rico.
February: Bahamas, Belize, Costa Rica, Cuba, Dominican Republic, El Salvador, Grenada, Guatemala, Haiti, Honduras, Jamaica, Mexico, Nicaragua, Panama, Puerto Rico.
March: Bahamas, Belize, Costa Rica, Cuba (peak time with April), Dominican Republic, El Salvador, Grenada, Guatemala, Haiti, Honduras, Jamaica, Mexico (peak time with April), Nicaragua, Panama, Puerto Rico.
April: Bahamas (peak time during second half of April), Barbados, Belize, Cayman Islands, Costa Rica, Cuba (peak time with March), Dominica, Dominican Republic, El Salvador, Guadeloupe, Guatemala, Haiti, Honduras, Jamaica, Mexico (peak time with March), Martinique, Montserrat, Nicaragua, Panama, Puerto Rico, St. Lucia, St. Vincent, Virgin Islands.
May: Barbados, Belize, Cayman Islands, Dominica, Dominican Republic, Guadeloupe, Haiti, Martinique, Montserrat, Panama, Puerto Rico, St. Lucia, St. Vincent, Virgin Islands.
June: Barbados, Cayman Islands, Costa Rica, Dominica, Guadeloupe, Martinique, Montserrat, Panama, St. Lucia, St. Vincent, Virgin Islands.
July: Costa Rica, Virgin Islands.
August: Costa Rica, Virgin Islands.
September: Bahamas, Costa Rica.
October: Bahamas, Cuba, Dominican Republic, Haiti, Jamaica, Puerto Rico.
November: Bahamas, Cuba, Dominican Republic, El Salvador, Guatemala, Haiti, Honduras, Jamaica, Puerto Rico.
December: Bahamas, Costa Rica, Cuba, Dominican Republic, El Salvador, Grenada, Guatemala, Haiti, Honduras, Jamaica, Mexico, Nicaragua, Puerto Rico.

Any birders fortunate enough to have a year to go birding in Central America and the Caribbean may find that the schedule outlined below could produce the best birding and the most birds. If anyone tries this please let the authors know how they get on. Better still, if there is a willing sponsor out there contact us immediately!

The beginning of the year is a fine time to visit most of the region for it is the driest period of the year and, while searching for the numerous endemics in Mexico and the Caribbean, it is also possible to see many of the North American species that winter in the region, notably a wide range of stunning warblers. So, at the start of what may well prove to be an epic journey why not begin in the extreme north, in Baja California in northwest Mexico, where in addition to a handful of endemics it is possible to see some seabirds such as Juan Fernandez Petrel. Once the Baja endemics have been seen work your way south through Mexico, in search of the rest of the country's 97 endemics, concentrating on the Barranca del Cobre, the San Blas area, the states of Jalisco, Colima and Oaxaca, El Triunfo, Palenque and the Yucatán Peninsula.

Generally speaking, the dry season in Central America lasts until April, so continue south from Mexico through Belize, Guatemala, El Salvador, Honduras, Nicaragua and Costa Rica during February and March, before arriving in Panama for April. Many resident Central American species breed at the end of the dry season so Panama's several endemics may be easier to locate then. Some Mexican endemics may prove impossible to find in the early part of the year, so it may be wise to try and see Panama's unique birds, including Beautiful Treerunner, as swiftly as possible, allowing time to return to Mexico for the breeding season, when any previously elusive endemics may be easier to find. It is important to concentrate on the more difficult Central American species during April because there will be plenty of time later in the year to return to the region and mop up the relatively common and widespread species.

Unfortunately, March is the month to visit Cuba, so the journey through Central America should be interrupted for a week or so, in order to visit the four main sites on the island where virtually all of the 24 endemics can be found. It would be a shame to miss Bee Hummingbirds at their best, as well as the low water levels in Zapata Swamp, which mean it may not be necessary to wade for Zapata Wren. Wintering New World warblers should still be present in good numbers in March, while summer visitors such as Antillean Nighthawk and Cuban Martin should have arrived.

Late April is the time to start birding the Caribbean in earnest. Begin in the Bahamas where the endemic swallow and yellowthroat, and near-endemic woodstar, should be easy to find, while the spring passage of species which breed in North America continues. Head for Jamaica in early May, where it is usually possible to see all 28 endemics and some other localised goodies in a week or so. The rainy season usually commences during May in the Caribbean but this is when many resident endemics begin breeding so it is a good time to track down the rarer and shyer species. Wintering birds from North America will have moved north but are, in any event, rather scarce away from Cuba and Jamaica, so in mid-May proceed to the Dominican Republic, where a week should be sufficient to see virtually all of the 28 Hispaniolan endemics, including Palmchat. From there hop east to Puerto Rico, where less than a week will be required to look for the 13 species unique to that island, including the superb Elfin-woods Warbler.

By the end of May, having visited most of Central America and the main islands of the Caribbean, the vast majority of the region's endemics could be under the belt, along with many other wonderful birds. There are another 25 endemics confined to the Lesser Antilles in the southern Caribbean however, so June, when many of these are breeding, is the time to search for them. In order to see all of these, 14 of which occur on more than one island and 11 of which are single-island endemics, it is necessary to visit, from north to south, Montserrat (endemic oriole), Guadeloupe (endemic woodpecker), Dominica (two endemic parrots), Martinique (endemic oriole), St. Lucia (endemic parrot, finch and oriole), St. Vincent (endemic parrot and warbler) and Grenada (endemic dove). Most are easy to find and there may even be time for the more adventurous to leave the beaten track behind and attempt to rediscover birds such as Semper's Warbler, a St. Lucian endemic that hasn't been seen for many years.

With six months gone it is time to relax and although the beginning of July is not the ideal time to be on the Cayman Islands it is a fine place to unwind and the only place on earth, apart from Swan Island off northern Honduras, where Vitelline Warbler occurs. Once this lovely bird has been added to what will already be an incredible list of New World warblers there will be plenty of time to enjoy the seabirds that breed in this beautiful archipelago, collapse on a beach and update your notebook, before a quick trip to San Andrés for the endemic vireo.

Although the long rainy season in Costa Rica commences in April there is usually a let-up in the daily downpours for a couple of weeks in mid-July, which, fortunately, coincides with the movement of such amazing birds as Resplendent Quetzal and Three-wattled Bellbird from the dense forests where they breed to wooded pastures, and the superb Snowcap from remote high-altitude forests to more accessible lowland forests. This break in the weather, known as *veranillo*, is unpredictable, but given that such birds are easier to see during July and August, it makes Costa Rica as good a place to be as any in the region at this time of the year. Indeed, there are so many birds in Costa Rica it is worth remaining in this tiny country until late September, if only on the Caribbean slope, where it is relatively dry during this month.

During October head back north through Nicaragua and Honduras to Belize for November, before completing what should have been a fantastic excursion through Central America and the Caribbean, in Mexico, where any endemics missed earlier in the year may wrap things up very nicely.

USEFUL ADDRESSES

Clubs and Conservation Organisations

American Birding Association (ABA), PO Box 6599, Colorado Springs, CO 80934-6599, USA (tel. (800) 850 2473 or (719) 578 9703; fax. (719) 578 1480; e-mail: member@aba.org; web site: www.americanbirding. org). This organisation publishes a monthly newsletter (*Winging It*), a bimonthly magazine (*Birding*) and, in alliance with the National Audubon Society (NAS), a quarterly magazine (*American Birds*), all of which contain occasional articles on Central America and the Caribbean.

BirdLife International, Wellbrook Court, Girton Road, Cambridge CB3 0NA, UK. Membership of this vitally important organisation costs from £25 per annum; members receive a quarterly magazine (*World Birdwatch*) and an annual report.

Caribbean Conservation Corporation (CCC), 4424 NW 13th Street, Suite #A1, Gainesville, FL 32609, USA (tel. (800) 678 7853 or (352) 373 6441; web site: www.cccturtle.org).

Neotropical Bird Club (NBC), c/o The Lodge, Sandy, Bedfordshire SG19 2DL, UK (e-mail: secretary@neotropicalbirdclub.org; web site: www.neotropicalbirdclub.org). This important club aims to foster an interest in the birds of the Neotropics and to increase awareness of the importance of support for conservation in the region. Its journal, *Cotinga*, is published biannually.

RARE Center for Tropical Conservation, 1616 Walnut Street, Suite 1010, Philadelphia, Pennsylvania 19103©5310, USA (tel. (215) 735 3510; fax. (215) 735 3515; e-mail: rare@rarecenter.org). This non-profit making organisation was founded in 1973 to protect endangered tropical wildlife and ecosystems, while enhancing the effectiveness of local conservation organisations.

Society for Caribbean Ornithology, c/o Jamaica Conservation and Development Trust, 95 Dumbarton Avenue, Kingston 10, Jamaica, West Indies (e-mail: JCDT@kasnet.com).

VSO's WorldWise Tourism Campaign, 317 Putney Bridge Road, London, SW15 2PN, UK (tel. (0208) 780 7233). This campaign aims to ensure local people benefit from tourism and provides information on how travellers can play their part.

Trip Reports

Dutch Birding Travel Report Service (DBTRS), PO Box 737, NL-9700 AS Groningen, Netherlands (tel. (50) 527 4993; fax. (50) 527 2668; e-mail: dbtrs@natuurschool.com; web site: www.natuurschool.com/dbtrs). To obtain a copy of the DBTRS catalogue, which lists a very extensive selection of reports covering most of Central America and the Caribbean, send £3 or US$5 to the address above.

Foreign Birdwatching Reports and Information Service (FBRIS), organised by Steve Whitehouse, 6 Skipton Crescent, Berkeley Pendlesham, Worcestershire WR4 0LG, UK (tel. (01905) 454541; e-mail: jwhite107@aol.com). To obtain a copy of the FBRIS catalogue, which includes over 450 trip reports and other privately published items, many of which deal with most of the birding sites in Central America and the Caribbean in great detail, send £1.20 in the form of a cheque, postage stamps or postal order, or a US$5 bill to the address above.

Tour Companies

Animal Watch, Granville House, London Road, Sevenoaks, Kent TN13 1DL, UK (tel. (01732) 811838; fax. (01732) 455441; e-mail: mail@ animalwatch.co.uk; web site: www.animalwatch.co.uk).

Avian Adventures, 49 Sandy Road, Norton, Stourbridge, DY8 3AJ, UK (tel. (01384) 372013; fax. (01384) 441340; e-mail: aviantours@argonet. co.uk; web site: www.avianadventures.co.uk).

Birdfinders, 18 Midleaze, Sherborne, Dorset DT9 6DY, UK (tel./fax. (01935) 817001; e-mail: Birdfinders@compuserve.com; web site: www. birdfinders.co.uk).

Bird Holidays, 10 Ivegate, Yeadon, Leeds, LS19 7RE, UK (tel./fax. (01133) 910510; e-mail: pjw.birdholidays@care4free.net).

Birding, Finches House, Higham Green, Winchelsea, TN36 4HB, UK (tel. (01797) 223223; fax. (01797) 222911).

Birdquest, Two Jays, Kemple End, Birdy Brow, Stonyhurst, Lancashire BB7 9QY, UK (tel. (01254) 826317; fax. (01254) 826780; e-mail: birders@ birdquest.co.uk).

Birdseekers, 19 Crabtree Close, Marshmills, Plymouth, Devon PL3 6EL, UK (tel./fax. (01752) 220947; e-mail: Bird@birdseekers.freeserve.co.uk).

Birdwatching Breaks, 26 School Lane, Herne, Herne Bay, Kent CT6 7AL, UK (tel. (01227) 740799; fax. (01227) 363946; e-mail: m.finn@ ndirect.co.uk).

Borderland Tours, 2550 W. Calle Padilla, Tucson, AZ 85745, USA (tel. (800) 525 7753; e-mail: rtaylor@borderland-tours.com; web site: www. borderland-tours.com).

Eagle-Eye Tours, PO Box 2090, Point Roberts, WA 98281, USA (tel. (800) 373 5678; e-mail: birdtours@eagle-eye.com; web site: www.eagle-eye.com).

Field Guides Incorporated, 9433 Bee Cave Road, Building 1, Suite 150, Austin, TX 78733, USA (tel. (800) 728 4953 or (512) 263 7295; fax. (512) 263 0117; e-mail: fieldguides@fieldguides.com; web site: www.fieldguides. com).

Goldeneye Tours, PO Box 1121, Helena, MT 59624, USA (tel. (888) 879 1765; e-mail: john@goldeneyetours.com; web site: www.goldeneyetours. com).

Great Glen Wildlife, Sherren, Harray, Orkney KW17 2JU, Scotland, UK (tel./fax. (01856) 761604; e-mail: davidkent@onetel.net.uk).

Greentours, Rock Cottage, High Street, Longnor, Buxton, Derbyshire SK17 0PG, UK (tel./fax. (01298) 83563; e-mail: enquiries@greentours.co. uk; web site: www.greentours.co.uk).

Island Holidays, Drummond Street, Comrie, Perthshire PH6 2DS, Scotland, UK (freephone 0800 253534; tel. (01764) 670107; fax. (01764) 670958; e-mail: enquiries@islandholidays.net; web site: www. islandholidays.net).

Limosa Holidays, Suffield House, Northrepps, Norfolk NR27 0LZ, UK (tel. (01263) 578143; fax. (01263) 579251; e-mail: limosaholidays@ compuserve.com).

Naturetrek, Cheriton Mill, Cheriton, Alresford, Hampshire SO24 0NG, UK (tel. (01962) 733051; fax. (01962) 736426; e-mail: info@naturetrek. co.uk; web site: www.naturetrek.co.uk).

Observ Tours Incorporated, 3901 Trimble Road, Nashville, Tennessee 37215, USA (tel. (615) 292 2739; e-mail: observinc@aol.com).

Ornitholidays, 29 Straight Mile, Romsey, Hampshire SO51 9BB, UK (tel. (01794) 519445; fax. (01794) 523544; e-mail: ornitholidays@ compuserve.com; web site: www.ornitholidays.co.uk).

Ornithology Expeditions, 6418 Wolcott Court, Dublin, Ohio 43017, USA (tel. (734) 850-9332; toll-free (N Am.) (877) 247-3397; e-mail: expeditions@belizebirds.com; web site: www.belizebirds.com).

Quest Nature Tours, 1170 Sheppard Ave W, Suite 45, Totonto ON M3K 2A3 (tel. (416) 633-5666; toll-free (800)387-1483; fax. (416) 633-8667).

Speyside Wildlife, 9 Upper Mall, Grampian Road, Aviemore, Inverness, PH22 1RH, Scotland, UK (tel./fax. (01479) 812498; e-mail: speyside-wildlife@msn.com).

Sunbird, PO Box 76, Sandy, Beds, Bedfordshire SG19 1DF, UK (tel. (01767) 682969; fax. (01767) 692481; e-mail: sunbird@sunbird.demon. co.uk; web site: www.sunbird.demon.co.uk).

The Travelling Naturalist, PO Box 3141, Dorchester, Dorset DT1 2XD, UK (tel. (01305) 267994; fax. (01305) 265506; e-mail: jamie@naturalist. co.uk; web site: www.naturalist.co.uk).

Turaco Tours, 15 Hillcrest Lane, Orono ON L0B 1M0 (tel. (905) 983-9384; e-mail: turaco@sympatico.com).

Victor Emanuel Nature Tours, 2525 Wallingwood Drive, Suite 1003, Austin, Texas 78746, USA (tel. (800) 328 8368 or (512) 328 5221; fax. (512) 328 2919; e-mail: info@ventbird.com; web site: www.ventbird. com).

Wildlife Worldwide, 170 Selsdon Road, South Croydon, Surrey CR2 6PJ, UK (tel. (0208) 667 9158; fax. (0208) 667 1960; e-mail: sales@wildlife-worldwide.com; web site: www.wildlife-worldwide.com).

Wildside Birding Tours, 14 Marchwood Center, Exton, PA 19341, USA (tel. (888) 875 9453; e-mail: wildsident@aol.com; web site: www. adventurecamera.com).

Wildwings, First Floor, 577/579 Fishponds Road, Fishponds, Bristol BS16 3AF, UK (tel. (0117) 9658 333; brochureline (0117) 9375 689; fax. (0117) 9375 681; e-mail: Wildinfo@wildwings.co.uk; web site: www. wildwings.co.uk). This is also a travel agency that specializes in arranging birding holidays.

Winchester Tours Limited, PO Box 706, New London, New Hampshire 03257, USA (tel. (800) 391 2473; e-mail: wintours@juno.com).

Wings, 1643 North Alvernon, Suite 105B, Tucson, AZ 85712©3350, USA (tel. (520) 320 9868; fax. (520) 320 9373; e-mail: wings@wingsbirds.com; web site: www.wingsbirds.com).

Zegrahm Expeditions, 1414 Dexter Avenue North, Suite 327, Seattle, WA 98109, USA (tel. (800) 628 8747 or (206) 285 4000; fax. (206) 285 5037; e-mail: zoe@zeco.com or zegrahm@accessone.com; web site: www.zeco.com).

Booksellers

NHBS Mailorder Bookstore, 2–3 Wills Road, Totnes, Devon TQ9 5XN, UK (tel. (01803) 865913; fax. (01803) 865280; e-mail: nhbs@nhbs.co.uk; web site: www.nhbs.com).

Subbuteo Books, The Rea, Upton Magna, Shrewsbury, Shropshire SY4 4UR, UK (tel. (0870) 010 9700; fax. (0870) 010 9699; e-mail: info@ wildlifebooks.com; web site: www.wildlifebooks.com).

Centurion Books (mainly antiquarian and secondhand), 2 Roman Quay, High Street, Fordingbridge, Hampshire SP6 1RL, UK (tel./fax. (01425) 657988).

Mapsellers

The Map Shop, 15 High Street, Upton upon Severn, Worcestershire WR8 0HJ, UK (tel. (01684) 593146; fax. (01684) 594559; e-mail: Themapshop@ btinternet.com; web site: www.themapshop.co.uk).

Stanfords, 12–14 Long Acre, Covent Garden, London WC2E 9LP, UK (shop tel. (0207) 836 1915; shop/mail order fax. (0207) 836 0189; mail order tel. (0207) 836 1321).

Audio CDs and Cassettes, Books, CD-ROMS, DVDs and Videos

American Birding Association (ABA), PO Box 6599, Colorado Springs, CO 80934-6599, USA. This organisation publishes a very detailed catalogue (toll free ordering tel. (800) 634 7736; other tel. (719) 578 0607); toll free ordering fax. (800) 590 2473; other fax. (719) 578 9705; e-mail: abasales@abasales.com; web site: www.americanbirding.org/ abasales/salecatal.htm).

BirdGuides, Jack House, Ewden, Sheffield, South Yorkshire S36 4ZA, UK (freephone 0800 919391; other tel. (0114) 283 1002; e-mail: sales@ birdguides.com; web site: www.birdguides.com).

WildSounds, Dept SP, Cross Street, Salthouse, Norfolk NR25 7XH, UK (tel./fax. (01263) 741100; e-mail: sales@wildsounds.com; web site: www. wildsounds.com).

Computer Software

Ideaform Inc., 908 East Briggs, Fairfield, IA 52556, USA (tel. (800) 779 7256 or (515) 472 7256; web site: www.birdwatching.com).

Perceptive Systems, PO Box 3530, Silverdale, WA 98383, USA (tel. (800) 354 7755; web site: www.avisys.net).

Santa Barbara Software Products, 1400 Dover, Santa Barbara, CA 93103, USA (tel./fax. (805) 963 4886; e-mail: sbsp@aol.com).

Wildlife Computing, 6 Fiddlers Lane, East Bergholt, Colchester CO7 6SJ, UK (tel. (01206) 298345 or 07768 348867; fax. (01206) 298068; e-mail: sales@wildlife.co.uk; web site: www.wildlife.co.uk).

RECOMMENDED BOOKS

Regional Birding Guides

A Birder's Guide to the Lesser Antilles. Sargeant, D., 1995. Privately published, but available from most specialist booksellers.

Regional Field Guides

A Guide to the Birds of Mexico and Northern Central America. Howell, S. N. G. and Webb, S., 1995. Oxford UP.

A Field Guide to the Birds of Mexico and Adjacent Areas: Belize, Guatemala and El Salvador. Edwards, E. P., 1998. Texas UP.

A Guide to the Birds of Costa Rica. Stiles, F. G. and Skutch, A. 1989. Cornell UP.

A Guide to the Birds of Panama with Costa Rica, Nicaragua and Honduras. Ridgely, R S. and Gwynne, J. A., 1989 (Second Edition). Princeton UP.

Birds of the West Indies. Raffaele H. *et al.*, 1998. Christopher Helm.

Collins Field Guide: Birds of the West Indies. Bond J., 1985 (Fifth Edition). HarperCollins.

A Photographic Guide to the Birds of the West Indies. Flieg, M. and Sander A., 2000. New Holland.

Field Guide to the Birds of Cuba. Garrido, O. H. and Kirkconnell, A., 2000. Cornell UP.

Birds of the Eastern Caribbean. Evans P., 1990. Macmillan.

A Field Guide to the Birds of North America. Scott S. (ed.), 1999 (Third Edition). National Geographic Society.

Collins Pocket Guide: Birds of North America. ABC, 1997. HarperCollins.

The North American Bird Guide. Sibley D., 2000. Pica Press.

Handbooks and Reference Works

Handbook of the Birds of the World. Volumes 1–6 and continuing to volume 12. del Hoyo, J. *et al.* (eds.), 1992 onwards. Lynx Edicions.

Bird Families

Seabirds. Harrison, P., 1985. Christopher Helm.

Seabirds of the World: A Photographic Guide. Harrison, P., 1996 (Second Edition). Christopher Helm.

Photographic Handbook of the Seabirds of the World. Enticott, J. and Tipling, D., 1998 (Revised Edition). New Holland.

Albatrosses. Tickell, L, 2000. Pica Press.

Cormorants, Darters and Pelicans of the World. Johnsgard, P., 1993. Smithsonian Institute Press.

Wildfowl: An Identification Guide to the Ducks, Geese and Swans of the World. Madge, S and Burn, H., 1988. Christopher Helm.

Photographic Handbook of the Wildfowl of the World. Ogilvie, M. and Young, S., 1998. New Holland.

Herons and Egrets of the World: A Photographic Guide. Hancock, J., 1999. Academic Press.

The Herons Handbook. Hancock, J. and Kushlan, J., 1984. Christopher Helm.

Storks, Ibises and Spoonbills of the World. Hancock, J., 1992. Academic Press.

Raptors of the World. Ferguson-Lees J. and Christie, D. A., 2001. Christopher Helm.

A Photographic Guide to North American Raptors. Clark, W., and Wheeler, B. 1995. Academic Press.

Rails. Taylor, B., 1998. Pica Press.

Shorebirds: An Identification Guide to the Waders of the World. Hayman, P., Marchant, J. and Prater, T., 1986. Christopher Helm.

The Hamlyn Photographic Guide to the Waders of the World. Rosair, D. and Cottridge D., 1995. Hamlyn.

Terns of Europe and North America. Olsen, K. M. and Larsson, H., 1995. Christopher Helm.

Terns and Skimmers. Wilds, C. and DiCostanzo, J., due 2001. Christopher Helm.

Skuas and Jaegers. Olsen, K. M. and Larsson, H., 1997. Pica Press.

The Auks. Gaston, A. J., 1997. Oxford UP.

Pigeons and Doves. Gibbs, D. *et al.*, 2001. Pica Press.

Parrots. Juniper, T. and Parr, M., 1998. Pica Press.

Owls (with accompanying CD). König, C *et al.*, 1999. Pica Press.

Nightjars (with accompanying CD). Cleere, N. and Nurney, D., 1997. Pica Press.

Swifts. Chantler, P. and Driessens, G., 2000 (Second Edition). Pica Press.

Trogons and Quetzals of the World. Johnsgard, P., 2000.

Kingfishers, Bee-eaters and Rollers. Fry, C. *et al.*, 1992. Christopher Helm.

Toucans, Barbets and Honeyguides. Short, L. and Horne, J., due 2001. Oxford UP.

Woodpeckers. Winkler, H. and Christie, D. A., due 2001 (Second Edition). Pica Press.

Cotingas and Manakins. Green, G. and Bushell, C., due 2001. Christopher Helm.

Crows and Jays. Madge S and Burn H, 1992. Christopher Helm.

Thrushes. Clement, P. and Hathway, R., 2001. Christopher Helm.

Wrens, Dippers and Thrashers. Brewer, D. and MacKay, B. K., 2001. Christopher Helm.

A Handbook to the Swallows and Martins of the World. Turner, A. and Rose, C., 1989. Christopher Helm.

Tits, Nuthatches and Treecreepers. Harrap, S. and Quinn, D., 1995. Christopher Helm.

A Field Guide to the Warblers of North America. Dunn, J. L. and Garrett, K. L., 1997. Houghton Mifflin.

New World Warblers. Curson, J. *et al.*, 1994. Christopher Helm.

Tanagers. Isler, M. L. and P. R., 1999. Christopher Helm.

New World Blackbirds: The Icterids. Jaramillo, A. and Burke, P., 1999. Christopher Helm.

Checklists

The AOU Checklist of North American Birds: The Species of Birds of North America from the Arctic through Panama, including the West Indies. AOU, 1998 (Seventh Edition). AOU.

A Checklist of the Birds of Mexico and Belize, El Salvador, Guatemala and Honduras. Principe, B., 1999.

A Birder's Field Checklist—Birds of The Lesser Antilles. Keith, A. R. and Loftin, H., 1992.

Birds of the World: A Check List. Clements, J., 2000 (Fifth Edition). Pica Press.

A Complete Checklist of the Birds of the World. Howard, R. and Moore,

A., 1991 (Second Edition). Academic Press.

Distribution and Taxonomy of the Birds of the World. Sibley, C. G. and Monroe B. L., 1991. Yale UP.

A Supplement to the Distribution and Taxonomy of the Birds of the World. Sibley, C. G. and Monroe, B. L., 1993. Yale UP.

World Bird Species Checklist (with alternative English and scientific names). Wells, M. G., 1998. WorldList.

Conservation

Threatened Birds of the World. Stattersfield, A. J. and Capper, D. R. (eds.), 2000. BirdLife International & Lynx Edicions.

Endemic Bird Areas of the World. Stattersfield, A. J. *et al.*, 1998. BirdLife International.

Biodiversity and Conservation in the Caribbean: Profiles of Selected Islands. Johnson, T. H., 1988. BirdLife International.

Status and Conservation of West Indian Seabirds. Schreiber, E. A. and Lee, D. S. (eds.), 2000. Society of Caribbean Ornithology.

Biogeography of the West Indies, Past, Present and Future. Woods, C. A. (ed.), 1989. Sandhill Crane Press.

General Reading

A Birder's West Indies: An Island-by-Island Tour. Wauer, R. H., 1996. Texas UP.

A Bibliography of Ornithology in the West Indies. Wiley, J. W., 2000. Western Foundation of Vertebrate Zoology.

A Neotropical Companion. Kricher, J. C., 1997 (Second Edition). Princeton UP.

The Islands and the Sea: Five Hundred Years of Nature Writing from the Caribbean. Murphy, J. A. (ed.), 1992. Oxford UP.

Other Wildlife

Collins Whales and Dolphins: The Ultimate Guide to Marine Mammals. Cawardine, M., 1998. HarperCollins.

Eyewitness Handbook: Whales, Dolphins and Porpoises. Cawardine, M., 1995. Dorling Kindersley.

The Sierra Club Handbook of Whales and Dolphins of the World. Leatherwood, S. and Reeves, R. R., 1983. Sierra Club.

Whale-Watching in the West Indies. Gricks, N., 1994. IRF.

A Field Guide to the Mammals of Central America and Southeast Mexico. Reid, F. A., 1997. Oxford UP.

Neotropical Rainforest Mammals: A Field Guide. Emmons, L. H., 1997 (Second Edition). Chicago UP.

National Audubon Society Field Guide to Tropical Marine Fishes: Caribbean, Gulf of Mexico, Florida, Bahamas, Bermuda. Smith, C., 1997. Knopf.

Caribbean Reef Fishes. Randall, J. E., 1996. TFH.

Butterflies of the Caribbean and Florida. Stirling, P., 1999. Macmillan.

The Butterflies of the West Indies and South Florida. Smith, D. S., 1994. Oxford UP.

Travel

Adventuring in the Caribbean. Fleming, C. B., 1996. Sierra Club.

Travel guides published by Footprint, Lonely Planet, Moon, Rough Guides and Vacation Work (Travellers Survival Kits) cover most of Central America and the Caribbean.

BIRD NAMES WHICH DIFFER BETWEEN *CLEMENTS* AND VARIOUS OTHER BIRD BOOKS

Only those name differences, which are not immediately obvious, are given.

Name used by *Clements*	Name used in other books	Scientific name
Common Loon	Great Northern Diver	*Gavia immer*
Band-rumped Storm-Petrel	Madeiran Storm-Petrel	*Oceanodroma castro*
Masked Booby	Blue-faced Booby	*Sula dactylatra*
Neotropic Cormorant	Olivaceous Cormorant	*Phalacrocorax brasilianus*
Northern Harrier	Hen Harrier	*Circus cyaneus*
Ridgway's Hawk	Hispaniolan Hawk	*Buteo ridgwayi*
Snowy Plover	Kentish Plover	*Charadrius alexandrinus*
Parasitic Jaeger	Arctic Skua	*Stercorarius parasiticus*
Scaly-naped Pigeon	Red-necked Pigeon	*Columba squamosa*
Eared Dove	Violet-eared Dove	*Zenaida auriculata*
Cuban Parrot	Rose-throated Parrot	*Amazona leucocephala*
Bay-breasted Cuckoo	Rufous-breasted Cuckoo	*Hyetornis rufigularis*
Cuban Screech-Owl	Bare-legged Owl	*Gymnoglaux lawrencii*
West Indian Woodpecker	Cuban Red-bellied Woodpecker	*Melanerpes superciliaris*
Cuban Woodpecker	Cuban Green Woodpecker	*Xiphidiopicus percussus*
Fernandina's Flicker	Cuban Flicker	*Colaptes fernandinae*
Sad Flycatcher	Dusky-capped Flycatcher	*Myiarchus barbirostris*
Bare-eyed Thrush	Bare-eyed Robin	*Turdus nudigenis*
St Andrew Vireo	San Andres Vireo	*Vireo caribaeus*
Jamaican Vireo	Jamaican White-eyed Vireo	*Vireo modestus*
White-winged Crossbill	Two-barred Crossbill	*Loxia leucoptera*
Green-tailed Warbler	(Green-tailed) Ground Warbler	*Microligea palustris*
Northern Stripe-headed Tanager	Western Stripe-headed Tanager	*Spindalis zena*
Yellow-shouldered Grassquit	Yellow-backed Finch	*Loxipasser anoxanthus*
Zapata Sparrow	Cuban Sparrow	*Torreornis inexpectata*

INDEX TO SPECIES

Page numbers in **bold** refer to illustrations in the text.

Index to species